Israel

the Bradt Travel Guide

Samantha Wilson

Updated by
Maria Oleynik

edition
3

www.bradtguides.com

Bradt Travel Guides Ltd, UK
The Globe Pequot Press Inc, USA

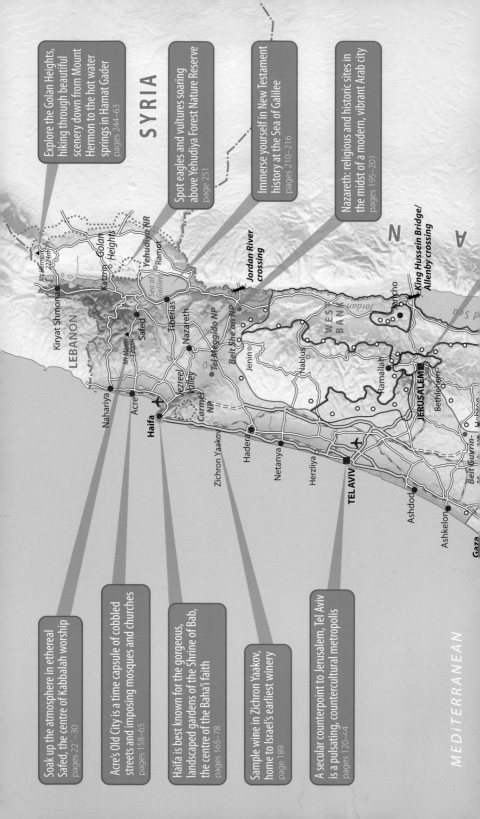

Explore the Golan Heights, hiking through beautiful scenery down from Mount Hermon to the hot water springs in Hamat Gader pages 244–63

Spot eagles and vultures soaring above Yehudiya Forest Nature Reserve page 251

Immerse yourself in New Testament history at the Sea of Galilee pages 210–216

Nazareth: religious and historic sites in the midst of a modern, vibrant Arab city pages 195–201

Soak up the atmosphere in ethereal Safed, the centre of Kabbalah worship pages 22 –30

Acre's Old City is a time capsule of cobbled streets and imposing mosques and churches pages 158–65

Haifa is best known for the gorgeous, landscaped gardens of the Shrine of Bab, the centre of the Baha'i faith pages 165–78

Sample wine in Zichron Yaakov, home to Israel's earliest winery page 189

A secular counterpoint to Jerusalem, Tel Aviv is a pulsating, countercultural metropolis pages 120–44

SYRIA

LEBANON

WEST BANK

MEDITERRANEAN

Mt Hermon 2224m

Golan Heights

Yehudiya NR

Katzrin

Ramot

Jordan River crossing

Kiryat Shmona

Sea of Galilee

Nahariya

Acre

Safed

Mt Meron 1208m

Tiberias

Nazareth

Jezreel Valley

Tel Megiddo NP

Beit She'an NP

Jenin

Carmel NR

Haifa

Zichron Yaakov

Hadera

Nablus

Jordan

Netanya

Herzliya

Ramallah

JERUSALEM

Jericho

King Hussein Bridge/ Allenby crossing

Bethlehem

Dead Sea

TEL AVIV

Ashdod

Ashkelon

Beit Guvrin-

Gaza

N

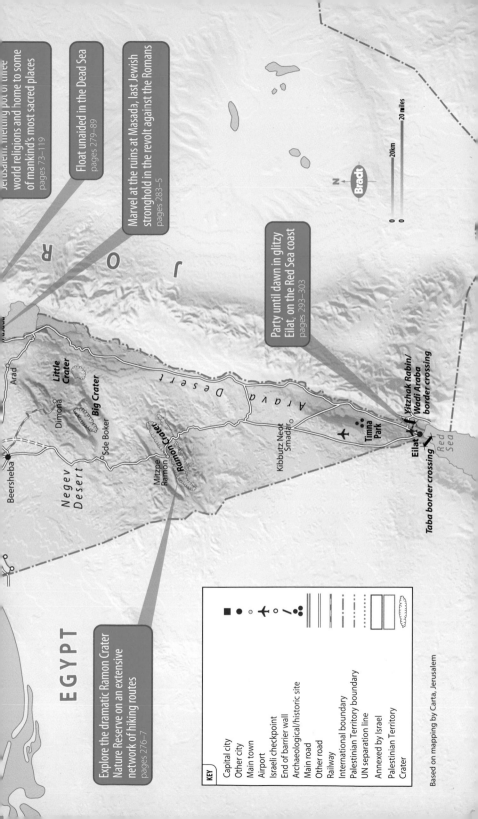

Israel
Don't
miss...

Dead Sea
The incredible buoyancy of this large saline lake makes for a surreal experience
(IG/IMOT) pages 279–89

Jerusalem
The majestic golden Dome of the Rock is the centrepiece of Temple Mount, the city's holiest Islamic site
(MO) page 104

Negev Desert
The barren beauty of this rocky desert is home to wildlife-filled oases and the vast Ramon Crater
(DT/IMOT)
pages 265–78

Sea of Galilee
The tranquil shores of this lake are steeped in New Testament history
(JA/A) pages 210–16

Tel Aviv
Israel's fun-loving beachside city sets itself apart with its striking modern architecture, eclectic restaurants and a buzzing nightlife
(IR/DT) pages 120–44

Israel
in colour

top

The Mount of Olives is dotted with Jewish, Christian and Muslim religious sites, including the frescoed Church of All Nations (r/S) pages 108–9

middle

Opening on to a bustling bazaar in Jerusalem's Old City, the Damascus Gate is a testament to Suleiman the Magnificent's fortification of the city in the 16th century (NC/IMOT) pages 105–6

bottom

The fine Benedictine Dormition Abbey is believed to have been built on the site where Virgin Mary fell asleep and was taken to Heaven (e/S) page 106

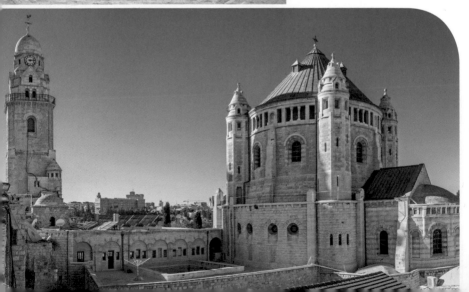

above left   Mahane Yehuda Market, established in the late 1880s, is iconic in Jerusalem and is one of the nicest places to spend a day savouring a variety of foods and spices (AB) pages 112–13

above right   Make sure to buy a souvenir, have a strong cup of Arabic coffee and try the homemade sweets in one of the narrow market alleys in Jerusalem's Old City (KS/AWL) pages 104–5

below   Located by the Old City's Jaffa Gate, the Citadel and Tower of David Museum is a fine example of Jerusalem's Mamluk and Ottoman heritage (NC/IMOT) pages 98–9

above left The Crusader-period Nimrod Fortress rises 800m above sea level amid the lush green hills and pastures of the Golan Heights (ZY/DT) page 262

above right The ancient port town of Caesarea has a wealth of well-preserved ruins, the legacy of phases of occupation by Phoenicians, Greeks, Romans, Crusaders and Mamluks (YB/DT) pages 188–92

below A visit to the remains of the ancient city of Beit Shean, with more than 4,000 years of history and impressive Roman architecture, is a highlight of a trip to northern Israel (IG/IMOT) pages 217–18

bottom Perched 400m above the Dead Sea and offering stunning panoramas over the surrounding arid land, the UNESCO-listed Masada archaeological site is a reminder of the Jewish resistance against Roman rule (PAN/S) pages 283–5

AUTHOR

Samantha Wilson spent several years living in Israel and is a regular visitor from her home in the UK. She has explored every corner of Israel's little land, meeting people, unearthing fascinating stories and learning about deep-rooted cultures. Along with the two previous editions of Bradt's *Israel*, she has authored many other guide and travel books and penned articles for a wide variety of publications including *National Geographic Traveller*. Samantha currently lives in  rural Somerset, from where she can write with views of rolling countryside. She makes regular trips back to Israel with her husband and young daughter to travel, research and visit the in-laws. For more of Samantha's work and publications, visit w samanthakwilson.com.

UPDATER

Maria Oleynik is an expert on the Middle East as well as an avid and endlessly curious traveller, linguist and freelance translator, including from Hebrew and Arabic. Since her first trip to the Middle East in 2003, she has returned regularly, ever expanding her knowledge of Arabic and the region. In the mid 2000s, she started learning Hebrew in order to be able to understand, appreciate and enjoy the Middle East in its entirety. She is currently studying Middle Eastern Language and Society at the University of Copenhagen.  Having updated guides for Iran and Kazakhstan for Bradt, Maria is experienced and methodical in her approach with an eye for tiny detail (ie: that miniature plaque in Hebrew across the street you did not know the meaning of) and discoveries she likes to share with readers.

AUTHOR'S STORY   *Sam Wilson*

It was by pure chance that I found myself living in the heart of the Middle East, a region I have grown to love for so many reasons. Perhaps it is its unconventionality, passion, staggering beauty or maybe even its drama; I couldn't say for sure. Friends and acquaintances would ask me why I lived in such a politically sensitive and volatile country, to me a sad opening question about life in Israel. There is so much more to this small yet incredibly fascinating place, and I was driven by this to share my intrigue and discoveries with others. And so I embarked on a thorough (and thoroughly enjoyable) exploration of every corner of Israel, from its mountain peaks to its Red Sea coast and every kibbutz in between. Along the way, my project and I were greeted with an enthusiasm, gratitude and assistance I could never have predicted, the people of Israel desperate for others to share in the country of which they are so fiercely proud. In this way, while I may have put pen to paper, this is truly the work of so many who share a common love of this vibrant and colourful little land.

Third edition published May 2018
First published January 2009
Bradt Travel Guides Ltd
IDC House, The Vale, Chalfont St Peter, Bucks SL9 9RZ, England
w bradtguides.com
Print edition published in the USA by The Globe Pequot Press Inc,
PO Box 480, Guilford, Connecticut 06437-0480

Text copyright © 2018 Samantha Wilson
Maps copyright © 2018 Bradt Travel Guides Ltd Includes map data © OpenStreetMap contributors
Where indicated, maps are based on sources provided by © Carta, Jerusalem
Photographs copyright © 2018 Individual photographers (see below)
Project Manager: Guy Jackson
Cover research: Pepi Bluck, Perfect Picture

ISBN: 978 1 78477 087 7 (print)
e-ISBN: 978 1 78477 536 0 (e-pub)
e-ISBN: 978 1 78477 437 0 (mobi)

British Library Cataloguing in Publication Data
A catalogue record for this book is available from the British Library

Photographs Adam Balogh (AB); Alamy: Jon Arnold (JA/A), Michelangelo Operandi (MO/A), Roger Hutchings (RH/A); AWL Images: Ken Scicluna (KS/AWL); Dreamstime: Gkuna (G/DT), Igor Rogkow (IR/DT), Rostislav Ageev (RA/DT), Yehuda Bernstein (YB/DT), Zova Yuzvak (ZY/DT); Israel Ministry of Tourism: Dafna Tal (DT/IMOT), Itamar Grinberg (IG/IMOT), Noam Chen (NC/IMOT); Maria Oleynik (MO); Shutterstock: eFesenko (e/S), Eve81 (E/S), FromMyEyes (F/S), Gershon Photo (GP/S), JekLi (J/S), Konstanntinn (K/S), leospek (l/S), Leonid Andronov (LA/S), Protasov AN (PAN/S), rasika108 (r/S), zebra0209 (z/S); SuperStock (SS)

Front cover Nubian ibex (MO/A)
Back cover Dome of the Rock, Jerusalem (z/S); the Dead Sea (IG/IMOT)
Title page The Greek Orthodox Church of the Seven Apostles at Capernaum (RA/DT); spices on sale at Mahane Yehuda Market, Jerusalem (AB); the Ramon Crater in the Negev Desert (DT/IMOT)

Maps David McCutcheon FBCart.S

Typeset by Ian Spick, Bradt Travel Guides Ltd
Production managed by Jellyfish Print Solutions; printed in India
Digital conversion by w dataworks.co.in

Acknowledgements

A book like this doesn't come together without the help of many people to whom I shall always be grateful. The interest, support and encouragement that I received when researching and writing the first edition of this guide have certainly continued, and I thank all my friends, in Israel and around the world, for that. I would also like to take this opportunity to thank all those who have read and used the guide, and who hopefully took away from their trip the same passion, intrigue and fun that I have always found researching and travelling in Israel.

To my family in Israel, thank you so much for all your wonderful hospitality, car loans, Shabbat dinners and of course your love and support – you have made Israel my second home. Thank you also to Allison Gosney for all her cheeriness and enthusiasm and for making all the pavement-pounding research so much fun. I would also like to thank Ami Dorfman for always giving up his time to share his knowledge and passion of the Galilee with me.

I would like to send my heartfelt thanks to my family, especially my parents, who are always my number one supporters. And of course to Niv, without whom I would have never have found my way to Israel and would certainly never have had the courage to pursue a career I so love. Thank you for your selfless help, encouragement and enthusiasm. Yet the biggest thanks for this third edition of the guide must go to Maria Oleynik, who did such a brilliant and thorough job updating it. Her incredible knowledge, hard work and hours on the road have brought new depth to the guide and made it what it is.

FEEDBACK REQUEST AND UPDATES WEBSITE

Israel is a modern country with a fast-paced way of living and, as such, things tend to change quickly in this little stretch of land. Today's trendiest bar or café is obsolete tomorrow, hotel prices fluctuate with the political situation, profound archaeological discoveries occur on a daily basis and public transport continues to improve and grow at a rate of knots. Everyone sees Israel in a different way, and I would love to hear from readers about their own experiences in the Holy Land, something that would help me to prepare for the next edition of this book. If you come across something that you feel should be included, a hotel that has lost its charm or a fantastic little restaurant nestled away somewhere, then please get in touch; be it good or bad, it all goes towards making the next edition that much better. Contact me via Bradt Guides on ☎ 01753 893444 or e info@bradtguides.com. I may post updates on the Bradt website at w bradtupdates.com/israel. Alternatively, you can add a review of the book to w bradtguides.com or Amazon.

Contents

LISTINGS Places to stay and eat are listed first by descending price code then alphabetically within each price code.

MAPS

Keys and symbols Maps include alphabetical keys covering the locations of those places to stay, eat or drink that are featured in the book. On occasion, hotels or restaurants that are not listed in the guide (but which might serve as alternative options if required or serve as useful landmarks to aid navigation) are also included on the maps; these are marked with accommodation (⌂) or restaurant (✖) symbols.

Grids and grid references Several maps use gridlines to allow easy location of sites. Map grid references are listed in square brackets after the name of the place or site of interest in the text, with page number followed by grid number, eg: [103 C3].

SPELLINGS For information about spelling conventions, see *Linguistic pointers* box, page 29.

WEB ADDRESSES A web address includes */en* when this offers a quick route to a version in English. Some websites might display the English version automatically or an English-language button on the home page.

LIST OF MAPS

Introduction

Israel is a land of dramatic and poignant contrasts, a land whose tumultuous existence often casts a shadow over the rich and vibrant life that beats beneath it. It is a land of incredible beauty, variety and character. Upon this soil have walked some of the greatest figures of our past, a ground that has seen the birth of some of the world's main religions and the passionate battles that ensued to protect them.

It is a sad yet realistic state of affairs that the word 'Israel' has today become synonymous with conflict, religious tension and political debate, and historically this tiny stretch of land has formed the gladiatorial arena where empires and faiths have risen and fallen, a fact that remains as true today as it did 2,000 years ago.

Yet behind the television cameras and glare of the international limelight, Israel's tourist appeal is simply enormous. From the snow-capped peaks that straddle the northern border with Syria, to its barren and eerily beautiful expanse of rock deserts that form the gateway to Egypt, the country leaves few landscapes unrepresented. As a meeting point between the cold steppes of Europe and the desert lands of the Syrian-African Rift Valley, Israel is a country geographically (and politically) divided. The swirl of green valleys, tree-studded hills and trickling streams that form the northern region are dotted with towns that have stood the tests of time, their inhabitants displaying a vibrant mesh of beliefs, traditions and cultures that remain proud and strong. In contrast are the arid lands of the south, vast craters, tiny isolated settlements and the inhospitable beauty of the Dead Sea swallowed up in their midst. The lively, cosmopolitan hub of Tel Aviv takes pleasure in its role as the country's economic, commercial and diplomatic centre, its wild beaches and secular way of life providing Jerusalem's diametric opposite. Jerusalem: few cities on this planet can attest to the life that this incredible city has lived, its willpower, determination and passion to survive having seen it rise above all that has come its way. Forming the cross on the map where the world's three biggest religions converge, it is a place like no other, one that leaves even the most religiously apathetic of visitors in awe.

Israel is a modern country that embodies, thanks to its millions of immigrants, countless faiths and innumerable cultures, a charm and uniqueness like nowhere else on earth. Combine this with its rich historic, geological and natural treasures, and it is instantly apparent why so many have fought for so long to keep it.

KEY TO SYMBOLS

Symbol	Description	Symbol	Description
— · — · — · —	International boundary	☆	Nightclub/casino
— · · — · · · —	Palestinian enclave boundary	⌂	Café
═══════	Motorway/main road	Å	Campsite
═══ ═ ═	Other road/4x4 track	♊	Male & female toilets
▦▦▦▦▦	Pedestrianised town street	✡	Synagogue
ⅠⅠⅠⅠⅠⅠⅠ	Stepped ways (paths)	☾	Mosque
═──═──═	Railway	†	Church/chapel/cathedral
═─═─═─	Metro/subway	⛪ ⓒ ⛨	Cemetery (Christian/Muslim/Jewish)
▭─○─▭	Cable car	🏛	Tomb
VI — — — V	The Stations of the Cross route	✿	Garden
· · · · · · · · · ·	National trail/footpath	∴	Archaeological/historic site
✈ ✦	Airport (international/domestic)	⅏	Waterfall
⛴ 🚗	Ferry (pedestrian/vehicle)	⌒	Cave/grotto
🚌	Bus station etc	❋	Viewpoint
🚕	Car hire/taxis	⋋⋌	Beach
ᨒ	Cycle hire	✒	Birdwatching area
🅿	Parking	✓	Scuba diving
⛽	Filling station/garage	🐪	Camel riding
•	Tram stop	⋯⋯⋯	Airport runway
🛈	Tourist information	⤛	Border crossing
🄴	Embassy/consulate	○	Hot springs
☗	Museum/art gallery	◎	Fountain
☺	Theatre/cinema	▲	Summit (height in metres)
▦	Important/historic building	●	Other point of interest
⌂	Castle/fort	⌒⌒	Crater edge
⌂⌂	Ancient city gate	⬭	Salt lake/pan
⚲	Statue/monument	⌐○	City wall
$	Bank/bureau de change	▨	Urban park
✉	Post office	▧	Urban market
✚	Hospital/clinic	▦	Shopping centre/mall
✚	Pharmacy/surgery/dentist	▬	Built-up area
⌂	Hotel/inn etc	▦	Forest park
✕	Restaurant	▨	Beach
⚱	Bar		

Part One

GENERAL INFORMATION

ISRAEL AT A GLANCE

Location Middle East
Neighbouring countries Lebanon, Syria, Jordan, Egypt and the Palestinian territories of the West Bank and Gaza Strip
Area 20,330km^2
Climate Varies according to latitude: temperate in central and northern regions, hot and dry in the south
Status Parliamentary democracy
Population 8,654,900 (Central Bureau of Statistics April 2017)
Life expectancy Women 84.4, men 80.6 (2016)
Capital Tel Aviv (de facto), Jerusalem (contested)
Other main towns Haifa, Ashdod, Beersheba, Netanya, Hadera, Nazareth, Eilat, Tiberias, Safed
Economy Cut diamonds, technology and agricultural products are the major exports
GDP Purchasing power parity US$297 billion; per capita US$34,800 (2016)
Languages Hebrew and Arabic are official languages. English and Russian are widely spoken.
Religion Judaism, Islam, Christianity, Druze
Currency New Israeli Shekel (₪/NIS)
Exchange rate (Feb 2018) US$1 = ₪3.5; £1 = ₪4.9; €1 = ₪4.4
National airline El Al
National airport Ben-Gurion International Airport
International telephone code +972
Time GMT +2
Electrical voltage 220V/50Hz
Weights and measures Metric
Flag White and blue with the Star of David in the centre
National anthem Hatikvah
National emblem Menorah
National memorial site Mount Herzl
National sport Football (soccer)
Public holidays Rosh Hashanah (September), Yom Kippur (September/October), Sukkot (September/October), Simchat Torah (September/October), Hanukkah (December), Purim (February/March), Passover (March/April), Holocaust Memorial Day (April/May), National Memorial Day (April/May), Independence Day (April/May), Shavuot (May/June), Tisha Bav (July/August). Dates vary according to the Jewish calendar.

1

Background Information

GEOGRAPHY AND CONSERVATION

Israel is located in the western fringes of the Middle East. The long, narrow strip of land is almost diamond shaped, coming to a point at the Red Sea in the south. It borders Lebanon and Syria in the north, Jordan in the east and Egypt in the southwest, with the western coast fringing the Mediterranean Sea. The Gaza Strip is located on the southern Mediterranean coast and the West Bank stretches centrally from the border with Jordan. Measuring just 470km in length and 135km at its widest point, the country is unique in that it has three highly contrasting geographical regions. In the west is the fertile coastal plain, home to major cities such as Tel Aviv and Haifa and the most densely populated region of the country. The forests, valleys, mountains and rivers that make up the north and east of the country incorporate the verdant Galilee region as well as the freshwater Sea of Galilee and Jordan River. More than half of Israel is desert, stretching all the way down to the Red Sea and the southern city of Eilat. The Dead Sea forms the eastern border with Jordan and stands as the world's lowest point at 400m below sea level. Sitting in the vast Syrian-African Rift Valley, its extreme salinity does not support any living organisms, the freshwater oases that dot the desert the only source of life to the flora and fauna of the region. Comprising the rocky Negev, Arava and Judean deserts, Israel's south is sparsely populated and transport links are few and far between.

NATIONAL PARKS Israel is today home to over 66 national parks and 190 nature reserves which are under the management of the Israel Nature and National Parks Protection Authority (INPA) (\ *3639, 02 5006261;* w *parks.org.il/sites/english*). In contrast to many other countries where the term 'national park' implies vast areas of open, protected land, in Israel the term is used to denote any protected area, be it a small archaeological site, vast canyon or landscaped hot spring park. Castles and fortresses, churches and synagogues, desert oases, caves, rivers, waterfalls and wildlife reserves grace the list of the country's national parks. Almost all parks charge an entry fee which goes towards continued conservation and management efforts. Discount cards can be bought at any of the park offices for ₪150 per person (the Orange Card), are valid for two weeks and provide access to almost all national parks and nature reserves in the country. There is also a ₪110 pass which grants access to six national parks of your choice.

FLORA The Bible describes the Holy Land as 'a land of wheat and barley, of vines and fig trees and pomegranates, a land of olive trees and honey'. This wealth of plant life is down to its varied climate, geology and geographical positioning. A total of 2,380 species of flora have been recorded, many endangered or endemic to Israel.

MOSHAV AND KIBBUTZ

About 8% of Israel's population lives in rural areas, divided between small towns, villages and two types of co-operative frameworks unique to the country. These co-operative frameworks, the *moshav* and the *kibbutz*, started appearing in the early part of the 20th century and today remain a key feature of the landscape and social structure of the country.

KIBBUTZ The word 'kibbutz' in Hebrew means 'gathering', and is used to describe a collective, self-contained farm settlement whereby members make decisions together for the good of the community, and wealth and property are shared out. The kibbutz appeared in Israel at the turn of the last century, created by Jewish settlers in Palestine, the first being Kibbutz Deganya Alef just south of the Sea of Galilee (page 215). For decades, the idealistic community living attracted non-Jews who came to volunteer and live within the enclosed settlements. Parents lived in separate quarters to children, meals were eaten communally and homes were owned by the community not the individual. These days, however, the original concept has mostly been lost and while kibbutz communities are still famously tight-knit and children and dogs run freely, many meals continue to be eaten in the communal dining room and a kibbutz-run business remains in each, members in most *kibbutzim* (the plural of kibbutz) are allowed to purchase their own homes, go out to work and live more independent lives. Today around 130,000 people (less than 2% of the population) live in some 270 kibbutzim, their main economies centring on agriculture, tourism, industry and services – indeed, kibbutzim produce 38% of Israel's farm produce.

MOSHAV Created in the early 1900s, the moshav settlement was a collective village based on agriculture. Each family maintained its own farm and household, and land was divided up between family members. Today there are 451 *moshavim* (the plural of moshav) housing 3.4% of the population, and while farming businesses still form the backbone of much of Israel's agriculture (in particular cattle rearing, dairy and poultry), families maintain a more independent lifestyle and generally work outside of the settlement. The safe, homely, family-oriented environment that abounds on these settlements is today much sought after and such property rarely comes on to the market. In many parts of the country, the incredible popularity of *zimmers* (page 62) – luxury, privately run essentially rural accommodation – has seen tourism begin to play an important part in the economies of the moshavim and has made them yet more sought after.

The Mediterranean region supports the densest concentrations, where alpine species thrive mainly along the Carmel Mountain ridge, in the Jezreel Valley and in the Galilee region. Plant life in the desert is sparse with the exception of small pockets of dense vegetation in oases such as Ein Gedi and Ein Avdat. In its accreditations, Israel is famed as being the northernmost limit for species such as the papyrus reed, the southernmost limit for plants such as the red coral peony and the only place where the Euphrates poplar still grows. The famed Madonna lily and Gilboa iris, rare Kermes oak trees and gnarled, ancient olive trees decorate the fertile northern terrain while towering date palms flourish in the arid, sub-Saharan soils of the desert.

WILDLIFE

Mammals Israel is home to 116 species of mammal, which, compared with the 140 species recorded in the whole of Europe, is vast. The country forms the crossroads for animals originating in the alpine European region to the north and those arriving from the desert regions of Arabia and Africa in the south. The largest inhabitants are mountain gazelles, wild boar, foxes, Nubian ibex, hyenas, jackals, wolves, onagers and the rarely seen leopards. The rock hyrax or rock badger, known in Israel as *shafan*, can often be seen between rocks and riverbeds. A large conservation effort is in play to reintroduce many biblical creatures long since

WALKING IN THE HOOFPRINTS OF ISRAEL'S BIBLICAL ANIMALS

Hai Bar is a nationwide organisation whose principal objective is to preserve the country's endangered animals and reintroduce indigenous species long since hunted to extinction back to their previous habitats. Lions, cheetahs, bears and crocodiles, some of Israel's more ferocious ancient inhabitants, are not, for obvious reasons, part of this scheme, but more mild-mannered species such as fallow and roe deer, Arabian oryx, Ethiopian ostrich and the onager (a type of wild ass) are being reintroduced to the delicate ecosystem. Several herds of onager have been released into the arid wilderness of the Arava Desert, with the Arabian oryx, whose impressive horns make them easily recognisable in the landscape, being another success story for the desert terrains. The **Yotvata Hai Bar Reserve** is home to many species which still roam the savannah-like lands of the south, and a delightful safari and conservation zoo makes a highly recommended trip. Hyenas, caracals, leopards, wolves, gazelle, sand and fennec foxes, desert hedgehogs and many birds and reptiles have all now been placed significantly lower down the endangered list thanks to ongoing efforts. On Saturdays at 11.00, reserve rangers run tours which include feeding the animals. There is a wide range of other tours on offer at this reserve.

The last native roe deer was shot in the Carmel Forest in 1912 and an intensive project has been under way to return them, and fallow deer, to their original habitat. Today, the **Carmel Hai Bar Wildlife Reserve** (\ 04 832 0648; ⊕ 08.00–16.00 Sat; admission adult/child ₪22/9), which hit headline news in December 2010 when a vicious wild fire reached the enclosure fences before being extinguished by hundreds of fire-fighters and volunteers, is home to the biggest population of fallow deer in the world, many of which have been successfully released. Wild sheep and goats, griffon, Egyptian vultures and Bonelli's eagles are also bred at the reserve which is located 300m south of Haifa University's main entrance on route 672. Another important griffon vulture sanctuary is located next to the hilltop fortress of **Kochav Hayarden** (pages 216–17).

Visitors are invited to enter the reserves to appreciate up close these biblical animals, the entry fees providing invaluable contributions to their continuing success. Many species, including the more fearsome contenders, can also be seen at the **Biblical Zoo** in Jerusalem, which is closely involved with the conservation efforts (page 115). There are also numerous smaller organisations around the Ramon Crater working to protect the endangered vulture populations in the area. For further details, contact the visitors' centre or The Green Backpackers in Mitzpe Ramon (page 275).

hunted to extinction from their natural lands. Jerusalem's Biblical Zoo and the Hai Bar nature reserves are at the centre of this scheme (pages 115 and 5).

Birds Sitting on the main migratory thoroughfare, Israel's skies and valleys seasonally fill with hundreds of species of birds who rest on their long journey south or north. A total of 510 bird species have been recorded, birdwatching reserves such as those in the Hula Valley, Eilat and Beit Shean Valley being prime places to see the splendid array of species that includes cranes, honey buzzards and pelicans. Of those who make their home in Israel are the highly endangered griffon and Egyptian vultures and imperial and spotted eagles. The Yehudiya National Park is the best place to see wild vultures soaring in the skies above, while the Israel Nature and National Parks Protection Authority has a research station and shelter next to Belvoir Castle in the Lower Galilee.

Reptiles There are 97 species of reptile and seven species of amphibian in the country, most others having disappeared because of urban and agricultural expansion and a loss of habitat. Scorpions are still prevalent in the desert while several snake species can be found across the country. Green turtles nest almost exclusively in Israel, Cyprus and Turkey, and researchers believe there are fewer than 1,000 females alive today. The more common loggerhead turtles, most populous in Greece, Cyprus and Turkey, also nest in Israel, Syria and North Africa, although numbers are dwindling.

Marine life Eilat's Red Sea coast is home to several species of tropical marine life although the once-flourishing coral reefs have been over-exploited and are now well past their prime. However, dolphins, octopuses, countless fish species and extremely occasionally whale sharks can be seen in the waters off Israel's southern coast.

CLIMATE

Israel has a 'Mediterranean', subtropical climate with hot summers and mild winters. Summer months are from April through October with temperatures peaking in July and August. Climatic conditions do, however, vary considerably. The Mediterranean coast suffers hot, humid summers and wet, mild winters, while the hilly regions of the north and east (including Jerusalem) are less humid in summer but have moderately cold winters and occasional snow. Mount Hermon is snow-capped almost year-round but snowfall has been significantly less in recent years. The desert is hot year-round, with exceptionally arid conditions. Rare flash floods can occur during heavy rains as water runs across the surface of the impermeable rock desert. Additional information and weather reports are available at the Israel Meteorological Service (w *ims.gov.il/imseng*).

CLIMATE CHART						
	Eilat	**Haifa**	**Jerusalem**	**Safed**	**Tel Aviv**	**Tiberias**
Mean temp Jan °C	10–21	9–17	6–12	4–9	10–17	9–18
Mean temp Aug °C	26–40	24–31	19–29	19–29	24–30	23–38
Days rainfall per annum	5	51	44	58	46	47
Annual rainfall (mm)	25	540	553	712	524	407

IN THE BEGINNING ... 'In the beginning God created the heavens and the earth.' And if you asked any observant Jew where Israel's history begins, it would be around this time. Historically, the land that is modern-day Israel has always stood on a great world crossroads, where empires, religions and cultures clashed or convened. In the 24th century BCE (Before Common Era, a term used in lieu of BC in non-Christian regions), it formed the cultural bull's-eye between Egypt, Assyria Mesopotamia and Asia Minor and in the 2nd millennium BCE various tribes began an invasion of the territory, at the time inhabited by the Canaanites. Around the 17th century BCE, the Hebrew Bible's Book of Genesis records the appearance of three Jewish patriarchs: Abraham, Isaac and Jacob, the last of whom was renamed Israel in the Book of Genesis. The Bible tells how Abraham was summoned to Canaan to unite a people who believed in 'One God'. When famine ravaged the land, the Israelites, the descendants of the 12 sons of Israel, relocated to Egypt where, according to biblical sources, they spent 400 years in slavery. Led by Moses they escaped to freedom and spent the following 40 years wandering the desert before resettling in Canaan. Every year the Jewish holiday of Pesach (pronounced *pesakh*; Passover) is celebrated in honour of this.

THE ISRAELITES AND THE IRON AGE (1200–586BCE) Throughout the next two centuries the Israelites conquered the land, a time known as the Period of Judges. During this time of fierce wars people made allegiances with many of the 'judges', who emerged as leaders at that time. The divided armies were weak and suffering from incursions from the Philistines, a tribe descended from Asia Minor who had settled along the southern coast. In 1020BCE, the Israelites received the gift of unification in the form of King Saul, the Jewish people's first monarch. Upon Saul's defeat against the Philistines, David ascended to the throne and it was under his reign that Jerusalem was conquered (from the Canaanite tribe of Jebusites) and declared capital of the realm. David was succeeded in 965BCE by his son Solomon who not only massively expanded the kingdom, but also commissioned the building of the First Temple from the cedar wood brought from present-day Lebanon. After Solomon's death civil unrest led to the division of the monarchy and the emergence of two kingdoms: Israel in the north, governed by ten tribes; and Judah in the south, led by two tribes. In 721BCE, the Assyrians conquered the Kingdom of Israel and its ten tribes fled, never to return. In 586BCE, the Kingdom of Judah suffered a similar fate at the hands of the Babylonians who destroyed Jerusalem and sacked the First Temple.

THE PERSIANS, ALEXANDER THE GREAT AND THE HASMONEANS (538–63BCE) After the Persians conquered Babylon in 538BCE, the tribe of Judah was granted permission by the Persian king Cyrus the Great to return to Jerusalem where in 515BCE they constructed the Second Temple. Throughout the Persian period the Jews prospered and strengthened, the Knesset Hagedolah (Great Assembly – page 23) owing its origins to this time. In 332BCE, however, Persian rule came to an end with Alexander the Great's conquest. His death in 323BCE led to battles over his legacy and right to the throne, a struggle that was eventually won by Seleucus I, founder of the Syria-based Seleucid dynasty. This period is characterised in history as the Hellenistic, whereby the remaining descendants of Alexander's Greek kingdom and its merging with the Persians resulted in the emergence of a distinctly Greek cultural phase, even under Seleucid rule. By this time synagogues had become the centre of the Jewish community and when the Seleucid rulers began suppressing the Jewish religion, imposing upon the population Greek-oriented culture, language and beliefs, the Jews in 166BCE rose in a revolt led by the Maccabees, a Jewish family of patriots (an event celebrated today with the festival of Hanukkah). This in turn led to the establishment of the Jewish Hasmoneans, who eventually ousted the Seleucids and imposed their own religion on the land. It was during this period of Jewish rule that religious tensions caused breakaway groups to emerge, most notably the Essenes who are the believed authors of the Dead Sea Scrolls found at Qumran in the West Bank on the eve of the 1948 Arab–Israeli War.

JESUS AND THE ROMANS (63BCE–212CE) In 63BCE, Roman statesman and general Pompey the Great captured Jerusalem, replacing the Seleucids as the region's great power, and demoting the Hasmonean king, Hyrcanus II, to acting king under Roman rule. The Jewish population was hostile to the new regime and rebellions eventually led to the final demise of the Hasmoneans, and the Roman rule over the Land of Judea. In 37BCE, Herod the Great was appointed king, becoming one of the Roman Empire's most powerful leaders. Under him the great coastal city of Caesarea exploded on to the scene as one of the world's most crucial seaports, the palace of Masada (pages 283–5) was built as his luxury playground and the temple was given a magnificent makeover. Despite (or perhaps in spite of) these achievements the Jews were displeased, and revolts led to the destruction of the Second Temple under Titus. A last attempt in 123CE (Common Era, used in lieu of AD) to claim Jewish liberation failed after an ambitious but unsuccessful uprising led by Shimon Bar Kokhba. According to Josephus Flavius, a 1st-century historian, hundreds of thousands of Jews were exiled and dispersed across the empire, an event known as the Jewish Diaspora. Jerusalem was razed to the ground and on it built a wholly Roman city named Aelia Capitolina. Judea thereafter was merged with Roman Syria into the Roman province of Syria-Palaestina.

Jesus of Nazareth was born in the early years of Roman rule. However, it would be a further 300 years until Christianity was legitimised by the Romans and became the official religion. Details of Jesus's life – especially his early years – are taken primarily from the Gospels, telling of his descent from the bloodline of King David, his mother Mary's Immaculate Conception and his birth in Bethlehem following a move made by Mary and Joseph in compliance with King Herod's census. The Gospels, however, mention nothing of Jesus from the age of 12 until he began his public ministry 18 years later, following his baptism by John the Baptist.

For the Jews, the remainder of the Roman period is characterised by the survival of their communities, now scattered across the land and beyond. The supreme legislative and judicial body, known as the Sanhedrin (successor to the Knesset Hagedolah) reconvened in 70CE in Tiberias, reinforced over time by returning exiles. During these exiled years the great texts of Judaism were scribed, the Mishnah (a book on Jewish oral law) in 210CE by Rabbi Judah Hanasi, and the Talmud (a commentary on the Mishnah) in 390CE.

THE BYZANTINES (313–636) In 313CE, Constantine the Great founded the Byzantine Empire and legalised Christianity. An influx of pilgrims and a huge building phase got under way with churches and monasteries appearing all over the land, more than 450 ecclesiastical buildings having been dated to this time. In 614, the Persians invaded Palaestina, aided by the Jews who as a sign of gratitude were granted permission to once again rule Jerusalem. But it was to be a short rule as three years later the Byzantine army ousted the Persians and once again expelled the Jewish inhabitants.

ARAB RULE (636–1099) Four years after the death of the Prophet Mohammed in 632, Omar Ibn Al-Khattab, also known as Omar I, the second *caliph* (Muslim ruler) of the emerging Islamic empire, conquered Jerusalem along with the lands of Mesopotamia, Syria, Palestine and Egypt. According to Muslim tradition, Mohammed ascended to Heaven from Jerusalem and as such it is considered Islam's third holiest city. In 638, caliph Omar I built the first mosque on the site of the destroyed Second Temple, which was enhanced by the construction of the Dome of the Rock in 691 by the fifth caliph of the Umayyad dynasty Abd Al-Malik (646/7–705). In the first years of Arab rule, Christians (and Jews) were allowed to enter Jerusalem, but this was stopped in the 11th century, prompting Pope Urban II to call for the crusade to free the Holy City from Muslim rule.

THE CRUSADES AND SALADIN (1099–1291) In the 200 years that followed, the country was dominated by waves of crusades that arrived from western Europe with the aim of returning the land to Christendom. The brutal and relentless First Crusade ended in 1099 with the capture of Jerusalem and the massacre of most of the city's Jewish and Muslim residents. Throughout the succeeding decades the Crusaders extended their power across the country either by diplomacy or, more often than not, brute force directed from their fortresses and castles that formed a fortified network across the land. The result was the founding of the Latin Kingdom of Jerusalem, first under Godfrey of Bouillon and then his brother Baldwin.

In 1187 Saladin, the Kurdish Muslim sultan of Egypt and founder of the Ayyubid dynasty, recaptured Jerusalem after victory at the mighty Battle of Hittin. Although his death four years later allowed the Crusades to gain another foothold in the country, they remained limited to their castles and fortifications, suffering countless incursions that ended with their defeat at Acre, their last stronghold, against the Mamluks.

THE MAMLUKS AND OTTOMANS (1291–1917) Throughout Mamluk rule the country descended into a dark era; governed from Damascus it became a peripheral province. The once-thriving port cities of Acre and Jaffa were closed through fear of more crusades and the economy suffered. By the end of the Middle Ages towns were dilapidated, Jerusalem was all but abandoned and the small Jewish, Christian and Muslim communities that remained were poverty-stricken. The dire situation was not aided by violent earthquakes and a devastating plague. Sources estimate that there were but 200,000 people left in the land by the time the Ottoman period began in 1517. The Ottoman Turks governed Palestine from their centre of power in Istanbul for the succeeding 400 years, until the onset of World War I. They divided Palestine into *senjaks* (districts) grouped into *vilayets* (provinces). Galilee was a senjak of Acre, and Samaria of Nablus, which were both part of the Beirut vilayet. The Jerusalem senjak was vast, encompassing a large part of the central area of present-day Israel, including northern Negev.

Suleiman the Magnificent (1495–1566), the Ottoman Empire's longest-reigning sultan, is credited with having constructed the great walls around Jerusalem. The small Jewish population known as the *yishuv* that had existed in Palestine when the Ottomans arrived, expanded quickly as immigrants from North Africa and Europe began to arrive, Safed becoming a major centre for Jewish learning (pages 222–3). However, after Suleiman's death in 1566, things took a turn for the worse and the country fell once more into decline.

At the beginning of the 19th century, the population of Palestine was around 250,000, of which 6,500 were Jews. Between 1831 and 1840, during the short reign of the Egyptian ruler Mohammed Ali Pasha, European countries were allowed to establish representatives in the Holy Land, thus opening Palestine to immigration from non-Muslim countries. Around the same period, as part of the expansive reforms in the Ottoman Empire between 1839 and 1876, known as *tanzimat*, foreigners were furthermore granted rights to purchase land across the empire, including in Palestine.

When World War I broke out, there were approximately 85,000 Jews living in Palestine, mostly Jerusalem, which at that time had a Jewish majority, and the newly built city of Tel Aviv, thus making up 12% of the total population.

ZIONISM Zionism refers to the nationalist movement of Jews in the 19th century to establish a Jewish homeland. Growing industrialisation in Europe allowed more Jews to travel and look for a better life, escaping growing anti-Semitism in eastern Europe and the pogroms in Russia's 'Pale of Settlement', territories at the Tsarist Empire's western borders where Jews had been allowed to settle permanently. The pogroms became known as *Suffot Banegev*, meaning 'storms in southern Russia'. The same year, in 1882, Dr Yehuda Leib Pinsker published his pamphlet entitled 'Auto-Emancipation', in which he advocated the establishment of a Jewish homeland, a territory where Jews could live as masters of their fate and not as a minority among the gentiles. The emerging Jewish press further enabled people from distant and remote places to be connected with their brethren elsewhere. Also in 1882, the first nationalist Jewish colony was established in Palestine, and Baron Edmond de Rothschild started ploughing money into Jewish settlements, founding Deganya, the first kibbutz.

It was, however, **Theodor Herzl** (1860–1904) who managed to appreciate the full extent of the emerging situation and formalise Jewish nationalist ideas into the Zionist movement. A bourgeois intellectual, he believed that a Jew could never be fully accepted, no matter how hard he or she tried to assimilate. It was with this conviction in mind that Herzl declared that Jews were a people, a nation, and in 1897 at the first World Zionist Conference in Basel, Switzerland, he proclaimed: 'At Basel I founded the Jewish state.' Herzl acutely felt the urgency of his project and the need to transform the movement from merely spiritual to political. He thus set about securing international, and in particular European, support for the establishment of a Jewish state. The idea proved to be very popular, especially among Jews in eastern Europe and British political circles. The Jewish Territorial Organisation (JTO) was established in 1905 with the purpose of finding a country for the Jews, transforming the Zionist movement in the process into a territorial as well as a nationalist movement. In support, British colonial secretary Joseph Chamberlain even suggested establishing the Jewish state in a part of East Africa (present-day Kenya), but this was rejected and Palestine had eventually become the main focus of the Zionist aspirations. In May 1916, Great Britain and France signed the secret Sykes–Picot Agreement, establishing their spheres of influence across the disintegrating Ottoman Empire. Syria fell under French control and Palestine under British. With the subsequent signing of the Balfour Declaration in 1917, the British foreign secretary Lord Balfour approved the establishment in Palestine of a 'national home for the Jewish people', with the condition that it did not prejudice the religious and civil rights of the non-Jews who lived there.

BRITISH RULE AND JEWISH IMMIGRATION (1918–48) In World War I, Turkey allied itself with Germany. Having already signed the Balfour Declaration, the British were at the same time allying themselves with the Arabs, pledging to support

Arab independence in exchange for them waging war against the Ottomans. The 1916 Arab Revolt, aided by T E Lawrence (of Arabia) declared war on the Ottomans, while only a year later in 1917, General Allenby entered Jerusalem to a warm welcome from the Jews, who saw the British as liberators.

In May 1916, France and Britain signed the secret Sykes–Picot Agreement to divide up the Middle East. According to the terms of the agreement, France received Lebanon and Syria, while Iraq, Palestine and Transjordan became Britain's sphere of influence. On 18 April 1920, at the San Remo Convention attended by the powers victorious in World War I, the League of Nations granted Britain the actual mandate over Palestine, which was of strategic importance as the overland route to India. Herbert Samuel was appointed as first high commissioner for Palestine. Although the British made it clear to the French that they intended Palestine to be under international control, the government in London thought otherwise. When Lloyd George became prime minister, he assisted the Zionists in their efforts to establish the Jewish state in the Holy Land. His foreign secretary at that time was Arthur Balfour, who had given his name to the Balfour Declaration of 1917. In 2017, celebrations to mark the centenary of the signing of the declaration were

THE IRANIAN SCHINDLER

Paris 1940, Anoshirvan Sepahbody, Iran's seasoned Minister Plenipotentiary in France, left the city for Vichy, entrusting the Iranian legation to his brother-in-law **Abdul Hossein Sardari** (1895–1981). This young and talented diplomat was a member of the Qajar Royal Family. In 1941, British and Russian troops invaded Iran, a German ally, and Iranian citizens in the Nazi-occupied territories had to seek protection from a third state, a role which Switzerland had agreed to take on.

Iranians, who the Nazis considered to be of the Aryan race, enjoyed a *carte blanche* on various matters. In an attempt to help his fellow countrymen, Sardari, a trained and eloquent lawyer, decided to use his position and challenge the Nazi ideology, arguing that Iranian Jews were not Semite, but like other Iranians, were Aryan. He prepared a document entitled 'Iranian followers of Moses', claiming that Jews of Iranian origin were of Mosaic faith and belonged to a distinct group of people, who, Sardari argued, were part of the Iranian race.

In August 1942, Sardari filed a letter containing a list of names of 'Iranians of Mosaic faith resident in Paris' with the German embassy in Paris. Following subsequent correspondence back and forth between the embassy and the Swiss consulate in Paris and the Swiss embassy and the German foreign ministry in Berlin, in September 1942 Iranian Jews had their 'Jew' stamp removed from their identity cards.

Despite objection from Adolf Eichmann himself, who had tried to discredit Sardari's efforts, calling them 'the usual Jewish tricks and attempts at camouflage', the Iranian diplomat had persevered and kept on expanding his list. In March 1943, he added two new categories – Iranians of the Zoroastrian and Karaite faiths. Having received Iranian passports the Jews whose names were on the lists submitted by Sardari were no longer obliged to wear the yellow patch. According to some estimates, thanks to Abdul Hossein Sardari's efforts, approximately 2,400 Jews had been issued with (illegal) Iranian passports by 1943.

held in London, where Israeli prime minister Benjamin Netanyahu met his British counterpart Theresa May as part of a five-day visit to the United Kingdom.

The British Mandate authorities granted the Jews – and to a far lesser degree the Arabs – the right to administer their own internal affairs. In 1929, as stipulated in the mandate, the Jewish Agency was formed. Throughout this period, Jewish culture flourished, and Hebrew was recognised as an official language alongside English and Arabic, much to the discontent of the Arab population, which was increasingly losing its land. Between 1929 and 1932, the yishuv population increased from 170,000 to 400,000, and the Arabs could no longer preserve the predominantly Arab character of the land. The Arab revolt against the British and the Jews in 1936 brought to the surface the underlying conflict. The unrest culminated in the Jaffa Riots and the subsequent issuing of a White Paper following the Peel Commission report in 1936 (which concluded that the British Mandate was unworkable), whereby the British imposed restrictions on the numbers of Jews allowed to immigrate.

By this time, Palestine had seen the first (1882–1903), second (1904–14), and the third *aliyah* ('moving up' or large-scale Jewish immigration; *olim* referred to the immigrants themselves) in the early 1920s from the Soviet Union and in the late 1920s from Poland. The fourth (1924–28), the fifth (1929–39) and last major wave of immigration (some 165,000 people) before the onset of World War II occurred in the 1930s, when Hitler rose to power in Germany.

Following the Holocaust, which saw the genocide of around six million Jews and subsequent mass immigration to Palestine (approximately two-thirds of Holocaust survivors immigrated to Israel), the British intensified their restrictions. Between 1945 and 1948, however, underground Jewish militias smuggled in an estimated 85,000 people in spite of naval blockades and border patrols. As a result of increasing friction between Jews and Arabs, and revolts from both sides against the British, in 1947 Britain decided to hand its mandate over Palestine back to the United Nations.

PARTITION, DECLARATION AND WAR On 29 November 1947, the United Nations General Assembly agreed to partition Palestine, whereby the land would be divided into one Jewish and one Arab state, with Jerusalem governed by the UN. Even the Soviet Union agreed to support the resolution in order to undermine the British standing in the Middle East, although the Soviets were in favour of a single binational state.

The Jews residing in Palestine were exuberant, while the Palestinians were in mourning. The day after the UN resolution, Palestinian Arabs started clashes and riots against the Jews, killing 250 people. The events that followed saw complete disintegration of the Palestinian Arab society and unity, while the exact opposite was taking place among the Jews. The British were now offering evacuation support to the communities, Jewish or Arab, who ended up being outnumbered and on the losing side in the battles for individual cities. By May 1948, around 300,000 Palestinian Arabs had fled.

On 14 May 1948, the same day the British Mandate in Palestine ended, Israel declared its independence. Within hours, Palestinian Arabs were joined by forces from Jordan, Egypt, Syria, Lebanon and Iraq, who retaliated against the declaration, and so began the 1948 Arab–Israeli War. The largest army was Egyptian, but the Arab Legion under the command of King Abdullah of Transjordan was the best-equipped. That said, King Abdullah had had numerous discussions with Jews since the 1930s and went into the war merely under pressure from the general public.

Despite their numerical advantage, the Arab armies, who were without clear guidance, training, equipment or even basic food supplies, were doomed to fail. In 1949, Israel and Egypt negotiated an armistice, and after the signing of the agreement on 24 February 1949, Egypt became the first Arab state to withdraw from the war. Jordan followed. An armistice with Lebanon was signed in return for the villages Israeli troops had occupied previously and, on 20 July 1949, Syria was the last to sign an armistice agreement with Israel. Although Israel successfully defended most of its new country, it submitted to the Egyptians in Gaza and the Jordanians in the West Bank, half of Jerusalem being absorbed into Jordan.

Thousands of Palestinians stormed into these Arab-controlled areas, creating crowded refugee camps. Today, the 1948 Arab–Israeli War is referred to by many as *Al-Nakba* (The Catastrophe), in reference to an estimated 15,000 Palestinians losing their lives and a further 700,000 becoming refugees. From the end of the war onwards, the army was instructed to prevent Arab refugees from returning to their old homes. Despite Israel's ultimate victory, it came at a cost, and over 6,000 Israelis died in the war.

THE STATE OF ISRAEL AND THE SUEZ–SINAI WAR After the war, Israel set about building a state: the first Knesset was elected on 25 January 1949, and Israel became the 59th member of the UN; David Ben-Gurion was democratically elected as the first prime minister; and between 1949 and 1951, some 700,000 Jews immigrated to Israel. Between 1948 and 1951, 270 new agricultural settlements were founded and the number of kibbutzim doubled. Agricultural production grew, investments flowed in, and the Israeli economy increased 15% annually. Overall, this period saw a tremendous economic boom, as Israel established close commercial links with the United States, and reparations from Germany started coming in following the agreement signed in September 1952 in Luxembourg. Although Israel does not have a constitution, a set of basic laws governing the national jurisprudence and legislation were established during this time.

In early 1949, armistice agreements between all warring countries (except Iraq) confirmed the situation reached at the end of the war, whereby half of Jerusalem and the West Bank fell under Jordanian control. In 1950, the Law of Return was enacted granting every Jew an unconditional right to Israeli citizenship. Secret underground organisations started disbanding and consolidating around the Israel Defence Force (IDF) which, with Ben-Gurion's support, had become the only army in Israel.

The armistice failed, however, to achieve lasting peace, and security issues in Israel heightened. Tensions at the Israeli borders were rising, and curfews were imposed. On 29 October 1956, an Israeli platoon commander was responsible for the killing of 47 Palestinian men, women and children returning home late to Kfar Kassem. The massacre has remained a stumbling block in Arab–Israeli relations. The secrecy surrounding what happened and the growing role of the defence establishment in the country's affairs were interpreted by opposition groups as an attack on Israel's democracy and a change in the ethos of the state.

The same year, Egypt's prime minister, Gamal Abdul Nasser, retaliated against the US and UK after they withdrew funding from his Aswan High Dam project following Nasser's association with the Soviet Union. In his retaliation in July 1956, he nationalised the Suez Canal, ousting French and British owners from its management. Blockades on Israeli-bound cargo, a massive increase in military preparations in the Sinai Peninsula, blockades of Israeli shipping via the Straits of Tiran and the signing of a tripartite military alliance between Egypt, Syria and Jordan resulted in the IDF allied by France and Britain initiating the Suez–Sinai

War. It was only France, however, that agreed to supply Israel with arms, including aircraft and tanks, which they delivered in 1956. In the course of an eight-day campaign, the IDF succeeded in capturing the Gaza Strip and the entire Sinai Peninsula, stopping just 16km short of the Suez Canal. On 30 October, as planned, Britain and France issued an ultimatum demanding Israel and Egypt relinquish control of the Suez Canal. Egypt refused, and on 31 October Britain and France responded by bombing Egyptian military bases, an act which put them back in charge of the canal. An urgent ceasefire demand issued by both the US and Soviet Union forced British, French and Israeli forces to relent, and Israel subsequently withdrew unconditionally from the Sinai. One of the consequences of the Suez–Sinai War was the increasing presence and involvement in the Middle East of the US, which was also looking for an ally in its operations in the region, a role eventually assumed by Israel.

THE SIX DAY WAR (1967) Enraged by the losses he suffered during the Suez–Sinai War, Nasser encouraged the Palestine Liberation Organisation (PLO) to continue its raids on Jewish settlements and formed a defence alliance with Syria that began preparations for war. Israel in turn attacked the West Bank village of Samu, burning 125 homes in the process, and violated Syrian airspace, flying over Damascus. Tensions were running high and following persistent Syrian artillery attacks in the north and the reimposition of the Tiran Straits blockade, Israel made a pre-emptive strike against Egypt on 5 June 1967, decimating the Egyptian air force in 170 minutes. King Hussein of Jordan was next to attack, but within two days the Israelis had taken Jerusalem and the West Bank. The following day saw the IDF once again reach the Suez Canal and the Egyptians pushed back, essentially now out of the war. That in hand, attentions turned to Syria, which had seen the destruction of two-thirds of its air force by IDF planes. Israeli forces penetrated the Golan Heights under orders from Moshe Dayan, one of Israel's most celebrated military leaders, and on 10 June Israel and Syria signed a ceasefire agreement.

The result of the Six Day War was a need to redraw the map of the Middle East. Despite the UN Resolution 242 adopted in November 1967 and calling on Israel to withdraw from the occupied territories, the West Bank (known in Israel as Judea and Samaria), Gaza, the Sinai Peninsula, the Golan Heights and all of Jerusalem (including the Old City) were now under Israeli control and administration.

The end of the war brought with it a new reality both socially and politically, as well as internationally. Dismayed by the defeat of its allies in the region, the USSR cut diplomatic relations with Israel. The relationship between the two states was only re-established in 1988. Control over the new territories gave Israel de facto responsibility for over a million Palestinians who found themselves cut off from Jordan, previously a major market for Palestinian produce, and now effectively dependent on Israel. This period also saw Orthodox Conservative groups gain ground and push vehemently for the idea of Greater Israel. All these developments put significant pressure on the secular Zionist ideas at the foundation of the State of Israel and 1968 saw Orthodox settlers for the first time defy government orders and settle in an Arab-populated area of the occupied territories, in the city of Hebron.

THE PLO AND FATAH After the Six Day War, the Palestinian refugee situation worsened and peace in the Middle East was very far away. The UN was not comfortable with the land gained by Israel and urged its return. Israel refused, agreeing only to consider returning the land in the cause of a comprehensive peace plan. Jordan was, in the meantime, in full control of the West Bank, underplaying the Palestinian identity and nationhood. To bring the Palestinian question back on the table, Yasser Arafat and Khalil Al-Wazir founded in 1959 a military organisation turned political party: Fatah (the 'conquest' or 'opening' in Arabic). Despite its explicit anti-Israeli agenda and insurgent activities, Israel was unable to retaliate. Fatah headquarters were in Syria, unconditionally supported by the Soviet Union, which Israel was not willing to alienate. The Palestine Liberation Organisation (PLO) was formed in 1964 at a summit meeting of the Arab League in order to provide a more organised form of Palestinian nationalism than that offered by the scattered *fedayeen* or Fatah. Ahmed Shukeiri became the first chairman of the new organisation.

The Arab states were calling for the destruction of Israel, and peace talks were by no means on any agenda. Putting their support behind the PLO, they urged them to continue their spate of terrorist attacks on Israel, attacks that were made from bases in Lebanon, Jordan, Syria, the West Bank and the Gaza Strip. In 1969, Fatah leader Yasser Arafat was elected chairman of the PLO. The raids on Israel executed from within Jordan both strained the fledgling secret peace talks between King Hussein and Israel and enabled the Palestinians to create a state within a state. In 1970, a short, bloody war between the Jordanian army and the PLO's fedayeen resulted in the latter fleeing to Lebanon. The heavy losses incurred by the Palestinians have come to be known as Black September. That said, at the Arab Summit in Rabat in 1974, the PLO was recognised as the sole representative of the Palestinian people. Later that year, the PLO was granted observer status, and in 2012 Palestine itself received a 'non-member observer state' status at the UN.

THE WAR OF ATTRITION (1969) In early 1969, as a consequence of the tense atmosphere in the region after the Six Day War, skirmishes between Egyptian and Israeli forces erupted along the Suez Canal, and these soon turned into the all-out War of Attrition, as it was called by Abdul Nasser. Backed by heavy military equipment from the Soviet Union, the humiliated Egyptian army sought revenge for the Six Day War and undertook a campaign which inflicted maximum casualties on Israeli troops. In response, Israel's new prime minister Golda Meir retaliated with even more force. The following year, Anwar Sadat succeeded Nasser and hostilities ceased, with the war-weary Egyptians looking towards the possibility of a pull-out from the Sinai Peninsula.

THE YOM KIPPUR WAR (RAMADAN WAR) (1973) Peace after the War of Attrition was not to be, however, and the Egyptians, Syrians (backed by Soviet weaponry) and Israelis (backed by military funding from the US) started to prepare their armies once again. Despite being warned by King Hussein of Jordan about the imminent attack, the government of Golda Meir remained passive. On Yom Kippur, 6 October 1973, Judaism's holiest day, Egypt and Syria executed a surprise attack on Israeli forces along the east bank of the Suez Canal and in the Golan Heights. By mid-October, however, despite heavy losses, the Israelis had pushed the Syrians back out of the Golan Heights and had come within 40km of Damascus. A similar scene was playing out in Suez, whereby Israeli forces had recrossed the canal and were now stationed a mere 100km from Cairo. Soviet leader Leonid Brezhnev, fearing the decimation of the encircled Egyptian Third Army would have dire consequences on the stability of the country, issued a veiled warning to the US to get Israel to back off or reap the repercussions of a Soviet intervention. US secretary of state Henry Kissinger subsequently received President Nixon's permission to put the country on nuclear alert. The stand-off was quickly defused, and on 25 October a fragile ceasefire agreement was signed.

Israeli society was in the meantime slowly changing, and so were the Palestinians in the West Bank and in Israel itself. Radicalisation was on the rise for a number of reasons, including social and economic. Despite a moderate government formed in 1974 by Prime Minister Yitzhak Rabin with Shimon Peres as Minister of Defence, a number of conservative settler groups emerged on the scene. In 1975, the full-scale settlement in the West Bank by Gush Emunim pioneers opened a new chapter in the settlement dynamics and the relationship between settlers and the government.

One of the major successes of this period was the Entebbe operation approved by the government in July 1976. The elite IDF unit Sayeret Matkal under the command of Jonatan Netanyahu (Benjamin Netanyahu's older brother) liberated hostages from a hijacked Air France airliner, which had departed from Tel Aviv but was diverted to Uganda after a stopover in Athens. Despite the complexity of the operation, there was only one IDF casualty, Jonatan Netanyahu himself.

CAMP DAVID ACCORDS AND THE DISENGAGEMENT For two years after the war, Kissinger travelled between Israel and the Arab states looking to achieve a peace accord. Egypt was seeking to reclaim the Sinai Peninsula and was starting to open up to the idea of peace talks. In the Geneva Peace Conference in December 1973, the US, Soviet Union, Israel, Egypt, Jordan and Syria signed an accord agreeing to relinquish parts of Sinai. Back in Israel, however, Israelis were angered by Golda Meir's disengagement decision and continued to settle in great numbers in the occupied lands. In May of the following year, much of Sinai was turned over to the Egyptians, the Golan Heights border was redrawn to the pre-1967 line and Golda Meir was forced to resign. In her place, Yitzhak Rabin (Labour Party) managed to halt settlement but his successor, Menachem Begin (Likud), funded and encouraged it.

By the late 1970s, Sadat was ready to talk peace and reclaim the remaining strip of Sinai coast still under Israeli control. He journeyed to Jerusalem and, in what became known as the Camp David Accords, an Egyptian–Israeli peace treaty was signed in 1979. Both Begin and Sadat received a Nobel Peace Prize as a result. The Sinai coast was returned to Egypt and normal diplomatic relations ensued. But the rosy picture was soon to turn dark, as the Arab League expelled Egypt, and Sadat was assassinated in 1981 by Islamist fundamentalists, although relations did continue even after Sadat's death.

THE FIRST LEBANON WAR (1982) The Camp David Accords, while finally achieving peace between the Egyptians and Israelis, did nothing for the situation with Syria and the PLO. The latter continued relentless terrorist activity from within Lebanon, and in June 1982, Israel, under minister of defence Ariel Sharon, and with support from Christian Lebanese militia, invaded Lebanon, occupying southern parts of the country. During what was known in Israel as Operation Peace for Galilee, Israeli troops bombarded and eventually occupied Beirut, driving out the bulk of the PLO, who fled to Tunis.

Despite the agreement of a draft peace treaty with Lebanon, approved by the newly elected president Amin Gemayel, the Lebanon War ended in a calamity and the indirect involvement of IDF soldiers in killings inside Lebanon; in particular the Sabra and Shatila massacre and the operation Grapes of Wrath led to the creation of an active anti-war movement in Israel and the rethinking of the IDF role.

In 1983, Israel started its gradual withdrawal, while Menachem Begin resigned. Only by 2000 did Israel withdraw fully across the international border with Lebanon. As a result of the war, 670 Israeli soldiers were killed, and twice as many Arab soldiers lost their lives. The total number of dead on the Lebanese, Syrian and Palestinian side was 18,000.

THE INTIFADA AND THE GULF WAR In December 1987, the first *intifada* ('shaking off' in Arabic) occurred when Palestinians in the West Bank and Gaza Strip rioted against the occupation by Israel. It was a popular uprising, and even the PLO was surprised by the extent of what was happening. Equally, it brought with it radicalisation of young people. The world once again turned its attention to the Palestinian situation and demanded a solution. In the meantime, following Iraq's invasion of Kuwait, the Gulf War erupted. An allied coalition of Western and Arab countries led by the US managed to expel Iraq from Kuwait, but in an attempt to gain support from the Arab states, Iraq launched 39 Scud missiles at Israel, encouraged by Yasser Arafat and the Palestinians, who sided with Iraq.

THE MADRID AND OSLO ACCORDS AND THE ASSASSINATION OF YITZHAK RABIN Following the Gulf War, what looked to be a glimmer of light in the dark clouds materialised when, in July 1991, Syria, Israel (following agreement to exclude the PLO), the US, Soviet Union, Lebanon, Egypt and Jordan convened at the Madrid Conference to openly discuss peace. Negotiations soon broke down, however, with the fate of Jerusalem proving to be the breaking point. In 1993, a breakthrough was finally made when Israel – once again under Yitzhak Rabin – and the Palestinians managed to come to a secret agreement known as the Oslo Accords. The accords set the way for the newly formed Palestinian National Authority (with Yasser Arafat as its president) to take over administrative control of the Gaza Strip and West Bank. At the same time, despite opposition from other Arab countries, Jordan's King Hussein opted to sign a peace treaty with Israel, one that has remained the most stable and lasting.

The Israeli–Palestinian agreement was not well received by everyone, however, and militant extremist groups on both sides undertook a series of terrorist activities. Hamas continued attacks on Israeli civilians and, in the midst of an Israeli peace rally in Tel Aviv, Yitzhak Rabin was assassinated by Yigal Amir, an Israeli student opposed to the peace process. His death is seen by many in the country as one of the darkest events in Israel's history.

ISRAEL AND PEACE TALKS THROUGH THE 1990S Following Rabin's assassination, Benjamin Netanyahu (Likud Party) ascended to the position of prime minister and peace talks took a nosedive. The tentative negotiations that had been sparked between Israel and Syria at the Madrid Accords dissolved, and despite withdrawing Jewish settlers from Hebron as part of the Oslo Accords, Netanyahu angered Arabs by encouraging settlement in Arab East Jerusalem. The opening in 1996 of the Western Wall tunnel sparked further animosity from the city's Arab residents. In turn, terrorist attacks on Israeli civilians were relentless, and peace talks once again came to an abrupt end. Netanyahu, under pressure both from some domestic factions (there are many who strongly oppose a land-for-peace accord) and from abroad, agreed to withdraw from more of the West Bank in return for cessation of terrorist attacks. Although this went through, negotiations broke down soon afterwards, and early elections in 1999 saw Ehud Barak (Labour Party) rise to become prime minister, which was the first time since the change to the electoral system in 1996 that Israelis voted directly for a prime minister.

THE NEW MILLENNIUM During the 1990s, Israel experienced probably its most significant social change since the establishment of the state. After the collapse of the Soviet Union, approximately 800,000 people immigrated to Israel. Although aliyah, which was technically only 75% Jewish, brought with it a wealth of knowledge and skills, it tilted national politics in a more conservative direction.

Despite continuing friction between Jews and Arabs, Christian pilgrims still flocked to the Holy Land, and Pope John Paul II made a historic visit in 2000. In the same year, Israel withdrew its forces from the security zone in southern Lebanon. Controversy arose, however, over the disputed 'Shebaa Farms', a 22km² area of land both countries lay claim to. Almost as soon as the Israelis withdrew, Hezbollah, an Islamist militant group and Lebanese political party, moved in.

In September 2000, Ariel Sharon caused outrage when he visited the Temple Mount, sparking the second (known as Al-Aqsa in Arabic) intifada, although Israel claims the violence was pre-planned and his visit used as an excuse. Amid a rapidly deteriorating Israeli–Palestinian situation, and after arduous attempts to sign a peace agreement with Syria had failed, Barak called for elections, only to lose to Ariel Sharon in 2001.

ARAFAT'S DEATH AND ISRAEL'S DISENGAGEMENT FROM GAZA In 2001, Sharon announced that, although he considered Arafat to be a hindrance to the peace process, he planned to execute a full withdrawal from the Gaza Strip. Later that year, following months of heavy terrorist activity, Sharon instigated the construction of a wall around the West Bank and the IDF surrounded Arafat's Ramallah home, in effect putting him under house arrest. It wasn't until 2004, shortly before his death, that he was allowed to leave to seek medical treatment in France. In November 2004, Mahmoud Abbas stepped in as leader of the Palestine National Authority (PNA). In the months leading up to the 2005 Gaza disengagement Israel found itself divided, with many residents strongly opposed. That summer the world watched as unarmed IDF soldiers dragged Israelis from Jewish settlements in Gaza and parts of the West Bank.

THE SECOND LEBANON WAR In 2005, Sharon left Likud and formed the Kadima Party which, after Sharon's stroke, went on to win elections in 2006 headed by Ehud Olmert. Later that year saw continued skirmishes on the border with Gaza, which erupted into full-scale war when Hamas entered Israeli territory, killing two soldiers and kidnapping a third. In the two months that followed, Israel bombarded Gaza with heavy forces, killing over 200 Palestinians and decimating the infrastructure. At around the same time, Hezbollah militants from south Lebanon also crossed the border to kidnap two IDF soldiers, killing others and shelling northern Israeli towns and villages. An attack on southern Lebanon ensued and soon escalated, drawing condemnation from the international community, who accused Israel of excessive force. Approximately 1,200 Lebanese civilians lost their lives and thousands more were displaced. Residents of northern Israel spent the summer in bunkers as rockets rained down, most concentrated on Haifa. In August 2006, the UN orchestrated a ceasefire and stepped in to man southern Lebanon.

THE 2006 LEBANON WAR In July 2006, Israel once again hit international headlines when military conflict broke out following Hezbollah's firing of Katyusha rockets at northern Israeli towns. The conflict raged for over a month, during which the residents of Haifa and much of the north of the country spent most of their time underground in bomb shelters and bunkers. The devastation caused by the conflict was massive, with 1,125 Lebanese and 159 Israelis (including 40 civilians) losing their lives in the month-long war. A UN ceasefire ended the shelling on 14 August, when the residents of Haifa and northern Israel finally emerged from their shelters. Apart from the vast economic and social impact of the conflict, several events caused catastrophic environmental damage that impacted on not just Israel but also Lebanon, Turkey and Cyprus. The IDF bombing of the Jiyeh power station in Lebanon resulted in the largest-ever oil spill in the Mediterranean Sea, while Hezbollah rockets caused numerous forest fires in northern Israel, destroying acres of forest that will take decades to recover.

THE GAZA CONFLICT In 2006, Hamas won Palestinian elections by a wide margin and an Israeli-imposed blockade was placed on Gaza. In response to rocket and mortar fire from Hamas, Israel launched an air strike and ground offensive on Gaza in December 2008. In the month that followed, about 1,400 Palestinians and 13 Israelis were killed before a ceasefire agreement was reached in January 2009. After a year of relative calm, tensions once again escalated dramatically when Israeli naval forces boarded a Turkish flotilla bound for Gaza. Following repeated warnings not to breach the imposed blockade on Gaza being ignored, the Israeli forces boarded the ships and killed nine Turkish activists. They maintain they acted in self-defence upon being attacked by those on board. A second 'Freedom Flotilla' attempted to sail in the direction of Gaza in 2011 from Greece, but was stopped by the Greek authorities. A third flotilla in 2011 was intercepted by the Israeli navy and forced to dock in Ashdod. The Gaza blockade remains in place, although it is less stringent. Its relaxation in 2011 brought with it the release of Gilad Shalit, an Israeli soldier who had been captured in 2006 just outside the Gaza Strip by Hamas militants. Following numerous attempts to negotiate his release that involved countless foreign governments and dignitaries including former US president Jimmy Carter and the French government (Shalit has dual French and Israeli citizenship), he was freed in October 2011 in exchange for 1,027 Palestinian prisoners.

In July 2014, a new Gaza offensive launched by Benjamin Netanyahu lasted 50 days and cost 2,100 Palestinian lives, mostly civilians. Israel lost 67 soldiers in this conflict.

THE CURRENT SITUATION Following Ehud Olmert's resignation and the failure of the Kadima Party's successor Tzipi Livni to form a coalition government, a general election was held in February 2009. Despite gaining a majority vote, Tzipi Livni and the Kadima Party had to relinquish power to Likud with Benjamin Netanyahu at its head, again due to the inability to create a coalition. Subsequently, the security discourse has tended to dominate politics, moving further in a conservative direction. In March 2014, the right-wing Likud Party, led by Benjamin Netanyahu, who first won a seat in the Knesset back in 1988, secured an overwhelming victory in the parliamentary elections. His assertive 2014 Gaza offensive followed shortly after. In 2015, Netanyahu took a further hard-line position, sharply criticising US president Barack Obama for the rapprochement with Iran and the resulting Nuclear Deal, which saw some sanctions against the Islamic Republic being lifted. Benjamin Netanyahu was first elected as prime minister in 1996, albeit for just a brief tenure. In March 2009, he again became prime minister and was subsequently re-elected in 2013. The 2015 election results have given him increased authority and power, although he remains a controversial figure in Israel itself. Overall, the political landscape in Israel is not short on tensions. In 2016, former prime minister Ehud Olmert was convicted in a number of corruption cases and imprisoned. He was subsequently released on parole in 2017, having served half of his sentence.

Making his contribution to an eventful year for Israel, the newly elected US president Donald Trump embarked on his first foreign trip as head of state in May 2017, travelling to Saudi Arabia and from there to Israel, promising a closer relationship with Benjamin Netanyahu's government.

The security situation around the world has changed drastically in the last few years and in addition to the existing underlying tensions in the region, new concerns have emerged. In 2017, Israel withdrew embassy staff from Cairo due to security concerns, heightened since the former embassy building was attacked in 2011. The two countries nonetheless collaborate closely on controlling the situation in the Sinai. Back in Israel, May 2017 saw more clashes between Palestinians and Israeli soldiers on the Gaza border as well as in Bethlehem in a sign of support for Palestinian prisoners on hunger strike in Israeli jails. Having ultimately secured better visiting rights, the prisoners ended the 41-day protest. This comes as a positive development from the right-wing government, which is for the time being there to stay. The next Knesset elections are scheduled for November 2019.

Today, the situation in Israel remains sensitive, and if history has taught us anything it's that peace in the Middle East is, at best, tenuous. In 2017, in protest against the UNESCO designation of the Old City of Hebron as a Palestinian World Heritage Site, Israel made the decision to leave the organisation. That said, and while Israel has received negative press over the years for being a danger zone, and governments often warn their citizens against travelling there, the increase in international terrorism has prompted potential visitors to look at the country in a new light. Israel's extreme security measures and experience with terrorist attacks has encouraged massive growth in tourism numbers. With obvious exceptions throughout the Second Lebanon War, the country has seen a steady influx of tourists and pilgrims coming not only to visit Jerusalem and the holy sites but also to take advantage of the natural and archaeological sites, health resorts, spas and beaches. And with home football games against England and Ireland and Giro d'Italia plans to start a cycling race in Israel in 2018, tourism is on the up and up.

TIMELINE

17th–6th centuries BCE	**Biblical period**
c17th century	Abraham, Isaac and Jacob settle in Canaan. Famine forces the Israelites to flee to Egypt.
13th–12th century	Israelites are led from Egypt by Moses and settle in Canaan
c1020	King Saul becomes the first Jewish monarch
c1000	Jerusalem becomes capital of King David's kingdom
c960	First Temple built by King Solomon
721	Israel falls to the Assyrians (Northern Kingdom)
586	Judea falls to Babylon (Southern Kingdom). Jerusalem and the First Temple destroyed.
538–142	**Persian and Hellenistic periods**
515	Jerusalem's Temple rebuilt
332	Alexander the Great conquers Persia. Hellenistic period begins.
166	Jewish revolt against the Seleucid dynasty and beginning of the Hasmonean period
63	Jerusalem captured by the Roman general Pompey
63BCE–313CE	**Roman period**
37BCE	Herod the Great appointed King of Judea
c8BCE	Jesus born
c26CE	Jesus begins his ministry after being baptised by John the Baptist
c30	Jesus crucified

66	Jewish revolt against the Romans
70	Destruction of Jerusalem and the Second Temple
132–135	Shimon Bar Kokhba leads the Jews in the Bar Kokhba uprising against the Romans
200	New Testament established in current form
c210	Mishnah (book on Jewish oral law) completed
313–636	**Byzantine period**
c390	Talmud (commentary on the Mishnah) completed
614	Persian invasion
636–1099	**Arab period**
691	Dome of the Rock built by Caliph Abd al-Malik
1099–1291	**Crusades (Latin Kingdom of Jerusalem)**
1187–93	**Ayyubid period under Saladin following Battle of Hittin**
1291–1516	**Mamluk period**
1517–1917	**Ottoman period**
1537	Suleiman the Magnificent constructs Jerusalem's walls
1897	Zionist Organisation founded by Theodor Herzl
1909	Tel Aviv and the first kibbutz, Deganya, founded
1917	British issue Balfour Declaration to establish a 'national home' for the Jews in Palestine
1918–48	**British rule**
1922	British granted Mandate for Palestine by League of Nations
1936–39	Arab Revolt
1939	Jewish immigration limited by British White Paper
1939–45	World War II. Holocaust in Europe.
1947	UN proposes a two-state (Arab and Jewish) solution
1948	
14 May	End of British Mandate
14 May	State of Israel declared
15 May	Beginning of Arab–Israeli War following attack by Egypt, Syria, Jordan, Iraq and Lebanon
1948–52	Mass immigration from Europe and Arab countries
1949	
July	Armistice agreements signed with Egypt, Jordan, Syria and Lebanon. Jerusalem divided between Israel and Jordan.
	Israel enters UN
1956	Suez–Sinai War
1964	PLO (Palestine Liberation Organisation) formed
1967	Six Day War – Israel occupies Gaza, Sinai, West Bank, Golan Heights and Jordanian-controlled Jerusalem
1969	War of Attrition
1970	Jordan expels PLO who resettle in Lebanon
1973	Yom Kippur War
1979	Peace treaty signed between Israel and Egypt
1982	First Lebanon War
1987	First intifada; violence between Israelis and Palestinians
1994	Israel–Jordan peace treaty signed
1995	Palestinian Authority established. Israel and PLO agree to mutual recognition (Oslo Declaration of Principles). Oslo Interim Agreement signed.

1

	Israeli prime minister Yitzhak Rabin assassinated by right-wing Jewish fanatic Yigal Amir
2000	Israel withdraws from southern Lebanon. Second intifada.
2001	Ariel Sharon (Likud Party) elected prime minister
2002	Israel constructs wall around West Bank following series of suicide bombings
2004	Palestinian Authority president Yasser Arafat dies in a Paris hospital
2005	Israel carries out Disengagement Plan and withdraws Jewish settlers from Gaza and parts of West Bank
2006	
January	Ariel Sharon suffers a stroke. Ehud Olmert becomes prime minister with new Kadima Party.
26 January	Radical Islamist Hamas movement wins election in Palestinian territories
12 July–14 August	Second Lebanon War
	Gilad Shalit, an Israeli soldier captured by Hamas in Gaza
2007	
February	Hamas and Fatah agree to share power in Palestinian Unity Agreement
June	Hamas ousts Fatah from Gaza
2008	
February	Hezbollah member Imad Moughniyeh killed by car bomb in Damascus
July	Israel frees five Lebanese prisoners in exchange for the remains of two soldiers captured by Hezbollah in July 2006
December	Israel embarks on heavy air and ground offensive in Gaza in response to rocket fire on southern Israeli towns
2009	
January	A ceasefire between Hamas and Israel is achieved
February	Benjamin Netanyahu (Likud) becomes Israel's prime minister despite a majority vote going to Tzipi Livni (Kadima)
September	An Israeli air force F16 crashes in training, killing pilot Assaf Ramon, son of Ilan Ramon, Israel's first astronaut who was killed in the space shuttle *Columbia* disaster
December	Ada Yonath becomes first Israeli woman to win a Nobel Prize (in chemistry)
2010	
May	Israeli soldiers board Turkish ships attempting to break the blockade on Gaza. Nine activists are killed – both countries claim self-defence.
August	Lebanese and Israeli troops exchange fire along the border
2–5 December	The country's largest forest fire rages across Mount Carmel, killing 44 prison officers in a bus and destroying hundreds of acres of land

2011	Gilad Shalit released by Hamas in exchange for 1,027 Palestinian prisoners
2013	Likud Party led by Benjamin Netanyahu overwhelmingly wins knesset elections
2014	Gaza offensive costs 2,100 Palestinian, mostly civilian, and 67 Israeli lives
2015	Zionist Union Party established
2016	Shimon Peres, a defining political figure in Israel and Nobel Peace Prize laureate dies
2017	A truck rams into a group of soldiers in Jerusalem, killing four and injuring 17 others

GOVERNMENT AND POLITICS

The State of Israel was declared on 14 May 1948 as a parliamentary democracy. The state is headed by the president, whose role is essentially symbolic. It is in effect managed by three authorities: the legislative authority (the Knesset), the executive authority (the government) and the judiciary. Although portrayed as a secular government, issues of religion and politics often find themselves tightly interwoven, the Jewish and Palestinian and Israeli–Arab conflict constantly giving rise to internal as well as external political tensions.

THE KNESSET AND GOVERNMENT The Knesset is the country's unicameral legislative body that took its name and declared its membership as 120 based on the Knesset Hagedolah (Great Assembly), the Jewish council that convened in Jerusalem in the 5th century BCE. The Knesset members, who represent a wide range of political parties, are chosen every four years through a nationwide election. Voters (of age 18 and over) cast ballots for political parties and not individual members (although the winning party is headed by the country's prime minister) and the entire country forms one electoral constituency. Election Day is a national holiday, and Israel has seen 77–90% of registered voters casting ballots. Likud, Labour and Kadima used to dominate the votes, but the 2013 elections brought a lot of changes to the Israeli political landscape.

Kadima, a centrist party focusing on civil and secular issues, was formed by Ariel Sharon in 2005, after he left the Likud Party. Following Sharon's stroke in January 2006, Ehud Olmert became prime minister and, after an election, Kadima extended an invitation to Labour to form a coalition. This resulted in Amir Perez, the first Mizrahi Jew to lead a major party, becoming defence minister. In February 2009, following Ehud Olmert's resignation, a general election saw the country torn and frustrated as Tzipi Livni (Kadima) received the majority vote, only to be ousted by Benjamin Netanyahu and the Likud Party when she couldn't form a coalition government. It has led to questions and scepticism in Israel over the state of parliamentary voting.

There are currently ten political parties which make up the Knesset with Likud, led by Benjamin Netanyahu, holding the majority (30 seats). The Kadima Party went from the largest in the 2006 elections to the smallest in 2013 and is effectively defunct. The second-largest party is the Zionist Union Party with 24 seats. It was established in 2015 and headed by Yitzhak Herzog, chairman of the Labour Party, and Tzipi Livni who in 2013 founded liberal-oriented Hatnuah. Ultra-Orthodox parties Shas and United Torah Judaism have seven and six seats respectively. Left-wing Meretz, advocating withdrawal from the Occupied Territories, has five seats.

1

THE IDF The Israel Defence Force (IDF), often referred to simply as the Israeli army (*tzahal*) comprises conscripts, reserve and career service personnel, the bulk of which is formed by reservists. Conscription is mandatory for men and women of 18 years, men serving three years and women 21 months. Those undertaking higher education courses, in big demand by the IDF, may defer entry but will serve after qualification. After completing their service men undergo 39 days a year of reserve training until the age of 51; employers and higher education institutions are bound under law to honour positions and not penalise workers and students for missed time. Because of the long periods of compulsory conscription, the army plays a huge part in the lives of most Israelis and service is regarded as heroic and honourable. Some Israelis, such as Orthodox Jews, Israeli-Arabs, new immigrants and Bedouin, may on some occasions, that are getting less frequent with time, be exempt from the military service. Given the choice, Druze and Bedouin residents opt to enter the IDF.

Military spending forms a considerable chunk of the country's outgoings, approximately 16.5% of government expenditure, with the United States providing in the region of US$2.4 billion per year in security assistance.

ECONOMY

Since its declaration of independence in 1948 Israel has struggled to cope with several major economic challenges thrown its way: security and the IDF, the immigration of two million Jews according to the country's Law of Returns and the need to establish modern infrastructure and public services. In its earlier years, heavy financial aid from Jewish organisations across the world as well as foreign governments (principally the US) supported the country's massively expanding population and increased security issues. Despite these pressures, Israel has managed in recent years to create a stable economic foundation through extensive privatisation as well as its free-trade agreements, and today its major industrial sectors are based on the production of metal products, electronic and biomedical equipment, processed foods, chemicals, transport equipment, and software development. Two other principal exports are cut and polished diamonds (in which it is the world's leading country) and agricultural products, namely fruit and vegetables, its total export income exceeding US$54.31 billion. In recent years tourism has begun to play an important role, which despite wars and conflict recovers rapidly.

Following the Israeli–Palestinian conflicts in 2001 and 2002 and the Second Lebanon War in 2006, the country's GDP growth took a nosedive but managed to get back on course and recover quickly. In 2010, Israel's GDP reached an estimated US$217.1 billion, with a per-capita figure of US$29,500, putting it on a par with European countries such as France and Italy. It had already experienced a 0.5% GDP growth in 2009 when many other Western countries saw a decline.

Currently, Israel ranks 32nd in the world in terms of GDP per capita (US$37,915 in 2016), which is three places up from 2005. The economy is doing very well overall, and consumer spending remains high.

ENERGY Israel has a fairly diverse energy sector. Not unlike other countries, it relies heavily on fossil fuels, but this is slowly changing. The government objective is that 10% of Israel's electricity will come from renewable energy sources by 2020, up from 2.5% at present. The Ashalim project in the Negev, which is currently underway and due for completion in 2018, will become Israel's largest renewable energy park, set to meet approximately 1.6% of the country's energy requirements. The project is so ambitious that it will see the construction of the world's tallest solar tower, 250m high.

Israel purchases gas from Egypt, although supplies have in the past been disrupted. The Israeli government therefore invests intensively in gas exploration in the Mediterranean Sea. So far, the major offshore fields (Dalit, Tamar and Leviathan) have been discovered approximately 80km off the country's northern coast and Mari B off the southern coast. Dalit is still being developed, while Tamar's commercial production started in 2013, and Leviathan is expected to convert Israel into a gas exporter thanks to the planned pipeline to Brindisi in Italy.

The 254km-long Trans-Israel Pipeline (Tipline) run by EAPC (Eilat Ashkelon Pipeline Co Ltd) is the longest operational crude oil pipeline in Israel, linking Ashkelon on the Mediterranean Sea to the Red Sea at Eilat (see the piers off the coast past the Dolphin Reef). Oil shale deposits in the Negev Desert are substantial, but extraction costs are too high to start commercial drilling.

Israel does not have a civil nuclear energy sector, but construction of a plant in the Negev by 2020 is still being discussed. The fact that Israel has not signed the Nuclear Non-Proliferation Treaty (NPT) further complicates the implementation of the project. The existing Dimona nuclear facility was finished in the early 1960s with help from France, which provided the necessary core for the reactor.

PEOPLE

The Israeli population is a jigsaw puzzle of religions, cultures and traditions. Today, the country's more than eight million-strong population is divided into 75% Jews (6,335,000), 21% Arabs (1,757,000) and 4% others (370,000). The Arab population is divided into Muslim (around 17%), Christian (around 2.3%, including Catholic, Orthodox and Maronite) and Druze (1.7%).

Within this varied framework, each religion is granted judicial rights over its people as well as administration of its own holy sites. Another interesting characteristic of Israel's diverse population is its incredible growth rate, highly unusual for a developed country. Long before Israel declared independence in 1948, Jews had been immigrating to the country, and following the declaration, this increased tenfold. In the last 60 years, the Jewish population has grown from 650,000 to over eight million. In 2015, for example, there were 28,000 olim to Israel, of which 25% came from France, 24% from Ukraine, 23% from Russia and 9% from the United States.

Culturally, the country is a melting pot of different traditions where immigration has led to the emergence of strong communities even within different religious groups. Many groups and nationalities live in Israel, yet retain their strong cultural traditions, languages and ways of life. For most of the Jewish population, who are third- or fourth-generation descendants of post-World War II immigrants, their cultural affiliation is most certainly Israeli, and while each is proud of their heritage, there is an undeniable feeling of nationalism and patriotism.

JEWS Since Israel's declaration of independence (and long before it), waves of immigration, known in Hebrew as aliyah or 'ascent', saw the country's Jewish population expand enormously. Between 1948 and 1952, it more than doubled, Holocaust survivors and refugees from Arab countries forming a large percentage of the total olim. Subsequent major waves of aliyah occurred in the mid 1950s and early 1960s from North Africa and Romania (350,000 people), in the 1990s from the former USSR (900,000 people) and in 1984 and 1991, when virtually all of Ethiopia's Jews were extracted and relocated to Israel.

Today, the percentage of Israeli-born Jews (*sabras*) has reached 70%, and while there are still pockets of strong culturally independent communities, intermarriage and cultural assimilation have blended the differences, whereby 'Israeli' culture most certainly prevails. The term *sabra* is an affectionate way of referring to generations of Jews born in early 20th-century Palestine. Sabra is a desert cactus with thorny skin, but sweet and juicy inside, said to characterise the brave and frank personality of the early generations.

Within the Jewish community, levels of religious observance form the biggest separation, and communities of like-minded residents have emerged. Orthodox *Haredim*, meaning devout Jews who strongly follow religious law and tradition, form 12% of Israel's Jewish population. Jews who would describe themselves as religious and devout in their day-to-day lives with respect to keeping *kosher*, attending synagogues, abiding by religious holidays and keeping Shabbat constitute 10%, while those who consider themselves traditional, as opposed to observant of religious rites, make up 35%, and secular Jews constitute 43% of the country's Jewish population.

Israel's Jewish background reaches from the far-flung corners of the globe, but the following form the greatest numbers of the population:

Ashkenazi Meaning 'German' or 'from Germany' in old Hebrew and referring to the Jews from the Rhineland. The term relates to Jews of German and eastern European descent, including Jews who had immigrated to North America, Australia and South Africa.

Sephardi Meaning 'Spanish' or 'from Spain' in Hebrew, the term relates to Jews who trace their lineage to Spain and Portugal in the 15th century, including those who had settled and spread across the Mediterranean after being expelled.

Mizrahi This term, meaning 'Eastern', loosely defines Jews of Middle Eastern, Persian and North African descent.

Beta Israel of Ethiopia Jews of Ethiopian origin refer to themselves as Beta Israel (meaning 'House of Israel'), while in Ethiopia they are known as *Falashas*, which means 'strangers' and has in past decades assumed a stigmatised connotation of lower status. In Israel, they are simply known as Ethiopian Jews.

Their exact ancestral link to Judaism is, however, unknown. Some suggest that Beta Israel are descendants of the Jews who left the conquered Kingdom of Judah for Egypt following the destruction of the First Temple in 568BCE. The most credible theory to date is that they descended from Menilek I, the son of Queen Sheba (Makeda) and King Solomon. This lack of clarity in ancestral lineage meant that Ethiopian Jews, whose right of return was recognised only in 1975, had been treated with suspicion.

Since 2013, there have been approximately 135,000 Ethiopian Jews in Israel, having been brought from Ethiopia in two huge operations: Operation Moses in 1984 (17,000 people) and Operation Solomon in 1991 (14,000 people), which together saw over 30,000 Ethiopian Jews airlifted to Israel. After 1991, migration from Ethiopia continued, but in smaller numbers. There are still Beta Israel Jews living in Ethiopia, but how many exactly remains unknown. In 2013, the Israeli government stopped the resettlement of Ethiopian Jews, claiming that those with legitimate Jewish heritage had already emigrated. In November 2015, it nonetheless agreed to accept 9,000 Ethiopian Jews for resettlement, which is yet to be implemented.

ARABS The largest non-Jewish population in Israel is Arab (21% or 1,757,000 according to the 2016 census), and communities vary considerably in heritage and religious practice.

Muslim Arabs Not counting Bedouin Arabs, Muslims (Sunni and Shi'a) make up about 70% of Israel's Arab population. Many hold close family ties with Palestinian Arabs in the West Bank and Gaza Strip and as such classify themselves as Palestinian Arabs (although they are referred to as Israeli Arabs by the Jewish community of Israel). They do not undertake military service in the IDF and live mostly in homogeneous communities in villages, towns and cities around the Galilee, eastern coastal plain and the northern Negev. There are also large communities in cities such as Haifa, Acre and Jerusalem.

Christian Arabs Christian Arabs comprise about 9% of Israel's Arab population, the largest concentration living in the Galilean city of Nazareth and also Haifa. Despite their differences in religion many Christian Arabs still consider themselves closely affiliated to the Palestinian people and as such rarely enlist in the IDF. However, personalities such as Salim Joubran, the first non-Jewish Arab judge to preside over Israel's Supreme Court, demonstrate a certain degree of cohesiveness between them and Jewish members of society.

DRUZE Druze (page 33) communities are spread mainly across the mountainous areas of Lebanon, Syria and Israel, in the last being concentrated in the northern Golan Heights and towns and villages across the Carmel Mountain range, notably Carmel City (better known as Isfiya and Daliat Al-Carmel). In Israel, the Druze community (which today numbers some 120,000 people, approximately 2% of the total population) is officially recognised as a separate religious entity and although their culture and language are both Arabic, their religious beliefs and affiliation to Israel (many serving in the IDF with the army draft rate of around 83%) separate them from the nationalism of other Arab communities. It is an integral part of the Druze faith to serve the country in which they reside, a fact that has seen families separated by Israel's capture of the Golan Heights in 1967 fight for opposing countries. Their loyalty to Israel, peaceful way of life and renowned hospitality has earned them great respect among Jewish members of society, a fact compounded by their presence in political, public and military positions. A notable member of the Druze in Israeli politics is Amal Nasr Al-Din, who served in the Knesset between 1977 and 1988. Druze men wear identifiable white caps, moustaches and wide trousers.

BEDOUIN The term 'Bedouin' generally applies to any member of an Arabic-speaking community of desert nomads in the Middle East. Historically, these communities would migrate with the seasons, herding their cattle, sheep, goats and camels to the desert regions during the rainy season. After World War II, however, most Middle Eastern countries, Israel included, prevented this movement by consolidating their borders. Following Israel's declaration of independence and the war that ensued, most Bedouin fled or were expelled from the country, approximately 11,000 of an estimated 65,000–90,000 remaining. In the 1950s and 1960s, the Israeli government relocated almost all of the Negev's Bedouin population to an area known as the *siyag* or enclosure, a relatively infertile area in the north of the Negev Desert. Despite legally being ordered to live in assigned towns, many Bedouin still preferred to live in makeshift villages, often having permanent structures torn down. The Israeli government also imposed mandatory school attendance on Bedouin children, which led to a rise in literacy. The offshoot of enforcing this sedentary lifestyle on a nomadic people who survived on a subsistence lifestyle, however, was that unemployment rose and poverty and crime in Bedouin towns increased. They have, however, benefited from the developed medical care in the country, often serve in the IDF (renowned for their tracking skills), retain strong cultural traditions and have one of the highest birth rates in the world. There are currently an estimated 125,000 Bedouin living in the Negev.

CIRCASSIANS There are approximately 3,000 Circassians living in Israel; all concentrated in the two Galilean villages of Kfar Kama and Reyhaniye. There used to be many Circassian villages in the Golan Heights, but none has remained. Although their religious affiliation is Sunni Muslim, the Circassians descend from the northwestern Caucasus and are not Arabs. Following the Russian–Circassian War that lasted from 1763 to 1864, large numbers of Circassians were deported to the Ottoman Empire while others settled in Russia. In the Middle East, the largest communities are found in Jordan and Syria, and throughout the French Mandate of the then Syrian Golan Heights, the members of the town of Quneitra (page 256) sought a national homeland for themselves in the area (it was not granted). Like the Druze, Circassian leaders have asked to be included in mandatory IDF conscription (although only for men), have strong cultural traditions and are officially recognised as a separate religious entity. Politically, the community overwhelmingly votes for Jewish parties, and Circassians identify themselves as patriotic Israelis.

SAMARITANS See page 35.

LANGUAGE

Hebrew and Arabic are the official languages of Israel. English is compulsory at school, which, combined with the lack of international television dubbing means most Israelis speak at least some English, mostly to a high level. As a result of the huge waves of immigration over the years, in particular from the former Soviet Union, Russian is widely spoken in Israel. French is also frequently spoken, as there are increasing numbers of olim from France, while Yiddish is the main spoken language in religious Jewish communities. For more information, see pages 304–13.

RELIGION

JUDAISM Judaism is one of the world's oldest existing religions (page 7), the foundations of which are based upon monotheism; specific laws and practices; ethnic and territorial identity; messianism and its belief in a special covenant with God. It began as the ancient religion of a small nation of Hebrews, and through thousands of years of suffering, persecution, diaspora and the occasional victory, has continued to be significantly influential both as a religion and a culture. Today, Judaism has approximately 14 million adherents, half of whom live in Israel, which they consider and believe to be the Jewish homeland.

The (mis)spellings and (mis)transliterations of Hebrew, Arabic and Latin alphabets in Israel could naturally cause some confusion. Below are a few linguistic pointers to help handle the situation.

Hebrew and Arabic are Semitic languages, and both have the definitive article *the*, 'ha' and 'al' respectively, but unlike English, the article is prefixed to the word itself. In Hebrew, for example, 'Hayarden Street' means 'the Jordan Street' while 'Rosh Hashanah' means 'the head/tip [of] the year'. In transliterations, the letter after 'ha' is often capitalised (ie: HaYarden), but in Hebrew itself no change occurs. It is worth noting that neither Hebrew nor Arabic has capital letters!

Arabic *the* is 'al' or 'el', depending on how a specific word is heard and pronounced. Spoken Arabic, in particular Levantine (Lebanese, Palestinian and Syrian) is very musical which makes matters more confusing. 'Al' is nonetheless the proper transliteration – *Al-Quds* (the Sacred [one]), and certainly not as 'es', ie: Souk Khan es Zeit (Al-Zeit). Another interesting fact is that unlike Turkish or Persian, Arabic does not have a 'p' sound, thus *Pasha* is pronounced as *Basha*. Palestine is actually pronounced *Falesteen*.

The word for 'eye/source [of a water spring]' in both Hebrew and Arabic is roughly the same, but it appears as 'en', 'ain' or 'ein' (eg: En Kerem, Ein Gedi). The sound often transliterated as 'kh' in Arabic, in Hebrew is often written as 'ch'. Thus 'Ronen Chen' is not a Jewish tailor from China, but an Israeli designer, and Chaim Bialik is pronounced as 'Khaim Bialik'. The preference for transliterating 'kh' as 'ch' in Hebrew comes from the way this sound is written down in German.

The transliterations used in this book have all been standardised to ensure conformity and ease of reference, which means that there may be discrepancies with the actual signage in Israel or alternative spellings elsewhere. The frequent use of the apostrophe (ie: Me'a She'arim) has been dropped in most places for the same reason.

On a different note, it comes in handy to know that *kfar* in Hebrew means 'village' (ie: Kfar Blum), *nahal* (*wadi* in Arabic) means creek (ie: Nahal Ayun), *tel* means 'archaeological mound', while *aviv* means spring (season of the year), suggesting exactly when Tel Aviv was founded.

The core belief of Judaism is that there is only one God, something that was unusual for the time the religion was born. According to tradition, God revealed this to Abraham, the founder of the Jewish people. Jewish identity arises primarily from belonging to an ancient people and an upholding of its ancient traditions, today seen as much as a culture as a religion. The following is designed to provide a brief overview of the practices and beliefs of Jewish religion and culture, but it is important to note that rituals and practices vary within different Jewish groups (Reform, who generally have a liberal view of Judaism; Conservative, devout interpretation of Judaism; and Orthodox, rigid and fervent interpretation of Judaism, often with a negative view of modern society).

Theology Textual tradition in Judaism is rich and old, the Torah (part of the Old Testament in Christianity) forming the core of this. The Talmud (the body of Jewish civil and religious law, including commentaries on the Torah) is divided into two parts: the Mishnah (the codification of laws) and the Gemara (a commentary on the Mishnah). One of the major concepts in Judaism is that of the **covenant**, or agreement, between God and the Jewish people. The agreement states that the Jewish people acknowledge God as their one and only king, and he in return will acknowledge the Jews as his 'chosen people' and take special care of them. One of the principal goals of Judaism is the patient wait for the **Messiah**, who will free the Jews and restore justice and peace to the world.

Rituals

Circumcision At eight days old Jewish boys are circumcised by a rabbi as a symbol of belonging to the covenant between God and Abraham (who self-circumcised at age 99).

Upsherin This is the ritual first haircut for three-year-old Orthodox boys held on the festival of Lag Baomer. Their hair is cut short with the exception of two pieces at the temples known as *payot*.

Bar and Bat Mitzvah At age 13 boys and girls celebrate their entering of adulthood (Orthodox Jews do not celebrate this).

Daily prayer Jews pray three times daily: *shaharith* in the morning, *minhah* in the afternoon and *maarib* in the evening. In Conservative and Orthodox groups synagogue prayer is attended daily.

Head coverings Jewish men and boys (in Conservative or Orthodox groups) wear a skull cap known as a *kippah* or *yarmulke* in order to demonstrate their submission to a higher being, God.

Tefillin This is a ritual practised by men only and usually only by Orthodox members. The *tefillin* consists of two small boxes containing biblical scriptures which are strapped to the forehead and left arm during weekday morning prayer.

Shabbat The day of rest and the seventh day of the Jewish week, which falls on a Saturday. An observant Jew is not supposed to engage in any kind of activity on this day, starting from Friday sundown and lasting until Saturday sundown. See box, page 41.

Kosher Referring to food and drink being suitable and prepared in accordance with the Jewish religious laws *kashrut*. See pages 64–5.

Holy places The Western Wall is the single holiest place in Judaism (pages 100–1) and stands as the last remnant of the Second Temple, destroyed by the Romans. The second holiest place is the tomb of Abraham in Hebron (today's West Bank). Abraham's son Ishmael is considered the ancestor of Islam, making this also a sacred site to Muslims. There are many other holy sites in Israel including the tombs of prominent rabbis and sages in Tiberias (pages 208–9), Beit Shearim (page 202), Safed (pages 227–8), Meron (see box, page 232) and the Mount of Olives (pages 107–10).

CHRISTIANITY Christianity is the world's largest religion with an estimated two billion followers. Founded in the 1st century CE, it has at its core the teachings, miracles, Crucifixion and Resurrection of Jesus of Nazareth (see box, pages

96–7), and in effect started as a messianic orientation of Judaism. The principal texts in Christianity are the Old and New Testaments, the first four books of the latter being known as the Gospels, written 20 to 100 years after the death and Resurrection of Jesus. He is believed in Christian tradition to be the Messiah, the son of God, the 12 Apostles appointed by him during his ministry being the first to believe this.

Jesus was arrested, tried and crucified in Jerusalem under the orders of the Roman leader Pontius Pilate, because he was seen as a threat to Judaism and Roman rule in the city. Today the Church of the Holy Sepulchre in Jerusalem's Old City is revered as the holiest site in Christianity, this being the place of Jesus's Crucifixion, burial and Resurrection (Golgotha in the New Testament). The Via Dolorosa (see box, pages 96–7) marks the traditional route taken by Jesus as he carried the Cross on his back to Golgotha and has been a site of pilgrimage for hundreds of years. Other holy sites include Bethlehem in the West Bank, where Jesus is believed to have been born, Nazareth (pages 195–201) where his mother Mary received news of the Immaculate Conception, and several sites around the Sea of Galilee (pages 210–15). While the core principles remain the same, Christianity has branched off into many different denominations, the three principal ones being Roman Catholicism, Eastern Orthodoxy and Protestantism.

Roman Catholicism Perceived by many as the 'original' Christian denomination, it is today seen as separate due to the emergence (and later acceptance) of other denominations such as Eastern Orthodoxy and Protestantism. Roman Catholicism has the largest number of adherents (more than one billion) and its spiritual centre is the Vatican City in Rome. The main differences between Roman Catholicism and other denominations are its appointment of a pope as leader of the Church, the belief that saints can intercede on behalf of believers and the concept of Purgatory (a place of purification before being allowed to enter Heaven). With respect to ritualistic practices, Roman Catholicism tends to be stricter than Protestantism, with the Eucharist (also known as Mass or communion) one of the central rites, celebrated weekly. Catholic nuns, monks and priests take a vow of celibacy, and rosary beads (prayer beads), crosses and the worship of saints are other distinctive features of the denomination. Monastic orders within Roman Catholicism include Jesuits, Dominicans, Franciscans and Augustinians. The Cross of the Custody of the Holy Land, also known as the Jerusalem cross, can be frequently seen at holy sites and buildings across Israel. It was originally a Crusader symbol of Jerusalem and eventually adapted by the Franciscans. The red Greek cross in the middle with four smaller crosses, one in each quadrant, symbolise the five holy wounds of the Crucifixion of Jesus.

Protestantism With an estimated 500 million followers, Protestantism is the second-largest branch of Christianity. Because of its numerous, wide-ranging denominations it is difficult to classify it as a single religious thought. In essence, the denominations differ in how much they denounce Roman Catholicism, ranging from conservative to very liberal. Most Protestant Churches adhere to two of the biblical sacraments, baptism and communion (as opposed to seven in Roman Catholicism). Throughout history different Protestant Churches have appeared, most in the 16th century. Presbyterians owe their origins to John Calvin, John Knox and the Church of Scotland; the Church of England to King Henry VIII; the Baptists to John Smyth and the Separatists; the Anglicans and Episcopalians to the Church of England; Evangelism and Methodism to a 17th-century Protestant movement; and Lutheranism to Martin Luther, whose Reformation movement celebrated its 500-year anniversary in 2017.

Eastern Orthodoxy Also known as Orthodox Christianity, it began in the Byzantine Empire (page 8) and today numbers some 225 million adherents living predominantly in Greece, Turkey, Russia, the Caucasus and the Middle East. Its separation formed in the 11th century when a divide between Western and Eastern Christian churches materialised, Roman emperor Constantine moving the Roman capital to Constantinople. The main differences lay in opinions relating to political, religious and cultural matters, with the use of icons and the date of Easter. Despite the glimmer of reconciliation between the Eastern and Roman Catholic churches during the Crusades (page 9), there have long since been tensions between the two. Since the 1960s, however, attempts have been made to recognise and respect each other's Churches and beliefs.

Major Eastern Orthodox denominations include the Greek, Russian, Armenian and Bulgarian Orthodox churches, the Church of Alexandria, the Church of Jerusalem and the Church of America. In contrast to Roman Catholicism and Protestantism, Eastern Orthodoxy's religious authority is the Scriptures as interpreted by the Seven Ecumenical Councils, and theology and philosophical thought play a bigger role.

Maronite Church Maronite religious thought belongs to the Eastern Rite of the Catholic Church and unlike Orthodox Christianity asserts union with the Catholic tradition. Maronites are in fact the only Orthodox Christians who have not separated from the Catholic Church. The spiritual father of the denomination was Saint Maron, a Syrian hermit monk (d 410CE), as well as Saint John Maron, patriarch of Antioch (a city in ancient Syria, now in modern-day Turkey) between 685 and 707. Maronite spiritual tradition is essentially monastic, and its adherents often reside in mountainous areas, in particular Lebanon, the spiritual centre of the faith and home to the largest Maronite community. The 'Patriarch of Antioch and all the East' resides in Bkerke, the see of the Maronite Church, in Mount Lebanon. Thanks to the protection of France, the community managed to preserve its religion and customs under Ottoman rule. In Israel there are approximately 12,000 Maronites, with the majority living in the Galilee (mainly in the small town of Jish), as well as in Jerusalem, Nazareth and Haifa.

ISLAM Islam is the world's second-largest religion with over one billion followers. It is based on the teachings of the Prophet Mohammed. Although the exact date of Mohammed's birth is not known, it is believed to be either 569 or 570. Born into the Quraishi tribe, who were rulers of Mecca at that time, he was orphaned at an early age. Mohammed's father died and he was taken from his mother to be raised among the wives of Bedouins. From the age of five, Mohammed was raised by his uncle, Abu Talib.

It was, however, in the 7th century, when he was 40 years old, that Mohammed became the prophet. For Jews and Christians alike, 40 is a special number – Moses spent 40 days on the mountain and Jesus 40 days in the desert. Gabriel delivered to Mohammed a message from God, which he spent the rest of his life spreading. Three decades after his death, Mohammed's life teachings were recorded in what became the spiritual text of Islam, the Quran. Islam, which means 'submission', is based on a submission to God's will and centres on the Five Pillars of Islam: confession of faith, daily prayer, fasting during Ramadan, pilgrimage and charity.

The three most sacred sites in Islam focus on the activities of Mohammed. The holiest site in Islam is the Kaaba in Mecca (Saudi Arabia), which tradition dictates is the mosque built by Abraham. Mohammed declared Mecca to be Islam's holiest site and that it should be towards this place that all prayers are directed (*qibla*). Performing the once-in-a-lifetime pilgrimage (*hajj*) to Mecca is one of the Five Pillars of Islam, and every year thousands of Muslims congregate here. The second holiest site is Medina or 'City of the Prophet' in Saudi Arabia and marks the spot to where Mohammed fled when he was exiled from Mecca and the place where his first followers joined him. In Jerusalem, the Al-Aqsa Mosque in the Al-Haram Al-Sharif (the Noble Sanctuary, known to Jews as the Temple Mount) is third in spiritual significance and, until Mecca was declared as qibla, it was to this mosque that Muslims directed their prayers. Islamic tradition states that this is where Mohammed ascended to Heaven following the Night Journey, and that the rock housed within the Dome of the Rock bears his last footprint. The stone is also considered holy to Jews, who believe it was the site upon which Abraham prepared to sacrifice his son Isaac to God, and over which the two temples were built.

Sunni and Shi'a When Mohammed died, a battle for the leadership of Islam ensued, a battle that rages to this day and forms a fierce divide between the two denominations that emerged. The dispute over who would become *khalif* (spiritual leader) was between those who believed that Mohammed had chosen Ali, his cousin and brother-in-law, and those who claimed allegiance to Abu Bakr, Mohammed's father-in-law and good friend. Ultimately, Abu Bakr became the first of four caliphs (the anglicised version of khalif) who are attributed with the great spread of Islam in the 7th century. Today, the vast majority of Muslims are Sunni, the name associated with those who followed Abu Bakr, while those who pledged allegiance to Ali are known as Shi'a, of which there are an estimated 120 million adherents. In contrast to the denominations in Christianity and Judaism, Sunni and Shi'a Muslims refuse to acknowledge one another; a fact that to this day causes a rift across the Islamic Middle East.

DRUZE The Druze (page 27) originated from the Ismaili sect of Shi'a Islam in the 11th century and today call themselves *muwahhidun*, or monotheists for their profound belief in the one God. The Druze religion is based on the belief that Al-Hakim, a caliph of the Fatimid dynasty of Egypt, was the incarnation of God. While most Muslims believe Al-Hakim died in 1021, the Druze believe he merely disappeared and is waiting to return to the world in the golden age for true believers. It is these beliefs that set the Druze aside from other Muslims (compounded by the fact that the Quran does not seem to play a role in their religious life), and it is apparent that the religion was strongly influenced by Gnostic elements from Judaism, Christianity, Hindu and Greek belief. Although the new religion was proselytised after its creation in the 11th century, this was short-lived and from 1050 has been closed to outsiders, the religion kept to this day a well-guarded secret.

The Druze believe in many prophets whom they consider embody the spirit of monotheism – Adam, Mohammed, Abraham, Noah, John the Baptist, Jesus and Solomon – as well as in the philosophies of Socrates, Plato, Pythagoras, Aristotle and Alexander the Great. Despite their acknowledgement of all three monotheistic religions, they believe that the performing of rituals and ceremonies has caused followers to move away from what they consider the 'pure faith'. They therefore do not (with the exception of fasting during the Islamic Ramadan) undertake any ceremonies, rituals, sanctification of physical places or organised prayer sessions, believing one should pray at all times to God. That said, popular gathering places have emerged whereby members will convene to discuss matters relating to the community. In Israel, there are several such places, one of the most important being Jethro's Tomb (Nabi Shuayb) at the Horns of Hittin (page 209), where the Druze gather on 25 April.

In keeping with the air of secrecy surrounding the Druze religion, the community itself is divided into two groups: the *Al-Uqqal* or 'knowers', and *Al-Juhhal* or 'ignorant ones'. The Al-Juhhal, who form about 80% of the population, do not have access to the religious literature and generally occupy political, military or administrative roles. The Al-Uqqal on the other hand are the keepers of the religion, and men and women are considered equal in their rights to become Al-Uqqal. Under Druze tradition, it is forbidden to eat pork, smoke or drink alcohol.

BAHA'I FAITH The Baha'i faith was founded in 19th-century Persia from Babism, a religion that developed out of the Shi'a branch of Islam. It is a monotheistic religion and, although Baha'is emphasise that God is ultimately unknowable, human knowledge of God can be achieved through his messengers. In 1844, Mirza Ali Mohammed declared himself Bab, the guide to divine truth, also declaring that 19 years later an even greater manifestation would come. In 1863, Mirza Hossein Ali Nuri, who after Bab's death in 1850 took the name Baha'u'llah, declared himself as this manifestation. Not long after, the Persians began persecuting the Babi (followers of Bab), Baha'u'llah and some of his followers being spared from death and imprisoned (to this day, Baha'i followers in Iran suffer considerable persecution). Sent by the Ottomans to the Palestinian city of Acre he remained under house arrest until his death. After he died, however, it was Baha'u'llah's son Abdul-Baha' who, once released from imprisonment in 1908, travelled extensively spreading the Baha'i word. Baha'u'llah is perceived as the last in a line of messengers that include Buddha, Jesus, Krishna and Mohammed.

Today, there are around seven million Baha'is worldwide, most residing in non-Muslim countries. In Israel, Baha'ism was officially recognised as a religion in 1986. The faith has no priesthood and spiritual authority rests with elected councils known as 'Spiritual Assemblies'. The ultimate authority, however, rests with the Universal House of Justice in Haifa, Israel therefore being the centre of this far-reaching religion. Taking pride of place in the country's third-largest city, Haifa's breathtakingly beautiful Shrine of the Bab and Persian Gardens (pages 175–6) is not only a site of pilgrimage for Baha'is but attracts admirers from all religions. While this may be the grandest Baha'i shrine, the most sacred is the Shrine of Baha'u'llah just outside Acre (page 165).

Baha'i claims to be a universal religion based on unity. Its key principles are unity of God, religion and mankind, harmony between races and religions, equality of the sexes, world peace, the elimination of prejudice, a universal language, education for all and the elimination of extremes of wealth and poverty. Gambling, gossip, alcohol, homosexuality and sexual relations outside marriage are forbidden and members over the age of 15 should pray daily. Women and men are allowed to pray together, and everyone does so in the direction of Acre. The Baha'i faith is widespread and firmly established in 247 countries with religious texts translated into hundreds of languages. To find out more, visit the official website of the Baha'i faith (w *bahai.org*). There are no Baha'is resident in Israel, so any you might encounter are either volunteers from the Baha'i World Centre or tourists themselves.

SAMARITANS The Samaritans are a small religious group who claim descent from the ancient Kingdom of Israel. While figures once numbered the Samaritans at over one million people in the 4th and 5th centuries, forced conversion to Islam and Christianity as well as persecution mean there are just 600 left today. Of these, half live in Kiryat Luza, close to Mount Gerizim, just south of Nablus in the West Bank, the remainder residing in the Holon district near Tel Aviv. Mount Gerizim is the holiest site in the Samaritan faith and the site of their 6th-century BCE temple, constructed following their break from Judaism. The Samaritans broadly practise a religion similar to that of the biblical Jews, with some elements of Islam added in. They write and speak in ancient Hebrew, abide by thousands-of-years-old traditions, recognise Moses as the one prophet and have one holy book, the Pentateuch (handed down by Moses).

EDUCATION

The Israeli workforce is well educated, having received many trained professionals through immigration, and today has a literacy rate of 97.1%. Its citizens enjoy a high standard of living with an unemployment rate of 7.6%. School attendance is mandatory from age five to 16 and free until the age of 18. The school system in Israel has created its own solution to the problems of differing social and religious backgrounds by forming different institutions to suit each group: state schools which are attended by the majority; state religious schools which emphasise Jewish studies and observance; Arab and Druze schools with classes in Arabic; and private schools. Israel has many higher education institutions attended by over 200,000 students at any one time. Back in 1948, there were only two higher educational institutions: the Hebrew University of Jerusalem and the Technion, the Israel Institute of Technology in Haifa. The Weizmann Research Institute was established much later. Higher education tends to start much later than in most other Western countries on account of the prolonged time spent in the army (and the subsequent year abroad that most Israelis undertake afterwards), with men often not beginning studies until their mid to late twenties. Religious Jews attend *yeshivas*, centres of Talmudic learning. There are hundreds of yeshivas across Israel and their number has been steadily growing since Ben-Gurion allowed for the rebuilding in Israel of yeshivas that were destroyed in Europe during the Holocaust. These centres enjoy generous government spending backed up by an increasing number of students thanks to a higher birth rate among religious Jews.

CULTURE, ENTERTAINMENT AND SPORT

ART Organised art in Israel can be traced back to 1906 and the Bulgarian professor Boris Schatz, who established the Bezalel Academy of Arts and Crafts in Jerusalem, years before Israel's declaration of independence. It encouraged talented Jewish artists to immigrate to the country and proved to be instrumental in the development of the rich artistic culture there today. To this day colonies such as **Ein Hod** and **Rosh Pina** flourish, the artists ranging from painters, sculptors, photographers and ceramicists, to those specialising in more unusual crafts such as weaving, glassblowing and calligraphy. Israel's art museums are world class, and Jerusalem's **Israel Museum** (pages 110–12) and the **Tel Aviv Museum of Art** (page 138) are held in the highest esteem internationally. Israel's multi-culturalism has provided for a range of styles, genres and traditions.

MUSIC With weekly sell-out performances and record-breaking numbers of season-ticket holders, the **Israel Philharmonic Orchestra** needs little introduction. Founded in Tel Aviv in 1936 as the 'Palestine Orchestra', it often plays host to guest conductors and musicians from around the world. The **Jerusalem Symphony Orchestra**, while not quite on a par with the Israeli Philharmonic, is still highly regarded and its concerts are broadcast on Israel's classical music stations. Other esteemed orchestras include the **Haifa Symphony Orchestra**, the Ramat Gan Orchestra, the Beersheba Simfonetta and the Israeli Chamber Orchestra. The Israeli Opera Company performs in the Merkaz Leomanuyot Habama near the Tel Aviv Museum, and its repertoire includes classical compositions and modern operas.

Modern music is also big business and many young Israelis have a rather deep passion for heavy trance. Rock, jazz and classic 1970s and 1980s hits also make their way into bars and clubs (and you might even hear the odd Christmas song thrown in during July for good measure). For more information about music events, see individual chapters.

THEATRE Israeli theatre comprises both large and small theatre troupes, the **Habima Theatre** in Tel Aviv, established in 1912 by immigrants from Russia, forming the national core of theatrical performances (page 135). The mesh of cultures that immigrated to the country in the early 20th century formed a unique blend of theatre that has lasted to this day. Jerusalem and Tel Aviv play host to the greatest number of theatres and productions (many of which provide English translation) whose styles and genres span a vast range.

DANCE Dance is gaining in popularity and institutions such as the **Suzanne Dellal Centre**, **Bat Sheva Dance Troupe** and the **Israeli Ballet** have become household names. However, they are still nowhere near as well established as theatre and classical music and as such performances are less frequent.

CINEMA Israeli cinema is more developed than most would imagine and several films have made their way along the red carpets of the Cannes Film Festival and even received Academy Award nominations as best international films. Cinematographic topics tend to centre on issues close to the hearts of Israelis and Jews, such as the Holocaust, the Israeli–Palestinian conflict and the IDF. The enormous **Jerusalem Cinematheque** (w *jer-cin.org.il/en*) is the best place for film aficionados to start, with its wealth of information, eclectic programme and educational courses, while the **Spielberg Jewish Film Archive** (**w** *en.jfa.huji.ac.il*) at the Hebrew University of Jerusalem is the world's largest centre for Jewish and Israeli film material.

SPORT If you look at Israel's medal-winning record in international events, you'd be forgiven for thinking that sport doesn't feature very highly in the country. That said, the 2016 Summer Olympics in Brazil saw Israel's largest delegation to date, which brought home two bronze medals in judo. Israel received its first (and to date only) Olympic gold medal in windsurfing in 2004 – bizarrely, the medal was inadvertently stolen in a run-of-the-mill burglary and was later found discarded in woodland and returned to the athlete. Israel has an impressive, for a small country, ranking in Paralympic Games. It is 16th in the overall medal standing.

Basketball, and in particular Maccabi Tel Aviv team is very popular and during a game the streets are the quietest they ever get. To add to Israel's basketball accolades, in 2009 Omri Casspi was selected by the Sacramento Kings for the NBA

> ### THE DARKEST DAY IN OLYMPIC HISTORY
>
> On 5 September 1972, the Munich Olympics were well under way when gunmen from the Palestinian terrorist group Black September stormed the athletes' village, killing two Israelis outright and taking hostage a further nine. Just 27 years after the Holocaust, Israeli participation in the event was seen as a significant and important step towards rebuilding Jewish morale and attempting to repair relations with Germany, yet the event was to be marred forever, and seen as one of the darkest days in Israel's history. The terrorists demanded the release of over 200 Palestinian prisoners from Israeli jails and free passage for themselves out of Germany, throwing the body of wrestling coach Moshe Weinburg out of the building as grim evidence of their intentions should their demands not be met.
>
> The Tunisian ambassador and members of the Arab League offered their help to the German authorities in negotiating with the terrorists, but it was to minimal avail, Israel standing firm on its policy of not negotiating with terrorists. At one stage in the negotiations, German officials offered to personally take the places of the Israeli athletes, such was their distress and horror that harm may come to the Jewish captives in their country so soon after the end of World War II. After more than 12 hours, the terrorists requested to leave the Olympic Village and were taken by helicopter to a military airport, handcuffed to the hostages. It was around this time that mounting pressure on the International Olympic Committee finally succeeded in getting the games halted, which until then had continued, seemingly oblivious to the events unfolding. At the airport, as the terrorists and their hostages walked across the runway to a waiting aircraft, German snipers attempted unsuccessfully to pick them off, an act that was to go horribly wrong and see the immediate murder of the Israeli athletes as the terrorists turned their guns on them. The remaining hostages were inadvertently killed when a German grenade was thrown into the helicopter in which they were waiting. At the end of the shocking and tragic day 11 Israeli athletes had lost their lives. In a move seen in Israel and many countries across the world as insensitive and disrespectful, just 24 hours after the shocking day had ended, the Olympics resumed.

Draft, making him the first Israeli to play in the NBA. He has since changed teams, but continues to play in the association.

Despite their notable sporting achievements being limited to basketball, Israelis love sport in general, and particularly extreme sports, such as skydiving, scuba diving, parasailing and kitesurfing. Soccer, judo and tennis also feature highly, while golf is limited to the Caesarea golf course (page 192). Rather surprisingly, Mount Hermon has a semi-decent ski slope, although in recent years this has been somewhat lacking in snow.

In the same style as the Olympics and the Commonwealth Games, every four years Israel hosts the **Maccabiah Games** (w *maccabiah.com*), where Israeli and Jewish athletes from across the world compete in the country's biggest sporting event. The games were founded in 1932. Over 7,000 participants from across the globe competed in the 2013 games, while the 2017 tournament featured 10,000 athletes.

2

Practical Information

WHEN TO VISIT

Israel's mild winter climate and brilliant sunshine mean that visiting the Holy Land at any time is possible. However, the extreme summer heat that permeates the entire country can often make sightseeing hard and exhausting work, so if you don't plan to spend a lot of your time on the beach then spring and autumn are prime tourist times. It is important to note that while getting the opportunity to experience Israel's national holidays (in particular Yom Kippur – see box, page 44) is a wonderful insight into the culture of the country, the collection of holidays that fall around the end of September and into October see the country barely open for business. Between the holidays and Shabbat, working days during that time can be very limited and as such many shops, restaurants, museums, national parks and sites of interest may be closed.

HIGHLIGHTS

Israel is a small country whose treasure trove of appeal reaches from religious interest and profound historical and archaeological discoveries to cosmopolitan cities and a varied and rich nature. So where do you start planning a trip and what are the must-sees? **Jerusalem** should be the first stop on any trip, its Old City the jewel in the crown of a fascinating, dramatic and poignant city. On the shore of the Mediterranean Sea is **Tel Aviv**, whose fun-loving residents and secular, relaxed way of life are a unique contrast to the Holy City, while the country's third-largest city, **Haifa**, perched on the edge of Mount Carmel and with the Baha'i Gardens forming its centrepiece, is a pleasant place to spend a few days. In the far south of the country is the resort city of **Eilat**, a mesh of great hotels and watersports resting on Israel's tiny stretch of Red Sea coast. The centuries of conquest, rebellion and settlement are represented in the bewitching old cities of **Nazareth**, famed as Jesus's birthplace; **Safed**, a Jewish Holy City, centre of Kabbalah learning and home to a burgeoning artists' colony; and **Acre**, the ancient Crusader port city, with its cobbled lanes, minarets and old city walls.

Historical and archaeological sites, including **Masada**, Herod's palace perched high on a desert cliff, and **Beit Shean**, the staggering remains of a prosperous Roman city shattered by an earthquake, are but the tip of the iceberg. Apart from the enigmatic modern cities, charming old cities and profound archaeological sites, Israel is a wonderful blend of hugely varied landscapes as it tumbles from the steppes of Europe down to the arid African deserts. The calm waters of the Sea of Galilee are surrounded by the lush, green fields, small kibbutzim and gently rolling hills of the Galilee, while the wild uplands of the **Golan Heights** are dotted with picturesque Druze villages, horse ranches, jagged peaks and gushing rivers.

Forming the southern half of the country are the great deserts, at their midst the Dead Sea, the lowest point on earth and a geological marvel.

SUGGESTED ITINERARIES

LONG WEEKEND – JERUSALEM AND DEAD SEA Spend one day getting lost in Jerusalem's Old City, a second day visiting the bustling Mahane Yehuda Market, finishing off day two with a trip to the Yad Vashem Holocaust Memorial Museum. Spend the third day taking a trip down to the Dead Sea.

ONE WEEK – JERUSALEM, DEAD SEA, TEL AVIV, SEA OF GALILEE AND ACRE As above plus a day or two in Tel Aviv and Jaffa, sitting in outdoor cafés, spending an afternoon on the beach, visiting the world-class art museums and exploring Jaffa Old City. From there head northwards and spend one day in Acre Old City, the ancient Crusader port city, today home to one of the country's largest Arab populations, a famous souk and countless historical buildings, sights and museums interwoven into the maze of cobbled lanes. Spend one day visiting the beautiful lower Galilee, at its midst the twinkling Sea of Galilee whose shores are adorned with pretty villages, rolling hills and churches commemorating Jesus's miracles.

TWO WEEKS – JERUSALEM, DEAD SEA, NEGEV DESERT, TEL AVIV, HAIFA, ACRE, NAZARETH AND SEA OF GALILEE Begin in Jerusalem and spend three days exploring the Old City, Mount of Olives, museum and neighbourhoods before dropping down to the Dead Sea. Spend two days at the Dead Sea and visit the archaeological site of Masada and Ein Gedi national park oasis. Continue down to Mitzpe Ramon and spend a day or two hiking in the Ramon Crater and getting to one with nature at one of the desert eco-lodges. Make your way up to Tel Aviv and enjoy three to four days relaxing on the beach, exploring Jaffa Old City and visiting the art museums. Head northwards to Haifa and spend at least two nights in the country's third-largest city with its pretty German Colony, Baha'i Gardens and museums. Spend the next day exploring the jumble of ancient lanes and buildings in Acre Old City and enjoy a fresh fish lunch and sweets from the souk. Head east into the Galilee and visit Nazareth Old City in the morning, with an afternoon by the shore of the Sea of Galilee.

THREE WEEKS – AS ABOVE ... BUT MORE With three weeks on your hands it is recommended that you follow the above itinerary (with a couple of days spent in Eilat on the Red Sea) but take your time and add in as many of the national parks, archaeological sites and array of activities as you can. Spend at least one night in a luxury rural zimmer (page 62), delve into the nature of the lower Galilee such as Beit Shean, Gan Hashlosha and Belvoir national parks, visit the crumbling relics of great Crusader castles in the upper Galilee or even spend a day cycling around the Sea of Galilee.

ONE MONTH – AS ABOVE WITH THE GOLAN HEIGHTS If time allows, do spend at least two to three days hiking in the Golan Heights. The area is so beautiful that exploring it on foot is one of the best ways to see it. Start in the north at Mount Hermon and visit Druze villages before moving southwards. Spend one day hiking through the Yehudiya National Park and a night in one of the rural villages of the highlands.

With the exception of Yom Kippur, Shabbat or the Sabbath is the holiest day in Judaism, and as it comes around every seven days there are a lot of them. According to the Ten Commandments and the Old Testament it was on this day that God rested during his creation of the world, and so man too must rest. Shabbat is seen as one of the great Jewish institutions and even the most secular of Israelis will greet each other with '*Shabbat Shalom*', meaning 'peace on the Sabbath'. In the Jewish calendar days begin not at midnight but at sunset, and each week Shabbat begins as the sun sets on Friday evening until one hour past sundown on Saturday. Shabbat practices vary considerably. Religious Jews abstain from most activities, including work, travel, switching electricity on or off (hence automatic elevators in some hotels), cooking or answering the telephone. For observant Jews it is a day of rest, most of which is spent praying. For the secular members of society, it still entails a day off work and as public transport, offices and many businesses are closed this limits movement. In cities such as the eternally secular Tel Aviv, the dawn of Shabbat sees the bars, cafés and beaches fill to bursting as Israelis take advantage of their free time in a country that works 5½-day weeks. Jerusalem, on the other hand, sees the city all but shut down. While there are still non-Shabbat observant restaurants and bars, a large majority abide by the day of rest, and as the sun sets on Friday, a calm settles over the normally bustling streets. Needless to say, in Arab communities, life continues as normal, the Muslim holy day being Friday, when many services and businesses close, and residents attend mosque prayer services.

PUBLIC HOLIDAYS AND FESTIVALS

The dates of Israel's national holidays change yearly according to the Jewish calendar, which coincides with the Gregorian calendar every 19 years. The following table provides the dates for the forthcoming years. It is important to note that holidays run from sunset to sunset, and as such the dates listed below will in fact begin the evening before. Holidays' eves are considered the same as Fridays (see box, page 95) with respect to all opening hours listed in the guide, while holidays will correspond to Saturdays. National sites, such as national parks, close 1 hour earlier on Fridays and public holidays. On Rosh Hashanah eve, Yom Kippur eve and Passover eve, these close at 13.00. Winter and summer times also vary, depending on the site.

TOURIST INFORMATION AND TOUR OPERATORS

For those who want hassle-free, well-organised excursions around Israel, there are many extremely good (and plenty of extremely bad) tour companies offering a great number of trips. The Israel Tour Operators Association (w *israeltravel.co.il/en*) and Israel Ministry of Tourism (w *gov.il/en*) have comprehensive lists. In addition, you can find hundreds of private licensed tour guides at w israel-guides.net. The tourist office at Ben-Gurion Airport (✆ *03 9754260*) is open round the clock daily.

LOCAL TOUR OPERATORS
Bein Harim Tourism Services Ltd
✆ 03 5422000; w beinharimtours.com. Big, professional multi-lingual company offering

countless private vehicle tours around Israel as well as to Bethlehem & the West Bank, Petra in Jordan & Egypt's Sinai.

Name	Description
Hanukkah (RH)	This festival is post-biblical and commemorates the victory of the Maccabees over the Seleucid rulers of Jerusalem (pages 7–8). It is celebrated by lighting eight candles, one on each day of the festival.
Holocaust Memorial Day (NH)	Commemorating the victims of the Shoah (Hebrew for the Holocaust), there is a 2-minute siren during which all vehicles stop, and people stand in silence.
Independence Day (NH)	Yom Haatzmaut is the national day commemorating the Declaration of Independence of Israel. It was originally the day – 14 June 1948 – when the British high commissioner left Palestine.
National Memorial Day (NH)	Yom Hazikaron in Hebrew, it is the national remembrance day for fallen soldiers and victims of terrorism, enacted into Israeli law in 1963.
Pesach (Passover) and Sukkot (RH)	These festivals celebrate the Exodus, when Moses freed the enslaved Jews from Egypt and spent the subsequent 40 years wandering in the desert. Pesach (NB: pronounced as *kh*) is celebrated with a meal (or *seder*) during which symbolic food is consumed and recitations from the Haggadah (book telling the story of the Exodus) are carried out. To commemorate the suffering of the Jews in Egypt, no leavened bread or cake may be consumed and as such, *matzeh* (unleavened bread) is a major feature.
Purim (RH)	This is the jolliest of Jewish festivals, celebrated in the name of Esther, when people dress in costume, partake in a joyous meal, drink alcohol freely and often give gifts.
Rosh Hashanah (RH)	This is the Jewish New Year, which is a day of remembrance rather than celebration, when it is common to hear the *shofar* or horn being blown 100 times in accordance with biblical traditions.
Shavuot (RH)	Marks the day when Moses received the Torah and the Ten Commandments on Mount Sinai.
Yom Kippur (RH)	This is the Day of Atonement, when most Jews fast and attend synagogue. It is considered the last day on which to repent any wrongdoings and change God's judgement for the coming year.
Simchat Torah (RH)	The day marking the end of the annual cycle of weekly Torah readings.

NH = national holiday; RH = religious holiday

2018	2019	2020
2–10 Dec	22–30 Dec	10–18 Dec
27 Jan	1 May	21 Apr
18 Apr	8 May	28 Apr
17 Apr	7 May	27 Apr
Pesach 30 Mar–7 Apr	**Pesach** 19–27 Apr	**Pesach** 8–16 Apr
Sukkot 23–30 Sep	**Sukkot** 13–20 Oct	**Sukkot** 2–9 Oct
1–2 Mar	21–22 Mar	10–11 Mar
9–11 Sep	29 Sep–1 Oct	18–20 Sep
19–21 May	8–10 Jun	28–30 May
19 Sep	9 Oct	28 Sep
2 Oct	22 Oct	11 Oct

Religious and national holidays in Israel are an emotional time, where raw passions of sorrow, celebration, faith and pride emerge. Of these, there are two particular times of the year when visitors can see Israeli patriotism and the resilience of the Jewish people come to light: the holy festival of Yom Kippur and the week in which Holocaust Memorial Day, National Memorial Day and Independence Day are celebrated. Yom Kippur, or the Day of Atonement, is the holiest day in Judaism, marking the end of the 'Ten Days of Repentance'. It is a day of fasting and prayer, for many secular Jews the only day of the year they attend the synagogue. Like a scene from a movie it is a fascinating sight to behold as not a single vehicle moves, children ride bicycles down the great motorways, the sounds of pigeons flap through the normally manic streets of Tel Aviv and the television and radio stations shut down.

In contrast to the country's most religious day, Holocaust Memorial Day and, exactly one week later, National Memorial Day, are times of great sorrow, where the raw pain of the world's worst genocide and the loss of the soldiers who have died in Israel's many wars comes bubbling up. Television stations play reels of the fallen soldiers' faces, families attend memorials and the country collectively mourns. Yet come 20.00 on the eve of National Memorial Day the country erupts into an almighty celebration of independence, relief from the pain of the previous week lifted from heavy hearts. Jerusalem, Tel Aviv and towns across the country explode into a vibrant party of fireworks, folk dancing, beer swilling, dancing and raucous, family fun.

CNairways Tours 09 9520520; e info@cnairways.com; w cnairways.com. Helicopter tours across Israel. Tours for up to 4 people include the Galilee (*2hrs/US$2,800*), Jerusalem & the Dead Sea (*6hrs/US$5,500*) which includes landing on Masada & lunch & spa at the Dead Sea & a winery tour (*4hrs/US$3,500*) which includes 2 landings at vineyards.

Desert Eco Tours 08 86326477; e angela@desertecotours.com; w desertecotours.com/english. Based in Eilat, they offer a multitude of trips around the country as well as to Jordan & Egypt. Well known for their adventure excursions.

Egged Tours 03 5271212–14; e israel-4-u@eggedtours.co.il; w www.eggedtours.com. In addition to their city tours, they also arrange fantastic, reasonably priced tours around the country.

Mazada Tours 03 5444454; e info@mazadatours.com; w mazada.co.il. Arrange tours & transport to Jordan & Egypt. There are daily buses to Amman (₪300) & Cairo (₪500) & a range of tours around Israel.

Noah Tours 02 5666601; e sales@noahtours.com; w noahtours.com. Offer day & multi-day tours within Israel as well as to Jordan & Egypt.

Society for the Protection of Nature in Israel (SPNI) 03 6388683; e bela@spni.org.il; w natureisrael.org. Offer trips ranging from 1 to 4 days that centre on hiking, environmentally friendly outdoor activities & guided tours to sites of interest.

United Tours 03 6173333; e united1@netvision.net.il; w unitedtours.co.il. One of the biggest tour companies in Israel offering many 1- & 2-day coach tours.

OVERSEAS TOUR OPERATORS

Holidays to Israel have long been seen as specialist travel, with many operators focusing on religious groups. These days though, Israel is a hugely popular place for all types of traveller, so there is a wide selection of tour operators around. Many of the big-name operators include Israel in their packages & numerous independent or specialist agencies have years of experience in tours to the Holy Land.

UK

El Al Superstar Holidays 020 3204 0490; e sales@elal.co.uk; w elal.com. El Al national airlines offers packages to Israel from London & Manchester.

Issta ☎020 8202 0855, 03 7777000; w is03ta.com (Hebrew only). Offer holidays to Israel from the UK, Holland, France & Ireland. Also have cheap flight options & last-minute deals.
On the Go Tours ☎020 7371 1113; e info@ onthegotours.com; w onthegotours.com. They have offices in the USA, Canada, New Zealand & South Africa, offering group holiday packages as well as individual & tailor-made tours to destinations around Israel.
Purple Travel (Longwood Holidays) ☎020 7993 9222; w purpletravel.co.uk. British tour operator specialising in Israel, Egypt, Jordan & Morocco. They offer package & tailor-made holidays.
Travelink ☎020 8931 8000; e info@travelinkuk. com; w travelinkuk.com. Specialist UK travel agent offering flights, holidays, tours & accommodation in Israel.

US & Canada
America Israel Tours ☎877 248 8687; w americaisraeltours.com. Specialising in Christian-themed trips to Israel from North America.
Pilgrim Tours ☎800 322 0788 (USA), 610 286 0788 (Canada); e mail@pilgrimtours.com; w pilgrimtours.com. North American organisation offering affordable trips to Israel, Jordan & Egypt.
Shalom Israel Tours ☎800 763 1948; w shalomisraeltours.com. North American-based agency specialising in Jewish-themed custom tours but with many other good packages also available.
Trafalgar ☎800 352 4444; w trafalgar.com. A well-established agency offering a variety of tours, including holiday packages to Israel combined with tours to Palestine.

RED TAPE

Citizens from the following countries will be issued with a tourist visa at their port of entry, valid for up to three months (a passport valid for six months from the date of entry will need to be provided). Citizens of all other countries should contact their local Israeli consulate or Israel's Ministry of the Interior (w *mfa.gov.il*).

EUROPE Austria, Belgium, Bulgaria, Cyprus, Denmark, Estonia, Finland, France, Germany, Gibraltar, Greece, Holland, Hungary, Iceland, Ireland, Italy, Liechtenstein, Luxembourg, Malta, Monaco, Norway, Portugal, Romania, Russian Federation, San Marino, Slovenia, Spain, Sweden, Switzerland, United Kingdom.

ASIA AND AUSTRALASIA Australia, Fiji, Hong Kong, Japan, New Zealand, Philippines, Singapore, South Korea.

AFRICA Central African Republic, Lesotho, Malawi, Mauritius, South Africa, Swaziland.

THE AMERICAS Argentina, Bahamas, Barbados, Bolivia, Brazil, Canada, Chile, Colombia, Costa Rica, Dominican Republic, Ecuador, El Salvador, Guatemala, Haiti, Jamaica, Mexico, Panama, Paraguay, St Kitts & Nevis, St Lucia, Surinam, Trinidad & Tobago, United States, Uruguay.

ISRAELI STAMP Israel does not hold diplomatic relations with most Arab and predominantly Muslim countries, so Israeli citizens are not permitted to travel to such places. Moreover, foreign nationals who have an Israeli visa stamp inside their passports will be refused or find it difficult to travel to many of these countries. This is, however, less of a problem now than a few years back. Currently, on arrival to Israel visitors are issued with a slip of paper with a bar code valid for three months. This effectively replaces the visa and needs to be kept in the passport, as it is often asked for in hotels and will be required for your tax refund and eventual departure from Israel. Other than that, there will be nothing left in the passport to suggest you have visited Israel.

EXTENDING VISAS Most tourist visas are issued for three months but can be extended at the Population and Immigration Authority offices in various cities:

Eilat 2nd Flr, City Centre 2 Hatemarin St; *3450, 02 6469597; e eilat_ashrot@piba.gov.il; ☺ 08.00–noon Sun–Tue & Thu
Haifa 15 Palyam St; *3450, 02 6469547; e haifa_ashrot@piba.gov.il; ☺ 08.00–noon Sun–Tue & Thu, 13.30–17.00 Wed, 14.30–17.00 Mon
Jerusalem 1 Shlomzion Hamalka St; *3450, 02 6469523; e jerusalem_ashrot@piba.gov.il; ☺ 08.00–noon Sun–Tue & Thu, 13.30–17.00 Wed, 14.30–17.00 Mon

Tel Aviv 125 Menachem Begin St; *3450, 02 6469578; e aviv_ashrot@piba.gov.il; ☺ 08.00–noon Sun–Tue & Thu, 13.30–17.00 Wed, 14.30–17.00 Mon
Tiberias 23 Al-Khadif St; *3450, 02 6469534; ☺ 08.00–noon Sun–Tue & Thu, 13.30–17.00 Wed, 14.30–17.00 Mon

EMBASSIES Since 1967 when Israel captured East Jerusalem (and the West Bank and Gaza Strip), the UN and much of the international community has been unwilling to recognise all of Jerusalem as Israel's capital. All countries therefore maintain embassies in Tel Aviv, although a few have consulate offices in Jerusalem, Eilat and Haifa. For contact details and opening hours of Israeli embassies abroad, see w embassies.gov.il.

⊕ Australia Discount Bank Tower, 28th Flr, 23 Yehuda Halevi St, Tel Aviv; \03 6935000; e telaviv. embassy@dfat.gov.au; w israel.embassy.gov. au; ☺ 08.00–12.30 & 13.00–16.30 Mon–Thu, 08.00–13.00 Fri
⊕ Canada Canada Hse, 3/5 Nirim St, Tel Aviv; \03 6363300; e taviv@international.gc.ca; w canadainternational.gc.ca/israel; ☺ 08.00–16.30 Mon–Thu, 08.00–13.30 Fri
⊕ France Embassy: 112 Herbert Samuel St, Tel Aviv; \03 5208300; w ambafrance-il. org; ☺ 09.00–noon Mon–Fri; Consulate: 5 Paul Emil Botta St, Jerusalem; \02 6298500; w consulfrance-jerusalem.org; ☺ 09.00–noon Mon–Fri
⊕ Germany 3 Daniel Frish St, Tel Aviv; \03 6931313; e info@tel-aviv.diplo.de; w tel-aviv.diplo.de; ☺ 08.00–16.00 Mon–Thu, 08.00–12.30 Fri

⊕ Jordan 14 Abba Hillel Silver St; \03 7517722; e tel-aviv@fm.gov.jo; ☺ 09.00–15.00 Mon–Fri
⊕ South Africa Sason Hogi Tower, 17th Flr, 12 Abba Hillel St, Ramat Gan; \03 5252566; w safis. co.il; ☺ 09.00–11.30 Mon–Thu, 14.00–15.00 Wed, 09.00–11.00 Fri
⊕ UK Embassy: 192 Hayarkon St, Tel Aviv; \03 7251222; ☺ 08.00–16.00 Mon–Thu, 08.00–13.30 Fri; Consulate: 19 Nashashibi St, Jerusalem; \02 5414100; e britain.jerusalem@fco.gov.uk; ☺ 08.00–16.00 Mon–Thu, 08.00–14.00 Fri
⊕ USA Embassy: 71 Hayarkon St, Tel Aviv; \03 5197575; w il.usembassy.gov; ☺ 08.00–16.00 Mon–Thu, 08.00–13.00 Fri; Consulate: 18 Agron Rd, Jerusalem; \02 6227230; e uscongenjerusalem@ state.gov; w jru.usconsulate.gov; ☺ 08.00–16.30 Mon–Thu

GETTING THERE AND AWAY

BY AIR Ben-Gurion International Airport (TLV) (*6663, 03 9723333; w iaa.gov.il/ Rashat/en-US/Airports/BenGurion) is Israel's main international airport, although more and more charter flights now go to Ovda Airport near Eilat (\08 6363888). Tel Aviv's velvet ropes came down in 2004 to reveal a plush, new terminal that Israelis are rightly proud of. There are good bus and train transport links with Tel Aviv (page 121) and Jerusalem (page 77), and 24-hour car-rental counters can be found on the first floor of the East Gallery in the arrivals terminal. If arriving on a Saturday, the only transport from the airport before 21.00 is a taxi. Note that when leaving Israel by plane, your checked-in luggage may be checked yet again after you leave it. There will always be a notice from Israeli airport security informing you of the additional screening.

El Al is Israel's national airline and flying with this famously security-conscious company is certainly an interesting experience. Since its conception in 1949 when it flew Israel's first president Chaim Weizmann home from Switzerland on its maiden voyage, it has had security at the forefront of its management. Post 9/11, El Al, and indeed Ben-Gurion Airport as a whole, has become a model for other airlines looking to improve their security standards. They are so confident of their security measures in fact, that after you have gone through their rigorous security checks they provide passengers with metal cutlery as a reward.

Embarking on a flight with El Al, however, needs some preparation, as even the most seasoned flyers will find things work a little differently. Firstly, check-in. In most airports across the world, El Al's check-in can be found at the furthest end of the terminal, cordoned off by barriers and surrounded by a selection of burly, heavily armed airport police. Only passengers may approach the cordoned-off area and passports and tickets must be shown to even get in line. At this point an Israeli El Al staff member, clipboard in hand, will approach and begin to ask rather a lot of questions. Who do you know in Israel? Why are you going there? Plus the standard 'did you pack your own bag?' questions. With the interrogation over you will then proceed to the enormous X-ray machine into which you will heave your suitcases. More often than not, your suitcase will then undergo an intensive search and rub down with a long, wand-looking object (which is in fact an explosive detector). After check-in comes phase two. As you approach the heart-sinkingly long queue to go through security you will suddenly be ushered down a different, El Al-only (and therefore considerably shorter) channel. Once through, there is another long walk to the gate, again the furthest the airport has to offer where you will finally board the plane. Most flights go by uneventfully unless you have yet to experience often large groups of Orthodox men praying fervently in the aisles, tefillin affixed to their heads and arms (page 30). While Israelis are notorious among airline staff for not abiding by seatbelt signs, as the wheels of the plane touch down a round of applause normally erupts in recognition of the pilot.

Israel's national airline is **El Al** (✆ *03 9714942–8;* w *elal.com; code LY*) and it operates regular flights to destinations all around the world. Owing to stringent security measures, prices were always notoriously high, although increased competition on flights to Israel has meant they are now mostly on a par with other major airlines. It is important to note that El Al does not fly on Shabbat and all meals are kosher (*glatt kosher* can be ordered in advance).

Tickets All airlines offer online ticket purchasing or tickets can be booked over the phone. Alternatively, travel agencies such as Issta or Ophir Tours (page 79) offer good budget deals and last-minute flights. From the **UK**, besides the daily services operated by British Airways (up to two a day) and Israeli national airline El Al (see above), budget airline easyJet offers up to two daily direct flights from London Luton (£124 one-way) and three flights a week from London Gatwick (£116 one-way). From the rest of **Europe**, national flag carriers, such as Air France, Iberia, Lufthansa, KLM and Alitalia offer fairly pricey tickets, while several low-cost airlines including Ryanair (flights to/from Belgium, Germany, Italy from €136 one-way), Air Baltic (three flights a week from Riga to Tel Aviv from €109 one-way) and WizzAir (flights to/from **eastern Europe** from €84 one-way) offer a convenient budget alternative, including for connecting flights. From **Russia**, Aeroflot offers five direct flights to Tel Aviv from Moscow daily and can be a good connection to east Asia. Travellers coming from **Australasia** and **South America** (or countries that do not have diplomatic relations with Israel) will need to change in Asia or Europe. El Al offers regular flights from **Hong Kong**, **Beijing** and **Bangkok** (around ₪3,000 return). Delta, El Al, Israir, Continental Airlines and American Airlines run regular flights between Tel Aviv and **New York** as well as **Los Angeles** and other major airports in the **United States** and **Canada**. Apart from **Jordan** and **Egypt**, **Turkey** is the only other Middle Eastern country with relations with Israel. It is in fact one of the top Israeli holiday destinations with cheap flights to Istanbul and Antalya operated by Turkish Airlines and Pegasus. Well-priced tickets to the Greek Islands and Cyprus can easily be found, especially in summer.

Airlines

✈ **Aeroflot** \03 7951555; w aeroflot.com
✈ **Air Baltic** \+371 6700 6006; w airbaltic.com
✈ **Air Berlin** \+49 30 3434 3333;
w airberlin.com
✈ **Air Canada** \03 6072111; w aircanada.com
✈ **Air France** \03 7630870; w airfrance.com
✈ **Alitalia** \03 7960700–66; w alitalia.com
✈ **American Airlines** \03 7548400; w aa.com
✈ **Arkia** \03 6902222; w arkia.com
✈ **Austrian Airlines** \03 5135353;
w austrian.com
✈ **British Airways** \03 6061555; w ba.com
✈ **Cathay Pacific** \03 9754047;
w cathaypacific.com

✈ **Delta** \03 5138000; w delta.com
✈ **easyJet** \03 7630561; w easyjet.com
✈ **Iberia** \03 9754067; w iberia.com
✈ **Israir** \03 7955777; w israir.co.il
✈ **Jet2** \+ 44 20 3059 8336; w jet2.com
✈ **KLM** \03 7630869; w klm.com
✈ **Lufthansa** \03 9058049; w lufthansa.com
✈ **Royal Jordanian Airlines** \03 5712826;
w rj.com
✈ **SAS** \03 9669339; w flysas.com
✈ **Turkish Airlines** \03 6945927;
w turkishairlines.com

BY LAND Of its neighbours Israel only has diplomatic relations with Jordan and Egypt and therefore it is only possible to travel overland (or by any other means for that matter) between these countries. While getting to either country under your own steam is perfectly achievable, Mazada Tours (page 125) arranges buses to Amman and Cairo from both Tel Aviv and Jerusalem. The Israeli Airports Authority has detailed information on all the border crossings (w *iaa.gov.il*).

To/from Egypt Despite several border crossings with Egypt, only the **Taba border crossing** in the south of the country near Eilat is open to tourists – the **Rafah border** is closed to foreign travellers for the foreseeable future owing to its proximity to Gaza. Depending on your nationality, you might not need to apply in advance to travel to Sinai or Egypt, though you should check visa requirements in advance with your Egyptian embassy. Instead, you can obtain one at the border crossing (US$25), which is open 24 hours, seven days a week, except Yom Kippur and Eid Al-Adha. It is a modern and well-run crossing. Rental cars cannot be taken into Egypt. Egged bus 15 runs from Eilat bus station.

To/from Jordan There are two border crossings with Jordan from Israel (Jordan River crossing and Wadi Araba crossing) and one from the Palestinian Territories in the West Bank at King Hussein/Allenby Bridge. Note that it is no longer possible – unless travelling with an Israeli tour group – to obtain a Jordanian entry visa at the border. Please contact the Jordanian embassy in Tel Aviv beforehand (see box, page 296). Your passport must be valid for at least six months.

Yitzhak Rabin/Wadi Araba border crossing (\ 6300555; ⊕ 06.30–20.00 Sun–Thu & 08.00–20.00 Fri–Sat; closed Yom Kippur & 1st day of Eid Al-Adha) Since January 2016, it has no longer been possible to obtain a Jordanian entry visa at the border, unless you are travelling with an Israeli tour group. This crossing was the first border between the two countries and is used mainly for day trips to Petra and Wadi Rum. There are no buses from Eilat, but it is a short taxi ride. On the way back, ask the Israeli guard at the gate to call you a taxi. There are a few taxis on the Jordanian side that will take you to Aqaba.

Jordan River crossing (Beit Shean; \ 04 6093400; ⊕ 08.00–21.00 Sun–Thu, 08.00–20.00 Fri–Sat) This border is convenient if you're travelling in the Galilee or coming from Jerusalem and Haifa. There is a 2km no-man's-land between the two terminals, but a shuttle service now operates on both sides. There are buses to the border from Beit Shean. A single-entry two-week Jordanian visa costs 40 dirhams (US$56) and can be extended at Jordanian police stations for up to three months.

BY SEA Ferry lines have been closed due to lack of traffic for several years, but it is still possible to get on one of the increasingly popular cruises departing from Haifa's port. Cruises to and from Turkey, the Greek Islands and Italy can be arranged through **Mano Tours** (2 Paliam St, Haifa; \ 04 8606677; e main@mano.co.il; w mano. co.il) or **Caspi Shipping** (76 Haatzmaut St, Haifa; \ 04 7962080; e info@caspitours. co.il; w caspitours.co.il, Hebrew only) and leave from the rather nice **Maritime Passenger Terminal** (\ 04 8518341; w haifaport.co.il).

HEALTH   with Dr Felicity Nicholson

Israel is a modern, developed country with Western standards of health, hygiene and medical facilities. Visitors do not need to have any vaccinations to enter the country although it is advisable to be up to date on tetanus, polio, rubella, mumps and diphtheria. Hepatitis A is usually recommended as there is a moderate risk of disease. It is also advisable to get children vaccinated against measles as outbreaks have occurred primarily in Orthodox neighbourhoods of Jerusalem where vaccination is opted against. Israel is home to several highly reputable and internationally renowned hospitals, in particular Ichilov in Tel Aviv, the Hadassah Ein Kerem in Jerusalem and Soroka in Beersheba (see the relevant chapters for details). Pharmacies are commonplace, well stocked with most Western-brand medicines and have pharmacists who speak a high level of English. Superpharm is the most widely distributed chain and most cities have several branches.

TRAVEL CLINICS AND HEALTH INFORMATION A full list of current travel clinic websites worldwide is available on w istm.org. For other journey preparation information, consult w travelhealthpro.org.uk (UK) or w wwwnc.cdc.gov/travel (US). Information about various medications may be found on w netdoctor.co.uk/ travel. All advice found online should be used in conjunction with expert advice received prior to or during travel.

HEALTH TOURISM With the increasing international popularity and awareness of the medicinal effects of the Dead Sea and its products, health tourism in Israel is growing by the year. Health clinics and spas that centre on natural resources such as the Dead Sea or hot springs have been claimed to help heal a whole host of ailments (see box, page 282).

INSURANCE As with all sensible travel, insurance is most certainly a requirement, but many policies do not cover injuries sustained through acts of terrorism so be sure to check the small print of your insurance company's documents. Most insurance companies only provide emergency dental treatment so if you have any concerns, get your teeth checked before leaving home. While Israel has good dental clinics, they come at a rather hefty price.

WATER Tap water is generally safe to drink in Israel and poses no health risks. It can occasionally have a rather chlorine-like taste so if your palate doesn't approve, bottled water is widely available and inexpensive.

HEALTH RISKS

Heat-related sicknesses Israel in general doesn't pose many health risks, with the exception of travel in the desert. Temperatures can reach as high as 45°C, which combined with the intense sunshine and arid conditions, poses **dehydration** risks. Be sure to always carry plenty of water when venturing into the southern desert region and stay hydrated. A hat, strong sunscreen and sunglasses are also important to minimise the effects of the relentless sun, both in winter and summer. For more details on safety around the Dead Sea, see box, page 279.

Mosquitoes and sand flies Israel does not suffer from malaria, so no antimalarial drugs are necessary. In summer, however, mosquitoes are out in their millions and can cause infections and irritations so be sure to use strong mosquito repellent such as those containing DEET. Likewise, sand flies along coastal regions can leave sore, itchy bites so apply repellent regularly. West Nile Fever is a viral infection transmitted by Culex mosquitoes. Most infections are asymptomatic and severe disease is rare. The risk of disease for most travellers is low.

Leishmaniasis is caused by the bite of a sand fly infected with *Leishamnia donovani* species. The sand flies bite mostly at night and live predominantly in forests or jungle areas. The disease is rare in travellers, but worth avoiding. Ways to reduce the risk of bites include ensuring that beds are raised off the ground, and bed nets should be impregnated with permethrin, as the sand flies are tiny enough to get through the holes in bed nets.

Stray animals and rabies Stray cats are a major problem in Israel and although most are not tame enough to be touched, some (mainly kittens) have got used to people and beg for food in outdoor restaurants. Despite their heart-breaking plight, it is best not to touch them as a variety of pests, infections and funguses can be transferred to you. Rabies is also present in Israel, although contained almost wholly in rural areas, so be attentive when camping and do not touch stray animals. If you get bitten, scratched or licked by mammals then wash immediately with soap and water and seek advice to ensure you get the appropriate treatment. If you are travelling to more rural areas of Israel then it is worth considering having a pre-exposure course of three rabies vaccines given over about a month. This will change the post-exposure management and make it more readily available within the country. Rabies is almost 100% fatal and is a hideous way to die.

Jellyfish While Israel's jellyfish do not cause any lasting harm and are not poisonous, they can leave you with a rather painful sting and red, whip-like mark. In general, those that wash on to the shores of the Mediterranean do so in waves between the months of June and August and, for the most part, the coast is clear. The small jellyfish that occasionally appear along Eilat's Red Sea coast, however, are sting-less and can be moved gently aside so as not to harm them while swimming.

Scorpions and snakes Scorpions are found in the desert and can have a nasty, painful bite. In general, the black scorpion bites are not life-threatening, but those inflicted by the yellow scorpion can be much more severe. Either way, seek medical advice if you get bitten. Be aware when moving rocks or stones and keep shoes on, especially at night. Israel is home to several species of venomous snakes but bites are rare. Don't stick your arms or hands into cracks, crevices or under rocks and if you're camping make sure you keep the tent flaps zipped closed at all times. If you do get bitten by a snake, immobilise the limb and place a bandage over the bite. Seek medical help as soon as possible.

Women's health As in any country, women travelling in warm climates or regions where sanitation levels may be low (camping in the desert, for example) should be aware of the possibility of contracting urinary tract, bladder or yeast infections, and should take necessary medication with them. Wearing loose-fitting clothing, drinking plenty of fluids and carrying toilet paper with you are preventative measures which can be taken to avoid these complications. If you do develop a gynaecological problem, over-the-counter medications are widely available, and most hospitals have women's health departments. Tampons, sanitary towels and condoms are available in all supermarkets, mini-markets and pharmacies, although not all brands are stocked so if you use something specific be sure to take enough with you. Contraceptive pills differ from country to country, so take a supply sufficient to last you your trip.

SAFETY

In general, visitors to Israel encounter few problems. **Crime** levels are low and while petty theft and pickpocketing do occur, violent crimes are rare. The most worrying safety threat for people considering a trip to Israel is terrorism, which despite considerable improvements over recent years, is unfortunately a part of life in the country. As the security situation in Israel and the Palestinian Territories can change rapidly, it is important to check with your country's foreign office (see the following list) before setting off.

Australia w smartraveller.gov.au
Canada w travel.gc.ca
Germany w auswaertiges-amt.de
Ireland w dfa.ie
New Zealand w safetravel.govt.nz
South Africa w www.dirco.gov.za
UK w fco.gov.uk
USA w travel.state.gov

TERRORISM Compared with many countries, Israel has a higher risk of terrorism, although stringent security measures have resulted in fewer bombings. Rocket fire from the Lebanon and Gaza borders has in the past been the biggest cause

2

for concern, as several people were killed or injured in the early 2000s. After a few years of relative calm, in April 2016 a bomb exploded on a bus in Jerusalem injuring 21 people, and in January 2017 a truck rammed into a group of soldiers in Jerusalem killing four and injuring 17 others.

Despite a decrease in indiscriminate suicide bombings, it is important to understand the danger and simply be aware. Bombers target crowded areas such as transport terminals, shopping centres, restaurants, markets and nightclubs. It is important to be vigilant and stay away from establishments that do not have security guards outside – it is common to be checked with a metal detector and be asked to open bags before entering most places. As situations can change quickly, it is a good idea to monitor media outlets and always follow the instructions of Israeli authorities. It is recommended to register at your country's consulate upon arrival, especially if staying in Israel for a long time, as they will be able to inform you of any changes to security issues.

BORDERS It is advisable not to travel to the **Shebaa Farms** area and **Ghajar** along Israel's northern border with Lebanon because of ongoing military operations over the highly disputed land. While problems along other sections of the Israeli/Lebanese border are rare these days, a clash between troops in August 2010 means tensions could spark unexpectedly. That said, the ongoing war in Syria has meant that Hezbollah, the main Israeli nemesis in Lebanon, have since focused their activities in Syria fighting ISIS and anti-Bashar Al-Assad government units. At the time of writing all but essential travel to within 12km of the border with the **Gaza Strip** was strongly warned against by Israeli and foreign authorities. While a tentative ceasefire is in place between Hamas and Israel, tensions are high and the area is hugely sensitive. Because of a breach in the Gazan/Egyptian border in March 2008, **route 10** running along the Egyptian/Israeli border is closed to civilian traffic until further notice. Live **minefields** along some border areas with Lebanon, the West Bank and Gaza remain in place, so it is important not to venture off marked roads or tracks. The disputed Golan Heights too has a number of live mine areas, remnants of past wars, and it is therefore imperative to stick to designated paths (page 244).

NATURAL DISASTERS Israel is located along an active earthquake zone and while most tremors go undetected (and it has been several hundred years since the last major earthquake), scientists and meteorologists have said the country may experience larger quakes in the future. Sandstorms and flash floods in winter months can become serious dangers in the desert regions so it is important to check with local national park authorities and meteorological stations before venturing off-road.

DRIVING Statistically you are considerably more likely to come to harm driving down Israel's fast and furious motorways than in a terrorist attack, and it is important to be aware of the somewhat haphazard driving techniques many Israelis have adopted. The idea that road traffic rules only apply to others, combined with aggressive driving techniques and high speeds, sadly results in hundreds of deaths a year. Tiredness on the long, straight, monotonous roads in the desert can also lead to accidents, so pull over and rest if you feel yourself start to tire.

CULTURAL CONCERNS Religious observances can often be the cause of serious negativity, so it is important to be aware of religious and cultural taboos and respect them. Serious issues include the following:

- **Being inappropriately dressed in religious neighbourhoods**. When entering ultra-Orthodox Jewish neighbourhoods, it is important to dress conservatively. This includes women not wearing trousers. Violent reactions towards those dressed or not behaving in accordance with Orthodox Jewish traditions have been reported.
- **Inappropriate conduct in religious neighbourhoods**. Shabbat is devoutly observed and therefore no cars should be driven through ultra-Orthodox neighbourhoods during these hours (see box, page 41). The stoning of vehicles not abiding by this is commonplace. Likewise, these neighbourhoods are best avoided during the holy day of Yom Kippur.
- **Public displays of affection in religious sites**. This applies to Jewish and Muslim religious sites as well as ultra-Orthodox neighbourhoods, and applies to both heterosexual and (considerably more so) to homosexual couples. Appropriate dress in any religious site should be adhered to (see box, page 93).
- **Public conduct on religious holidays**. Fasting during both the Muslim holiday of Ramadan and the Jewish holiday of Yom Kippur is strictly followed and you should abstain from eating, or drinking alcohol (and in the case of Muslim areas during Ramadan, smoking) in public areas during these times.
- **Taking photos of military or police installations**. This is prohibited and enforced for security reasons.

WOMEN TRAVELLERS As in any country, women travelling alone can incur unwanted attention and face additional security risks. On the whole, Israel is safe for women and violent crimes are rare, but sensible precautions should be taken to ensure you have a hassle-free trip. In particular at Ben-Gurion Airport, solo female travellers can incur unwanted attention and face additional security risks. Wearing a wedding ring, dressing modestly, excercising caution if hitchhiking, staying in well-lit areas at night, letting someone know where you are going, carrying cash on you for a taxi or phone call, staying in women-only dormitories and ignoring male advances can all help avoid unwanted confrontations.

GAY/LESBIAN TRAVELLERS In recent years, Tel Aviv has well and truly established itself on the gay travel scene, and its residents and tourism board are fully embracing and encouraging this trend. The annual Gay Pride parade (page 133) attracts party-goers from around the country and the world, and there is a burgeoning nightlife scene aimed at homosexual revellers. The Tel Aviv Endless Summer is a weekend of parties, events and festivals aimed at the gay community and visitors. The city is liberal and secular, and as such it is common to see open displays of affection. The Russian-speaking gay community in Israel has its own website (w *gayisrael.org*) with information about events. It's in Russian only, but your web browser might well offer you a decent English translation.

In complete contrast is Jerusalem, whose predominantly religion-abiding residents are less used to, and therefore less tolerant of, homosexuality. While in the modern city it is sometimes fine to be openly affectionate, in religious neighbourhoods, the Old City or near any religious buildings this will not be well received, and violence has been reported in the past. In 2005, a Haredi Orthodox Jew attacked marchers on a Gay Pride parade in Jerusalem with knives, and in 2009 a gay centre was attacked in Tel Aviv by Jewish Orthodox fanatics and two teenagers were killed. In 2015, having served his ten-year sentence for the attack in 2005 (page 18), Yishai Schlissel attacked five people at the annual Gay Pride parade in Jerusalem, but no-one was killed. These sorts

TRAVELLING WITH CHILDREN

Israelis love children and having a large family is common practice, and as such your little ones will be welcomed into most venues with open arms. What many foreign parents often find a little disconcerting to begin with, however, is the tendency of complete strangers to come up and pinch cheeks, pick up, cuddle or play with children, something not accepted in many more reserved Western countries. While obvious precautions should always be taken with regards to your children, do not be alarmed by these acts as they are almost always offered in the most tender way and are purely an outpouring of affection that most Israelis, men and women alike, hold for babies and young children. Being stopped in the street and given 'helpful' advice as to whether your child should be wearing a hat, be given more water or needs a nap are also common, and while few parents appreciate advice from strangers, this is again not meant to offend.

of incidents are extremely rare, however, and Israel's government is encouraging homosexual visitors to the country. The rest of the country can be divided into either the Tel Aviv or Jerusalem category, with cities such as Haifa, Eilat and predominantly secular cities generally more respectful of homosexuality, with religious neighbourhoods and cities such as Safed, Nazareth and Acre strongly and vociferously opposed.

TRAVELLING WITH A DISABILITY Israel is a modern country and as such it is well geared towards travellers with disabilities. Increasing numbers of establishments, national parks and public transport have disabled facilities, wheelchair accessibility and assistance, and the Israeli government is working on schemes and projects to increase this number. Access Israel (w *aisrael.org*) offers detailed, up-to-date information on accessible tourism sites, hotels, tours, events, restaurants and car rental, as well as ideas on touring routes.

SECURITY CHECKLIST The following are recommendations as to how best to minimise potential problems while travelling in Israel:

- Organise a variety of ways to obtain money, for example credit cards, cash, travellers' cheques, etc.
- Make two copies of your documents (passports, insurance details, credit cards, etc). Give one set to a relative or friend at home and keep the other set with you but separate to the originals.
- Leave expensive jewellery behind to minimise the risk of theft.
- Steer clear of political demonstrations that can occasionally turn violent.
- Be vigilant in crowded areas (page 52).
- Register with your consulate upon arrival if you are planning an extended stay.
- Be prepared to undergo lengthy questioning and bag searches on arrival in and particularly departure from Israel. Your checked-in luggage may be searched without your knowing (in which case you will find a security note inside when you open it at home).
- Abide by cultural and religious traditions in certain areas.
- Avoid travel to within a 12km radius of the border with the Gaza Strip.
- Check Foreign Office warnings before leaving home.

The UK's **gov.uk** website (w *gov.uk/guidance/foreign-travel-for-disabled-people*) provides general advice and practical information for travellers with disabilities preparing for overseas travel. **Accessible Journeys** (w *disabilitytravel.com*) is a comprehensive US site written by wheelchair users who have been researching wheelchair-accessible travel full-time since 1985. There are many tips and useful contacts (including lists of travel agents on request) for slow walkers, wheelchair travellers and their families, plus informative articles, including pieces on disabled travelling worldwide. The company also organises group tours. **Global Access News** (w *globalaccessnews.com/index.htm*) provides general travel information, reviews and tips for travelling with a disability. The **Society for Accessible Travel and Hospitality** (w *sath.org*) also provides some general information.

Specialist UK-based tour operators that offer trips to Israel include: **Disabled Holidays** (w *disabledholidays.com*), **Can Be Done** (w *canbedone.co.uk*) and **Disabled Access Holidays** (w *disabledaccessholidays.com*).

- Do not venture off marked roads and footpaths to avoid live minefields and army training zones.
- Beware of flash floods in desert regions. Abide by ranger instructions, avoid ravines, narrow gorges and caves and monitor weather conditions before setting off.

WHAT TO TAKE

While there are few things that you cannot buy in Israel, prices for many products are equal to, if not more expensive than, other Western countries, and considerably more expensive than in developing countries. Shopping malls, big chain stores and vast supermarkets generally stock all the necessities you may have forgotten, but while camping and outdoor shops are well stocked, they are expensive and you're best buying any equipment before leaving home. Summers are hot and humid so bring lightweight clothing and some long-sleeved shirts and trousers, or a light shawl, for entering religious sites. Sunscreen, sunglasses and a hat are essential items whatever the time of year, especially if you're travelling in the desert region. A wet-weather jacket is a good idea during the autumn, winter and even spring months when rain is likely, and if travelling during the winter months a warm jacket and winter attire will be necessary for Jerusalem and the mountainous areas. It is also highly recommended to wear good shoes, in particular for walking around the Old City in Jerusalem or Nazareth. Stone alleyways can be slippery. Electricity is 220V and while most power sockets have three pinholes, they will usually work with standard European two-pin plugs. Plug adapters are cheap and most mini-markets and pharmacies will stock them.

MONEY, BANKING AND BUDGETING

The first currency in Israel was the Israeli lira which was introduced in the summer of 1948 and replaced in 1980 with the New Israeli Shekel (₪) (NIS), referred to simply as shekels; anything under a shekel is known as an agora (plural *agorot*). The supposedly original shekel is the Hebrew coin referred to in the Bible. There are coins of five, ten and 50 *agorot* and one, five and ten shekels as well as notes of 20, 50, 100 and 200 shekels. Exchange rates in February 2018 were US$1 = ₪3.5; £1 = ₪4.9; €1 = ₪4.4. Most major credit cards are widely accepted in stores, tour agencies, restaurants, hotels, etc, and ATMs are commonplace. Be sure to use ATMs which are specially marked as accepting international cards, since some only accept debit cards issued in Israel.

CHANGING MONEY AND TRAVELLERS' CHEQUES There is no limit on the amount of money allowed into Israel, be it in cash, travellers' cheques or credit cards. Most major currencies and travellers' cheques can be exchanged for shekels at the airport, banks, post offices, many hotels or licensed exchange booths dotted around most towns and cities. To exchange travellers' cheques, you will need to show your passport. Exchange rates vary, and you will often get the best rate from the exchange booths in city centres, but it is a good idea to shop around a little, especially if you are changing large sums. All public services such as banks and post offices are closed on Shabbat, so be sure to arrange your finances before Friday evening. At the end of your trip, it is possible to change money from shekels only at the airport. A maximum of US$500 (or equivalent in other currencies) can be changed, or up to US$5,000 if you have the receipt for the original conversion.

TIPPING AND BARGAINING In a country that tends to complain loudly about most things, it is a surprising fact that bad service is rarely reported and tips are still given to sullen staff. It is customary to tip about 12% in restaurants, cafés and sit-down bars as well as bellboys and other service providers. Tips are expected, so do not be surprised if you are gently reminded that service is not included in the bill. In general, taxi drivers are not tipped, although it is common to tell the driver to round up the fare to the nearest appropriate number (for example a ₪18 fare would be rounded to ₪20). Taxi drivers are required by law to run the meter, and those who refuse are highly likely to be overcharging you. Bargaining is standard procedure only in open markets.

VAT AND TAX RETURN Israel has a VAT rate of 17%, which the city of Eilat is exempt from thanks to its special status as a free-trade zone. The purchase must cost at least ₪400 to be eligible for a tax refund. Carry a copy of your passport with you to have the form completed in the shop, where it must be stamped, otherwise it will not be valid. To obtain VAT refunds in Tel Aviv Ben-Gurion Airport, you will need to present your completed form to the VAT Refund kiosk in the departures area before the security check. The refund amount can then be collected in cash or on credit card in the Duty Free area of the airport. Bulky goods must be shown before the security check and can then be checked-in with your other luggage. Jewellery must be presented at the desk when collecting the refund. If claiming tax back in cash, Milgam Financial Services (✆ 03 7280123; e vat.info@milgam.co.il; w milgam.co.il) charge a commission of 1.99% on the refundable amount. VAT refunds are not given on food, drinks, tobacco, electrical appliances or photography equipment.

BUDGETING Israel isn't a cheap country in which to travel and you'll find that without keeping a close eye on your expenditure, money can fly out of your pocket at a rate of knots. One of the biggest expenses is ultimately accommodation. Although the country has thankfully seen a big boom in hostels thanks to increasing numbers of independent travellers and backpackers, there is little in between these and the hugely pricey hotels. Prices tend to be around ₪80 for a dormitory bed and ₪300 for a private room. Outside of the big cities, zimmers (page 62) form the core of rural accommodation and while these are small and privately owned, they come under the luxury category and are therefore at the higher end of the price bracket (₪500–800 average). In the desert regions there are many eco-lodges and hostels that provide reasonably priced accommodation options. When booking your accommodation online do remember to state your country of origin, as non-Israelis are exempt from the 17% VAT on the accommodation bill. Food is less of a problem if you're travelling on a tighter or shoestring budget as Israeli/Arabic fast food is healthy, widely available, filling, delicious and extremely cheap (falafel costs around ₪20 and a hummus meal ₪25–40; see box, page 64) so you won't be reduced to the likes of McDonald's. For self-catering, prices are comparable with western Europe, a loaf of bread costing ₪3.45 and litre of water ₪5, for example. If you're renting a car then petrol, not the rental itself, will be your biggest expenditure. Diesel and regular petrol cost ₪6/6.02 per litre respectively. If you shop around then some petrol stations sell even cheaper diesel/95/98 for ₪5.74/5.71/7.23 respectively. Alcohol in bars and pubs is also expensive in Israel so you're best off opting for the perfectly good local Goldstar or Maccabee beers (₪22–25 for half a litre) rather than imported brands. Spirits are also pricey, and a single shot of Baileys will set you back ₪40.

Many of Israel's top archaeological and natural sites are managed by the Israel Nature and National Parks Protection Authority who offer an 'Orange Card' ticket that can save you huge amounts of money on entry. They can be purchased for ₪150 per person at any park ticket office and are valid for two weeks. Likewise, the Tel Aviv and Jerusalem city municipalities offer free guided tours around their cities, which are a good and cost-effective way to be introduced to the cities. Students and senior citizens can get discounts on entry to most sites of interest as well as on public transport (see below) by showing an international student card or identification respectively.

GETTING AROUND

Israel is wonderfully compact, making travel easy, affordable and free of draining, long-distance journeys. It is in fact possible to drive from Israel's northernmost point in the Golan Heights to the southernmost tip of Eilat on the Red Sea in about 8 hours. While public transport is good in most urban regions, travelling around areas such as the Golan Heights and Negev and Arava deserts can be arduous and time-consuming without your own wheels, so renting a car is highly recommended to get the most out of your time in these beautiful, wild and remote regions. It is important to note that, with the exception of some services in Haifa (page 171), none of Israel's public transport runs on Shabbat or religious holidays.

BY BUS Buses are the most commonly used form of public transport in Israel, and both inter- and intra-city networks are very developed. **Egged** (w egged.co.il) provides the bulk of bus lines, although some regions have their own inter-city companies (see individual chapters), eg: **Nateev Express** (w nateevexpress.com), **Superbus** (w superbus.co.il), **NTT** (w ntt-buses.com) and **Metropoline** (w metropoline. com). **Dan** (w dan.co.il/eng) for example, serves Tel Aviv and surrounding urban areas. Conditions are good, and although inter-city buses can get crowded, all are air conditioned, clean and comfortable (in particular long-distance coaches, for which seats need to be reserved). Tickets can be purchased either at ticket booths inside bus stations or from the driver. Discounts for students and senior citizens are available. Egged has recently translated its online timetable (w *egged.co.il/eng*), and it is now possible to search for routes, prices and bus numbers. Alternatively, you can search for timetables online via w bus.co.il or download the Moovit mobile phone app (w *moovitapp.com*). It is also recommended to get a RavKav travel card, which is valid on all public transport (including trains) across Israel and gives the holder an automatic 20% discount. RavKav is issued at the central bus station in Tel Aviv free of charge (page 121). Remember that Israeli bus drivers strictly observe bus stops and will not pick up or drop off passengers on request anywhere other than the designated stop.

BY TRAIN Although bus travel still forms the core of public transport, Israel's train network is growing extremely quickly and, with massive rush-hour congestion problems around all main cities, it is becoming a very popular commuter option. Routes serve only main cities such as Tel Aviv, Haifa, Acre and Nahariya as well as connecting with Jerusalem, Ben-Gurion Airport and Beersheba, but train services are particularly useful for those travelling up and down the Mediterranean coast and between Jerusalem and Tel Aviv (via the airport). Tickets can be purchased at either ticket booths or automated vending machines (also in English) at all train stations. Israel Railways has complete schedules and ticket pricing (\03 577 4000; w *rail.co.il/en*).

BY METRO Israel's one and only underground system is located in Haifa, the country's third-largest city. Designed to help residents navigate the steep geography of the city, it has five stops running between Paris Square near the port and the Central Carmel area (page 172). Two metro systems are in their fledgling development phases in Tel Aviv and Jerusalem but it will be many years before they are fully functional.

BY TAXI All major towns and cities have large numbers of taxis which can be hailed from the street, telephoned for or found at taxi ranks. Rates start at ₪11.50 and an average inter-city ride costs around ₪25. Rates increase by 25% during Shabbat and between 21.01 and 05.29. Taxi drivers almost always try to negotiate a price with foreigners and are reluctant to run the meter. Insist they use the meter or find another taxi. There is no need to tip taxi drivers, although it is common to round up.

HITCHHIKING THE ISRAELI WAY

Hitchhiking, in particular in the Golan Heights, is standard practice in Israel, and you are unlikely to see a bus stop without a small gaggle of youngsters and soldiers pointing at the floor. In contrast to most countries where a smile and a thumbs-up are your best hope of getting a free lift from a stranger, in Israel the technique is to look aloof and carefree while casually pointing at the ground with an index finger. While it needs to be said that hitchhiking always comes with certain risks, they are minimal in Israel, and you needn't worry about giving it a go. Indeed, in some of the more remote parts of the country, it may be your only option.

Stretching from Kibbutz Dan in the far north of the country to Eilat in the south, the Israel National Trail (Shvil Israel) was created to incorporate some of the most stunning natural landscapes, pristine countryside and national treasures that Israel has to offer. The entire trail is approximately 940km in length and winds its way through varied terrains with verdant, green hills rolling down to the Sea of Galilee, where the sandy Mediterranean coast sweeps through the metropolitan cities, which in turn explode into the vast, barren beauty of the Negev Desert. To undertake the entire trail takes seasoned hikers between 30 and 50 days, although cutting the Israel National Trail into bite-sized chunks is a more realistic choice and offers hikers the opportunity to experience some of the best sections. The trail is clearly marked by tri-colour markers in orange, blue and white, but good hiking maps are an essential piece of kit to have in your backpack before embarking on long sections. *Hike the Land of Israel* is an English-language guide to hiking the trail and contains 67 topographical maps as well as places to stay, what to look for and a wealth of other information. The third edition was published in 2016 and is available from major book and camping shops in Israel as well as online. There is currently a set of 16 maps that, although in Hebrew, are still usable to non-speakers, and which cost around US$20 each. There is a good forum on the official website (w *israeltrail.net*) which allows prospective hikers to chat to those who have walked the trail. Please be extremely careful with fire when hiking; the 2016 wildfires that spread from the Dead Sea to the Mediterranean are believed to have been caused by hikers.

In addition to this well-established hiking trail, the **Israel Bike Trail** (w *ibt. org.il/en*), with a similar idea in mind, is currently in the planning stage, but once completed, the route is expected to cover 1,200km across the country's varied lands.

Sherut Shared taxis, known as *sherut*, run along the main intra- and inter-city bus routes and consist of small minibuses that generally only depart when full. Their appeal is that apart from being marginally cheaper, they can be stopped anywhere along the route and often run on Shabbat, albeit charging a little more than on weekdays. The number of the bus route they correspond to is normally posted in the front window and fares are paid to the driver once the journey is under way (normally passed down the bus via the other passengers).

BY DOMESTIC FLIGHTS The country's diminutive size means that often internal flights are unnecessary and almost always more expensive than other forms of transport. Some companies do, however, offer special deals at certain times of the year so it is worth asking if you're pushed for time. It is really only worth flying between Eilat and Tel Aviv or Haifa. The following companies offer internal flights between Tel Aviv (Sde Dov and Ben-Gurion airports) and Eilat and between Haifa and Eilat.

✈ **Arkia** 📞 03 6909698; w arkia.com   ✈ **Israir** 📞 03 5109589; w israir.co.il
✈ **El Al** 📞 03 9716111; w elal.com

BY CAR If your budget runs to it, renting a car is the best way to get the most out of your trip to Israel, especially in regions where public transport is sparser.

Practical Information   GETTING AROUND   **2**

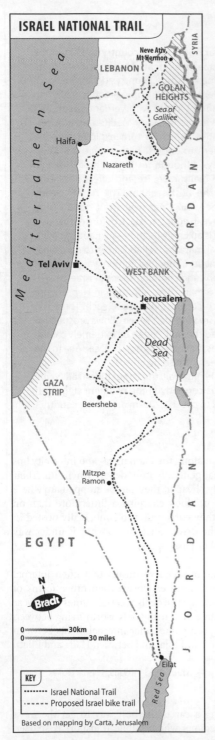

ISRAEL NATIONAL TRAIL

SYRIA
LEBANON
Neve Ativ,
Mt Hermon
GOLAN
HEIGHTS
Sea of
Galilee
Haifa
Nazareth
Mediterranean Sea
Tel Aviv
WEST BANK
Jerusalem
JORDAN
Dead
Sea
GAZA
STRIP
Beersheba
Mitzpe
Ramon
EGYPT
N
Bradt
0 ————— 30km
0 ————— 30 miles
Eilat
Red Sea

KEY
------- Israel National Trail
- - - - - Proposed Israel bike trail
Based on mapping by Carta, Jerusalem

Most international and national rental companies have offices at Ben-Gurion Airport (page 123) and in major towns and cities (see the relevant chapters). To rent a car you must be over 21 years of age and be in possession of an international driving licence. Driving in Israel is on the right-hand side of the road and most signs are in Hebrew, Arabic and English. However, the quality of English spelling can vary drastically and be a bit confusing at times, a classic example being Safed, which can be seen on road signs spelt Safed, Tsfat and Zefat. It is the law to wear seatbelts and using mobile phones while driving is strictly illegal and subject to fines of ₪500 (some car-rental companies offer hands-free sets). Carta (w carta.co.il) have produced a good English-language road map designed especially for tourists which can be bought in any branch of Steimatzky bookshops or from their website.

You can also opt to rent an RV or camper van from **Laofek Caravan & Camping Centre** (6 Hayetsira St, Petah Tikva; ☏ 03 7443344; e info@laofek. co.il; w laofek.co.il) and explore Israel at leisure. Campsites and parking for large vehicles are plentiful.

BY SEA Israel's ferry links are sadly not what they used to be and at the time of writing there are no passenger ferries into and out of Israel, but it is possible to get to Turkey, Italy and Greece aboard cruises that depart from Haifa (pages 170–1).

ACCOMMODATION

While it may appear that Israel has more than its fair share of hotels, statistics released by the government have revealed that the country is close to bursting with respect to availability of rooms versus the number of visitors. Needless to say, booking ahead in the height of summer and national holidays is highly recommended, especially in Jerusalem, Tel Aviv and Eilat. Other areas are slightly less pressured, so you are more likely to find somewhere at the last minute. In general, however, the higher-end establishments seem to fill up fastest. Rooms in hotels and private guesthouses are approximately ₪200 cheaper on weekdays and can be twice as much on national holidays. Accommodation options in this book are listed according to price from luxury to basic.

Israel has a sweeping array of accommodation types, and although luxury hotels, cabins and resorts still form the vast majority of options, an increase in backpackers means more hostels and budget choices are slowly appearing.

One of the greatest problems facing travellers is the policy of almost all zimmers and many hotels to have a two-night minimum stay on weekends; this generally doesn't apply to hostels or campsites. It is worth taking this into account when making travel plans. Having said that, there is no public transport on Shabbat, and services and attractions close early or don't open at all, so settling somewhere nice for the weekend is a good idea.

CAMPING Camping is an extremely popular activity in Israel, both with youngsters and families who pitch giant tents, set up the compulsory barbecue and settle in for a long weekend. There are many campsites dotted around the country that range from lovely grassed areas inside national parks, kibbutz and moshav to the beaches of the Sea of Galilee, Dead Sea and Mediterranean to Bedouin-style encampments in the desert. Some beaches, particularly in Eilat and along the Mediterranean where turtles nest, do not allow camping, but these will be signposted. While Israelis love being pampered, they are essentially outdoor types and all big towns and cities have camping shops aplenty and equipment is easy to come across (although expensive). Safety issues arise when pitching tents outside designated campsites, which while it is possible and legal, needs to be approached with caution. Beware of army training zones (in the desert and Golan Heights) and minefields (in the Golan Heights), which pose obvious dangers. Rabies and poisonous snakes exist in Israel, which are important safety considerations when camping. Camping prices start at ₪60 per tent, but often depend on the season and location. Expect to pay on average ₪85 per person per night.

HOSTELS For many years hostels and decent budget accommodation were extremely limited, but in recent years an increase in the number of foreign backpackers and budget travellers has resulted in countless new hostels being opened. Israel's hostels can be divided into those belonging to Hostelling International (HI) (\1 599510511; w iyha.org.il) and privately run establishments. HI hostels can be somewhat sterile and attract large groups of teenagers on organised trips but do offer good value for money and are always clean. Private hostels are more hit and miss but on the whole are full of character, reasonably priced and friendly. ILH Israel Hostels (w hostels-israel.com) is a group of 30 independent hostels spread around the country offering great budget accommodation, a good ambience and a host of other facilities. Enjoy a 5% discount on your ILH booking by collecting a discount card at the hostel where you are staying then presenting it at the next one. A dorm bed costs approximately ₪80, but some hostels charge up to ₪150 (eg: Odem in the Golan Heights). Abraham Hostels and Tours (w abrahamhostels.com) is a growing chain of hostels across Israel geared towards young and budget travellers. Booking a room with them comes with some perks, such as discounts at museums or restaurants. They also have a good network across the country and can arrange trips and tours around and about.

ZIMMER Israel has, over recent years, been overtaken by zimmer fever. The zimmer (based on the German word for 'room' and pronounced *tzimeh*) is essentially a luxury rural cabin built in the owner's back garden or on their land. There are quite literally thousands of them found in every part of the country and, while some can be slightly questionable, most are beautifully decorated, set in stunning locations and run by friendly owners as a little side earner. A key attraction of the cabin experience is the jacuzzi bath, and no self-respecting Israeli would book a zimmer without such a feature. There are approximately 1,500 zimmers across Israel; although most are rural, there are some notable and worthy city exceptions, in particular the breathtaking zimmer in Nazareth (page 198). Prices range from ₪400 per night for a standard zimmer up to ₪800 or more for something more luxurious during peak season, or over weekends and holidays.

The whole of the Galilee, in particular, is blanketed with zimmer accommodation. It is possible to drive through the small moshavim and kibbutzim and look for signs advertising good last-minute deals. Alternatively, websites such as w zimmeril.com and w zimmer.co.il have comprehensive, region-by-region listings.

HOTELS Hotel standards in Israel are high, and most major international chains are represented. National chains such as Dan, Isrotel and Rimonim also have numerous high-quality hotels dotted around the

ACCOMMODATION PRICE CODES	
Price of a double room (hotel)/dorm bed (hostel) per night:	
$$$$$	₪801+
$$$$	₪601–800
$$$	₪351–600
$$	₪201–350
$	up to ₪200

country, while the European chain Leonardo, a company affiliated to Israeli Fattal Hotels, has a hotel in most cities in Israel. In addition, spa resorts have become big business in the Holy Land, especially along the Dead Sea, as well as 'boutique hotels' found mainly in Tel Aviv that blend modern Art Deco with classy (if sometimes a little pretentious) service. Room prices can often be surprisingly high. Expect to pay approximately ₪200 less per night on weekdays.

EATING AND DRINKING

FOOD With such a diverse population, there is not really such a thing as 'Israeli food'. Culinary styles have blended together from all across the world to leave a rather eclectic mix of cuisines. Apart from the insuppressibly popular Middle Eastern fast foods such as hummus and falafel (see box, page 64), both kosher and non-kosher restaurants are well and equally represented. Tel Aviv is undoubtedly the culinary centre of the country, and is home to the bulk of non-kosher restaurants. Seafood, fish and French-style gourmet are found alongside traditional Indian food, steakhouses and Japanese sushi bars. That isn't to say that Jerusalem doesn't offer good food, as it most certainly does. While it may be considered a little more conservative than experimental, secular Tel Aviv, it has a wonderful mixture of cuisines, including some creative vegetarian places. Haifa too has benefited from its varied population and offers a wealth of great eateries. For rustic country food, juicy, succulent steaks and age-old, traditional Druze dishes the wilds of the Golan Heights, with its cattle ranches, farming communities and sweeping lands, is the best bet, while Eilat offers the complete opposite with themed restaurants and beach bars. The website w restaurants-in-israel.co.il often has vouchers and discounts for many restaurants throughout the country so it is worth checking beforehand.

DRINKS Israelis love their coffee, so you will find cafés in the most unlikely of places. The new café chain Aroma has countless shops all over the country, including in service stations. Another hugely popular Israeli invention is Cofix. Founded in 2013, it already has branches in Copenhagen, Moscow and plans to open stores in London. Cofix's marketing concept is to sell everything in the store, including good coffee, at a fixed price, originally ₪5, but currently ₪6. The company is extremely popular and ideal for budget travellers. Cofizz is a later arrival arduously trying to take a chunk of the Cofix market share; the concept is the same, and even the price is the same.

Apart from the European brews, be sure to try the strong, aromatic Arabic coffee that is hugely popular in Israel. A word of warning, however: avoid drinking the entire contents of the cup as a thick layer of coffee sediment sits at the bottom, which is rather unpleasant to swallow. In the height of the sweaty summer fruit-juice bars will freshly squeeze you your own fruity concoction and most kiosks sell inexpensive, creamy iced coffee. While Israelis aren't particularly big drinkers, they love the whole bar scene and most alcohols are represented. The local beers are Goldstar and the better known, but less popular Maccabee; both are more or less respectable, but they pale in comparison to a very good, albeit a little commercialised, Jem's or other more low-key brews of the booming craft beer industry. Beer enthusiasts will feel particularly at home in Tel Aviv,

RESTAURANT PRICE CODES	
Average price of a main course:	
$$$$$	₪121+
$$$$	₪91–120
$$$	₪71–90
$$	₪31–70
$	up to ₪30

Israel is a virtual casserole dish of cultures, traditions, culinary styles, religions and nationalities yet if you were to pinpoint the single unifying ingredient, one that has become the unofficial national symbol of the country, it would undoubtedly be the modest chickpea, or more specifically hummus and falafel. Israelis eat these two inexpensive, fast food-style dishes by the bucket load and there is unlikely to be a fridge in the country that doesn't have an emergency pot of hummus inside. The good news for visitors is that the country's cheapest food is also some of its best and no trip would be complete without several helpings of creamy hummus, puffy pitta, moist falafel, crunchy salad, crisp aubergine, roasted lamb or seasoned goat cheese. Below is a guide to the best of Israel's fast-food dishes:

HUMMUS A traditional Levantine Arab dip, hummus is a thick, creamy mixture of chickpeas, tahini, oil, lemon juice and garlic served with pitta. It can be eaten hot or cold, lumpy or smooth, and with a variety of toppings.

FALAFEL Another Levantine Arab invention of spiced chickpea balls deep-fried and served piping hot in fresh pitta with hummus, tahini and a selection of salads.

SABICH (pronounced *sabikh*) Believed to have come to Israel with Iraqi Jews, it is a huge favourite and a typical Israeli dish. Pitta is stuffed with fried aubergine, a hard-boiled egg, hummus, tahini and a variety of salads.

SHAWARMA Known in other countries as doner kebab, gyros and a whole host of other names, it consists of slow-roasted, spiced lamb on a large skewer, finely sliced and eaten in pitta with a choice of sauces and salads.

BUREKAS AND SAMBUSAK Thin pastry parcels stuffed with a variety of fillings such as spinach, potato, cheese, mushroom or meat. *Sambusak* are in effect big *burekas*.

LABNEH Soured, creamed, goat's cheese usually eaten by scooping with pitta alongside salad, hummus and chips.

TAHINI A thick sauce made from sesame seeds that is a crucial ingredient of hummus. It can also be eaten on its own with pitta.

SHAKSHOOKA While not exactly considered fast food, this cheap, filling dish is a big Israeli favourite and was brought to the country by Jews from North Africa. It involves a big mash of eggs, tomatoes, onions, green and red peppers and garlic cooked in a frying pan and eaten by scooping it on to bread.

where some bars specialising in local beer have an endless variety on offer (pages 133–4). Israel is furthermore a proud producer of excellent quality wines, regularly winning prizes at international fairs; for details of wineries, see box, page 189.

KOSHER When asked the reason behind kosher laws most Jews will reply that it is for health issues. While several of the laws do indeed seem to have positive health effects, there are others that do not appear to have relevance. In fact, the reason behind kosher laws (or kashrut) is that the Torah says it should be so. It doesn't, however, elaborate as to reasons why these laws were put in place, but for devout Jews there doesn't need to be. Kosher is upheld to varying levels of strictness in Israel, the secular barely abiding by it all, or simply eliminating pork from their diet. There is no law in Israel that restaurants need to be kosher and as such a large proportion of those in secular cities such as Tel Aviv choose the 'not' option. While seafood and meat and dairy dishes are widely available on non-kosher menus, pork is the lasting taboo and doesn't often feature in Israel.

General rules

- Certain animals cannot be eaten. Of mammals, only those that chew their cud and have cloven hooves are considered kosher. Pigs, camels and rabbits are not kosher. Marine life must have fins and scales, therefore shellfish is not kashrut. The Torah mentions only birds of prey as not being edible along with rodents, reptiles, amphibians and insects.
- Of permitted animals, they must be slaughtered in accordance with kashrut (the laws of kosher). This includes not consuming animals that have died of natural causes.
- No blood of any animal must be consumed. Slaughtered animals must be drained of blood so as to ensure none of the animal's spirit is left.
- Certain parts of an animal may not be eaten including certain fats and nerves.
- Meat and dairy must be separated. Not only can they not be eaten together, but they cannot be cooked or come into any contact with each other. A time period of 3–6 hours must elapse between consuming the two foods.
- Cooking utensils must be kept kosher. This involves reserving one set for cooking with dairy ingredients and another for preparing meat. Kitchen work surfaces, towels and even dishwashers are included in this rule.
- Wine must be made only by Shabbat-observant male Jews and all preparatory instruments must be kept kosher.

SHOPPING

One of the favourite Israeli pastimes is shopping, and more specifically shopping in malls. In fact, Israel has one of the highest mall-to-population ratios in the world. Malls and high-street shops are comparable to any western European country and you can find pretty much anything you can at home, with many major international brands represented, particularly in Jerusalem and Tel Aviv. That said, Israel, and in particular Tel Aviv, has a wonderful selection of handcrafted goods, clothes and shoes. For many tourists, however, the vibrant markets are one of the main shopping appeals, where bargaining, noise, hustle and bustle and Middle Eastern charm are the main draws.

MEDIA AND COMMUNICATIONS

POST The Israel Post Office has several branches in all major cities and towns which are denoted by their red sign with the white logo of a gazelle inside. While branches do differ slightly, most are open 08.00–noon and 15.30–18.30 Sunday, Tuesday and Thursday, 08.30–12.30 Wednesday and 08.00–noon Friday (the last includes the eve of holidays). Postal services include express, registered mail and EMS. EMS is a quick, international service that allows for tracking of parcels and includes insurance. All post offices in Israel offer a poste restante service to tourists for up to three months. They will hold post for up to 30 days and identification needs to be shown to collect mail.

TELEPHONE Telephone connections in Israel are reliable, convenient and modern, and international calls can be made with ease. Most hotel rooms come with direct-dial telephones, but be aware that prices can be grossly over-inflated. As in Europe, public phones are rarely in use or even in existence, although an old device occasionally pops up on a street corner. Mobile phones are big business in Israel, and you are unlikely to find an Israeli, young or old, who doesn't have one. You may like to purchase an Israeli SIM card for the duration of your stay. The most convenient provider at the time of writing was HOT mobile (w *hotmobile.co.il*). The ₪85 package includes a SIM-card with an Israeli number, unlimited calls and texts within Israel (no calls abroad are possible) as well as 6GB of data for a period of 30 days. The SIM can be purchased in convenience stores around the country. Within Israel, mobile numbers have eight digits starting with three indicating the service provider (eg: 050 or 052). Landline numbers have seven digits with the first two indicating the region code (eg: 02 for Jerusalem, 03 for Tel Aviv), and all seven digits have to be dialled when calling from a mobile number or a different area. There is also another type of eight-digit landline number starting with 077. Less frequent, but often used by larger organisations (eg: Egged) for customer and other enquiries are *0000 (star followed by four digits) numbers operated by Pelephone, Cellcom, Partner-Orange and Mirs. These can be dialled only within Israel. At the time of writing, there were no specific premium-rate prefixes to be avoided, unless of course you are calling about a product using a number that explicitly states additional phone charges.

INTERNET Israel is easily the most Wi-Fi-connected country you will ever travel through. There is free Wi-Fi almost everywhere, from the streets of Tel Aviv to the beaches of Eilat. You'll find it on buses, in cafés and shopping malls and even at some archaeological and camping sites. Otherwise, with an Israeli number you can connect to a 3G or 4G network with excellent coverage even in the desert.
With regards to tourist information and websites in this guide, over the past couple of years a lot of official tourist information has been gathered under the w new. goisrael.com website or regional municipal information internet pages (eg: for Acre and the Mediterranean Coast; w akko.org.il/en). Should any of the websites mentioned in this guide change within the next few years, it is most likely because they have been merged with the central hubs.

NEWSPAPERS AND MEDIA In a country with such a tumultuous existence, it is perhaps unsurprising that most Israelis are fanatical about reading, watching, listening to and talking about current affairs and the news. Because of the country's wide-ranging cultural and linguistic differences, television and newspapers offer a plethora of languages and topics to suit the eclectic mix of the population. There are currently seven daily **newspapers** published in Hebrew, the one with the highest circulation being *Yediot Aharanot* (*Latest News*), with approximately two-thirds of all newspaper readers in the country, closely followed by *Israel Hayom* (*Israel Today*). *Haaretz*, which is also published in English, is the country's oldest daily, founded in 1919, and it enjoys a wide circulation. In addition, there are several publications printed in Russian and French, as well as the internationally renowned *Jerusalem Post* (formerly the *Palestine Post*), which is published in English in Israel and North America, and in French in western Europe. *Al-Ittihad* (*The Union*) is the main Arabic-language daily, and there are also several periodicals.

Radio is an integral part of Israeli life and Kol Yisrael (Voice of Israel) is responsible for eight stations, broadcasting in countless languages and covering a wide range of genres. Radio Reka offers foreign-language broadcasts for new immigrants. One of the most popular stations is Gal Galatz, a predominantly music and news headline station run and hosted by the IDF.

In 2017, the Israeli government closed the state-funded Israel Broadcasting Authority, prompting the country's withdrawal from the Eurovision Song Contest, which it won three times over 40 years of participation. A new public broadcaster, the Israeli Public Broadcasting Corporation (abbreviated to Kan), has since taken on the IBA's role and some of its programming. Channel 2 was subsequently split into two separate channels, bringing the total number of public channels in Israel to seven. BBC and National Geographic are available as satellite options.

While freedom of the press is an important institution in Israel, military censorship is in place that deals with stories considered a threat to national security, and some stories undergo governmental screening before release.

BUYING PROPERTY

The religious significance of land in Israel, combined with a rapidly growing economy, has seen a large demand for land acquisition. The majority of property purchases tend to be new constructions, as families often live in the same house for their lifetime and pass it on to children. This is especially the case in the pretty moshavim where property rarely comes on the market. With the right amount of money (starting at €1 million) it is also possible to purchase a Bauhaus-listed property in Tel Aviv. Such opportunities are not frequent, but they do crop up from time to time. There are no restrictions on the purchase of property by foreigners, and when buying property expect to pay around 8% in fees, divided into 2% commission (which the buyer and seller both have to pay), 1% lawyer's fees and purchase tax of 3.5–4.5%. Foreign non-residents can apply for mortgages, 60% being the norm for resale properties and up to 80% on new constructions. It is important to note that homes are advertised on the basis of the number of rooms, which includes bedrooms and living rooms, and areas are expressed in *dunams*, one dunam being equivalent to 1,000m².

CULTURAL ETIQUETTE

With such a diverse population it is unsurprising that customs and etiquette are also hugely diverse within Israel. Most customs arise from religious significance but within secular society there is no strict etiquette and Israelis are, for the most part, well travelled and knowledgeable of others' customs and cultures. The following points will help you understand the culture of the country and be respectful towards its residents:

- **Greetings** Handshakes are common, although observant male Jews are not permitted to touch women; men should wait for a hand to be extended to ensure no awkward situations. Shalom is the usual greeting, although on Shabbat Shabbat Shalom is used.
- **Communication** Israelis can be very loud, direct and to the point, which other nationalities can occasionally interpret as rude or aggressive. It almost always isn't intended that way and they will appreciate honesty and directness. Touching on the arm is common and a sign of friendliness, and the use of hands and hand gestures is a major part of communication.

- **Men and women** With the exception of religiously observant communities, men and women have equal rights in Israel and women hold equal roles in government, the IDF and business. Religiously observant women rarely work outside of the home.
- **Taboos** Within the Muslim culture it is offensive to show the sole of your foot. The left hand is considered unclean so only shake hands or eat with your right hand. Dressing appropriately in religious neighbourhoods and sites (see box, page 93) is important and strictly adhered to.

BUSINESS ETIQUETTE

Israel's business etiquette can be described as casual and relaxed. Meetings are often held over food and involve a lot of chatting beforehand to get to know one another. Dress is usually casual, trousers and shirt for men, and a suit or blouse and skirt for women. Ties and suits are worn only in formal situations. If engaging in business with observant Jews, women are best advised to wear less revealing attire. Most business people speak English, first names are used, and Israeli hosts often like to take their clients or guests on a short tour of the country or at least Jerusalem.

As Hebrew is read from right to left, books, leaflets or folders will also open in reverse (from the back cover). The working week is from Sunday to Thursday, although many businesses will open Friday morning. Shabbat (see box, page 41), which runs from Friday sunset to Saturday sunset, is observed broadly, depending on the level of religious adherence, but no business will occur during that time. In Muslim communities, the holy day is all of Friday.

TRAVELLING POSITIVELY

SUSTAINABLE TRAVEL AND ECOTOURISM In a world that is seeing a huge boom in all things 'eco', where green travel and responsible holidays are a growing trend, Israel stands as one of the foremost countries in this arena. For decades schemes and projects have been in place to return the land to its former, pre-Ottoman glory and natural abundance. Today this cascades from the higher echelons of government, through the Israel Nature and National Parks Authority and their ongoing conservation efforts down to the tiny kibbutzim and moshavim that dot the countryside and which are embracing organic farming, recycling projects and a communal way of life. Israel is fast becoming one of the most popular, genuine eco-vacation spots in the world (w *ecotourism.org.il*).

The rural regions are undoubtedly the most ecologically aware, and tourism infrastructure, both for Israelis and foreigners, is plentiful. The wild desert lands, Galilee and the Golan Heights play the most pivotal roles, and small, family-run ecological cabins have become a super-trend across rural Israel, where organic food is served and horseriding and hiking opportunities are plentiful. In the deserts, several kibbutzim including Lotan (page 291), Yahel and Ketura practise sustainable living, farming and building practices, as well as offering workshops, guest accommodation, meditation and massage. Likewise, the eco-lodges scattered across the desert lands (see the Negev and Arava chapters) have been created from organic, locally sourced materials and aim to enlighten visitors about the fruits of the desert and how to live sustainably. Even in big cities, giant hotel chains are subject to strict environmental policies and engage in the use of solar power, low-flush toilets, grey water and recycling programmes. In 2010, the Israel Ministry of Tourism launched the '100 Years of Green' campaign, which aims to promote this unique side of Israel, including activities from hiking to cycling to rafting and horse- and camel-trekking. Indeed, thanks to efforts by the Keren Keyemet L'Israel (KKL) – the Jewish National Fund – the Israel National Trail (see box, page 59) is soon to have a cycling version running the entire length of the country.

The infrastructure is in place, the knowledge is there, and the potential is enormous to make Israel a true example of sustainable travel, from luxury to budget trips. The author urges you to take full advantage of these resources, to consider your options and select carefully, and to make your trip count both personally and environmentally. Tell others of your experiences, suggest ideas to hostel and restaurant owners and let them – and the tourism bureau – know what you enjoyed or would have preferred on your trip to help them in future endeavours.

CHARITIES

Israel Cat Lovers' Society w isracat.org.il/english. Feral street cats are a major problem in Israel's cities & their numbers increase exponentially every year. The CWSI is one of the biggest animal welfare institutions in the country committed to educating people, rescuing, neutering & caring for feral or unwanted cats. In 2004, during Israel's disengagement from Gaza & parts of the West Bank, thousands of street cats that survived on handouts or scavenging in rubbish bins were left as Jewish settlers moved out. In 2016, they also endeavoured to save pet animals fleeing the Haifa fires. The CWSI lobbied the government for access to the Gaza Strip & went in to capture hundreds of animals. Today they reside in a shelter in Hadera, & as most cannot be rehomed, will remain cared for there. Visitors can volunteer their time at the shelter, raise awareness in their home countries, donate blankets & equipment or sponsor a cat for US$25/month. They also have an internet shop where you can buy a 'I helped save a Holy Cat!' T-shirt.

Meir Panim w meirpanim.org. Israel's ongoing conflict, political problems & the cost of supporting the IDF has led to government cuts in social welfare, payments, health & education: & as such the lowest-paid & unemployed members of society suffer most. Meir Panim is a national organisation dedicated to providing a range of welfare care including free kitchens, meals on wheels to elderly members of the community, youth clubs, vocational training, homes for abused women & centres for the elderly. Volunteers are always needed, to help prepare & hand out food at the 30 free restaurants around the country, as are donations.

Safe Haven for Donkeys w safehaven4donkeys.org. In many rural areas of Israel, working donkeys are still very much a part of life. Yet, because of their cheap purchase price, those that get sick or old are just left abandoned, many to suffer considerably. British-born Lucy Fensom arrived in Israel many years ago & vowed to do something to help these 'beasts of burden'. She founded an enormous shelter for abused & abandoned donkeys that today is home to over 100 animals. The enormous costs of running shelters in Israel & Palestine are difficult to maintain & donations are always needed.

ISRAEL ONLINE

For additional online content, articles, photos and more on Israel, why not visit w bradtguides.com/israel?

Part Two

THE GUIDE

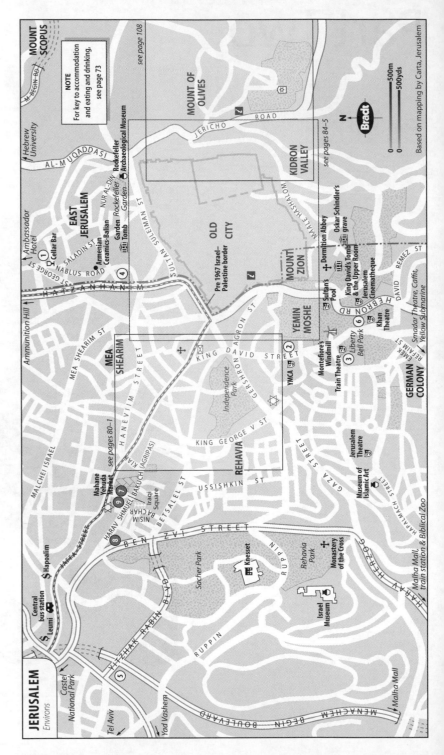

JERUSALEM
Environs

MOUNT SCOPUS

NOTE
For key to accommodation and eating and drinking, see page 73

see page 108

MOUNT OF OLIVES

Hebrew University

AL-MUQADDASI

EAST JERUSALEM

Ambassador Hotel

Cellar Bar (1)

Saladin St

Armenian Ceramics-Balian

NABLUS ROAD (4)

NUR AL-DIN

Rockefeller Archaeological Museum

Garden Tomb

Rockefeller Garden

ST GEORGE ST

Ammunition Hill

HATZANHANIM

SULTAN SULEIMAN ST

Pre 1967 Israel–Palestine border

OLD CITY

KIDRON VALLEY

JERICHO ROAD

see pages 84–5

MALE HASHALOM

MOUNT ZION

Dormition Abbey

Oskar Schindler's grave

King David's Tomb & the Upper Room

Jerusalem Cinematheque

DAVID REMEZ ST

MEA SHEARIM

MEA SHEARIM ST

HANEVIIM STREET

see pages 80–1

KIA (AGRIPAS)

Mahane Yehuda Market

Iraqi Square (9)(7)

NISIM BACHAR

BETSALEL ST

SHMUEL BARUCH

HARAV SHMUEL

(8)

BEN ZVI STREET

USSISHKIN ST

REHAVIA

King David Street

Independence Park

GERSHON AGRON ST

YMCA (2)

Montefiore's Windmill

Train Theatre

Liberty Bell Park (3)

Sultan's Pool

YEMIN MOSHE

HEBRON RD

Khan Theatre (6)

EMEK REFAIM ST

GERSHON V ST

KING GEORGE V ST

GAZA STREET

Jerusalem Theatre

Museum of Islamic Art

RADAK STREET

GERMAN COLONY

Smadar Theatre, Caffit, Yellow Submarine

HAPALMACH

EMEK REFAIM ST

MALCHEI ISRAEL

Central bus station

Leumi

Hapoalim

YITZHAK RABIN BLVD

Sacher Park

RUPPIN

Knesset

Israel Museum

Rehavia Park

Monastery of the Cross

RUPPIN

HARAV HERZOG

Malha Mall, train station & Biblical Zoo

Castel National Park

Tel Aviv

MENACHEM BEGIN BOULEVARD

Yad Vashem

Malha Mall

N

0 500m
0 500yds

Bradt

Based on mapping by Carta, Jerusalem

72

3

Jerusalem

Telephone code 02; population 865,700

In 1967, Israel occupied East Jerusalem, including the Old City, and declared the entire city as its undivided capital. The annexation was legally approved in Israel in 1980. The occupation of East Jerusalem is considered illegal under international law. However, for the purposes of this guidebook and the ease of use to travellers, it has been included in one chapter. See **Palestine: the Bradt Guide** *for a more comprehensive description.*

As the sun sets over Jerusalem's white-stone buildings, it is impossible to imagine the millions of people who have stood and witnessed the very same event. For centuries, Jerusalem (Yerushalaym in Hebrew, Al-Quds in Arabic) has stood as the single most revered, contested and loved city in the world. Its many different inhabitants have given it a cultural and religious make-up like no other place on earth, a place pilgrims flock to and residents defend to the bitter end. To define the city is impossible, as it is above all else a city of contrasts. A city where Judaism, Christianity and Islam meet; where ancient neighbourhoods tumble into shiny new ones; where both the devout and the secular find their own place; and where modern and traditional somehow flourish together.

At its core sits the Old City, a remarkable and awe-inspiring area. Yet despite its historic, archaeological and religious treasures, its centuries of turmoil and conflict, and its political tensions, Jerusalem is first and foremost a vibrant, living city. Outside its walls, the city is a mesh of modern neighbourhoods, efficient transport networks, bustling souks, world-famous museums and high-class universities. Jewish Orthodox, secular and Arabic neighbourhoods each maintain their own traditions, for the most part respecting each other's day-to-day lives.

Visitors to the city find they leave changed. For the spiritually minded, the almost overwhelming wealth of holy sites is humbling and moving, while the more religiously apathetic find themselves stirred. A history that seemed so distant is now as real as the present. For Jerusalem has always marked the final battle for the land, a fact that remains as true today as it did thousands of years ago. The stumbling block over which peace negotiations fall, Jerusalem sits unwittingly in the midst of an international drama, the world watching every move out of the corner of its eye. Yet for those who live

JERUSALEM *Environs*
For listings, see pages 82–8

⌂ **Where to stay**
1   American Colony Hotel
2   King David
3   Inbal Jerusalem
4   Jerusalem
5   Park
6   St Andrew's Scottish
    Guesthouse

✕ **Where to eat and drink**
7   Azura
8   Ima
9   Machaneyuda
Off map
    Caffit

Jerusalem

3

73

there, and for those who get the chance to visit, the tensions and turmoil are put to the back of the mind as they witness first hand the reasons so many want to call it home.

HISTORY

THE CANAANITES AND THE ISRAELITES Although evidence points to occupation in the Stone Age, by c4000BCE the more technologically advanced Canaanites had taken over the area we now know as Jerusalem. In the 15th century, the Egyptians conquered, ruling until the Israelites took control of the region in 1250BCE. While they managed to capture most of the realm, the fortified Jerusalem didn't fall for another 200 years. During this time David was declared the first King of Israel and in 1004BCE he finally stormed the city, declaring it capital of his kingdom and renaming it the City of David.

THE FIRST TEMPLE PERIOD (1006–586BCE) Following David's conquest, the city soon became the political, religious and cultural centre of the kingdom. He constructed a great palace, installing in it the sacred Ark of the Covenant. The construction of the First Temple is attributed to Solomon, David's son, who at the same time enlarged the city. Soon after Solomon's death the kingdom split in two, the northern Kingdom of Israel forming a new capital, while the southern Kingdom of Judah retained Jerusalem as its centre. In 586BCE, however, Jerusalem fell to the Babylonians who exiled the Jews and destroyed the temple.

THE SECOND TEMPLE PERIOD (536BCE–70CE) Shortly afterwards, the Persians came to rule and the Jews were once more allowed to return. During the following years they constructed the Second Temple and reignited the religious and spiritual fervour that had been flourishing before the Babylonian incursion. When Alexander the Great conquered the Persian Empire and, in 333BCE Jerusalem with it, the city entered a period of Greek and Hellenic cultural influence. Upon Alexander's death a fervent battle for the great city took place, the Syrian ruler Antiochus IV emerging as victor and installing Seleucid rule over the land. Subjugation of the Jews and the destruction of the Second Temple instigated a great revolt under the leadership of the Maccabees, a Jewish family of patriots. This in turn led to the establishment of the Hasmoneans, who eventually ousted the Seleucids, beginning an 80-year period of Jewish independence.

THE ROMANS AND THE HERODIAN ERA (63BCE–96CE) In 63BCE, Roman general Pompey conquered Jerusalem and in 37BCE, Herod ascended the throne. His reign saw the city expand northwards and a massive phase of building get under way. Herod constructed the second wall of the temple, today part of which is the Western Wall. He is also attributed with giving the temple a magnificent makeover and constructing the Antonia Fortress, Citadel, numerous palaces, markets, a theatre and a hippodrome.

It was during this time that Jesus of Nazareth was also active. After gathering support and naming his Apostles in the Galilee, Jesus made his way to Jerusalem where, according to the New Testament, he was tried and crucified by Pontius Pilate as a threat to Roman rule and religious order for his increasing numbers of followers. Herod's death and the subsequent iron-fisted rule of the Romans led to a Jewish revolt, which ended in Roman victory. The Jewish residents were once again expelled, the Second Temple destroyed and Jerusalem burnt to the ground.

THE ROMAN BYZANTINE PERIOD (135–638CE) In 135CE, Emperor Hadrian named his new conquest Aelia Capitolina, a new city layout was installed (the main streets of which still form the central cross-section through the Old City), Roman buildings appeared everywhere, paganism prevailed, Jerusalem became a backwater city and Jews and early Christians were forbidden to enter. Until, that is, Constantine assumed power in 303CE. Constantine was the first Roman ruler (by this time Byzantine after the break-up of the western Roman Empire) to be converted to Christianity, and throughout his rule Jerusalem exploded on to the scene as a pilgrimage destination, hundreds of churches, including the Church of the Holy Sepulchre, owing their origins to this time. Over the next three centuries Christianity became the official religion of the Byzantine Empire, marking a crucial chapter in Jerusalem's history. In 614, Jerusalem fell to the Persians who massacred the city's inhabitants and decimated many of the holy sites. Although the Emperor Herclius managed to reclaim the city six years later, it was not to last and Jerusalem fell once again, this time to the rising force of the Arab Islamic Empire.

THE EARLY MUSLIM PERIOD (638–1099) In 638, Jerusalem came under Muslim rule following Calpih Omar's conquest of the kingdom. Although the Quran does not mention Jerusalem by name, the Hadith (a collection of sayings and traditions of Mohammed) specifies that it was from here that the Prophet ascended to Heaven in the Night Journey. The conquest was bloodless and Christians and Jews were granted permission to continue practising their faiths unhindered. By the end of the 7th century, Jerusalem was recognised as the third holiest site in Islam (after Mecca and Medina) and, shortly afterwards, Umayyad ruler Abd Al-Malik built the Dome of the Rock above the stone said to be both where Mohammed ascended to Heaven, and the site of the former First and Second temples. A short distance away the grand Al-Aqsa Mosque was also built. While the Umayyad period brought prosperity, the subsequent Abbasid and Fatimid rulers showed significantly less interest in the city and Jerusalem lost its importance.

THE CRUSADES AND SALADIN (1099–1250) In the 11th century, the city came under the harsh rule of the Turkish Seljuks, an event that saw Pope Urban II call for the Crusades. Led by Godfrey of Bouillon, European Christians travelled to Jerusalem with the aim of liberating it from Islamic control. In 1099, they captured the city, naming it the capital of the Latin Kingdom of Jerusalem. It was a vicious and bloody conquest and most of Jerusalem's Jewish and Muslim residents were slaughtered. Jerusalem entered a new cultural phase whereby European customs and language became commonplace and where Christianity prevailed. Churches were restored and the holy sites on the Temple Mount (pages 103–4) became Christian, the Knights Templar (an order of monastic knights) installing their headquarters there. Even though the Kingdom of Jerusalem lasted until 1291, the capital fell to Saladin, a powerful Islamic hero, in 1187. Saladin allowed worship by all religions and during this time many exiled Jews returned. Despite attempts by Richard the Lionheart to recapture the city in the Third Crusade, it remained under Saladin's control until the Mamluk conquest in 1260.

THE MAMLUKS AND OTTOMANS (1250–1917) A somewhat peripheral city, Jerusalem fell into a period of decline and poverty. A respite from the dire situation was offered when the city was incorporated into the Ottoman Empire and Sultan Suleiman took the reins. Under his rule the great Old City walls were erected along with gates and an aqueduct. Following his death, however, things took a turn for the worse and the succeeding 300 years are seen as a dark era in Jerusalem's past. Poverty, neglect and a static population blighted the once-great city and it wasn't until exiled Jews fled to the land in the 15th and 16th centuries that things began to improve. By the 19th century, as the Ottoman Empire weakened, Jerusalem was taking on a more Europeanised outlook. During the short reign (1831–40) of the Egyptian ruler Mohammed Ali Pasha, Europeans were granted permission to establish representations in Palestine, and by the time the Ottomans re-established their control of the lost territory, European powers were intensely involved in building their presence in the Holy Land. The ban on building in the Holy City, in place since the 16th century, had thus been abrogated, and Russia, France, Germany, Austria-Hungary and Great Britain started purchasing property and building in Jerusalem and its surroundings. Foreign consulates, schools, hospitals and churches were established, trade links flourished, the population grew rapidly and neighbourhoods burst out of the Old City walls. The population at the time was divided into four major communities: Jewish, Christian, Muslim and Armenian, each concentrated around its respective religious shrine.

THE BRITISH MANDATE, THE ARAB–ISRAELI WAR AND A CITY DIVIDED

(1917–48) Towards the end of World War I and the collapse of the Ottoman Empire, Jerusalem surrendered to British forces and on 11 December 1917 General Allenby marched through Jaffa Gate as a sign of respect to the Holy City. By this time the patchwork of cultures and religions across the Old and New cities had expanded considerably, but was lacking any sort of planning. With the advent of the 1922 mandate granted to the British by the League of Nations, they set about developing plans for its growth. The use of the white sandstone façades that are today one of the city's most endearing features was made law, while buildings such as the Hadassah Medical Centre, Hebrew University, King David Hotel and Jewish Agency headquarters owe their origins to this period. Yet as the city expanded, the separation between Jews and Palestinians once observed in the Old City again began to materialise. The struggle for religious and political control escalated and tensions heightened. This culminated in the 1920s riots and the Arab Revolt of 1936–39. Following the departure of the British (and the dissolution of the Partition Plan), Israel declared independence on 14 May 1948. Less than 24 hours later, neighbouring Arab nations invaded the fledgling country and so ensued the 1948 Arab–Israeli War. The end of the war found the city divided: Jordan had control of East Jerusalem and the Old City, Israel of West Jerusalem. From this time until the Six Day War in 1967, fences and landmines separated the two halves of the city.

A UNITED CITY OF DIVIDED PEOPLE The 1967 Six Day War saw Israel capture the Jordanian-controlled half of Jerusalem and in 1980 the Knesset officially declared the united city its capital, a declaration highly contested by the UN and international community to this day. The Moroccan area of the Old City was demolished, and in its place the Western Wall Plaza was built. The Waqf (the Supreme Muslim Religious Council) was granted administration of the Temple Mount and Jews forbidden (both by Israel and the Waqf) from praying there. Over time clear divisions appeared between West and East Jerusalem, both culturally and economically. Money was poured into West Jerusalem and the Old City given a makeover, yet East Jerusalem, now populated by almost equal numbers of Jews and Arabs, was suffering. To this day the UN and much of the international community do not recognise the annexation of East Jerusalem (and the West Bank and Gaza Strip) and all countries maintain embassies in Tel Aviv, with the exception of some consulates.

JERUSALEM TODAY Under Israeli control, members of most religions are granted access to their holy sites, the exceptions being those Palestinians living in the West Bank and Gaza Strip. Jews are forbidden to pray or study inside the Temple Mount although entrance is permitted. Inside this fragile and highly sensitive city, where political and religious tensions are on a knife-edge, conflicts do arise. Events such as the arson attack on the Al-Aqsa Mosque in 1969 by a Christian fundamentalist; rioting following the digging of an exit to the Western Wall tunnels in the Muslim Quarter; Jewish opposition to the Waqf's excavations inside the Temple Mount, and the igniting of the second intifada by Ariel Sharon's visit to the Islamic holy site in 2000 being but some examples. Jerusalem has always been the stumbling block over which any form of peace negotiations break: Israel lays claim to the entire city; the Palestinians to at least the eastern half including the Old City. Ancient districts remain more or less segregated and police are more in evidence here than anywhere else in the country. Old City street names are also being reinvented and transliterated, causing silent discontent among the original residents. As the conflict continues with little sign of a solution on the horizon, it must be said that for travellers, the Old City at least displays a certain aura of calm.

GETTING THERE AND AWAY

BY BUS AND SHARED TAXI (SHERUT) Jerusalem's **central bus station** (*Jaffa St;* ✆ *5304704;* ◷ *06.00–21.30 Sun–Thu, 06.15–15.45 Fri*) has buses running all over the country. Buses to the Palestinian Territories leave from outside the Damascus Gate [84 C2].

BY TRAIN The **Jerusalem Malha train station** (*Yitzhak Modai;* ✆ **5770, 03 6117000;* w *rail.co.il/en*) is located in the southwest of the city near the Jerusalem Malha Mall. Western Israel's train network is still in its fledgling stage and you therefore need to change once in Beit Shemesh on the way from Tel Aviv's Hahaganah train station. Trains depart hourly (*1hr 20mins/₪20*). There is also a station at the Biblical Zoo, a few minutes from the main station.

BY AIR Ben-Gurion Airport is located between Tel Aviv and Jerusalem and can be accessed easily (*approx 30mins*) by car or a combination of bus and train (change to the train at El Al junction).

DIRECT ROUTES RUN BY EGGED TO AND FROM JERUSALEM CENTRAL BUS STATION				
To	**Frequency**	**Bus no**	**Duration**	**Price (₪)**
Beersheba	15mins	446, 470	1hr 40mins	27
Ben-Gurion Airport				
(El Al junction)	30mins	947, 950	36mins	21.50
Eilat	07.00/10.00/14.00/17.00	444	4hrs 40mins	70
Ein Gedi	1hr	444, 486/7	1hr 20mins	34
Haifa	20mins	940, 947	3hrs	37.50
Katzrin	08.30/12.15/17.30	966	4hrs	42.50
Kiryat Shmona	06.50/13.45/18.40	963	3hrs 10mins	42.50
Nazareth	16.15/18.20	955	2hrs 40mins	37.50
Tiberias	45mins/1hr	959, 961/2	2hrs 45mins	37.50
Tel Aviv	15mins	405	1hr	16

BY BUS AND LIGHT RAIL The Holy City has a reliable light rail and bus network connecting the city's mountainous, higgledy-piggledy neighbourhoods quite efficiently. A one-way ticket to anywhere costs ₪5.90. Tram tickets have to be purchased before boarding. At present there is only one light rail/tram line running along Jaffa Street all the way to Mount Herzl, stopping at Mahane Yehuda and the central bus station. Useful Egged bus routes are as follows:

- **#1** Runs from the Old City (Western Wall) past the Rockefeller Museum, down Malchei Yisrael and past Mea Shearim before terminating at the central bus station.

- **#18** Runs from the central Malha train station along Jose San Martin Street then heads down to the German Colony, along King David Street, past Mahane Yehuda market and terminates on Shazar Boulevard.

- **#19** Runs from Hadassah Hospital (Ein Kerem) along Golomb and Azza streets past Mea Shearim neighbourhood, then turns into Haneviim Street (near Damascus Gate) and terminates at Hebrew University on Mount Scopus (East Jerusalem).

BY SHERUT Sheruts generally follow the lines of the major bus routes but can be hailed from anywhere along those routes. They cost marginally less than the buses and are a convenient option on Shabbat when the buses stop running. Sheruts to Tel Aviv, Haifa, Eilat and all the stops along the way leave from the central bus station.

BY CAR Most of the car-rental agencies can be found along King David Street and there are offices of most major national and international companies at Ben-Gurion Airport (page 123). Parking in the city can be difficult and expensive and parking illegally will result in your car being towed away. Cars are not an ideal way to get around Jerusalem but are by far the best option for exploring the country at large. You must be over 21 to rent a car anywhere in Israel (page 60).

Car-rental companies

🚗 **Avis** [81 F8] 19 King David St; ✆6249001; w avis.co.il; ⏱ 08.00–18.00 Sun–Thu, 08.00–13.00 Fri

🚗 **Budget** [81 G7] King David Hotel, 23 King David St; ✆03 9350015; w budget.co.il/en; ⏱ 08.00–18.00 Sun–Thu, 08.00–14.00 Fri

🚗 **Eldan** [81 F8] Eldan Hotel, 24 King David St; ✆6252151/2; e jer_hotel@eldan.com; w eldan.co.il/en; ⏱ 08.00–17.00 Sun–Thu, 08.00–13.00 Fri

🚗 **Hertz** [81 F8] 18 King David St; ✆*9678, 6231351; e hertzjerusalem@hertz.co.il; w hertz.co.il/en; ⏱ 08.00–18.00 Sun–Thu, 08.00–14.00 Fri

🚗 **Sixt** [81 F7] 8 King David St; ✆6250833; w sixt.com; ⏱ 08.00–18.00 Mon–Fri, 08.00–18.00 Sun

BY TAXI Taxi fares are calculated by a meter (page 58) which drivers are obligated by law to run. If they refuse, get out and look for another one, otherwise you will no doubt be overcharged. There are several taxi companies, including Bar Ilan (✆ 5866666), Gilo (✆ 6765888), Hapalmach (✆ 6793333) and Nesher (✆6257227).

ℹ Christian Information Centre [84 C5] Jaffa Gate; ☏6272692; e cicinfo@cicts.org; w cicts. org; ⊕ 08.30–17.30 Mon–Fri, 08.30–12.30 Sat. Offers information on Christian sites in & around the Old City.
ℹ Tourist Information Centre [84 C5] Jaffa Gate; ☏6271422; w tourism.gov.il;

⊕ 08.30–17.00 Sat–Thu, 08.30–13.30 Fri. Offers a wealth of information including free maps, hotel reservations & tour guide recommendations.
ℹ The Mount of Olives Information Centre [108 B3] ☏*6033; w mountofolives.co.il/en, w cityofdavid.org.il/en

OTHER TOURIST INFORMATION There are some good web resources you can check out before setting off: the **Ministry of Tourism** (w *tourism.gov.il*) and the **Municipality of Jerusalem** (w *jerusalem.muni.il*), which also has a 24-hour hotline 106 (from landlines). The Jerusalem Post (w *jpost.com*) is an English-language newspaper that has lots of practical information and entertainment listings about Jerusalem and Tel Aviv for tourists and foreign residents. *Haaretz* (w *haaretz.com*), Israel's leading newspaper, is also printed in English daily. Another good publication to pick up is the *Tours and Sites* booklet produced by the Municipality of Jerusalem Tourism Department. *Time Out* magazine now has a Jerusalem edition (w *timeout.com/israel/jerusalem*) to add to its popular Tel Aviv publication.

CITY TOURS The sheer volume of things to see in Jerusalem means that taking guided tours is a good way to get orientated and expand your understanding. Apart from those listed below, the tourist information office (see above) can supply a list of licensed tour guides. The **Jerusalem Municipality** [80 G4] (*1 Safra Sq*; ☏6296666/7777; w *jerusalem.muni.il*) offers a wide range of information on tours and what to see and do in Jerusalem. Do check their website for events and festivals. **Sandeman's New Europe** offers a somewhat insouciant, but potentially informative free tour leaving from Jaffa Gate (*11.00 daily & 14.00 Sun–Thu; 3hrs; donations welcome*; w *newjerusalemtours.com*). There are also **hop-on-hop-off sightseeing buses** on City Tour Bus line 99 [84 B5] (☏5238818). Although infrequent (*5 buses daily Sun–Thu*), the red, open-top double-decker bus does a circuit of Jerusalem's major sites (*adult/child ₪80/68 or 2hr tour ₪60/48*) and can be an option for tired legs. Buses stop at Jaffa Gate at 09.30, 11.30, 14.00, 16.15 and 18.30.

Smart Tour ☏*9678, 5618056; e info@ smart-tour.co.il; w smart-tour.co.il. Offering a variety of unusual tours on Segway bikes, this is a unique & eco-friendly way to see the city (*2hr long; ₪195pp*). Tours include a 20min lesson on using the 2-wheeled Segway bikes.

Zion Walking Tours [84 C5] Jaffa Gate; ☏6277588; w zionwt.zapages.co.il; ⊕ 09.00–18.00 Sun–Fri. Zion are 30-year veterans of tours around the Old City. Don't let the dusty little shop put you off – these guys know their way around. There's a wide range of tours (*approx 2–3hrs; US$20*), including to the Mount of Olives (*10.00 Mon & Wed*), Judean Desert (book in advance) & Western Wall Tunnels (*10.00 Mon & Wed*).

TRAVEL AGENCIES
Issta [80 F2] 31 Haneviim St; ☏6213600; w issta.co.il; ⊕ 09.00–18.00 Sun–Thu, 08.30–13.00 Fri. Israel's biggest agency. Specialises in budget travel.

Ophir Tours 3 Yanai St; ☏5269422; e henriette_h@ophirtours.co.il; w ophirtours. co.il; ⊕ 08.30–18.00 Sun–Thu, 09.00–12.30 Fri

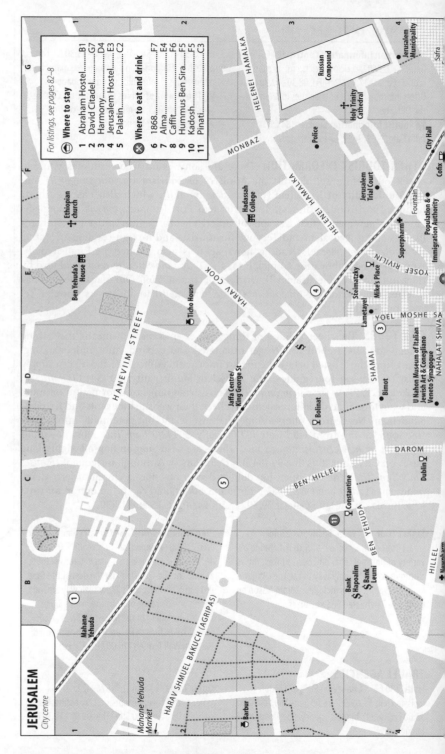

JERUSALEM
City centre

For listings, see pages 82–8

◐ **Where to stay**
1 Abraham Hostel........B1
2 David Citadel..........G7
3 Harmony...............D4
4 Jerusalem Hostel......E3
5 Palatin...............C2

✕ **Where to eat and drink**
6 1868..................F7
7 Alma.................E4
8 Caffit...............F6
9 Hummus Ben Sira......F5
10 Kadosh..............F5
11 Pinati..............C3

Russian Compound

Holy Trinity Cathedral ✝

Police ●

HELENEI HAMALKA

MONBAZ

Jerusalem Trial Court

Jerusalem Municipality ●

Safra

City Hall ●

Cofix ●

Fountain

Superpharm ✝

Population & Immigration Authority

YOSEF RIVLIN

HELENE HAMALKA

Hadassah College 🏛

HARAV COOK

Ethiopian church ✝

Ben Yehuda's House 🏛

Ticho House 🏛

E

Steinmatzky

Mike's Place

Lametayel

YOEL MOSHE SA

U Nahon Museum of Italian Jewish Art & Conegliano Veneto Synagogue

NAHALAT SHIVA

SHAMAI

Bimot ●

DAROM

Dublin 🍴

④

③

HANEVIIM STREET

Jaffa Centre/ King George St ●

Bolinat 🍴

BEN HILLEL

Constantine 🍴

⑤

⑪

BEN YEHUDA

DAROM

Bank Hapoalim $

Bank Leumi $

HILLEL

Newbarm ✝

Mahane Yehuda ●

①

Mahane Yehuda Market →

HARAV SHMUEL BAKUCH (AGRIPAS)

Barbur 🍴

80

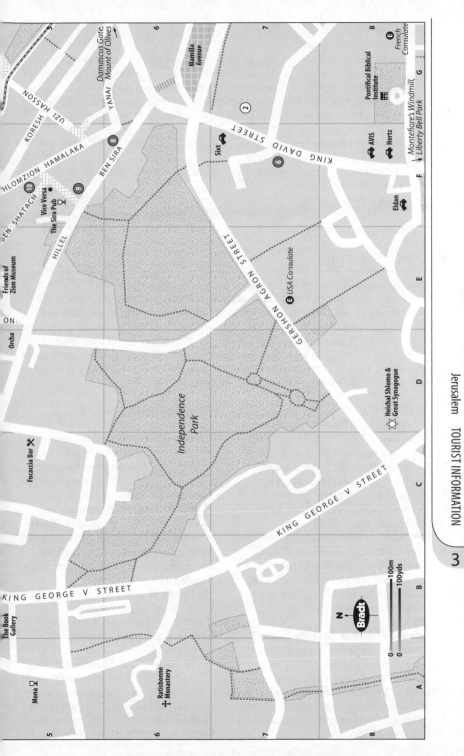

MP3 tours are growing in popularity across the world, and Jerusalem is an excellent candidate for do-it-yourself walking tours. By simply downloading the tour to your iPad, iPhone or MP3 player and printing out the associated map, you can tour the city's maze of cobbled lanes in your own time, stopping to take photos or enjoy a coffee break without the rush of an organised tour.

Jerusalemp3 w www1.jerusalem.muni.il/jer_sys/tour/VoiceTour/all.html; free. Excellent tour offered by the Jerusalem Municipality.
Trek Exchange w trekexchange.com; US$11.95. Some 4hrs of recorded tour information covering the whole of Jerusalem.
Tower of David w tod.org.il/en; admission free. The museum now offers the chance to download their 90min tour for free before your visit, saving you money on renting the audio headsets.

WHERE TO STAY

Accommodation options in Jerusalem are endless. Staying in the Old City is of course the highlight of a trip, although budget accommodation here might not be to everyone's taste. Old houses and hostels have poor ventilation so those looking for comfort might want to try the more luxurious or mid-range hotels in the new city districts, in particular around Jaffa Street. It is highly recommended to book in advance if coming to Jerusalem for Easter or other religious holidays as on these occasions, the Old City simply cannot accommodate everyone. At other times of the year though, booking a room is relatively easy.

CITY CENTRE

David Citadel Hotel [81 G7] (384 rooms) 7 King David St; ☎6211111; w thedavidcitadel. com. One of Jerusalem's hotel greats, it is 2nd in line to the throne after the King David Hotel (see box, opposite). It combines Old City views, traditional Jerusalem architecture, plush, modern facilities (including a swimming pool) & fresh, contemporary décor. $$$$$

Harmony Hotel [80 D4] (50 rooms) 6 Yoel Moshe Salomon St; ☎6219999; w atlas.co.il/ harmony-hotel-jerusalem. Kitsch chic brings a different kind of stay in the Holy City. Spacious, funky rooms, excellent b/fast & 10min walk to the Old City make it a great package. $$$$$

Inbal Jerusalem Hotel [map, page 72] (283 rooms, with 50 more to be added by 2018) Liberty Bell Park, 3 Jabotinsky St; ☎6756666; w inbalhotel.com. Sophisticated, understated elegance & wonderful New or Old City views from every room. Israeli b/fast buffet included, & there is a choice of world cuisine restaurants as well as a luxury spa. $$$$$

Mount of Olives Hotel [108 D2] (55 rooms) 53 Mount of Olives Rd; ☎6284877; w mtolives.com. Its proximity to the Christian sites on the Mount of Olives has made this simple but comfortable family-run hotel a favourite with small pilgrim groups. It offers great views over the Mount & Old City. $$$

Palatin Hotel [80 C2] (200 rooms) 4 Agripas St; ☎6231141; e info@palatinhotel.com; w palatinhotel.com. Opened in 1936 & excellently located between the sights of the Old and New cities, it offers Jerusalem family-run charm, quality & comfort. $$$

Park Hotel [map, page 72] (210 rooms) 2 Vilnay St; ☎6582222. Fantastic-value hotel offering comfort & style & a range of facilities including AC, an Israeli b/fast & big, open-air dining room. $$$

St Andrew's Scottish Guesthouse [map, page 72] (19 rooms) 1 David Remez St; ☎6732401; e info@scotsguesthouse.com; w scotsguesthouse. com. One of the few buildings constructed by the British during the Mandate period, St Andrew's Guesthouse & Church stand on the Valley of

The King David [map, page 72] (23 King David St; ☏ 6208888; e kingdavld@
danhotels.com; w danhotels.co.il; $$$$$) stands as Israel's most prestigious
and luxurious hotel, frequented by politicians and royalty from across the
globe. With five restaurants, a fitness centre, swimming pool, tennis courts and
flawless, elegant rooms it doesn't get much better than this. More than just
a hotel, however, the King David is a Jerusalem landmark, with a tumultuous
and dramatic history. The hotel was founded in 1931 and afforded asylum to
King Alfonso VIII of Spain, Emperor Haile Selassie of Ethiopia and King George
II of Greece who were all exiled from their countries. The British Mandate
period saw the King David act as the headquarters of British rule in Palestine
until it was bombed by the Irgun Zionist group in July 1946. Throughout the
1948 Arab–Israeli War the hotel became a Jewish stronghold, only to find
itself poignantly isolated between Israeli- and Jordanian-controlled lands.
When Israel captured Jerusalem in 1967, the hotel was restored to its former
grandeur and elegance and has since stood as the jewel in Jerusalem's royal
crown. It was also here that Menachem Begin and Anwar Sadat met for an
unofficial conversation on 19 November 1977 and pledged to each other
their commitment to peace between Israel and Egypt.

Hinnom; a beautiful, castle-like building offering
refined elegance & a taste of classic Jerusalem.
$$$

🏠 **Abraham Hostel** [80 B1] (40 rooms)
67 Haneviim St; ☏ 6502200; e infojlm@
abrahamhostels.com; w abrahamhostels.com.
Excellently geared towards budget independent
travellers, it offers big communal areas, single-sex
& mixed dorms & private rooms as well as a wide
range of social events & activities. Great location
next to the bustling Mahane Yehuda Market. The
hostel opened its doors in 2010 as the brainchild of
a group of avid travellers & nomads from Abraham
Hostels & Tours. **$$**

🏠 **Jerusalem Hostel** [80 E3] (14 rooms) 44
Jaffa St; ☏ 6236102; e reservation@jerusalem-
hostel.com; w jerusalem-hostel.com. What the
rooms lack in character the hostel makes up for
in cleanliness & great location. Well-equipped
kitchen, roof terrace & helpful staff. **$$**

OLD CITY

🏠 **Gloria Hotel** [84 C5] (100 rooms) 33 Latin
Patriarchate St; ☏ 6282431/2; e gloriahl@netvision.
net.il; w gloria-hotel.com. Opened in 1957, it
has retained all its Old City charm combined with
modern facilities. A rustic, stone-arched lounge
& bar is the perfect place to rest after a day of
sightseeing. Rooms have AC & TV. **$$$$**

🏠 **Knights Palace Hotel** [84 B4] (50
rooms) Freres St; ☏ 6282537; e kp@actcom.co.il;
w knightspalace.com. Nestled in a quiet corner
of the Muslim Quarter is this charming hotel
steeped in Old City elegance with vaulted ceilings
& arched windows. It has comfortable rooms, a
nice restaurant & bar, Wi-Fi throughout, AC & cable
TV. **$$$$**

JERUSALEM Old city
For listings, see pages 82–8

😴 **Where to stay**
1	Al-Arab Hostel	D3
2	Armenian Gueshouse	E3
3	Austrian Hospice	E3
4	Gloria	C5
5	Hashimi	D3
6	Jaffa Gate Hostel	C5
7	Knights Palace	B4
8	Petra Hostel	C5

Where to eat and drink
9	Abu Shukri	E3
10	Al-Mufti Café	D3
11	Armenian Tavern	C6
12	Askadinya	C1
13	Eucalyptus	B6
14	Jaber Coffee Shop	F1
15	Lutheran Guesthouse Café	D5
16	Nafoura	B5
17	Shahin' Kebabs	D4
18	Shawar's Bakery	D3
19	Versavee Bistro, Bar & Café	C5
	Viennese Café	(see 3)
20	Te'enim	A6

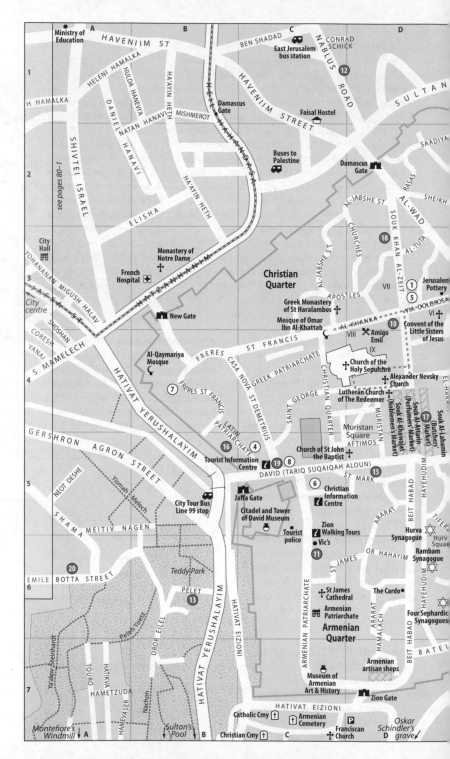

A

- Ministry of Education
- HAVENIIM ST
- HELENI HAMALKA
- HULDA HANEVIA
- H HAMALKA
- DANIEL HANAVI
- NATAN HANAVI
- HA'AYIN HETH
- SHIVTEI ISRAEL
- MISHMEROT
- see pages 80–1
- ELISHA
- HA'AYIN HETH
- City Hall
- YOHANANAN MIGUSH HALAV
- French Hospital
- HATZANHANIM
- City centre
- JAFFA ST
- SHOSHAN
- CORESH
- YANAI
- S MAMELECH
- New Gate
- Al-Qaymariya Mosque
- ⑦
- FRERES ST FRANCIS
- HATIVAT YERUSHALAYIM
- GERSHRON AGRON STREET
- NEOT DESHE
- SHAMA
- Yismah Melech
- MEITIV NAGEN
- ⑳
- EMILE BOTTA STREET
- Teddy Park
- Yaakov Steinhardt
- Peleth Yoetz
- PELET
- ⑬
- TOURO
- HATIKVA
- HAMETZUDA
- HAMEVASER
- Nachon
- DROR EILEL
- Monteﬁore's Windmill

B

- BEN SHADAD
- Damascus Gate
- HAVENIIM STREET
- Buses to Palestine
- Monastery of Notre Dame
- HATZANHANIM
- FRERES CASA NOVA ST
- ST FRANCIS
- LATIN PATRIARCHATE
- GREEK PATRIARCHATE
- ST DEMETRIUS
- ⑯
- ④
- Tourist Information Centre
- ⑲ ⑧
- DAVID (TARIQ SUQAIQAH ALOUN)
- ⑥
- Christian Information Centre
- City Tour Bus Line 99 stop
- Jaffa Gate
- Citadel and Tower of David Museum
- Tourist police
- Vic's
- ⑪
- Zion Walking Tours
- ARMENIAN PATRIARCHATE
- ST JAMES
- OR HAHAYIM
- St James Cathedral
- Armenian Patriarchate
- Armenian Quarter
- Museum of Armenian Art & History
- HATIVAT YERUSHALAYIM
- HATIVAT EIZIONI
- Sultan's Pool
- HATIVAT EIZIONI
- Catholic Cmy
- Christian Cmy
- Armenian Cemetery

C

- East Jerusalem bus station
- ⑫
- NABLUS ROAD
- CONRAD SCHICK
- Faisal Hostel
- Damascus Gate
- AL-JABSHE ST
- AL-JABSHE ST
- CHURCHES
- SOUK KHAN AL-ZEIT
- ⑱
- Christian Quarter
- APOSTLES
- Greek Monastery of St Haralambos
- Mosque of Omar Ibn Al-Khattab
- AL-KHANKA
- VIA DOLOROSA
- VII
- VIII
- Amigo Emil
- IX
- Church of the Holy Sepulchre
- CHRISTIAN QUARTER
- SAINT GEORGE
- Lutheran Church of The Redeemer
- Muristan Square
- AFTIMOS
- MURISTAN
- Church of St John the Baptist
- ST MARK
- ⑮
- ST JAMES
- OR HAHAYIM
- Hurva Synagogue
- Hurva Squa
- Rambam Synagogue
- ARARAT
- BEIT HABAD
- HAYEHUDIM
- The Cardo
- ARARAT
- HAMALACH
- Four Sephardic Synagogues
- BEIT HABAD
- Armenian artisan shops
- Zion Gate
- Franciscan Church
- Oskar Schindler's grave

D

- SULTAN
- SAADIYA
- RASAS
- AL-WAD
- SHEIKH
- AL-TUTA
- Jerusalem Pottery
- ①
- ⑤
- VII
- VI
- ⑩
- Convent of the Little Sisters of Jesus
- Alexander Nevsky Church
- EL-HAKARI
- Souk Al-Lahamin (Butchers' Market)
- Souk Al-Khwajat (Noblemen's Market)
- Souk Al-Attarin (Perfumers' Market)
- ⑰
- HAYEHUDIM
- TIFER
- HURVA
- BATEI
- Oskar Schindler's grave

1
2
3
4
5
6
7

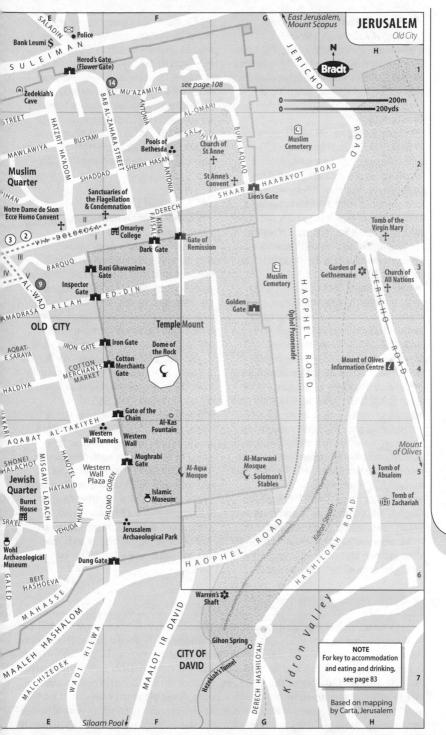

JERUSALEM
Old City

East Jerusalem, Mount Scopus

N

Bradt

see page 108

0 ——————— 200m
0 ——————— 200yds

Bank Leumi 💲
● Police
✉

SULEIMAN

SALADIN

Herod's Gate
(Flower Gate)

Zedekiah's
Cave

⑭

EL MU'AZAMIYA

BAB AL-ZAHARA STREET

ANTONIA

AL-OMARI

SALAHIYA

BURJ LAQLAQ

Muslim
Cemetery

STREET

MAWLAWIYA

HATZRIT HAADOM

BUSTAMI

SHADDAD

SHEIKH HASAN

Pools of
Bethesda

Church of
St Anne

**Muslim
Quarter**

Sanctuaries of
the Flagellation
& Condemnation

St Anne's
Convent

SHAAR HAARAYOT ROAD

Lion's Gate

Notre Dame de Sion
Ecce Homo Convent

③ ②

VIA DOLOROSA

II

I

DERECH

Omariye
College

Dark Gate

Gate of
Remission

Tomb of the
Virgin Mary

KING FAISAL

ANTONIA

III

BARQUQ

Bani Ghawanima
Gate

Muslim
Cemetery

Garden of
Gethsemane

Church of
All Nations

IV

V

⑨

AL-WAD

Inspector
Gate

ALLAH ED-DIN

Golden
Gate

Ophel Promenade

HAOPHEL ROAD

JERICHO ROAD

AMADRASA

OLD CITY

AQBAT-
E SARAYA

IRON GATE

Iron Gate

Temple Mount

Dome of
the Rock

Mount of Olives
Information Centre

HALDIYA

COTTON
MERCHANTS
MARKET

Cotton
Merchants
Gate

AQABAT AL-TAKIYEH

Gate of
the Chain

Al-Kas
Fountain

*Mount
of Olives*

SHONEI
HALACHOT

Western
Wall Tunnels

Western
Wall

Tomb of
Absalom

MISGAVI LADACH

HAKOTEL

Mughrabi
Gate

Western
Wall Plaza

SHLOMO GOREN

Tomb of
Zachariah

**Jewish
Quarter**

HATAMID

HALEVI

Al-Aqsa
Mosque

Al-Marwani
Mosque

Solomon's
Stables

Burnt
House

YEHUDA

Islamic
Museum

SRA'EL

Wohl
Archaeological
Museum

Jerusalem
Archaeological Park

GALED

BEIT
HASHOEVA

Dung Gate

HAOPHEL ROAD

Kidron Stream

HASHILOAH ROAD

MAHASSE

MAALEH HASHALOM

MALCHIZEDEK

WADI HILWA

MAALOT IR DAVID

Warren's
Shaft

**CITY OF
DAVID**

Gihon Spring

Hezekiah's Tunnel

DERECH HASHILO'AH

Kidron Valley

NOTE
For key to accommodation
and eating and drinking,
see page 83

Based on mapping
by Carta, Jerusalem

Siloam Pool

E   F   G   H

🏠 **Armenian Guesthouse** [85 E3] (27 rooms) 36 Via Dolorosa; ✆6260880; e armenianguesthouse@hotmail.com. A gem of a place, housing church, convent & hotel in the same grounds. Staff are wonderful, rooms are classic but simple, & the smell of frankincense in the inner courtyard after a church service is comforting & pleasant. **$$$**

🏠 **Austrian Hospice** [85 E3] (34 rooms) 37 Via Dolorosa; ✆6265800; e office@austrianhospice.com; w austrianhospice.com. Beautiful building in the beating heart of the Muslim Quarter. Impressive collection of modern & classical art plus high ceilings, a rich history & antique furniture. There is also a lovely café (page 88), garden & great view from the roof terrace (⊕ *10.00–18.00; admission ₪5*). Rooms are simple but enormous & the b/fasts (included) are wonderful. **$$$**

🏠 **Hashimi Hotel** [84 D3] (39 beds) 73 Khan Al-Zeit St; ✆6284410; e hashimi123@gmail.com; w hashimihotel.com. Previously a hostel, the revamped hotel (it has an elevator now) offers private rooms only. Although the new design isn't to everyone's taste, the location & view from the spacious rooftop terrace are simply wonderful. **$$**

🏠 **Al-Arab Hostel** [84 D3] (8 rooms) 61 Khan Al-Zeit St; ✆6273539; m 052 3688846. At the time of writing, renovation work on the upper floors & roof terrace was promising. Tucked away amid the city bazaars, the hostel offers surprisingly spacious common areas. Lower floor rooms come with small windows (a rare luxury here) overlooking the narrow Old City streets. **$$–$**

🏠 **Jaffa Gate Hostel** [84 C5] (12 rooms) Jaffa Gate; ✆6276402; e jaffa_gate_hostel@yahoo.com; w jaffa-gate.hostel.com. Family-run hostel offering both dorms & private accommodation. Ground-floor rooms don't have windows, which is typical of the Old City, but rooms on the 1st floor are definitely airier. The family running the place are friendly & helpful. The location is great & the terrace offers beautiful views over the Old City. **$$–$**

🏠 **Petra Hostel** [84 C5] (40 rooms) David St; ✆6286618; e newpetrahostel@yahoo.com; w newpetrahostel.com. Bohemian backpacker hostel in the Christian Quarter market. Dorms are good value for money with small balconies overlooking the Old City although private rooms are a bit shabby. Located upstairs past an exchange kiosk as you enter the market street from Jaffa Gate. **$$–$**

EAST JERUSALEM

🏠 **American Colony Hotel** [map, page 72] (92 rooms) 23 Nablus Rd; ✆6279777; e reserve@amcol.co.il; w americancolony.com. The breathtakingly beautiful building & grounds exemplify the elegant, classic charm that Jerusalem stands for. Its long history has seen it rise in the ranks of prestige from the home of a Turkish pasha to today acting as the temporary home of visiting diplomats, journalists & UN officers. It was from this building that the 'white flag' now housed in London's Imperial War Museum was flown, an act signifying Jerusalem's surrender in World War I. The epitome of elegance, service & top-of-the-range facilities. **$$$$$**

🏠 **Jerusalem Hotel** [map, page 72] (14 rooms) Nablus Rd; ✆6283282; e raed@jrshotel.com; w jrshotel.com. Run by the same family since 1960 & rebuilt following its devastation in 1967. This traditional Arabic mansion hotel has retained its age-old Palestinian charm & character. Decorated with Islamic & Andalusian furniture & antiques throughout & boasting an indoor dining room & beautiful Kan Zeman restaurant. Facilities include AC, balconies, TV, Wi Fi, travel arrangements & classical Arabic music evenings. **$$$$**

✖ WHERE TO EAT AND DRINK

Israelis love to eat out and accordingly the country is awash with fabulous restaurants serving more cuisines than you'd find at a UN dinner party. Jerusalem's restaurants are generally kosher and abide by Shabbat opening hours, although it is possible to find plenty that are open during this time, notably in East Jerusalem and the Muslim Quarter of the Old City. Outside Shabbat, restaurants, cafés and fast-food joints stay open until the small hours. Most places to eat in the Old City are simple falafel/hummus eateries, while the city centre has a variety of mid-range options. The most exclusive restaurants are in the western part of the city, towards the King David Hotel. The German Colony, although mainly residential, also has a number of restaurants to choose from along Emek Refaim Street.

CITY CENTRE

✖ **1868** [81 F7] 10 King David St; ☎6222312; w 1868.co.il; ⏰ noon–15.00 & 17.00–23.00 Sun–Thu, end of Shabbat–23.30. Kosher. Prime ingredients are cooked to perfection in succulent traditional French cuisine. Meals don't come cheap, but you're paying for top quality & an atmosphere of elegance & sophistication. **$$$$$**

✖ **Eucalyptus** [84 B6] 14 Hativat Yerushalayim St; ☎6244331; w the-eucalyptus.com; ⏰ noon–midnight Sun–Thu, 10.00–Shabbat Fri, end of Shabbat–late Sat. Chef Moshe Basson has spent over 20 years resurrecting traditional biblical foods & has received many awards for his contribution to the culinary arts. Try starters such as stuffed figs or eucalyptus salad & mains such as lamb with green fava beans in almond milk, or the famous taster menus. **$$$$$**

✖ **Te'enim** [84 A6] 12 Emile Botta St; ☎6251967; w teenim.rest-e.co.il; ⏰ 10.00–22.00 Sun–Thu, 08.30–14.30 Fri. Kosher. Unique vegetarian restaurant with wonderful views of the Old City walls. The French-Algerian owner-chef has created colourful dishes influenced by styles from across the globe. Cosy, unpretentious restaurant in an old 3-storey stone building behind the King David Hotel. **$$$**

✖ **Alma Restaurant** [80 E4] 18 Yosef Rivlin St; ☎5020069; ⏰ 11.00–midnight daily. Kosher traditional hearty Israeli dishes. Opened in 2014 in the heart of the city centre, Alma's specialities are traditional *kubbeh* (dumplings filled with meat) soups, which are more than suitable for a cool evening. **$$**

✖ **Caffit** [map, page 72] 35 Emek Refaim St, German Colony; ☎5635284; ⏰ 08.00–01.00 Sun–Thu, 07.00–14.00 Fri, end of Shabbat–01.30 Sat. Kosher. Although it may appear under the title 'café', this is a great option for a relaxed meal, & b/fasts are particularly good. The menu includes fresh sandwiches, pies, salads, grilled fish & gooey desserts, & there is a breezy little terrace on which to enjoy them. Another branch at Shlomzion Hamalka [81 F6]. **$$**

✖ **Kadosh** [81 F5] 6 Shlomzion Hamalka St; ☎6254210; ⏰ 07.00–midnight Sun–Thu. Easily the best bakery in central Jerusalem, Kadosh has been serving mouth-watering desserts & light

meals since 1967. Equally popular with locals dropping in for a cup of coffee or business people for a professional lunch. **$$**

✖ **Hummus Ben Sira** [81 F5] 3 Ben Sira St; ☎6253893; ⏰ 09.00–02.00 Sun–Thu. A relatively new but very hip addition to the Israeli hummus scene. The hummus is creamy, & side dishes are excellent. B/fast is also good, with superb shakshooka. Very busy in the evenings. **$**

✖ **Pinati** [80 C3] 13 King George V St; ☎6254540; m 057 9438531; ⏰ 07.00–19.00 Sun–Thu, 07.00–before Shabbat. Kosher. Opened more than 60 years ago & considered one of the best hummus/falafel joints in Jerusalem as attested to by the queues of salivating customers lining the street outside. **$**

MAHANE YEHUDA MARKET

The market & Harav Shmuel Baruch St (formerly Agripas St, but both names are used interchangeably) have dozens of tiny eateries & cafés nestled amid the bustling stalls. Most are as old as the market itself & serve traditional Middle Eastern foods, but there is a new influx of trendy yet relaxed places too. The market developed in the late 1880s, with the first 16 shops set up in 1920. After the 1930s, it expanded & the little Iraqi market, which is now the small square with eateries, opened up. The market as it appears today was renovated in the late 1980s. It is full of character & packed with sights, smells & welcoming shouts from its traders. Food stalls & bars are numerous, & you could easily spend the whole day walking amid the smell of oriental spices, fresh parsley & garlic.

✖ **Ima** [map, page 72] 55 Shmuel Baruch St (189 Agripas St); ☎6246860; w ima-rest.co.il/en; ⏰ 11.00–23.00 Sun–Thu, 11.00–Shabbat Fri. Kosher. Ima translates as 'mother', & this is exactly the sort of hearty food Jewish mamas cook up for their offspring: salads, soups, stuffed vegetables & various meat dishes. Big portions of Israeli/Middle Eastern food. **$$$**

✖ **Machaneyuda** [map, page 72] 10 Beit Yaakov St; ☎5333442; ⏰ 18.30–late Sun–Thu, 21.00–late Fri–Sat. One of the trendiest places on the block. The menu changes every day & reflects all manner of international cuisine from gazpacho soup to amberjack fish to oxtail & Jerusalem artichoke. $$$

✗ Azura [map, page 72] Iraqi Market Sq; ✆6235204; e shabiazura@gmail.com; ◷ 09.00–16.00 Sun–Thu, 08.30–Shabbat start Fri. Kosher. Situated in the delightful square, where old men while away the hours playing backgammon, this is a true local joint. Named after Erza (Azura) Shaftai, this family restaurant has expanded from a small stall set up by Erza in 1952 to 2 restaurants in the Iraqi Market & another in Tel Aviv. When seated you're served a plate of pickles, a spicy mix & pitta bread. Once every 3 weeks there is a house special worth enquiring about – *sinnia* – a stew of minced meat with potatoes, tomatos, zucchini & spices. $$

OLD CITY AND EAST JERUSALEM

The Old City specialises in traditional, home-cooked food that reflects the origins of those who make & serve it. Aromas of warm, fresh hummus, falafel, shawarma, spices, nuts, aromatic coffee & sticky pastries waft down the narrow streets of the Muslim Quarter souks, while the Jewish Quarter sports the more sedate cafés & bakeries along the leafy **Tiferet Yisrael Boulevard**. There are also some cheap eateries around **Muristan Square** in the Christian Quarter.

✗ Armenian Tavern [84 C6] 79 Armenian Orthodox Patriarchate St; ✆6273854; ◷ 11.00–22.00 Mon–Sat. One of the most atmospheric places to enjoy a meal in the Old City. Housed inside a Crusader-era cellar with rustically elegant décor, traditional Armenian dishes & comfortable ambience. $$$

✗ Askadinya Restaurant & Bar [84 C1] 11 Shimon Hatzadik St; ✆5324590; ✆noon–midnight Wed–Mon, 19.00–midnight Tue. An old East Jerusalem favourite; it is easy to see why people come again & again. A comfortable family atmosphere, hearty Italian & Middle Eastern food all set in a traditional cobbled stone building. There is live music on Thu. $$$

✗ Nafoura [84 B5] 18 Latin Patriarchate St; ✆6260034; w nafoura-rest.com; ◷ 12.30–23.00 daily. Middle Eastern & Mediterranean meats are served in this delightful Christian Quarter restaurant. The stone courtyard is particularly pleasant & there's a good-value buffet. $$

✗ Versavee Bistro, Bar & Café [84 C5] Greek Catholic Patriarchate Rd, Jaffa Gate; ✆6276160; w versavee.com. A classy yet unpretentious bistro, bar & café. Steeped in Old City charm & set inside a 2,000-year-old building, it is one of the favourites among international journalists & tourists. Meals consist of salads, hot & cold sandwiches & simple, but filling mains. $$

✗ Abu Shukri [85 E3] 63 Al-Wad St; ✆6271538; ◷ 08.30–18.00 daily. Located where the Via Dolorosa crosses Al-Wad St this is one of the best, if not *the* best, hummus joints in the city. It is easy to spot by the throngs of people queuing for their turn at the little plastic tables inside. $

✗ Shahin' Kebabs [84 D4] 76 Souk Al-Lahamin; ◷ 10.00–18.00 daily. A simple meal in this rudimentary eatery might just be the best you will have in the Old City. Shahin himself prepares succulent kebabs & meatballs mixed with spices & served with a meze set. $

✗ Viennese Café [85 E3] Austrian Hospice, 37 Via Dolorosa; ✆6265800; ◷ 07.00–22.00 daily. Take afternoon tea away from the hubbub of the Muslim Quarter in the tranquil gardens of the Austrian Hospice. Traditional, delicate Viennese cakes, teas, coffees & liqueurs are all home baked & superb. You're also in for a treat here if you fancy a hearty Austrian meal with potato salad. $

⎕ Al-Mufti Café [84 D3] Via Dolorosa between the 6th & 7th stations; ◷ 10.00–22.00 daily. A friendly tiny place serving strong Arabic coffee with cardamom & traditional sweets. $

⎕ Jaber Coffee Shop [85 F1] Bab Al-Zahara St. As good & Arab as it gets. Located in the vicinity of the Herod's Gate, the coffee here is strong, the locale is nostalgic & the crowd (essentially men) are friendly & welcoming. Spending an evening here enjoying a game of backgammon is a must! $

⎕ Lutheran Guesthouse Café [84 D5] St Mark St; w luth-guesthouse-jerusalem.com; ◷ 10.00–16.00 daily. Somewhat hidden, this place is worth looking for. An idyllic café on a leafy terrace on the Osman Mosque rooftop. The drinks menu is simple, but the location beats it all. Can be accessed either via the guesthouse itself or via the stairs from Habad St. $

⎕ Shawar's Bakery [84 D3] 54 Khan Al-Zeit St; ✆6280004. A cosy bakery with a coffee shop tucked away in a traditional building inside the bazaar. Coffee is good & all pastries & sweets are homemade. $

BARS AND CLUBS

Jerusalem's bars are not quite on a par with its naughty neighbour Tel Aviv, but then again, they don't try to be. Watering holes tend to be more refined & less rowdy, attracting those who want to enjoy some sociable drinks with friends in pleasant surroundings, & many double as restaurants. There are, however, several places where you can let your hair down to live music, have one too many & enjoy a good dance. The Zion Sq/Nahalat Shiva area is teeming with small bars, cafés, pubs & restaurants & is a good place to head for a night out. Ben Yehuda St is another popular area.

♀ **Bolinat** [80 D3] 6 Dorot Rishonim St; 6249733; ⊕ 24hrs daily. Friendly, relaxed bar & restaurant that attracts the 20-something Jerusalemites. Music styles vary but you are unlikely to hear Abba on the stereo. Rich, feel-good meals & a good selection of beers is another big draw. Abraham Hostel guests receive a 15% discount.

♀ **Cellar Bar** [map, page 72] 23 Nablus Rd; 6279777; ⊕ 19.00–midnight daily. Housed within the famous American Colony Hotel, this is a favourite watering hole of foreign journalists. The intimate, charming ambience is perfect for sipping a glass of smoky red wine & discussing the current situation in the Middle East.

♀ **Constantine** [80 C4] 3 Hahistadrut St; 6221155; ⊕ 21.00–late daily. The enormous bar/club has been decked out in flashy modern décor & offers live performers, a huge drinks menu & a selection of bar food. Themed nights all week.

♀ **Dublin** [80 C4] 4 Shamai St; 6223612; ⊕ 17.00–03.00 Sat–Thu, 17.00–05.00 Fri. Friendly, relaxed Irish-style pub. Modern Hebrew & Irish music, rock performances & DJ nights all week. You have to be 22 years old to enjoy a pint here.

♀ **Mike's Place** [80 E4] 37 Jaffa St; m 054 9292551; w mikesplacebars.com; ⊕ 16.00–late daily. This quintessential British pub has branches in Jerusalem & Tel Aviv & remains ever popular. Live rock, jazz, blues & acoustic performances & open mic every night.

♀ **Mona** [81 A5] 8 Shmuel Hanagid St; 6222283; w monarest.co.il; ⊕ 19.00–midnight Sat–Thu. Mona is predominantly a restaurant specialising in fish & meat, but its rustic charm & wide bar has seen it become popular with those

looking for a comfortable place to enjoy a cool beer. Popular also with journalists. Located inside the Jerusalem Artists' House.

♀ **The Sira Pub** [81 F5] 4 Ben Sira St; 6234366; ⊕ 16.00–03.00 Sun–Thu, 14.00–05.00 Fri–Sat. This smoky & intimate bar is the perfect place to mingle & chat. The crowd here is very diverse, but mostly bohemian & hip.

♀ **Smadar Theatre Bar** [map, page 72] 4 Lloyd George; 5617819; w lev.co.il; ⊕ 08.00–00.30 daily. Situated in the artsy Smadar Theatre which shows films (one at a time), it attracts a bohemian crowd who come as much for the bar/café as the films. In 2017, the bar & theatre were due to close for renovation, but were still open at the time of writing. Enquire in advance.

☆ **Bar 17** [map, page 72] 17 Haoman St; 6781658. Considered the best club in the city, attracting international DJs & playing house & techno.

☆ **Yellow Submarine** [map, page 72] 13 Harechivim Rd; 6794040; w yellowsubmarine.org. il. Shows get going late (after 22.00) & finish early; admission ₪30–90. Known across the country for its live rock, punk, jazz & acoustic performances, this is Jerusalem's hottest spot to catch up-&-coming artists (despite its rather inconvenient location in the Talpiyot Industrial District).

FESTIVALS

Israel Festival May–Jun; w israel-festival.org/ en. Theatre, dance & classical music performances in theatres & concert halls around Jerusalem.

Jerusalem Film Festival Jul; w jff.org.il/en. International, avant-garde, Israeli directed & modern films & documentaries shown in theatres & cinemas around the city.

Jerusalem International Book Fair Jun; w jbookfair.com/en. Browse, buy & read hundreds of genres of books at this internationally respected book fair.

Latin Patriarch Procession Dec. The procession heads from Jerusalem to the Church of the Nativity in Bethlehem.

International Puppet Festival Aug; Train Theatre; w traintheater.co.il/en. Jerusalem has become the international centre for puppetry & this week-long festival is the culmination of the most colourful performances of this rare art form.

Wine Festival Sep; Israel Museum; w www.imj. org.il/en/events/wine-festival. Started in the late 2000s, this festival hosts numerous wineries which offer wine tasting & food in the Art Garden of the Israel Museum.

PERFORMING ARTS

Israel has long been high in the world rankings of classical music, producing a continuous stream of top-class musicians & orchestras. The arts remain incredibly popular & getting tickets to many of the concerts & theatre performances can be difficult, but can purchased at **Bimot** [80 D4] (*8 Shamai St;* ✆*6237000;* w *bimot.co.il*) box office.

✆ **Barbur** [80 A3] 6 Shirizli St; w barbur.org. A non-profit space created by artists for artists offering regular concerts & showings of differing music genres, art, architecture, dance & cinema.

▄ **Gil** Malha Mall; ✆6788448. A multiplex with 8 screens showing the latest releases of the mainstream cinema industry.

✆ **Jerusalem Centre for Performing Arts (Jerusalem Theatre)** [map, page 72] 20 David Marcus St; ✆5605755; w jerusalem-theatre. co.il. Houses the Jerusalem Theatre, Henry Crown Auditorium & Rebecca Crown Hall that show a collection of Israeli plays, Hebrew translations of classic plays & concerts by the Jerusalem Symphony Orchestra, the Israel Chamber

Ensemble, & occasionally the world-renowned Israel Philharmonic Orchestra whose permanent home is in Tel Aviv.

▄ **Jerusalem Cinematheque** [map, page 72] 11 Hebron Rd; ✆5654333; w jer-cin.org.il/ en. Shows a mixture of classical, avant-garde, Hollywood & experimental films.

✆ **Khan Theatre** [map, page 72] 2 David Remez Sq; ✆6303600; w khan.co.il. One of the most popular venues for new Hebrew theatre performances ranging from Israeli pieces to translations of international classics. There are also regular chamber & jazz concerts, Israeli folklore nights & occasional English performances.

✆ **Sultan's Pool** [map, page 72] Between Jaffa Gate & Mount Zion. Often acts as the beautiful & dramatic setting for modern rock, classical, jazz & theatre performances in the summer months.

✆ **Ticho House** [80 E2] Has regular music performances, art exhibitions & poetry readings (page 116).

✆ **Train Theatre** [map, page 72] Liberty Bell Park; ✆5618514; w traintheater.co.il/en. The home of the world puppetry centre & has regular performances.

✆ **YMCA** [map, page 72] 26 King David St; ✆5692692. Has a regular stream of Israeli music concerts & folk dancing performances. Seats cannot be reserved in advance so get there early.

SHOPPING AND SOUVENIRS

Jerusalem's modern shops and malls are comparable to those found in Europe, with their marble-floored glitzy walkways, fashionable clothes shops and plethora of eateries. **Malha Mall**, also referred to as 'the Kanyon', stands as the country's biggest shopping centre. Its closest equivalent in central Jerusalem is **Mamilla Avenue** [81 G6], just outside the Jaffa Gate in the Old City. The **Nahalat Shiva** neighbourhood, founded in 1869 as the third Jewish settlement outside the Old City, together with the pedestrianised **Ben Yehuda Street** are a hub of fun, full of bustling cafés, bars, fast-food kiosks and overpriced souvenir and Judaica shops. A popular Jewish souvenir is a *mezuzahme*, a small parchment scroll which is fixed to the entrance or front door of a building. Jaffa Street **evening market** is also recommended; the atmosphere is wonderful and there are some great handicrafts to choose from. At the lower end of the nearby **Shlomzion Hamalka Street**, there are a few antique and handicraft shops worth a look. For **camping and outdoor equipment**, try Lametayel [81 E4] (*5 Yoel Salomon St;* ✆*077 3334509;* ⊕ *10.00–20.00 Sun–Thu, 10.00–14.00 Fri*), a big branch of the nationwide chain of camping and travel shops, or the smaller Orcha [81 D5] (*31 Hillel St;* ✆*6240655;* ⊕ *09.00–20.00 Sun–Thu, 10.00–14.00 Fri*).

For more cultural shopping experiences, you can't beat the colourful **Old City souks** (page 104) and **Mahane Yehuda Market** (pages 112–13). Despite the sous' obvious tourist appeal, they are undoubtedly among the main attractions of the Old City, each quarter selling wares that reflect the ethnic origins of the vendors. The **Cardo** [84 D6] in the Jewish Quarter is one of the best places to buy quality Judaica, jewellery and Israeli art, although it is important to note that most Judaica stores do not give refunds, so make sure you compare prices first. Bargaining is not the done thing here, but you can politely ask for a 'discount'. Other good areas for buying Judaica include **Yochanan Migush Halav Street**, the **Mea Shearim neighbourhood** and for more modern styles, the **German Colony**. The Muslim Quarter souks are known for their vibrant, bustling atmosphere and are certainly more 'alive' than their Christian Quarter counterparts, which cater wholly to tourists. At the bottom of Armenian Patriarchate Road in the Armenian Quarter are some good, little-known **craft and pottery stalls** that sell handmade products for a fraction of what you'll pay in the Muslim Quarter. To buy the unique turquoise and blue-patterned tiles and ceramics like those adorning the Dome of the Rock, look no further than **Armenian Ceramics-Balian** (*14 Nablus Rd;* ✆ *6282826;* w *armenianceramics.com*) or **Jerusalem Pottery** [84 D3] (*15 Via Dolorosa;* ✆ *6261587;* w *jerusalempottery.biz;* ⊕ *09.30–17.00 Mon–Sat*) that specialise in authentic, hand-painted wares in a range of geometric patterns, floral motifs and animal designs. Outside **Damascus Gate** [84 D2] is East Jerusalem's busiest shopping area, where local residents come to buy and sell a wide range of products, from food to homewares to Arabic-style embroidered clothes. Another recommended shop for Armenian ceramics is **Vic's** [84 C6] (*77 Armenian Patriarchate Rd;* ✆ *6280496;* e *lepejian_vic@hotmail.com;* ⊕ *09.00–19.00 daily*) in the Armenian district of the Old City. It has a fine selection of pieces handmade by Vic Lepejian. The pomegranate (*rimon* in Hebrew) is the symbol of fertility in the Middle East and central Asia and is a very common ceramic theme all over Israel.

As with the rest of the country, shopping hours in West Jerusalem are 08.30–13.00 and 16.00–19.00 Monday to Thursday and 08.30–14.00 Friday. Stores tend to reopen on Saturday evenings after Shabbat. In Muslim areas such as East Jerusalem and the Muslim Quarter of the Old City, many shops will be open during Shabbat but will often close or have shorter working hours on Fridays, the Muslim holy day. Likewise, shops in the Christian or Armenian quarters will likely close on Sundays.

When you are making purchases, bear in mind that it may be possible to get a tax refund (page 56) on items over US$100, so be sure to ask the vendor for a special receipt or voucher which can be submitted upon departure from Israel at Ben-Gurion Airport.

BOOKSHOPS

The Book Gallery [81 B5] 6 Schatz St; ✆6231087; w bookgallery.co.il; ⊕ 09.00–19.00 Sun–Thu, 09.00–14.00 Fri. A treasure-trove of secondhand, rare & antique books in many languages.
Munther's Book Shop 1 Louis Vincent St; ✆6279777; ⊕ 09.00–21.00 daily. Friendly, fascinating little bookshop opposite the American Colony Hotel. Stocks many English books including maps, bestsellers, history & politics.

Steimatzky [80 E4] 33 Jaffa St; ✆6250155; ⊕ 08.00–19.00 Sun–Thu, 08.00–14.00 Fri. This was the flagship shop in this now incredibly popular nationwide chain & has been open since 1925. Big selection of English novels, non-fiction, maps & travel guides.
Vice Versa French Bookstore [81 F5] 1 Ben Shatach St; ✆6244412; w viceversalib.com; ⊕ 09.00–19.00 Sun–Thu, 09.00–13.30 Fri. Has a good French & Hebrew selection & occasional literary events & readings.

OTHER PRACTICALITIES

The central **post office** is located on 23 Jaffa Street [80 F4] (📞*6290676;* ⏲ *08.00–18.00 Sun–Thu, 08.00–noon Fri*), but the postal authority's website can provide a list of all branches in the city (📞*035 385909;* w *israelpost.co.il*). The nearby Assicurazioni Generali building is now home to the **Population and Immigration Authority** [80 F4] (*1 Shlomzion Hamalka St;* 📞**3450;* w *piba.gov.il;* ⏲ *14.30–17.00 Mon, 08.00–noon Sun–Tue & Thu, 14.30–17.00 Wed*). With regards to **money**, it is important to note that there are no **ATMs** for international cards in the Old City. Numerous **exchange** shops (including one inside the Damascus Gate) offer a cash withdrawal service but charge a percentage which varies from one kiosk to another. The exchange rate offered is fair, but it is best to use one of the ATMs on Jaffa Street. **Newpharm pharmacy** [80 B4] (*27 King George V St;* 📞*6259999;* ⏲ *08.30–19.30 Sun–Thu, 08.30–14.00 Fri*) and **Superpharm pharmacy** [80 F4] (*3 Hahistadrut St;* 📞*6246244;* ⏲ *08.00–midnight Sun–Thu, 08.00–15.00 Fri, 19.00–midnight Sat*) are located in the centre. The nearest **hospitals** are Hadassah (*Ein Kerem;* 📞*6777111*) and Shaare Zedek Medical Centre (*12 Beit Shmuel St;* 📞*6666666*), which both entail a 20- to 30-minute bus ride.

WHAT TO SEE AND DO

OLD CITY In a city of such religious and historic poignancy, Jerusalem's Old City sits like the jewel in the crown. Within the grand city walls, a living, breathing museum of sacred buildings, fervent worshippers, ancient architecture and centuries-old traditions abounds. The Old City is but 1km² in size, yet its reach extends across the world, Jews, Christians and Muslims worshipping here with passion and zeal. The Western Wall, Church of the Holy Sepulchre and Temple Mount may stand as the three most ideologically and conceptually opposing religious sites, yet they are by no means the extent. A jumble of buildings fall into four rough quarters: Christian, Armenian, Jewish and Muslim forming an array of ornate architectural styles from every century of the city's long life. Holy men, pilgrims, tourists and street vendors together wander the cobbled alleyways, bazaars and souks, their customs and dress adding yet more colour to this eclectic mini-city.

Christian Quarter Located in the northwest quadrant of the Old City, the Christian Quarter is characterised by its ancient churches, bustling bazaars and representation of most Christian denominations. Its centrepiece, the Church of the Holy Sepulchre, is the holiest place in Christianity and marks the final stop on the Via Dolorosa pilgrimage walk, an approximation of the footsteps of Jesus on his path to Golgotha (see box, pages 96–7). The quarter is accessed by the New and Jaffa gates, the latter being the Old City's busiest visitors' entrance. Of the 4,200 people who reside within the Christian Quarter, the vast majority belong to the Greek Orthodox Church, its architectural and cultural influence being clearly visible, while Arabic remains the predominant language.

Jaffa Gate [84 C5] This is located on the border between the Armenian and Christian quarters to the left of the Citadel of David. At the time of its construction it marked the beginning (or end) of the highway leading to the thriving port city of Jaffa. The gate has gone by a number of names over the years, notably the Arabic Bab Al-Khalil (Hebron Gate), named after the road leading to the city of Hebron. It is the name still used in Arabic. A closer inspection reveals two entrances: one an arched L-shape and next to it a wider one created in 1898 to allow Kaiser Wilhelm II to enter the city without alighting from his carriage. Today the gate is accessed from the main Jaffa Road, and steps on the left lead up to the beginning of the Ramparts Walk (see box, page 107).

Church of the Holy Sepulchre [84 D4] (⊕ *04.30–19.00 daily*) This awe-inspiring church is the traditional site of Jesus's Crucifixion, burial and Resurrection and is the single most important shrine in Christendom. From the exterior, the church looks rather shabby, its scaffolding a long-lasting remnant of the conflict of ownership between the countless religious sects that have laid claim to it. To preserve the peace among these numerous religious communities, the key to the church has remained in the hands of a Muslim family since Ottoman times. Today, the church is divided among the Greek Orthodox, Armenian Orthodox and Roman Catholic denominations, their different ecclesiastical styles and ornate methods of worship forming a fascinatingly beautiful blend within the ancient church.

Following Constantine the Great's adoption of Christianity, his mother Queen Helena arrived in the Holy Land in search of Jesus's site of Crucifixion and burial. She is attributed with having discovered what is believed to be the rock of Golgotha and nearby tomb, known as Anastasis (Greek for resurrection). Constantine commissioned a shrine above the site in 330CE, later destroyed by the Persians in 614. Most of the building we see today dates to the 12th-century Crusader period as well as later renovations following a series of earthquakes and fires.

What to see and do The **Unction Stone** is located immediately inside the entrance and commemorates the preparation of Jesus's body for burial. The ornate lamps that hang over the stone belong to each of the different denominations that are represented within the church.

Calvary (Golgotha) is the traditional site of Jesus's Crucifixion and is accessed by narrow steps to the right of the entrance. It is the most extravagantly decorated area of the church and comprises three parts: the Chapel of the Nailing of the Cross (station 11 along the Via Dolorosa) to the left of the altar, the Statue of Mary (station 13) marking the spot where Jesus's body was removed from the cross and given to his mother and, next to this, the Rock of Calvary (station 12). It was around this rock that the church was built and is today encased in glass, a small hole allowing visitors to touch it.

The Rotunda (Anastasis) is the church's *pièce de résistance*, located to the west of the entrance beneath the vast dome. In the centre sits the edicule, revered as the tomb of Christ. It is housed within a rather unsightly wooden structure, supported

MODEST DRESS

Jerusalem is first and foremost the religious centre of three world faiths, and walking around the Jewish, Christian and Muslim sites it is important to respect dress codes. Wearing revealing clothing such as sleeveless shirts, shorts or skirts above the knee will result in you not being allowed entry into many religious buildings. In Jerusalem's cold winters this isn't a problem but come the stifling hot summer months dressing up can be more uncomfortable. Loose, baggy clothing is recommended, or alternatively carry a shawl or shirt with you to put on as you enter religious buildings. Men must wear *yarmulkes* (Jewish caps) on entering synagogues and to approach the Western Wall, but paper versions are provided on entry free of charge.

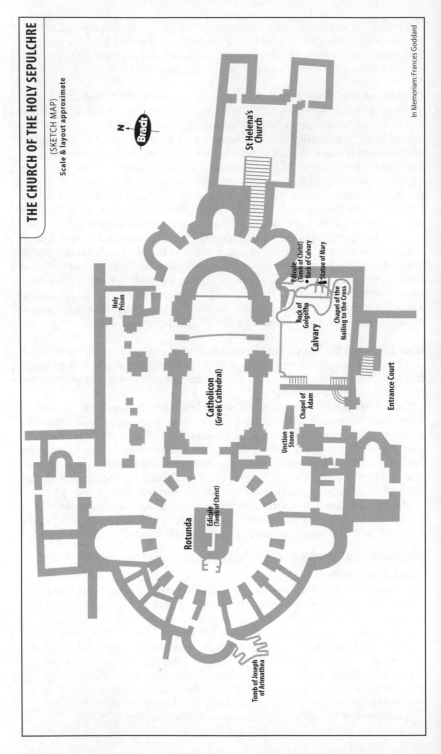

THE CHURCH OF THE HOLY SEPULCHRE

(SKETCH MAP)
Scale & layout approximate

N Bradt

St Helena's Church

Holy Prison

Catholicon
(Greek Cathedral)

Rotunda

Edicule
(Tomb of Christ)

Tomb of Joseph
of Arimathea

Edicule
(Tomb of Christ)
Rock of Calvary
Statue of Mary

Rock of
Golgotha
Calvary

Chapel of the
Nailing to the Cross

Chapel of Adam

Unction
Stone

Entrance Court

In Memoriam: Frances Goddard

by scaffolding to protect it against earthquakes. Inside, the Chapel of the Holy Sepulchre (station 14) contains the tomb of Jesus, marked by a marble slab.

Other notable sights within the church include the **Chapel of Adam**, which houses the cracked rock said to have been caused by the earthquake that occurred at the moment of the Crucifixion; the **Holy Prison** where tradition has it Jesus was kept before the Crucifixion; and **St Helena's Church**, a vast underground complex containing the Chapel of the Finding of the Cross. Also of note is the small **tomb of Joseph of Arimathea**, whose discovery proved this area was once used as a burial site and, according to Christian tradition, that it was the site of Jesus's death, burial and Crucifixion, although the Garden Tomb (page 114) is another, later contender.

Church of St John the Baptist [84 D5] (*Muristan Sq*) The silver-domed Church of St John the Baptist stands as the oldest in Jerusalem, and is the original 'Hospital of St John' after which the Knights Hospitaller were named. The present church was built on the site of a 5th-century chapel, possibly because of the presence of the relics of St John the Baptist, and belonged to a pilgrim hospice. In 1099, Christian knights wounded in the battle for Jerusalem were cared for in the church, many of whom, upon recovery and subsequent defeat of the Crusaders, dedicated themselves to caring for the sick and protecting pilgrims of the Holy Land. They called themselves the Knights Hospitaller, and so the order was formed. They later developed into the military order that played a crucial role in the defence of the Holy Land. The church can be seen from the fountain in the middle of **Muristan Square** (from Persian *bimaristan* meaning 'hospital'). With the exception of the simple façade and its two bell towers, the church remains as it has for 1,000 years, and is an integral part of Jerusalem's Christian history. The entrance is located along Christian Quarter Street in Muristan Square. It is signposted in Greek only but a small blue painting of St John indicates you are in the right place. The church doesn't keep regular opening hours, but you can ask the Greek Orthodox priest who resides in the adjacent monastery to open it for you.

Alexander Nevsky Church [84 D4] (*Souk Al-Dabbagh;* ✆*6274952;* ⊕ *09.00–18.00 daily*) Named after the legendary Russian commander and prince Alexander Nevsky (1221–63), the church was built on land purchased by Russia from the Coptic Church in 1859. It is famous for housing the remains of an impressive Roman arch believed to be the 'Justice Gate' as well as remnants from the 4th-century Holy Sepulchre Church.

The Via Dolorosa (Way of Sorrow or Suffering in Latin) is one of Christianity's most celebrated devotional routes and follows what tradition states was Jesus's path from his condemnation to his Crucifixion in Golgotha. Today the route begins near the Lion's Gate in the Muslim Quarter and ends in the Church of the Holy Sepulchre in the Christian Quarter. Every Friday at 15.00 Christian pilgrims, led by Italian Franciscans, walk the course, which is marked by 14 Stations of the Cross (nine located along the route and five within the Church of the Holy Sepulchre). Stations III, IV, V, VI and VII are open only on Friday afternoons. During Holy Week, thousands of pilgrims join the procession that winds down the narrow alleys of the Old City, a moving and impressive sight to behold.

HISTORY Pilgrims began to trace the route taken by Jesus when open Christian worship became permitted during the Byzantine period. Over the years the route has changed along with the Old City's jumbled façade, and would have looked very different during Jesus's time. From the 14th to 16th centuries, pilgrims followed what was known as the Franciscan route, which began in the Church of the Holy Sepulchre and included eight stations. At the same time, the tradition of 14 stations was emerging in Europe, and so as not to disappoint European pilgrims, six more were included. Although members of different denominations follow their own routes, the most widely accepted is that of the early Byzantine Christians. Eight of the 14 stations along the Via Dolorosa are described in scriptures, while the other six are traditional. It is important to note that the stations are not historical sites but commemorate religious events.

Station I – Jesus is condemned to death [85 E4] Located on the left, 300m from Lion's Gate, is the large courtyard of the **Omariye College** [85 F3] (⊕ *14.30–18.00 Mon–Thu & Sat, 14.30–16.00 Fri*) that marks the beginning of the Via Dolorosa. The minaret that stands in the distance is traditionally named the 'Antonia Tower' after historian Josephus's description of the ancient Roman fortress where Jesus was condemned to death by Pontius Pilate. The college is still used as a school and can be visited at limited times.

Station II – Jesus takes up the cross [85 E3] Across the street in a large courtyard are the **Sanctuaries of the Flagellation and Condemnation** [85 F2] (⊕ *08.00–11.45 & 14.00–18.00 daily, 08.00–11.45 & 13.00–17.00 between 1 Oct & 31 Mar*) where according to tradition, Roman soldiers flogged Jesus and placed a crown of thorns on his head. A few metres further along is the **Notre Dame de Sion Ecco Homo Convent** [85 E3] where steps lead down to what has long been claimed to be the **Lithostratos (Pavement of Justice)** (⊕ *08.30–17.00*), the section of paving stones where Pilate condemned Jesus (it has since been dated to the 2nd century CE). A little further on, and spanning the route, is the **Ecce Homo Arch** named after Pilate's words 'Behold the man!' upon Jesus being presented to the crowd. The arch is a traditional symbol, having also been built in the 2nd century CE.

Lutheran Church of the Redeemer [84 D4] (*Muristan Sq*; ☏ *6276111*; ⊕ *09.00–13.00 & 13.30–15.00 daily; admission ₪15*) The current Protestant church, consecrated by Kaiser Wilhelm II on 31 October 1898, was built upon land granted to the German emperor by the Ottomans as a symbol of alliance. It has formed the seat of the Lutheran community in Jerusalem ever since. While

Station III – Jesus falls under the cross for the first time [85 E3] This traditional station is marked by a small 19th-century **chapel** that was funded by Catholic soldiers of the Free Polish army during World War I. Walk to the corner of Al-Wad Street and turn left. The chapel is immediately on the left with a relief of Jesus falling, above the door.

Station IV – Jesus meets his mother [85 E3] The station is marked by a small Armenian chapel located a few metres along from Station III. Blue iron doors, above which is a bas-relief of the Virgin Mary comforting Jesus, mark the entrance.

Station V – Simon of Cyrene is forced to carry the cross [85 E3] The event, where Simon of Cyrene (a north African pilgrim) was compelled by Roman soldiers to help Jesus carry the Cross, is mentioned in three of the Gospels. The station is marked by a **Franciscan oratory** and is located on the corner of Al-Wad Street and the Via Dolorosa.

Station VI – Veronica wipes the sweat from Jesus's face [84 D3] A hundred metres further up is the chapel of the **Convent of the Little Sisters of Jesus**. The chapel is the traditional house of Veronica from where she emerged to wipe the sweat from Jesus's face.

Station VII – Jesus falls for the second time [84 D3] This station traditionally marks the place where Jesus passed beneath the Gate of Judgement on his way to Golgotha. Today a large Roman column housed within a **Franciscan chapel** commemorates the event. Walk to the crossroads at the end of the Via Dolorosa. The chapel is located on the northwest corner where Souk Khan Al-Zeit Street and Al-Khanqa Street meet.

Station VIII – Jesus consoles the women of Jerusalem [84 D4] A stone embedded in the outer wall of the **Greek Monastery of St Haralambos** [84 C3] commemorates the point where Jesus met the daughters of Jerusalem, who wept over his fate. According to Luke's Gospel he replied: 'Do not weep for me; weep for yourselves and for your children.' In Jesus's time this would have been an open field between the city wall and Golgotha. The monastery is located 30m up Al-Khanqa Street on the opposite side to Station VII.

Station IX – Jesus falls for the third time [84 D4] Walk back to Souk Khan Al-Zeit Street and turn right. After 50m a stairway on the right leads to a Coptic church within which is a Roman column painted with a Latin cross. This marks the traditional spot where Jesus fell for the third time. A doorway to the left of Station IX leads on to the roof of the Chapel of St Helena, where an Ethiopian church is located.

Stations X–XIV [84 D4] The final five stations are located within the Church of the Holy Sepulchre. From the Ethiopian chapel walk down the stairs, which will bring you out in the courtyard of the church (pages 93–5).

the history of the site is undoubtedly significant, the view from the top of the bell tower (⊕ *10.00–17.00 Sat–Mon; admission ₪15*) is most certainly its most charming feature. Climb the narrow, circular stone steps past the vast bell to the top of the tower for a 360° panoramic view over the Old City. While it is rather demanding, those who undertake the hike will reap the rewards of Jerusalem's best viewpoint. The bell rings daily at noon so visitors (in the interest of preserving their eardrums) cannot ascend between 11.45 and 12.20. English services are held on Sundays at 09.00.

Bazaars In contrast to the Muslim Quarter souks (Arabic for 'bazaar') that remain an active part of local daily life, those in the Christian Quarter cater only for the throngs of visitors who pour in through Jaffa Gate. Packed into the narrow, cobbled alleys, stores sell an interesting mix of religious items, the vendors happy to promote rosary beads alongside yarmulkes with a few novelty T-shirts thrown in for good measure. Handicrafts, jewellery, pottery, Arabic-style home decorations and spice stalls compete for space amid the crowds that weave through the alleyways, and yet somehow, despite its obvious tourist appeal, the souk is a fascinating and lively place to explore. There are a couple of shops selling exquisite and very distinct Syrian furniture and they can arrange for shipment abroad. Prices are predictably over-inflated so if you wish to purchase, bargain hard! Stores are generally open ⊕ 09.00–19.00 Monday–Saturday with limited opening on Sundays.

New Gate [84 B3] New Gate was not one of Suleiman's original seven gates (hence the name) but was built in 1887 by Sultan Abdul Hamid to link the houses in the northwest with the Old City. The adjacent Tancred's Tower, named after the Latin Kingdom ruler who is believed to have commissioned it, is built from stones originally prepared for Herod's palace. During the Crusader period, the stones were removed and used to build the tower. The tower is known in Arabic as Qasr Jalud (Goliath's Castle) after a legend that it was near here that David killed Goliath.

Armenian Quarter The Armenian Quarter is the smallest area of the Old City and is today home to some 2,200 residents. The area centres on the ornate Armenian cathedral and has its own schools, seminary, library and residential areas, all occupying what was once the site of Herod's great palace. The Armenians have formed part of the city's demographic make-up since the 1st century when the Roman emperor Titus brought Armenian traders, artisans and soldiers to the Holy Land. They were the first to adopt Christianity in the 4th century and within 100 years, following an influx of pilgrims, had erected over 70 monasteries in Jerusalem. The Armenians are an ancient people whose history dates back over 4,000 years, their rich cultural value and dramatic history often being overlooked in favour of their more vocal Old City neighbours. As an exiled people who have suffered great persecution and a devastating genocide, the small community in Jerusalem has a strong sense of cultural identity and independence, and has largely managed to avoid the battles and wars that have ravaged the rest of the Old City.

Citadel and Tower of David Museum [84 C5] (✆ 6265333; w tod.org.il/en; ⊕ 10.00–16.00 Sat–Thu, 10.00–14.00 Fri; admission adult/child ₪40/18) The Tower of David Museum occupies the imposing citadel that forms one of the Old City's most recognisable landmarks. Throughout Jerusalem's tumultuous past, the citadel stood as the main line of defence to the north and west, being reinforced and rebuilt by each generation of invaders. The area was hugely fortified by the Hasmonean kings and, in 24BCE, refortified by King Herod. Throughout the ages the citadel was used as a garrison for Roman soldiers and, with the adoption of Christianity, a quasi-monastery. It once again resumed its military role throughout the Muslim conquest and Crusader rule, during which time its large moat was constructed. It also became the seat of the Crusader king of Jerusalem. The fortress in its present form dates from the Mamluk period, and later underwent changes during the Ottoman period when a large mosque was built, its towering minaret later dubbed the 'Tower of David' by 19th-century European travellers (which has caused considerable confusion over the years). When the British army entered the city in December 1917, it was from the platform outside the citadel that General Allenby addressed the people of Jerusalem, declaring freedom of worship. Today the citadel is home to the Tower of David Museum, one of the city's top attractions and a valuable tool in piecing together Jerusalem's past. Displays are spread throughout the network of guardrooms and cover the 5,000 action-filled years of Jerusalem's history. Exhibits present the city's chronological story with the aid of models, visual aids and multi-media displays. The walls and ramparts of the citadel provide some fantastic views of both the Old City and modern city.

Show and tours Every evening (except Fri) the citadel hosts the *son et lumière* show, a light display depicting the city's history (*admission adult/child ₪55/45*). Free guided tours in English leave the main entrance at 11.00 Sunday to Thursday and a free downloaded MP3 tour is available on the website. A two-in-one-entry ticket is available (*admission adult/child ₪70/55*).

St James Cathedral [84 C6] (⊕ *08.00–17.00 daily*) Amid such an abundance of ecclesiastical buildings within the Old City, St James Cathedral is sadly often overlooked. Tradition has it the cathedral was named after both Jesus's brother and James the Apostle, both of whom are said to be buried within. Jesus's brother is believed to be buried within the central nave, while St James the Apostle rests under the exquisitely decorated shrine behind large wooden doors. Hundreds of gold and silver lanterns hang in the cathedral illuminating the domed ceiling. If possible, try to visit during Armenian Orthodox mass. Afternoon mass is signalled by the priest clanging wooden bars in the porch. The entrance to the monastery is located approximately 200m along Armenian Patriarchate Street from Jaffa Gate on the right.

Museum of Armenian Art and History [84 C7] (*Armenian Orthodox Patriarchate St;* ✆*6282331;* ⊕ *09.30–16.30 Mon–Sat; admission ₪5*) Heading south towards the Zion Gate, pass under the narrow bridge and turn left after 30m. The museum is located on the right of a large, 200-year-old courtyard. Displays are simple yet informative, depicting the lives, history, culture and art of the Armenian community in Jerusalem. The most moving and horrifying exhibit depicts the Armenian genocide in Turkey during World War I, a graphic and powerful display of photographs and personal descriptions.

Zion Gate [84 D7] The gate leads out of the Armenian Quarter and provides access to and from Mount Zion. It remains in the original 'L' shape, designed to prevent horse-mounted soldiers from charging, and to slow the battering rams used in attacks during the Ottoman period. Cars slowly weave their way through the awkwardly shaped pass and a resident camel often sits in the corner. The gate bears the scars from the 1948 Arab–Israeli War in the form of bullet marks on its outer edge. It is known in Arabic as Bab el Nabi Daoud (Gate of the Prophet David) because of the traditional site of David's tomb just outside (pages 106–7).

Jewish Quarter The Jewish Quarter is undoubtedly the most serene area of the Old City, where Jerusalem's oldest synagogues stand, where bougainvillea flowers creep over brick walls, and where an air of religious learning permeates the quiet cobbled alleys. During Herod's reign, this was the city's most affluent neighbourhood, inhabited mainly by aristocratic and priestly families. It also formed the core of the Roman city of Aelia Capitolina with the grand Cardo, the city's main thoroughfare, beginning here. The quaint Hurva Square sits at the centre of the quarter and is fringed by outdoor cafés and bakeries. At the eastern edge of the Jewish Quarter, the vast plaza stretches the length of the Western Wall, the last remaining icon of the Second Temple, and the holiest Jewish site.

Western Wall [85 F5] The Western Wall is the single most sacred site in Judaism. It stands as the last remnant of the Second Temple and has been a site of pilgrimage for Jews from all over the world since the Ottoman period, who come to lament over the loss of their temple, their emotional and sorrowful prayers awarding it the name 'The Wailing Wall'. Today it remains the heart of the Jewish faith and one of the most religious and politically sensitive sites on the planet.

History The wall, or Hakotel, was built by King Herod in 20BCE as part of the Temple Mount complex and is all that remains from the Roman destruction of the temple in 70CE. From the Ottoman period, Jewish pilgrims flocked to the wall, at the time accessed by a narrow alley – 3.6m wide and 28m long – embedded in the surrounding Muslim neighbourhoods. Throughout the 19th century, conflict hummed around the wall and several prominent Jews, including Baron Rothschild (see box, page 186) and Sir Moses Montefiore, attempted unsuccessfully to gain control of it. During the British Mandate period there were numerous clashes between Jews and Muslims and from December 1947 Jews were banned from approaching the wall, a restriction which, following the capitulation of the Jewish Quarter in May 1948, lasted 19 years. After the 1967 Six Day War the wall once again fell into Jewish hands and was greatly expanded to create the vast plaza that we see today.

The wall and tunnels The Western Wall lies at the end of the 56m-long, sloping **Western Wall Plaza** and is the principal site of Jewish pilgrimage, where worshippers come to slip prayer notes in between the ancient stones. The plaza itself is a great place to people-watch, especially during religious celebrations or the Shabbat prayer sessions. Inside the men's area the cavern-like **Wilson's Arch** serves as the main place of prayer (particularly in summer when it is air conditioned). It once formed part of the great bridge linking the Upper City and temple. To the left of the men's prayer area is the beginning of the **Western Wall Tunnels** [85 F5] (✆ *5958, 6271333;* w *thekotel.org;* ⏰ *07.00–last tour booking Sun–Thu, 07.00–noon*

<table>
<tr><td>VISITING THE WESTERN WALL</td></tr>
</table>

There are three entrances to the plaza, one from Shlomo Goren (near the Dung Gate), another from the base of the steps leading down from the Burnt House and Western Wall viewing platform and the third from Hakotel Street that leads off Chain (Bab Al-Silsila) Street. Modest dress is mandatory and bared shoulders or legs above the knee are forbidden. Shawls are supplied at the entry points. Men are supplied with paper yarmulke if needed. Visitors of all faiths are in theory welcome to approach the wall provided they respect religious rules. On the Sabbath, taking photographs, using mobile phones and smoking are forbidden inside the plaza.

Fri; admission adult/child ₪30/15), excavated to reveal buried sections of the original temple wall and stretching as far as the Via Dolorosa. Guided tours (in English, 1¼hrs, must be booked in advance) are a fascinating insight into the wall's complex layers of history. Tours take visitors along the narrow **Secret Passage** to the Herodian Wall, once a beautiful public building. The **Large Hall** leads to the **Largest Stone**, a 570-tonne building stone that is the last remaining foundation block and the largest stone to be unearthed in the country. **Warren's Gate** (there are also three other ancient gates: Wilson's, Barclay's and Robinson's) is named after the prominent 19th-century researcher of Jerusalem and leads to a **small alcove** that is part of the wall closest to the temple. Known as 'the holy of holies', it is separated from the foundation stone (located beneath the Dome of the Rock) by a mere 100m. From here the tunnels lead to the **Herodian Wall**, which during temple times was a bustling shopping street, past a **quarry** and **aqueduct** and emerge along the **Via Dolorosa** in the Muslim Quarter. The **Chain of Generations Centre** (❀ *5958, 6271333; w thekotel.org; ⊕ 08.00–last tour Sun–Thu; admission adult/child ₪25/15) is a good accompaniment to the tunnel tour, relating the story of the Jewish people throughout the past 3,500 years using a combination of music, sculpture, archaeology, glass, light effects and holographic images. It was seven years in the making and is a revolutionary museum experience.

The Cardo [84 D6] The Cardo formed the main north–south thoroughfare of Roman Jerusalem, which was modelled on the structure of typical Roman cities. The street was excavated for 200m and today a small section at its southern end has been restored to reveal the parallel columns that ran its length and would have supported a wooden roof. The 22.5m-wide thoroughfare was flanked by shops, but later had a row of buildings erected down the centre. The street now comprises two lanes: Chabad and Hayehudim. The street is bordered by cafés, art galleries and age-old bakeries and is one of the busiest areas of the Jewish Quarter. A section of the Cardo has been rebuilt as a modern shopping area comprising mainly pricey Judaica stores and art galleries, and is a far cry from the original shops selling grain, spices and olives, but it is nevertheless a pleasant place to stroll around.

Synagogues The **Hurva Synagogue** [84 D5] (*hurva* meaning 'ruins') was originally commissioned by Rabbi Yehuda Hanassi who arrived in Jerusalem in 1701 with 500 Ashkenazis. Following his death, the synagogue fell into disrepair and wasn't fully rebuilt until 1856. From then until its destruction during the 1948 war it acted as the spiritual core of Jerusalem's Ashkenazi Jews. After the Israeli capture of Jerusalem in 1967, plans were discussed to rebuild the ancient synagogue, but weren't put into action until 2006 when its signature arch was dismantled. A US$6.2 million budget saw it rebuilt it to its former neo-Byzantine splendour, and it was completed in early 2010.

The **Rambam Synagogue** [84 D6] is named after Rabbi Moshe ben Nachman (the Rambam) who arrived in Jerusalem in 1267 following the decimation of the city in the battle between the Crusaders and the Mamluks. He established a synagogue amid the destruction, a poignant event seen by Jews as the beginning of the reconstruction of Jerusalem. In the 16th century, the Muslims commandeered the building, and between 1949 and 1967 it was used to house livestock. Only after Israel gained control of the city was it returned to its original purpose. Since then, it has superseded the Hurva Synagogue as the most important Jewish house of worship within the Old City. It has been well restored and marks a key point on the Jewish history trail.

The **Four Sephardic Synagogues** [84 D6] (✆ *6280592;* ⊕ *09.30–16.00 Sun–Thu,
09.30–12.30 Fri*) is a complex of four Jewish houses of prayer, each representing
different histories, religious requirements and prayer practices. Following
the arrival of Sephardic Jews expelled from Spain in the 17th century, a new
synagogue was built, becoming the first since the Ottoman period. It was named
the **Yochanan ben Zakai Synagogue** after the notable sage who is attributed with
later establishing the Sanhedrin (Jewish school of biblical studies). Another wave
of Sephardic immigrants arrived from Istanbul, Turkey, later in the 17th century
who constructed the adjacent **Istanbuli Synagogue**. Named after Elijah the Prophet,
the third, **Eliyahu Hanavi Synagogue** was used solely for Torah study. In the centre
of the three buildings, a courtyard formed, which during the 18th century was
converted into the **Emtsai** (or **Middle**) **Synagogue**. The complex is also attributed
with being the last position held by Jewish defenders before the fall of the Jewish
Quarter to the Jordanians in 1948.

The Herodian Quarter During the Second Temple period, the Upper City (the
present-day Jewish Quarter) housed the most affluent of Jerusalem's residents and
was the last section to be razed to the ground by the Romans in 70CE. The **Burnt
House** [85 E5] (✆ *6287211;* ⊕ *09.00–17.00 Thu–Sun, 09.00–13.00 Fri; admission adult/
child ₪25/12*) stands as a testament to the day the Upper City was burnt and those
within lost their lives. Finds discovered in the house include an arm bone seemingly
reaching for a nearby spear, coins, and many household objects including a set of
weights inscribed with the name 'Bar Kathros'. This find proved to be the most telling,
possibly identifying the occupants as being of the priestly family known from the
Talmud to have lived at the time of the Second Temple. Inside the house there is a
short film (every 40mins) that delves into the history of the site and Upper City. A
visit to the house is more interesting for what it represents than for the finds inside.
    The **Wohl Archaeological Museum** [85 E6] (*1 Hakaraim St;* ✆ *6265900;* ⊕ *09.00–
17.00 Sun–Thu, 09.00–13.00 Fri; admission adult/child ₪15/7*) contains remains
of Jewish mansions and houses from the affluent Upper City, which was mostly
occupied by Jewish Temple priests. On display are luxury relics ranging from
mosaic floors to expensive glassware that provide an insight into the Herodian
Quarter and its wealthy residents. Today, the quarter lies 3–7m below street level, a
staircase leading up from the submerged museum ending abruptly and providing a
clear reminder of the devastation caused by the Roman destruction. The museum
contains three sections, the most impressive being the **Palatial Mansion**, the most
complete of the Herodian houses on display.

Jerusalem Archaeological Park [85 F5] (✆ *6277550;* w *archpark.org.il;*
⊕ *08.00–17.00 Sun–Thu, 08.00–14.00 Fri; admission adult/child ₪30/16*) This
covers the area surrounding the Western Wall Plaza and southern wall of the
Temple Mount complex, and has been extensively excavated to reveal substantial
remains from the Second Temple period. Jumbled remains from the Byzantine,
early Islamic, Crusader and Mumluk periods provide an interesting glimpse into
Jerusalem's layers of occupation and are best appreciated by first paying a visit to
the Davidson Centre which displays historic exhibits and virtual reconstructions.
A 1-hour guided tour costs ₪160 and must be booked in advance.

Dung Gate [85 F6] The Jewish Quarter is accessed by the Dung Gate located on
its southern wall. A bus stop at the top of Shlomo Goren Street that passes through
the gate is directly outside the southern entrance to the Western Wall Plaza. It

also provides access to the visitors' entrance to the Temple Mount and Jerusalem Archaeological Park. There are conflicting theories as to the origins of the name of the gate, the most plausible being that it was where rubbish was brought out of the city from the 2nd century onwards.

Muslim Quarter What the Christian, Jewish and Armenian quarters have in historic buildings, state-of-the-art museums and ecclesiastical marvels, the Muslim Quarter has in vivacity. It is undoubtedly the liveliest of the four quarters, the Damascus and Herod's gates opening into the thriving Arab neighbourhood of East Jerusalem. Its markets are incomparable: a hub of activity, noise, aromas and traditional Arabic merchandise, a wonderful contrast to the more serene streets elsewhere in the quarter. But the area is not without its historic gems: the vast, walled Temple Mount complex occupies the most prized piece of real estate in the country, its majestic golden Dome of the Rock forming the centrepiece of the Old City. As the call of the *muezzin* echoes across the city signalling the beginning of Friday prayer sessions, swarms of worshippers pour down the lanes towards the mount, while from its easternmost gate begins the Via Dolorosa, Christianity's holiest processional.

Temple Mount [85 F4] (✆ 6283292; ◷ 07.30–10.00 & 12.30–13.30 Sun–Thu; admission free) Rising above the city, the golden Dome of the Rock (Qubba Al-Sakhra) forms the centrepiece of Jerusalem's holiest Islamic site, the Temple Mount. Known to Muslims as Al-Haram Al-Sharif (Noble Sanctuary), the heart of the Temple Mount is Al-Aqsa Mosque, which is believed to be the site from where Mohammed began his Night Journey to Heaven and today ranks as the third holiest Islamic site in the world after Mecca and Medina. To Jews, this is also the pinnacle of holiness, the site where the First and Second temples stood, where the Foundation Stone upon which the world was built stands, where Adam was created and where Isaac was almost sacrificed by Abraham. In a city that has seen more than its fair share of turmoil and tension, the Temple Mount is today still a raw and sensitive point, often acting as the centre of unrest between Jews and Muslims. For the most part, however, the area is a peaceful and tranquil place of worship and as you wander around the wide, open complex, it is hard to envisage the 3,000 years of turmoil that have surrounded it.

History The history of the Temple Mount spans 3,000 years, seven periods of time, three world religions and five cultures. Upon land bought by King David, Jerusalem's First Temple was built by his son King Solomon and stood until the Babylonians destroyed it in 586BCE. Not long after, Jews returning from exile rebuilt it and so the Second Temple came into being. Following the Roman destruction of the city in 70CE, the temple (bar the Western Wall) was left in ruins until the Muslim conquest in 638 when Caliph Omar built the first mosque upon the site. Fifty years later, during the reign of Caliph Abd Al-Malik, the Dome of the Rock and Al-Aqsa Mosque were erected.

In 1099, the Crusaders captured Jerusalem, whereby holy sites on the Temple Mount were declared Christian, and the area became the seat of the Knights Templar. In 1187, Saladin put an end to Crusader rule, reconverting churches to mosques.

Safety issues Following the 1948 Arab–Israeli War, Jerusalem remained divided, with the Old City and Temple Mount under Jordanian rule. After Israel captured the city during the 1967 Six Day War, the Waqf was allowed to retain administration of the site on the proviso that non-Muslims be allowed to enter. In order to prevent rioting and religious unrest, the Israeli government has banned any non-Islamic praying on the site. Modest dress is compulsory and open displays of affection are not appreciated. The Dome of the Rock, Al-Aqsa Mosque and Islamic Museum are closed to all non-Muslims. Some Jews do enter the Temple Mount but often limit themselves to the perimeter wall. During times of political unrest it is best to check government warnings on the advisability of visiting the complex, although entry is generally prohibited if threats arise. During the relatively short opening times, queues for entry can be long so it is best to arrive early.

What to see and do While the most impressive and alluring structure within the Temple Mount is undoubtedly the Dome of the Rock, the 144,000m² **Al-Aqsa Mosque** [85 F5] is the holiest part of the complex. It was the earliest mosque constructed in Palestine and is today one of Islam's most important houses of prayer, believed to be the place referred to in the Quran as 'Al-Aqsa' (the furthermost). Although the mosque has suffered great tragedy over the last century, being, *inter alia*, the site of King Abdullah of Jordan's 1951 assassination, it is today a mostly peaceful and active centre of prayer holding up to 4,000 worshippers at any one time. In the southeast corner of the temple esplanade are the scanty remains of **Solomon's Stables** [85 G5] (part of a more extensive underground hall area), which contrary to their name were not in existence in Solomon's time, but acted as stables during the Crusader occupation. Just north of the mosque, the circular **Al-Kas Fountain** [85 F4] dates to 709 and is used by Muslims for the ritual washing prior to prayer sessions. Directly ahead lies the octagonal **Dome of the Rock** [85 F4], crowned by its gold-leafed dome, a million-dollar gift from Saudi Arabia in 1965. It stands as the oldest Islamic shrine in the world (dated to 688) and also boasts the world's oldest-surviving *mihrab* (niche indicating the direction of Mecca). Extensive decoration from a variety of periods including mosaics, painted wood, marble, coloured tiles, carpets and carved stone covers both the interior and exterior of the building, most of the blue and gold exterior tiles laid under Suleiman the Magnificent. Muslim pilgrimage to Jerusalem is known as *taqdis* and marks the final destination on the main pilgrimage (hajj). The **Islamic Museum** [85 F5] (⊕ *08.00–11.30 Sat–Thu*) although currently not open to non-Muslims, has interesting displays on Islamic art, the Quran and architectural items.

Bazaars (⊕ *09.00–19.00 daily, with limited hours on Fri*) The Muslim Quarter bazaars are among the most fascinating places to visit in the Old City, a clear demonstration of the thriving Arab communities who call this area (and the neighbourhoods in East Jerusalem) home. Beginning at the swarming Damascus Gate two market streets branch off southwards: **Al-Wad Street** and **Souk Khan Al-Zeit**. A third street, **Souk Al-Qattanin** (Cotton Market), is located at the southern end of Al-Wad Street, and is probably the most ancient and intriguing market, with its stone-arched roof and rudimentary stalls. It was established in 1336 by Tankiz, Mamluk viceroy of Syria. An atmosphere of effervescent hubbub surrounds the markets where colourful shops, cafés and food stalls squeeze into any available space. Compared with the Virgin Mary statues and Stars of David that attract tourists and pilgrims in the Christian Quarter markets, the Muslim markets form the centre of daily life in the Arab community. Spices, leather goods, Arabic-style clothes, carpets, butchers, bakers and candlestick makers all have their place. From Jaffa Gate, walk straight ahead and enter **David Street** (Tariq Suqaiqah Aloun in Arabic), the busiest Christian Quarter souk. At the end, three streets lead off to the left: **Souk Al-Lahamin** (Butchers' Market), **Souk Al-Attarin** (Perfumers' Market) and **Souk Al-Khawajat** (Noblemen's Market).

Bargaining is customary in all of the markets, so don't be shy or you'll pay over the odds. Expect to pay in the region of three-quarters of the vendor's opening price (you can offer half and go from there). It is a lively and fun activity and a smile goes a long way. You will no doubt get offered strong Arabic coffee or mint tea so take it – it's a great way to get to know the people and a more relaxing way to bargain.

Church of St Anne and the Pools of Bethesda [85 F2] (✆*6283285;* ⏰ *08.00–noon & 14.00–17.00 Mon–Sat; admission ₪10*) The vast church complex is located on the right of Shaar Haarayot Street 30m from Lion's Gate. Entering through the large wooden gate, the Church of St Anne is located at the rear of a small garden (on the right) and the excavations of the Pool of Bethesda lie opposite.

The Pool of Bethesda was documented in John's Gospel account as the site where Jesus healed a man who had suffered illness for 38 years (John 5:2–9). Until 1871, proof was based on faith alone, then excavations unearthed remains of a colonnaded pool matching John's description. It is now considered by archaeologists and Christians to be the exact site described in the Gospel. The Pool of Bethesda is today a series of impressive submerged dry relics, but during Jesus's time was a site of healing, where legend had it an angel moved the waters and cured the sick.

The Church of St Anne and ruins are located within peaceful, quiet gardens that are often thronged with pilgrims who come to sing hymns in the beautiful 12th-century Crusader church renowned for its acoustics. The church was erected over the traditional site of the birthplace of St Anne, the mother of Mary. The Crusader church that stands today was built over an earlier Byzantine church, which was later converted by Saladin into a Muslim theological school (an inscription above the church commemorates this). The church was eventually abandoned until, in 1856, the Ottomans donated it to France, who restored it to its former beauty, although most of what you see today is in fact original. From within the church, stone steps lead down to the cavern, traditionally regarded as St Anne's birthplace.

Notre Dame de Sion Ecce Homo Convent [85 E3] (✆ *6277292;* w *eccehomopilgrimhouse.com;* ⏰ *08.00–17.00 daily, Good Friday prayer only; admission adult/child ₪9/6*) The convent is situated on Via Dolorosa after the Church of the Condemnation. In 1857, ruins dating back to the Roman era were discovered inside. The convent was built on top of a water reservoir and Roman pavement, laid by Hadrian as a market place area on the ruins of Jerusalem.

Zedekiah's Cave [85 E1] (✆ *6277550;* ⏰ *09.00–17.00 Sat–Thu*) Located 100m east of Damascus Gate, Zedekiah's Cave (also known as Solomon's Quarries) is believed to be the vast quarry from which the building blocks of the First Temple were unearthed. While there isn't an awful lot to see inside, the cave's interest lies in its history and as the site of ritual ceremonies of the Freemasons, the order claiming spiritual ancestry from the founders of Jerusalem's Temple.

Damascus Gate [84 D2] At the northern end of the main Muslim Quarter souk and leading on to Sultan Suleiman Street, the Damascus Gate is in fact known by three names: the Christians refer to it as Damascus as it marks the beginning of the highway that led through Israel to Syria; it is known in Hebrew as Shaar (gate of) Shechem after the biblical city (modern-day Nablus) that was accessed by a road crossing the Damascus route; Arabs refer to it as Bab Al-Amud (Gate of the Pillar) after the remains of the 2nd-century wall discovered beneath. The gate is the main entrance into and out of the Muslim Quarter and a constant buzz of activity surrounds it, where merchants and worshippers stream through on their way to the souk or Al-Aqsa Mosque. There is a great view of the Muslim Quarter from the top of the gate, which can be accessed by steps on its eastern side.

Golden Gate [85 G3] (closed) The sealed gate that is today located along the eastern wall of the Old City in the Temple Mount complex dates to 640CE and was built either by the last Byzantine rulers or the first of the Arab conquerors. Jews claim that it is through this gate that the Messiah will pass on his way to the Old City and it is said to have been sealed by the Muslims during Suleiman the Magnificent's reign in an attempt to prevent the Messiah from entering. Today the closure of the gate is not considered by most Jews to be a sensitive point. Many jokingly claim that if the Messiah can get this far, he will find a way to get in.

Lion's Gate [85 G2] Tradition states that Sultan Suleiman the Magnificent dreamed of being eaten by lions, and that to prevent this the walls of Jerusalem had to be rebuilt. On either side of the gate are reliefs of leopards, which are mistakenly referred to as lions. The gate also goes by the name St Stephen's Gate, as, according to tradition, this was the site where the first Christian martyr Stephen was stoned to death. In Arabic the gate is known as Bab Sitti Maryam, Gate of the Virgin Mary. The gate once again entered the history books when, during the Six Day War, Israeli soldiers from the 55th Paratroop Brigade marched through and raised the Israeli flag, signalling the conquest of the Old City.

Herod's Gate (Bab Al-Zahara) [85 E1] Located on the northern side of the city, the gate faces the vibrant Arab area of East Jerusalem. During the British Mandate period it became the principal entry point to the Old City and had its L-shape removed to allow for an easier flow of traffic. It was called Herod's Gate by 16th- and 17th-century pilgrims who mistakenly believed a house located just inside it was that of Herod Antipas, Herod the Great's son. It was also at Herod's Gate that at midday on 15 July 1099 the Crusaders breached the wall and took Jerusalem, declaring it part of the Latin Kingdom.

Mount Zion Accessed by the towering, bullet-ridden Zion Gate that leads from the Armenian Quarter, Mount Zion's wealth of religious and historic relics sees it incorporated into any tour of the Old City. It is a small, easily navigable area but often crowded with Jewish and Christian tour groups who make the pilgrimage to the holy sites concentrated here.

Dormition Abbey [map, page 72] (✆5655330; 08.30–noon & 12.40–18.00 Mon– Fri, 08.30–noon & 12.40–17.30 Sat, 10.30–11.45 & 12.40–17.30 Sun; information leaflet ₪1) Easily recognisable by its blue conical roof, this beautiful church was commissioned in 1906 by Kaiser Wilhelm II, its robust architecture and conical corner towers evoking images of medieval European castles. According to the Roman Catholic and Eastern and Oriental Orthodox churches, this is the site where the Virgin Mary fell asleep and was taken to Heaven (the Assumption of Mary). In the basement of the cavernous church is a statue of the Virgin. The church is frequented by hordes of tour groups so be prepared for a squeeze.

King David's Tomb and the Upper Room [map, page 72] These two holy sites, located one above the other, attract vast crowds of quite varying religious backgrounds. To the Jews this is the site of King David's cenotaph, located on the ground floor of the building complex. It is one of the most venerated Jewish sites in the world and high

To get a completely different view of the Old City, a wonderful walk around the great stone walls that encompass the maze of alleys and jumble of buildings is a lovely way to spend an afternoon, or indeed an evening, when the walls are illuminated. The present Old City walls date from the 16th century. Completed during the reign of Sultan Suleiman the Magnificent, who was afraid of Crusader attacks, the walls include 35 watchtowers; however, half of these were never completed. Begin at the **Jaffa Gate** [84 C5] and climb the steps on to the ramparts and head northwest (right if you're facing out of the gate). The wall leads around the quiet corner of the Christian Quarter, over the New Gate and continues along the north wall to the bustling Damascus Gate, which is a great place to stop and watch the milling throngs of market-goers below. Continue along the ramparts where you'll have the busy Sultan Suleiman Street of East Jerusalem on one side and the quieter parts of the Muslim Quarter on the other. At the corner of the wall is an impressive lookout over the Mount of Olives and Kidron Valley. Head down the east wall until you reach Lion's Gate and the beginning of the Temple Mount complex, and descend the steps. Exit the gate and carry on along the outside of the east wall on the **Ophel Promenade** [85 G4] that runs through the Muslim cemetery. At the end of the Temple Mount wall the promenade stops and you will need to walk along the road for about 350m until you reach the Dung Gate. Ascend the steps back on to the ramparts, which will then lead you past the tumble of white stone buildings of the Jewish Quarter and then past the quiet lanes of the Armenian Quarter. In 2017, the walk ended at the Herod's Gate, but it could in theory reopen. The **ticket office** is at the Jaffa Gate (✆ 072 2157000; ⏱ 09.00–16.00/17.00 (winter/summer) Sun–Thu & Sat; ₪10). Make sure you keep the ticket until the end of the walk.

on the pilgrimage list, particularly on Shavuot, the traditional day of David's death. The vast ornate sarcophagus is located within a stone-cut tomb. To Christians, the **Upper Room** (or Coenaculum) (⏱ *08.00–17.00 daily*) is the site of Jesus's Last Supper, the establishment of the rite of the Eucharist and the location of his last appearance to the Apostles. The room, today accessed by a flight of steps, was once a part of the Crusader Church of Our Lady of Mount Zion but is now located above various Jewish yeshivas (schools of Torah study). There isn't a lot to see inside the room bar some sparse examples of Crusader architecture. Guides direct visitors to one or other of the rooms, managing to successfully ascertain their religious preference by a mere glance.

Montefiore's Windmill [map, page 72] Born in Italy, Moses Montefiore (1784–1885) was a British-Jewish businessman, renowned for his Zionist dreams, Jewish philanthropy and establishment of the Yemin Moshe neighbourhood to the west of the Old City walls. Today, the unmistakable Montefiore's Windmill is a lasting legacy to his tireless efforts, although it was never actually used on account of a distinct lack of wind in this area.

Mount of Olives and the Kidron Valley
City of David [85 F7] (✆ *6262341;* w *cityofdavid.org.il/en;* ⏱ *08.00–19.00 Sun–Thu, 08.00–14.00 Fri; admission adult/child ₪28/14*) The City of David referred to in the Bible lies outside the modern-day walls in the Kidron Valley. In the area between the

Temple Mount and Mount of Olives, excavations have revealed the original capital of Jerusalem, built by King David more than 3,000 years ago to unify the tribes of Israel. For most, the highlight of a trip to the archaeological park is taking a 30-minute wade through the 2,700-year-old **Hezekiah's Tunnel** [85 F/G7] that leads from the **Gihon Spring** [85 G7] to the **Siloam Pool** [85 F7] further down the valley (although there is a dry route for those less disposed to getting wet). The spring was the principal water source of the city and its waters are mentioned in countless events in the Bible. In the 8th century BCE, under Assyrian threat, King Hezekiah had the water flow diverted underground in an attempt to protect this important source. Today, the 533m-long tunnel can be traversed (be sure to wear appropriate clothing as water reaches knee height). Other important sites include the extensive **Area G** excavation zone and **Warren's Shaft** [85 G6]. A guided tour is well worth it to gain a better understanding of the complexities of the site (*adult/child* ₪*60/45*), which includes the **3-D Movie** depicting the history of the City of David (*normally* ₪*10 with entry ticket*).

Church of All Nations and the Garden of Gethsemane
At the foot of the Mount of Olives is the **garden** [108 B2] (\6283264; ⊕ *08.30–noon & 14.00–17.30 daily*), known in Christian tradition as the site of Jesus's agony, prayer, betrayal

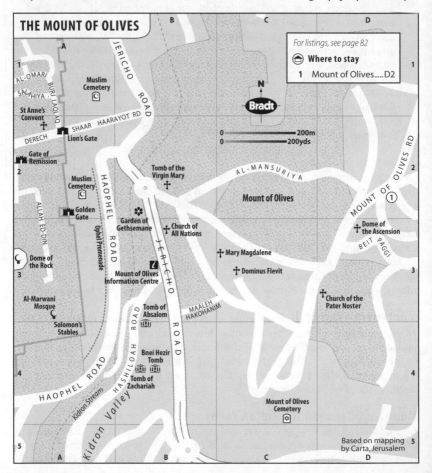

THE MOUNT OF OLIVES

For listings, see page 82

Where to stay
1 Mount of Olives.....D2

N

Bradt

0   200m
0   200yds

AL-OMARI/
SA...HIYA
St Anne's Convent
DERECH
Gate of Remission
Muslim Cemetery
Golden Gate
ALLAH ED-DIN
Dome of the Rock
Al-Marwani Mosque
Solomon's Stables
HAOPHEL ROAD
Ophel Promenade
HASHILOAH ROAD
Kidron Stream
Kidron Valley

JERICHO ROAD
SHAAR HAARAYOT RD
Lion's Gate
Muslim Cemetery
Garden of Gethsemane
Mount of Olives Information Centre
Tomb of Absalom
Bnei Hezir Tomb
Tomb of Zachariah
MAALEH HAKOHANIM
JERICHO ROAD

Tomb of the Virgin Mary
Church of All Nations
Mary Magdalene
Dominus Flevit

AL-MANSURIYA
Mount of Olives

Mount of Olives Cemetery

Dome of the Ascension
BEIT PAGGI
Church of the Pater Noster
MOUNT OF OLIVES RD

Based on mapping by Carta, Jerusalem

Oskar Schindler (28 April 1908–9 October 1974) was a German businessman and member of the Nazi Party who is renowned for saving his Jewish workers from entering concentration camps during the Holocaust. He established a factory as a sub-camp of the Plazow labour camp, employing his Jewish workers and keeping them safe from execution. In 1944, he relocated his factory, opening it under the ruse of manufacturing tank shells. Through contacts and bribery, he instead spent his fortune buying medicine and food for his Jewish workers. Following the war, Schindler found himself ostracised from his native homeland and moved to Argentina. In 1962, he was invited to plant a tree in the Avenue of the Righteous in Jerusalem, an act that brought his World War II acts to light and subjected him to abuse and harassment from Nazi sympathisers. He became the only member of the Nazi Party to be recognised as a 'righteous gentile' in Israel, and shortly before his death in 1974 he declared his wish to be buried there. He died a poor man in Germany, and his remains were transported to Jerusalem, where his coffin was carried through the streets and buried in the Mount Zion Protestant Cemetery. He is credited with having saved 1,200 Jews from persecution and was venerated in the Booker Prize-winning *Schindler's Ark* by Thomas Keneally. The book was adapted by Steven Spielberg in the Academy Award-winning movie *Schindler's List* (1993), with Schindler played by Liam Neeson.

Today the cemetery appears long forgotten. Overgrown and dishevelled, its tombstones are untended and have fared badly with the passage of time. At the bottom of the cemetery, Oskar Schindler's grave [map, page 72] stands out, tiny white stones lined along its clean slab. The custom of piling stones dates to biblical times when they were used to mark graves. Today they represent a more permanent symbol than flowers to show love and respect.

by Judas and subsequent arrest. The name Gethsemane derives from the Hebrew *gat shemen* meaning 'oil press', a reference to the ancient olive trees that remain standing to this day, believed by botanists to pre-date Christianity. Within the tranquil, shady garden stands the magnificent **Church of All Nations** [108 B3] (also known as the Basilica of the Agony). The church, with its vast fresco adorning the façade, was rebuilt in 1924 on the site of earlier Byzantine and Crusader churches, thanks to contributions from Catholic communities all over the world. Inside the church mosaic symbols of each of these communities are present in the domes. Inside, the **Rock of the Agony** is said to be the stone where Jesus prayed. Services in English are at 11.00 on Sundays.

Tomb of the Virgin Mary [108 B2] (⏰ *06.00–12.30 & 14.00–18.00 daily*) The cavernous church, which dates to the Crusader period, is the traditional burial site of Jesus's mother. While this event is unrecorded in the Bible, belief in this site dates back to the 2nd or 3rd century CE. Muslims also worship this spot in the belief that the Prophet Mohammed saw a light shine over Mary's tomb on his Night Journey from Mecca. A wide marble staircase leads down to the eerily beautiful, grotto-like church, the ceiling of which is adorned with hundreds of ornate lanterns. Mary's tomb is located at the bottom of the steps to the right past a Greek Orthodox altar. To the right of the tomb is a Muslim prayer arch dating to medieval times. The church is the Greek Orthodox rival to the Dormition Abbey on Mount Zion as the site of Mary's assumption.

Dominus Flevit [108 C3] (☉ *08.00–noon & 14.30–17.00 daily*) To find the church, turn left off Jericho Road and then right up the extremely steep and narrow lane that runs along the edge of the cemetery. Continue almost to the top and the entrance to the church is on the left through a large gate. Inside is a small, well-kept garden within which is a teardrop-shaped chapel, designed to represent the tears shed by Jesus as he lamented over the future destruction of Jerusalem.

Dome of the Ascension [108 D3] (*admission ₪5*) This small octagonal chapel is the traditional site of Jesus's Ascension to Heaven. A church once stood on the site but today a mosque covers the rock believed to be indented with Jesus's last footprint, the church taken and destroyed by Saladin in 1187 (Islam recognises Jesus as a prophet although does not accept the Christian belief that he was the son of God). It is but one of the contenders for Jesus's ascension, the Russian Orthodox Church and the Church of the Pater Noster also being in the running. Opening hours vary but access can normally be gained during the mornings (ring the doorbell outside to gain entry).

Mount of Olives Cemetery [108 C4] (☉ *08.00–16.00 Sun–Thu, 08.00–13.00 Fri*) The Jewish cemetery that blankets the side of the Mount of Olives resides on some of the country's prime real estate, and for good reason. According to Jewish belief, the resurrection of the dead will begin here upon the coming of the Messiah. Although the cemetery dates to the First Temple period, most of the tombs that we see today are from the 15th century. During the Jordanian rule, a road leading to Jericho was built over the graves, many gravestones being smashed, destroyed or used in construction. Following the 1967 Six Day War and Israel's conquest of Jerusalem, the government went to great lengths to restore the tombstones to their original positions. The **visitors' centre** [108 B3] (*Jericho Rd;* ☎ *6275050;* w *mountofolives.co.il/en;* ☉ *09.00–17.00 Sun–Thu*) is located on Jericho Road, 200m from the Lion's Gate traffic lights and provides information on finding some of the most prominent graves, including among many, Eliezer Ben-Yehuda, Shmuel Yosef Agnon (awarded the Nobel Prize for literature) and Menachem Begin. The website shows an aerial photograph of the site and a database of all graves and tombs within it as well as routes for self-guided tours through it.

Tomb of Absalom [108 B4] In past centuries devout Jews, Muslims and Christians would pelt stones at the magnificent stone structure that holds pride of place in the Kidron Valley, a symbol of their contempt for King David's son who rebelled against his father. Today, however, the tomb has been dated to almost a millennium after Absalom and is believed by some to be the tomb of Jehosophat, King of Judah. A recent hidden inscription has also led to claims that this was the true tomb of the priest Zachariah, father of John the Baptist, although this is hotly contested. Rather confusingly, the rock-cut **Tomb of Zachariah** is located a few metres away. The adjacent **Bnei Hezir Tomb** dates back to the 2nd century BCE and is an example of the influence of Greek architecture in Jerusalem.

CITY CENTRE
Israel Museum [map, page 72] (*11 Ruppin Rd;* ☎ *6708811;* w *imj.org.il;* ☉ *10.00–17.00 Sun–Mon, Wed–Thu & Sat, 16.00–21.00 Tue, 10.00–14.00 Fri; admission adult/child ₪48/36; free to under 17s Tue & Sat*) This is Israel's largest, and one of the world's leading, archaeology and art museums. Its exhibits cover a wealth of topics, housed within the vast complex, interconnected pavilions and surrounding gardens.

The elegant golden domes of the Mary Magdalene Church [108 C3] (↘6284371; ☉ 10.00–noon Tue–Thu) stand as glittering landmarks on Jerusalem's skyline, unmistakable in their position halfway up the Mount of Olives. Yet the church, built in 1888 in traditional Russian style in honour of Tsar Alexander III's mother Maria Alexandrovna Empress of Russia, is not just a pretty face. This is the final resting place of two rather prominent royal women: the Grand Duchess Elizabeth Fyodorovna and Queen Alice of Battenberg. The grand duchess was the granddaughter of Britain's Queen Victoria, and she is said to have been so inspired by the beauty of the Holy Land that she requested it to be the place of her burial. Upon the assassination of her husband, Elizabeth retreated into a monastic life, giving away her possessions and dedicating her life to caring for Moscow's needy. In 1918, Elizabeth and her family were exiled and murdered by the Bolsheviks. Her remains were buried in the crypt in the Mary Magdalene Church and she was canonised by the Russian Orthodox Church in 1992.

At around the same time, Elizabeth's niece, Princess Alice of Battenberg (the mother of Britain's Prince Philip) married the Prince of Greece and lived in Athens until the royal family's exile in 1917. Alice was born deaf, and in 1930 diagnosed with schizophrenia, and institutionalised. After recovering, she separated from her husband and cut off ties with her family and, like her aunt before her, dedicated her life to serving God and the poor. In 1938, Alice returned to Athens and lived in a small, cramped apartment where she helped the poor, serving the Red Cross and risking her life throughout World War II. Upon the Nazi occupation of Athens, Princess Alice was approached by Rachel Cohen and her children, a Jewish family who had helped King George I of Greece in 1913. In return for this help, Alice saved the family and was posthumously honoured as 'Righteous Amongst the Nations' in Jerusalem, a ceremony attended by Prince Philip. The princess finally left Athens in 1967 and moved to Buckingham Palace in England where she died two years later. In accordance with her wishes, her body was interred (20 years later) in the Mary Magdalene Church alongside her aunt.

The Judaica and Jewish Ethnography Wing consists of the world's largest collection of Jewish religious objects gathered from communities across the globe. The Shrine of the Book and Model of Jerusalem in the Second Temple period is the museum's most famous exhibit, housing the Dead Sea Scrolls discovered at the isolated site of Qumran in the West Bank. Today, the scrolls are kept inside their very own display hall. Dating from between the 3rd century BCE and 68CE, the scrolls are older than any other surviving biblical manuscripts by almost 1,000 years. Their discovery by a Bedouin shepherd in 1947 gave rise to almost a decade of intensive excavation, as archaeologists and historians were desperate to discover the authors and age of the thousands of fragments (totalling 800–900 scripts) that were found. The onion-shaped roof of the pavilion was designed to reflect the jar in which the scrolls were discovered.

On the lower level of the building are displays of the letters written by Simon Bar Kokhba during the Second Jewish Revolt and artefacts discovered in Masada (page 283). The Art Pavilion proudly displays works by artists such as Corot, Monet, Renoir, Degas, Gauguin and Matisse, along with the beautifully landscaped Billy Rose Art Garden containing classical and modern pieces by, among others, Rodin, Picasso, Henry Moore and Chana Orloff. The newly renovated archaeology wing houses significant artefacts spanning all of the land's countless time periods, eras and invasions. Free tours are arranged in English starting at the Entrance Pavilion (\6708811; *reserve in advance*). Alternatively, free audio guides are available from the entrance.

U Nahon Museum of Italian Jewish Art and Conegliano Veneto Synagogue [80 D4] (*25 Hillel St;* \6241610; w *ijamuseum.org;* ⊕ *10.30–16.30 Sun, Tue, Wed, noon–19.00 Thu, 10.00–13.00 Fri; admission adult/child* ₪25/15) The small museum and adjacent synagogue have fine, delicate Italian architecture. The highlight is the carved wooden and finely decorated Holy Ark from the original Conegliano Veneto synagogue dating back to the 16th and 17th centuries CE. Transported from Italy, it is now the centrepiece of the present synagogue, completed in the 1990s. The museum also offers an interesting insight into the life of the Italian Jewry.

Knesset [map, page 72] (*Rothschild St;* \6753420; w *knesset.gov.il*) The Knesset is the seat of Israel's parliament, a vast building holding pride of place in Jerusalem's centre. An interesting tour can be arranged illuminating not only the workings of the country's political centre but also offering a fascinating insight into the history, culture and heritage of the Jewish people. Tours include architecture, art, the magnificent menorah (which can be seen outside the main complex), divisions of the Knesset, the library, archives and synagogue. Guided tours must be booked in advance (in English at 08.30, noon & 14.00 Sun & Thu), while sessions can be viewed with no need for advance reservation (16.00 Mon–Tue, 11.00 Wed). The Knesset operates a strict dress code and no jeans, shorts, skimpy tops and sandals for men are permitted. Passports must be shown on entry.

Museum of Islamic Art [map, page 72] (*2 Hapalmach St;* \5661291; w *islamicart. co.il/english;* ⊕ *10.00–15.00 Mon–Wed, 10.00–19.00 Thu, 10.00–14.00 Fri–Sat; admission adult/child* ₪40/20) This privately owned museum houses a varied selection of Islamic artistry from every corner of the globe and depicts the history and religious beliefs of Islam. Exhibits include weaponry, glass, jewellery, pottery and carpets from the last 1,400 years. Guided tours can be arranged in advance in Hebrew, English and Arabic.

Monastery of the Cross [map, page 72] (\6790961; ⊕ *10.00–16.30 Mon–Sat*) This beautiful, castle-like church sits in the middle of what is today referred to as the Valley of the Cross (Rehavia Park) near the Knesset. According to biblical belief, Lot planted branches from pine, fir and cypress trees, which grew into one tree, later used to make the cross upon which Jesus was crucified. The monastery dates to the Byzantine period, built by Greek Orthodox monks with funding from the King of Georgia. Almost all the complex is open to the public, the kitchen in particular providing a rare and insightful view of daily monastic life.

Mahane Yehuda Market [map, page 72] This covered food market is one of the city's liveliest spots, especially on a Friday before Shabbat when all and sundry come to buy their weekend groceries. Everything from fruit and vegetables to meats, cheeses, spices, olives and nuts are sold as well as household items and clothes. It also contains some tiny, rustic, traditional eateries serving Middle Eastern dishes that have become some of the 'in' places in Jerusalem. The market as we see it now dates to the British Mandate era, although its roots go back much further to 1887 when the neighbourhood was first established. It is a hugely worthwhile trip both for the excellent food and to gain a real insight into local daily life, and a chance to get away from museums and history for a while.

Mea Shearim neighbourhood The ultra-Orthodox neighbourhood was founded in 1874 by eastern European Jews. Easily recognisable in their traditional black clothes, felt hats (*streimel*) and side curls (*payot*), most speak Yiddish, an old Jewish variant of German, reserving Hebrew only for prayer. Signs plaster the walls surrounding the neighbourhood's entrances requesting those entering to dress appropriately (those who don't heed the warnings often find themselves at the receiving end of

HAREDIM

Haredim are the ultra-Orthodox Jews whose origins date back to 19th-century eastern Europe. At that time, following pressure from the proponents of Jewish Enlightenment (Haskalah) and European governments forcing Jews to assimilate, a small community of rabbis, afraid of losing their religious identity, insisted on a return to the original interpretation of Judaism, strictly following and observing the writings of the Torah. The term *haredi* comes from the Book of Isaiah, meaning those 'who tremble before God'. Many Haredim have, over time, left for the United States and many settled in Israel.

The daily life of a Haredi man is devoted to studying the Torah, on average 17 hours a day, six days a week. The same applies to children, who learn the Torah in yeshivas from 07.30 to 17.30. One hour of their daily curriculum is spent on a secular subject. On completion of yeshiva studies, they graduate to a *kollel*. According to the Haredi belief, women are not permitted to read from or touch the Torah, so women tend to be the primary breadwinners, not only going to work, but also taking care of household chores and children. Men receive a government stipend to aid them in their studies.

In addition to strict obedience with the word of God, Haredim devotedly follow the word of a rabbi, which explains the existence of numerous Jewish movements focused on the teachings of a single rabbi. Haredim believe that Hebrew is a holy language and can only be used for praying, thus they mainly use Yiddish as their spoken language. In 1947, there were around 30,000 Haredim in Israel. Today, there are 800,000, which is roughly 10% of the population and, according to the National Bureau of Statistics, by 2059 this figure will reach 27% due to high birth rates within the community.

Haredim have evolved from an apolitical community to one active in national and local politics. Many of them harbour strong anti-Zionist feelings, believing that only God could bring about the State of Israel, and certainly not a secular Jewish movement. That said, the Deputy Mayor of Jerusalem, Itzhak Pindrus, is a Haredi rabbi, Aryeh Deri, one of the founders of the ultra-Orthodox Shas Party, acts as the Minister of the Interior, and Yaakov Litzman from the United Torah Judaism Party is the Minister for Health.

A non-traditional and small (around 1,000 people) Haredim group is the Na Nachs. These dancing Haredim wear a distinctive yarmulke with a pompon on top and follow the teachings of Rabbi Nachman. Na Nachs believe that one comes closer to God by being happy and not by simply reading the Torah. They drive around spreading their daily *hafatza* by dancing and singing *Na Nach Nachma Nachman Mehuman*.

verbal abuse and anger). Short sleeves or the baring of legs is not allowed at any time, women are advised to wear long skirts and not trousers, and photographing the residents is also not permitted. Within the area are numerous synagogues, ritual baths, Judaica stores and Talmudic schools, including Mir Yeshiva, one of the largest Haredi (see box, page 113) yeshivas in the world, founded in 1815 in Lithuania. The neighbourhood is also home to the Neturei Karta, a group which does not recognise the State of Israel as it was not founded by the Messiah. A visit to the neighbourhood is unarguably fascinating, and provides a deeper understanding of devout Judaism, and it should be treated with the utmost respect. While it is possible to visit during Shabbat, it is advised not to for religious laws are many, and the chances of those not familiar with them getting it wrong are high. Visiting midweek still demands a level of awareness and religious respect, but is less sensitive than on Fridays and Saturdays.

German Colony After creating an impressive and – for the time – developed neighbourhood in the heart of Haifa (page 171), the German Templars moved to Jerusalem where, in the late 1800s, they settled in the Emek Refaim area of the city. Built in the styles reminiscent of their homeland, the Christian Templars, who had moved away from the Protestant Church, were later ousted from Jerusalem during the British Mandate period, but left in their wake a pretty neighbourhood of much sought-after real estate. Today the main street through the neighbourhood is Emek Refaim, home to countless popular restaurants, cafés and bars, and is home to a big English-speaking population.

EAST JERUSALEM
Rockefeller Archaeological Museum [map, page 72] (*27 Sultan Soleiman St;* ✎*6708011;* w *www.imj.org.il/en;* ✆ *10.00–15.00 Sun–Mon & Wed–Thu, 10.00–14.00 Sat; admission adult/child ₪26/12*) Formerly the Palestine Archaeological Museum and located opposite the northeast corner of Herod's Gate, the museum is easily recognisable by its massive, limestone tower. It was commissioned by John D Rockefeller in 1927 following a growing need for an appropriate home for finds being unearthed throughout Palestine at the time. For those embarking on a trip around the country, the museum is best saved as a finale, where finds from great sites such as Caesarea, Acre, Beit Shean, the Carmel and the Galilee can be envisioned in their original context. Among the most impressive exhibits are the relief carving from the Church of the Holy Sepulchre, the 200,000-year-old skull excavated from the Carmel Caves, wooden beams from the Al-Aqsa Mosque and Egyptian and Mesopotamian material unearthed from Beit Shean.

The Garden Tomb [map, page 72] (*Conrad Schik St;* ✎*6272745;* w *gardentomb. com;* ✆ *09.00–noon & 14.00–17.30 Mon–Sat; admission free*) The Garden Tomb is the second contender for the site of Golgotha, and couldn't be further removed from the grand Church of the Holy Sepulchre. Tombs discovered by the British general Charles Gordon in 1883 have led many to believe this is the spot mentioned in the Bible. Some archaeologists, however, date the tombs to Old Testament times. Today it is a pretty place of quiet, simple prayer and reverence visited predominantly by Protestant pilgrim groups.

GREATER JERUSALEM
Yad Vashem (✎*6443420;* w *yadvashem.org;* ✆ *09.00–17.00 Sun–Wed, 09.00–20.00 Thu, 09.00–14.00 Fri; admission free; under 10s not allowed*) The Holocaust was one of the most horrific and devastating events in human history. Over six million Jews lost

their lives in unthinkable ways, and many more suffered unimaginable trauma and loss. In Israel, remembrance of the Holocaust is as raw today as it was immediately after World War II, and it drives the underlying strength and social unity of the country. The **World Holocaust Remembrance Centre** was created to keep alive the memory of those who suffered and to tell the story through their eyes. Originally, Yad Vashem was established in 1953 as the Holocaust Martyrs and Heroes Remembrance Authority, and the museum, which depicts the human story behind the Holocaust, was inaugurated in 1957 by Israeli heads of state, with dignitaries from 40 other nations in attendance. The triangular concrete museum hall takes visitors on a walk through history, each room depicting a different stage in the events leading up to and during the Holocaust. Displays include authentic artefacts, testimonies, personal letters, documentary evidence, films, art and, chillingly, mountains of hair and shoes, and they are pieced together to tell the wider picture evoked by these personal stories.

At the end of the museum, the **Hall of Names** has been given a different home. The circular hall is covered with the faces of those who perished and is a moving finale. In a separate room, the **Central Database of Shoah** (Holocaust) **Victims' Names** can be accessed, allowing visitors to search for relatives. It can also be accessed through the website (page 114).

Castel National Park (*Mivasseret Zion;* \ *5342741;* ☉ *08.00–17.00 Sat–Thu, 08.00–16.00 Fri, closes 1hr earlier in winter; admission adult/child ₪14/7*) Although its history stretches from biblical times to the Crusades, the Castel Fortress is most poignantly remembered for its role in the 1948 Arab–Israeli War, when the crucial route leading to Jerusalem was being fiercely contested. For five days, Jewish forces fought off attacks from Arab troops, and, despite drastic and almost total loss of life, they gained an eventual victory. Models, exhibits and a great view from the fortress's 790m elevation make it a worthwhile trip. The park is located 15 minutes from the city centre near the village of Mivasseret Zion on route 1.

Ammunition Hill (*Givat Hatachmoshet;* \ *5828442;* w *www.g-h.org.il/en;* ☉ *09.00–17.00 Sun–Thu, 09.00–13.00 Fri; admission free*) The Ammunition Hill memorial site stands as a long-lasting reminder and tribute to members of the IDF Paratrooper Regiment who died in one of the Six Day War's bloodiest battles. The hill, a Jordanian army stronghold, was seen as a crucial strategic point in the battle for Jerusalem and, on 6 June 1967 in a battle that lasted 4 hours, 36 men lost their lives in the capture of the hill. Visitors can join the throngs of young IDF soldiers who frequent the site in exploring the battleground, which includes a tour of the tunnels and bunkers.

Biblical Zoo (\ *6750111;* w *jerusalemzoo.org;* ☉ *09.00–19.00 Sun–Thu, 09.00–16.30 Fri, 10.00–18.00 Sat; admission adult/child ₪55/42*) Complete with its very own Noah's Ark, the Biblical Zoo aims to preserve endangered and rare animals from across the world. This non-profit zoo concentrates mainly on animals from Israel's past, most especially those mentioned in the Bible.

Ein Kerem This picturesque, tranquil village is tucked into the green hills, terraced hillsides and olive groves southwest of Jerusalem. Famous in Christian tradition for being the birthplace of John the Baptist, Ein Kerem is home to impressive churches, a burgeoning artists' colony and a few cafés and restaurants. The village, whose name literally means 'Spring of the Vineyard', was named after the spring at its centre, which nowadays is located under the building of a former Ottoman mosque

Formed out of Jerusalem's oldest neighbourhoods that grew outside the Old City walls, the centre of the New City covered in this walk is today a fascinating example of the unique atmosphere that characterises the city, where ancient and modern have continued to develop alongside one another. From the ultra-Orthodox neighbourhood of Mea Shearim where biblical times have stood still, to the vibrancy and noise of the Mahane Yehuda food market, a day's walk leads you through the present and past of the city centre.

Start in the irrepressibly fascinating ultra-Orthodox neighbourhood of **Mea Shearim** (pages 113–14). Leave the neighbourhood and walk down the narrow Ethiopia Street towards Haneviim Street. On the left of the narrow road, lined with stone mansions you will find the lovely, circular **Ethiopian church** [80 E1] (⊕ *07.00–18.00*). Built in 1896, it is believed to have been a gift to the Ethiopian Queen Sheba from King Solomon. Directly opposite the large church and marked by a plaque on the wall outside is **Ben Yehuda's House** [80 E1], where he lived and did much of his work on the revival of the Hebrew language.

At the bottom of Ethiopia Street cross Haneviim Street and walk down Harav Kook Street. On your left is the **Rothschild Hospital** [80 F3], today the Hadassah College, which was built in 1888 by funds from the baron (see box, page 186) and became the first Jewish hospital to be built outside the Old City. Across the street is the delightful **Ticho House** [80 E2] (✆ *6244186;* ⊕ *10.00–17.00 Sun–Mon & Wed–Thu, 10.00–22.00 Tue, 10.00–14.00 Fri*), one of Jerusalem's earliest buildings outside the walls. It belonged to Dr Avraham Ticho, a German optometrist and his wife Anna who in 1924 opened an eye clinic, which operated until his death in 1960. Anna worked as both his assistant and landscape artist until she passed away in 1980. Upon her death, the house was converted into a museum, library and art gallery. Walk to the end of Harav Kook Street and turn right on to Yafo Street.

and known as **Mary's Spring**. It also appears in the Mishnah as the site from where the stone for the altar of the First Temple was taken. For more details, download the excellent audio tour from w einkaremtour.com/en.

Getting there and away There is no direct bus to Ein Kerem. The easiest way to get here is to go by tram from Jaffa Street in central Jerusalem to the Yefe Nof stop from where you cross the road to catch bus 28/28x to the centre of the village. Alternatively, go by tram to the terminus of Mount Herzl, from where it is a 20-minute walk down to the village. To visit the Gornensky Convent, take bus 19 from Jerusalem city centre to the Hadassah Hospital, then walk for 5 minutes to the entrance gate.

What to see and do The main sight in Ein Kerem is the **Church of John the Baptist** (⊕ *Apr–Sep, 08.00–noon & Oct–Mar, 14.30–17.45 & 08.00–noon & 14.30–16.45*) – not to be confused with the Eastern Orthodox church of the same name – said to have been built over the grotto in which John the Baptist was born to Elizabeth and Zachariah. The present structure was built over Byzantine and Crusader ruins in the second half of the 19th century and completed in 1920. Inside, the walls of the church are unusually decorated with white and blue ceramic tiles.

A short walk away from here is the Franciscan **Visitation Church** (⊕ *Apr–Sep, 08.00–11.45 & 14.30–18.00 Oct–Mar, 08.00–11.45 & 14.30–17.00*), which is also

Take a mildly strenuous 25-minute uphill walk until you reach the unmistakable **Mahane Yehuda Market** (pages 112–13). Exit the market at the southern end on to Harav Shmuel Baruch Street (formerly Agripas Street) and turn right on to Eliash Street. Follow the road until you get to Shmuel Hanagid Street (crossing Ben Yehuda Street). Follow it to where it meets Bezalel Street, where you will see the **Ratisbonne Monaster**y [81 A6] (⊕ *08.00–16.00 Mon–Thu, 08.00–14.00 Fri*). Founded in 1876 by Father Ratisbonne, a Jewish aristocratic banker turned monk, the monastery was built as a French Catholic monastery and vocational school. Today, the building remains as impressive as when it was first erected, its tower believed to be one of 16 that stretched from Jaffa to Jerusalem, each acting as part of a chain of smoke signals announcing the arrival of merchant ships. Continue walking to the end of Shmuel Hanagid Street and right on to King George V Street. A short distance away, on the left, is the **Heichal Shlomo and Great Synagogue** [81 D8], the former seat of the Israeli Rabbinate and Supreme Rabbinical Court. The magnificent synagogue next door was designed to reflect architectural features of the First Temple. From here continue across **Independence Park** (Gan Haatzmaut) [81 D6], the eastern part of which is a pre-1948 Muslim cemetery. Graves can still be spotted among the shrubbery. Exit on to Shlomzion Hamalka Street and turn left. At Yafo Street turn left and immediately right on to Cheshin Street. At the top is the **Russian Compound**, whose green-domed late 19th-century Holy Trinity Cathedral [80 G3] (⊕ *09.00–13.00 & 15.00–18.00 Tue–Thu, 09.00–13.00 Fri, 07.30–noon & 16.30–19.30 Sat*) takes pride of place. The compound was built in 1860 to accommodate thousands of Russian pilgrims who flocked to Jerusalem until the 1917 Russian Revolution. Today, most of the buildings are occupied by various government institutions, including the central police station on Moscow Square in front of the cathedral.

one of the more prominent sights in Ein Kerem. Its name commemorates the Virgin Mary, while pregnant, visiting the house of the parents of John the Baptist, whose mother, Elizabeth, was Mary's cousin. On one wall of the church are the words of the Magnificat, the hymn Mary traditionally sang at the time, in 62 languages. The gates are closed on Saturdays, so ring the bell for entry. Not far from the church is **Mary's Spring**, the traditional site of Mary and Elizabeth's meeting and from where the village received its name.

Amid the greenery of the surrounding hills of the **Moskobiya** district, right behind the Visitation Church, rise the five golden onion domes of the **Cathedral of All Saints of Russia** (⊕ *Apr–Sep 10.00–13.00 & 15.30–18.00, Oct–Mar 10.00–noon & 15.00–17.00, closed Sun & Orthodox holidays*) of the **Gornensky Convent** of the Russian Ecclesiastical Mission in Jerusalem. Founded in 1871, the privacy of the convent is strictly preserved and although signs and people in Ein Kerem may suggest otherwise, the only way up here is down from the Hadassah Hospital. The cathedral itself is relatively new, completed only in 2007, although construction started back in 1911. The views from the convent over Ein Kerem are spectacular.

AROUND JERUSALEM

LATRUN The area of Latrun most likely owes its name to the almost completely dilapidated remains of a **Crusader fortress** 'Le Toron des Chevaliers' (The Tower of the Knights), an integral part of the many battles that took place here during the Crusades. Latrun is an area of the Ayalon Valley stretching between Tel Aviv and Jerusalem that, for hundreds of years, has formed one of the country's most important strategic routes. Much of the fortress, located behind the monastery, is still underground and awaiting excavation, so tread with care as some areas can be unstable and dangerous.

The **Latrun Monastery** has over recent decades become known for its wine and its thriving vineyards sweeping up the valley to the doorstep of the beautiful building inhabited by monks of the French Trappist order. In 2006, the monastery shot into a different spotlight as the unlikely setting for the much-anticipated Roger Waters concert, which attracted thousands of Pink Floyd fans from around the country. Opposite the monastery is the **Armoured Corps Museum** (*Yad Laahiryon, Latrun;* \ *08 6307400;* ⊕ *08.30–16.30 Sun–Thu, 08.30–12.30 Fri, 09.00–16.00 Sat; admission adult/child ₪30/20*), a British-built police fort used to control the passage between Tel Aviv and Jerusalem. After the British Mandate period, control of the fort passed to Arab forces, an act that resulted in a siege of Jerusalem during the 1948 Arab–Israeli War. After Israel declared independence, forces led by ex-prime minister Ariel Sharon stormed the stronghold, suffering two brutal and bloody defeats. Today, the police fort and its environs act as a tank museum and memorial site.

Just up from the police station is the **Mini Israel Park** (\ *08 9130000–10;* w *minisrael.co.il;* ⊕ *summer 10.00–22.00 Sat–Thu, winter 10.00–17.00 Sat–Thu, 10.00–14.00 Fri; admission ₪59*), where visitors can feel like Gulliver in the Holy Land. Impressive reconstructions of the country's most prolific religious, architectural and geographical places occupy an area designed to resemble the Star of David.

Getting there and away Egged buses 403/4 and 433/4 from Jerusalem central bus station stop at the Hativah Sheva junction from which all sites are within walking distance (*20mins/₪16*).

SOREQ CAVE (*Near Beit Shemesh;* \ *9911117;* w *parks.org.il;* ⊕ *08.00–17.00 Sat–Thu, 08.00–16.00 Fri; admission adult/child ₪28/14*) The Stalactite Cave Nature Reserve is unique in that its relatively small area (the cave measures 82m by 60m) is home to the vast majority of cave formations known throughout the world. As old as five million years, some of the formations measure up to 4m in length, occasionally meeting up with their stalagmite counterparts rising off the cave floor. A visit to the cave involves a guided tour and slide show. Photography is permitted only on Fridays, when there are no tours.

Getting there and away The cave is located 2km east of Beit Shemesh. From Jerusalem, buses 417/8/9 run every 20 minutes to Beit Shemesh (*1hr/₪14.5*), from where you can take a taxi for the final short stretch. The train from Jerusalem Malha also stops in Beit Shemesh.

ABU GHOSH About 20 minutes' drive from Jerusalem, located just off route 1, is the little Arab town of Abu Ghosh, best known across Israel for its Middle Eastern restaurants. Indeed, in 2010, it got itself into the *Guinness Book of Records* for producing the world's largest plate of hummus, weighing over 4,000kg (since topped by Lebanon). One of the best eateries is **Lebanese Restaurant** (*88 Hashalom St;* \ *5702397;* ⊕ *09.00–23.00 daily;* **$$**), where the queues of people waiting for a seat in the enormous, rustic restaurant testify to its incredible popularity. This most certainly isn't a quiet meal in the countryside, as children race about, the chatter reaches high decibels, running waiters fling piles of fresh hummus, pitta, salads, grilled skewered meats and ice-cold lemonade on to tables, and pans clatter in the busy, open kitchen.

The grand, sturdy **Crusader castle** that stands in the village dates back to the 12th century and displays traditional architecture of that time with thick and strong walls. In 1899, it was bought by the French government, who gave it to the Benedictine order. It makes a nice visit to walk off a hearty hummus lunch.

BEIT GUVRIN–MARESHA NATIONAL PARK (✆ *08 6811020; w parks.org.il; ☉ 08.00– 17.00 Sat–Thu, 08.00–16.00 Fri, closes 1hr earlier in winter; admission adult/child ₪28/14)* Often overlooked by visitors to Israel, this national park with its unique caves is certainly worth the time and effort of getting there. The park is cut in two by route 35, leaving the Roman Amphitheatre on one side (by Kibbutz Beit Guvrin) and the remaining sites on the other. The extensive archaeological area is a UNESCO World Heritage Site and contains 3,500 underground chambers. Inside the chambers have been found remains from human development over a 2,000-year period. The foundation of the earliest settlement of Maresha (today it is the remains of Tel Maresha in the centre of the site) goes back to the 8th century and continued through to the Crusaders. Inside the caves are residential chambers with oil presses and baths, places of worship as well as *columbaria* (dovecots). The *columbarium* caves were built solely for raising doves, and there are around 2,000 niches. The most spectacular caves, however, are the bell caves, so called because of the unique quarrying method used for their creation, whereby a round shaft was cut through the rock surface and enlarged in the soft chalk layers underneath it. The bell caves were quarried between the 4th and 9th centuries CE and produced significant amounts of chalk, making Beit Guvrin an important commercial centre at that time. When walking around, it is important to stick to the marked routes, as there remain numerous pits scattered across the park.

Getting there and away The easiest way of getting to the park is by car, as public transport is not frequent. From Jerusalem, Dan South have numerous buses to Kiryat Gat, from where bus 66 *(20mins/₪5.90)* goes to the entrance of the park. You can also reach Kiryat Gat from Beersheba with frequent Metropoline 367/8/9 and 371 services *(40mins/₪15)*.

UPDATES WEBSITE

You can post your comments and recommendations, and read feedback and updates from other readers online at w bradtupdates.com/israel.

4

Tel Aviv and Jaffa

Telephone code 03; population 432,900

Tel Aviv is the black sheep of the family. In a country of such profound historical importance, passionate religions, political struggles and strict traditions, Tel Aviv stands out and knows it. Where Jerusalem is proud of its biblical history, architectural beauty and devout religiousness, Tel Aviv's pride is found in the opposites. This colourfully loud and flamboyant city has an almost hedonistic atmosphere, where the main concerns are what to wear, where to be seen and where to party.

Tel Aviv, whose name translates as 'Hill of Sprint' or 'Spring Mound', is the economic, financial and commercial heart of Israel. A recent boom in international business has seen the city flourish, with a big international airport, seafront overlooked by large five-star hotels, a highly profitable diamond exchange and the emergence of modern high-rise buildings standing as testament to this. While few would describe Tel Aviv as beautiful, a closer look will reveal the world's largest collection of Bauhaus buildings, a pre-Nazi German architectural style, granting it UNESCO World Heritage status in 2004.

In a country steeped in centuries-old history, Tel Aviv has managed to make its mark on the country in just six decades. Today, it epitomises the average Israeli. The fast-paced, hard-working and fun-loving way of life has drawn people from all over the country and abroad to make money and have plenty of fun spending it. While it may be easy for visitors to overlook Tel Aviv, using it as a gateway to the more traditional sights in Jerusalem, the Dead Sea and Galilee, a trip to Israel would most certainly be a biased one without a stop in this, the most Israeli of Israel's cities.

Merely a few kilometres down the coast sits Jaffa, one of the most beautiful, charming and ancient places in Israel. Jaffa's Old City and port form the historic core of this predominantly Arab neighbourhood, its artists' houses, cobbled alleys, breathtaking views and old-worldly atmosphere having become a magnetic draw for visitors to the country. The once-thriving fishing port, in bygone days one of the most crucial seaports in the world, is today a tranquil area where small boats chug in and out of the harbour, old men sit patiently fishing and aromatic smells waft out of the countless restaurants. In 'modern' Jaffa, the streets are abuzz with everyday hustle and bustle, the flea market, Middle Eastern eateries, mosques and Arabic culture providing a contrast with Tel Aviv so stark you would be forgiven for thinking you had crossed a border into another country.

TEL AVIV

HISTORY Modern Tel Aviv was officially founded by 66 Jewish families in 1909 and was a small garden town with only 2,000 people. The idea was to create a Jewish commuter suburb on the outskirts of Jaffa, the 4,000-year-old fortified port city located approximately 3km from Tel Aviv's centre. In 1914, a population of 40,000, 15,000 of whom were Jews, called the city home and it became the centre for waves of Jewish immigrants moving to the Holy Land. By 1931, Palestine had witnessed four *aliyot* (plural of *aliyah*), including mass immigration during the British Mandate period, and the population of the 'first Hebrew city' had reached 46,000. Already in its early years, Tel Aviv earned a reputation for being bourgeois, with a love for aesthetics. A lot of Jews coming to Palestine during this time were considered to be secular 'people of means', giving preference to the pleasant surroundings of the new city as opposed to the more religious Jerusalem or the harsher country lifestyle led elsewhere in the yishuv. By the 1930s, it was already the place to window-shop for the latest European fashions and watch Bauhaus architecture emerge in reflection of the bourgeois tastes of Tel Avivians. On 14 May 1948, the city was chosen to host the signing of the Declaration of Independence of the State of Israel. In 2016, the population of Tel Aviv stood at almost 500,000, but it remains a garden city at heart with numerous parks and leafy boulevards in which to savour its *joie de vivre* and charm.

GETTING THERE AND AWAY Tel Aviv forms the hub of Israel's transport network, with good-quality bus and/or train links to most places in the country.

By bus Tel Aviv has two main bus stations: the **central bus station** [130 G7] (*106 Levinsky St;* `6948888`); and **Merkaz bus station** [126 G4] that is adjacent to the train station (both are often referred to as Arlozorov stations). Most buses arrive and depart from the central bus station although many of them will also stop at Merkaz bus station. Egged (**w** *egged.co.il*) and Dan (**w** *dan.co.il/eng*) bus companies form the core of bus travel, with the former providing most of the long-distance services. The free **RavKav** transportation card can be issued on the spot from the office on the sixth floor of the central bus station (⊕ *07.00–19.00 Sun–Thu, 07.00–13.00 Fri*), and gives the holder an automatic 20% discount on the entire transport network, including trains and buses, both city and regional.

By sherut Inter-city sherut taxis to Jerusalem, Haifa, Eilat, Nazareth and all stops along the way leave regularly from the central bus station. Some sheruts run on Shabbat.

By train Tel Aviv forms the centre of Israel's growing train network and is an affordable, comfortable and convenient way of avoiding the coastal traffic. The city has four train stations running from south to north: Hahaganah [130 H7], Hashalom [126 G4], Savidor Centre (Central Station) [122 G1] and University.

DIRECT ROUTES RUN BY EGGED TO AND FROM TEL AVIV CENTRAL BUS STATION				
To	**Frequency**	**Bus no**	**Duration**	**Price (₪)**
Afula	20mins	825	1hr 50mins	27
Eilat	10 departures daily	390, 394	5hrs 20mins	70
Golani junction	40mins	836, 840	2hrs 15mins	37.50
Haifa	20mins	910, 921	1hr 40mins/3hrs	21.50/27
Jerusalem	15mins	405	1hr	16
Katzrin	09.45/14.00/17.00	843	4hrs	42.50
Kiryat Shmona	40mins/1hr	845	3hrs 30mins	42.50
Nazareth	20mins	826	2hrs 30 mins	34
Safed	17.30	846	3hrs 30mins	42.50
Tiberias	40mins	836	2hrs 30mins	37.50

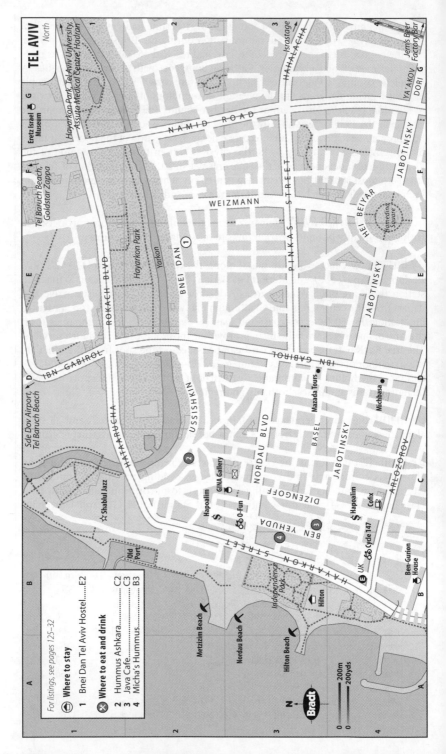

TEL AVIV
North

Eretz Israel 🏛 G
Museum

Hayarkon Park, Tel-Aviv University,
Assuta Medical Centre, Hadran

Tel Baruch Beach,
Goldstar Zappa

Sde Dov Airport,
Tel Baruch Beach

NAMID ROAD

WEIZMANN

ROKACH BLVD

Hayarkon Park

Yarkon

BNEI DAN

HATAARUCHA

IBN GABIROL

USSISHKIN

P I N K A S   S T R E E T

H A H A L A C H A

Israstage

JABOTINSKY

HEI BEIYAR

Dizengoff
Square

IBN GABIROL

NORDAU BLVD

BASEL

Mazada Tours

JABOTINSKY

JABOTINSKY

Michbasa

DIZENGOFF

BEN YEHUDA

Cofix

ARLOZOROV

Shablul Jazz ☆

Old
Port

HAYARKON STREET

Hapoalim 💲

GINA Gallery

O-fun

Hapoalim 💲

Cycle 147

UK

Ben-Gurion
House

YA'AKOV G
DORI

Jem's Beer
Factory Bar

Metzizim Beach

Nordau Beach

Independence
Park

Hilton

Hilton Beach

Where to stay

ⓘ **1** Bnei Dan Tel Aviv Hostel......E2

✕ Where to eat and drink

2 Hummus Ashkara............C2
3 Java Cafe.........................C3
4 Micha's Hummus..............B3

For listings, see pages 125–32

Bradt

N

0 ___ 200m
0 ___ 200yds

122

There are regular services to and from Nahariya (*1hr 50mins/₪39.50*), Haifa Hof Hacarmel (*55mins/₪27.50*), Haifa Bat Galim, Haifa Merkaz Hashmona and Acre (*1hr 30mins/₪35.5*) along the way. Trains stopping at Atlit (*55mins/₪27.50*) leave Tel Aviv once every hour. A shorter line runs as far as Caesarea (*Pardes-Hana; 50mins/₪22*), stopping at Herzliya (*18mins/₪8.50*), Netanya (*40mins/₪13.50*) and Hadera (*40mins/₪20.50*). A direct line runs to and from Jerusalem (*1hr 30mins/₪20*) and services south run as far as Beersheba (*1hr 20mins/₪27*) and Dimona (*1hr 40mins/₪31.50*). Trains running between Tel Aviv and Ben-Gurion Airport (*12mins/₪13.50*) depart every half-hour.

By air Tel Aviv is home to Israel's only international airport, Ben-Gurion (page 46), approximately 25km to the east. Domestic flights depart from Sde Dov Airport in the north of the city [122 D1]. **Israir** (✆*5109589;* w *israir.co.il*) runs regular flights between Tel Aviv (Sde Dov) and Eilat for around ₪250 each way, while **Arkia** (✆ *6903333;* w *arkia.com*) offers flights between Ben-Gurion Airport and Eilat starting from ₪86 each way.

GETTING AROUND

By bus Dan (w *dan.co.il/eng*) operates Tel Aviv's intra-city buses, and fares around town cost ₪5.90. At the time of writing, Tel Aviv light rail construction was underway, causing some traffic restrictions and delays, but work is set to be completed in 2021. The following bus routes run along most major streets and stop at the main attractions:

- **#4** Runs every 5 minutes from new central bus station up Allenby and Ben Yehuda streets and past the Carmel Market.
- **#5** Runs every 5 minutes from new central bus station up Rothschild and Dizengoff streets to the Dizengoff Centre, then turns right and goes down Nordau, Pinkas and Weizmann streets and finishes at the central train station.
- **#10** Runs every 15 minutes from the central train station along Arlozorov Street, then turns left to go down the coast along Ben Yehuda, Herbert Samuel and Kaufman streets to Jaffa.

By sherut Sherut taxis operate along the main Dan bus routes and will have the same bus number in the front window. The fare is marginally lower than that of the buses, and you can get on or off anywhere you choose. Routes 4, 5 and 16 (among others) also run on Shabbat.

By car Cars are not an ideal way to get around but are by far the best option for exploring the country at large. Parking in the city can be difficult and expensive, and parking illegally will result in your car being towed in the blink of an eye. Most car-rental agencies can be found along Hayarkon Street [126 A3], near the bottom of Frishman and Gordon streets, and in Ben-Gurion Airport. Most of them also have mopeds to rent. You must be over 21 to rent a car anywhere in Israel.

🚗 **Avis** 113 Hayarkon St; ✆5271752; w *avis. co.il;* ⏰ 08.00–18.00 Sun–Thu, 08.00–14.00 Fri; Ben-Gurion Airport; ✆9712315; ⏰ 24hrs
🚗 **Budget** 99 Hayarkon St; ✆9350012; w *budget.co.il;* ⏰ 08.00–18.00 Sun–Thu, 08.00– 14.00 Fri; Ben-Gurion Airport; ✆9712315; ⏰ 24hrs

🚗 **Dollar Thrifty** 80 Hayarkon St; ✆6335252; w *thrifty.com;* ⏰ 08.00–18.00 Sun–Thu, 08.00– 13.00 Fri & holidays
🚗 **Eldan** 114 Hayarkon St; ✆5271166; w *eldan. co.il/en;* ⏰ 08.00–18.00 Sun–Thu, 08.00–14.00 Fri; Ben-Gurion Airport; ✆9773400; ⏰ 24hrs

Hertz 144 Hayarkon St; ☎5223332; w hertz.
co.il/en; ⏰ 08.00–18.00 Sun–Thu, 08.00–14.00
Fri; Ben-Gurion Airport; ☎9772444; ⏰ 24hrs
Motogo 109 Hayarkon St; ☎9226753;
w motogo.co.il; ⏰ 08.00–17.00 Sun–Thu,
08.00–13.00 Fri

Sixt 122 Hayarkon St; ☎9773500; w sixt.
co.il; ⏰ 08.00–18.00 Sun–Thu, 08.00–noon Fri;
Ben-Gurion Airport; ☎5244935; ⏰ 24hrs

By taxi

Tel Aviv has no shortage of taxis, except on Shabbat, when the buses and trains stop and it can take a little longer to hail one. To order a taxi, call **Kastel** (☎*6991296*) or **Ichilov** (☎*6967070*).

By bicycle

Cycling around Tel Aviv is very pleasant – the weather certainly encourages it – and safe. There are a few options to consider, from standard bikes to electric. Pick one with a basket to bring your lunch to the beach with you.

Cycle 147 [126 B1] Ben Yehuda St;
☎5293037; w cycle.co.il; 10.00–18.00 Sun–Thu,
10.00–13.00 Fri; ₪35/hr, ₪70/day
O-Fun Rent a Bike 2 branches: [122
C2] 197 Ben Yehuda St (cnr of Nordau Bd);
☎5442292; w ofun.co.il; ⏰ 09.30–19.00 Sun–
Thu, 09.30–14.00 Fri; ₪25 or 50/hr, ₪75 or 150/
day, depending on the type of bicycle; & [130 C1]
32 Allenby St; ☎6332506; ⏰ 10.00–19.00
Sun–Thu, 10.00–14.00 Fri. City bikes from
₪25/hr, electric bikes from ₪35/hr,

w/end & weekly rates are ₪130/200 &
₪450/650 accordingly.
Pole Position [130 C1] 13 Ben Yehuda St;
☎5252134; w polepositiontlv.com/en; ⏰ 10.00–
19.00 Sun–Thu, 10.00–16.00 Fri. Best-priced
option ₪30/hr for electric bikes.
Tel-O-Fun w tel-o-fun.co.il/en. Their green
bicycle-rental stands installed around the city in
2014 are convenient, albeit pricey; daily access
fee ₪17, first 30mins free, up to 1hr ₪6, up to
90mins ₪12, up to 270mins ₪152.

GUIDED TOURS

There are a number of guided tours in English to choose from. Some are free, though a tip is welcome, while a small fee is charged for others.

Bauhaus Tour 10.00 Fri, leaving from the Bauhaus Centre Tel Aviv, 77 Dizengoff St; ☎5220249;
e info@bauhaus-center.com; w bauhaus-center.com; ⏰ 10.00–19.30 Sat–Thu, 10.00–14.30
Fri. Run by expert guides from the Bauhaus Centre, this unique tour provides a wonderful insight
into this fine architectural style. Advance booking is recommended.
Tel Aviv by Night 20.00 Tue. Meeting point: where Rothschild Bd & Hertzl St meet.
Incorporating a bit of everything, this tour details some of the city's history as well as shedding
light on its restaurant, bar & café scene. It centres on the lively & hip southern Rothschild Bd &
Nahalat Binyamin St, & it's a great way to find out what's 'in' & trendy in the city that never sleeps.
Tel Aviv 14.00 Wed & Sat (₪75/70 adult/student), 11.00 daily (free of charge). Meeting point:
clock tower, Yefet St, Jaffa. Run by Sandeman's New Europe, you can choose between a free daily
tour (although tips are expected & encouraged by guides) or a twice-a-week option at a fee. The
tour starts in Jaffa & goes past the charming Neve Tzedek district & classic Tel Aviv boulevards.
Sandeman's tours can be hit or miss, as presentation quality depends on the person leading a
tour on a specific date. Either way, one is welcome to leave at any time during the tour.
Old Jaffa 11.00 & 14.00 daily. Meeting point: clock tower, Yefet St, Jaffa. The Sandeman's New
Europe tour takes in the best of the quaint Old City of Jaffa including the flea market, cobbled
alleyways, views of Tel Aviv from Hapigsa Gardens & the area's archaeological sites. Tips are
welcome. There is no need to reserve a spot in advance, just show up at the meeting point & join in.

TOURIST INFORMATION AND LOCAL TOUR OPERATORS

Tourist information

ℹ Tourist Information Centre [130 B2] 46 Herbert Samuel St, ✆5166188; w visit-tel-aviv.com; ⏲ 09.00–17.00 or 18.30 (09.30–13.00 or 14.00 Fri), depending on the season
Tourist police [130 B2] Cnr Herbert Samuel & Geula; ✆5165382

Local tour operators and travel agencies

Dan City Tour ✆6394444; e information@dan.co.il; w dan.co.il/eng; adult/child ₪65/56. Runs an open-top tourist sightseeing bus around Tel Aviv & Jaffa taking in the major sights from the port area to Jaffa's Old City. Buses run hourly (*09.00–19.00 Sun–Thu, 09.00–14.00 Fri*) & it is possible to hop on & off all day. Audio information is in several languages. The tour begins at the Dan bus station on Hataarucha St, but you can join at any point.

Mazada Tours [122 D3] 51 Basel St; ✆5444454; e info@mazadatours.com; w mazadatours.com. Organises trips around Israel, as well as to Jordan & Egypt.
Yarkon Tours [126 A4] 14 Allenby St; ✆7965020; w yarkon.co.il. Specialise in Jewish & Christian pilgrimage tours.
Issta [126 B2] 109 Ben Yehuda St; ✆6216100; e customerserv.issta@issta.co.il; w issta.co.il; ⏲ 09.00–18.00 Sun–Thu, 08.30–13.00 Fri. Part of Israel's biggest travel agency chain. Staff can be decidedly officious, so try not to take it personally.
Ophir Tours [122 G1] Tel Aviv University, Music Academy Bldg; ✆6429001; w ophirtours.co.il; ⏲ 09.00–18.00 Sun–Thu, 09.00–13.00 Fri. Friendly, budget-oriented agency.

🛏 WHERE TO STAY

🏠 **David Intercontinental** [130 B4] (555 rooms) 12 Kaufman St; ✆7951111; w intercontinental-telaviv.com. Renowned as being Tel Aviv's most prestigious & luxurious hotel. Located equidistant from Jaffa & central Tel Aviv, beautiful beachfront location & views, immaculate rooms & an indulgent b/fast. **$$$$$**

🏠 **Poli House** [130 C2] (40 rooms) 62 Allenby & 1 Nahalat Binyamin St; ✆7105000; e hotel@thepolihouse.com; w thepolihouse.com. Known as Polishuk House, the Bauhaus-listed property was built & designed in 1934 & only recently converted into this gem of a boutique hotel. Pastel colours & fine décor finishes are completed with a rooftop swimming pool & terrace. **$$$$$**

🏠 **Center Hotel** [126 C3] (54 rooms) 2 Zamenhof St; ✆5266100; e reservations@atlashotels.co.il; w atlas.co.il. Part of the growing chain of Atlas hotels, this is a fashionable & trendy boutique hotel in Bauhaus architecture. Fresh, minimalist décor with each room sporting a different painting by up-&-coming artists. B/fast included & free bicycle rental. **$$$$**

🏠 **Isrotel Tower** [126 A4] (90 rooms) 78 Hayarkon St; ✆5113636; w isrotel.com. This cylindrical 30-storey hotel is one of the most eye-catching buildings in the city. Located in the heart of the city centre, it affords great views of the sea & is within walking distance of most attractions. Its rooftop swimming pool is fabulous, but perhaps not if you're afraid of heights. **$$$$**

🏠 **Nordoy** [130 D3] (20 rooms) 27 Nahalat Binyamin St; ✆2727279; e info@hotelnordoy.com; w hotelnordoy.com. Opened in Apr 2017, this is another Bauhaus property turned hotel. With a lovely terrace overlooking the market stalls at the Nahalat Binyamin, rooms are airy & exclusive, & some come with private balconies. **$$$$**

🏠 **Prima Tel Aviv** [126 A3] (60 rooms) 105 Hayarkon St; ✆5206666; e primatlv@prima.co.il; w prima-hotels-israel.com. Tel Aviv's representative in this nationwide chain of reputable hotels is located on the seafront in front of Frishman Beach, 15mins' walk from the city centre. The recently renovated rooms are elegant, breezy & modern with the complete range of facilities. B/fast included & there is a swish bar & lounge area. **$$$$**

🏠 **Hotel de la Mer** [130 B1] 62 Hayarkon St; ✆5100011; w zvielihotels.com. Elegant boutique hotel, with tasteful, unpretentious décor designed using the principles of feng shui. Rooms are spacious & comfortable (some with jacuzzi), & there is a lovely spa. Excellent value. **$$$**

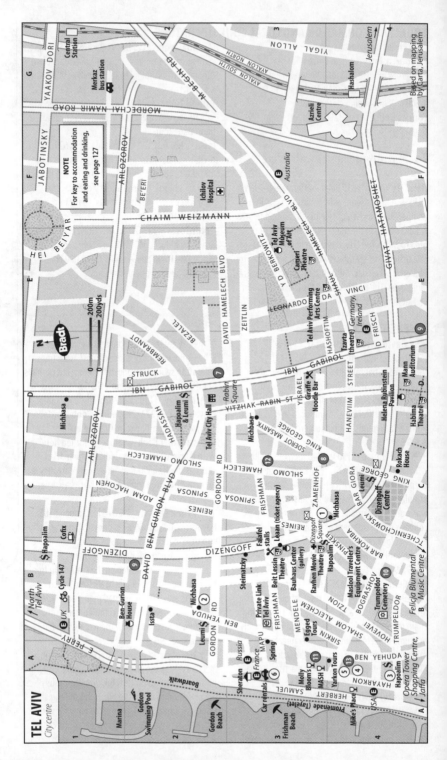

TEL AVIV
City centre

NOTE
For key to accommodation and eating and drinking, see page 127

Based on mapping by Carta, Jerusalem

TEL AVIV *City centre*
For listings, see pages 125–32

Where to stay

Where to eat and drink

Maxim Hotel [126 A4] (71 rooms) 86 Hayarkon St; 5173721; w telavivmaxim.com. Well-priced hotel with fantastic location on Hayarkon St. Comfortable, well-equipped rooms are exceptionally well priced. Israeli b/fast & laundry service. **$$$**

Miguel Hotel and Bistro [126 A4] (21 rooms) 88 Hayarkon St; 5107744. Resembling the elegant, family-run hotels of France & Italy, Miguel's abounds in character & finesse. On the seafront 10mins from the city centre. Rooms are equipped with AC, TV & Wi-Fi. Downstairs is a gourmet French-style restaurant & bar (⊕ noon–17.00 Sun–Thu; **$$**) serving fresh fish & meat dishes. **$$$**

Abraham Hostel [130 E4] (350 rooms) 21 Levontin St; 6249200; e infotlv@ abrahamhostels.com; w abrahamhostels.com. The latest addition to the Abraham Hostels & Tours family, this new hostel opened in 2016 has a variety of rooms, including a studio & a 2-bedroom apartment on offer. Rooms are simple, but pristine & there is an upbeat vibe in communal areas. It is a good place in central Tel Aviv to start exploring Israel from – Abraham Hostels & Tours can advise & organise trips around the country. **$$**

Gordon Inn Hotel & Guesthouse [126 D2] (27 rooms) 17 Gordon St; 5238239; e gordoninn@gmail.com; w gordoninn.hostel. com. A welcoming & friendly little guesthouse located a few mins' walk from the beach. Dbl rooms (shared bathroom or en suite) have TV & coffee facilities & are pleasantly decorated & extremely clean. Guests receive 10% discount in the Gordon Inn pub next door. **$$**

Hayarkon 48 Hostel [130 B1] (36 rooms) 48 Hayarkon St; 5168989; e info@hayarkon48. com; w hayarkon48.com. This is undoubtedly Tel Aviv's best hostel & unsurprisingly often booked to capacity. Located a few mins' walk from the beach, it is immaculately clean & offers a fabulous array of services & facilities including a well-equipped kitchen, lively lounge, complete with pool table & TV, free safe, b/fast & a breezy rooftop balcony overlooking the Mediterranean. The bright yellow building used to be the Geula School. **$$**

Bnei Dan Tel Aviv Hostel (HI) [122 E2] (45 rooms) 36 Bnei Dan St; 02 5945655; e telaviv@iyha.org.il; w iyha.org.il. A member of the Hostelling International group, this large hostel is located near the Hayarkon Park & River. Immaculately clean rooms have AC & bathrooms. Kosher b/fast included. Often frequented by large groups. **$$–$**

WHERE TO EAT AND DRINK Tel Aviv takes pride in its gastronomic prowess and thriving restaurant culture and is a big player on the international culinary scene. Israelis are real foodies and hearty meat lovers, and nowhere manifests this better than here. Mediterranean-influenced food is the most popular, generally cooked in a gourmet, fusion style. Restaurants and eateries are numerous, the variety is endless and the standard is high. You will rarely leave dissatisfied, although the customer service often leaves a little to be desired. Restaurants such as Giraffe Noodle Bar, Focaccia Bar or Burgersbar have successfully established good and reliable chains across Israel. There are also plenty of sandwich bars on leafy boulevards. The best budget options are the Israeli staples of hummus, falafel, shawarma and sabich, but if you've had enough of chickpeas for a few days, there are also plenty of small pizza places (although some are decidedly shabby, so choose carefully), sandwich bars, burekas, bakeries and cheaper-end restaurants. Most bars and pubs also serve cheap snacks for a late-night meal.

Tel Aviv and Jaffa TEL AVIV

4

As you explore, take time to notice the street names; it's a great way to put some of the country's complex history into context. Almost without exception, names are dedicated to those who remain close to the hearts of Israelis and Jews the world over.

ALLENBY Sir Edmund Henry Allenby (1861–1936) was a British World War I commander who is best known for his Middle East campaign. He battled the Turks in Palestine, capturing Gaza and Jerusalem in 1917. In 1918, he won the vicious battle on the plain of Meggido and later took Damascus and Aleppo.

ARLOZOROV Haim Arlozorov (1899–1933) was a Ukrainian-born Zionist who represented the yishuv at the League of Nations in Geneva and rose to become head of the political party of the Jewish Agency. He was assassinated in 1933 on Tel Aviv Beach, two days before he was to negotiate the Ha'avara (transfer) agreement with the Nazi government.

BEGIN Menachem Begin (1913–92) was Prime Minister of Israel from 1977 to 1983. Founder of the Likud political party, Begin negotiated the 1979 Israeli–Egyptian Peace Agreement with Anwar Sadat.

BEN-GURION David Ben-Gurion (1886–1973) was Israel's first prime minister following the formation of an independent state in 1948 (page 13).

BEN-YEHUDA Eliezer Ben-Yehuda (1858–1922) was one of the first Zionists, and responsible for reintroducing the Hebrew language as the spoken tongue of Israel.

DIZENGOFF Meir Dizengoff (1861–1936) was the first mayor of Tel Aviv from 1911 until his death in 1936.

FRISHMAN David Frishman (1859–1922) was one of the first major writers of modern Hebrew literature. His most famous work is the *Bar Midbar* (1923), a series of fictional biblical tales.

HERZL Theodor Herzl (1860–1904) was the founder and first president of the World Zionist Organisation.

Restaurants

✖ **Manta Ray** [130 A5] Alma Beach; ☎5174773; w mantaray.co.il; ⏱ 09.00–23.00 daily. Wonderful fresh fish & seafood cooked in a Middle Eastern style. They also serve big, hearty b/fasts in a setting of laid-back beach charm. $$$$$

✖ **Onami** [130 G2] 18 Haarbaa St; ☎5621172; ⏱ noon–late Sun–Fri, 13.00–late Sat. One of the city's best & longest established sushi spots. The restaurant consists of a sushi bar, Yakituri grill & Japanese dishes. The business lunches are a good way to sample the variety (⏱ noon–18.00 Sun–Fri; $$$$). $$$$$

✖ **Brasserie** [126 D3] 70 Ibn Gabirol St; ☎6967111; w brasserie.co.il; ⏱ 24hrs daily. Chic, French bistro facing Rabin Sq. This has long been a huge favourite in the city serving elegant, hearty dishes of good Mediterranean food. Different b/ fast, lunch & dinner menus have a wide choice of meals & prices. $$$

✖ **Max Brenner** [130 E4] 45 Rothschild Bd; ☎5604570; w maxbrenner.com; ⏱ 09.00–late Sun–Thu, 08.00–late Fri–Sat. Chocolate is the name of the game at Israel's sweetest restaurant. It has become one of the country's most popular exports, making chocolate waves in the US,

IBN GABIROL Solomon Ibn Gabirol (1021–58) was a Jewish poet and philosopher.

JABOTINSKY Vladimir Evgenevich Jabotinsky (1880–1940) led the Revisionist Movement which seceded from the Zionist Organisation and in 1920 organised and led the Haganah, a Jewish militia.

NAMIR Mordechai Namir (1897–1975) was a Knesset member, government minister, one of the heads of the Labor Zionist Movement and Mayor of Tel Aviv.

RABIN Yitzhak Rabin (1922–95) was the Prime Minister of Israel between 1974–77 and 1992–95. He undertook secret negotiations with the PLO, which led to the signing of the peace agreement between Israel and Palestine (page 17).

ROTHSCHILD Baron Edmond Benjamin James de Rothschild (1845–1934) was a member of the wealthy Rothschild family and a supporter of Zionism. He made extensive purchases of land in Palestine, contributing to the establishment of Jewish settlements and eventually the State of Israel (page 13).

SADEH Yitzhak Sadeh (1890–1952) was Commander of the Palmach and one of the founding members of the Israel Defence Force (IDF).

SAMUEL Sir Herbert Samuel (1870–1963) was the British High Commissioner for Palestine from 1920 to1925. He became the first Jew to govern the Holy Land in 2,000 years.

SHAUL HAMELECH (pronounced *hamelekh*) Saul the King was the first king of the ancient Kingdom of Israel as recorded in the Old Testament and the Quran. He reigned from c1020 to 1000BCE.

WEIZMANN Chaim Weizmann (1874–1952) was the first President of Israel from 1949 to 1952, President of the World Zionist Organisation and founder of the Weizmann Institute of Science.

Australia, Philippines & Singapore. Outlandish, gooey recipes have been created that are rich & calorie-laden but any sweet tooth's dream come true. A good selection of salads, sandwiches, chicken dishes, pasta & crêpes form the savoury menu, but be sure to leave room for dessert. **$$$**

✘ **The Thai House** [126 A4] 8 Bograshov St; ✆5178568; w thai-house.co.il; ⊕ noon–23.00 daily. Authentic, traditional Thai food cooked by Thai chefs. The décor is simple, with bamboo, trees & candles adding a flavour of the oriental. Regional dishes range from hot & fiery to coconut creamy. **$$$**

✘ **Azura** [130 E4] 1 Mikveh Israel St; ✆5015050; e azuratlv@gmail.com; ⊕ 11.00–17.00 Sun–Fri. A recently opened branch of the popular family-run Azura restaurant in Jerusalem's Mahane Yehuda Market, it serves filling & zesty Middle Eastern dishes in a slightly more modern locale. **$$**

✘ **Goocha** 171 Dizengoff St [126 B2] & 14 Ibn Gabirol St [126 E4]; ✆5222886, 6911603; ⊕ noon–02.00 daily. Having earned its reputation for fresh fish, seafood & pasta at unusually reasonable prices, Goocha have now opened 2 new branches. The paper cone of calamari & shrimp is a great take-out. **$$**

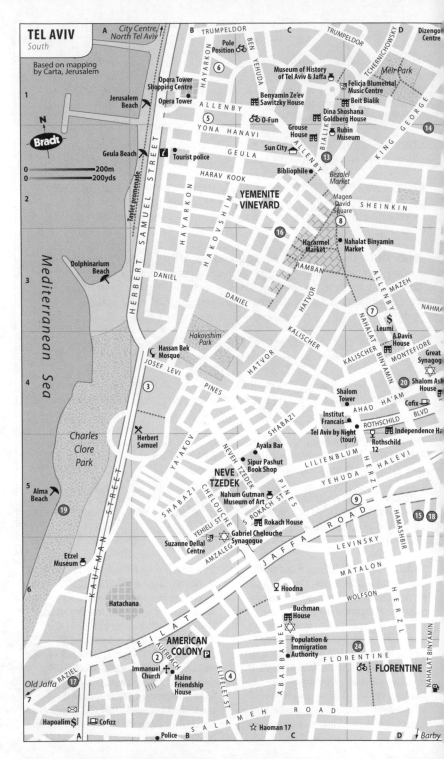

TEL AVIV
South

Based on mapping
by Carta, Jerusalem

Bradt

Mediterranean Sea

0 ————— 200m
0 ————— 200yds

Charles
Clore
Park

Alma
Beach 19

Etzel
Museum

Hatachana

Old Jaffa

Hapoalim $ Cofizz

A
City Centre/
North Tel Aviv

Jerusalem
Beach

Opera Tower
Shopping Centre
Opera Tower

Geula Beach

Tourist police

Tayelet promenade

HERBERT SAMUEL STREET

KAUFMAN STREET

Dolphinarium
Beach

Hassan Bek
Mosque

JOSEF LEVI
PINES
3

Herbert
Samuel

YA'AKOV

SHABAZI

CHELOUCHE

YEHIELI ST

AMZALEG

EILAT

AUERBACH

Immanuel Church
Maine
Friendship
House

RAZIEL

ELIFELET ST

Police

B
TRUMPELDOR

HAYARKON

BEN YEHUDA

Pole
Position 6

Benyamin Ze'ev
Sawitzky House

O-Fun

ALLENBY

YONA HANAVI

GEULA

HARAV KOOK

HAYARKON

HAKOVSHIM

YEMENITE
VINEYARD

16

Hakovshim
Park

DANIEL

DANIEL

HATVOR

NEVEH TZEDEK

Ayala Bar

Sipur Pashut
Book Shop

Nahum Gutman
Museum of Art

S ROKACH ST

Rokach House

Gabriel Chelouche
Synagogue

Suzanne Dellal
Centre

AMERICAN
COLONY 2

4

SALAMEH

Museum of History
of Tel Aviv & Jaffa

Grouse
House

Sun City

Bibliophile

TRUMPELDOR

TCHERNICHOWSKY

Felicja Blumental
Music Centre

Beit Bialik

Dina Shoshana
Goldberg House

Rubin
Museum

BIALIK

ALLENBY

13

Bezalel
Market

Magen
David
Square

8

Hacarmel
Market

RAMBAN

Nahalat Binyamin
Market

KALISCHER

HATVOR

KALISCHER

NEVE
TZEDEK

PINES

SHABAZI

LILIENBLUM

YEHUDA

JAFFA ROAD

LEVINSKY

MATALON

WOLFSON

Hoodna

Buchman
House

Population &
Immigration
Authority

ABARBANEL

FLORENTINE

24

ROAD

Haoman 17

D
Dizengoff
Centre

Meïr Park

KING GEORGE

14

SHEINKIN

ALLENBY

MAZEH

NAHMA

NAHALAT BINYAMIN

7

Leumi $
A Davis
House

MONTEFIORE

Great
Synagog

20

Shalom Ash
House

Cofix

ROTHSCHILD BLVD

Shalom
Tower

Institut
Francais

Tel Aviv by Night
(tour)

AHAD HA'AM

Independence Ha

Rothschild
12

HERZL

HALEVI

9

HAMASHBIR

15 18

HERZL

FLORENTINE

Barby

130

NOTE
For key to accommodation
and eating and drinking,
see page 132

E   Entertainment ▲
    venues

Helena
Rubinstein
Pavilion

F   Charles Bronfman
    Auditorium

Habima
Theatre

BOGRASHOV

MARMOREK

Cinematheque

HAARBAA ST

26   22

HAHASHMONAIM

AHAD HA'AM

ROTHSCHILD BOULEVARD

MELCHETT

25

SHEINKIN

LINCOLN

CARLEBACH

JAFFA ROAD

HAMASGER

SHONTZINO STREET

Tmuna

YITZAKH SADEH

Armadillo

MAZEH

HA'AM

HALEVI

Krieger
House

Nosen Chen

Jov Hershkowitz

BEZALEL YAFFE

AHAD

Michbasa

MAZEH

NAHMANI

YEHUDA

21

HARAKEVET

11   1

HAMASGER

Levontin 7

LEVONTIN ST

ELECTRIC
GARDEN

ROAD

JAFFA

HASHOMRON

SALOMON

Old central
bus station

HARAKEVET

ROSH PINA

12

Y L PERETZ

LEVINSKY

MATALON

HAALIYA

TCHLENOV

BNEI BRAK

MATALON

LEVINSKY

Tel Aviv
Mall

New central
bus station

BEN GUVIN

HAYIM

SCHLOMO   ROAD

MISALANT

ISRAEL

AYALON SOUTH

AYALON NORTH

Hahaganah
railway station

🛏 **Where to stay**

⊗ **Where to eat and drink**

✕ **Ma Pau** [130 D4] 59 Nahalat Binyamin St; ☎7739797; ⏲ 11.00–23.00 Sun–Fri. A new addition to the food scene in Tel Aviv, this small Indian restaurant serves excellent thali & Mumbai-inspired dishes. $$

✕ **Orna & Ella** [130 E2] 33 Sheinkin St; ☎6204753; ⏲ 10.00–midnight daily, kitchen closed Fri between 16.30 & 17.30. Easy to find by the queues of young Tel Avivians waiting their turn inside one of the city's most well-known & well-established café-restaurants. There are plenty of vegetarian options including a selection of quiches & sandwiches, & they serve great coffee. Meals are light, so not the place to go for a big slap-up dinner. On w/ends be prepared to wait to be seated or make a reservation in advance. Vegan-friendly. $$

✕ **Piccola Pasta** [126 A3] 53 Ben Yehuda St; ☎5290643; ⏲ 18.00–00.45 Sun–Fri. This tiny rustic-style Italian restaurant is family-run & has been around since 2000. It is the best place to go if you are looking for classic Italian dishes slightly infused with Israeli culinary ingenuity. $$

✕ **Tony Vespa** [130 G2] 8 Haarbaa St; ☎*2045; ⏲ noon–03.00 daily. One of the city's favourite pizza haunts. Pizzas are priced by weight & there is a huge variety of toppings. $$

Cafés Café culture is huge in Tel Aviv & come Fri morning every seat in the city will be full, with chic Tel Avivians sipping cappuccinos, wearing big sunglasses & soaking up the sun. You don't have to look very far to find a decent café serving good-quality coffee, Israeli b/fast (eggs, salad, bread, muesli, fresh fruit & yoghurt) & a range of salads & sandwiches. The biggest concentrations can be found along the sides of Rabin Sq & along Ibn Gabirol St, down the length of Rothschild Bd & along Sheikin & Bograshov streets. There are a number of **Cofix** shops around town & **Aroma Café** is another good choice.

☕ **Arcaffè** [130 E4] 31 Rothschild Bd; ☎5660259; 35 Basel St; ☎5467001; ⏲ 07.00–midnight daily. Branches of this popular chain are dotted all over the city. Their delicate pastries, fresh baguettes & sweets are what pull in the crowds. $

☕ **Café Bialik** [130 D1] 2 Bialik St; ☎6200832; ⏲ 08.00–late Sun–Fri, 11.00–late Sat. Well-loved & well-established café on trendy Bialik St. It has a full menu ranging from b/fasts to sandwiches to full meals & often hosts live music. $

☕ **Garden Café Sonia** [130 D2] 18 King George St; ☎077 5261234; ⏲ 09.00–midnight daily. This bohemian-chic café has a delightful garden patio covered with plants & flowers. There is a well-stocked menu of light meals. $

☕ **Java Cafe** [122 C3] 196 Ben Yehuda St; ☎7440466; ⏲ 08.00–midnight Sun–Thu. Opened in 2014, this breezy café-restaurant has secured its client base, & lunchtime queues are not uncommon. Shakshooka is particularly good here. $

☕ **Shine** [126 C3] 38 Shlomo Hamelech St; ☎5276186. Ultra-trendy café attracting the brunch-eating, soya latte-drinking crowd. If you can get a seat, sit outside for the real chic Tel Aviv experience. Selection of salads, sandwiches & light meals served. $

☕ **Tika** [130 E2] 41 Sheinkin St; ☎6201099; ⏲ 07.30–midnight Sun–Thu, 07.30–20.00 Fri. Rustic & comfortable, this is one of the most fashionable cafés along Sheinkin St, without the pretension of some of its neighbours. A small wooden balcony provides the perfect viewpoint for people-watching while you enjoy an iced coffee & sandwich. $

I lummus and falafel are a godsend to those on a budget or those who simply want to savour the staple foods of the Middle East. Tel Aviv and Jaffa are teeming with small restaurants and kiosks selling freshly cooked falafel, pitta, hummus, salads, shawarma and sabich, but the following are particularly recommended:

✖ **Falafel Hakosem** (The Wizard) [126 C3] 1 Shlomo Hamelech St; ☎ 5252033; ☉ 09.00–23.00 Sun–Thu. This is the best falafel you will find in Tel Aviv. Be prepared to queue but expect rare customer service from the lively owner. Shawarma, schnitzel & sabich also served. **$**

✖ **Hummus Ashkara** [122 C2] 45 Yermiahu St; ☎ 5464547; ☉ 24hrs. 40-year-old veteran of the Tel Aviv hummus circuit serving lightly spiced hummus, plus soups in winter. **$**

✖ **Hummus Shlomo** [130 C3] Hacarmel Market; ☉ 08.00–14.30 Sun–Fri. 50-year-old hummus hideaway in the depths of the Hacarmel Market – ask any vendor to point you in the right direction. **$**

✖ **Mashwesha** [126 B4] 40 Pinsker St; ☎ 6293796; ☉ 11.00–23.00 Sun–Thu, 11.00–17.00 Fri, noon–23.00 Sat. Rudimentary little eatery just off Bograshov St; get there early before the hot, chunky hummus runs out. **$**

✖ **Micha's Hummus** [122 B3] 191 Ben Yehuda St; m 052 4689856; ☉ 11.00–19.00 Sun–Thu, 08.00–16.00 Fri. Serves delicious hummus with a modern twist & various toppings. **$**

ENTERTAINMENT AND NIGHTLIFE

Festivals Tel Aviv is a cultural hub of the country and as such there are countless festivals and events throughout the year, from modern and classic music to theatre, film and food. Tel Aviv City (**w** telavivcity.com/eng) has a review of all festivals. **Taste of the City** (*ta'am ha'ir* in Hebrew) is held in May in the Hayarkon Exhibition Centre; the city's best restaurants cook up and serve their finest dishes for ₪20 each in this festival of food, offering a true culinary bonanza. The **Gay Pride Parade** (**w** gaytelavivguide.com) starts around Rabin Square in June, and is a fun and raucous procession attended by thousands that leads through the streets to Hayarkon Park.

Bars While in most countries it is easy to differentiate between a bar and a nightclub, in Tel Aviv the line seems to have become a little blurry. Come 01.00, dance fever will have overtaken most bars and there will be people packed into every space bopping away. Bars generally get going late and stay open until the last person staggers out. They tend to cluster in Tel Aviv, and the list below is merely a taste of what the city has to offer night-owls. Simply head to one of the popular areas – **Dizengoff Street**, **Lilinblum**, **Jaffa Flea Market** or the old port, for instance – and see what's on offer.

The flea market in Jaffa has become one of the hangouts in the city and is a really wonderful experience for visitors, who get to appreciate the trendy side of young Tel Avivians in the setting of a funky, authentic old market. In summer, the bars and cafés that surround the central market area come alive with antique hunters, the young and chic and the bohemian, and on Thursdays the market stays open until midnight.

✖ **Jem's Beer Factory Bar** [122 G4] 15 Hamagshemim St, Petach Tikvah; ☎ 9195366; e beer@jems.co.il; w jems.co.il/en; ☉ noon–midnight, closed Fri evening until Sat evening.

Finding your way here takes time, but it's worth it. The newly opened bar has an excellent menu (the homemade sausages are delicious) & it epitomises the style & coolness of Tel Aviv. You can also, of course, savour all Jem's beers, easily the best craft beer in Israel.

♀ Levontin 7 [130 E5] 7 Levontin St; ☏ 5605084; w levontin7.com; ⊕ 19.00–late daily. Funky music bar in the charismatic Levontin neighbourhood. They often host live music nights, usually of the indie genre, & it is frequented by a relaxed, casual crowd.

♀ MASH [126 A3] 98 Hayarkon St; ☏ 6051007; ⊕ 17.00–04.00 daily. MASH has been attracting sports buffs & expats for over 25 years, & while it can get decidedly rowdy during televised sporting events it's a far cry from the rest of the city's glitzy, chrome-decorated bars.

♀ Mike's Place [126 A4] 90 Herbert Samuel St; ☏ 5106392; ⊕ 16.00–late daily. Although from the outside it may look better suited to a Costa del Sol holiday resort, the inside actually has quite a lot of charisma. It hit international headlines when it was the target of a suicide bombing in 2003 but was subsequently rebuilt. It is a great place to see live sporting events & they have live music most nights of the week.

♀ Molly Bloom's [126 A3] 100 Hayarkon St; ☏ 5221558; w molly-blooms.com; ⊕ 16.00– 02.00 Sun–Wed, 16.00–midnight Fri, 15.00–02.00 Sat, 16.00–02.00 Sun. Eternally popular, Tel Aviv's first Irish pub is a little rough around the edges but manages it in a charming kind of way. Not a lot of seating room on w/ends. Beers include draught Guinness & Kilkenny. Selection of good, simple pub foods.

♀ Rothschild 12 [130 D4] 12 Rothschild Bd; ☏ 5106430; w rothschild12.co.il; ⊕ 07.00–late Sat–Thu. Popular night-time bar in the style of a French saloon. It is a chic place, where the glitz-&-glamour set come to socialise.

Nightclubs and live music
Israelis have a penchant for hardcore trance music, and raves and one-off parties are big business, although in the city centre you're more likely to find a mixture of rock, techno, dance and plenty of 1980s hits. Tel Avivians have a lot of partying stamina (mainly because of the small amount of alcohol they consume) and go out late, so don't even consider a nightclub before midnight. Live music clubs range from rock to alternative to South American drums to jazz and R&B. Admission charges tend to vary depending on who's playing.

☆ Barby [130 D7] 52 Qibbutz Galuyot Rd; ☏ 5188123; w barby.co.il; admission varies with performer. This is the place to see big-name rock musicians & bands in concert. The bunker-like club is generally packed with crowds of eccentrically dressed youngsters spilling on to the street.

☆ Goldstar Zappa [122 F1] 24 Raoul Wallenberg St; ☏ 7626666; w zappa-club.co.il; ⊕ daily for evening performances; admission ₪50–150. One of the city's leading live music venues, it hosts Israeli & international artists covering a wide spectrum of music genres.

☆ Haoman 17 [130 C7] 15 Abarbanel St; ☏ 5189131; ⊕ 23.00–late daily; admission ₪70– 140. This is the younger sibling of the immensely popular Haoman/Bar 17 club in Jerusalem. Equally popular in Tel Aviv, this is the place to blow your budget in a single evening (drinks are exorbitant) & have a hell of a time doing it.

☆ Shablul Jazz [122 C1] Hangar 13, Tel Aviv Port; ☏ 5461891; w shabluljazz.com; ⊕ 20.00–late daily; admission free–₪80. Swanky jazz bar with regular jam sessions & open mic nights as well as an impressive wine list & gourmet menu.

Cinemas
The **Tel Aviv Cinematheque** [130 G1] (*Haarbaa St*; ☏ *6060800*; w *cinema.co.il/english*; *admission ₪36*) shows an arty selection of films, ranging from classics to avant-garde and experimental pieces. Annual film festivals are shown so check at the box office for upcoming events. The cinema is often at the centre of Israeli debate thanks to its decision to show politically sensitive films. For new releases and blockbusters (subtitled in Hebrew) try the **Lev Cinema** [126 C4] (*Ground Flr, Dizengoff Centre*; ☏ *6200485*; *admission ₪36*) or **Ravhen Movie Theatre** [126 B3] (*Dizengoff Sq & Azrieli Towers*; ☏ *5282288*; *admission ₪37*).

Performing arts To find out what's on in the city's theatres, galleries and concert halls, and to buy tickets for upcoming events, contact one of the following **box offices** (note that some are in Hebrew only): Hadran [122 G1] (*101 Rokach Bd;* ✆*5215200;* w *hadran.co.il*); Leaan [126 B3] (*7 Frug St;* ✆*5247373;* w *leaan.co.il*); or Israstage [122 G3] (*22 Tuval St;* ✆*6023619;* w *israstage.com*).

Theatre Theatre has had a long & rich history in Tel Aviv & even today still enjoys regular sell-out performances.

⚇ **Arab-Hebrew Theatre** [147 E2] 10 Mifratz Shlomo St; ✆5185563; e info@jaffatheatre.org. il; w arab-hebrew-theatre.org.il. In Jaffa, this theatre is housed inside an ancient stone building & comprises 2 groups that produce plays in both Hebrew & Arabic.

⚇ **Beit Lessin** [126 B3] 101 Dizengoff St; ✆7255333; w lessin.co.il. Small theatre that has performances most weeks although mostly in Hebrew.

⚇ **Cameri Theatre** [126 E3] Golda Meir Centre, 19 Shaul Hamelech Bd; ✆6060960; w cameri.co.il. This theatre offers English translation & has a good website for upcoming events.

⚇ **Habima Theatre** [130 F1] Habima Sq, Tarshat Av; ✆6295555; w habima.co.il. This is not only Israel's national theatre but also the one that has made the greatest contribution to Israeli & Jewish theatrical culture over the past century. It was founded in 1918 in Moscow & relocated to Tel Aviv in 1931 & today comprises 80 actors who perform 4 plays daily. Plays are in Hebrew but there is simultaneous English translation available.

⚇ **Tzavta** [126 D4] 30 Ibn Gabirol St; ✆6950156; w tzavta.co.il. This swings between avant-garde theatre performances, Israeli folk music nights & classical performances (Hebrew only).

Music and dance

⚇ **Charles Bronfman Auditorium** [130 F1] Habima Sq; ✆6211777. Home of the world-renowned Israeli Philarmonic Orchestra.

⚇ **Felicja Blumental Music Centre and Library** [130 C1] 26 Bialik St; ✆6201185; w fbmc.co.il. Hosts regular classical music performances.

⚇ **Israel Ballet** ✆6046610; w iballet.co.il/eng. This company has regular performances of the great classics.

⚇ **Suzanne Dellal Centre** [130 B5] 6 Yehieli St; ✆5105657; w suzannedellal.org.il/en. This is the country's foremost dance centre & home of the nationally acclaimed Bat-Sheva Dance Group. Check their website for upcoming shows & ticket booking.

⚇ **Tel Aviv Performing Arts Centre** [126 E3] 19 Shaul Hamelech Bd; ✆6927777; w israel-opera. co.il/eng. Home of the New Israel Opera.

⚇ **Tmuna** [130 H3] 8 Shontzino St; ✆5611211; e tmu-na@tmu-na.org.il; w tmu-na.org.il. This small performing arts centre is a place where you can sit back with a drink & watch up-&-coming young musicians, actors, dancers & singers.

SHOPPING Tel Aviv is a shopper's paradise and pretty much anything you're looking for can be found in the city's malls, shopping streets, boutiques and markets. For more mainstream shops, the city's major shopping centres are your best bet. The **Azrieli Centre** [126 F4] (*123 Menachem Begin St;* ✆*6081179;* ⊕ *10.00–22.00 Sun– Thu, 09.30–17.00 Fri, 20.00–23.00 Sat*) is the Disneyland of shopaholics, home to an enormous selection of moderate and expensively priced stores (page 138).

Spread across both sides of the constantly busy street of the same name, **Dizengoff Centre** [126 C4] (*cnr of Dizengoff & King George sts;* ✆*6212416;* w *dizengof-center. co.il/en;* ⊕ *09.00–midnight Sun–Thu, 09.00–16.00 Fri, 20.00–midnight Sat*) is a throwback to the early 1970s when it was built. The maze-like centre seems to be designed to provide shoppers with the maximum amount of walking, and is decidedly confusing. It is still, however, one of the busiest shopping spots in the city and home to most of Tel Aviv's big-name stores and countless food outlets. The weekend **food market** (⊕ *16.00–22.00 Thu, 10.30–16.00 Fri*) sees the walkways of the mall fill with stalls selling home-cooked, reasonably priced food, including meatballs, couscous, stuffed peppers, cakes, pies and a whole host of traditional fare. The long, narrow Dizengoff Street that stretches from the Azrieli buildings to the Hayarkon Park is one of the main arteries of central Tel Aviv.

For one-of-a-kind boutiques and a variety of shoe shops, funky **Sheinkin Street** (page 141) is the place to go, while if it's shoes and boots you're after, **Dizengoff Street** is teeming with a rather strange combination of cheap and expensive shoe shops, and a gaudy selection of wedding dresses. At the other end of town, **Allenby Street** is a fun, if rather shabby street of cheap shoes and clothes, although you might have to look a bit harder for the good stuff. Where Allenby Street meets the seafront is the plush **Opera Tower Shopping Centre** [130 B1] (*1 Allenby St;* ⧵*5107496;* ☺ *10.00–22.00 daily*). For a totally different experience, the **Hacarmel Market** (page 143) offers a feast of super-cheap clothes, homewares, fresh produce and sweets and is a must-see in the city. Souvenir shopping can be slightly harder in Tel Aviv, and one of the best places to visit is the small **Spring** shop [126 B3] (*65 Ben Yehuda St;* ⧵*5223759*), which sells a good selection of Ahava Dead Sea products as well as nice gift ideas, souvenirs, novelty T-shirts and postcards. **Ayala Bar** [130 C5] (*36 Shabazi St;* ⧵*5100082;* e *ayalabar.art@gmail.com;* w *ayalabar.com;* ☺ *10.00–20.00, Fri 18.00*) is a modern version of Middle Eastern taste in jewellery and is now even available in Europe.

Alternatively, the twice-weekly **Nahalat Binyamin Market** (page 143) has a great selection of arts and crafts, and it is always possible to pick up a bargain or two at Jaffa's **flea market** (page 150). In addition, many of the museum gift shops sell high-quality souvenirs and crafts. The area known as the **Electric Garden** (Gan Hahashmal) [130 E5] is an up-and-coming zone in which trendy boutiques are opening by the dozen and vying for space in this much-sought-after neighbourhood.

For travel and camping equipment, **Lametayel** [126 C4] (*3rd Flr, Dizengoff Centre;* ⧵*077 3334508;* ☺ *10.00–21.00 Sun–Thu, 10.00–14.30 Fri*) stocks a wide range of camping gear plus a great selection of maps and travel guides, while **Maslool Traveller's Equipment Centre** [126 B4] (*47 Bograshov St;* ⧵*6203508;* ☺ *09.00–23.00 Sun–Thu, 09.00–17.00 Fri, 19.30–22.30 Sat*) offers a huge variety of camping, backpacking and outdoor equipment, with sleeping bags and boots downstairs.

Bookshops There are plenty of big chain stores and small secondhand shops selling Hebrew and English books as well as books in French, German and Russian.

Bibliophile [130 C2] 87 Allenby St; ⧵6299710; ☺ 09.00–19.00 Sun–Thu, 09.00–14.00 Fri. This warren-like used bookstore has a big selection of tatty books in a variety of languages.
Sipur Pashut [130 C5] 36 Shabazi St; ⧵5107040; w sipurpashut.com/english; ☺ 10.00–20.00 Sun–Thu, 09.30–16.00 Fri. Opened in 2003, this is a small & stylish bookshop, worth a visit for something a bit different.
Steimatzky [126 B3] 109 Dizengoff St; ⧵5233415; ☺ 08.30–21.30 Sun–Thu, 08.30–15.00 Fri. Has a big English-language section including Carta maps. There's a smaller branch at 50 Dizengoff St in the Dizengoff Centre.

OTHER PRACTICALITIES

Money There are countless currency-exchange shops around the city centre that offer commission-free money exchange. While some of them may look a little shady, they all offer pretty much the same rate, are above board and have shorter queues than in the post offices and banks. They are also open later. There are a number of exchange shops inside the central bus station, plus several branches along Hayarkon and Ben Yehuda streets and King George Street near the Dizengoff Centre. Some offer Moneygram or Western Union facilities, as does the post office.

Travellers' cheques can be changed at most banks and at the post office for no commission. There are branches of all the major banks dotted around the city, but the following are the most convenient:

$ Bank Hapoalim [126 D2] 71 Ibn Gabirol St; ☏6532407; ☉ 08.30–14.00 Sun & Tue–Wed, 08.30–13.45 & 16.00–17.00 Mon & Thu. Other useful branches can be found at 205 Dizengoff St [122 C4]; 19 Ben Yehuda St [126 A4]; 19th Flr, Round Bldg, Azrieli Centre [126 F4]; 217 Ben Yehuda St [122 C2].

$ Bank Leumi [126 C4] 50 Dizengoff St; ☏9544555; ☉ 08.30–14.00 Sun & Tue–Wed, 08.30–13.00 & 16.00–18.30 Mon & Thu. Other useful branches are on 1 Jerusalem St, Jaffa; 87a Ben Yehuda St [126 B2]; 71 Ibn Gabirol St [126 D2]; 43 Allenby St [130 D3].

Post

✉ **Post office** [126 D2] 108 Ibn Gabirol St; ☏5228009; ☉ 08.00–18.00 Sun–Thu, 08.00– noon Fri. This is the main branch, but there are also useful branches on 60 King George St [126 C3]; 286 Dizengoff St [122 C2]; 12 Jerusalem St, Jaffa; 4th floor of the central bus station.

Medical

✚ **Assuta Medical Centre** [122 G1] 20 Habarzel St; ☏7644444
✚ **Ichilov Hospital** [126 F2] 6 Weizmann St; ☏6974000

✚ **Superpharm** [126 C4] Ground Flr, Dizengoff Centre; ☏6203798; ☉ 09.30–22.00 Sun–Thu, 09.00–15.30 Fri, 06.30–23.00 Sat

Laundry Almost all automatic laundries are open 24 hours and charge around ₪15 to wash and dry one load. **Michbasa** has branches at 102 Ben Yehuda Street [126 B2]; 95 Yehuda Halevi Street [130 F3]; 109 Ibn Gabirol Street [122 D4]; 88 Frishman Street [126 D3]; and 6 Dizengoff Square [126 C4].

Media The *Jerusalem Post* (w *jpost.com*) is an English-language newspaper that has lots of practical information and entertainment listings about Jerusalem and Tel Aviv for tourists and foreign residents. *Haaretz* (w *haaretz.com*), Israel's leading newspaper, is also printed in English daily. The monthly *Time Out Tel Aviv* (w *timeout.com/israel*), which is produced in English and Hebrew, also lists what's on in the city.

WHAT TO SEE AND DO
City Centre

Rabin Square [126 D2] Few people around the world will have escaped seeing Rabin Square on the news at some time in its 40-year history. For it is in Tel Aviv's largest public square that celebrations, festivals, rallies, protests and exhibitions are held. The most shocking event to take place here, however, was the assassination of Israeli prime minister Yitzhak Rabin in 1995 by a Jewish student, Yigal Amir, who wanted to disrupt the Oslo peace process. Today, a small memorial to the right of the rather unsightly City Hall (when facing it) marks the spot upon which he was killed. Following his assassination, the square, then known as Kings of Israel Square, was renamed in his memory. Yitzhak Rabin is buried in the Mount Herzl Cemetery in Jerusalem and his funeral was attended by over 80 heads of state. At the time of writing, Yigal Amir was serving his life sentence in Ayalon Prison, which from 2006 included conjugal visits with his wife, Larisa Trembovler, something seen by most Israelis as a sore and angering concession. While there isn't an awful lot to see when there isn't an event taking place, the square can nonetheless be a good people-watching spot, where people come out to play frisbee, walk their designer dogs or just sit and chat. During events, however, this is the place to see some real Israeli patriotism, memorial and mourning, gay pride, artistic flair or political aggression.

Dizengoff This is the name given to both central Tel Aviv's main thoroughfare and the country's first **shopping mall** (page 135). Northwards from here, once ultra-trendy shops line the pavements, today selling mainly shoes and gaudy, Cinderella-style wedding dresses. Just north of the mall is **Dizengoff Square** [126 C3] with its kitsch, all-singing, all-dancing water fountain, which is decidedly unattractive but makes the locals strangely proud. The square is home to several boutique hotels, a few cafés and a cinema, and it plays host to an antique market (⊕ *14.00–16.00 Tue, 09.00–16.00 Fri*).

Azrieli Centre [126 F4] (*123 Menachem Begin St;* ☏*6081179;* ⊕ *10.00–22.00 Sun–Thu, 09.30–17.00 Fri, 20.00–23.00 Sat*) Constructed in the late 1990s, the complex of Azrieli buildings quickly became one of Tel Aviv's most recognisable landmarks. The round, square and triangular structures are home to not only one of the Middle East's biggest business centres but also the country's largest mall (page 135). One of its key attractions is the **Azrieli Observatory** (*49th Flr, Round bldg;* ☏*6081179;* ⊕ *winter 09.30–18.00 daily, summer 09.30–20.00 Sat–Thu, 09.30–18.00 Fri; admission adult/child ₪22/17*), which offers, without a shadow of doubt, the best view of the city. A 3D movie on Tel Aviv and an audio guide to help you pinpoint the major sites on the horizon will certainly aid you in getting your bearings.

Tel Aviv Museum of Art [126 E3] (*27 Shaul Hamelech Bd;* ☏*6077020;* w *tamuseum. org.il;* ⊕ *10.00–16.00 Mon, Wed & Sat, 10.00–21.00 Tue & Thu, 10.00–14.00 Fri; admission adult/child ₪50/free*) Having been in its current location since 1971, the museum started from humble beginnings in 1932 in the home of Tel Aviv's first mayor Meir Dizengoff, several years before the State of Israel was founded. It was in that first building that the signing of the declaration of independence took place and is today known as **Independence Hall**. The museum's collection is impressive even to an art novice, its permanent exhibitions proudly displaying pieces by Picasso, Miro, Monet, Renoir, Cézanne, Matisse and Chagall, to name but a few. Standing as one of the world's foremost art museums, it is the *pièce de résistance* of Israel's art scene and an integral part of the country's cultural heritage. Be sure not to miss the photography collection, which has some beautiful photographs of 19th-century Palestine, and the temporary exhibitions that often display works based upon contemporary Israeli issues such as the disengagement from Gaza in 2005.

Helena Rubinstein Pavilion [130 F1] (*6 Tarsat Bd;* ☏ *5287196;* ⊕ *10.00–16.00 Mon, Wed & Sat, 10.00–21.00 Tue & Thu; 10.00–14.00 Fri; admission ₪20*) The pavilion displays works by well-known Israeli artists who have made their niche in both the international and national art scenes. The gallery was established in 1959 to serve as an overflow of the Tel Aviv Museum of Art, but has developed into a highly reputable space in its own right. Exhibitions change regularly, some of which are free while others can be accessed using the Tel Aviv Museum entrance ticket.

Rubin Museum (Beit Rubin) [130 C2] (*14 Bialik St;* ☏ *5255961;* w *rubinmuseum.org.il/en;* ⊕ *10.00–15.00 Mon, Wed, Thu & Fri, 10.00–20.00 Tue, 11.00–14.00 Sat; admission adult/child ₪20/free*) One of Israel's most acclaimed artists, Reuven Rubin (1893–1974) bequeathed his house to the city upon his death and it has now been converted into a gallery displaying many of his famous works. His pieces stand alongside other works by Israeli artists and there is an audio-visual presentation on his life.

Bialik Museum (Beit Bailik) [130 C1] (*22 Bialik St;* ℡*5254530-3403;* ⊕ *09.00–17.00 Mon–Thu, 10.00–14.00 Fri–Sat; admission adult/child ₪20/10*) Dating from 1925, this is the nicely restored former home of the much-acclaimed Jewish poet Chaim Bialik, who lived here until his death in 1934. All the information inside the house is in Hebrew, but many of his personal rooms have been restored or recreated and are interesting in themselves.

Museum of History of Tel Aviv and Jaffa (Beit Ha'ir) [130 C1] (*27 Bialik St;* ℡ *5253403;* ⊕ *09.00–17.00 Mon–Thu, 10.00–14.00 Fri–Sat; admission adult/child ₪20/10, varies throughout high season*) Located in the old town hall building, originally built in 1925, this museum is an impressive piece of white, modernist architecture. Dedicated to the history of the city it has permanent exhibitions on Meir Dizengoff, the city's first mayor, as well as temporary exhibits of photos and art. An interactive display showcasing the city's timeline is a good way to gain some historical insight.

Bauhaus architecture In 2003, Tel Aviv was awarded UNESCO World Heritage status because of its abundance of buildings built in the Bauhaus architectural style. Today, around 2,000 Bauhaus buildings are the pride and joy of an otherwise architecturally drab, grey city and have earned Tel Aviv the nickname 'the White City'. The pre-Nazi Germany school of Bauhaus architecture produced several renowned architects who later settled in Tel Aviv before the founding of the State of Israel and who put their names to the buildings that many years later have come to define the city. As an architectural form, Bauhaus is simple, striking and unadorned and is based on functionality rather than glamour. Signature features of the style are its small, elongated balconies and rounded corners. While Bauhaus buildings can be found dotted all over the city centre, there are well-preserved concentrations along the length of Rothschild Boulevard, Dizengoff Square, Bialik Street and Kalisher Street as well as some buildings around the Sheikin Street area.

There is usually a small plaque outside a Bauhaus-listed property with historical facts. Some of the buildings, such as Polishuk House (page 125) have been converted into boutique hotels and can be visited, while others have been carefully restored and are used for residential or commercial purposes. A few that you are likely to pass by are **Nordoy Hotel** [130 D3] (*27 Nahalat Binyamin St*), **A Davis House** [130 D4] (*39 Nahalat Binyamin St*), **Dov Hershkowitz** [130 E4] (*41 Ahad Ha'am St*), **Nosen Chen** [130 E4] (*45 Ahad Ha'am St*), **Krieger House** [130 E3] (*71 Rothschild Bd*), **Benyamin Ze'ev Sawitzky House** [130 C1] (*36 Allenby St*), **Shalom Ash House** [130 D4] (*114 Allenby St*), **Grouse House** [130 C2] (*9 Bialik St*) and **Dina Shoshana Goldberg House** [130 C1] (*15 Bialik St*).

Ben-Gurion House [126 B2] (*17 Ben-Gurion St;* ℡*5221010;* w *ben-gurion-house. org.il;* ⊕ *08.00–15.00 Sun & Tue–Thu, 08.00–17.00 Mon, 08.00–13.00 Fri, 11.00–14.00 Sat; admission free*) Israel's first prime minister once stated: 'I bequeath to the State of Israel my home in Tel Aviv', and to this day that home stands as it did when David and Paula Ben-Gurion lived there. They alternated between this abode and their later home in Sde Boker (page 271), which is also a museum. In the house adjacent are exhibitions about the life, history and achievements of Ben-Gurion.

Trumpeldor Cemetery [126 B4] (⊕ *06.30–19.00 Sun–Thu & 06.30–14.00 Fri & holidays in summer, 06.30–17.00 Sun–Thu & 06.30–14.00 Fri & holidays in winter*) Hidden away amid the city centre's buildings is the old cemetery. The final resting place of countless Tel Avivian greats, it is a quiet place to reflect on those who contributed to the creation of the country and added their stamp on this enigmatic city. Haim Bialik, Shimon Rokach, Haim Arlozorov and Max Nordau are among just some of the notable graves.

North city centre

GINA Gallery [122 C3] (*255 Dizengoff St;* \5444150; w *ginagallery.com;* ⊕ *noon–21.00 Mon–Thu, 10.00–14.00 Fri; admission free*) Founded in 2003, this Gallery of International Naïve Art is delightful, showing exhibits from international and Israeli artists. Naïve art is created by artists who reject conventional forms, which results in a variety of bold colours and shapes. The works on display are also available for sale. Avraham Kan, an artist whom you are likely to meet in the Old Jaffa Hostel, has a number of his works exhibited here.

Hayarkon Park [122 D2–G1] Tel Aviv's biggest park spreads out from the Yarkon River that pours into the Mediterranean at the northern end of the city. The park is in effect divided into two sections, the larger and more developed being to the east of the Ayalon Highway where, in addition to the river, a manmade lake has been dug and the grounds nicely landscaped. It is a lovely place to go and escape the urban buzz, especially in the warmer months, but be warned – half of Tel Aviv will also have the same idea. For children in particular the park has a wealth of activities including boating (₪150/hr) or canoeing (₪70/hr) on the lake, countless playgrounds and activity parks and sprawling lawns on which to set up an afternoon picnic. If it's sports you're after head down to the area directly to the east of the Ayalon Highway bridge where locals will be happy to let you join in with football, basketball, table tennis or tennis; a great way to see real Tel Avivian life and a step off the tourist trail. Alternatively, on the northern side of the river in the west of the park is the **Sportek**. A **climbing wall** (w *kir.co.il;* ⊕ *17.00–22.00 Sun–Thu, 14.00–20.00 Fri, 11.00–21.00 Sat; day admission ₪55*) and **skateboard park** (⊕ *16.00–20.00 Sun–Thu, 11.00–20.00 Fri–Sat; admission ₪28*) can be found in the park as well as plenty of packed grassy areas to throw a ball or frisbee around.

Eretz Israel Museum [122 G1] (*2 Hayim Levanon St;* \6415244; w *eretzmuseum. org.il/e;* ⊕ *10.00–16.00 Mon–Wed, 10.00–20.00 Thu, 10.00–14.00 Fri, 10.00–16.00 Sat; admission adult/child ₪52/free*) Spread across the greenery of the Hayarkon Park, the museum is a tell-all of Israel's history and culture. Permanent and temporary exhibits range from archaeology and ethnography to Judaica, folklore and traditional crafts, and these are presented in a multitude of different ways. Impressive collections of ancient glass, coins and metallurgical pieces can be found in the permanent collection as well as the highly interesting Ethnography and Folklore Pavilion at the southern end of the museum complex. Mosaics, a 1945 New York fire engine and a full reconstruction of an ancient olive oil plant are also among the huge variety of exhibits. The Planetarium has several daily showings (in Hebrew only).

Old Port [122 B2] Long since closed to sea traffic, the Old Port has been remodelled and reshaped into a hub of recreation, good food, nightclubs, wooden promenades and great views. Located in the north of the city near the Yarkon River estuary, the area benefits from being situated away from urban areas, its pumping clubs able to make as much noise as they wish all night long. During the daytime the port is a pleasant place to come for a stroll, light lunch or relaxing afternoon in one of the countless cafés. A nice walk starts in the centre of the port and heads southwards past the old warehouses and workshops to the old pier where there is a lovely view south. Likewise, views from the stone pier are worth seeing. For something a bit different, the **Antique Fair and Organic Market** (⊕ *10.00–20.00 Fri, market 10.00–18.00*) makes for a pleasant couple of hours perusing old knick-knacks and a whole range of organic foods. At night, the area really comes into its own, with more bars and clubs than you can shake a cocktail stick at (pages 133–4). While there is a good selection of music genres and types of bar, the majority tend to be 'pick-up' bars, attracting the young and good-looking in all their Lycra finery.

Diaspora Museum (Beit Hatefusot) [122 G1] (*Tel Aviv University;* \7457808; w *bh.org.il;* ⊕ *10.00–19.00 Sun–Wed, 10.00–22.30 Thu, 09.00–14.00 Fri, 10.00–15.00 Sat; admission* ₪*45*) Located in the southeast corner of the university grounds, the museum has risen to international renown as the first and largest museum dedicated to Jewish history. The permanent exhibition depicts the story of the Jewish people through video clips, drawings, reconstructions, models and computer generations. Exhibits include 'The Jews', 'The community', 'Faith' and 'The return to Zion'.

South city centre

Great Synagogue [130 D4] (*110 Allenby St;* \5604905) Just east of the Shalom Tower on Allenby Street is the Great Synagogue which, as its name implies, is the largest of Tel Aviv's 350-odd synagogues. Built in 1926, it underwent a major overhaul in the 1970s in an attempt to recreate the former glory of the ornate pre-Holocaust synagogues of Europe. Relative to the distinctly unadorned, plain synagogues that are a feature of Judaism, a huge domed roof and stained-glass windows have given some beauty to the building. Shabbat services are open to the public, but appropriate modest dress must be worn by both men and women.

Sheinkin Tel Aviv has many areas frequented by those who think they're a cut above the rest, and there is nowhere more so than Sheinkin Street. This ultra-trendy, yet slightly bohemian street, is the place to go during the week to buy the boutique fashion that you will then wear on a Friday while sunning yourself outside one of its countless cafés. Many Israeli designers have set up shop here, selling pricey but highly individual outfits, and there are more shoe shops than you could shake a stiletto at.

Neve Tzedek Its name meaning Abode/House of Justice in Hebrew, this is one of Tel Aviv's most delightful neighbourhoods and was the first to appear outside the Old Jaffa walls in 1887, forming the centre of Tel Aviv as the city grew up around it. It eventually fell into decline and became a dilapidated and tired area full of run-down, shabby buildings. A major overhaul in the 1980s, however, put Neve Tzedek back in the fashionista limelight, and it is now one of the city's trendiest and most enchanting areas. It was originally settled by many Jewish artists, and today its heritage has been honoured by the galleries that line the main streets, as well as the famous **Suzanne Dellal Centre** (page 135). The small streets that weave through the area are packed with a fascinating selection of shops selling art, designer clothes, pottery and jewellery, as well as countless cafés and restaurants for when you feel the need to recharge your batteries. While you wander, look out for the **Rokach House** [130 C5] (*36 Shimon Rokach St*), which was one of the first houses built

The **Tayelet** (promenade) that runs the length of Tel Aviv's coastline (whose official name is **Herbert Samuel Promenade**) is one of the top additions to the city and the wide, paved pedestrian walkway is one of the best spots in the country to witness the true cross-section of Israeli culture. In the hot and humid height of summer the beach is standing room only, where Tel Avivians and tourists take refuge from the smoggy heat and congestion of the day. From the young groups of teenagers to families and the old, the white sands lining the clean waters of the Mediterranean are bursting at the seams. Probably the most prominent group, however, is the young 20-somethings. This is where Israeli men come to strut their stuff and young women revel in watching them do it. *Matkot* (bat and ball) has become a very popular, highly competitive game where egos are made and destroyed. Bronzed Israeli girls wearing next to nothing parade the promenade in a catwalk fashion to rival the south of France. But somehow Tel Aviv has almost managed to escape the arrogance of other cities with such a strong beach culture. Here 'each to their own' seems to be the motto, a place where people from all walks of life converge. From the glamorous and fashionable, the large gay population, the religious and the Orthodox, to families, tourists and business people, foreign immigrants and students, they curiously and surprisingly live harmoniously in a city they have grown to love for its freedom and tolerance.

in the area. Also of interest is the **Nahum Gutman Museum of Art** [130 C5] (*21 Shimon Rokach St;* ☏*5161970;* w *gutmanmuseum.co.il/en;* ⊕ *10.00–16.00 Mon–Thu, 10.00–14.00 Fri, 10.00–15.00 Sat; admission adult/child* ₪*24/free*), located in one of Neve Tzedek's traditional buildings, which displays works by Gutman, a renowned Jewish artist who immigrated to the country in 1905. His work encompassed oil paintings, sculpture, mosaics and engravings, as well as writing and illustrating children's books.

Rothschild Boulevard Running from the Habima Theatre in the north to the Neve Tzedek neighbourhood in the south, the leafy, tree-lined Rothschild Boulevard is Tel Aviv's pride and joy, and rightly so. It forms the heart of not only Bauhaus architecture but also weekend recreation and leisure. The long, wide boulevard with its central pedestrian walkway and bicycle lane is dotted with sandwich bars that have become an unlikely super-trend. Come Friday, young, chic Tel Avivians (and their designer dogs) come to strut their stuff, lounge on the grass or pull up a chair at one of the street's innumerable open-air cafés. The entire length of the street is a mass of restaurants and cafés (pages 128–32), ranging from the moderately pricey to the downright extortionate, but then you pay for the location.

Located at number 16 is **Independence Hall** [130 D4] (☏*5106426;* ⊕ *09.00–17.00 Sun–Thu, 09.00–14.00 Fri; admission adult/child* ₪*24/16*), the site where Israel's declaration of independence was signed. The museum hall has been left as it was on 14 May 1948, with cameras, flags and broadcasting equipment *in situ*, and is a poignant and stirring dedication to Israel's heritage. On the wall is the famous photograph of Ben-Gurion reading the declaration to a large crowd, above which is a photograph of Theodor Herzl, the grandfather of Zionism. The building later became the home of Tel Aviv's first mayor, Meir Dizengoff, and the first site of the Tel Aviv Museum of Art (page 138). The small, one-room museum is surprisingly simple for a country so fiercely proud of its ancestry but worth a visit if you're passing by.

Yemenite Vineyard [130 C2] (*Kerem Hateimanim*) The tiny web of streets that form the Yemenite Vineyard (which actually isn't a vineyard in any shape or form) is one of the most rustically charming neighbourhoods in the city. It was established at the turn of the last century by immigrants from Yemen, and until its huge facelift in the early 1990s, it was little more than yet another run-down neighbourhood. Since its major cosmetic surgery, however, it has become one of the trendiest places to live, and its restored houses are now highly sought after (and increasing in price by the day). The narrow streets are laid out in a gridiron pattern unusual to the city, and houses are small and low-rise. Its proximity to the seafront and the Hacarmel Market makes it the ideal place to set up home, while for visitors to the city, the neighbourhood offers a pleasant stroll and a selection of small, traditional Yemenite restaurants. Yemenite Jews originally came to Israel with the first aliyah and later as part of the 'Magic Carpet' airlift in 1949. They were accompanied by their exquisite jewellery-making technique, zesty food recipes and musical traditions.

Hacarmel Market [130 C3] (⊕ *08.00–17.00 daily*) On the southern side of the junction where Sheinkin, Allenby and King George streets converge is the northern entrance to the tunnel-like Hacarmel Market. This is the city's busiest fruit and vegetable (and everything else you can think of) market, and it's a bustling, noisy and lively part of traditional Tel Avivian life. All and sundry come to buy their weekly fresh produce, shop for cheap trinkets and stock up on socks, and it's a delightful insight into the less chic side of the city. Apart from selling food, homewares and cheap clothes, it is a good place to buy Dead Sea products for discounted prices, but be prepared to haggle. Hidden behind the clothes stores that are found at the Allenby Street end of the market are some fantastic bureka and baklava shops, so look carefully to avoid missing out.

Nahalat Binyamin Market [130 C3] (⊕ *10.00–17.00 Tue & Fri*) On market days, artists and artisans come to display their handmade works on small stalls set up along the paved section of Nahalat Binyamin Street near Allenby Street. To make it even more special, the market's council handpicks the artists allowed to participate in an attempt to keep away the mass-produced, money-making pieces and retain the cultural diversity of the market. In addition to the stalls, there are clowns, fortune tellers and performers who often show up to entertain the crowds, creating a lively and bohemian atmosphere.

Etzel Museum [130 A6] (*15 Goldman St;* \5177180; ⊕ *08.00–16.00 Sun–Thu; admission adult/child ₪10*) Etzel was a Zionist military organisation involved in the fight for free immigration for Jews to Palestine, battling with both the Palestinians and British Mandate Authority. They were responsible for the attack on Jerusalem's King David Hotel (see box, page 83). The small museum has artefacts, films, videos, photographic displays and information on Etzel and their campaigns within Palestine.

Hatachana (Manshia train station) [130 A6] (\609995; w *hatachana.co.il;* ⊕ *10.00–22.00 Sat–Thu, 10.00–17.00 Fri; admission free*) Since its reopening and redevelopment, the city's oldest train station has become one of the most popular cultural zones in Tel Aviv. Built in 1892 in Ottoman-era style, the station

Tel Aviv's beaches are wonderful. Wide and sandy, they are clean, relaxed and thanks to coastal barriers, much calmer than some of the wild stretches further up the coast. If there is a downside, it is the sheer number of people who flock to them on summer weekends, when you will be hard pushed to find a square metre of sand on which to lay your towel.

TEL BARUCH BEACH [122 D1] This is Tel Aviv's most northerly beach and is actually well beyond the urban areas. Located just north of Dov Airport, it is a bit of a schlep from the city centre, but worth it for the wild sands, natural feel and isolation. Once notorious for prostitution, it has been cleaned up in recent years and is now a wholesome family beach. Plans to extend the nearby airport may scupper the tranquillity of the area in the future, but for now it is a great expanse of soft white sand and rolling waves.

METZIZIM BEACH [122 B2] While it would be difficult to call the view from Metzizim Beach beautiful, it is in fact one of the funkiest places to hang out both during the day and at night (when it's even harder to see the power station and old port works). The wide beach, chilled bars and relaxed atmosphere are a refreshing change from some of the younger, more raucous beaches further south.

HILTON BEACH [122 B3] Named unsurprisingly after the nearby Hilton Hotel, this beach is frequented predominantly by three very different groups of sun-seekers. The northernmost end is the only section of Tel Aviv's coastline where dogs can run free. While it is a heart-warming sight to see over-excited pups chasing each other and crashing in and out of the waves, it isn't as much fun if you're lying on a beach towel as they do it. Further down from the doggy area is a patch of sand that has become the unofficial gay beach of the city, mainly with men. Tight swim shorts, hunky bodies and a lively atmosphere are its key characteristics. The Hilton Beach is also famed for being the city's best surfing beach, as an offshore reef causes waves to break nicely on their way towards the coast. Surfers of all ages flock to the seas, and the **Sea Centre** surfing club (✆6503000) operates from here.

NORDAU BEACH [122 B3] Known as the Religious Beach, this is Tel Aviv's contribution to single-sex swimming. The beach is surrounded by a high wall and is more often than not near-deserted. Women looking for that all-over tan have been known to come on women's days without the fear of being leered at, something that doesn't seem to bother the conservatively dressed religious

was Jaffa's gateway to Jerusalem. For 60 years, it was in a state of disrepair, but a major renovation project has seen it returned to its former glory, and now an entire complex of buildings boasts galleries, boutiques, cafés, weekly markets, jazz concerts, art exhibitions and festivals.

JAFFA AND AROUND

Jaffa (Yafo in Hebrew and Yafa in Arabic) is a world in itself. Often included in Greater Tel Aviv as its southern district and absorbed by the ever-expanding de women. Women's days are Sunday, Tuesday and Thursday while men's days are Monday, Wednesday and Friday.

GORDON AND FRISHMAN BEACHES [126 A2/3] These are the quintessential Tel Avivian beaches, where muscular bronzed soldiers, tiny tots in rubber rings, sunburnt foreigners and everyone in between come to enjoy the summer sun and refreshing Mediterranean waters. Their central location means they are never empty, but midweek is certainly less crowded than summer weekends. Lifeguards, shower and bathroom facilities, huge beach bars and cafés and plenty of shade add to their appeal. At the northern end of Gordon Beach is the city's marina, a small, rather quaint area that incorporates the delightful **Gordon Swimming Pool** [126 A1] (\ *7623300;* w *gordon-pool.co.il;* ⏱ *13.30–20.00 Sun, 06.00–21.00 Mon & Thu, 06.00–20.00 Tue–Wed, 06.00–19.00 Fri, 07.00–18.00 Sat; admission adult/child ₪60/50 midweek, ₪72/65 w/end*), which was fully renovated in 2009. Like the beaches, the big, refreshing saltwater pools attract hundreds of Israeli families on weekends, but weekdays are considerably quieter.

JERUSALEM BEACH [130 B1] This is another wide, pleasant beach with several cafés, plenty of space to throw a frisbee around and shallow, clean water. Across Herbert Samuel Street are countless ice-cream parlours, fast-food joints and the beginning of the enigmatic Allenby Street.

GEULA BEACH [130 B2] Unofficially and more commonly known as Banana Beach after the highly popular bar-restaurant-café located here, this is one of the funkiest and most bohemian beaches along the coast. The **Banana Beach** (\ *5107958;* ⏱ *24hrs*) is a great place to enjoy a meal at any time of the day or simply cool off with an iced coffee or fruit smoothie. The food is relatively simple but does the trick if your budget runs to it – you're paying for the location and experience anyway. During the summer, big screens often show live sporting events or movies, which is a fun and chilled-out evening's entertainment in true Tel Aviv style.

DOLPHINARIUM BEACH [130 A3] Named after the old dolphin tank that used to be here, the beach attracts the hippy set who come to smoke *nargileh* pipes, juggle fire balls, play the guitar or meditate. Friday afternoons see the beach turned into the setting for a huge jam session, where budding musicians come to drum out a beat in the open air. There is also a watersports club, **Surf Point** (\ *1 599567888;* w *surf-point.co.il;* ⏱ *09.30–dark daily*) where you can rent equipment for (or do courses in) windsurfing, scuba diving, kite-surfing, surfing and kayaking.

facto capital of Israel, Jaffa is a buoyant and lively town with a fascinating history and welcoming atmosphere.

The town was mentioned several times in the Bible but flourished during the 19th century when its city walls were built, trade markets established, its main mosque was erected and the great trunk road to Jerusalem constructed in 1869. Jaffa grew into a major trading port city through the Egyptian and Ottoman rule, and after the opening of the Suez Canal in 1869 saw the appearance of vast cargo ships from Europe. In 1880, its population was only 10,000 people, but the town kept on growing thanks to the Jaffa–Jerusalem railway completed in 1892, which made it easier to export 'Jaffa' oranges from the surrounding Arab groves. The clock tower face was even set to European time so as to aid merchants arriving in the port. Yet it wasn't just trade that disembarked in Jaffa; scores of early pilgrims trudged up and down the road to Jerusalem's holy sites, and German Templar and American colonies were established near the Old City. Following near-abandonment during World War I, Jaffa recovered to become an almost wholly Palestinian city with Tel Aviv housing most of the Jewish population. Before the 1948 Arab–Israeli War, there were 100,000 Arabs living in Jaffa, known at that time as the 'Bride of Palestine'. The town flourished until the 1936–39 rebellion, which saw the closure of the once-prosperous port in favour of the new one in Tel Aviv. In 1948, Arab forces in Jaffa shelled nearby Tel Aviv, an attack quickly countered by Jewish forces who captured the Old City, poignantly two days before Israel's independence was declared. After Jaffa fell to the Jews in 1948, most of the 65,000 Palestinians left the city and in 1950 Jaffa was incorporated into the Municipality of Tel Aviv.

Currently, various religious communities call Jaffa home. In addition to old mosques, there are a number of churches of all denominations tucked away amid narrow, leafy alleys and neighbourhoods. The charming residential area around Hadolfin Street has several churches, including Maronite, and historical buildings, and it is simply wonderful to wander around after a hummus meal in the nearby Ali Karavan (page 148). In the vicinity of the Old City on Raziel Street, there are a few modern art galleries, and the flea market is undoubtedly a must anytime on any day in Jaffa.

GETTING THERE AND AROUND From the central bus station, bus 83 (look for the Levinsky Street exit inside the station) goes all the way to Jaffa. A taxi from central Tel Aviv takes under 15 mins and walking is also an option, in particular along the seafront all the way to the Old Town.

TOURIST INFORMATION The **Tourist Information Centre** [147 G2] (*2 Marzuk-Ve-Azar St*; w *visit-tel-aviv.com*; ⊕ *Apr–Oct 09.30–18.30 Sun–Thu, 09.30–16.00 Fri, 10.00–16.00 Sat, 09.30–14.00 holiday eves, Nov–Mar 09.30–17.30 Sun–Thu, 09.30–14.00 Fri*) is behind the New Saraya Building on Clock Tower Square.

⌂ WHERE TO STAY
Jaffa

⌂ **Andromeda Hill** [147 D3] (50 apartments) 38 Yefet St; ☎ 6838448; e omri@andromeda.co.il; w andromeda.co.il. Newly built holiday apts in a prime location in Old Jaffa. Out of 150 units, 50 are used as a hotel, the rest are private & some are for sale. Beautiful, luxury studios & apts with access to swimming pool, gym, jacuzzi, solarium, games room & café. Discounts for longer stays. $$$$

⌂ **The Market House Hotel** [147 G2] (44 rooms) 5 Beit Eshel St; ☎ 7974000; e markethouse@atlashotel.co.il; w atlas.co.il. Opened in 2015, this classically designed hotel is located in a historic building that was used as Shin Bet headquarters between 1948 & 1970. Lobby area is spacious & tasteful; you can see the ruins under the present building through a glass floor.

Rooms are immaculate & some even come with small balconies. $$$$

⌂ **Beit Immanuel Guesthouse** [130 B7] (16 rooms) 8 Auerbach St; ☎ 6821459; e welcome@beitimmanuel.org. w beitimmanuel. org. This family-oriented pilgrim's guesthouse has captured the serenity & atmosphere of the area with its leafy garden & sunny balcony. The décor is a little old-fashioned but seems somehow apt for this part of the city & rooms are clean & comfortable. Most rooms are private, but dorms are available for large groups when booking together. $$$

⌂ **Old Jaffa Hostel** [147 F2] (20 rooms, including private & dorms) 13 Amiad St; ☎ 6822370; e ojhostel@shani.net;

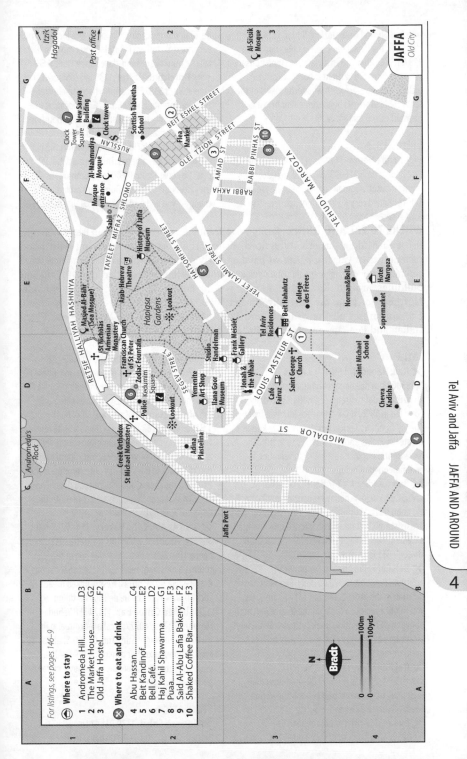

JAFFA
Old City

For listings, see pages 146–9

🛏 **Where to stay**

1 Andromeda Hill................D3
2 The Market House............G2
3 Old Jaffa Hostel...............F2

🍴 **Where to eat and drink**

4 Abu Hassan.....................C4
5 Beit Kandinof..................E2
6 Bell Café.........................D2
7 Haj Kahil Shawarma........G1
8 Puaa...............................F3
9 Said Al-Abu Lafia Bakery..F2
10 Shaked Coffee Bar...........F3

Tel Aviv and Jaffa   JAFFA AND AROUND

4

147

w telaviv-hostel.com. Oozing Old Jaffa's rich character, the hostel has been in operation since 1987. It is located within an ancient stone house just mins from the harbour & beach. Facilities include a roof terrace with wonderful views of the sea & cobbled streets below, excellent b/fast & pleasant communal space. **$**

Florentine

🏠 Rena's House [130 D5] (24 rooms) 3 Simtat Beit Habad; m 058 6999669, 052 5457026; e renashousetlv@gmail.com; w renashouse.co.il. Self-contained cosy & very bright apartments

decorated in modern urban style. The location is very good & staff are helpful. Guests can rent a bicycle from the ground-floor Sapeh Café. **$$**

🏠 Florentine Hostel [130 B7] (65 beds) 10 Elifelet St; ✆5187551; e rafi@florentinehostel. com; w florentinehostel.com. Great location in the increasingly trendy Florentine neighbourhood. Rooms are bright, albeit not so spacious, communal areas including the kitchen & the big open terrace are spotless. This is a party hostel; b/fast is served from 09.00 to accommodate all the late-night dwellers. Dorms are probably the cheapest you will find in the city. **$**

✕ WHERE TO EAT AND DRINK Jaffa's restaurants are known for their freshly caught fish and Middle Eastern-influenced dishes. The port area is teeming with good restaurants of varying price, so have an early evening stroll around and see what catches your eye. There are also several small restaurants nestled into the ancient buildings around Kedumim Square which, come summer, lay tables outside. Northeast of Jaffa, the **Levinsky Market** (🕓 *08.00–18/19.00 Sun–Thu, 08.00–15.00 Fri*) epitomises all the gourmet and flavourful culture of the Middle East. From Indian and Persian to vegan and pizzas, the market is a delight.

Jaffa

✕ Itzik Hagadol [130 A7] 3 Raziel St; ✆6830033; e itzikhagadol1@gmail.com; w itzikhagadol.co.il/en; 🕓 11.00–23.30 daily. Founded in 1996, this is the place for meat lovers. The joy comes at a price, but the chef sure knows his steaks, & there are great wines to match. The restaurant is popular, so advance reservation is recommended. **$$$$**

✕ Beit Kandinof [147 B2] 14 Hatsorfim St; m 052 2693654; e nadav.rapoport@gmail.com; 🕓 noon till last customer, daily. This newly opened artists' studio, restaurant & bar rolled into one is an excellent place for an evening drink after a stroll through Old Jaffa. **$$**

✕ Bell Café [147 B2] 10 Kedumim Sq; ✆5109670; 🕓 09.30–23.00 daily. Excellent location in the heart of Old Jaffa. If you are lucky, you might even get a table on the terrace perched above the 17th-century Greek Orthodox St Michael Monastery overlooking the sea. Hearty b/fasts & good coffee. **$$**

✕ Haj Kahil Shawarma [147 G1] Clock Tower Sq; ✆6812947; 🕓 09.00–midnight daily. Incredibly fresh turkey, beef & lamb shawarma. Great fillings to go on top. **$$**

✕ Puaa [147 F3] 8 Rabbi Yohanan St; ✆6823821; w puaa.co.il; 🕓 09.00–01.00 Sun–

Fri, 10.00–00.30 Sat. Established in 1999, this much-loved restaurant offers great atmosphere & an excellent traditional menu, including sabich & shakshooka. Gets very busy in the evenings. **$$**

✕ Abu Hassan (Ali Karavan) [147 C4] 1 Hadolfin St; ✆6820387; 🕓 07.45–14.45 Sun– Fri. Renowned for the best hummus in the Tel Aviv area since its opening in 1966, this rudimentary eatery is packed day in & day out. Hummus is the extent of the menu, but that's all you need. The 18 Shivtai St branch is open all day (or until the hummus runs out). **$**

✕ Said Al-Abu Lafia Bakery [147 F2] 7 Yefet St; ✆6834958; 🕓 24/7. This was Jaffa's 1st bakery, opened in 1880 & remains today one of the country's most famous & well-loved snack shops. Arabic-style pizza, pittas, freshly baked breads & sticky baklava are cheap, delicious & filling. **$**

☕ Shaked Coffee Bar [147 F3] 8 Yehuda Margoza St; ✆5740777; w shakedcoffee.co.il; 🕓 07.00–midnight Sun–Thu, 07.00–Shabbat start. A popular kosher café since 1993 with a pleasant outdoor seating area to enjoy a coffee & people-watch. **$**

Florentine

✕ Gormeh Sabzi [130 D5] 47 Levinsky St; ✆5080709; 🕓 10.00–18.00 daily. To try something different, this little Persian restaurant offers excellent authentic cuisine. *Gormeh sabzi* (Iranian bean & meat stew) is recommended. $ **✖ Kaymak** [130 D5] 49 Levinsky St; ⊕ 11.00–23.00 Sun–Thu, 11.00-16.00 Fri. A popular yet tiny vegetarian restaurant serving generous portions. Each day there is something new on the menu & you can ask for half portions to try a couple of different dishes. The food is delicious. $

♀ Beer Bazaar [130 E5] 13 Zvulun St; m 052 8689732; ⊕ 10.00–late Sun–Thu. Tired of Maccabi & Goldstar? Then this is the place to head to. There are more than 100 kinds of craft beer in this funky, easy-going bar. **♀ Shuffle Bar** [130 D7] 19 Florentine St; ⊕ 18.00–02.00 Sun–Thu, 14.00–04.00 Fri–Sat. A very popular bar in the heart of the Florentine district, offering a great selection of drinks. There is also a good food menu & some table games to enjoy. Happy hour is 18.00–20.00.

SHOPPING Shopping in Jaffa generally is a joy, and shopping for souvenirs and curios is even more thrilling. Souvenir shops sell items made of Roman glass – a treat for the eye, a danger to the wallet, but still worth having a look at. Many exclusive stores sell designer jewellery. **Yemenite Art** [147 D2] (3 *Mazal Dagim St;* ✆ 6812503; e office@yemenite-art.com; w yemenite-art.com; ⊕ 09.00–22.00 Sun–Fri, 18.00–20.00 Sat) is of particular interest for its delicate gold-plate Yemenite pieces crafted by David Ben-Zion. The tradition of Jewish Yemenite craftsmanship is centuries old, and Israel is now the only place to enjoy it fully. **Adina Plastelina** [147 C2] (23 *Netiv Hamazalot St;* ✆ 5187894; w adinaplastelina.com) shop and studio are a must and highly recommended on a visit to Old Jaffa. There are also numerous exquisite handmade clothes and shoe stores. The quality and creativity put into the pieces is worth the price tag. **Norman&Bella** [147 E4] (30 *Yehuda Margoza St;* ✆ 6813626; w normanandbella.com) is particularly recommended.

OTHER PRACTICALITIES There are two **exchange shops** on Clock Tower Square: the one on the corner is open from 09.00 to 17.00, and the one opposite the clock tower is open from 10.00 to 20.00; both closed on Saturdays. Jerusalem Boulevard has a **post office** [147 G1] (11 *Jerusalem Bd;* ⊕ 08.00–20.00 Sun, Tue & Thu, 08.00–13.30 Mon & Wed, 08.00–noon Fri) and a **copy centre** (⊕ 09.00–20.00 Sun–Fri, 09.00–13.00 Fri). In the vicinity on Salameh Road is the district **police** headquarters [130 B7] (✆ 6802222) and **Population and Immigration Authority** [130 C7] (✆ *3450; w piba. gov.il; ⊕ 08.00–noon & 14.30–17.00 Mon, 08.00–noon Sun & Tue–Thu, 13.30–17.00 Wed). Jaffa's **tourist police station** is located in the narrow alley off Kedumim Square [147 D2] (m 050 6270666; ⊕ 16.00–19.00 Sun, 08.00–11.00 Tue). There are a couple of **laundrettes** on Jerusalem Boulevard and another copy centre two blocks down from the Scientology building.

WHAT TO SEE AND DO
Clock Tower Square [147 F1] Jaffa's clock tower, which stands in the middle of the square, is the centrepiece of the Old City. It was built at the beginning of the 20th century to commemorate the reign of the Ottoman sultan Abdul Hamid II and returned to its former glory after a major overhaul in 2006. Directly opposite it is **Al-Mahmudiya Mosque** [147 F1] (*between Yefet St, Olei Tzion;* ✆ 5272691), which is also known as Masjed Al-Kabir. Its Ottoman origin is testified by the *tughra* (calligraphic seal carving) at the top of the central façade. Built in the early 18th century, the mosque's minaret is a Jaffa landmark. The buildings have grown around it, and while the architecture is impressive (there are columns from Caesarea), it takes a little investigating to see it fully. It is open to non-Muslims, but be discreet and dress appropriately. The entrance is at the back of the mosque to the right of a

well-preserved *sabil* (public water fountain) for performing ablutions. The former police station building adjacent to the mosque will soon be transformed into a luxury hotel.

Yefet Street Formerly Ajami Street, this is the central artery running through Jaffa all the way to the Ajami neighbourhood. There are some wonderful historic houses on both sides of the street, which is a pleasant walk. **Scottish Tabeetha School** [147 F2] (*21 Yefet St;* w *tabeethaschool.org*), which was founded in 1863 for poor girls, still functions as an educational institution but is now an all-inclusive multi-denominational school for boys and girls. The somewhat neglected building across the street is the **Beit Hahalutz** (*34 Yefet St*), meaning 'Pioneers' House' dating from 1920. It was originally a hostel for Jewish immigrants but was relocated to Allenby Street after the Jaffa riots. The house is named after the Hahalutz youth movement founded in 1905 for settling Jewish immigrants in Palestine; Joseph Trumpeldor was one of its leaders. The Hebrew term *halutzim* was used essentially as part of the Zionist rhetoric to describe Jewish avant-garde idealists in Palestine at the start of the 19th century. **College des Frères** [147 E3] (*25 Yefet St;* w *collegedesfreresjaffa.com*) is another school facing Louis Pasteur Street. Established in 1882 by the Brothers of the Christian Schools (Lasallian Brothers), it accepts children from all religious denominations and prepares them for the French leaving certificate (BAC). Just a few metres from College des Frères, the new Andromeda Hill residential development conceals the small Greek Orthodox **Saint George Church** [147 D3] (*3 Louis Pasteur St*) with its distinctive bell tower. Built in the late 19th century, it is still operational, albeit open for services only, and has a cemetery in its grounds.

Flea Market (Shuk Hapishpeshim) [147 F/G2] (*between Olei Tzion & Beit Eshel*) Although the name conjures up images of cheap tack, Jaffa's flea market is in fact a great place to find yourself an antique bargain (and a lot of cheap kitsch). While wandering among the mountains of furniture, fabrics, knick-knacks, Judaica, brassware, carpets and nargileh pipes and enjoying the lively, Middle Eastern ambience and noisy chatter, you're a world away from the chic cafés in Tel Aviv. Haggling is a must, and you're more likely to get a good deal on a Friday, when the market is busiest.

Kedumim Square (Kikar Kedumim) [147 D2] This is the central square of Old Jaffa and marks the starting point for the labyrinth of cobbled lanes and alleys amid the old buildings. The wide square is surrounded by artists' galleries, expensive restaurants and craft and jewellery shops, and it's one of the most charming and delightful places in all Tel Aviv-Jaffa. The alleys weave their way through the maze of houses downhill to the **port**, and the best way to explore is to simply get lost among them. You'll end up in the port one way or another.

Around the History of Jaffa Visitors' Centre [147 D2] (⊕ *10.00–18.00 daily; admission adult/child ₪30/15*) The long history of Jaffa is told through displays and audio-visual presentations at this museum, who also hand out free maps. On your way to the museum from the artists' quarter, you will pass the imposing – but sadly deteriorating – landmark of the **Franciscan Church of St Peter** [147 D2] (⊕ *08.00–11.45 & 15.00–17.00 daily; modest dress*), built in 1894 on the ruins of an earlier 16th-century church and said to have been visited by Napoleon during its years as a hostel. Just off to the right of the square, a small alley leads to the **Greek**

Orthodox St Michael Monastery [147 E2] (closed to visitors at the time of writing), displaying the traditional bright colours and architecture of Greek ecclesiastical buildings. Further towards the sea is the small but picturesque **Sea Mosque** (Masjed Al-Bahr) [147 E1]. The exact date of its construction is unknown, but the carving on the façade says that it was renovated in 1995. It is not open to visitors.

Hapigsa Gardens [147 E2] The gardens form the summit of the hill upon which Jaffa's Old City sits, and countless small paths weave their way through the greenery and rockeries. A small wooden bridge leads from the square to the gardens, within which is an amphitheatre where summer concerts are held, and a monument depicting scenes from the Bible. This is such a beautiful viewpoint northwards along the coast of Tel Aviv that it's worth visiting once during the day and again at night. The gardens are also home to the Theatre of Jaffa and the Old Saraya and Soap Factory (at present being restored), which date back to the early 19th century and were at one point a grand palace of the Ottoman governor Mohammed Agha Al-Shami, known as Abu Nabbut. He was the one who built the Jerusalem Gate in Jaffa, hence why it's also known as Abu Nabbut Gate.

Artists' quarter Mazal Dagim Street forms the heart of the artists' quarter along which you will find several art galleries including the **Ilana Goor Museum** [147 D2] (*4 Mazal Dagim St;* \6837676; w *ilanagoormuseum.org/eng;* ⊕ *10.00–16.00 Sun–Fri, 10.00–18.00 Sat; admission ₪30*). The museum and gallery have been created in a space within Goor's beautiful home and are worth a visit, partly for the artwork and partly to appreciate the classical architecture of the building. A little further along is the **Studio Handelman** [147 D2] (*14 Mazal Dagim St;* \6819574; ⊕ *10.30–22.30 Sun–Thu, 10.30–Shabbat Fri, end of Shabbat–22.30 Sat*) which designs and sells silk paintings, while the **Frank Meisler Gallery** [147 D3] (*25 Mazal Arie St;* \5123000; w *frank-meisler.com;* ⊕ *09.00–23.00 Sun–Thu, 09.00–16.00 Fri, 18.00–23.00 Sat*) displays a memorable, expensive selection of metalwork figurines and Judaica.

BRESLOV

As the sound of loud, pumping music permeates the relaxed, summery atmosphere of Tel Aviv's seafront, you would be forgiven for rolling your eyes and looking around for the local boy-racer, his small hatchback and oversized stereo interrupting everyone's leisurely day. Yet, upon turning around, you will find that the noise culprit is not a testosterone-fuelled youngster but in fact a minivan full of bearded, white-robed Hassidic Jews. These fun-loving men of God are members of an Orthodox Hassidic group known as Breslov, who originated from Ukraine and are today a joyous addition to Israeli life. Founded by Rebbe Nachman of Breslov (1772–1810), their ethos is to create an intense relationship with God through happiness, joy and living life to its fullest. Equipped with loud stereo systems, groups of Breslov drive around the streets in white vans, some sitting cross-legged on the roof, their long hair and beards blowing in the wind. As the van comes to a halt at traffic lights, the back doors swing open in a style reminiscent of the A-Team and out burst Breslov men, who proceed to dance enthusiastically until the lights change and they tumble back in and move on. The Breslov are received in Israel with amusement and affection, their contagious happiness bringing smiles to the faces of those around.

On the outskirts of the city, this is a zoo in a safari park (*Ramat Gan;* 6320222; w *safari.co.il;* ⊕ *09.00–14.00 Fri all year, winter 09.00–14.30 Sat–Thu, summer 09.00–17.00 Sat–Thu; admission ₪70).* Visitors (who in summer arrive in their thousands) drive through the African savannah-like lands past big herds of animals and then park up and enter the main part of the zoo. There is a safari bus if you don't have your own transport. The admission charges are used to promote and develop new conservation techniques and the safari park is involved with several programmes that aim to reintroduce endangered species back into the wild. The area outside the zoo is a big weekend favourite with hundreds of barbecuing Israeli families, giving it a nice, if extremely crowded, ambience. Buses 45 and 60 from central Tel Aviv stop near the park.

Port As the waves gently lap against the ancient rock walls and old men stand patiently, fishing rods in hand, it is hard to imagine that this was once one of the busiest ports in the country. The fact that fishing boats still chug in and out of the port on a regular basis has awarded it the distinction of being one of the oldest active ports in the world. It has not, however, been used for cargo since 1965. Just beyond the sea wall are several rocks, the darkest said to be **Andromeda's Rock** [147 B1]. According to Greek mythology, Andromeda was chained to this rock by her father King Cepheus as a sacrifice to Poseidon's sea monster. As the legend goes, she was saved by the hero Perseus, who slayed the monster and took her hand in marriage.

American Colony In the heart of the American Colony, with its traditional wooden houses amid greenery and flowers, is a small **Lutheran Immanuel Church** [130 B7] (6829841–0654; w *immanuelchurch-jaffa.com;* ⊕ *10.00–14.00 Tue–Fri; advance booking for groups required).* Built in 1904, it holds regular concerts and is the centre of the Lutheran congregation in Jaffa and Tel Aviv. Just around the corner from the church is **Maine Friendship House** [130 B7] (6819225; w *jaffacolony. com;* ⊕ *noon–14.00 Fri–Sat)* established in 1866, but subsequently demolished. The building was restored and opened to the public in 2005 and now functions as the museum of the American Colony in Jaffa.

5

Mediterranean Coast

Telephone code 04

Israel's western coastline marks the end of the shimmering Mediterranean waters that stretch from the border with Lebanon to the Gaza Strip and Egypt. Great port cities have flourished along these shores for centuries, ancient Caesarea and Acre's Old City gracing the history books and providing a glimpse into the turbulent, magnificent and dramatic past, where empires were won and lost. The Phoenicians produced a vibrant and much-sought-after purple dye from the marine snails that inhabit the coast, and they enjoyed a flourishing economy along the Mediterranean, stretching from present-day Syria and Lebanon down to Acre. In modern times, Haifa, Israel's third-largest city, has bloomed into a *découpage* of colourful neighbourhoods that tumble down Mount Carmel's northern slopes. The undulating hills of the Carmel mountain range are blanketed with a carpet of green, as they roll alongside the coast. Upon these hills, where the Prophet Elijah battled the priests of Baal, ancient biblical deer once again roam freely and the irrepressibly picturesque town of Zichron Yaakov stands as a living memorial to Edmond de Rothschild, the grandfather of Zionism.

For visitors to the country, the Mediterranean coast offers sweeping sandy beaches, majestic archaeological sites and a mesh of Jewish, Druze, Baha'i, Christian and Muslim traditions. Combine this with a wealth of tourist facilities and the best of the country's public transport, and you get Israel's most relaxed, sun-soaked and culturally rich region.

NAHARIYA   *Population 54,300*

The northern coastal town of Nahariya holds claim to a rich history. On these soils Canaanites stamped their mark, Byzantine finds were unearthed, Romans marched along their paved roads, and it was a crucial stop along the great Via Maris highway. Unfortunately, little of Nahariya's ancient glamour has managed to find a place in the modern version of the town, and today this rather gaudy seaside resort is characterised by neon-lit eateries and cafés, a developed beachfront and groups of holidaying families. Outside the summer season there is not a lot to entice anyone to Nahariya, but the warmer weather allows for plenty of sporting and water activities, and visitors are attracted by its hotels and decent restaurants. A long seaside promenade stretches to the fringes of Acre and makes for some lovely cycling or walking opportunities. The clean and sandy (but often overcrowded) Municipal Beach forms the hub of summer activities, where beach volleyball, a large playground and a whole host of standard seaside activities are enjoyed.

Most facilities in Nahariya can be found along the main Hagaaton Boulevard, which runs from north to south. The train station, the last stop along the Tel Aviv line, is at the northernmost end of the street, alongside the central bus station.

GETTING THERE AND AROUND Nahariya is a small town and it is an easy 10-minute walk down central Hagaaton Boulevard from the train or bus station to the seafront. Taxis can also be hailed from outside the stations.

By train Trains run from Tel Aviv (*1hr 50mins/₪39.50*), Acre (*9mins/₪7.50*) and Haifa (*50mins/₪17.50*) to Nahariya train station (*1 Hagaaton Bd;* ☏*8564446*). Departure and arrival frequency is approximately every hour 05.20–20.20 Sunday–Thursday, 06.10–14.10 Friday and 09.15–noon Saturday.

By bus Nateev Express buses arrive at and depart from Nahariya central bus station (*3 Hagaaton Bd;* ☏*9923434*) every 20 to 30 minutes to and from Acre (*15mins/₪8.50*) and Haifa Merkazit Hamifratz (*1hr/₪12.50*).

TOURIST INFORMATION The **Tourist Information Centre** (*19 Hagaaton Bd;* ☏ *9879800;* ⏲ *08.00–13.00* & *16.00–19.00 Sun–Wed, 08.00–13.00 Thu–Fri*) is located on the square near the Municipal Building. Most of the big hotels offer tours to surrounding areas, so it is worth enquiring at their receptions.

⌂ **WHERE TO STAY** *Map, page 156*
Nahariya doesn't have a lot in the way of mid-range accommodation so it's a choice between the four-star complexes or shabby, family-run guesthouses. Prices tend to be inflated, especially during peak seasons and the surrounding moshavim and kibbutzim offer lovely zimmer, which are much better value for money.

⌂ **Carlton Nahariya** (200 rooms) 23 Hagaaton Bd; ☏ 9005555; w carlton-hotel.co.il/en. Recently renovated with a good range of services, including large swimming pool, sun terrace, spa, restaurant, bar & children's club. 4x4 & boat tours can be arranged through their travel service. **$$$**

⌂ **Hotel Frank** (49 rooms) 4 Haaliyah St; ☏ 9920278. Spacious, tidy rooms are clean &

well equipped with TV, AC & big windows. A bar, outdoor terrace & buffet b/fast are also offered. **$$$**

⌂ **Hotel Rosenblatt** (14 rooms) 59 Weizmann St; ☏ 9920051. While in dire need of a makeover, the hotel is clean, well located, & even has an outdoor swimming pool (in summer only). Rooms have AC & TV. **$$**

�eat **WHERE TO EAT AND DRINK** *Map, page 156*
Hagaaton Boulevard is teeming with eateries, cafés and bars. Pizza joints and shawarma stands are your best budget options.

✗ **El Poncho** 33 Hagaaton Bd; ☏ 9928635; ⏲ 11.00–23.00 daily. This Argentinian restaurant is decked out in traditional gaucho-style décor, mimicking the cowboy saloons of the rural homeland. **$$$$**

✗ **Penguin Restaurant** 31 Hagaaton Bd; ☏ 9928855; w penguin-rest.co.il; ⏲ 08.00–

midnight Sun–Fri, 09.00–midnight Sat. The ever-popular Penguin Restaurant & attached Penguin Café serve a rather theme-less selection of meals, but all are well cooked & portions are generous. Salads, hamburgers, chicken, soups, pasta & Chinese dishes can be followed by a great choice of shakes & ice creams. **$$**

OTHER PRACTICALITIES Hagaaton Boulevard running from the seafront to route 4 (direction Rosh Hanikra) is the centre of the town's life and activities. There are several branches of all Israel's major **banks** with ATMs, exchange kiosks (⏲ *standard opening hours 09.00–19.00 Sun–Thu, 09.00–14.00 Fri*), **pharmacies** and a **post office** (*40 Hagaaton Bd;* ☏*9920180;* ⏲ *08.00–18.00 Sun* & *Thu, 08.00–*

12.30 & 15.30–18.00 Mon–Tue, 08.00–13.30 Wed, 08.00–noon Fri) on the square near the Municipal Building. The nearest **police station** (*5 Ben Zvi St;* ✆ *9920344*) is on Ben Zvi Street, as is the **Galilee Medical Centre** (✆ *9107107;* w *gmc.org.il*). Avis **car rental** is located in the Hamed Centre (✆ *9511880;* w *avis.co.il;* ⊕ *08.00–17.00 Sun–Thu, 08.00–13.00 Fri*). For shopping and cafés, or if you simply need to kill some time waiting for the bus, there is a newly opened **Arena Mall** (w *arenastar. co.il/mallone/en*) a few hundred metres from the central bus station.

WHAT TO SEE AND DO
Municipal Museum (Beit Liebermann)
(*Nahariya Town Hall, 21 Hagedud St; Flrs 5, 6 & 7;* ✆ *9821516;* ⊕ *09.00–13.00 Mon–Thu, 10.00–14.00 Sat, 09.00–16.00 Sun; admission adult/child ₪10/8*) Opened in 1971, this simple municipal museum contains several displays, including a substantial collection of locally discovered fossils and shells. An art exhibition is housed on the fifth floor, while the seventh floor is dedicated to the history of the town since 1934. Ring in advance, as opening times may change.

Canaanite temple (*Hamaapilim St; admission free*) Located a few metres from the Municipal Beach are the remains of a Cannanite temple. It is believed the temple was dedicated to Astarte, goddess of the sea, and dates to around 1500BCE. The ruins form part of the Municipal Museum, so ask at the reception if you wish to have a look around.

Byzantine church (*Bielefeld St;* ✆ *9879800; admission free; call ahead to arrange entry*) Beautifully preserved mosaics make visiting the church a worthwhile activity. The 4th- to 7th-century mosaic floors are some of the best examples of their kind in the country discovered to date.

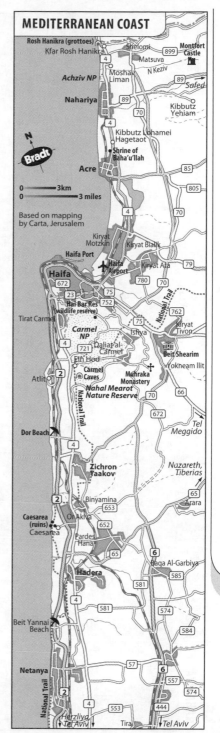

MEDITERRANEAN COAST

Rosh Hanikra (grottoes)
Kfar Rosh Hanikra
Shelomi
Montfort Castle
899
Matsuva
Achziv NP
Moshav Liman
N Keziv
89
Safed
Nahariya
89
70
Kibbutz Yehiam
Kibbutz Lohamei Hagetaot
Shrine of Baha'u'llah
Acre
85
805
0 ——— 3km
0 ——— 3 miles
Based on mapping by Carta, Jerusalem
Kiryat Motzkin
Kiryat Bialik
Haifa Port
Haifa Port
Haifa Airport
Kiryat Ata
79
Haifa
672
780
70
23
75
Hai-Bar Res (wildlife reserve)
752
762
Tirat Carmel
75
Kiryat Tivon
Carmel NP
Isfiya
4
721
Daliat al-Carmel
Beit Shearim
Ein Hod
Carmel Caves
Muhraka Monastery
Yokneam Ilit
Atlit
Nahal Mearot Nature Reserve
70
66
672
Tel Meggido
Dor Beach
4
Nazareth, Tiberias
Zichron Yaakov
2
Binyamina
653
65
Arara
Caesarea (ruins)
Or Akiva
Caesarea
652
Pardes Hana
6
Baqa Al-Garbiya
65
Hadera
581
585
4
581
574
Beit Yannai Beach
584
Netanya
57
6
557
574
2
4
553
444
Herzliya
Tira
Tel Aviv
Tel Aviv

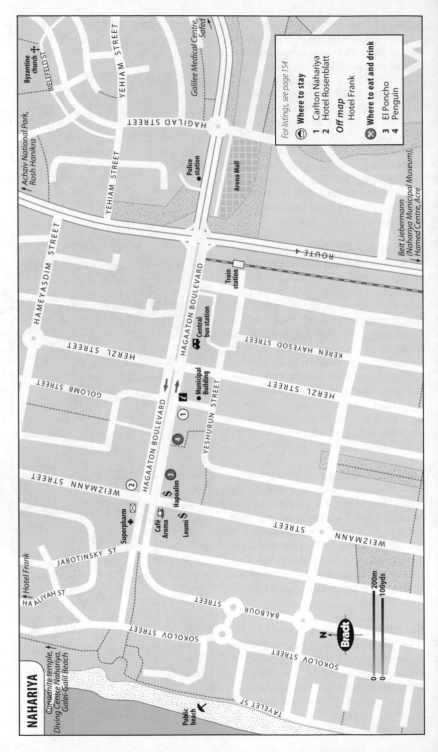

NAHARIYA

Rosh Hanikra
Achziv National Park,

Canaanite temple,
Diving Centre Nahariya,
Galei-Galil Beach

TAYELET ST

Public beach

SOKOLOV STREET

SOKOLOV STREET

BALBOUR STREET

WEIZMANN STREET

HA ALIYAH ST

Hotel Frank

JABOTINSKY ST

Superpharm

Café
Aroma

Leumi $

Hapoalim $

WEIZMANN STREET

GOLOMB STREET

HERZL STREET

HAMEYASDIM STREET

HAGAATON BOULEVARD

HAGAATON BOULEVARD

② ④ ① ③

YESHURUN STREET

Municipal
Building

HERZL STREET

KEREN HAYESOD STREET

Central
bus station

Train
station

HAGAATON BOULEVARD

ROUTE 4

Beit Liebermann
(Nahariya Municipal Museum),
Hamed Centre, Acre

YEHIAM STREET

YEHIAM STREET

HAGLIAD STREET

Police
station

Arena Mall

BIELEFELD ST

Byzantine
church

Galilee Medical Centre,
Safed

N Bradt

0 ___ 200m
0 ___ 100yds

For listings, see page 154

Where to stay
1 Carlton Nahariya
2 Hotel Rosenblatt

Off map
Hotel Frank

Where to eat and drink
3 El Poncho
4 Penguin

156

Scuba diving As far as Mediterranean dive sites go there are a few interesting ones around Nahariya. The most well known is the intentionally sunk Ahi Kidon Military Craft, which acts as a memorial site for members of the IDF water commando unit.

Dive trips to the Rosh Hanikra Grottoes and Achziv Cave can also be arranged through the dive centres, a good choice of which is the **Diving Centre Nahariya** (*8 Hamaapilim St;* ✆ *9511503;* e *club@putsker.co.il;* w *putsker.co.il;* ☉ *08.00–13.00 & 16.00–19.00 Sun–Thu, 08.00–17.00 Fri–Sat; 2-tank dive ₪170, equipment rental ₪130/dive).*

Galei-Galil Beach (☉ *May–Oct 08.00–18.00 daily; admission ₪20*) Renowned for its cleanliness and safety, it offers many sporting activities, eateries and cafés. The outdoor and indoor pools are included in the entry price.

AROUND NAHARIYA

ROSH HANIKRA (RAS AL-NAQOURA) (✆ *073 2710100;* ☉ *summer 09.00–18.00 daily, winter 09.00–16.00 daily; admission adult/child ₪45/35*) At the northernmost point of Israel's Mediterranean coast and exactly 205km from Jerusalem and only 120km from Beirut, the large chalk grottoes and emerald waters of Rosh Hanikra (meaning 'tip of the chiselled slope') are today a popular tourist destination. As the crashing waves eroded the soft rock over thousands of years, they formed a series of large, watery caves at the base of the high cliff. Today visitors can experience these unusual geomorphological structures via a short, steep cable car that leads down to the entrance of the grottoes, providing magnificent views over the sea and along the jagged coastline, which continues on towards the small village of Al-Naqoura in southern Lebanon.

Historically, Rosh Hanikra's prime location straddling the border with Lebanon made it an important strategic thoroughfare. During the 3rd and 4th centuries BCE, it marked the extent of the Israelite tribes and later became a crucial point along the trade route between Lebanon and Syria, and Palestine, Egypt and north Africa. In 333BCE, Alexander the Great entered the country here, supposedly leading his Greek army through tunnels dug out of the chalk. During the world wars, the British army invaded Lebanon, digging a railway tunnel to connect Haifa–Beirut–Tripoli. The 250m-long tunnel – which is partially open to have a peek in when visiting the grottoes – and connecting bridges provided a means of transport for supplies and troops, and also created access for the *haapala* (immigration) of Jews fleeing Nazi Europe. During the 1948 Arab–Israeli War, Israeli forces destroyed the bridges, fearing an insurgence from Arab forces through Lebanon.

Today, the southern tunnel and half of the middle tunnel are in Israeli territory, the remainder in Lebanon. A 15-minute sound and light show on the site provides some further insight into the history and geology of the area.

Getting there and away From Nahariya, bus 31 (direction Matsuva) stops at Rosh Hanikra (*20mins/₪6.80*) but it runs only every 90 minutes. You can also get on any of the numerous and frequent buses headed to or from Shelomi and get off at the Betset junction (Tzomet Betset), from where it is a 2.3km walk to the visitors' centre. Alternatively, it is a pleasant 90-minute walk along the shore from Achziv National Park (page 158) past the scenic Rosh Hanikra Beach. The rocky coastline is popular with fishermen.

ACHZIV NATIONAL PARK (☏9823263; ⊕ *Apr–Jun & Sep–Oct 08.00–17.00 daily, Jul–Aug 08.00–19.00 daily; admission adult/child ₪35/21*) The ancient town of Achziv (pronounced a*khziv*) has had a long and prosperous past. An Old Testament settlement, it belonged to the tribe of Asher and was also mentioned in the Talmud and Mishnah. During the Crusader period, Achziv was known as Castle Imbert after the Crusader knight Hombertus de Pacci, until it was conquered by the Mamluk sultan Baibars in 1271.

Today, however, the park is loved not for its historical distinction, but for its shimmering turquoise waters that attract bathers and sea turtles alike. From the rocky coast, wide sandy beaches lead towards the sheltered bays and deep natural pools that have formed along the length of the coast. The park has camping facilities by the beach (*adult/child ₪63/53*) built around the old Arab fishing village of Al-Zib, whose residents fled during the 1948 Arab–Israeli War. The village ruins are closed to visitors, but it is a picturesque backdrop for a day of swimming.

For something a bit different, make your way to Achzivland, run by Eli Avivi and his wife Rina (signposted off the main road to 'Eli Avivi'). This hamlet lies between the national park and the old Arab cemetery. A tiny, self-governing community since 1971, the houses and wooden cabins of Achzivland do not lack charm. Avivi was born in Iran in 1930 and has lived here since the 1950s, becoming a well-known character throughout Israel. As a teenager, he was a member of the Palyam underground Jewish navy, helping to bring illegal Jewish immigrants into Palestine, and he was a Shin Bet agent in his later years. Achzivland is known as a hippy paradise and has even hosted a rock music festival. Of more interest for the visitor, however, is the collection of ancient artefacts assembled by Avivi from the bottom of the sea and the surrounding area. It is currently on display in the house of a former Arab chief from Al-Zib.

Getting there and away The park is located on route 4 between Nahariya and Rosh Hanikra. From Nahariya, Nateev Express bus 31 (direction Betset/Matsuva) or any of the buses towards Shelomi (22, 23, 24, 28, 36) or Shatula (27) stop on request outside the park.

⌂ **Where to stay and eat** The nearby **Moshav Liman** provides good food and zimmer accommodation. Although prices are a little steep compared with nearby Nahariya, you certainly get what you pay for, and these are a much nicer alternative to the rather shabby choices in the city. The **Shpan Motel B&B** (☏ 9822255; **$$$**) offers a lesser degree of luxury than some of its neighbours at more affordable prices. Pretty gardens and outdoor eating areas make it a pleasant spot and self-catering apartments are good for families or couples.

At the northern end of the moshav is the kosher **Morgenfeld Steak House** (☏ 9524333; ⊕ *noon–23.00 Sun–Thu, noon–15.00 Fri, end of Shabbat–23.00 Sat;* **$$$$**), which combines hearty chunks of prime meat with à la carte fine dining. Entrecôte, Argentinian *asado*, juicy ribs and a mouth-watering selection of desserts are just some of the treats on offer in a romantic, candlelit atmosphere.

ACRE (AKKO/AKKA) Population 47,700

Within the ancient walls, sheltered from modernisation, development and change, Acre's Old City remains today as it has done throughout its long years of existence. It is undoubtedly one of Israel's most picturesque and historically fascinating places to visit, and a must-see on any itinerary. A jumble of cobbled lanes snake around,

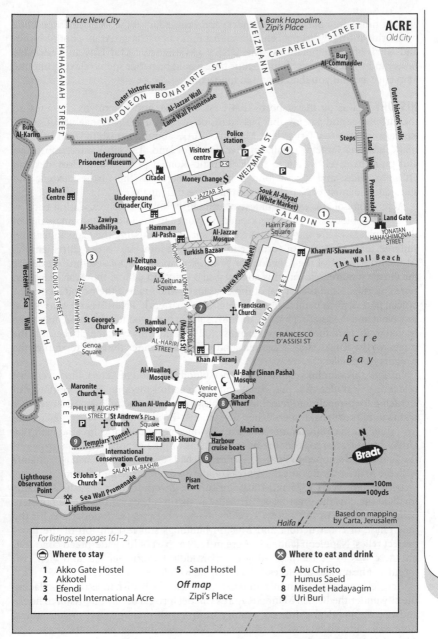

↑ Acre New City

↑ Bank Hapoalim,
Zipi's Place

Outer historic walls

HAHAGANAH STREET

CAFARELLI STREET

WEIZMANN ST

Burj
Al-Commander

NAPOLEON BONAPARTE ST

Al-Jazzar Wall
Land Wall Promenade

Outer historic walls

Burj
Al-Karim

Police
station

Steps

Land Wall Promenade

Visitors'
centre

Underground
Prisoners' Museum

Citadel

④

P

Baha'i
Centre

Underground
Crusader City

Money Change $

AL-JAZZAR ST

P

Souk Al-Abyad
(White Market)

SALADIN ST

①

② Land Gate

Zawiya
Al-Shadhiliya

Hammam
Al-Pasha

Al-Jazzar
Mosque

Haim Farhi
Square

YONATAN
HAHASHIMONAI
STREET

Turkish Bazaar

⑤

Khan Al-Shawarda

③

Al-Zeituna
Mosque

Marco Polo (Market)

SIGURD STREET

The Wall Beach

KING LOUIS IX STREET

HABAHAIM STREET

Al-Zeituna
Square

RICHARD THE LIONHEART ST

⑦

Franciscan
✝ Church

Acre

Western Sea Wall

St George's
Church

Ramhal
Synagogue ✡

B. METUDELA ST (Market St)

FRANCESCO
D'ASSISI ST

Bay

HAHAGANAH STREET

Genoa
Square

AL-HARIRI
STREET

Khan Al-Faranj

Al-Muallaq
Mosque

Al-Bahr (Sinan Pasha)
Mosque

Maronite
Church ✝

Venice
Square

Ramban
Wharf

PHILLIPE AUGUST
STREET

Khan Al-Umdan

⑧

N

P

St Andrew's
✝ Church

Pisa
Square

Marina

Bradt

⑨ Templars' Tunnel

Khan Al-Shuna

Harbour
cruise boats

International
Conservation Centre

⑥

SALAH AL-BASHRI

0 ————— 100m
0 ————— 100yds

Lighthouse
Observation
Point

St John's
✝ Church

Pisan
Port

Sea Wall Promenade

Lighthouse

Haifa ↙

Based on mapping
by Carta, Jerusalem

For listings, see pages 161–2

🛏 **Where to stay**
1 Akko Gate Hostel
2 Akkotel
3 Efendi
4 Hostel International Acre
5 Sand Hostel

Off map
   Zipi's Place

✕ **Where to eat and drink**
6 Abu Christo
7 Humus Saeid
8 Misedet Hadayagim
9 Uri Buri

through and past ancient stone buildings, piled one upon another; majestic, vibrant mosques and churches stream with devout worshippers; immaculately preserved relics remain, left by the city's passionate invaders; people crowd into the aromatic souks; and the tranquil waters of the ancient sea port lap against the old sea walls. It was on this small peninsula where empires were battled over, where religions clashed and where cultures merged. Acre was one of the most crucial cities of ancient times on a par with Alexandria and Troy, a fact difficult to envisage while wandering the lively yet peaceful alleys that today house large Arab – both Muslim and Christian – populations. The UNESCO-designated Old City is a veritable maze, and while maps are handy, your time would be better spent relaxing into the ambience around you than trying to follow one.

HISTORY It was on these shores that west met east, and few towns can attest to the turbulence and passion that passed inside Acre's walls. The Canaanites, Greeks, Romans, Byzantines, Crusaders, Mamluks, Turks and the British have all left their mark, however large or small, on this stretch of land. The city's most impressive and prominent relics date to the Hellenistic–Roman periods and Crusader and Ottoman rules, and it will forever be remembered as the furthest extent and subsequent demise of Napoleon's Middle Eastern campaign.

Acre is one of the world's oldest continuously inhabited cities, dating back as far as 1504–1450BCE. It was mentioned only once in the Old Testament as one of the few places where the Israelites did not succeed in ousting the Canaanites, and suffered three centuries of torment in the years leading up to the Christian era. At the time a part of the Kingdom of Israel, Acre was incorporated into Alexander the Great's empire following his conquest in 332BCE. In 638CE, the Arabs captured Acre and ruled until the arrival of the Crusaders, who made it their capital city. The crucial port city was named the Crusaders' headquarters in Palestine and was witness to violent and devastating battles. In 1187, Saladin managed to take Acre, only to be ousted by Richard the Lionheart's troops in 1191. Under his rule, the city became the capital of the Kingdom of Jerusalem and was placed under the directorship of the Knights Hospitaller.

In 1291, the Mamluks embarked on their bloody invasion of Acre, killing every last remaining Crusader, thus putting an end to the Latin Kingdom. The once-powerful city fell into disrepair and remained virtually ruinous for the following 500 years. It wasn't until provincial leader Daher Al-Omar Al-Zaydani (1690–1775) made Acre his capital in the 18th century that the city once again began to breathe with life. Under his rule, Acre's economy boomed, thanks to the export of cotton grown in the Galilee and shipped to France. Al-Zaydani had successfully reached agreements with the Maltese pirates attacking ports on the Mediterranean and disrupting trade.

Between the years 1775 and 1804, the Turkish governor Ahmad Pasha Al-Jazzar fortified the city, the great Al-Jazzar Mosque that has become the symbol of Acre owing its origins to this time. Crusader remains became the foundations for the new phase of construction, and Muslim buildings still rest on top of the near-perfect relics. Napoleon landed in Acre in 1799 as part of his widespread conquest, but Acre was to be the beginning of his Middle Eastern demise, and after two months of heavy and unsuccessful battling he withdrew to France.

Acre fell under Ottoman rule until their defeat by the British in 1918, thus placing the city under the British Mandate. Acre's Citadel fortress became a prison to house and execute political prisoners, mainly from Jewish underground organisations. Acre was captured by Jewish forces on 17 May 1948 during the Arab–Israeli War. Almost 75% of its Arab inhabitants fled the city.

GETTING THERE AND AWAY The **central bus station** is on Haarbaa Street in the New City, adjacent to the **train station**, which is on David Remez Street. While buses arrive from Tel Aviv, Haifa and Nahariya regularly, trains are considerably faster and more convenient. Buses 251, 271/2, 282, 361 and 371/2 (Nateev Express) leave and arrive approximately every 30 minutes to and from Haifa Merkazit Hamifratz bus station (*50mins/₪11.50*). Trains from Haifa Carmel station (*35mins/₪13.50*), Tel Aviv (*1hr 28mins/₪35.50*) and Nahariya (*8mins/₪7.50*) run every 30 minutes.

There is now a regular **cruise ferry line** between Acre Marina and Haifa (*passenger terminals 4 & 7, near Hashmona train station, Haatzmaut St*; **w** *akko.org.il/en*). Departure times are indicated below but may change subject to weather conditions, so it's worth clicking on the ferry web page in advance. Tickets can be purchased at the ticket office in Acre Marina up to 30 minutes prior to departure. Tickets for the cruise can also be combined with tickets for various other sites in Acre.

Departure	From Acre	From Haifa	Fare one-way/return
Weekdays	10.00	11.00	₪30/55
	15.00	16.00	
Saturday	09.30	11.00	
	12.30	14.00	
	15.30	16.30	

GETTING AROUND Acre Old City is small and almost wholly pedestrianised so the only way to navigate the labyrinthine alleys is on foot. There are signs to the main sites all around the city, so it's hard to get lost. From the New City and bus station, taxis can drop you at the visitors' centre (*approx ₪10*). Alternatively a few buses (including 361 to Safed) stop at Yehonatan Hahashmonai Street, which is a walk of only a few minutes from the Old City.

TOURIST INFORMATION The Acre Old City **visitors' centre** (*1 Weizmann St;* **** *9956706;* **w** *akko.org.il/en;* ⊕ *winter 08.30–17.00 Sun–Thu & Sat, 08.30–14.00 Fri, summer 08.30–18.30 Sun–Thu & Sat, 08.30–15.00 Fri*) is located on the right as you enter the citadel through the visitors' car park. It is very well run, and they sell combination tickets to all of Acre's sites, book hotels and can also arrange tour guides as well as full-day excursions to attractions in the area. The centre should be your first port of call in the Old City. You can purchase city maps for ₪3 here or at any of the other major sights in the Old City. Since 2017, in an attempt to centralise tourist information, most of the hotels, restaurants and tourist attractions listed in this chapter have been incorporated into the visitors' centre website.

↳ **WHERE TO STAY** *Map, page 159*

⌂ **Akkotel** (16 rooms) Saladin St; **** 9877100; **e** info@akkotel.com; **w** akkotel.com. Beautiful boutique hotel located in the Old City. The 250-year-old building exudes Acre charm, & rooms come with AC, TV, minibar, plush beds & sofas. A roof terrace café provides wonderful views of the ancient buildings below & there is a Mediterranean restaurant serving freshly caught fish. **$$$$**

⌂ **Efendi Hotel** (12 rooms) Louis IX St; **** 074 7299799; **e** reservation@efendi-hotel.com; **w** efendi-hotel.com. 2 traditional mansions formerly owned by an *effendi* (an Ottoman title, meaning 'a noble man') were combined into this gem of a boutique hotel. Syrian wooden furniture on various floors, 2 rooftop terraces, a spa &

beautiful rooms make this authentic & exquisite. **$$$$**

⌂ **Akko Gate Hostel** (12 rooms) 14 Saladin St; **** 9910410; **e** walid.akko.gate@gmail.com; **w** akkogate.com. Traditionally decorated family-run hostel offering an excellent budget option in the Old City. Rooms on the newly extended side of the building are a bit more spacious & modern. **$$**

⌂ **Hostel International Acre** (76 rooms) 2 Weizmann St; **** 02 5945711; **e** acre@iyha.org.il; **w** iyha.org.il. Located in the Old City across the street from the citadel, the structure is bulky & a little unsuited to the surroundings, but rooms are bright & modern. **$$–$**

⌂ **Zipi's Place** (20 beds) 10 Bilu St; **m** 050 7901447; **e** zipi503@walla.co.il. A 20min walk from the Old City is this cosy, family-run guesthouse. Facilities include laundry & communal kitchen, & there's a choice of dormitory beds or private rooms. **$$–$**

🏠 **Sand Hostel** (14 rooms) m 050 9083402. A traditional hostel that has been around for more

than 30 years. Located in an old building opposite the Turkish Bazaar, it embodies the very character of the Old City, although facilities & rooms need some freshening up. Ask for Hammudi when phoning to book. **$**

✗ WHERE TO EAT AND DRINK Map, page 159

Fish and seafood play a big part in the menus of the more upmarket restaurants, while hearty, traditional Middle Eastern food dominates the cheaper eateries. Plastic-chaired, reasonably priced restaurants along **Al-Jazzar Street** are good for a quick bite of shawarma, hummus, French fries and salads and there are some fabulous bakeries, sweet cakes, spices and nuts in the **souk**. For an evening drink or light meal, **Khan Al-Shawarda** public square is a good place to start; a few bars are also open, albeit with somewhat irregular hours, in the **Turkish Bazaar** (w *acre-turkish-bazaar.com*), which was nicely restored in 2011.

✗ **Uri Buri** Hahaganah St; ✆9552212; w uriburi.co.il; ⏰ noon–midnight daily. Often considered one of the best fish & seafood restaurants in the country. Although the fruits of the deep sea will burn a deep hole in your pocket, it is money well spent – the food is fabulous. Informal, classy atmosphere & a great location next to the lighthouse. **$$$$$**

✗ **Abu Christo** South Sea Promenade; ✆9910065; ⏰ noon–23.00 daily. Established in 1948, a well-respected fish & meat restaurant that boasts the best view in the Old City. The menu includes plenty of elegantly prepared Greek- & Arabic-style salads, seafood & steaks. **$$$$**

✗ **Misedet Hadayagim (The Fisherman's Restaurant)** Harbour entrance; ✆073 7569540;

⏰ noon–midnight daily. Rustic little restaurant serving incredibly fresh fish at incredible prices. Head to the fish market next door, choose your fish, then head back into the restaurant, where they'll cook it up on the spot. A buffet selection of salads with drink costs ₪60 including the fish. Simply wonderful. **$$$**

✗ **Hummus Saeid** Market St; ✆9913945; ⏰ 06.00 Sun–Fri until the food runs out, usually around 14.30. Queues down the street attest to the incredible popularity of this tiny hummus bar. Known across the country, this is normally the first port of call for any visitor to old Acre. But don't expect a leisurely meal, as you'll have the eyes of the next customer in line boring into the back of your neck willing you to hurry up. **$**

ENTERTAINMENT AND NIGHTLIFE In July, the Crusader Hall plays host to concerts performed by the renowned **Haifa Symphony Orchestra**, the echoing hall providing the perfect accompanying acoustics and a unique setting. Around the Jewish holiday of Sukkot (the Harvest Festival which falls around October) is the **Acco Festival of Alternative Israeli Theatre** (w *accofestival.co.il*), consisting of theatre performances by national theatre groups. These are mainly in Hebrew, but there are some productions in English. Ask at the visitors' centre (page 161) for a list. Alternatively, take an evening walk along the Sea Promenade in the Old City and spice it up with a boat ride for ₪10 per person.

OTHER PRACTICALITIES Note that there are no ATMs in the Old City, although exchange shops (⏰ *09.30–18.30 daily*) are plentiful. The nearest **Bank Hapoalim** branch is on 6 Ben Ami Street (✆*03 6532407*; ⏰ *08.30–13.15 Sun–Thu, 16.00–18.30 Mon & Thu*). The **police station** (*Weizmann St*; ✆*9876736*) is also nearby. There's a **post office** near the entrance to the citadel (*13 Al-Jazzar St*; ✆*9910171*; ⏰ *08.00–12.30 & 15.30–18.00 Sun–Mon & Wed–Thu, 08.00–13.00 Tue, 08.00–12.30 Fri*), while you'll find the central post office (*11 Haatzmaut St*; ✆*9910023*; ⏰ *08.00–18.00*

Sun & Thu, 08.00–12.30 & 15.30–18.00 Mon–Tue, 08.00–13.30 Wed, 08.00–noon Fri) in the New City. **Mizra Hospital** (✆9959595) is located north of the New City.

WHAT TO SEE AND DO
Underground Crusader City (✆ 9956706; ⊕ 08.30–18.00 Sat–Thu, 08.30–17.00 Fri, closes 1hr earlier in winter; admission adult/child combination tickets from ₪25/22) Resting under the foundations of Al-Jazzar's citadel, this was the headquarters of the Knights Hospitaller during the Crusades. Excavated in the 1950s to reveal a maze of rooms, the subterranean city is a fascinating place to explore. A vast hall, believed to be a refectory, leads to what was once a secret tunnel that emerged 350m away in Acre's harbour. The tunnel has only partially been excavated and now leads to the Bosta, a large room used by the knights as a refuge for pilgrims. The crypt of St John, displaying a poignant and telling fleur-de-lis that dates the room to Louis VII's era, was once used as the knights' banqueting hall.

The citadel Looming over the submerged Crusader City below, the Ottoman citadel has been engraved in history books mainly through its role as a high-security prison during the British Mandate. It was in this supposedly impenetrable fortress that members of Jewish Zionist underground organisations were held and several executed. On 4 May 1947, it became the scene of one of the most famous prison escapes in history, when members of the Irgun militant Zionist group broke through its defences in an attempt to free the prisoners. While few escaped alive, it was seen as a major failure on the part of the British and marked a significant blow to their control. Today the citadel holds a wealth of sights, most notably the **Underground Prisoners' Museum** (✆9911375; ⊕ 08.30–16.30 Sun–Thu; admission adult/child ₪8/4). The prison has been left in its original daunting and oppressive state and huge, high ceilings and thick walls make it easy to imagine the horror of being locked up here. The Gallows Room contains the noose from which the nine Jewish resistance fighters were hanged, and photographs and documents commemorating the prisoners who were kept here, including the first prisoner and Israeli hero Z Jabotinsky, are on display. In addition, the **prison cell of Baha'u'llah**, the Baha'i faith's founder, can be visited. He was imprisoned by the Ottoman government and spent the best part of his adult life within the walls. Outside is the **enchanted garden**, a replica of the one believed to have existed during the Crusader era.

Al-Jazzar Mosque (⊕ 08.00–18.00 Sat–Thu, 08.00–11.00 & 13.00–18.00 Fri, closes 1hr earlier in winter; admission ₪6) The beautiful, green-domed Al-Jazzar Mosque is hard to miss. Built on the site of Acre's Crusader cathedral, it is not only the largest of the city's four mosques, but the third-largest mosque in the country. The submerged cathedral was later flooded and served as a reservoir, which is today accessible from a door at the end of the compound (signposted). Many of the building materials, notably the ornate Roman columns in the courtyard, were taken from the ancient coastal city of Caesarea (pages 188–92) while inside the mosque is said to be housed a strand of hair from the Prophet Mohammed's beard. The entrance to the courtyard is up a flight of stone steps and through a small gate located on the lively Al-Jazzar Street just behind the citadel. Visitors are welcome outside prayer times, provided they dress appropriately and respect Muslim religious traditions. A small, simple domed building on the right of the entrance contains the sarcophagi of Ahmed Al-Jazzar and his successor Suleiman Pasha.

Hammam Al-Pasha (or Al-Basha) (☏ 9551088; ☉ *winter 08.30–17.00 Sat–Thu & 08.30–14.00 Fri, summer 08.30–18.00 Sat–Thu & 08.30–17.00 Fri; admission adult/ child ₪25/18; can be included in combination tickets*) This was built in the 1780s by Al-Jazzar as part of his vast mosque complex, and was modelled on Roman bathhouse styles. There are three rooms: one a dressing room, one functioning like that of a Roman *tepidarium* (warm room) and the last a hot steam room. The baths served as more than a place of religious purification, forming an important social centre where meetings were conducted and people came to relax. Colourful lighting on the intricate ceramic tiling and marble statues combined with trickling water sounds and the multi-media **Story of the Last Bath Attendant** (a rather soapy bath attendant who regales lively tales of the history of Acre) detract somewhat from the historic significance of the place but are tolerable if you have 15 minutes to spare. The entrance to the baths is along Al-Jazzar Street, opposite the citadel and a little way up from the Al-Jazzar Mosque.

Khan Al-Umdan Translating as 'Pillar's Inn', the first glimpse of Acre's most impressive ancient merchants' inn will reveal why it was named thus. Built in the late 18th century, the *khan* (inn) was built on a series of large granite columns and acted as storeroom and hotel for merchants arriving at Acre's thriving port. The tiny entrance to this vast courtyard is easily missed, but it is certainly worth ferreting out. Look for the minaret of the **Al-Bahr (Sinan Pasha) Mosque** on the harbour's edge and the entrance is opposite. At the time of writing it was undergoing renovations and was closed to the public, but could still be glimpsed through the gates.

The city walls The sturdy, pentagon-shaped wall that today surrounds Acre was built in 1750 by Daher Al-Omar upon the remains of the Crusader structures, and later fortified by Al-Jazzar. When completed it encircled Acre on both land and sea perimeters. From the Weizmann Street entrance, steps on the left lead up on to the **Land Wall Promenade** and on to the **Land Gate**, which was built in the 13th century and during the Ottoman period served as the only point of entry to the city. The **Burj Al-Commander** located on the northeast corner of the wall was the tower said to have defeated Napoleon in 1799 and offers a fabulous view southwest over the rambling buildings of the Old City. The **Sea Wall Promenade** is accessed by steps located a few metres along from Abu Christo Restaurant in the south of the Old City and leads to the **Lighthouse Observation Point**. To see the walls from an invader's viewpoint, countless boats do tours leaving throughout the day. **Malkat Acre Cruises** (*Leopold the Second St;* ☏ 9913890; *admission adult/child ₪20/15*) operate boat tours around the walls (*40mins*) as well as to Haifa and Rosh Hanikra. Boats leave from the marina hourly throughout summer and tickets can be bought at the dock.

Templars' Tunnel (☉ *winter 08.30–17.30 daily, summer 09.30–18.30 Sat–Thu & 09.30–17.30 Fri; admission adult/child ₪15/12*) The 350m-long tunnel, which was opened to the public in 1999, was built in the 12th century by the Knights Templar and leads from the port in the east to their long-since destroyed and submerged fortress in the southwest of the Old City. The arched tunnels are well lit and not especially narrow, making this little-known attraction a worthwhile detour. There are two entrances to the tunnel: one through the rather dilapidated **Khan Al-Shuna** opposite the Khan Al-Umdan, and the second near the lighthouse car park.

Market Street (☉ *until 17.00 daily*) Running from north to south, Market Street is noisy, busy and crowded. It is also, however, one of the most fascinating parts of the present-day Old City, where stalls selling sweet pastries, dried fruit, fish, spices and household items squeeze together, the sights, sounds and smells accentuated in the narrow tunnel-like maze. At the end of the street and up a small lane on the right is the **Ramhal Synagogue** (☉ *09.30–18.00 Sun–Thu & Sat, 09.30–15.00 Fri*), named after the Italian sage Rabbi Moshe Haim Luzatto (the Ramhal), who is best known for his moral guide *Mesilat Yesharim*.

AROUND ACRE

SHRINE OF BAHA'U'LLAH (*gardens:* \ *8313131;* w *ganbahai.org.il;* ☉ *09.00–17.00 daily; shrine:* ☉ *09.00–noon Sun–Fri; admission free; modest dress*) The Shrine of Baha'u'llah is the holiest site for members of the Baha'i faith, topping even the vast Shrine of Bab, Haifa's most recognisable landmark. This is the final resting place of Baha'u'llah, founder of the Baha'i faith and the principal pilgrimage site for members of the religion. Following his death on 29 May 1892, Baha'u'llah was interred in the ornate shrine erected next to the **Mansion of Bahji**, where he spent his final days. It is in the direction of the shrine that worshippers face when reciting daily prayers. The shrine is surrounded by immaculately kept, manicured gardens where not a blade of grass can be found out of place. There are free tours every day except Wednesday.

GHETTO FIGHTERS' HOUSE (BEIT LOHAMEI HAGETAOT) (*Kibbutz Lohamei Hagetaot:* \ *9958080;* ☉ *09.00–16.00 Sun–Thu, 09.00–13.00 Fri; Yad Layeled:* ☉ *10.00–17.00 Sun–Thu; admission adult/child ₪20/10*) The vast museum complex was established by a group of Holocaust survivors who aimed to tell the story of the Jewish people throughout the 20th century and in particular remember those who died and suffered in the Holocaust. It focuses on Jewish resistance throughout World War II, exhibitions including 'The Warsaw Ghetto Fights Back' and 'Ghettos and Deportations'. The moving Yad Layeled (Children's Museum) focuses on the children of the Holocaust, and is a combination of informative displays, symbolic objects and audio-visual presentations.

Getting there and away Both the above sights are located along route 4 between Acre and Nahariya. The Shrine of Baha'u'llah North Gate entrance is approximately 2km from Acre, and bus 271 between Nahariya and Haifa stops outside the entrance to the shrine. The Ghetto Fighters' House is in Kibbutz Lohamei Hagetaot.

HAIFA *Population 279,000*

Cascading down the slopes of Mount Carmel towards the sandy beaches of the Mediterranean, Israel's third-largest city is often overlooked as a tourist destination. Yet the city has a lot going for it, and is a great place to spend a few days. Haifa has grown tremendously since its foundation, when Allenby Street used to be called Zeytoon (Olive) Street in honour of the olive trees and farms, which have today given way to a modern residential area.

Haifa is probably best known for its harmonious interaction among its different faiths, where Jews, Muslims, Druze, Christians and Baha'is exist contentedly alongside one another. The vast, landscaped gardens of the Shrine of Bab, the centre of the Baha'i faith, form the unexpected centrepiece of the city, while its thriving port is the largest in the country. Prosperous industries, a large hilltop university, countless religious and historic sights, neighbourhoods old and new, a fascinating

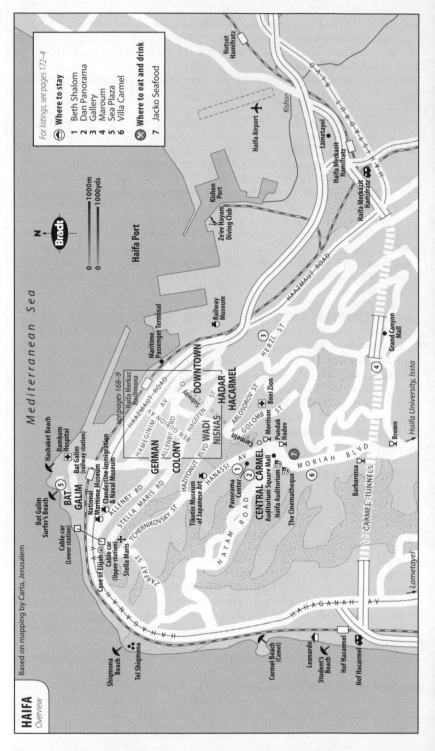

HAIFA
Overview

Based on mapping by Carta, Jerusalem

Mediterranean Sea

Bradt

N

0   1000m
0   1000yds

For listings, see pages 172–4

Where to stay
1 Beth Shalom
2 Dan Panorama
3 Gallery
4 Maroum
5 Sea Plaza
6 Villa Carmel

Where to eat and drink
7 Jacko Seafood

Hashaket Beach

Rambam Hospital

Bat Galim
(railway station)

National Maritime Museum

Clandestine Immigration & Naval Museum

BAT GALIM

Cable car (Lower station)

Cave of Elijah

Cable car (Upper station)

Stella Maris

Shigmona Beach

Tel Shigmona

Haifa Port

Maritime Passenger Terminal

Haifa Merkaz Hashmona

Railway Museum

Kishon Port

Ze'ev Hayam Diving Club

Haifa Airport

Kishon

Hutsot Hamifratz

Lametayel

Haifa Merkazit Hamifratz

Haifa Merkazit Hamifratz

Grand Canyon Mall

Haifa University, Issta

Brown

DOWNTOWN

HADAR HACARMEL

WADI NISNAS

GERMAN COLONY

Tikotin Museum of Japanese Art

Haifa Auditorium

Auditorium Square Mall

Panorama Center

CENTRAL CARMEL

The Cinematheque

Barbarossa

Carmelit

Morrison

Pundak Hadov

Bnei Zion

HERZL ST

ARLOSOROV ST

GOLOMB

MORIAH BLVD

HAAZMAUT ROAD

HAAZMAUT ROAD

HAMEGINIM AV

BEN GURION AV

ALLENBY RD

HAGEFEN ST

HAZIYONUT BLVD

HANASSI AV

HAYAM ROAD

ALLENBY RD

STELLA MARIS RD

TCHERNIKOVSKY ST

ZAFAT ST

HAHAGANAH AV

HAHAGANAH

Bat Galim Surfer's Beach

Leonardo

Student's Beach

Carmel Beach (Camel)

Hof Hacarmel

Lametayel

CARMEL TUNNELS

see pages 168–9

collection of museums and a lively restaurant and bar scene make Haifa a firm favourite among Israelis and a pleasant contrast to Jerusalem and Tel Aviv.

HISTORY Finds discovered across the city date from the Stone Age to the Ottoman period, while Roman and Greek discoveries attest to occupation, although by no means comparable to the thriving port city at Caesarea. While not mentioned in the Bible, Haifa appears in the Talmud as an established Jewish settlement, which during the Middle Ages grew into a shipping centre.

The Crusaders and the Carmelites In 1099, Haifa was conquered by the Crusaders who slaughtered the Jewish residents almost in their entirety. During their occupation of the region, groups of religious hermits began to live in caves dotted across the Carmel area in honour of Elijah the Prophet. Over the next 100 years they formed the Carmelite order, which spread as far as Europe. While the order continued to thrive in Europe, the founders on Mount Carmel were exiled when, in 1265, the city fell to the Mamluk sultan Baibars. From 1750 until the beginning of World War I, Haifa remained under Turkish rule. Around this time, the modern city of Haifa was founded by Daher Al-Omar Al-Zaydani (see box, page 205), who laid the city's foundations approximately 3km from the original settlement and built a seaport. The Turks were ousted in 1799 by Napoleon, but this was short-lived following his poignant defeat at Acre. In 1830, the first Jewish settlement was established in the city.

The German Templars In 1868, the German Templars established a colony in Haifa which today remains one of the city's most picturesque areas (page 177). The German Templars have been credited with the rapid development of the small, insignificant town they founded. It was, however, at around the same time that the Baha'u'llah, founder of the Baha'i faith, arrived in Haifa, a factor contributing to its development boom at the time. The Templar Society was founded in Germany in 1861 as a result of the severe socio-economic conditions in southwest Germany, and was formed with the aspiration of promoting messianic ideas as a path to salvation. They purchased lands in Haifa and set up an agricultural community, constructing a beautiful, wide boulevard. The Templars' contribution to the development of Haifa was dramatic: they were the first to use horse-drawn carriages to transport goods and people to Acre; they built modern buildings; a road up to the Carmel; brought with them tools; and introduced new agricultural techniques.

The British Mandate and post 1947 During the British Mandate, the city renewed its development, with the construction of Jewish neighbourhoods and factories (including the oil refinery), Technion College, the first technical tertiary institution in the Middle East, having opened in 1912, while the city was still under Ottoman control. After World War II, the port at Haifa became the site of several notorious confrontations between the British and Jews attempting to enter Palestine. The Haganah Zionist organisation operated fervently in the area, smuggling in immigrants and Holocaust survivors. The *Af-Al-Pi-Chen*, a ship used by the British in their blockades, today resides as a lasting reminder outside the Clandestine Immigration and Naval Museum (page 178). The Irgun equally left their mark when, in 1938, the organisation set off a bomb killing dozens of Arabs at the market in Haifa. In the city's post-independence history, the 1950s were marked by ethnic tensions between the local population and new immigrants, resulting in the Wadi Salib riots in 1959.

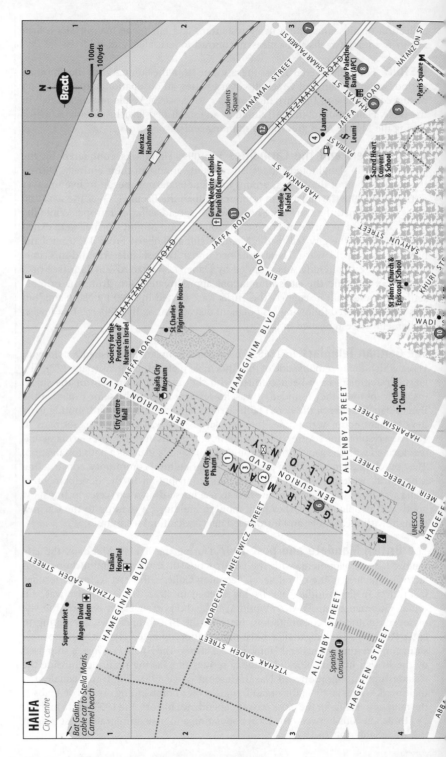

HAIFA
City centre

Bat Galim,
cable car to Stella Maris,
Carmel beach

Merkaz
Hashmona

Supermarket
Magen David
Adom

Italian
Hospital

Society for the
Protection of
Nature in Israel

St Charles
Pilgrimage House

City Centre
Mall

Haifa City
Museum

Green City
Pharm

Spanish
Consulate

Greek Melkite Catholic
Parish Old Cemetery

Michelle
Falafel

Students
Square

Laundry

Anglo Palestine
Bank (APC)

Leumi

Paris Square

Sacred Heart
Convent
& School

St John's Church &
Episcopal School

Orthodox
Church

UNESCO
Square

HAMAL STREET

HAATZMAUT ROAD

SHAAR PALMER ST

KHAYAT ROAD

NATANZON ST

JAFFA ST

PATRIA ST

HABANKIM ST

SAHYUN STREET

KHURI STR

WADI S

HAPARSIM STREET

MEIR RUTBERG STREET

ALLENBY STREET

HAGEFE

HEGEFEN STREET

JAFFA ROAD

EIN DOR ST

HAMEGINIM BLVD

BEN-GURION BLVD

GERMAN COLONY

MORDECHAI ANIELEWICZ STREET

YTZHAK SADEH STREET

ALLENBY STREET

HAMEGINIM BLVD

YTZHAK SADEH STREET

HAATZMAUT ROAD

JAFFA ROAD

BEN-GURION BLVD

ABB

N

Bradt

0   100m
0   100yds

168

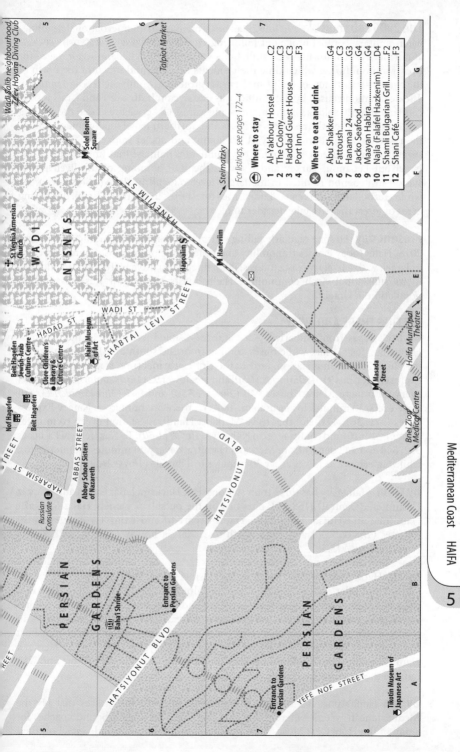

For listings, see pages 172–4

ⓘ Where to stay

1	Al-Yakhour Hostel	C2
2	The Colony	C3
3	Haddad Guest House	C3
4	Port Inn	F3

✕ Where to eat and drink

5	Abu Shakker	G4
6	Fattoush	C3
7	Hanamal 24	G3
8	Jacko Seafood	G4
9	Maayan Habira	G4
10	Najla (Falafel Hazkenim)	D4
11	Shamli Bulgarian Grill	F2
12	Shani Café	F3

Wadi Salib neighbourhood,
Zeev Hayam Diving Club

Talpiot Market

✝ St Yeghia Armenian
Church

WADI

NISNAS

Solel Boneh
Square

Beit Hagefen
Jewish-Arab
Culture Centre
● Clore Children's
Library &
Culture Centre

HADAD ST

WADI ST

Haifa Museum
of Art

SHABTAI LEVI STREET

HANEVIIM ST

Hapoalim Ⓢ

Ⓜ Hanevim

Nof Hagefen

Beit Hagefen

ABBAS STREET

STREET

HAPARSIM ST

Russian
Consulate Ⓔ

Abbey School Sisters
of Nazareth

Steimatzky

Ⓜ Masada
Street

Haifa Municipal
Theatre

Bne Zion
Medical Centre

HATSIYONUT

BLVD

PERSIAN
GARDENS

Entrance to
Persian Gardens

Baha'i Shrine

HATSIYONUT BLVD

PERSIAN GARDENS

Entrance to
Persian Gardens

YEFE NOF STREET

Tikotin Museum of
Japanese Art

The 2006 Lebanon War In July 2006, Israel once again hit international headlines when military conflict broke out following Hezbollah's firing of Katyusha rockets at northern Israeli towns. The conflict, known as the 2006 Lebanon War, raged for over a month during which time the residents of Haifa and much of the north of the country spent most of their time beneath ground in bomb shelters and bunkers. The devastation caused by the conflict was massive on both sides and Israel lost 43 civilians and 120 soldiers in the month-long war. A UN ceasefire ended the shelling on 14 August when the residents of Haifa and northern Israel finally emerged from their shelters. Apart from the vast economic and social impact of the conflict, several events caused catastrophic environmental damage that impacted not just Israel but Lebanon, Turkey and Cyprus. The IDF bombing of the Jiyeh power station in Lebanon resulted in the largest-ever oil spill in the Mediterranean Sea while Hezbollah rockets caused numerous forest fires in northern Israel, destroying acres of forest that will take decades to recover.

Present day Despite regularly falling victim to forest fires, including in 2010 and 2016, Haifa today exudes tranquillity and peace. One of the most interesting cities in Israel, with a lively mix of cultures, it is a finer alternative to Tel Aviv. In addition to its substantial Arab community, Haifa boasts the largest Russian-speaking population in Israel.

GETTING THERE AND AWAY

By bus Buses from Nahariya, Acre and the Galilee terminate in the Merkazit Hamifratz bus station, while buses coming from the south and Jerusalem stop at the Hof Hacarmel bus station, next to the Hof Hacarmel train station. To Tel Aviv, express Egged bus 910 (*90mins/₪21.50*) and the slower 921 (*2hrs20mins/₪27*) depart every 20 minutes. Direct buses 940 (*2hrs/₪37.50*) and 947 (*2hrs45mins/₪37.50*) leave every 30 minutes for Jerusalem. To Acre, there are numerous Nateev Express buses (271, 361, 471, etc) that leave Merkazit Hamifratz station every 10 minutes (*50mins/₪9.10*) and continue on to Nahariya (*1hr/₪11.50*). To Nazareth, NTT buses 332, 340 and 342 depart from Merkazit Hamifratz every 20 minutes (*45mins/₪16*), while Superbus 432 leaves every 30 minutes to Tiberias (*1hr/₪21.50*).

By train Haifa City has three train stations: Hof Hacarmel, Bat Galim and Merkaz Hashmona (Central) [168 F2], plus two on the outskirts, namely Haifa Merkazit Hamifratz and Hutsot Hamifratz. Trains depart to and from Tel Aviv every 20 minutes (*1hr/₪27.50*) and head north to Nahariya hourly (*30mins/₪17.50*) via Acre (*22mins/₪13.50*).

By air Haifa Airport (☎8476100) ranks as Israel's third-busiest airport after Ben-Gurion and Eilat and offers decently priced domestic flights to both cities. **Arkia** (☎03 6902222; w arkia.com) offers flights to and from Eilat starting at ₪210 one-way. **Lahak Aviation** (☎8555224; w lahakaviation.com) based in the airport can organise private jets and helicopter travel throughout Israel. Public transport to the airport is limited, but Egged bus 58 from Karyot bus station or Merkazit Hamifratz runs hourly. **Monitax taxis** (☎8664343) also serve the airport and wait outside the terminal building.

By sea Haifa's port has become a popular addition to the cruises that ply the Mediterranean waters, where passengers hop on to Jerusalem-bound coaches for a day in the Holy City. Most of the major cruise lines now include Israel on their itineraries. Cruises to Turkey, the Greek Islands and Italy can be arranged through **Mano Tours** (*2 Hapalyum St;* ✆*8606666;* w *mano.co.il*) and leave from the rather nice **Maritime Passenger Terminal** (✆*8518245;* w *haifaport.co.il*). Now there is also a **cruise ferry line** between Acre (Marina) and Haifa with daily departures (page 161).

ORIENTATION Haifa is divided into three distinct zones ranked one above another both in terms of geography and wealth. The **downtown area (Ir Hatahitt)** with its Old City, harbour and coastal areas is the lowest zone; the central zone is made up of the **Hadar Hacarmel district**, the city's main shopping and commercial hub and home to some of the older neighbourhoods; and **Central Carmel** in the upper reaches of the city, which comprises the richest residential neighbourhoods and luxury hotels and restaurants. The **University of Haifa** occupies the highest point and furthest reaches of the city where buildings meet the sweeping greenery of the Carmel National Park.

Walking around the city is possible, but tough going. The steep slopes are linked by thousands of steps that make a nice downhill tour (see below) and a cable car operates from **Bat Galim** to just below the **Carmelite monastery**. The city is also home to Israel's only subway system, the **Carmelit underground railway**. The unmistakable gardens of the **Shrine of Bab** lead down to the **German Colony** at its base, where countless restaurants and cafés line the main **Ben-Gurion Boulevard**. The major downtown roads are **Haatzmaut** and nearby **Jaffa Road**, both running along the coast, while the **Old City** is located one block back. Life in the Central Carmel district centres on **Hanassi Boulevard** with its pricey restaurants and trendy bars. In between these, **Herzl Street** forms the hub of activity in the Hadar Hacarmel, an area in serious need of a makeover. While it is the busiest shopping district in the city, it doesn't have an awful lot else going for it. Cheap eateries and budget hotels often attract those on a tighter budget, while **Nordau Pedestrian Precinct** has become the Russian centre of the city, inhabited by scores of immigrants who have added their stamp to the area.

GETTING AROUND Haifa's city centre cascades down Mount Carmel's northern slope, making for some interesting, but tiring, topography. Walking downhill is always an option but you'll soon run out of steam if you try and travel by foot. Thankfully Haifa has several good public transport options to combat foot fatigue, and it is also the only city in Israel where public transport runs on Shabbat (albeit limited services).

By bus Intra-city buses operate 05.00–23.30 Sunday–Thursday, 05.00–16.30 Friday, and a limited service runs 09.00–midnight Saturday. Fares within Haifa are ₪5.90. For more information, call ✆8549131. There are three express Metronit buses departing every 6 minutes during the week and every 20 minutes on Saturdays and holidays. Note that tickets for these three routes must be purchased/validated using a RavKav card at the bus stop before boarding.

- **#1** (Metronit) From Hof Hacarmel bus station along Hahaganah and James De Rothschild boulevards past Ben-Gurion Boulevard and Hashmona railway station, then on to Merkazit Hamifratz via Wadi Salib, terminating at Krayot Central bus station.
- **#2** (Metronit) From Bat Galim railway station along James De Rothschild Boulevard past Ben-Gurion Boulevard and Hashmona railway station, then on to Merkazit Hamifratz via Wadi Salib and heading east to Kiryat Ata along Yoseftal Boulevard.

- **#3** (Metronit) From Krayot Central bus station along Jerusalem Boulevard and Haitstadyon Street via Merkazit Hamifratz, then down Haneviim Boulevard.
- **#43** (Egged) Begins at Bat Galim railway station and runs along James De Rothschild Boulevard on to Hahaganah Boulevard, then on to Hamelekh Shlomo Street, terminating in Hof Hacarmel bus station.
- **#24** (Egged) Runs to the university on the fringes of the city. The route takes buses along Pika Road, past the Grand Canyon Mall, Rupin Road and Arlozorov Street. It then continues on to Hameginim and James De Rothschild boulevards past Hahaganah Boulevard and finishes at Hof Hacarmel bus station.
- **#99x** (Egged) Begins at Haaliyah Hashniya Street (Stella Maris cable car) and runs along James De Rothschild Boulevard and on to Stella Maris Road. From there it makes its way to Hanassi Boulevard.

By underground The Carmelit underground railway (✆*8376861;* **w** *carmelithaifa. com; trains run 06.00–22.00 Sun–Thu, 06.00–15.00 Fri; fare ₪6.60 one-way, ₪15 day ticket*) is Israel's one and only underground metro system and is a great way of avoiding the steps of central Haifa. The line starts at Paris Square in the downtown [169 G4] area and finishes at the Gan Haem Park in the Carmel Centre. There are four stations in between: Golomb Street, Masada Street, Neviim Street and Solel Boneh Square.

By cable car The Haifa cable car (✆ *8335970;* ⊕ *summer 09.00–20.00 daily, winter 10.00–18.00 daily; fare one-way/return ₪19/28*) consists of three little bubbles which zip up and down the steep slope between Bat Galim and the Stella Maris, offering lovely views over the harbour.

TOURIST INFORMATION AND TOUR OPERATORS Many of the nationwide tour operators arrange trips to and around the Haifa and Carmel region. A free **MP3 Haifa city tour** can be downloaded from **w** gpsmycity.com.

🛈 **Haifa Tourist Board** [168 B4] 48 Ben-Gurion Bd; ✆8535606; **w** visit-haifa.org; ⊕ 09.00–17.00 Sun–Thu, 09.00–13.00 Fri, 10.00–15.00 Sat. Can organise museum tickets, guides & accommodation.
Egged Tours ✆03 9203992; **w** eggedtours.com. These operate informative city bus tours that pass Haifa's top sights.

Issta Travel Agency ✆8118888; **w** issta.co.il. Has several branches around town, including in Haifa University, & can book budget air tickets.
The Society for the Protection of Nature in Israel (SPNI) [168 D2] 90 Jaffa Rd; ✆8553860; **e** bela@spni.org.il; **w** natureisrael.org. Has good hiking maps & can arrange trips to the Carmel National Park.

🏠 **WHERE TO STAY**
🏠 **Dan Panorama Hotel** [map, page 166] (267 rooms) 107 Hanassi Bd; ✆8352222; **e** t.panormamahaifa@danhotels.com; **w** danhotels.com. Modern, contemporary décor, swish rooms & fabulous bird's-eye views over Haifa & the harbour. It is linked to the flashy Panorama Shopping Centre & has 2 restaurants, a café & bar, fitness centre & sauna. **$$$$**
🏠 **The Colony Hotel** [168 C3] (40 rooms) 28 Ben-Gurion Bd; ✆8513344; **e** info@colony-hotel.

co.il; **w** colonyhaifa.com. Located in a restored 100-year-old building in the picturesque German Colony at the base of the Baha'i Gardens, this boutique hotel exudes classical elegant charm. A wide range of in-room facilities exists, as well as a full b/fast, café, bar, spa room & sun roof. **$$$$**
🏠 **Villa Carmel** [map, page 166] (16 rooms) 1 Heinrich Heine St; ✆8375777; **e** info@ villacarmel.co.il; **w** villacarmel.co.il/en. Classically elegant, newly renovated boutique hotel. Rooms

come with all mod cons & jacuzzi bath, & there is a restaurant & rooftop sun terrace. **$$$$**

⌂ Beth Shalom Hotel [map, page 166] (30 rooms) 110 Hanassi Bd; ☎8377481; w bethshalom.co.il. Perched high on Mount Carmel, this simple hotel is well tended, comfortable & good value for money. Rooms are uninspiring but clean & airy & come with TV, AC & phone. A small, leafy courtyard is a welcome spot to rest after a day of sightseeing. **$$$**

⌂ Gallery Hotel [map, page 166] (40 rooms) 61 Herzl St; ☎8616161; e gallery@hotelgallery.co.il; w haifa.hotelgallery.co.il. Boutique hotel decked out in minimalist elegance in Bauhaus architectural style. Luxury packages include room, gourmet b/fast & massages. Full range of facilities includes spa centre, money change & guided tours of the city. **$$$**

⌂ Haddad Guest House [168 C3] (11 rooms) 26 Ben-Gurion Bd; ☎077 2010618; e reservation@haddadguesthouse.com; w haddadguesthouse.com. Simple, clean rooms in a fantastic location in the heart of the German Colony come with kitchenette, TV, AC, etc. **$$$**

⌂ Marom Hotel [map, page 166] (48 rooms) 51 Palmach St; ☎8254355; e htlmarom@gmail.com; w marom.yolasite.com. Set on the outskirts

of the city amid spacious green gardens, the hotel offers good value. A gym, jacuzzi, spa & lovely outdoor seating areas make it a quiet & refreshing change from the hubbub of the city. **$$$**

⌂ Seaplaza Hotel [map, page 166] (42 rooms) 6 Bat Galim Bd; ☎8552222; e info@seaplaza.co.il; w seaplaza.co.il. A newly opened hotel offering holiday-style self-contained apts a few metres from the sea promenade & beach. There's also a pleasant rooftop terrace. **$$$**

⌂ Port Inn [168 F3] 34 Jaffa Rd; ☎8524401; e port_inn@yahoo.com; w portinn.co.il. Big, bright, airy rooms & a port view make this a refreshing option. Comfy lounge area with cable TV, fully equipped kitchen & dining room, laundry facilities, tourist information & a shady sun terrace make it one of the best budget choices. B/fast included. Private rooms & dorms. **$$–$**

⌂ Al-Yakhour Hostel [168 C2] (50 beds) 24 Ben-Gurion Bd; ☎077 6570928; e alyakhourhostel@gmail.com; w alyakhourhostel.com. An excellent new hostel in the heart of the German Colony. Rooms are clean & spacious. Facilities include communal kitchen & laundry. There is a bar with a good selection of refreshments at reasonable prices, & the outdoor courtyard is the perfect place to enjoy an evening drink. **$**

✗ WHERE TO EAT AND DRINK The **Turkish Market** area is a popular place to get a drink in the evening, and there are also a few good places to eat. The **Wadi Nisnas** district is famous for excellent falafel and hummus, while its souk that forms the core of the neighbourhood abounds with traditional Arabic fare at extremely low prices. The **German Colony** boasts a number of elegant dining options, trendy cafés and wonderful ice-cream parlours, while **Central Carmel** is renowned for being the *pièce de résistance* of eating out in Haifa. The best restaurants can be found alongside five-star hotels with views over the city and harbour.

✗ Hanamal 24 [168 G3] 24 Hanamal St; ☎8628899; ◷ noon–midnight Mon–Sat. Haifa's most exclusive eatery has elegant, classic décor & a hugely varied menu composed of prime meats (including ostrich), exotic & local fish & sumptuous pastas. **$$$$$**

✗ Fattoush [168 C3] 38 Ben-Gurion Bd; ☎8524930; w fattoushhaifa.com; ◷ 09.00–01.00 daily. Great location in the German Colony with a lovely shady terrace. Arabic menu of big b/fasts, salads, hummus & traditional meals. Lovely décor & ambience at any time of the day. **$$$**

✗ Jacko Seafood [168 G4] 12 Kehilat Saloniki St; ☎8102355; ◷ noon–midnight daily. First

branch of this 30-year-old chain of well-loved fish & seafood restaurants. Countless different fish, shellfish & seafood cooked any way you like it. There is another branch at 11 Moriah Bd [map, page 166]. **$$$**

✗ Maayan Habira [168 G4] 4 Natanzon St; ☎8623193. An excellent place for a meal or a drink in the heart of the Turkish Market. Has indoor & outdoor seating. The menu ranges from Israeli food to Russian *pelmenis*. Excellent beer selection. **$$$**

✗ Shamli Bulgarian Grill [168 F2] 56 Jaffa Rd; ☎8529842; e shamli1876@hotmail.com; w 2eat.co.il/shamli; ◷ noon–17.00 Sat–Thu, noon–

15.00 Fri. Founded in Sofia, Bulgaria in 1876, this authentic gem is managed by 2 brothers, Yossi & Moshe Shamli, who relocated the 5-generation family business to Israel in the 1990s. The recipe for the succulent meatballs (*ktitza*) & kebab prepared on charcoal is a closely guarded family secret. The eatery is tiny, but look out for the large Bulgarian flag in the window. $$

✘ **Abu Shakker** [168 G4] 29 Hameginim Bd; ⏱ 06.00–18.30 daily. Tiny hummus joint that is super popular with locals. Squeeze on to one of the 7 tables & enjoy a meal of hummus, chips, salad & *mejadra*, a bowl of hot rice & lentils. $

✘ **Najla (Falafel Hazkenim)** [168 D4] 18 Wadi St; ⏱ 08.00–19.00 Mon–Sat. Tiny place in the heart of Wadi Nisnas. Best falafel in town since 1950. $

▱ **Shani Café** [168 F3] 55 Haatzmaut Rd; ⏱ 05.30–17.30 daily. Open since 1964, this small place, although lacking in décor, sells amazing pastries. Good for a quick coffee or take-away. $

ENTERTAINMENT AND NIGHTLIFE
The arts

▣ **Haifa Auditorium** 138 Hanassi Bd; ☏ 8353506; w ethos.co.il. Seating up to 1,200 people, the auditorium plays host to concerts & events throughout the year. Buses 21, 22, 23, 28 & 37 stop outside, or take the Carmelit railway to Gan Haem station.

▣ **Haifa Municipal Theatre** 50 Pevsner St; ☏ 8600555, box office 8605000. Has regular performances, but few are in English.

▣ **Haifa Symphony Orchestra** 7 Mahanayim St; ☏ 8338888. One of the country's top orchestras with national & debut performances.

▰ **The Cinematheque** 142 Hanassi Bd; ☏ 8338888; w haifacin.co.il; ⏱ 18.00–20.00 daily. The hub of all things cinematic. Twice-daily showings of non-mainstream films, cinema courses & a huge auditorium are on offer.

Bars Haifa offers plenty of decent & varied bars & pubs. The main cluster of bars is along Moriah Bd, which turns into Hanassi St.

▽ **Barbarossa** 8 Hapika St; ☏ 6895589; w barbarossa.co.il; ⏱ 18.00–late daily. Modern meat & seafood restaurant with a great bar atmosphere. They offer 9 types of beer, 110 types of whisky, some wonderful Italian appetisers & a mean hamburger ($$$). Attracts a slightly older crowd.

▽ **Brown** 131 Moriah Bd; ☏ 8112391; w brown-bar.com; ⏱ 19.00–06.00 daily. Leather-seated booths, wooden tables & cosy lighting make this a good choice for a relaxed beer & light meal. Music ranges from 1980s hits to Israeli & international rock.

▽ **Morrison** 115 Yefe Nof St; m 052 2722787; ⏱ 20.00–late daily. Highly popular rock/pick-up bar that hosts Mon open mic nights, Tue live performances (starting at 22.00) & Wed student nights.

▽ **Pundak Hadov (The Bear)** 135 Hanassi Bd; ☏ 8381703; ⏱ 17.00–late Sat–Wed, 11.00–late Fri. Cosy pub with indoor & outdoor seating, an extensive cocktail menu, decent pub food & a mellow atmosphere. Often shows live sporting events (when the atmosphere is a little less mellow).

SHOPPING The awkward city layout is not conducive to window-shopping, and as such Haifa has become known for its numerous malls and shopping centres. The gargantuan **Grand Canyon Mall** (*Simcha Golan Way, Neve Shaanan;* ↘ *8121111;* ⊕ *10.00–22.00 Sun–Thu, 10.00–15.00 Fri, end of Shabbat–22.30 Sat*) is one of Israel's largest shopping centres with 150 shops, an indoor amusement park, countless food outlets and a spa. Although built in 1986, the **Panorama Center** (*109 Hanassi Bd;* ↘ *8375011;* ⊕ *09.00–20.00 Sun–Thu*), located in the Carmel Centre, remains a firm favourite and has a great variety of shops, cinemas and cafés. A similar grand shopping centre is the **Auditorium Square Mall** (*134 Hanassi Bd;* ↘ *8103980;* ⊕ *09.00–21.00 Sun–Thu, 09.00–14.00 Fri*) located just a few blocks away next to Haifa Auditorium. The **City Center** [168 D1] (*6 Ben-Gurion Bd;* ↘ *8530111;* ⊕ *10.00–20.00 Sat–Thu, 09.30–14.00 Fri*) is considerably smaller than the others, but it's useful if you're in the German Colony area and has more high-end shops.

Away from the malls, **Talpiot Market** [169 G6] sells a lovely array of spices and fresh fruit and vegetables and is a nice alternative to the glitzy malls, while **Herzl** and **Nordau streets** are your best bet for shopping. On Friday and Saturday mornings around Feisal Square, there is a **flea market** (*Wadi Salib bus stop*) for curios and bric-a-brac. For **camping supplies**, Lametayel (*2 Kdoshei Yassi St;* ↘ *077 3334508*) stocks a good range. At Steimatzky [169 F7] (*16 Herzl St;* ↘ *8665042;* ⊕ *08.30–19.00 Sun–Thu, 08.30–14.00 Fri*), you'll find plenty of English-language **books** and newspapers. Haifa **museum shops** have an excellent selection of handicrafts, souvenirs and jewellery.

OTHER PRACTICALITIES The central **post office** is located at 22a Haneviim Boulevard [169 E7] (↘ *8304351;* ⊕ *08.00–18.00 Sun–Thu, 08.00–noon Fri*), while other branches can be found at 19 Hapalyam Boulevard, 152 Jaffa Road, 63 Herzl Street and 7 Wedgewood Boulevard. There are numerous **banks** with **ATMs** in the city, of which **Bank Hapoalim** [169 E6] (*18 Haneviim Bd;* ↘ *03 6532407;* ⊕ *08.30–13.15 Sun & Tue–Wed, 08.30–13.00 & 16.00–18.30 Mon & Thu*) and **Bank Leumi** [168 F3] (*21 Jaffa St;* ↘ *03 9544555;* ⊕ *08.30–14.45 Sun–Thu, 08.30–noon Fri*) are the most convenient. **Hospitals** nearest to the centre are **Bnei Zion** (*Rothschild*) (*47 Golomb St;* ↘ *8359359*), **Rambam** (*Bat Galim;* ↘ *8543111*), **Italian Hospital** [168 B1] (*106 Hameginim Bd;* ↘ *8514294*) and emergency service **Magen David Adom** [168 B1] (*10 Yitshak Sadeh St;* ↘ *8512233*) is located around the corner from the Italian Hospital. The most central pharmacy is **Green City Pharm** [168 C2] (*97 Hameginim Bd;* ↘ *8333633;* ⊕ *09.00–21.00 Sun–Thu, 09.00–19.00 Fri*). **Superpharm** has numerous stores in town, including in the City Centre Mall [168 D1] (*6 Ben-Gurion Bd;* ↘ *8507755;* ⊕ *09.00–22.00 Sun–Thu, 09.00–16.00 Fri, 08.00–23.00 Sat*) and Auditorium Haifa Mall (*134 Hanassi Bd;* ↘ *8104844;* ⊕ *08.30–10.30 Sun–Thu, 08.00–17.00 Fri, 08.00–23.00 Sat*).

WHAT TO SEE AND DO
Baha'i Shrine and Persian Gardens [169 B6] The immense golden dome of
the Shrine of Bab (⊕ *09.00–noon daily; admission free; modest dress: women & men must cover shoulders & knees*) and Persian gardens (↘ *8313131;* ⊕ *09.00–17.00 daily except 9 Jul & 2 May; admission & tour free*) dominate Haifa's skyline and are the world centre and one of the holiest sites of pilgrimage for members of the Baha'i faith. The gardens were designed by the Iranian-Canadian architect Fariborz Sahba and completed in 2001. The land and buildings on the present site have been gradually purchased and built using private donations. The first structure was built in 1953 over the burial place of Sayyed Ali Mohammed Shirazi, known as 'the Bab',

founder of the faith. Overall, there are 19 terraced gardens created for 18 disciples and the Bab himself which are adorned with 2,200 lamps to commemorate the time spent by the Bab in a Persian prison starved of light.

The gardens are divided into three levels, each with its own entrance. The **southern entrance** [169 A7] is located just below Yefe Nof Street, where grand marble steps stretch through immaculate gardens and past vibrant flowerbeds amid terracotta pieces. It is at this entrance that the daily English-language tour starts at noon. The tour is general, but nonetheless provides a good introduction to the site and is the only way to see the second level of terraces in full. It concludes at the **middle entrance** [169 B6] at Hatsiyonut Boulevard from where you enter to visit the shrine itself. Inside the shrine on the wall is the Tablet of Visitation prayer. There are public and Baha'i visiting hours in order to allow for praying time. The **northern entrance** [168 B4] is at the UNESCO Square at the top of Ben-Gurion Boulevard.

The world centre in Haifa is also the administrative centre and archive for the followers of the faith. In Baha'ism, there are no priests and all matters are decided collectively at the gathering of the faith's representatives.

Wadi Nisnas Translated as 'Mongoose Valley', Wadi Nisnas remains the effervescent heart of the city. This pleasant Arab neighbourhood is a fascinating place to visit. There are various communities living here, Muslim and Christian, and the market and narrow alleys are buzzing with life, Arabic sweet shops, and hummus. Wadi Nisnas is also home to an Armenian community who settled in Haifa to escape the Armenian genocide. **St Yeghia Armenian Church** [169 E5], hidden amid the narrow alleys, is the religious heart of the community here. Every year in December, the neighbourhood puts on the **Hag Hahagim** (Festival of all Festivals) in which Jews, Christians and Muslims take part in a celebration of Hanukkah, Christmas and Ramadan. The **Beit Hagefen Jewish-Arab Culture Centre** [169 D5] (*33 Hatsiyonut Bd;* ✆ *8525252;* w *beit-hagefen.com;* ⊕ *08.00–13.00 & 16.00–20.00 Sun–Thu, 08.00–13.00 Fri, 10.00–13.00 Sat*) arranges various art exhibitions, events and tours of Wadi Nisnas, and it is best to call in advance.

Tel Shiqmona Although somewhat neglected and overgrown, the ruins of the Byzantine settlement will surprise you with the mosaics they hide. They are located to the left of the National Institute of Oceanography but can be tricky to find. To return to the city, walk along the shore to Bat Galim for a pleasant stroll. Alternatively, bus 1 departs from the Ein Hayam stop and departs every 6 minutes in the direction of either of the two main bus stations.

Cave of Elijah (*230 Allenby Rd;* ✆ *8527430;* ⊕ *08.00–18.00 Sun–Thu (17.00 in winter), 08.00–13.00 Fri; admission free; modest dress*) According to tradition, Elijah the Prophet spent many years living in a cave nestled into Carmel Mountain and many significant events in his life are said to have happened here. It was in this cave that he lived and meditated before defeating the Priests of Baal at Al-Muhraka (page 183); he took refuge here from King Ahab and his wife Jezebel; and established his school here on his return from exile. It is also said to be the place where the Holy Family took shelter on their return from Egypt. Today the cave is worshipped by Jews, Christians, Druze and Muslims (who had a mosque here until 1948), who all venerate Elijah. Inside the cave is a small altar, illuminated by candles which can be bought for ₪2 from vendors at the base of the steps leading up to the cave. The steps and entrance are located on Allenby Road, 100m from the Maritime Museum but signposted in Hebrew only.

Stella Maris (*Mount Carmel;* ☏*8337758;* ⊕ *06.20–12.30 & 15.00–18.00 Mon–Sat; admission free; modest dress*) The 19th-century Carmelite monastery is located high on the slopes of Mount Carmel, offering fabulous views over the bay of Haifa and north towards Lebanon. Members of the 12th-century Carmelite order were exiled following the conquest by the Mamluk sultan Baibars, and didn't return until the 18th century when the monastery was commissioned. During Napoleon's unsuccessful attack on Acre, an earlier monastery on the grounds was used as a hospital for wounded French soldiers who were promptly slaughtered by the Turks upon Napoleon's retreat. In front of the monastery is a **monument** to the soldiers who died. The beautiful church that stands today is constructed of bright white marble, and the dome is adorned with paintings depicting stories from the Old Testament. The **cable car** (☏*8335970;* ⊕ *10.00–18.30 Sat–Thu, 10.00–17.30 Fri & public holidays; fare one-way/return ₪25/35*) makes its final stop opposite the monastery next to the **lighthouse**. The street opposite the Stella Maris hit the headlines in 2006 when it became the first place in Haifa to be struck by a Hezbollah Katyusha rocket.

German Colony The main street through the recently renovated colony is Ben-Gurion Boulevard, which begins at the base of the Baha'i shrine and runs south to Hameginim Avenue. The 30m-wide boulevard is lined with stone houses, courtyards, large, leafy trees, trendy restaurants, outdoor cafés and ice-cream parlours, and is one of the undoubted highlights of any trip to Haifa. In the evening when the Persian Gardens are illuminated it makes for a lovely setting in which to sip on an iced coffee and enjoy the ambience.

University The university has claim to some of the prime real estate in Haifa, with fantastic views over both the harbour and city and Carmel Mountain range. The 30th floor of the Eshkol Tower has been converted into an **observatory** and is unarguably the best viewpoint in the city. The **Hecht Museum** (☏*8257773;* w *mushecht.haifa.ac.il;* ⊕ *10.00–16.00 Sun–Mon & Wed–Thu, 10.00–16.00 Tue, 10.00–19.00 Fri, 10.00–14.00 Sat; admission free*) is located within the university grounds, and features, apart from archaeological collections, 19th- and 20th-century paintings and sculptures, including works by Monet, Pissarro and Van Gogh.

Museums A combination ticket for many of Haifa's museums can be purchased at the museums' box offices for ₪60 for adults and ₪35 for children. Each museum has a good shop with an excellent selection of souvenirs and handicrafts.

Haifa Museum of Art [169 D5] (*26 Shabtai Levi St;* ☏*9115997;* ⊕ *10.00–16.00 Sun–Wed, 16.00–19.00 Thu, 10.00–13.00 Fri, 10.00–15.00 Sat; admission adult/child ₪45/30*) The museum incorporates the Museum of Modern Art and the Museum of Ancient Art and has departments dedicated to ethnography, folklore and Jewish ritual art. There are good archaeological exhibits of finds from Haifa and Caesarea and a collection of over 7,000 international and Israeli contemporary art pieces. Originally an English School for Girls that operated between 1930 and 1948, the building was converted into the museum in 1978.

Haifa City Museum [168 D2] (*11 Ben-Gurion Bd;* ☏*9115888;* w *hms.org.il/eng;* ⊕ *10.00–18.00 Sun–Wed, 16.00–19.00 Thu, 10.00–13.00 Fri, 10.00–15.00 Sat; admission adult/child ₪35/23*) A small city museum in the heart of the German Colony tells the story of Haifa from its foundation by Daher Al-Omar Al-Zaydani and has exhibitions of personal stories of Haifa's residents.

National Maritime Museum (*198 Allenby Rd;* ✆*8536622;* ⏰ *10.00–16.00 Sun–Thu, 10.00–13.00 Fri, 10.00–15.00 Sat; admission adult/child ₪35/23*) The museum depicts the maritime history and development of shipbuilding in the region. Four floors of collections cover a whole spectrum of themes including maritime mythology, piracy, the Greeks and Romans, scientific instruments, naval ships and shipping over the past 5,000 years.

Tikotin Museum of Japanese Art (*89 Hanassi Bd;* ✆*8383554;* ⏰ *10.00–16.00 Sun–Thu, 10.00–13.00 Fri, 10.00–15.00 Sat; admission adult/child ₪35/23*) The museum displays a unique collection of ancient and modern Japanese art.

Clandestine Immigration and Naval Museum (*204 Allenby Rd;* ✆ *072 2798030;* ⏰ *10.00–16.00 Sun–Thu; admission adult/child ₪15/10*) is easily identified by the large British blockade ship the *Af-Al-Pi-Chen* outside, which was at the centre of skirmishes between British officials and immigrants attempting to land in the country following World War II. The museum, opened in 1969, is devoted to Israeli naval history and the clandestine immigration (haapala), but pales in comparison with the National Maritime Museum.

Railway Museum (*1 Hativat Golani St;* ✆*8564293;* ⏰ *08.30–15.30 Sun–Thu; admission adult/child ₪20/15*) The picturesque old train station dates to the Ottoman period, and has been restored complete with a steam train to make a pleasant museum complex. It also depicts Israel's funicular history.

BEACHES AND ACTIVITIES Beaches in Haifa can be divided into two types: official, with bars, restaurants and the full set of facilities; and unofficial, which have none of these. The younger set tends to enjoy the unofficial beaches, where the wild sands and sea are facilities enough, while families often opt for the official beaches. **Carmel Beach** marks the beginning of the unofficial beaches, from which uninterrupted sand sweeps the length of the coast as far as Atlit naval base. Just south of Carmel Beach is the ever-popular **Student's Beach**. Official beaches are located between Carmel Beach and the Meridien Hotel and around Bat Galim. **Bat Galim Surfers' Beach** and **Shiqmona Beach** are the most popular with surfers, windsurfers and kite surfers but often too rough for swimming. Opposite the Clandestine Museum is a **windsurfing centre** where equipment can be hired. The religious **Hashaket Beach** is one of the quietest in the city, with pond-like waters and plenty of shade. Men and women have separate swimming days except Saturdays when it is open to all (*women: Sun, Tue, Thu; men: Mon, Wed, Fri*). The **Ze'ev Hayam Diving Club** (*Kishon Port;* ✆*8323911, 8662005;* ⏰ *08.00–17.00 daily*) offers dive trips to sites in and around Haifa, where several wrecks have created reefs. **Harbour cruises** (*Kishon Port;* ✆*8418765; fare adult/child ₪30/25*) operate tours three times a day during Passover, Sukkot and summer school holidays. There is a possibility of getting on group-booked cruises at other times of year, but you need to call ahead.

MOUNT CARMEL

Mount Carmel is a 23km-long limestone mountain ridge extending from Haifa in the north to the Galilee in the east and as far as the coastal Plain of Sharon in the south. Its rich, fertile soils have long been a draw for settlers, taking advantage of its lush greenery and thriving plant and animal species for as long as 200,000 years.

MEDITERRANEAN COAST

Gordon, Frishman and Bograshov beaches The city centre's most popular beaches are frequented by the complete cross-section of Tel Aviv's eclectic population. A wealth of amenities, cafés, restaurants, lifeguards and beach beds combined with the wide, golden sands make this the best city beach in the country.

Beit Yannai About 20 minutes north of Netanya is this wild, sweeping stretch of pristine coast which is the pride and joy of the residents who live in the cosy little moshavs nearby. With a definite neighbourhood feel, high rocky cliffs, scampering dogs, a rustic little café and miles of open sand, it exemplifies Israeli beach culture.

Achziv With the crumbling ruins of an old Arab fishing village (page 158) forming the backdrop, this northern Mediterranean beach is a hidden paradise. Sheltered pools have been carved out of the rocky shoreline, their warm, shallow waters glimmering a vibrant turquoise under the summer sun.

Dor Beach Sheltered lagoons of shallow, turquoise waters make Dor Beach (page 184) one of the most picturesque spots in which to take a dip (although during summer holidays it is hugely crowded).

SEA OF GALILEE

Ein Gev Resort Village Beach As the biblical waters of the Sea of Galilee lap against the green-grassed shores, an air of tranquillity and spirituality descends over the private resort village. In contrast to its more rambunctious neighbours along the coast, the Ein Gev Beach and those just to the south of it, characterise the air of mysticism that most hope to find.

DEAD SEA With its sulphur pools, the beach at the **Ein Gedi Sea of Spa** (page 283) is a great way to enjoy the richness of minerals from the Dead Sea. There are a few wild beaches along the coast, but getting to some of them requires an arduous hike or a 4x4 vehicle.

RED SEA

Coral Beach Reserve The aquatic, fish-laden tropical garden of Eilat's Coral Beach Reserve is the best-preserved stretch of Israel's Red Sea coast. Rainbow-coloured fish, swirling corals and the year-round warm, gentle waters make this one of the prettiest beaches in the country.

The area is today under the umbrella of the Mount Carmel National Park (\8231452; *admission ₪33/car, free on foot*) which is wholly dedicated to the preservation of this natural heritage and the indigenous habitat of the area.

The Carmel was designated a national park in 1971 and incorporates (among a whole host of picturesque and historically significant sites) the **Hai Bar Wildlife Reserve**, **Ein Hod** artists' village, **Muhraka Monastery** and **Carmel Caves**. You can easily spend days exploring the area and it is certainly a justifiable expenditure of your time, although the devastating forest fire in December 2010 destroyed a great portion of the park (see box, page 181). The area also sustained significant damage during the wildfires in November 2016 that engulfed vast stretches of Israel from the Dead Sea to the Mediterranean.

The Mediterranean scrub forest, with its carob and rare kermes oak trees, provides for some wonderful walks, picnic and camping spots, cycling, jeep trips and nature spotting, and it is a strong favourite with weekending Israelis. Several streams flow through the mountains, including Nahal Mearot, which can be accessed through the Nahal Mearot (Carmel Caves) Nature Reserve, and Nahal Galim.

HISTORY Sacred to Christians, Jews, Muslims and Baha'is alike, the Carmel region has seen its fair share of triumphs and defeats over the past 200,000 years. From the skeletal remains of a Neanderthal couple that were unearthed from one of the caves that dot the landscape, to World War I when the area's strategic prowess was drawn upon, a wealth of stories emerges. The 20th-century Battle of Meggido that took place on the head of the ridge saw British general Allenby lead his troops to victory, a battle considered a turning point in the war against the Ottoman Empire.

Even as early as Canaanite times, the region was considered holy, and Baal of Canaan was worshipped from the hilltops. According to Jewish, Christian and Islamic belief, it was here that Elijah battled the prophets of Baal in a contest to determine the rightful ruler of the Kingdom of Israel and where, upon his victory, fire rained from the skies. The Assyrians conquered the area in 732BCE, restoring the worship of Baal of Canaan, who was associated by the Greeks with the god Zeus and was known to the Romans as Deus Carmelus. The 12th-century Carmelites, a Catholic religious order, founded a monastery at the site of Elijah's victory which, during the Crusades, was converted into a mosque, hence its present-day name Muhraka, meaning 'place of burning'. It was later restored (page 183). In some Christian traditions, it is celebrated that at this site Mary, mother of Jesus, gave the Scapular of Our Lady of Mount Carmel (a symbolic devotional cloth) to a British Carmelite.

GETTING THERE AND AROUND Buses from Haifa's city centre will drop you at the park's northern entrance near Haifa University. The rest of the park runs parallel with the coast and can be entered from any point (see individual sites for more transport directions). Renting a car is by far the best way to get the most out of a trip to Carmel National Park as public transport runs only along main arteries and does not delve into the heart of the park itself.

WHERE TO STAY Carmel National Park covers a wide area and accommodation options are found scattered throughout the small settlements within it. Good choices for the quintessential picturesque Carmel experience are **Ein Hod** (page 182), **Dor Beach** (page 184) and **Zichron Yaakov** (pages 185–8). Campsites are also dotted throughout the park.

WHERE TO EAT AND DRINK Druze villages dot the landscape and their hospitality (and food) is well renowned among Israelis. Small, makeshift stalls can be found in clearings by the side of the road, huddled between the trees for shade from the summer sun. They sell locally made olive oil in rudimentary bottles as well as freshly made *labneh* cheese balls, pitta and *zatar*; you haven't experienced the Carmel until you've sat on their small plastic stools and wolfed down a traditional Druze meal. Zichron Yaakov and Ein Hod both have some high-quality restaurants as well as funky little cafés.

On 2 December 2010, a ferocious fire broke out on the Carmel Mountain just south of Haifa and spread quickly through the region, raging for four days. It is believed the fire started near the Druze town of Isfiya, but it is not fully clear why or how the fire began. Extremely dry conditions and little annual rainfall combined with flammable scrub and pine forests meant the fire moved quickly, decimating entire stretches of the beautiful mountain ridge and claiming 44 lives – making it the worst fire in Israeli history. Thirty-seven prison service cadets were trapped and killed in their minibus when the flames engulfed the area and several firefighters lost their lives.

The Israel fire and rescue services, along with the police, IDF soldiers and volunteer firefighters battled to control the blaze, but eventually Israel had to request international help. Firefighting teams, helicopters and planes from the US, Turkey, Greece, the Netherlands, Switzerland, Cyprus, Russia and the UK were dispatched and help from countless other countries was offered.

The damage wreaked by the fire is extensive. Entire villages have been destroyed, acres of land reduced to ashes, sensitive ecological areas have vanished and an estimated 1.5 million trees burnt down. Some 17,000 people were evacuated in a mass operation, and villages such as Kibbutz Beit Oren, Ein Hod and Nir Etzion were severely affected.

WHAT TO SEE AND DO
Nahal Mearot (Wadi Al-Mughara) Nature Reserve (✆ *9841750;* w *parks.org. il;* ⊕ *summer 08.00–17.00, winter 08.00–16.00 (closes 1hr earlier on Fri); admission adult/child ₪22/9)* Nahal Mearot Nature Reserve, as it is officially known, sits amid the lush vegetation of the Carmel Mountain range and centres on three large caves. The site, which was added to the UNESCO World Heritage List in 2012, has proved to be of crucial importance in prehistoric archaeological investigations, finds indicating that the caves were settled continuously for 200,000 years. This almost unprecedented discovery has highlighted three different prehistoric cultures and a great many artefacts, and has contributed greatly to the study of human evolution. The caves are perched a short walk from the visitors' centre. The first of the three is the Oven Cave, which displays a chronology of the long life of the area, while the smaller Carmel Cave has a reconstruction display of life during the Mousterian period (40,000–100,000 years ago). The last and most impressive Al-Wad Cave is 70m long and provides visitors with an insight into prehistoric life with the aid of an audio-visual presentation and some resident bats flapping overhead.

A network of signposted trails leads from the centre of the reserve through the surrounding countryside and along the Carmel range. In spring and summer, the area is awash with wild flowers, whose scents fill the air, and it makes for some delightful and undemanding walks. Helpful and knowledgeable guides can take you on hikes or point you in the right direction, and maps are available in the visitors' centre.

Getting there and away The site is located a 10-minute walk from the Ein Carmel junction (*Tzomet Ein Carmel*). Bus 921, operated by Egged between Haifa Merkazit, Hof Hacarmel and Tel Aviv central bus station every 30 minutes, stops here on request. From the junction walk approximately 500m south, cross the road and follow signs to the park (350m).

Mediterranean Coast MOUNT CARMEL

5

EIN HOD The tiny artists' village of Ein Hod lies hidden in a sea of deep green, nestled against Carmel Mountain and surrounded by pine forests and olive groves. Whether you're an art lover or not, the picturesque beauty of this unique little village shouldn't be missed. With stunning views over the Mediterranean, visitors can spend anything from a few hours to several days immersing themselves in the creativity that emanates from every household. Painting, sculpting, ceramics, acting, stained-glass printing, photography and glass blowing are just some of the artistic techniques that visitors can observe, or partake in (workshops are designed for all levels).

Getting there and away Bus 921 runs between Tel Aviv and Haifa and is the closest to Ein Hod that you can get on public transport. Ask the driver to stop at the Nir Etzion junction from where it is a 1km walk east. Alternatively, the village lies on the Israel National Trail and is a pleasant and relatively easy hike (*5.3km, approx 1hr 30mins*) from the Nahal Mearot (Wadi Al-Mughara) Nature Reserve (page 181).

Tourist information The **Ein Hod Information Centre** (m *054 4811968*; w *einhod.info*) can book **guided tours** and help make reservations for accommodation and workshops.

🏠 **Where to stay** Bed-and-breakfast accommodation is plentiful, luxurious and pricey.

🏠 **ArtRest Zimmers** (2 rooms) m 054 3548466; e arma@netvision.net.il. Clearly designed by an artistic hand, these beautiful suites are reminiscent of a royal boudoir, oozing class & minimalist elegance. AC, TV & DVD, fully fitted kitchen, herb garden, private entrance, sea views & a huge mosaic bath. **$$$$**

🏠 **Yakir Ein Hod** (3 rooms) ✆9842656; m 050 5543982; e yakir_g@zahav.co.il; w yakireinhod.

co.il/en. Fully equipped luxury zimmers complete with private balcony with sea view & swimming pool. **$$$$**

🏠 **Batia and Claude** (1 room) ✆9841648; m 050 5319266; e batjan@research.haifa.ac.il. The cheapest of 3 rustic stone cottages. Simple & clean with a very pleasant garden, private entrance, AC, shower & TV. **$$$**

✗ **Where to eat and drink** There are three restaurants in the village: **Doña Rosa** (m *053 9345530*; ☉ *12.30–22.30 Mon–Sat*; **$$$**) boasts prime Argentinian meat dishes; **Abu Yaakov** (✆*9843377*; ☉ *11.00–21.00 Mon–Sat*; **$**) serves Middle Eastern salads, meats and hummus; **Café Ein Hod** (m *054 4801985*; ☉ *08.30–19.00 Tue–Sun, until late Thu*; **$$**) offers a bohemian caffeine kick with a splash of secondhand arts and crafts blended in, plus Indian-style food and big breakfasts. For locally brewed beer, the **Art Bar** (✆ *9840071*; ☉ *10.00–15.00 Sun & Tue, 10.00–15.00 & 20.00–midnight Mon & Thu–Fri*) produces the perfect accompaniment for lounging under the shade of an ancient olive tree.

What to see and do

Janco Dada Museum ✆9842350; w jancodada.co.il; ☉ 10.00–15.00 Sun–Thu, 10.00–14.00 Fri, 10.00–15.30 Sat; admission adult/child ₪24/12. Celebrates Marcel Janco, Ein Hod's founder & a member of the Dada movement of modern art. The tree at the entrance to the museum was planted in 1983 by Haim Herzog, President of Israel.

Artists' Gallery ✆9842548; ☉ 10.00–17.00 Sun–Thu, 10.00–14.00 Fri, 11.00–16.00 Sat. Exhibits one of the country's largest collections of Israeli art.
Nisco Museum of Mechanical Music m 052 4755313; ☉ 10.00–17.00 daily; admission adult/child ₪30/20. Displaying antique music boxes. There are guided tours every hr.

Isfiya and Daliat Al-Carmel These once separate towns merged in 2003 to become what is now officially known as Carmel City (although they are still commonly known by their original names). Located about half an hour from Haifa, the first one you arrive at is **Isfiya**. The populations are predominantly Druze and the people's legendary hospitality draws locals and foreigners alike to bargain in the markets, eat in the traditional Middle Eastern restaurants and experience the unique atmosphere of their secretive religion. Older men wear the traditional long gowns and headdresses, often sporting a large bushy moustache while the younger set has adopted a more modern style. In keeping with other Druze settlements square, Arabic-style houses characterise the architecture, the affluence and industriousness of its rural inhabitants clearly displayed. Unfortunately the big fire in 2010 (see box, page 181) destroyed much of the surrounding countryside here and with it the once-lovely views over the green hills and terraced fields.

Historically, it is possible that Isfiya, built on the ruins of an earlier Byzantine settlement, formed the centre of Crusader rule in the area, judging by extensive excavated finds. The 5th-century Jewish settlement of Husifah was excavated, which included a synagogue and mosaic floor bearing the inscription 'Peace be upon Israel', while copious amounts of gold coins dating from the Roman period demonstrate the town's extent at that time. The modern city of Isfiya was founded in the 18th century, when residents prospered from a flourishing agricultural economy. Today, the population of Isfiya alone is 9,000, 70% being Druze, the remainder Christian and Muslim.

Daliat Al-Carmel is the largest and most southerly of all Israel's Druze towns. The 13,000 Druze residents have traced their ancestry back to Aleppo (Halab in Arabic) in Syria, which explains their strong accents and the frequency of the surname Halabi. Today, Daliat Al-Carmel, whose name means 'Vine Branches of the Carmel', boasts a large central market selling handmade Druze crafts and products, and its streets teem with rudimentary yet delectable local eateries. Markets are closed on Fridays.

Getting there and away Bus 37/37x leaves Haifa Bat Galim bus station several times a day (*40mins/₪6.40*). Sheruts leave Haifa regularly between 06.00 and 18.00, departing from the Hadar at the corner of Shemaryahu Levin and Herzl streets.

Muhraka Monastery (m *052 8779686;* ⊕ *Apr–Sep 08.00–12.30 daily, Oct–Mar 14.30–17.00 daily; admission ₪3*) Just south of the Druze town of Daliat Al-Carmel, a winding mountain road leads through a dense oak and pine forest to Muhraka, today the site of a Carmelite monastery. Tradition states that it was at this site that the Prophet Elijah battled the priests of Baal amid fire that rained down from the heavens. Elijah then had the priests taken to Tel Kasis (the 'priests' mound' in Arabic) at the foot of Mount Carmel along the Kishon Stream, where they were slaughtered.

The Carmelite monastery that now stands on the site was constructed during the Crusades, and the four monks residing there today tend the quaint, peaceful gardens. The view from the top of the monastery is unrivalled. It is possible, especially on clear days, to see right across the Galilee to the Jezreel Valley, Nazareth, Mount Tavor and even Mount Hermon. While of obvious biblical significance, the true magic of Muhraka lies in the picturesque landscape and staggering vista, a strong contender for the best in Israel.

The area around Muhraka provides for some fantastic walks, where the only other people you are likely to bump into are goat herders and their flocks. The Society for the Protection of Nature in Israel (page 44) in Haifa sells good hiking maps of the Carmel range.

Getting there and away Bus 37a from downtown Haifa will take you to Daliat Al-Carmel where it is a half-hour walk to the site. By car, follow signs from Daliat Al-Carmel and take a right when the forest road forks.

Atlit The **Atlit Detention Camp for Illegal Immigrants** (✆ *9841980;* w *eng.shimur. org;* ⊕ *09.00–17.00 Sun–Thu, 09.00–13.00 Fri; admission adult/child ₪17/14*) was set up by British Mandate authorities in 1938 to house immigrants arriving in Palestine. The immigrants included refugees and Holocaust survivors from the Nazi regime as well as people escaping anti-Jewish persecution in Arab countries. The historic site, located on the original grounds of the camp, commemorates those who were kept here, and educates people of their plight. The emphasis is on personal stories, and a large archive has been commissioned to record individual tales. Stories of heroism, escape, and a battle for freedom are depicted through the restored barracks. The ship seen from the highway on the approach to the camp belongs to the site and was one of the 130 vessels used to transport the refugees to Israel. Guided tours can be arranged but you need to book in advance.

Nearby, perched at the end of Atlit's promontory, is an impressive UNESCO-listed **Crusader fortress**. Built in 1218, its main function was to control the coastal road with the aim of recovering Jerusalem. While the site has roots in prehistoric, Roman and medieval times, it was during the Crusader occupation of the area that the fortress and promontory were strongly fortified, and these are the remains we see today. While not comparable to the great fortresses of Montfort (pages 234–5) and Belvoir (page 216), its coastal location nonetheless makes it a nice place to explore if you're in the area.

Atlit is also home to some of the area's loveliest **beaches**. Those at the southern end of the small town are easily accessed, but the northern stretches are part of a naval base and thus out of bounds. It is, however, possible to walk all the way to Atlit from Haifa along the beach, a distance of 15km.

Getting there and away The easiest way to get to Atlit is by train from Haifa, which leave every 30 minutes (*20mins/₪13.50*).

Dor Beach Dor Beach (*admission ₪20–25*) is a strong contender for best Mediterranean beach in the country and, out of peak season, makes for an idyllic, tranquil holiday experience. Three sheltered bays have been carved out of the rock to form shallow natural pools, and still, turquoise waters and white sands complete the checklist. The **Dor Holiday Village** (✆ *6399121;* e *dortantura@walla. com;* w *dortantura.co.il;* **$$$$–$$$** *depending on season*) is located to the left of the beach as you enter the car park and provides unusual, igloo-shaped huts dotted like anthills amid bright-green lawns only a few metres from the beach. A campsite (**$**) and more pricey bungalows (**$$$$**) are also on offer within the complex. The igloos and cottages have air conditioning, kitchenettes and cable television and can sleep two–five people. Two-person igloos have jacuzzi baths. Facilities include restaurants, a bar and watersports. Kayaks can be rented on the beach (*30mins/₪20*).

Getting there and away There are no direct (or indirect) buses to the beach so it is highly recommended to hire your own car for this area. Bus 921 heading up and down route 4 between Haifa Merkazit Hof Hacarmel and Tel Aviv central bus station will stop at the Dor junction every half an hour, from where it is a long 3km walk to the beach.

above   The Mount of Beatitudes is believed to be where Jesus gave his Sermon on the Mount (IG/IMOT) page 213

right   Israel's largest Arab city, Nazareth is known for it's New Testament history and is today a centre of Christian pilgrimage (DT/IMOT) pages 195–201

below   Tel Meggido, or Armageddon, certainly has a battle-weary past: this trading town was destroyed and rebuilt 25 times in its 4,400-year existence (IT/IMOT) pages 201–2

above left The Via Dolorosa has been a one of the most celebrated devotional routes for Christians of all denominations since the Byzantine era (SS) pages 96–7

above right The single holiest place in Judaism, the Western Wall is a symbol of longing and belonging among Jews across the world (AB) pages 100–1

below The site of Jesus's crucifixion, the Church of the Holy Sepulchre is arguably the single most important shrine in Christendom where pilgrims from all over the world come to pray (AB) pages 93–5

above   Israel is home to more than 100,000 Bedouins, Arabic-speaking Nomads who lead a traditional desert lifestyle predominantly around the Negev area (DT/IMOT) pages 27–8

right   The Druze community is a close-knit religious group, residing mainly in the Golan Heights and around Mount Carmel (IG/IMOT) page 27

below   Israel's relatively recent success as a wine producer owes much to the award-winning Cabernet Sauvignon and Merlot of the Golan Heights Winery (RH/A) page 189

above Planted squarely in the middle of Israel's 14km sliver of Red Sea coast, Eilat's scores of resort hotels are a draw with partygoers and dedicated scuba divers alike (DT/IMOT) pages 293–303

left Inside Safed's Abuhav Synagogue, the world centre of Kabbalah, where you'll find a Torah scroll that is the source of many traditions and legends (IG/IMOT) page 228

below Only a few kilometres apart, Tel Aviv and Jaffa are strikingly different: one is a hedonistic, determinedly modern metropolis, the other a tranquil port city steeped in Arabic culture (J/S) pages 120–52

above The UNESCO-listed Old City of Acre is a historically significant Crusader and Ottoman-period walled town of narrow cosy alleyways, traditional small restaurants and markets; pictured here, the Sinan Basha mosque (LA/S) pages 158–65

right The massive dome of the Shrine of Bab, one of the most important pilgrimage sites for members of the Baha'i faith, dominates the Haifa skyline (E/S) pages 175–6

below The charming moshav of Zichron Yaakov is Israel's longest-serving wine producer (K/S) pages 185–8

above   Dead Sea beaches and spas are hugely popular for the therapeutic properties of their mineral-rich salt and mud (G/DT) pages 279–89

left   Located 25km north of Eilat in the Negev Desert, Timna Park offers a stunning diversity of geological and archaeological formations (DT/IMOT) page 293

below   Picturesque Ein Avdat National Park is a highlight on the Israel National Trail, with windy hiking routes and leafy oases (FME/S) pages 272–3

above The waterfalls at Banias are the most spectacular sight in Hermon National Park (I/S) pages 262–3

right Besides its religious importance to both Jews and Christians, Mount Tavor offers stunning scenic views over the Jezreel Valley in the Lower Galillee (IG/IMOT) page 217

below The rich and fertile lands of the Golan Heights not only provide Israel with 30% of its water resources, but is also home to some of the best wineries in the **region** (G/DT) pages 244–63

above Yotvata Hai Bar Reserve in southern Israel is home to a large number of species, including addax (above left), desert-adapted African antelope and wild ass (above right) (DT/IMOL) page 5

left Dolphin Reef in Eilat offers a fantastic opportunity to get up close and personal with these wonderful and human-friendly mammals (DT/IMOT) pages 301–2

below The verdant Hula Valley in northern Israel is the best place to witness great bird migrations, especially cranes (PAN/S) pages 236–7

Founded in 1882 by Romanian Jews during the first aliyah, Zichron Yaakov has managed to come a long way without losing its quaint charm and old-worldly atmosphere. In the year following its founding the village came under the patronage of Baron Edmond de Rothschild (see box, page 186) who named it Zichron Yaakov (Memory of Jacob) after his father. Rothschild had extensive vineyards planted, the country's first, which today are considered among the top wine producers in the country and recognised internationally. Winemaking soon became the primary economy within the moshav, and in the 1950s new immigrants to Israel flocked in great numbers to Zichron Yaakov to settle.

Zichron Yaakov boasts a proud pioneering history and is Edmond de Rothschild's final resting place. Home of the renowned botanist and spy Aaron Aaronson, it is the centre of the secret Nili intelligence organisation.

In recent decades, the town has developed a second crucial economy: tourism. Israelis flock to the beautiful leafy, cobbled lanes strewn with outdoor cafés, restaurants and art galleries; traditional gas lamps adorn the pavements, and red shingle buildings and blossoming almond trees combine with the modern development to produce a truly unique Israeli town. In November 2016, various neighbourhoods of Zichron Yaakov were affected by wildfires, a number of homes burnt down, and ten people were hospitalised, but thankfully there were no fatalities. The town has since recovered and makes a pleasant stop on a journey through this part of Israel.

GETTING THERE AND AWAY Egged bus 872 between Tel Aviv and Zichron Yaakov runs several times a day (*1hr 45mins/₪21.50*), while buses 202 and 222 make the journey to and from Haifa (*30mins/₪14.50*).

GETTING AROUND Zichron Yaakov is a small town and most of its interest lies in the single street that runs through its centre; Hameyasdim Street (also known as the Wine Road). Public transport is certainly not necessary to cover the small area and on foot it takes 10–15 minutes to walk from the cemetery and Founders Memorial at one end to the far end of Hameyasdim Street.

TOURIST INFORMATION The **Tourist Information Centre** can be found behind the Founders Memorial (\6398811, 6398892; w *zy1882.co.il*; ⏾ *08.30–13.00 Sun–Thu*) across the road from a cemetery.

WHERE TO STAY At the main entrance to the town by the cemetery, there is an elegant, intimate boutique hotel and spa, **Achouzat Zamarin** (*16 Hameyasdim St*) which, at the time of writing, was undergoing renovation and was closed without a set reopening date. Reopen it shall, so do bear it in mind and contact the tourist office (above) to ask for their new number.

🛏 **Smadar Hotel & Winery** (4 rooms) 31 Hameyasdim St m 050 6551155; w smadar-inn.com. A cosy boutique hotel with a rustic homely feel. Conveniently located in the heart of town, it offers spacious rooms with high ceilings. Facilities include a swimming pool & excellent b/fast as well as a selection of wines made from their own grapes. **$$$$**

🛏 **Hotel Beit Maimon** (25 rooms) 4 Tzahal St; \6290999; w maimon.com. Lovely little hotel in a quiet street offering fabulous views of the sea; AC, breezy, modern rooms, a range of reasonably priced spa treatments & a heated jacuzzi. Lunch & dinner menus available (*₪85*) with a good selection of local wines. **$$$$–$$$**

✕ WHERE TO EAT AND DRINK Hameyasdim Street is lined with delightful cafés and restaurants, each one as quaint as the next. Come the weekend the pedestrian street and every seat lining it are packed full, but this rather adds to the carefree atmosphere in the town. Prices are predictably high so if you're on a tight budget then eat elsewhere and then splash out on a coffee while sitting on one of the leafy terraces.

✕ Haneshika 37 Hameyasdim St; ✆6390133; w haneshika.com; ⏱ 09.00–22.00 Mon–Sat. Situated in the quaint back garden of one of Zichron's old stone houses, this is one of the most prestigious & pricey restaurants around. The menu is changed regularly but can always be counted upon to be the best of the best. Book in advance especially on w/ends. **$$$$$**

✕ Nachman Hummus 37 Hameyasdim St; ✆6390133; ⏱ 10.00–18.00 Sun–Thu, 08.00–15.00 Fri. Part of the Haneshika restaurant & café chain, this recently opened, informal hummus bar is a real treat. Nachman special bean hummus is simply delicious & recommended. **$$**

✕ Tishbi 33 Hameyasdim St; ✆6290280; w tishbi.com; ⏱ 08.00–23.00 Sun–Thu, 09.00–15.00 Fri. This is not only a great place to enjoy an Israeli b/fast or a meal of locally produced wine & cheese, but is also one of the oldest houses in Zichron Yaakov. The coffee house is owned by the local winemaking Tishbi family. **$$**

BARON EDMOND BENJAMIN JAMES DE ROTHSCHILD

Born into the powerful Rothschild banking family in 1845, Edmond was not interested in financial matters, preferring instead the more artistic side of life. He was an avid and prosperous art collector, with many notable works in his collections, including several Rembrandt pieces later donated to the Louvre Museum in Paris, his home city. But it is his successful endeavours to help the Jews fleeing the pogroms of eastern Europe, and to establish a haven for them in the Holy Land for which he is most widely and affectionately remembered in Israel.

His early offers of help soon grew into a desire to create a self-sufficient Jewish homeland and later, state. His financial support of settlements destined for monetary ruin awarded him the nickname 'Father of the yishuv', but in the 1890s disagreements with Theodor Herzl and the Zionist organisation Hovevei Zion over the interpretation of 'political Zionism' resulted in the creation of 12 settlements under the Rothschild's Jewish Colonisation Association (ICA). In 1924, the Palestine Jewish Colonisation Association (PICA) was established, under the patronage of his son James Armand de Rothschild, who arrived in Palestine as a British soldier with General Allenby towards the end of World War I.

Rothschild was awarded honorary presidency of the Jewish Agency in 1929 and made countless visits to Palestine during his lifetime. Upon his death in Paris in 1934, he had purchased 500km^2 of land and funded the creation of almost 30 settlements at an estimated cost of US$50 million. He was interred in Paris until, in 1954, his and his wife's remains were transported to Israel. After a state funeral held by Israel's first prime minister David Ben-Gurion they were reburied in the Ramat Hanadiv Memorial Gardens near Zichron Yaakov. His famous statement 'the struggle to put an end to the Wandering Jew, could not have as its result, the creation of the Wandering Arab', was perhaps a foresight and warning to future generations of the political turmoil that was to engulf this country and region from his early days to the present.

OTHER PRACTICALITIES There's a Bank Hapoalim with an **ATM** (*49 Hameyasdim St;* ⊕ *08.30–13.00 & 16.00–18.30 Mon & Thu, 08.30–13.15 Tue–Wed, 08.15–12.30 Fri*), located in the former house of Zeev Lupo Neiman, one of the pioneers of Mount Zamarin and a talented violinist. There is also a small **Steimatzky** (*53 Hameyasdim St;* ⊕ *09.00–20.00 Sun–Thu, 08.30–15.00 Fri*) bookshop and a **post office** (*17 Hanadiv St;* ⊕ *08.00–20.00 Sun, Tue & Thu, 08.00–13.30 Mon & Wed, 08.00–noon Fri*).

WHAT TO SEE AND DO
The Wine Road There is plenty to see in Zichron Yaakov, most of which can be found by taking a very pleasant stroll along Hameyasdim Street (also referred to as the Wine Road), which is located in the heart of the small town. This was the pioneering colony's first street and has undergone heavy but meticulous reconstruction over recent years to return it to its former glory, with Rothschild's characteristic architectural features such as wooden window frames, tiled roofs, stone posts and traditional building façades having been fully restored. The Wine Road starts at the cemetery in the south end of town and finishes at the Carmel Winery in the north.

Ramat Hanadiv Memorial Cemetery and Gardens (✆ *6298111;* w *ramat-hanadiv.org.il/en;* ⊕ *08.00–16.00 Sun–Thu, 08.00–14.00 Fri, 08.00–16.00 Sat; admission free*) Rothschild expressed a strong desire to be buried in the old cemetery in Zichron Yaakov, a wish that was eventually fulfilled. It wasn't until 1954, 19 years after his passing, that the baron and his wife Adelheid were transported aboard a naval frigate from Paris and reinterred in this cemetery located at the entrance to Hameyasdim Street (the Wine Road) opposite the Founders Memorial and tourist information office. They received a state funeral presided over by former prime minister David Ben-Gurion. Rothschild's simple yet impressive mausoleum can be found in the centre of the cemetery, while a stone-carved map showing the extent of his colonies can be found in the western part of the beautifully tended memorial gardens, which spread over 17 acres. The formal gardens are a perfectly tended maze of flowers and fountains, and they sit in the heart of the nature park. Wander slowly along the paths, set off on a longer circular hike or drop into the visitors' centre, which was certified as the first green building in the country. The Samaria Observation Point is located between the Rose and Palm gardens and definitely worth the trip.

Founders Memorial This remarkable building is located next to the town's central bus station a little way up from the cemetery. Its construction is unique in that it has been designed to resemble an open scroll. A fascinating ceramic relief decorates the walls and depicts the story of Zichron's founding.

Aaronson House (*40 Hameyasdim St;* ✆ *6390120;* w *nili-museum.org.il;* ⊕ *09.00–16.00 Sun–Thu, 09.00–noon Fri; admission adult/child ₪26/20*) Zichron Yaakov was home to the Nili group, an anti-Turkish spy ring that supplied the British with intelligence during World War I. The name Nili stands for 'Netzah Yisrael Lo Yishaker', which translates as 'The eternal one of Israel will not be false'. Aaron Aaronson, an internationally reputed agronomist, and his sister Sarah were at the centre of the group's operations and spent several years living in the house that now acts as their memorial. Sarah Aaronson has become one of the country's most well-loved martyr heroines, a reputation strengthened by her refusal to divulge secret

information upon her capture and brutal inquisition. She took her own life while in the captivity of the Turks. Aaron Aaronson was killed in a plane crash at the end of World War I. There is an impressive collection of photographs and documents on display depicting their heroic story.

Benjamin's Pool Water Tower Located on the right as you walk up Hameyasdim Street is the settlement's first water tower, built by Rothschild and inaugurated in 1891. Its outer façade has been designed to resemble that of an ornate ancient synagogue. A climb to the top offers a wonderful panoramic view over the green hills and valleys of the Carmel.

First Aliyah Museum (*2 Hanadiv St;* ✆*6294777;* ◷ *09.00–14.00 Sun–Fri; admission adult/child ₪15/10*) Dedicated to the groups of pioneering families that arrived between 1882 and 1904, the museum illuminates their role in the founding of the State of Israel. The museum is housed in the 110-year-old council building built by Rothschild, at its time considered the most impressive in the country. Displays depict the history of the early settlers, its most precious relic being that of a short black-and-white film shot in 1913, which is believed to be the oldest film depicting life in the yishuv. Long believed lost, it was discovered in 1997 in a Paris film archive and shows, among others, Joseph Trumpeldor (page 240).

Ohel Yaakov Synagogue Named after Rothschild's father Jacob (Yaakov) the synagogue was, at the time, the largest and most beautiful synagogue in all of the baron's colonies. It was founded in 1886 and has been carefully restored to its former elegance.

Carmel Winery (w *carmelwines.co.il/en*) A centre for wine culture, the wine cellars and plush bistro make for a real viticultural treat. There is also a small cinema, shop, tasting rooms and workshops, and tours can be arranged (see box, opposite).

CAESAREA

Resting on the shores of the glittering Mediterranean Sea, Caesarea offers a wealth of attractions and luxury activities. The modern town is a sprawling series of wealthy, leafy neighbourhoods, where large, mansion-like houses sit amid green lawns and expensive cars line the driveways. Caesarea has been home to VIPs such as the ex-president Ezer Weizmann. Yet the area is best known not for its well-to-do residents, but for the staggering ancient ruins that lie just south of it. The ruins at Caesarea, where successive phases of occupation have left a treasure trove of archaeological remains, most notably the Crusader City and Roman theatre, are worth visiting if archaeology is of interest. Around the national park, Israel's finest golf course, several wide, sandy swimming beaches and a luxury spa make this a five-star stopover.

HISTORY The site at Caesarea was first settled in the 4th century BCE by the Phoenicians, who built a small harbour city named Straton's Tower. After Alexander the Great's conquest of the country in 332BCE, the city flourished under Greek rule. The Roman Conquest in 63BCE saw the city undergo a major phase of construction, and under Herod was renamed Caesarea, in honour of the Roman emperor. The Temple of Augustus, deep-sea harbour, hippodrome, theatre, bathhouses, public buildings, wide roads, markets and state-of-the-art water supply all owe their origins to this time. It has been recorded that Roman procurators Pontius Pilate and Felix

A BOTTLE OF ISRAEL'S FINEST

Winemaking has been known since pre-biblical times; indeed Noah's first task after completing the Ark was to plant vines. In more recent history, however, the first attempts at viniculture in Palestine date back to 1885 when, during his struggle to make *moshavot* profitable, Rothschild brought experts from France to help plant vineyards in Zichron Yaakov. The experiment was unsuccessful, but Israel has since managed to put itself on the prestigious wine map and now competes favourably with the giants of the wine world.

Yet only in recent years has Israel been regarded as a producer of quality wine, a development owed mainly to the creation of the Golan Heights Winery which opened in 1983. From the outset the winery was a success, with its second wine, a 1984 Cabernet Sauvignon, winning the gold medal at the International Wine and Spirit Competition. Its Yarden series is considered its most reputable and prestigious, notably the Cabernet Sauvignon and Merlot. Today the country's largest winemaker is the Rothschild-founded Carmel Winery in Zichron Yaakov (page 188). It produces over 13 million bottles a year and has three main series: the Selected, the Vineyard and the prestigious Rothschild, which includes Merlot, Cabernet Sauvignon, Chardonnay and Emerald Rieslings. Much of the wine purchased in Israel and exported is kosher. While there are several rules that need to be abided by, there is no conflict of interest in the production of good wine and it remaining kosher. For example, grapes may not be used until their fourth year of growth, equipment must be kept kosher clean and only Sabbath-observant male Jews can take part in the wine-producing process.

TOURS Most of Israel's wineries offer tours, although you may need to book ahead. While the main attraction is the winemaking process and wine tasting, the wineries tend to be located within some of the country's most stunning landscapes. For more information, visit w winesisrael.com/en.

Carmel Zichron Yaakov Wine Cellars Zichron Yaakov; \04 6290977; w carmelwines.co.il/en
Domaine du Castel Yad Hashmona, between Tel Aviv & Jerusalem; \02 5358555; w castel.co.il/en
Galil Mountain Winery Kibbutz Yiron; \04 6868740; w galilmountain.co.il
Golan Heights Winery Katzrin, Golan; \04 6968420; w golanwines.co.il/english (page 251)

Hamasrek Winery (kosher) Beit Meir, near Jerusalem; \02 5701759; w hamasrek.com
Neot Smadar Winery Neot Smadar, Negev Desert; \08 6358111; w neot-smadar. com/neot-smadar-winery
Sde Boker Winery Sde Boker, Judean Desert; m 050 7579212
Tavor Winery Kfar Tavor, Lower Galilee; \04 6760444; w twc.co.il/en
Yatir Winery Tel Arad, Judean Desert; m 052 8308196; w yatirwinery.com/en

resided in Caesarea, and it was here the Apostle Paul was imprisoned and sent to Rome for trial. It was also the site of Paul's baptising of the Roman officer Cornelius. The Jewish uprising of 66CE was repressed by Vespasian who was later declared Emperor of the Roman Empire in Caesarea and the city became one of the most important in the eastern part of the Roman Empire, classified as 'Metropolis of the Province of Syria Palestina'. Following the Bar Kokhba revolt, its leader Ben Akiva was tortured and died in the city in 135CE.

Caesarea prospered during the Byzantine period until the Arab conquest of 637. The Crusaders captured the city during the First Crusade, but it wasn't until 1251 that Louis VI fortified the city, constructing high walls and a deep moat. The fortifications were breached shortly afterwards, however, by the Mamluk sultan Baibars, who captured the town. The once-flourishing port had by this time completely silted over. The city fell into ruins and remained desolate until the 19th century, when Bosnian refugees were settled on the land. It was later resettled in 1940, with the establishment of the nearby Kibbutz Sdot Yam, but abandoned for a brief period during the 1948 Arab–Israeli War.

GETTING THERE AND AWAY There are no direct buses from Haifa or Tel Aviv. Get any number of regular buses heading north or southbound and get off at the Or Akiva junction 2km from Caesarea, where you can walk or hitch the final stretch. Trains leave regularly from Tel Aviv and Haifa to Caesarea-Pardes Hana railway station, which is about 8km from Caesarea. Kavim bus 80 (w *kavim-t.co.il*) departs from outside the train station once every 90 minutes (*20mins/₪6.90*), terminating at the entrance to the national park. If you're driving here, be aware there is absolutely no continuity with the English spelling of Caesarea on road signs. It can range from Qesariya, to Kesariya, to Quesariyya, so try to be imaginative and keep an eye open.

🏠 **WHERE TO STAY**

🏠 **Dan Caesarea Hotel** (114 rooms) ☎1700 505080. Part of the luxury chain of Israeli hotels, the Dan Caesarea represents the country-manor member of the Dan family. Located on the fringe of the Caesarea golf course & its velvet lawns, the hotel prides itself on immaculate service & top-quality facilities. **$$$$$**

✖ **WHERE TO EAT AND DRINK** Restaurants in the archaeological park tend to be a bit pricey but are generally of good quality. The **Crusaders Restaurant** (☎ *6361679; ⊕ 10.00–midnight daily; $$$$*) serves a wide selection of meat, fresh seafood and fish, while **Hellena** (☎*6101018; w hellena.co.il; ⊕ noon–23.00 daily; $$$$*) specialises in Middle Eastern cuisine.

WHAT TO SEE AND DO
Caesarea Maritime National Park (☎*6267080; w caesarea.com; ⊕ 08.00–18.00 Sat–Thu, 08.00–16.00 Fri, closes 1hr earlier in winter; admission adult/child ₪39/24*) Although described as a national park, the area around Caesarea archaeological site is a modern development of luxurious apartments set amid fine lawns and gardens. Nothing other than the ruins of the ancient city is likely to detain a visitor here.

Theatre This symbol of Caesarea has been fully restored and converted into a modern music venue. Seating up to 4,000 people, it once again hosts concerts, operas and summer events and has been designed so that audiences have a view over the Mediterranean Sea behind. At some point after its original construction, the theatre was extended to form a quasi-amphitheatre, where it is likely gladiatorial battles would have taken place. It is located south of the Crusader City near the Herodian south wall.

Promontory Palace Jutting out into the sea, the high promontory located in the south of the Roman city was the site of King Herod's exquisite palace. The excavated complex, 110m by 60m in size, contained a large central saltwater pool and was surrounded by ornate porticoes. On display within the palace is a replica of a stone mentioning Pontius Pilate, the only physical evidence discovered bearing his name. The original is in the Israel Museum in Jerusalem.

Hippodrome A major feature of the Herodian town, it was here that great sporting events were played out and legendary gladiator games were hosted. The arena housed up to 15,000 spectators and was 250m long and 80m wide. It has yet to be excavated and is overgrown, but its shape and extent are still clear.

Bathhouses The excavated 4th-century bathhouses are a wonderful example of Roman architecture. A series of courtyards and rooms, many containing exquisite mosaics, made up the large bath complex that formed the core of Roman social life.

Byzantine Street Along the ancient shopping street are two headless statues, located near the entrance. Dated to the 2nd or 3rd centuries, one is made of white marble and the other from reddish, purple-coloured porphyry. It is believed the latter is the figure of an emperor, most likely Hadrian.

Crusader City Entrance to the city is via the imposing East Gate. To the left of the gate are remains of houses while within the fortified area remnants of the ancient water supply and drainage system, the Temple of Augustus and the still-standing Crusader cathedral can be found. The cathedral was dedicated to St Paul and built on the site of an earlier Byzantine church. Near the cathedral is the mosque built by Bosnian settlers in the 19th century.

Aqueduct The aqueduct was commissioned by Herod to bring fresh water from Carmel Mountain 15km away and represents an incredible feat of ancient architectural engineering. The aqueduct was built on arches and the gradient precisely measured, allowing for a constant flow of water into the city. It was later extended by Hadrian and the Crusaders. Today part of the aqueduct is inside the national park on the beautiful Caesarea Beach, and sections can be spotted along the entire coastal region to its source.

Underwater Archaeological Park (Caesarea Dive Club) (✆ 6265898; e *divingc@inter.net.il;* w *caesarea-diving.com/en*) Most of what remains of the deep-sea port today lies under the emerald waters of the Mediterranean Sea and has become an underwater park frequented by scuba-diving enthusiasts and archaeology buffs from around the world. Diving here is open to professionals and amateurs and a reputable dive centre operates informative and insightful expeditions to the ruins of the Roman and Crusader naval port, including several ancient shipwrecks.

BEACHES The **Harbour Beach** (*admission adult/child ₪25/20*) is a lovely, well-kept beach that boasts shimmering green waters as its view and the ancient buildings of Caesarea as its backdrop. Parking, lifeguards, changing rooms, parasols and sunbeds are available. There is also a pleasant beach bar (complete with grill). The incredibly picturesque **Aqueduct Beach** just outside the national park perimeter is free and a tranquil place to go swimming. Facilities are limited, however, so families with small children are best advised to opt for the Harbour Beach.

OTHER CAESAREA ATTRACTIONS Located within the boundaries of the national park (but not included in the entry price) are the Caesarea Experience, Caesarea's Stars and the Time Tower (*admission adult/child ₪40/35 including park admission*)

– three state-of-the-art, multi-media experiences aimed at illuminating Caesarea's tumultuous and fascinating past and the people who lived there.

Many people don't venture too far outside the archaeological park, but there are several expensive and luxurious activities in which to participate, if your budget runs to it. The **Caesarea Golf Club** (↘*6109600*) is Israel's one-and-only 18-hole golf course and is set within beautiful sea-view grounds complete with bird lake. It is located at the entrance to Caesarea in grounds donated by the Rothschild family. The nearby **Ralli Museum** (*Rothschild Bd;* ↘ *6261013;* w *rallimuseums.com/en;* ⊕ *10.30–17.00 Mon–Tue, Thu & Sat, 10.30–15.00 Fri; admission free*), housed in a vast mansion, displays a selection of modern and ancient paintings, and it includes a gallery devoted to Salvador Dalí. The **Caesar Spa** (↘*6266669*) set within manicured grounds, takes pampering to a new dimension. For those with deep enough pockets, this luxury complex offers everything one could need to relax and unwind: massages from mud to Thai, wraps, aromatic peeling, and face and body treatments.

HERZLIYA *Telephone code 09; population 91,900*

Twenty minutes away from Tel Aviv's city centre is the town of Herzliya which, over recent years has become one of the major night-owl hotspots. In fact, all bars, restaurants and clubs centre on the expensive, oh-so-trendy area known as Herzliya Pituach, the strip running along the seafront to the left of the highway (the other part of town being purely residential). In contrast to Tel Aviv's Old Port area, Herzliya's marina is still very much active, being home to small, private yachts around which has appeared the **Arena Mall** (⊕ *10.00–22.00 Sun–Thu, 09.30–16.00 Fri, 11.00–23.00 Sat; cinema stays open later*), as well as dozens of cafés, restaurants and pubs. A wide, sandy beach 100m from the marina has a young, laid back atmosphere, with beach volleyball, a relaxed bar and plenty of towel space, while the strip 0.5km back from the seafront is packed with good restaurants, swanky bars and pubs and, come the small hours, pumping nightclubs.

GETTING THERE AND AWAY There are numerous Egged buses (502, 525, 531 etc), departing every 15 minutes from Tel Aviv central bus station to Herzliya central station (*1hr/₪9.30*) and stopping on the way at the major junction by the highway. From there, it is a 10-minute walk to central Herzliya Pituach, but to get to the beach and marina you will need to find a taxi.

🏠 WHERE TO STAY

🏠 **Dan Accadia Hotel** (200 rooms) Herzliya Beach; ↘9597070; e accadia@danhotels.com; w danhotels.com. Great beachfront setting & all the facilities & quality associated with the Dan chain & a 5-star resort hotel. **$$$$$**

🏠 **Shizen Spa Resort** (40 rooms) Herzliya Beach; ↘9520808; w shizenhotel.com. Oriental-themed boutique hotel where Zen, tranquillity & feng shui are the name of the game. A 1st-class spa, gourmet restaurants & artistic rooms with sea view. **$$$$$**

✖ WHERE TO EAT AND DRINK

✖ **Segev** 16 Shenkar St (cnr of Hahoslim St); ↘077 4142025; w segevchef.com; ⊕ noon–16.00 & 19.00–23.00 Sun–Thu, noon–15.30 & 19.00–23.00 Fri, 13.00–17.00 & 19.30–23.00 Sat. It has been decorated to resemble the Neve Tzedek neighbourhood of Tel Aviv, giving it a cosy, friendly

atmosphere. Cuisine is widely international & very varied. The 3-course business lunch (*₪115*) is good value. **$$$$$**

✖ **Tapeo** 9 Shenkar St; ↘9546699; ⊕ noon–14.00 & 18.00–01.00 Sun–Thu, 18.00–01.00 Fri, noon–01.00 Sat. Huge Spanish restaurant where

booking ahead at w/ends is a must. Despite the size, it has a romantic, candlelit feel & serves garlicky, rich tapas at reasonable prices. $$$$
♀ **Hattori Hanzo** 1 Sapir St; ↖9514045; ⏱ 21.00–late daily. A veteran of raucous, pumping party nights, this bar-cum-nightclub is the ultimate 'pick-up' place.
♀ **Murphy's Pub** Marina; ↖9569495; ⏱ 16.00–late Sun–Thu, noon–late Fri–Sat. Irish-style pub

that's a bit softer around the edges than those in Tel Aviv. Live music on Tue & Wed & live sporting events on big screens. Big portions of nice bar food. Outdoor seating opposite the marina.
♀ **Yam Bar** Akadia Beach; ↖9597102; w yambar. co.il; ⏱ 24hrs daily. Perched on the cliff edge above the beach with fantastic views & a gentle breeze, this is a relaxed watering hole attracting the chilled-out surfer types.

WHAT TO SEE AND DO

Marina and beach Herzliya Pituach is first and foremost a leisure town where a plethora of bars, cafés, restaurants and beachside activities converge. The marina is a pleasant place to spend an evening sipping drinks after a full day on the huge expanse of white sand. Sailing, surfing, scuba diving, beach volleyball and countless other active pursuits can all be arranged from Acadia Beach.

Apollonia National Park (Tel Arsuf) (*Coastal plain north of Herzliya Pituach;* w *parks.org.il;* ⏱ *08.00–17.00 Sat–Thu, 08.00–16.00 Fri, closes 1hr earlier in winter; admission adult/child* ₪*22/9*) The site contains the recently excavated remains of a once-prosperous Crusader City and fortress. It is easy to see why the Crusaders chose this spot – both defensively and aesthetically – and resting on a cliff overlooking the Mediterranean it makes for a pleasant afternoon exploring the ruins and piecing together the site. The entrance is located just outside Herzliya Pituach. Turn right on to Wingate Street when heading towards the town at the second set of traffic lights.

Sidni Ali Mosque The mosque complex, which is today both a school and active mosque, in fact houses the shrine of the Mamluk chief for whom it was built and who died in battle on this hill – Sidni Ali. It is dated to the 13th century CE, the time of the great battles between the Mamluks and Crusaders.

Herzliya Museum of Contemporary Art (*4 Habanim St;* ↖ *9550010;* w *herzliyamuseum.co.il;* ⏱ *10.00–14.00 Mon, Wed & Fri–Sat, 16.00–20.00 Tue & Thu; admission* ₪*20*) The museum houses collections of Israeli and international contemporary art, focusing on works that offer an alternative angle to the political and social issues within the country. Exhibits change regularly.

Mediterranean Coast   HERZLIYA

5

6

Lower Galilee

Telephone code 04

The 1st-century historian Flavius Josephus once wrote of the Lower Galilee: 'One may call this place the ambition of nature.' Stretching from the sweeping, fertile plains of the Jezreel Valley (or simply 'Haemek', 'The Valley') in the south to the natural border of the Jordan River in the east, and up to the more rugged terrains of the Upper Galilee, it is a land of true diversity. Agriculturally, the area has been the beating heart of the country for centuries, its fertile valleys seasonally blanketed with crops. The delicate microclimate of the region, coupled with its diverse geography account for its eclectic mix of produce. Almonds, citrus fruits and olive trees grow in the Beit Shean and Herod valleys, cotton and grain prosper in the warm fields of the Jezreel Valley while flowers and herbs blossom alongside the Jordan River. The Sea of Galilee's abundant fish stocks have long complemented agriculture in the vicinity of the sea, called thus through tradition rather than definition. Throughout the time of Jesus up until today a thriving fishing industry has prospered, forming the economy of many of today's kibbutzim that concentrate in the valleys. The country's pioneering kibbutz, Deganya Alef, is on the shores of the sea, and the area is now home to most of the country's kibbutz settlements. Nazareth, the heart of Arab life and culture in the region, together with the countless Arab villages that dot the landscape, denoted by their minarets and typical jumbled street planning, are home to one million of Israel's Arab residents, whose traditional way of life and close cultural ties flourish.

Historically, nowhere outside Jerusalem can compete with the Lower Galilee for drama, passion and religious tenor. The scene of legendary battles, it was on these soils that empires were won and lost. At the Battle of Hittin in 1187, the revered Arab leader Saladin defeated the Christian Crusader armies, a battle that marked the beginning of the conquest of Jerusalem and prompted the Third Crusade. Under the shadow of Mount Tavor, the prophet and heroine Deborah, alongside Barak, defeated the Canaanite captain Sisera, marking the first great Israelite victory since the days of Joshua, and the last battle they would ever have with the Canaanites. After this, during the Hasmonean period, the entire Galilee region was controlled by several empires and emerged as a Jewish stronghold, a claim that remained for five centuries after the demise of the Second Temple. The highly contested lands changed hands countless times throughout the succeeding centuries: Arabs, Crusaders, Mamluks and Ottomans all ruled at times throughout the Galilee's colourful past.

Sacred in the hearts of Christians and Jews the world over, the region is the destination for thousands of pilgrims. From the magnificent churches and picture-postcard cobbled alleys of Nazareth's Old City where Jesus's life began, to the sites of his numerous miracles that dot the shores of the Sea of Galilee, biblical stories abound. Tiberias, one of Judaism's four Holy Cities and often considered the capital of the Lower Galilee, was once the seat of the Jewish Sanhedrin, school of Jewish learning, and home to Rabbi Judah Hanassi as he compiled the Talmud. Tiberias's party-going streets today belie the importance of the city in Judaism's history, the

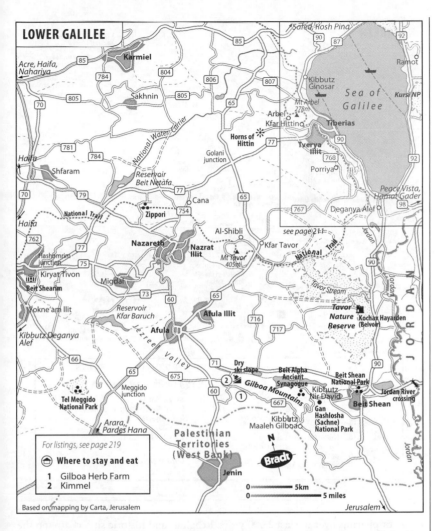

LOWER GALILEE

Acre, Haifa, Nahariya

Karmiel

Sakhnin

Haifa

Shfaram

Reservoir Beit Netofa

National Trail

Zippori

Cana

Al-Shibli

Nazareth

Nazrat Illit

Hashomrim junction

Kiryat Tivon

Beit Shearim

Migdal

Yokne'am Illit

Reservoir Kfar Baruch

Afula

Afula Illit

Kibbutz Deganya Alef

Meggido junction

Tel Meggido National Park

Arara, Pardes Hana

Palestinian Territories (West Bank)

Jenin

For listings, see page 219

◉ Where to stay and eat
1 Gilboa Herb Farm
2 Kimmel

Based on mapping by Carta, Jerusalem

Safed, Rosh Pina

Kibbutz Ginosar

Mt Arbel 278m

Arbel

Kfar Hitting

Horns of Hittin

Golani junction

Tverya Illit

Porriya

Sea of Galilee

Kursi NP

Tiberias

Ramot

Peace Vista, Hamat Gader

Deganya Alef

see page 211

National Trail

Kfar Tavor

Mt Tavor 405m

Tavor Stream

Tavor Nature Reserve

Kochav Hayarden (Belvoir)

Dry ski slope

Gilboa Mountains

Beit Alpha Ancient Synagogue

Kibbutz Nir David

Gan Hashlosha (Sachne) National Park

Kibbutz Maaleh Gilboa

Beit Shean National Park

Beit Shean

Jordan River crossing

JORDAN

Jerusalem

N

Bradt

0 — 5km
0 — 5 miles

---

quiet tombs of some of the great philosophers and rabbis scattered around the city acting as reminders to this secular settlement.

One hour's drive from Jerusalem and Tel Aviv, it is easily accessible and thus regularly frequented by Israeli holidaymakers and day trippers, who escape the cities to unwind in the national parks, hot springs and lakeside beaches. Tour buses, laden with pilgrims and sightseers, trek through the valleys and hills, fuelling the region's ever-growing tourism economy. Be it by the rich history, spiritual allure or thriving flora and fauna that abound in the valleys and hills of the Lower Galilee, few could fail to be enchanted by the beauty and historic appeal of the region.

NAZARETH *Population 75,700*

Nazareth – Israel's largest Arab city – rests atop, between and around five hills that form the end of the Galilee Mountains presiding over the Jezreel Valley below. Outside the country, it is probably most well known as being the childhood home of Jesus and

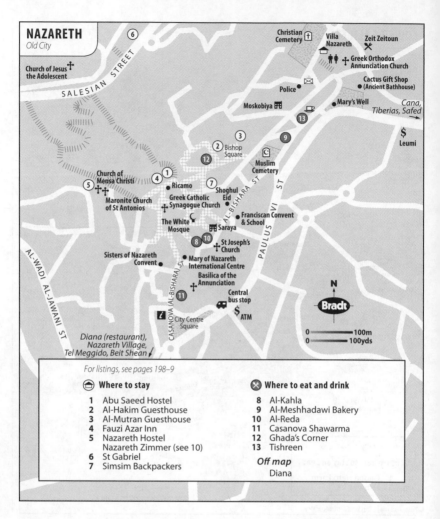

NAZARETH
Old City

Church of Jesus the Adolescent

SALESIAN STREET

Church of Mensa Christi

Maronite Church of St Antonios

Ricamo

Greek Catholic Synagogue Church

The White Mosque

Saraya

Sisters of Nazareth Convent

Mary of Nazareth International Centre

Basilica of the Annunciation

City Centre Square

Diana (restaurant), Nazareth Village, Tel Meggido, Beit Shean

Bishop Square

Muslim Cemetery

Shoghul Eid

Franciscan Convent & School

St Joseph's Church

Central bus stop

ATM

Christian Cemetery

Villa Nazareth

Zeit Zeitoun

Greek Orthodox Annunciation Church

Police

Cactus Gift Shop (Ancient Bathhouse)

Moskobiya

Mary's Well

Cana, Tiberias, Safed

Leumi

N

Bradt

0 ———— 100m
0 ———— 100yds

For listings, see pages 198–9

🏠 **Where to stay**

1 Abu Saeed Hostel
2 Al-Hakim Guesthouse
3 Al-Mutran Guesthouse
4 Fauzi Azar Inn
5 Nazareth Hostel
  Nazareth Zimmer (see 10)
6 St Gabriel
7 Simsim Backpackers

❌ **Where to eat and drink**

8 Al-Kahla
9 Al-Meshhadawi Bakery
10 Al-Reda
11 Casanova Shawarma
12 Ghada's Corner
13 Tishreen

Off map
Diana

a site for pilgrims over the last 2,000 years. Religious and historic sites centre on the Old City in the heart of Nazareth, where preconceived images of quaint cobbled stone alleys and bustling markets are fully realised. Outside the Old City, however, Nazareth is a hectic, modern and vibrant Arab city where the aromas of strong coffee, spices and sweets drift along the streets and where the loud chatter and the sounds of car horns dull only marginally at prayer times. Arabs make up around 22% of the population of Nazareth and are represented by Muslim and Christian religious communities, including Maronites. Inconceivably to many other Palestinians living in Israel and certainly those living in the West Bank, the people of Nazareth are content with their situation, where Arab life and culture most certainly prevail. Modest dress is highly recommended – particularly for women – both in the Old City and outside. There are directions everywhere in the Old City and orientation is easy.

HISTORY On account of its absence from both the Old Testament and Talmud, it is likely that Nazareth was a small and insignificant settlement during Jesus's time and that the city as it is known today flourished and grew alongside the spread of

Christianity. Among the Christian sites in Israel and across the world, Nazareth holds its claim to being 'where it all began'. It was here that Jesus spent most of his early life and where the Bible states that Mary was told of the Annunciation by the Angel Gabriel, hence the high number of churches claiming to be the location of the event around here. The fact that Nazareth was mentioned in the Quran suggests existence of the Muslim community here as early as the 7th century CE.

From the Muslim Conquest of Palestine in 637CE throughout the First Crusade and long-lasting conflict, power changed hands regularly, which had a great impact on the religious balance of the population. In 1099, the Galilee was captured by the Crusader Tancred, and Nazareth was appointed as capital of the area. Following Saladin's victory at the Battle of Hittin in 1187, Muslim control was re-established in Nazareth, where it lasted until it was once more returned to Christian hands, during part of the Sixth Crusade. In 1263, however, the Mamluk sultan Baibars had all Christian buildings destroyed and its people evicted, their absence lasting until 1620, when a Druze leader from Mount Lebanon, Fakhr Al-Din II, allowed their return. Throughout Ottoman rule, Nazareth flourished, and it is well documented as a time of affluence for the city. Testament to this are the traditional two-storey mansions constructed during this period at the base of the Nabi Sa'in cliff rising behind the city.

In the late 19th and early 20th century, Nazareth was a small village of a few thousand people, divided into three religious neighbourhoods: the central Muslim Quarter around the White Mosque, the Latin Quarter located westwards from the Basilica of the Annunciation and up to the Mensa Christi Church, and the Greek Orthodox Quarter stretching towards the Greek Orthodox Annunciation Church. In its more recent history, the city emerged from the 1948 Arab–Israeli War almost unscathed. During the battle for Nazareth, the city's Arab residents capitulated and Ben-Gurion himself forbade Jewish troops from expelling its inhabitants, which greatly contributed to the city's authentic Arab character being preserved. There are currently some Jews living in Nazareth, although the main Jewish town is the satellite Nazareth Illit, founded in 1957.

GETTING THERE AND AWAY Nazareth is fairly accessible by bus from most major cities. Regional bus company Nazareth Transport & Tourism (w *ntt-buses.com*) has a wide network of routes to and from the city. Buses and sheruts stop at several bus stops along Paulus VI Street. When you're coming to Nazareth, make sure the bus is headed for the original Old City (Natzrat Haatika in Hebrew) and not Natzrat Illit, the nearby Jewish satellite town built much later. Egged bus 826 has 11 daily departures between Tel Aviv and Nazareth (*2hrs 10mins/₪34*), stopping in the Old City. NTT buses 332 and 342 leave Haifa every 30 minutes to the central bus station (*35mins/₪16*). Egged bus 955 leaves Jerusalem at 16.15 and 18.20 (*2hrs 45mins/₪37.50*) and for Jerusalem at 05.18 and 08.48. NTT bus 431 runs hourly between Tiberias and Nazareth (*25mins/₪16*).

GETTING AROUND Nazareth suffers from dire congestion problems and weaving your way through the dusty, strangely organised roads is an arduous task. If you're arriving by car, it's recommended to park outside the Old City area and either walk or take a taxi into the centre. The worst of the traffic centres on Paulus VI Street, which during rush hour is bumper to bumper. Most of Nazareth's sights are within the Old City and within easy walking distance of each other. Sights are well marked, but finding a specific street name may prove to be a challenge as most streets in the Old City do not have names, but numbers instead, which are supposedly used in lieu, but only exist on the maps. In reality, trust your senses and enjoy wandering around the old stone alleys and endless steps.

TOURIST INFORMATION The **Tourist Information Centre** (*58 Casanova St;* \ *6570555;* e *ronnye@tourism.gov.il;* ⊕ *08.30–17.00 Mon–Fri, 09.00–14.00 Sat*) is small, but well equipped with most helpful staff. Maps and itinerary booklets are available in a variety of languages and are free of charge. Tours can also be arranged here. Alternatively, **Fauzi Azar Inn** (below) offers a daily 2-hour tour of the city (*09.30; free of charge for inn guests, ₪20 pp for everyone else*).

🏠 WHERE TO STAY *Map, page 197*

🏠 **Nazareth Zimmer** (1 room) 21 Al-Bishara St. Perched on the top floor under the arched roof of a traditional Arab mansion across the street from St Joseph's Church, this self-contained large open space is easily the nicest in all of Israel. Traditional classic furniture, Middle Eastern carpets & a terrace overlooking the Basilica of the Annunciation & the entire Old City, everything here breathes taste & style. To book this gem, contact Daher Zaydani (\ *6084404*), owner of the Al-Reda Restaurant (below). **$$$$$**

🏠 **Al-Hakim Guesthouse** (10 rooms) Bishop Sq; \ 6545990; e alhakimguesthouse@gmail. com. Opened in 2015, this charming family-run boutique hotel is tucked into the old building & is tastefully decorated. It has been a family property since 1932, & Bassam Hakim, the manager, has converted his grandfather's carpentry shop into 10 rooms named after family members. There is a small 1st-floor inner terrace to enjoy the sunshine. **$$$**

🏠 **Al-Mutran Guesthouse** (11 rooms) \ 6457947; e info@al-mutran.com; w al-mutran. com. Charming, traditional decoration & a wide range of facilities & room options (from a 6-bed private, en-suite room to dbl en suites, shared bathrooms & a dormitory) in this Old City gem. The house itself is more than 150 years old & is wonderfully preserved. The hotel sometimes holds cultural events & even *oud* lessons in the adjacent House of Culture & Art. **$$$**

🏠 **Nazareth Hostel** (7 rooms) m 052 8766053; e info@nazareth-hostel.com. Confusingly called a hostel, this new guesthouse, which opened in 2013, offers private accommodation in a traditional house in the Old

City. On the ground floor, there is a small leafy terrace & café, while the upper terrace offers great views over Nazareth. **$$$**

🏠 **St Gabriel Hotel** (60 rooms) 2 Salesian St; \ 6572133; e nazsgh@yahoo.com; w stgabrielhotel.com. Perched high on the hill behind the city with fabulous views, especially from the b/fast patio. Furnished in plush, Middle Eastern design, it once housed a congregation of Catholic nuns & its exterior has retained its ecclesiastical splendour. Often caters to big groups. Rooms are comfortable & bright, & some even come with great views over the Old City. **$$$**

🏠 **Fauzi Azar Inn** (10 rooms) \ 6020469; e info@fauziazarinn.com; w fauziazarinn. com. A very good, mid-range option in town. Located in the true heart of the Old City & souk & housed in a 200-year-old Arab courtyard house, it offers unparalleled comfort, character & ambience, as well as a variety of differently priced accommodation options, including dorms. The guesthouse is now operating as part of the Abraham Hostel chain. **$$$–$**

🏠 **Simsim Backpackers** (ILH) (5 private rooms & 3 dorms) Old City; \ 077 5517275 (ILH). Located in a late 19th-century building, the hostel is right in the heart of Nazareth. It has a wonderful ground-floor Liwan Culture Café (e *liwan. nazareth@gmail.com*) serving food & organising cultural events in the city. **$$–$**

🏠 **Abu Saeed Hostel** (8 rooms) \ 6462799; e hajmosmar.ramzi@gmail.com; w abusaeedhostel.com. Opened in 2008, this budget option is tucked away in the Old City, but follow signs in the streets to locate this family-run hostel. Rooms are spacious & clean. **$**

✖ WHERE TO EAT AND DRINK *Map, page 197*

✖ **Al-Reda** 21 Al-Bishara St; \ 6084404; ⊕ 19.00–02.00 Mon–Sat. Situated in an old

Arab mansion house with an arched roof, heavy wooden furniture & a small garden, this is one of the nicest restaurants in Nazareth. The food combines Arabic style with contemporary flavours. The succulent meats are highly recommended, especially the lamb, while vegetable dishes such as stuffed mushrooms or artichokes are also excellent. Run by simply wonderful Daher Zaydani. **$$$**

✖ Diana 51 Paulus VI St; ✆6572919; ⏰ 11.00–midnight daily. Ask anyone in the country to recommend a restaurant in Nazareth & this is where you'll be sent, & justly so – it is simply terrific. Don't be put off by the unimpressive exterior or simple decoration; the food is top-notch, freshly prepared Middle Eastern cuisine. Ordering the salad (meze) will result in 22 different dishes being piled on your table – & that's just for starters. The kebabs are succulent & just mouth-watering. **$$$**

✖ Tishreen Hamaayan Sq; ✆6084666; ⏰ 11.00–midnight Mon–Sat, 18.00–midnight Sun. Delightful restaurant serving up creative, aromatic foods & sweet black coffee. Lovely ambience & ornate décor. **$$$**

✖ Al-Meshhadawi Bakery Al-Bishara St; ⏰ 04.00–late daily. This small bakery is easily missed but worth looking for. It serves freshly baked bread & pastries. Try spinach-filled buns with sour cheese spread & spicy toppings (جبنة). **$**

✖ Casanova Shawarma Casanova St; ✆6554027; ⏰ 07.00–19.00 daily. Without a doubt the best falafel in the city. A tiny take-away stall halfway up Casanova St, it is unassuming & easily missed. Serving falafel with an array of varied, fresh salad accompaniments, shawarma & freshly squeezed orange juice. **$**

▭ Al-Kahla Al-Bishara St; ⏰ 10.30–18.00 daily. Opened in 2015 across the street from St Joseph's Church, this café & bar serving tea, coffee & excellent Palestinian wine is adjacent to Al-Reda Restaurant, which it accompanies. Run by Razan, a local architect & wonderful host. **$$**

▭ Ghada's Corner ✆9869116; e bouloscompany@gmail.com. ⏰ 10.00–16.00 daily. A tiny cosy café serving strong Arabic coffee & light pastries. There are also handmade souvenirs to browse too. The owner, Ghada, is a certified tour leader (w ghadaboulos.com). **$**

OTHER PRACTICALITIES Most sites in Nazareth are either inside or within easy walking distance of the Old City. The city keeps hours in accordance with Muslim and Christian holy days (Friday to Sunday). For **shopping**, a newly opened handmade jewellery store **Ricamo** (m 050 3008305; e wafazaher@hotmail.com) opposite Fauzi Azar Inn offers a nice selection of traditionally designed pieces, all fairly priced. For handmade Palestinian souvenirs and dresses, **Shoghul Eid** (Al-Bishara St, ✆6537989; ⏰ 09.00–19.00 daily) run by friendly Samr and her father beats every other store for quality, selection and price. Note that there are no **ATMs** in the Old City and the closest is a **Bank Leumi** branch on 14 Hagalil Street (✆ *5522, 03 9545522; ⏰ 08.30–13.00 & 16.00–18.15 Mon & Thu, 08.30–14.15 Tue–Wed, 08.30–13.00 Fri). Paulus VI Street has money-changing bureaus. The **post office** and **police station** in the city centre are side by side on 6077 Street. Nazareth has three main **hospitals**: French St Vincent Hospital (✆6509000), Holy Family Hospital (✆6508900) and Nazareth Hospital (✆6571501–2).

WHAT TO SEE AND DO The **Old City** (Al-Balda Al-Qadima in Arabic) provides the backdrop for most of the main religious and historic sites of interest. The **Salesian School** and the **Church of Jesus the Adolescent** overlook the Old City from the hill up above and are visible from afar. Narrow alleys and winding streets reveal the city's numerous churches. Some are tourist magnets, while others are discreet and usually open for Sunday service only, but they still present a beautiful reminder of the city's past and present. The **Maronite Church of St Antonios**, built in 1774, is one such example. Located just a few metres down the street from it is the **Church of Mensa Christi**. At the end of the 18th century, Franciscans built a chapel here to commemorate the meal of Jesus with his disciples after his Resurrection. The present church was reconstructed in 1860. In the lower part of the Old City is the **Saraya**

Ottoman administrative building, dating from the 18th century. It is closed currently but until 1991 functioned as the Nazareth Municipality Office. The **Moskobiya** building, as the name suggests, was a Russian pilgrims' house, built in 1904 and named after Grand Duke Sergey Alexandrovich of Russia, founder of the Russian Orthodox Pilgrims' Society. The building had accommodation for 1,000 people, a hospital and a school which was attended by the Palestinian cultural elite. The Moskobiya belonged to the Russian Empire until the 1917 October Revolution, and later until 1948 served as Nazareth's administrative centre. It is currently a police building and there are plans to change its function yet again. Closer to the touristy heart of the city is **Mary of Nazareth International Centre** (⊕ *09.30–noon & 14.30–17.30 daily*). Besides a small archaeological site at the entrance, it has a café and a beautiful rooftop terrace which is open to visitors free of charge, though a donation is welcome on exit. The centre has also an excellent, albeit overpriced, gift shop and offers a multi-media tour and visit of the archaeological site for ₪15.

Basilica of the Annunciation (*Casanova St;* ⊕ *08.00–18.00 Mon–Sat, 14.00–17.30 Sun & hols; admission free*) This is the most prominent and easily identifiable site in the Old City, and makes for a good starting and orientation point. The modern Catholic church stands 55m tall, the entrance of which is located up Casanova Street just off the main Paulus VI Street. Today's modern church – designed in the shape of the Madonna lily, a symbol of the Virgin Mary – was built in 1969 over the remains of earlier Byzantine and Crusader churches, and contains the **Cave (or Grotto) of the Annunciation**, where tradition states the Virgin Mary received news from Gabriel of Jesus's conception. Remains of the earlier churches are still visible in the lower stone cave. The unusual geometric design and grey stone walls dotted with stained-glass windows of the basilica, located up the spiral staircase on the right of the main entrance, are eerily impressive.

St Joseph's Church (⊕ *07.00–18.00 daily*) Located 50m from the northern exit of the basilica, this is the early traditional site of Joseph's carpentry shop, and later the 'House of Joseph'. The current church was built in 1914 on the site of an earlier 12th-century one. In its heyday caves, granaries and wells – which today are located down the stone stairs from within the church – were used by early Nazarene inhabitants. It was later, when Christian pilgrims were appearing in greater numbers, that it turned into a site of worship.

Greek Orthodox Annunciation Church (⊕ *08.00–17.00 Mon–Sat, noon–14.00 Sun; admission free*) This church is another contender for the site where the Virgin Mary received news from Gabriel of Jesus's Annunciation. The church, the Orthodox equivalent to the Basilica of the Annunciation, was built over the spring said to be where Mary was fetching water at the time of Gabriel's appearance. The present church, built in 1750 along the south side of the chapel containing the spring, can be visited, although is often overcrowded with large groups of pilgrims. Descending from the small upper church into the lower chapel downstairs, a single, narrow aisle leads to the northern end where it is possible to look over an altar into the running spring.

Greek Catholic Synagogue Church From the top of the main souk street turn left and then take the next right. The small, stone entrance is easily missed. This is said to be the synagogue where Jesus preached to the people of Nazareth. It became a popular place of Christian worship after influxes of pilgrims, during which

time the church was built. The building is extremely quaint and stands like an old grandfather clock, snuggled into the maze of souk streets.

Mary's Well and Ancient Bathhouse The well and bathhouse are fed by the spring gushing through the Church of St Gabriel, and is a site whose importance in daily life and religious connotations is undeniable. Christian tradition states that it was here, while Mary was collecting water from the well, that Gabriel appeared to her and divulged news of the Annunciation. In the 1990s, beneath an adjacent souvenir shop, profoundly impressive remains of a bathhouse were discovered. Believed to be Roman, they would therefore have been built at around the time Jesus lived in Nazareth. Tours to the well-preserved remains can be organised through the **Cactus Gift Shop** (*Mary's Well Sq;* \6578539; ⊕ *09.00–19.00 Mon–Sat; admission ₪120 for up to 4 people, which covers the 30min tour & a light refreshment*).

Nazareth Souk As one of the largest markets in the country the souk is a well-trodden corner of the city, frequented by people from all over the Galilee. Its entrance is located at the top of Casanova Street where tight, winding cobbled lanes weave through a large part of the Old City, crammed to the hilt with stalls selling pretty much everything. A huge restoration project has seen the market returned to its original glory, where mansion houses, mosques, churches and squares compete for space.

The White Mosque (Al-Masjed Al-Abyad) The mosque was built between 1799 and 1808 to commemorate the end of the Ottoman governor Al-Jazzar's heavy-handed rule. White was chosen to signify purity and the peaceful coexistence of religions in Nazareth. The mosque is located in the heart of the Old City and is easily identifiable by its colour and thin, elegant minaret. The mosque is open for visitors to have a look inside, but dress modestly. Women must cover their heads, and a guardian will provide a headscarf if you don't have one.

Nazareth Village (\6456042; w *nazarethvillage.com*; ⊕ *09.00–17.00 Mon–Sat; admission adult/child ₪50/25*) The village is a reconstruction of Jewish Nazareth as it would have appeared during Jesus's time and provides a kitsch yet entertaining step back in time. Agricultural techniques, food presses, traditional costumes, food and even animals set this time capsule back 2,000 years.

AROUND NAZARETH

TEL MEGGIDO (ARMAGEDDON) (\6590316; w *parks.org.il*; ⊕ *08.00–17.00 Sat–Thu, 08.00–16.00 Fri; admission adult/child ₪28/14*) According to Christian tradition, Tel Meggido is the site where the battle for the world will take place and, judging by its tumultuous past, it seems a likely enough spot. Destroyed and rebuilt 25 times in its long existence, Meggido was a crucially important strategic site along the great trunk road leading trade caravans from Syria and Mesopotamia down to Egypt. Extensive excavations have revealed the remains of 20 phases of occupation dating from 4000BCE to 400BCE, while its battle scars continue on into the 20th century and World War I. Perhaps rather poignantly, it was here that Israeli prime minister Levi Eshkol and Pope Paul VI chose to meet on the Pope's 1964 visit to Israel.

Meggido's location on the fertile plains of the Jezreel Valley would have given its rulers and occupants access to the Via Maris trade highway. It would have been here that the often miles-long camel caravans would have stopped off to trade in the city's abundant and flourishing marketplaces.

Today, the park provides but a mere glimpse into the city's prosperous and ever-changing past, and of the mighty battles that ensued here. Partial reconstructions of some of the major features of the park do help in putting together what can sometimes be, to the untrained eye, a mass of stones (tours can be arranged from the park office). A short but insightful video is screened at regular intervals in English or Hebrew at the request of the majority.

The Chariot City and tunnel remain the most impressive relics in the park. A 30m-long water system built during King Solomon's reign was constructed to enable the fortified city's occupants access to fresh water throughout times of conflict. Today, visitors can enter the tunnel by descending 183 steps, which are located at the southwest corner of the park. The tunnel leads outside the park boundaries, where a 600m walk will bring you back to the car park.

Getting there and away The park entrance is located approximately 3km from the Meggido junction on route 66. Egged bus 825 runs every 30 minutes/1 hour between Tel Aviv (*1hr 40mins/₪27*) and Afula (*11mins/₪9.10*) and will stop at the Meggido junction if hailed. NTT bus 750 from Nazareth (*30mins/₪14.50*) stops at the junction on the way to Kfar Qara. You would then need to walk for about 20–25 minutes along the hard shoulder of the road until the turn-off to the site.

BEIT SHEARIM (*between Hashomrim & Hatishbi junctions;* ✆*9831643;* w *parks.org. il;* ⊕ *08.00–17.00 Sat–Thu, 08.00–16.00 Fri, closes 1hr earlier in winter; admission adult/child ₪22/9*) Extensive excavations that began in 1871 and have proceeded up until today, have revealed the ancient Jewish settlement of Beit Shearim and, more significantly to Jewish history, the underground cemetery built at its foot. The Sanhedrin – Jewish school of learning – was located here, and at its head was the much-revered Rabbi Yehuda Hanassi. After many years in Beit Shearim, Rabbi Hanassi relocated to the nearby city of Zippori, only to be returned posthumously in 220CE. Word of the rabbi's death spread the length and breadth of the Middle East and a fervent desire to be buried close to his grave became paramount to many. Beit Shearim hence became the holiest Jewish burial site throughout the Mishnaic and Talmudic periods.

The voluminous caves and countless graves shoehorned into every potential space that we see today are merely the tip of the iceberg of the possibly thousands who are buried in the surrounding hills. Large stone sarcophagi inscribed in Hebrew, Aramaic and Greek show Jewish symbols as well as secular images of figures and animals, and also families that derived from as far as southern Arabia and Syria. The catacombs are impressive and certainly worth visiting. Cut out of the hillside, they contain dozens of sarcophagi, some caves being up to 30m deep and several metres high. Free tours, offered by volunteers from the nearby moshav, are certainly instrumental in making sense of the mounds of tombs and the intricate messages inscribed on them.

Getting there and away The site is located off routes 75 and 722, between Hashomrim and Hatishbi junctions 20km southeast of Haifa. There is no direct transport to the park, but Superbus operates numerous services including 74, 190 and 193 (*30mins/₪12.50*) between Haifa Merkazit Hamifratz and nearby Kiryat Tivon, from where it is a 2km walk to the entrance.

ZIPPORI (SEPPHORI) (✆ *6568272;* w *parks.org.il;* ⊕ *08.00–17.00 Sat–Thu, 08.00–16.00 Fri, closes 1hr earlier in winter; admission adult/child ₪28/14*) Zippori was once a splendid city and a much-contested site throughout the Galilee region's dramatic past. Excavations that began in 1931 unearthed remains dating from the First Temple period, through the Roman conquest and Herod the Great's reign to the Byzantine period and beyond. Zippori was appointed capital of the Galilee region shortly after the Roman conquest in 63BCE and changed hands many times amid fierce battles and revolts. It wasn't until the 3rd century CE that the Jews finally retook control of Zippori and it was during this time that textual and archaeological evidence points to the arrival of Rabbi Judah Hanassi and the Sanhedrin Jewish lawmakers. Rabbi Judah lived out his final 17 years here and it was during this time that, in c200CE, he drafted the Mishnah.

The Sanhedrin remained in Zippori until its relocation to Tiberias at the end of the 3rd century CE, and the city's frequent appearance in the Talmud testifies to its significance in Jewish history. Zippori was razed to the ground by a violent earthquake in 363CE, shortly after the beginning of the Byzantine period and rapid spread of Christianity. The city was rebuilt and flourished as a Christian city – the population of which was still predominantly Jewish – until the beginning of the Arab period. Throughout the Crusader period, Arab revolt of 1936–39 and 1948 Arab–Israeli War, Zippori was contested, battled over and conquered.

Today the excavated ruins are fairly scanty. To the untrained eye, there is little to be gleaned from the piles of stones and masonry walls, with the exception of the rather impressive mosaic floors and Roman theatre. The remains are best appreciated through an arranged tour, which can be organised through the park office. A circuitous route through the park's antiquities offers panoramic views over the surrounding area and takes you past relics of street patterns, a marketplace, bathhouses, Jewish and Christian ecclesiastical buildings and a Crusader fortress.

Getting there and away NTT bus 353 between Nazareth (*20mins/₪9.10*) and Acre (*1hr 30mins/₪21.50*) stops every 1½ hours at the Zippori junction from where you will have a 4km walk to the entrance of the park. To reach the site by car from Nazareth head north out of the city on route 79 and turn right after 4km towards Moshav Zippori. Upon entering the moshav, follow signs to the antiquities park.

CANA (KFAR CANA) Today 8,500 people – 83% of whom are Muslim, 17% Christian – call Cana home. The small town is located approximately 8km north of Nazareth, and is a likely candidate for the biblical site of the same name, where Jesus performed his first miracle of turning water into wine. Jewish tradition also believes this to be the site of the tomb of the sage Rabbi Shimon ben Gamliel.

The town itself is characterised by several churches commemorating the miracle located on Churches Street, running through central Cana. The **Franciscan Wedding Church** (⊕ *08.00–noon & 14.00–18.00 Mon–Sat; admission free*) was established in 1883 and is the traditional site of the home where Jesus performed his miracle. Next door, in the **Greek Orthodox Church of St George** visitors are shown an ancient-looking glass jar, purportedly – under Orthodox belief – one of the ten water containers involved in the miracle.

Further along Churches Street is the **Nathanael Chapel**. It was built towards the end of the 19th century in honour of Nathanael, later to become St Bartholomew, one of Jesus's most vocal opponents who later ended up being one of his disciples. The ruins of the ancient village of Cana rest atop a nearby hill, which is only accessible by foot or 4x4. It is a demanding walk, but those who undertake the challenge will be rewarded by panoramic views of the southern Galilee region.

Getting there and away NTT buses 28, 29, 30, 332, 340 and 431 (direction Tiberias) all stop in Cana (*20mins/₪9.10*). To reach Cana by car, head north on route 754 for approximately 8km. The turning to the town is signposted on the right.

TIBERIAS *Population 42,600*

Tiberias is the hub of eastern Galilean life and often considered the capital of the region. Named in honour of the Roman emperor Tiberias, the city has seen its share of proverbial ups and downs. In more recent times, an extensive clean-up operation has been under way to create a Tiberias that offers more than tacky seaside attractions, shabby hotels and littered beaches. The project has seen some success and, while Jewish and Christian pilgrims never halted their yearly processions to the city, visitors now seem to want to stick around a little longer.

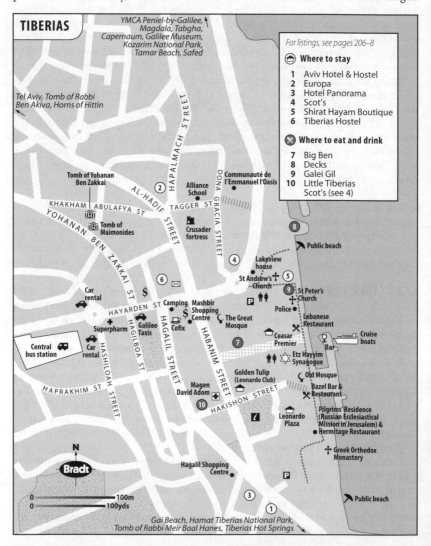

TIBERIAS

YMCA Peniel-by-Galilee,
Magdala, Tabgha,
Capernaum, Galilee Museum,
Kozarim National Park,
Tamar Beach, Safed

For listings, see pages 206–8

⌂ **Where to stay**
1 Aviv Hotel & Hostel
2 Europa
3 Hotel Panorama
4 Scot's
5 Shirat Hayam Boutique
6 Tiberias Hostel

✕ **Where to eat and drink**
7 Big Ben
8 Decks
9 Galei Gil
10 Little Tiberias
   Scot's (see 4)

Tel Aviv, Tomb of Rabbi
Ben Akiva, Horns of Hittin

Tomb of Yohanan
Ben Zakkai

KHAKHAM ABULAFYA ST

YOHANAN BEN ZAKKAI ST

HAPALMACH STREET

AL-HADIF STREET

TAGGER ST

DONA GRACIA STREET

Alliance
School

Communauté de
l'Emmanuel l'Oasis

Crusader
fortress

Tomb of
Maimonides

Lakeview
house

St Andrew's
Church

Public beach

St Peter's
Church

Car
rental

HAYARDEN ST

HAGILBOA ST

HASHILOAH STREET

Camping

Superpharm

Galilee
Taxis

Cofix

Mashbir
Shopping
Centre

The Great
Mosque

Police

Lebanese
Restaurant

Cruise
boats

Central
bus station

Car
rental

Ceasar
Premier

Bar

HABANIM STREET

HAGALIL STREET

Etz Hayyim
Synagogue

Golden Tulip
(Leonardo Club)

Old Mosque

HAPRAKHIM ST

Magen
David Adom

HAKISHON STREET

Bazel Bar &
Restaurant

Leonardo
Plaza

Pilgrims' Residence
(Russian Ecclesiastical
Mission in Jerusalem) &
Hermitage Restaurant

Greek Orthodox
Monastery

N

Bradt

Hagalil Shopping
Centre

0   100m
0   100yds

Public beach

Gai Beach, Hamat Tiberias National Park,
Tomb of Rabbi Meir Baal Hanes, Tiberias Hot Springs

While beaches in the near vicinity of urban areas are still overcrowded and littered in peak summer months, international restaurants, outdoor cafés and an improved standard of accommodation have gradually appeared. Tiberias has long been a top holiday spot with Israeli teenagers in search of a party atmosphere, and hence the school summer holiday months are the city's busiest. Yet pilgrims and partygoers have always seemed to coexist in relative harmony in this city, where beer and the Bible are the main attractions for two very different kinds of visitors.

HISTORY Tiberias was founded in c20CE by Herod Antipas, son of Herod the Great, and the city was soon forcibly populated by reluctant Jews. Over time Tiberias became one of the country's four Holy Cities and was the seat of the Sanhedrin and centre of Jewish learning for many years after the Roman destruction of the Temple of Jerusalem. It was here that the Mishnah, which later grew into the Talmud – dictating Jewish civil and religious laws – was believed to have been compiled between the 3rd and 5th centuries CE.

The Jewish community continued to thrive throughout Byzantine and Arab rule, until the Middle Ages when wars and earthquakes ravaged the city and it fell into rapid decline. Throughout the Crusades, it was the central city of the Principality of Galilee in the Kingdom of Jerusalem until, in 1187 during the Battle of Hittin on the outskirts of Tiberias, Saladin defeated the Crusaders, and the city was all but abandoned. It was at this time that the present-day city was established, just north of its ancestor.

The first modern Jewish area in the city dates back to 1740, when Tiberias was under the rule of Daher Al-Omar Al-Zaydani, who nominated Tiberias as capital of Galilean territory (which lasted until his assassination in 1775). The city prospered

DAHER AL-OMAR AL-ZAYDANI (1690–1775)

Born to a Galilean family of Qaysi notables, Daher Al-Omar Al-Zaydani is considered to be the first independent ruler in Palestine after establishing an autonomous territory in the Galilee. Originally appointed as an Ottoman tax collector, Al-Zaydani's diplomatic skills and administrative policies brought him support from the people along with prosperity to the Galilee. In 1768, the Ottomans acknowledged his success, awarding him the title of 'Sheikh of Acre, Amir of Nazareth, Tiberias, Safed, and Sheikh of all Galilee'.

In 1730, Al-Zaydani fortified Tiberias and negotiated with Bedouin tribesmen to stop incursions against the city. A tolerant ruler, he encouraged Jews to settle in Tiberias and developed and maintained good relations with the Greek Orthodox Church in Nazareth and Acre, thus securing support from Russia, which was expanding its presence in Palestine.

However, all his achievements, which included the founding of the modern city of Haifa and the fortification of Tiberias and Acre, meant that Al-Zaydani secured unprecedented autonomy, which the Ottoman authorities tried on numerous occasions to curb. Confrontations resulted in the siege of Tiberias in 1742–43, organised by the Governor of Damascus, from which Al-Zaydani emerged victorious. Subsequently, in 1750, he took control of Haifa and Tantura. The years that followed saw him engage in a war against the Ottomans in Egypt as well as in Palestine and present-day Lebanon and Syria. However, as the Ottoman–Russian War of 1768–74 came to an end, the Ottomans once again tried to restore their control of the area and besieged Acre. Al-Zaydani died a year later in 1775, during an attempt to flee his captured capital.

thanks to its abundance of fertile agricultural lands and mild climate and today continues to play a pivotal role in Galilean life and Israeli tourism. In the 1948 Arab–Israeli War, Tiberias became the first mixed Arab–Jewish city to fall to the Jews.

GETTING THERE AND AWAY The **central bus station** is located down a small side road off Hayarden Street, just past Hashiloah Street. Egged buses 959, 961 and 962 depart to and from Jerusalem hourly (*2hrs 40mins/₪37.50*), and 836 and 840 run every 20 minutes to and from Tel Aviv (*2hrs 20mins/₪37.50*). Superbus 432 has regular services to Haifa (*1hr 15mins/₪37.50*) and also operates the 450 to Safed (*1hr/₪37.50*) and 28 shuttles regularly to and from Beit Shean (*40mins/₪37.50*). NTT bus 431 runs hourly between Tiberias and Nazareth (*25mins/₪16*). There is a bus service around the Sea of Galilee departing every 2 hours from Tiberias (page 210). Golan buses 57 and 147 leave Tiberias once every three hours, going anticlockwise around the Sea of Galilee to Katzrin (*1hr 30mins/₪29*) and stopping at Deganya Alef, Lavnun Beach, Kursi junction, Ramot junction and Yehudiya junction. Golan bus 52 has only two departures per day and runs clockwise around the Sea of Galilee.

GETTING AROUND With the exception of those mentioned above, buses to and from sites and beaches around the Sea of Galilee are few and far between, and taxis can be exorbitant if you're using them regularly. There is a taxi rank outside the Leonardo Hotel, next to the tourist information centre. Alternatively, **Galilee Taxis** (\5720353) has a small office on the corner of Hayarden and Hagilboa streets. The most convenient and economical means of getting around is by **renting a car.** You'll find **Dollar Thrifty** (*3537; ⊕ *08.00–18.00 Sun–Thu, 08.00–13.00 Fri*) at the central bus station. **El Dan** (*Habanim St;* \03 5579004; ⊕ *08.00–17.00 Sun–Thu, 08.00–13.00 Fri*) and **Avis** (*2 Haamakim St;* \6722766; ⊕ *08.00–17.00 Sun–Thu, 08.00–14.00 Fri*) rent cars from ₪150 per day. **Bicycles** can be rented for ₪75 per day from the **Aviv Hotel** (page 207).

TOURIST INFORMATION The **Tourist Information Office** (*9 Habanim St;* \6725666; ⊕ *08.00–16.00 Sun–Thu, 08.00–19.00 Fri*) is located in the small archaeological park directly in front of the Leonardo Hotel.

Local tour operators
Lido Cruises Lido Beach; \6710800; w lido.co.il. Operates 30min cruises around the Sea of Galilee. Schedules change from day to day so call ahead to find out sailing times. During the summer months there are regular sailings, so it is possible to just show up at the dock.

Tour Plan Israel \08 6316860; e info@ tourplanisrael.com; w tourplanisrael.com; ⊕ 08.00–22.00 Sun–Thu. Offers day tours around the Sea of Galilee (*departs 08.00 Tue; US$149*), to the Golan Heights & Upper Galilee (*departs 08.00 Wed; US$149*) & to Safed, Meron & Peki'in (*departs 08.00 Thu; US$159*).

🏠 **WHERE TO STAY** *Map, page 204, unless otherwise stated*
Tiberias is small, but there is a good range of higher-end hotels, some good mid-range options and some much-improved budget choices too. Come the Jewish and summer holidays all are booked to capacity, so if you plan on visiting around those times be sure to book well in advance.

🏠 **Scot's Hotel** (69 rooms) 1 Gdud Barak St; \6710710; e info@scotshotels.co.il; wscotshotels.co.il/en. The Scot's Hotel is the jewel

in Tiberias's hotel crown. Built as a hospital by Scottish missionary Dr David Torrance in 1894, the castle-like building was converted in 2004 into a 5-star hotel. While all rooms are faultless, the so-called 'antique rooms' are especially charming (& considerably pricier). Manicured lawns, a swimming pool, lake views & a gourmet restaurant clinch the deal. Prices based on HB. $$$$$

🏠 **Europa Hotel** (30 rooms) 3 Hapalmach St; ☎ 6169999; e info@europa1917.com; w europa1917.co.il. Opened in 1917, it was one of the 1st buildings to be built outside the Old City walls. The hotel has also housed the British Regimental Office in Palestine, but that was eventually closed in 1939. The new boutique hotel was rebuilt preserving Ottoman charm & style. Original stairways, beautiful airy rooms & an outdoor terrace make it one of the nicest hotels in Tiberias. $$$$

🏠 **Shirat Hayam Boutique Hotel** (11 rooms) 1 Hayarden St; ☎ 6721122; e info@shirathayam. org.il; w shirathayam.co.il/en. A boutique hotel by the sea, set in a historic building dating back to 1850. The wonderful Umm Kulthum, one of the greatest-ever Arab musicians, stayed here in 1946. Rooms are classically decorated & come with small balconies overlooking the Sea of Galilee. $$$$

🏠 **YMCA Peniel-by-Galilee** [map, page 211] (13 rooms) Route 90 north; ☎ 6720685; w ymca3arches.com. Just 5km up the coast from Tiberias is this secluded YMCA hostel. Nestled amid palm trees & shady gardens, the 1920s stone building exudes Middle Eastern charm. Located on the shore of the Sea of Galilee, it has private beach access & a hot-spring pool as well as a Middle Eastern terrace restaurant. Rooms are simple but with views like these you won't be looking at them anyway. All northbound buses stop directly outside. $$$

🏠 **Aviv Hotel & Hostel** (30 rooms) 66 Hagalil St; ☎ 6720007; e avivhotel@walla.com. Located a short walk from the centre & offering a selection of clean, fresh rooms ranging from dorms to dbl & twin rooms. $$

🏠 **Hotel Panorama** (40 rooms) 56 Hagalil St; ☎ 6724811, 6720963; e rafizaharur@gmail. com. Not the most charismatic hotel in the city & in need of a lick of paint, but it offers decently priced dbl rooms, nice sea views & good central access. $$

🏠 **Tiberias Hostel** (18 rooms) Rabin Sq; ☎ 6792611; e tiberiashostel@gmail.com; w hosteltiberias.com. Don't judge a book by its cover springs to mind here as the outside of the building is shabby & ramshackle but inside is a hostelling treat. Both the 4-bed dorms & private rooms come with en-suite bathrooms, AC & strong Wi-Fi. There is a great rooftop terrace, travel information & a well-equipped communal kitchen. $

✕ WHERE TO EAT AND DRINK *Map, page 204*

Most places serve up a pleasant grilled St Peter's fish, the Sea of Galilee's local produce, or grilled meat and salad. The pedestrianised Hakishon Street is lined with cafés, restaurants and late-night bars and is a good place to soak up the summer resort atmosphere. For light bites there are falafel stalls, bakeries and pizzerias dotted around the main streets, especially along north Hagalil Street.

✕ **Scot's Hotel Restaurant** 1 Gdud Barak St; ☎ 6710710; e info@scotshotels.co.il; w scotshotels.co.il/en. Enjoying a sunset dinner on the terrace of this regal restaurant is a true Tiberias treat, with views over the fragrant gardens & still waters of the Sea of Galilee. The menu changes regularly to incorporate seasonal specialities but expect fresh, home-grown vegetables & herbs, St Peter's fish & a selection of speciality cheeses. To top it off, the wine cellar is first rate & offers some local boutique bottles. 3-course meal $$$$$

✕ **Decks** Gdud Barak St; ☎ 6721538; ⊙ 19.00–late Sun–Thu, end of Shabbat–late Sat. Kosher. Picturesque location on a wooden deck jutting out into the lake, this restaurant specialises in expertly prepared meats & fish grilled over wood renowned for its aromatic properties. The lamb, duck & local fish are highly recommended. $$$$

✕ **Little Tiberias** Hakishon St; ☎ 6792806; w littletiberias.com; ⊙ noon–midnight daily. Cosy, home-style cooking in the middle of the busy pedestrian thoroughfare. Wide selection of meats & seafood & some cheaper pasta dishes if the budget doesn't quite run to the seafood platter. $$$$

✕ **Galei Gil** Promenade; ☎ 6720699; ⊙ 11.00–midnight daily. With perfect views over the lake & a menu chock-full of grilled meats, locally caught fish & salads, this is a great place to while away an evening. $$$

✖ Big Ben Midrahov; ☏6722248; ⏰ noon–late daily. An old Tiberias favourite, Big Ben pulls in the crowds with decently priced beer, a chilled-out atmosphere & plenty of live televised sporting events. Standard pub food fills a hole even if it's not particularly exotic. $$

ENTERTAINMENT AND NIGHTLIFE Tiberias's nightlife centres on the pedestrianised Hakishon Street leading down to the seafront. Throughout the busy summer months, this is where people congregate to chatter noisily amid the pumping bar sounds, street vendors and abundance of late-night restaurants.

SHOPPING For camping and hiking, **Camping** (*cnr of Hagalil & Hayarden sts;* ☏*6723972;* ⏰ *08.30–19.00 Sun–Mon & Wed–Thu, 08.30–14.00 Tue & Fri*) offers a wide range of equipment. **Steimatzky** (*Hagalil Shopping Centre, Hagalil St;* ☏ *6791288;* ⏰ *08.00–19.30 Sun–Thu, 08.00–14.00 Fri*) has a good selection of English-language books, magazines and newspapers, while the **Galilee Experience Gift Shop** (page 210) has plenty of souvenirs to choose from.

OTHER PRACTICALITIES Tiberias is a small and easily navigable city, with an even smaller centre, which radiates out from the seafront promenade. Most services and facilities are located on Habanim Street, running parallel to the sea. There are numerous **exchange shops** (*standard opening hours 08.30–14.00 & 16.00–18.30 Sun–Mon & Wed–Thu, 08.30–13.30 Tue & Fri*) around Habanim Street as well as banks with **ATMs**. The **post office** is also located nearby (*Rabin Sq;* ☏*6790066;* ⏰ *08.00–20.00 Sun, Tue & Thu, 08.00–13.30 Mon & Wed, 08.00–noon Fri*). Superpharm has a **pharmacy** on 42 Hayarden Street (☏*6676663;* ⏰ *08.00–22.30 Sun–Thu, 08.00–20.00 Fri, 10.00–23.00 Sat*), and emergency service **Magen David Adom** is on 1 Hakishon Street (☏*6790101/111*). The nearest **hospital** is Porriya, 7km from Tiberias centre; bus 39 from the central bus station stops outside.

WHAT TO SEE AND DO

Tombs As the seat of the Sanhedrin and home to numerous Talmudic scholars over the years, Tiberias's hills are scattered with the tombs of influential men who had a profound impact on Judaism throughout the 2nd and 3rd centuries. Modest dress is required to enter all and yarmulkes for men can be obtained at the entrances. About 300m from the northern end of Hagalil Street are several tombs including that of **Maimonides** (also known as Rambam). Born in Spain in 1135, he fled his country from persecution and travelled to Cairo where he worked as Saladin's personal physician. During this time he rose to rabbi and leader of the Jews in Egypt and made significant contributions to the Mishnah. After his death in 1204 his body was transported to Tiberias. There is very little to see at the tomb except the 14 pillars encircling it, which represent the 14 sections of the Mishnah Torah. Plans to improve the site are under consideration in an attempt to raise Maimonides's tomb to the status that other tombs enjoy. One such tomb belongs to **Rabbi Meir Baal Hanes**, whose grandiose shrine is on the hill behind the city in the Hamat Tiberias National Park. Tradition has it that illnesses can be cured in the hot springs adjacent to the tomb. Near the tomb of Maimonides rests the tomb of **Yohanan Ben Zakkai** who was responsible for the relocation of the seat of the Sanhedrin from Jerusalem following its destruction in 70CE. The story of his escape from the capital hidden within a coffin, only to emerge in front of Roman general Vespasian, is legendary. Upon announcing to Vespasian that he was now the Caesar following the death of the Roman leader, he was granted one wish: he chose to found the Jewish learning centre, which was to become the Sanhedrin. In the areas now swallowed up by the modern city's sprawl is the tomb of **Rabbi Ben Akiva**, located just off the main road near the police station. Ben Akiva, one of the rabbis who is credited in the Talmud as being among those who carried Rabbi Yohanan Ben Zakkai out of Jerusalem, believed Bar Kokhba to be the Messiah and was finally executed after his rising in 135CE.

Crusader fortress The dilapidated remains of the 12th-century fortress are on the northern edge of the Old Town and worth a visit if only for the views over the lake. The fortress was rebuilt in the local black basalt stone in 1745 by Daher Al-Omar Al-Zaydani, ruler of the Galilee. Right across the street from the fortress is the former **Alliance School**, established in 1898 and relocated here in 1925 as the first Jewish school outside the Old City.

St Peter's Church (✆6720516; w *saintpeterstiberias.org;* ⊕ *08.00–12.30 Sat–Mon*) The apse of the church was designed in the form of a ship's bow, representing Peter's fishing boat. The present building was fully restored in 1870, although the church itself dates from the Crusader period. The entrance is tiny and hidden from view next door to Galei Gil Restaurant.

St Andrew's Church (m *054 2446736;* w *standrewsgalilee.com*) The Church of Scotland has just two churches in Israel, as well as a school and a guesthouse under its patronage. In Jerusalem is the St Andrew's Scots Memorial Church and in Tiberias is the relatively recent (1930) St Andrew's Church, which is essentially closed to visitors, but holds a service in English every Sunday at 18.00. It also often functions as a venue for concerts organised by the nearby Scot's Hotel.

Greek Orthodox Monastery Built in 1837 on top of the ancient ruins believed to belong to a Hashala synagogue, this seafront monastery is essentially open for pilgrims only, but there is no harm in trying to see if the entrance door is open. Inside, there is a lovely inner courtyard and a prayer niche below ground level. The tower rising above the monastery was erected by Daher Al-Omar Al-Zaydani. Across the alley is the Russian pilgrims' house dating from roughly the same period.

Horns of Hittin To put ancient Tiberias into perspective, the somewhat exerting hike of approximately an hour to the top of the hill allows for views over the entire Galilee region and beyond into present-day Jordan. It was here that Saladin defeated the Crusaders in 1187, signalling the beginning of the end for the Crusader kingdom in the Holy Land. It is also an important Druze gathering site. The trail starts at the main road leading west out of the city or can be reached by bus 42.

Tiberias Hot Springs (*Eliezer Kaplan Bd;* ✆ *6123600;* w *chameytveria.co.il;* ⊕ *08.00–20.00 Sun–Mon & Wed, 08.00–22.00 Tue & Thu, 08.00–16.00 Fri, 08.30–16.00 Sat*) Seventeen different springs emerge here and a whole menu of treatments and massages is offered. There are indoor and outdoor mineral pools, several restaurants and a fitness centre. Opposite the complex, which is now part of the Rimonim Hotel chain, is the **Hamat Tiberias National Park** (✆6725287; w *parks.org. il;* ⊕ *08.00–17.00 Sat–Thu, 08.00–16.00 Fri; admission adult/child ₪14/7*), which pays homage to the natural springs that played a crucial part in the development of Tiberias. Throughout the Roman period, thousands of people came to bathe in the therapeutic waters that flowed from the ground, and a large synagogue was built on the site indicating that it played a central role in the proceedings of the Sanhedrin. Within the ruins is an ornate mosaic, the oldest in Israel.

The Midrahov This is the place (a pedestrian walkway) where it all happens. Tourists can choose to relax in one of the countless bars, cafés or restaurants, soak up the sun, sea and spirituality of the lake or partake in one of the various activities. Boat trips can sometimes be organised from the dock although there is no set timetable for their departure. The tourist information office will be able to tell you what's what with respect to boat-trip departures on specific days. For those of us not able to walk on water, self-drive motorboats can be rented (*30mins/₪120*) from **Tiberias Water Sports**. Banana boats, water skiing and a range of other watersports are available from the offices on the dock throughout summer.

The Galilee Experience (✆ *6723620;* ⊕ *09.00–22.00 Sun–Thu, 09.00–15.00 Fri;* w *thegalileeexperience.com; admission adult/child ₪25/20*) Located on the second floor of the marina building, it has regular showings of a 38-minute movie depicting 4,000 years of Galilean history. There is also an impressively stocked gift shop and café.

Beaches Tiberias's beaches leave a lot to be desired and people looking for the quintessential Sea of Galilee swimming experience are better off heading to the beaches further along the coast or on the eastern shore (pages 214–16). If you decide to opt for a beach closer to home then the **Gai Beach** belonging to the **Gai Beach Resort Spa Hotel** is your best option. The **Gai Beach Water Park** (✆ *6700713;* ⊕ *Passover–Oct 09.30–17.00 daily; admission ₪70*) is a big hit with kids and has an assortment of slides and pools as well as beach access. Hotel guests get free entry.

THE SEA OF GALILEE (LAKE KINNERET)

While Tiberias itself is not an unpleasant place to spend a couple of days, most visitors use it as a jumping-off point to the sights around the Sea of Galilee. Steeped in New Testament history, the sea was the site of many of Jesus's miracles, with small churches dotting the shoreline commemorating these events. For hundreds of years Christian pilgrims have made their way to the gently lapping shores of the Sea of Galilee (known in Hebrew as 'the Kinneret') to soak up the abounding tranquillity, gaze down at ancient lands and walk in Jesus's footsteps. Today is no different, and despite the scores of tour buses that make regular stops along the sea, it has managed for the most part to avoid a mass-produced, over-touristy feel and there is a tranquil vibe with banana plantations and mango trees lining the pretty coastline. This, however, doesn't apply to the Sea of Galilee's beaches which are extremely popular with young Israeli teenagers. It is also worth avoiding the very good, but extremely busy **St Peter's Restaurant** between 13.00 and 15.00 (*buffet ₪80;* ✆ *6791888, 6712372;* ⊕ *noon–16.00; map, page 211*), when dozens of coach tours stop here. The following sights have been arranged in a clockwise direction starting from Tiberias, and recommended accommodation has been included under each site where appropriate. Beach campsites (pages 214–16) are good budget options, especially on weekdays and out of the school holiday season.

GETTING THERE AND AWAY Golan buses 52, 57, 142 and 147 have frequent departures to Katzrin from Tiberias, driving clockwise around the northern shore of the Sea of Galilee and stopping at the sights along the way. Golan buses 51 and 57 do the anticlockwise circuit, stopping at Kibbutz Deganya Alef, Ein Gev

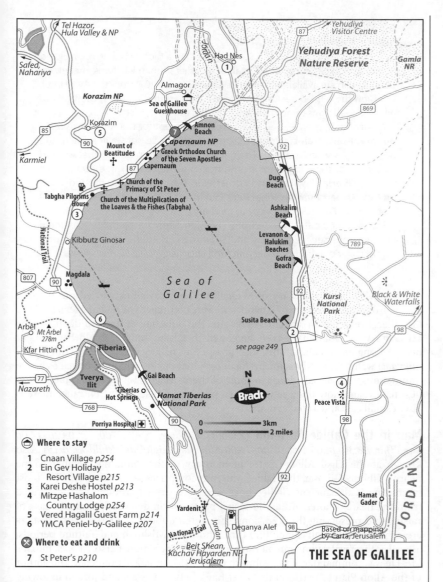

Where to stay

1 Cnaan Village *p254*
2 Ein Gev Holiday
     Resort Village *p215*
3 Karei Deshe Hostel *p213*
4 Mitzpe Hashalom
     Country Lodge *p254*
5 Vered Hagalil Guest Farm *p214*
6 YMCA Peniel-by-Galilee *p207*

Where to eat and drink

7 St Peter's *p210*

THE SEA OF GALILEE

Beach, Lavnun Beach and Kursi junction before continuing to the Golan Heights. Since 2010, there has been a **circular Kinneret bus** service (✆ *55477*; w *kineret. org.il*), which departs from Tiberias (Hagalil Shopping Centre on Hagalil Street) and drives around the lake stopping at major tourist sights. There are two lines: green (clockwise) and blue (anticlockwise) with the following departure times: 10.00/14.00/18.00 and noon/16.00/20.00 respectively.

WHAT TO SEE AND DO

Magdala (✆ *6209900*; w *magdala.org*; ⊕ *08.00–18.00 daily; admission adult/child ₪15/free*) Located approximately 6km north of Tiberias and clearly signposted, this small archaeological site by the Sea of Galilee is believed to be the birthplace of Mary Magdalene (or Mary of Magdala). The excavations carried out by Juan Salana from the University of Anahuac in Mexico (hence the flag of Mexico which flies there) revealed an ancient synagogue, the only one of its kind dating to the 1st century CE. Some have even suggested that Jesus himself could have taught here. Among the remains of this once-prosperous fishing village are *mikvah* (plural *mikvaot*) water installations for performing ritual purity ablutions as well as house foundations with mosaic floors in some of them. Magdala is a popular pilgrimage destination and now has a new modern pilgrims' house. At the entrance there is also a small café and a souvenir shop.

Man in the Galilee Museum (*Kibbutz Ginosar;* \ *6727700;* ☉ *08.30–17.00 Sun–Thu, 08.30–14.00 Fri, 08.00–16.00 Sat; admission adult/child ₪20/15*) Also known as the Yigal Allon Centre in memory of the founding member of the nearby Kibbutz Ginosar, the Galilee Museum comprises several sections. The most interesting is the ancient Galilee boat, a 1st-century CE wooden ship excavated from the nearby shores. An audio-visual presentation depicts the arduous task of raising and preserving the 8.2m-long ship, often dubbed the Jesus Boat. Upstairs are exhibitions on Galilean culture throughout the Mishnah and Talmud periods, as well as the Yigal Allon remembrance room offering a more personal peek into his life. He was commander of the Palmach (page 315), an Israeli politician, and author of the Allon Plan to partition the West Bank between Israel and Jordan following the Six Day War. Head to the roof of the five-storey building for a fabulous view over the lake. The museum is adjacent to the large tourist village of **Nof Ginosar** (\ *6700320;* e *nofginosar@ginosar.co.il;* w *ginosar.co.il.* **$$$**), which offers 162 rooms with excellent facilities, including access to the beach and a swimming pool.

Tabgha Benedictine Monastery and the Church of the Multiplication of the Loaves and the Fishes (☉ *08.00–16.45 Mon–Fri, 08.00–14.45 Sat, 11.00–16.45 Sun; admission free; modest dress; car parking ₪10*) The church's rather long-winded title does in fact sum it up pretty nicely. This is the site believed to be where Jesus performed one of his most well-known miracles: the Multiplication of the Loaves and Fishes and the Feeding of the Five Thousand. The church, located in the minute village of Tabgha, was consecrated in 1982 and is a far descendant of the original, built in the 4th century CE. Remains of a large Byzantine monastery, devastated during the Arab Conquest, were discovered when the area was excavated in the 1980s. After restoration to its Byzantine glory (including sections of the original figurative mosaic, the church's highlight) it is now one of the top spots along the sea's pilgrimage route. Tradition has it the block of limestone under the altar is 'the table of the lord', where Jesus performed the miracle. Located just south of Tabgha is the **Karei Deshe Hostel (HI)** (*65 rooms;* ☎ *5945633;* **e** *kdeshe@iyha.org.il;* **w** *iyha.org.il;* **$$$–$$**; *map, page 211*), which is perfectly located for exploring the sites along the north shore of the lake. Rooms have two, four or six beds (dorms **$**), air conditioning, television and en-suite bathroom. Kosher breakfast is included; sprawling lawns lead down to private beach access; often fully booked long in advance by groups.

Church of the Primacy of St Peter (*🕒 08.00–noon & 14.00–17.00; admission free; modest dress*) Just along from Tabgha, the modest Franciscan church marks the site where, tradition has it, Jesus appeared to his disciples for the third time, and where he confirmed the Apostle Peter. The black basalt chapel is small and simple and pales in contrast to its more elaborate ecclesiastical counterparts along the coast. Aside from its religious connotations there isn't an awful lot here, but its tranquillity and beachside location make it a worthwhile stop.

Mount of Beatitudes (*🕒 08.00–noon & 14.40–17.00; admission free; car parking ₪10; modest dress*) While the exact location of Jesus's Sermon on the Mount is a much-contested topic, with potential sites including the Horns of Hittin and Mount Arbel, Mount Eremos just up from the Church of the Multiplication has been the site of commemoration and pilgrimage for the past 1,600 years. With funding from Italy, more specifically from Benito Mussolini, whose name plaque was later removed from the doorstep, a beautiful Catholic church was built in 1938. The church oozes numerical symbolism, its octagonal shape representing the eight virtues. Within the church hangs Pope Paul VI's cloak, a memento of his visit to Israel in 1964. Despite the regular stream of tour buses clogging the car park, the church and its shaded, serene gardens remain a quiet and tranquil place of worship. Here there is also a convent and a **guesthouse** run by the Franciscan Sisters of IHM (*43 rooms;* ☎ *6711223–6;* **e** *ospbeat@netvision.net.il.* **$$$**).

From the car park, offering a fabulous view southwards over the ancient biblical lands and Sea of Galilee, a somewhat Herculean but worthwhile walk is possible. A steep path leads downhill towards the lake, likely part of the great trunk road coming from Damascus. Rain makes the path extremely slippery so you will need sturdy walking shoes.

Capernaum A little confusingly, there are two sites along the lakeside that go by the name Capernaum. In fact, the 5km stretch of coast that begins at Tabgha is classified under the umbrella title **Capernaum National Park**. The park's headquarters (*🕒 08.00–16.00 Sat–Thu, 08.00–15.00 Fri; admission free*) form the northern boundary from where there is a beautiful view across the lake towards the Golan Heights. Privately hired boats leave the dock at irregular intervals but if there is space and if you talk nicely to the captain he might let you hop on board. Boats normally head towards Ein Gev Beach on the eastern shore. Alternatively, you can take one of several truly serene and picturesque walks along a stretch of lake that remains today as it did hundreds of years ago. The opulent, red-domed **Greek Orthodox Church of the Seven Apostles** (*🕒 08.00–noon; admission free; modest dress*) can be accessed by the path leading west from the car park. A little further south of the church is the archaeological site of **Capernaum** (☉ *08.00–17.00 daily; admission free; modest dress*), best known through the New Testament as the centre of Jesus's Galilean activities after his departure from Nazareth. Today a church stands over an earlier Byzantine one, erected over the spot believed to be the birthplace of St Peter. A little north of this are the remains of a once-grand, white limestone synagogue, possibly dating to the 3rd century CE.

Korazim National Park About 5km north of the lake between the villages of Korazim (also spelt Corazim and Chorazim) and Almagor lie some impressive archaeological remains (✆ *6934982*; w *parks.org.il*; ☉ *08.00–17.00 Sat–Thu, 08.00–16.00 Fri, closes 1hr earlier in winter; admission adult/child ₪22/9*), sadly often overlooked by many visitors to the region. The ruins are spread over a broad area and include residential buildings, streets, ritual baths, olive presses (some of which have been reconstructed) and the site's *pièce de résistance* – a large, highly ornate synagogue. The city is recorded from the Second Temple period and is mentioned in the Mishnah and Talmud as a flourishing agricultural hub. Korazim also appears in the New Testament in conjunction with Capernaum and Bethsaida as the three cities condemned by Jesus for their lack of belief in his preachings.

Just off the Korazim junction is the lovely **Vered Hagalil Guest Farm** (*route 90 north*; ✆ *6935785*; w *veredhagalil.com*; *up to half price off-season midweek*; **$$$$**; *map, page 211*), which offers country wood cabins and suites complete with jacuzzi and a lovely deck perfect for morning coffee. A delightful rustic yet elegant **restaurant** (☉ *08.00–22.00 Sun–Wed, 08.00–23.00 Thu–Sat*; **$$$$$**) serves sumptuous grilled meats and fish on a wisteria-covered terrace. The farm offers guided horseriding treks, ATV tours, a café and spa, which are open to non-guests as well.

Beaches The pebbly beaches around the Sea of Galilee have long been a top destination for holidaying families and groups of teenagers who come all summer long to pitch their tents, light up a barbecue and soak in the mild waters of the lake. While pollution and plummeting water levels are two of the problems facing the lake, thankfully the one that aggrieved the Israelis most – the illegal privatisation of the beaches – has been resolved. Now almost all beaches are once again public, with a fixed entry rate of ₪57. Unfortunately it has also meant that swimming is prohibited at almost all the beaches, as there are no longer lifeguards on duty. While almost all the beaches provide access for the set fee, there are still charges for camping. As a general rule, the beaches on the eastern shore are considerably better than the dirty, litter-strewn ones around Tiberias.

Amnon Beach Lovely beach located along the quieter northern strip of the sea that is one of the few privately owned beaches left. Despite the fact that swimming is not permitted, there are windsurfing rentals and toilet and shower facilities. **Camping** is possible (*₪120/car*). The Kinneret Trail passes through the beach and from here a path leads to Capernaum (2km) and the Jordan Estuary (2km).

Duga Beach (*₪55/car, free on foot*) Perfect for some quiet Sea of Galilee reflection. Swimming is prohibited and there aren't any grassy areas but the beach is not crowded, is clean and undeveloped.

Ashkalim Beach (*₪55/car, free on foot*) Despite its huge popularity and crowded car park, the beach is probably the wildest of all the Sea of Galilee beaches. A path leads through sand dunes down to the shore (no swimming) where kite surfers by their dozens fly through the sky and whizz across the waves. There are plenty of picnic spots but very few facilities.

Levanon (Lavnun) and Halukim beaches (♦*6732044; ₪55/car, free on foot*) Located right next to each other, these beaches are popular with big groups of raucous teenagers in summer holidays, but lovely and quiet the rest of the time. Facilities include a small pebbly swimming beach with lifeguard, watersports, grass area for **camping** (included in the entry price), toilet and shower facilities and a snack-food kiosk.

Gofra Beach (*₪70/car, free on foot*) Family-oriented beach where sound systems are prohibited. Swimming is also prohibited but the area is clean and has bathroom facilities.

Ein Gev Beach If your budget stretches to a night at the **Ein Gev Holiday Resort Village** (*184 rooms;* ♦*6659800;* e *resort@eingev.org.il;* w *eingev.com;* **$$$$**; *map, page 211*), this is probably the Sea of Galilee's most beautiful, albeit private, beach. The four-star complex is set with green lawns and eucalyptus trees on the edge of the lake, and spacious rooms come with all the trimmings. Just south of the resort village are several kilometres of shady beaches, which are particularly pleasant midweek when there are fewer sun-seekers (*admission ₪14 pp*). If you are on a tighter budget, the campsite at nearby **Susita Beach** is an excellent alternative.

Kibbutz Deganya Alef Often referred to as the 'mother of kibbutzim', this is Israel's founding collective farm settlement, located to the east of Yardenit. It was established in 1910 during Ottoman rule by 12 Jews from surrounding areas.

In 2006, the kibbutz decided to go 'private', relinquishing their long-standing collective system and opting for the increasingly popular style of living that allows people to seek jobs and own property. The small museum in the Pioneers' Courtyard (♦*6608273;* ⊕ *09.00–noon Sun–Thu; admission free*), built inside what was the original dining room, depicts the life and times of this small but nationally renowned kibbutz; ask for an English transcript of the information boards at reception. A destroyed Syrian tank remains in the grounds, serving as a reminder of the 1948 Arab–Israeli War.

Several eminent Zionist names crop up in Deganya's past, many of whom are interred in the cemetery. Among these are the national poet Rachel, A D Gordon (an early Zionist figure) and General Moshe Dayan (general, politician and the kibbutz's second-born child). Albert Einstein and his wife also paid Deganya a visit.

Yardenit (♦*6759111;* e *info@yardenit.com;* w *yardenit.com;* ⊕ *08.00–18.00 Sat–Thu, 08.00–16.00 Fri, closes 1hr earlier in winter; admission free*) Just south of the lake, Yardenit is the traditional Christian baptismal site on the Jordan River. The strikingly green, fish-laden waters trickle through the northern valleys only to end up in the over-developed site of Yardenit. While the site has an obvious religious and spiritual draw for many, baptism by bulk seems a more apt description than peaceful confirmation. The site has, however, opened up the surrounding areas, so it is possible – and recommended – to get away from the crowds, gift shops and food outlets and walk along the banks of the river for some getting to one with nature, history and quiet reflection. While the site may be a little on the touristy side, a visit during a service, where up to 1,000 pilgrims clothed in white robes

MOUNT ARBEL

Mount Arbel's silhouette is one of the most unmistakable landmarks in the southern Galilee region. Its flat summit and drastically sloping edge is the result of a violent earthquake that shattered it into the two separate mountains we see today. A lookout at its peak proffers views over the Galilee region towards the Golan Heights, but even for seasoned hikers, getting to the top is difficult (but possible). The trail starts in the Valley of Doves at 206m below sea level and ascends directly up the sheer face of the cliff for 384m. Steps and handrails have been erected by the Israel Nature and National Parks Authority, which does ease things somewhat. Vertigo sufferers, however, would be best advised to drive up through Moshav Arbel and walk the short distance to the summit. Many believe that the graves of some of Jacob's children – whose 12 sons comprised the Tribes of Israel – are located here, in the caves that dot the cliff face. The caves – also used as shelter by Jews throughout the Roman and Greek periods – were again inhabited in the 17th century by the Druze. The scanty ruins of an ancient Jewish settlement include what little is left of a 4th-century synagogue dug into the cliff.

In the nearby Moshav Arbel, the excellent **Arbel Guesthouse** (\6794919; e arbelguest@4shavit.com; w en.4shavit.com; $$) is a great choice just outside the hubbub of Tiberias in the beautiful Galilee countryside. It is a lovingly run family place that has a real community feel. There are five apartments that can comfortably house between two and eight people and each has kitchenette, air conditioning and television. There is also a small swimming pool and lovely gardens.

stand knee-deep in the river, is anything but touristy, and is a moving experience whether you're a believer or not. Call in advance for baptismal bookings.

AROUND TIBERIAS AND THE SEA OF GALILEE

KOCHAV HAYARDEN NATIONAL PARK (BELVOIR) (*Yissahar Ridge, 15km north of Beit Shean;* \6581766; w *parks.org.il;* ☉ *08.00–17.00 Sat–Thu, 08.00–16.00 Fri, closes 1hr earlier in winter; admission adult/child* ₪22/9) It is immediately apparent when climbing the steep, winding road of the Yissahar Ridge up to the Kochav Hayarden Crusader fortress why such a site was chosen. With breathtaking views over the Jordan Valley, it offered strategic and defence capabilities that surpassed anywhere else in the region and thus became one of the most important fortresses in the country. Today, the heavily moated fortress has been fully excavated, the only such example from the Crusader period in Israel.

Though it was inhabited for a mere 21 years (1168–89), other residents have called Kochav Hayarden their home for a lot longer. Egyptian vultures, indigenous to the area, have lived in the Galilee and Golan regions for centuries. The practice by farmers of illegally poisoning calf carcases against predators, however, has led to severe decreases in their numbers. A sanctuary, erected 30m left of the castle, has given home and hope to several crippled birds. In 2007, a rare birth was celebrated, the baby chick destined for the wild when strong enough.

Getting there and away Getting there without a car is not easy. The steep 6km uphill walk from the main road is not for the faint-hearted; better, perhaps, to hitchhike from the bottom. Superbus 28 from Tiberias to Beit Shean will drop you off on the main road at the small junction. By car from Tiberias head south on route 90 for approximately 12km and turn right at the Kochav Hayarden junction. Follow the road 6km up the ridge, turning left at the T-junction at the top.

MOUNT TAVOR, AL-SHIBLI AND KFAR TAVOR Mount Tavor is the most easily recognisable feature in the Jezreel Valley landscape. Almost completely symmetrical, the 405m-high domed mountain affords staggering views of the valley and surrounding areas. The mountain holds importance in both Christian and Jewish biblical history, although the scores of pilgrims who make the regular trip are predominantly Christian. While hotly contested, the **Church of the Transfiguration** (⏰ *08.00–noon & 14.00–17.00 Sun–Fri; admission free; modest dress*), holding pride of place on the summit, is the site many believe to be where Jesus was recognised as the Son of God. Jewish tradition places the battle between Deborah and Barak and Sisera on the slopes of the mountain. Cars and buses are no longer permitted up the road so the options are by foot or bicycle – both quite exerting. Walkers can ascend using the 4,300 steps built in the 4th century CE for pilgrims.

Ascend Mount Tavor through the Bedouin village of **Al-Shibli**, a dusty, rather nondescript place whose friendly residents are descended from a nomadic tribe who made Mount Tavor their permanent home.

Catering to the abundance of hiking and cycling trails in this area is one of the most popular hostels in the country, located in the pleasant village of Kfar Tavor, 2km north of the turn-off to Mount Tavor on route 65. The **HooHa Cyclist's House** (*7 rooms; 7 Hacharuvim St; Kfar Tavor;* 📞 *077 7080542;* w *hooha.co.il; $$–$*) is fully geared towards those arriving on two wheels or two feet and offers a huge pool, bicycle storage, repairs and rental, cycling guides, free internet and spa and massage services. There is also a big garden, fully equipped kitchen and library. It is exceptionally popular so book ahead.

Getting there and away The village of Kfar Tavor is located just north of the turn-off to Mount Tavor on route 65 between Afula and the Golani junction. By car from Nazareth or Tiberias make your way to the Golani junction on route 77, turning south on to route 65. Continue south to the Kfar Tavor junction. The mountain road will be signposted on the right. The road north of Al-Shibli is steep, narrow and badly paved, but traversable with caution. Buses 442, 541, 542, 821 and 959 (*22mins/₪14.55*) run regularly between Afula (for Nazareth) and Tiberias, stopping at Kfar Tavor junction for walking (or hitching) up the mountain, or at the following Gazit junction for the short walk to Al-Shibli.

BEIT SHEAN NATIONAL PARK (📞*6587189;* w *parks.org.il;* ⏰ *08.00–17.00 Sun–Thu, 08.00–16.00 Fri, 08.00–17.00 Sat, closes 1hr earlier in winter; admission adult/child ₪28/14*) Beit Shean was put on the ancient map owing to its strategic importance along the great north–south trade route, with the area's abundant fertile lands an added incentive for residents, who first settled in the 5th century BCE. Today, the town of Beit Shean is a rather unappealing place. A small, unprosperous settlement, it seems to escape being forgotten only through the extremely impressive national archaeological park situated on its fringes.

The remains are awe-inspiring. Beit Shean's timeline spans 4,500 years, the decades following the Roman conquest truly its glory days, when it became one of ten cities that formed the Decapolis, a federated alliance, and the only one west of the Jordan River. It flourished through Hadrian's reign and, after the Bar Kokhba revolt, under Antonius Pius and Marcus Aurelius. Rapid and extravagant development saw the construction of statues, governmental buildings and after the adoption of Christianity, the amphitheatre, bathhouses and fountains, which remain Beit Shean's most striking features. The enormous amphitheatre is in fact but a fraction of its original size and is today honoured by live summertime concerts held within it. The **Shean Nights** (*Mar–Oct*) evening light show walks visitors through the site, illuminating features with displays on the natural canvas of the hill behind. In daylight hours, a trip up the hill's steep steps affords a fabulous view over the ruins. Visit the national park's website to book tickets.

In the middle of the park, a single standing pillar, the only erect structure unearthed, acts as a poignant reminder of the fateful fall of a once-magnificent city when it was ravaged by a violent earthquake in 749CE.

In the town itself is the **Beit Shean Hostel (HI)** (*62 rooms; 129 Menachem Begin Bd;* \5945644; e *beitshean@iyha.org.il;* w *iyha.org.il;* **$$$–$**). Housed in a vast, modern building, it even boasts its own swimming pool. Catering to large groups, it does have a rather mass-produced feel but is exceptionally clean. Single or double rooms have air conditioning, shower and television and kosher breakfast is included.

Getting there and away Buses heading to and from Jerusalem and Tiberias will pass through Beit Shean. Be sure to ask the driver if the bus stops there, as express services often don't. Buses 943, 961 and 966 depart hourly to and from Jerusalem (*2hrs/₪37.50*). Bus 843 to and from Tel Aviv leaves three times a day at 09.45, 14.00 and 17.00 (*2hrs 30mins/₪37.50*). From Tiberias, Superbus 28 departs every 30/45 mins (*2hrs 20mins/₪14*). There are no direct buses from Nazareth or Haifa, but Superbus services 411 and 412 leave Afula every 30 minutes (*30mins/₪10*), where you can connect to both.

GAN HASHLOSHA (SACHNE) NATIONAL PARK (\6586219; w *parks.org.il;* ⊕ *08.00–17.00 Sat–Thu, 08.00–16.00 Fri, closes 1hr earlier in winter; admission adult/child ₪39/24*) Most Israelis would vote Gan Hashlosha one of the most beautiful national parks in the country, and rightly so. The crystal-clear spring waters weave through the park's numerous pools and waterfalls, framed by well-kept lawns and vegetation. The surprisingly impressive, albeit small **Museum of Regional and Mediterranean Archaeology** (\6586352; ⊕ *10.00–14.00 Sun–Thu & Sat*), barbecue areas, changing rooms, lifeguards and children's play areas have unfortunately meant that the park is also one of the most visited sites in the country, especially in the peak summer months and weekends. Needless to say, it is a different kettle of fish on weekdays and

---

THE BIG ONE

Both seismologists and the Bible warn that Israel, sitting precariously on the fault line that stretches the length of the Syrian–African Rift Valley, is due for 'the big one', an earthquake to beat all others. Throughout history, violent earthquakes have devastated great cities and buildings the length and breadth of the country, many of which were never rebuilt. Beit Shean, Capernaum, Safed Old City and Jerusalem's Church of the Holy Sepulchre are but some of the casualties of Mother Nature's power. While Israel feels the effects of dozens of tremors and small quakes every year there is no need to panic yet – we could still be eons away from the devastating quake that experts believe is ultimately inevitable.

out of the school holiday season, and the constant 27°C waters mean swimming is possible any time of the year (although only one pool is full in the winter months). Early risers will most certainly be rewarded with solitude and tranquillity. An exact replica of the Tel Amal tower and stockade settlement that once stood on this spot is also worth a visit. The lovely little **Muse on the Water** (✆ 6588097; ⊕ noon–23.00 Sat–Thu, 10.00–16.00 Fri; $$$) is a kosher vegetarian restaurant serving an array of quiches, salads, pasta and fish. They also have a book exchange. Inside the adjacent and extremely pretty **Kibbutz Nir David** are plenty of **zimmer** bed and breakfasts that make a nice choice for a couple of days' stay.

Getting there and away The park is located next to Kibbutz Nir David on route 669 next to the petrol station. Buses 411 and 412 from Afula to Beit Shean stop every 30 minutes outside the kibbutz.

GAN GAROO AUSTRALIAN ZOO (*Adjacent to Kibbutz Nir David;* ✆ 6488060, 6488952; ⊕ 09.00–20.00 Sun–Thu, 09.00–15.00 Fri, 09.00–17.00 Sat, 09.00–16.00 Sun–Thu in winter; admission ₪45, 25% discount on Gan Hashlosha entry ticket) This relatively small but well-kept animal park was made possible by contributions from the Australian embassy in Israel and has now joined the ranks of only seven other zoological parks outside Australia to house koala bears. The nearby Kibbutz Nir David grows eucalyptus plants especially for their distinguished guests. Children and animal lovers enjoy the relative freedom given to the Australian

MOUNT GILBOA

The 500m-high Mount Gilboa ridge stretches for 18km across the southeastern part of the Jezreel Valley just south of Beit Shean. Every spring Israelis make their way up the mountain to see the blossoming of the famed purple Gilboa iris and hike in its abounding beauty. Mount Gilboa was the site where King Saul, the first king of Israel, and his sons died fighting the Philistines, a tragic event in Jewish history. The well-paved Gilboa scenic route (route 667), which runs the entire length of the ridge, offers magnificent views in all directions, as well as countless opportunities for hiking, picnicking and cycling. From here it is possible to see the ancient city of Beit Shean, the hill of Moreh where the Philistines assembled to fight King Saul, Mount Tavor and the Jordan Valley. While the mild year-round weather means visiting at any time is possible, the clearest views are during spring when the whole mountain is alive with blossom. At the eastern end of the Gilboa range is the **Gilboa Herb Farm** (✆ 6531093; w thegilboaherbfarm.rest-e.co.il; ⊕ noon–22.30 Mon–Sat; $$$; map, page 195), a rustic farm building perched atop the mountain. The farm specialises in the growing (and exporting) of fresh herbs, which their delightful restaurant takes delicious advantage of. Housed in a charmingly simple wood building (if the weather is nice be sure to sit outside), it serves rustic French, Italian and Middle Eastern-style foods. Also on the eastern end of the mountain is the new **Kimmel Restaurant** (✆ 6895566; m 054 9100091; e kimmelbagilboa@gmail.com; w kimmelbagilboa.co.il/en; ⊕ noon–late daily; $$$$; map, page 195), which offers excellent views over the valley below amid a rustically elegant setting. Just outside is the newly constructed **dry ski slope** that is a rather unusual addition to the mountain but one that is becoming increasingly popular with weekending Israelis.

animals, which include free-hopping kangaroos, kookaburras and flying foxes. The park is recognised by the Australian Wildlife Protection Authority and offers a small education centre, albeit mostly in Hebrew.

Getting there and away The park is adjacent to Kibbutz Nir David on route 669 just outside the entrance to Gan Hashlosha next to the petrol station. Buses 411 and 412 from Afula to Beit Shean stop outside the kibbutz every 30 minutes.

BEIT ALPHA ANCIENT SYNAGOGUE (*Kibbutz Hefzibah;* \ *6532004;* w *parks.org. il;* ① *08.00–17.00 Sat–Thu, 08.00–16.00 Fri, closes 1hr earlier in winter; admission adult/child* ₪*22/9*) Although under the care of the Israel Nature and National Parks Protection Authority, Beit Alpha can't really be described as a park. The site itself houses the ruins of an ancient synagogue dating to the 6th century CE. Its crowning glory and *raison d'être* is the elaborate and well-preserved mosaic floor, which can be viewed from raised platforms encircling it. Lights accentuate the significant features of the mosaic throughout a 15-minute video presentation detailing the history of the area and synagogues within Israel. It is a little pricey for the short time it takes to visit the park, but those with a national park combination ticket should definitely make the short detour.

Getting there and away The park is located next to the Kibbutz Beit Alpha on route 669. Buses 411 and 412 from Afula to Beit Shean stop every 30 minutes outside the kibbutz.

7

Upper Galilee

Telephone code 04

The landscape of the Upper Galilee provides the biggest surprise to visitors to Israel, who arrive expecting the barrenness of the Negev Desert, the cobbled lanes of Jerusalem's Old City and the white-sand beaches of coastal Tel Aviv. It is difficult to decide where the magic of the Upper Galilee region lies: in its tranquil, rural lifestyle perhaps, or in its abounding natural beauty, with roaring rivers, dense green forests and winding valleys. Yet perhaps its mystical (Note: this word is used a lot when describing Safed due to its centre as a place of Kabbalah worship) atmosphere arises from the Holy Jewish city of Safed, from its long-abandoned Crusader fortresses or its impressive archaeological ruins, the ghosts of the past retelling their stories through the remains of once-great sites.

With a landscape reminiscent of the verdant valleys of western Europe, the Upper Galilee is perfectly suited to a plethora of activities that you wouldn't necessarily associate with Israel, and plenty that you would. From kayaking down the bubbling Jordan River to inhaling the mysticism that abounds in Safed Old City's cobbled alleys, from witnessing the great bird migrations as they rest in the lush Hula Valley on their way south to getting swept up in the passionate celebration of Lag Baomer at the tomb of Rabbi Shimon bar Yokhai, this region is steeped in rural charm. Tiny villages dot the countryside, their family-run guesthouses a far cry from the chain hotels of the Mediterranean coast. Intertwined cultures and religions cohabit in a land that has seen its fair share of turmoil, its long border with Lebanon acting as a launch pad for Hezbollah rockets throughout a number of wars and battles. Yet as you watch the sun set over the majestic Montfort Castle or listen to the breeze gently whistling through the leaves of Rosh Pina's enigmatic little artists' quarter, it is difficult to imagine it in any way other than simply enchanting.

SAFED   *Population 33,400*

Through all of its countless names and spellings, from Tzfat, Tsfat, Safad, Tzefat, Zfat, Zefat to Zephath, there is but one name that stands out as the perfect fit: 'The Mystical City'. Perched high on the green, wooded slopes of the Upper Galilee mountains, Safed's clean, fresh air seems to whisper the secrets of the past, where Jewish mysticism abounds and whose spirit is still so clearly present. Cobbled stone alleyways, small cottages dotted with blue doors and windows and an abundance of ancient synagogues form the Old City, where today artists show off their talents in open studios.

Safed is regarded as one of Judaism's four Holy Cities (along with Jerusalem, Tiberias and Hebron) and was home to some of the religion's true greats. Scholars, spiritual leaders and religious philosophers gathered in the 16th century and together they gave Safed its proud status as a world centre for Jewish mysticism, Kabbalah. Today, they rest atop the mountain in the ancient cemetery, whose views befit their status as the 'righteous ones'. With the swift rise in Kabbalah's popularity

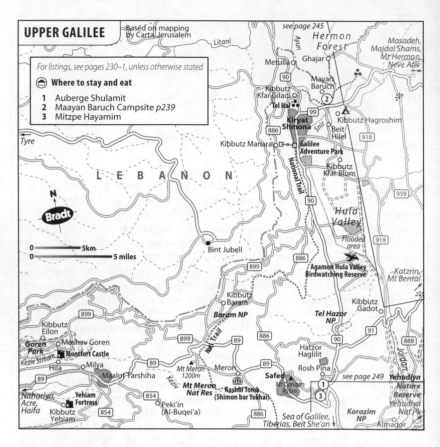

see page 245

UPPER GALILEE Based on mapping by Carta, Jerusalem

For listings, see pages 230–1, unless otherwise stated

⌂ **Where to stay and eat**
1 Auberge Shulamit
2 Maayan Baruch Campsite *p239*
3 Mitzpe Hayamim

see page 245

Litani

Hermon Forest

Masadeh, Majdal Shams, Mt Hermon, Neve Ativ

Metulla Ghajar Ayun

Mayan Baruch

Kibbutz Kfar Giladi

Tel Hai

Kiryat Shmona

Kibbutz Hagroshim

Beit Hilel

Kibbutz Manara **Galilee Adventure Park**

Kibbutz Kfar Blum

L E B A N O N

National Trail

Hula Valley

Flooded area

Tyre

Bint Jubell

Agamon Hula Valley Birdwatching Reserve

Katzrin, Mt Bental

Kibbutz Baram

Baram NP

Tel Hazor NP

Kibbutz Gadot

Kibbutz Eilon

Moshav Goren

Goren Park

Montfort Castle

Keziv Stream

Hila Milya

Maalot Tarshiha

Mt Meron 1200m Meron

Mt Meron Nat Res

Rashbi Tomb (Shimon bar Yokhai)

Hatzor Haglilit

Rosh Pina

Safed

Mt Canaan 955m

see page 249 **Yehudiya Nature Reserve**

Yehudiya Nat Pk

Nahariya, Acre, Haifa

Yehiam Fortress

Kibbutz Yehiam

Peki'in (Al-Buqei'a)

Sea of Galilee, Tiberias, Beit She'an

Korazim NP

Almagor

0 —— 5km
0 —— 5 miles

across the world, the quiet little town of Safed has suddenly found itself the centre of a budding spiritual tourism industry. Followers flock to study in the multitudinous centres of learning, where the substantial Hassidic Orthodox presence lends an air of antiquity, as though time has stood still. But somehow Safed's charm and sacred atmosphere have not been weakened (within the Old City at least), and it is an alluring and enchanting place to explore.

HISTORY Although legend has it that Safed was founded by one of Noah's sons after the Flood, the first textual mention is in the Roman period. The city is not mentioned in the Bible and didn't make its mark as one of Judaism's holiest centres until the 16th century. A large Crusader citadel fell to the Muslim conqueror Saladin in the 12th century and in 1266 the Mamluk leader Baibars made Safed one of his administrative centres, killing or dispelling much of the population in the process.

In 1492, the same year that Columbus set sail for the Americas, Spanish Jews fled to Palestine escaping persecution. Top Jewish scholars and rabbis congregated, and Safed was transformed into a centre for Jewish mysticism, Kabbalah. Rabbi Isaac Luria, Kabbalah's principal proponent, was a key figure in its creation, along with many other notable sages and Kabbalists. Groups came from many parts of Europe and North Africa and by 1550 a Jewish population of 10,000 was thriving. Throughout the 18th and 19th centuries Jewish residents suffered plagues, repeated Druze attacks and a severe earthquake that killed 5,000 people. Influxes of Jews

WHAT IS KABBALAH? Kabbalah is an aspect of Jewish mysticism that relates to a set of esoteric beliefs and practices that supplement the traditional Jewish interpretations of the Bible. It deals with the nature of divinity, the creation and the origin and the fate of the soul.

WHAT DOES KABBALAH MEAN? 'Kabbalah' literally means 'receiving', and is often used synonymously with the word 'tradition'.

WHERE AND WHEN DID KABBALAH ORIGINATE? While many Orthodox Jews date Kabbalah back to a system of interpretations of the scriptures handed down orally from Abraham, the system of Kabbalah seems to have been given its organised form in 11th-century Spain and arrived in Israel when Jews were expelled from the country. It centres on the Zohar, the principal source of Kabbalah.

WHAT EXACTLY IS THE ZOHAR? The Zohar is the principal book of Kabbalah written in the 13th century by Moses de Léon, a Spanish Kabbalist, but attributed to 2nd-century rabbi Shimon bar Yokhai, also known as the Rashbi. It provides a commentary on the first five books of the Torah and a cosmic-symbolic interpretation of Judaism based on the view of God as the dynamic flow of force through ten *sefirot* (planes or realms). These sefirot are symbols for everything in the world of creation.

WHO PRACTISES KABBALAH? Traditional Kabbalists are generally Hassidic Orthodox Jewish men, many aspects of this mystical practice are meaningless outside the realms of Judaism. What are often referred to as Hermetic Kabbalists range from Jews who prefer this form to the traditional practice, as well as non-Jews.

WHAT EXACTLY IS HERMETIC KABBALAH? Hermetic Kabbalah is a variant on traditional Kabbalah and dates back several hundred years. It is an esoteric, mystical tradition that draws on influences such as traditional Kabbalah, astrology, tarot, alchemy, pagan religions, Gnosticism, Freemasonry and tantra. It is usually spelt 'Qabbalah' to distinguish it from the traditional form. It has become increasingly popular over recent years because of celebrities such as Madonna and Demi Moore promoting its attributes.

HOW CAN I STUDY KABBALAH? This depends on which form of Kabbalah you wish to learn. Traditional Kabbalah is considerably more complicated, a long-standing belief being that when a student is ready, a teacher will appear. However, there are workshops, centres and meetings you can attend. A good grasp of Hebrew is essential for this and only male Jews may study it (although some women have been allowed). For those wishing to learn more about Hermetic Kabbalah, the internationally known Kabbalah Centre (w *kabbalah.com*) has branches all over the world (the Los Angeles branch being where celebrity followers convene). Within Israel there are branches in Tel Aviv, Jerusalem and Haifa that offer classes, meetings and information.

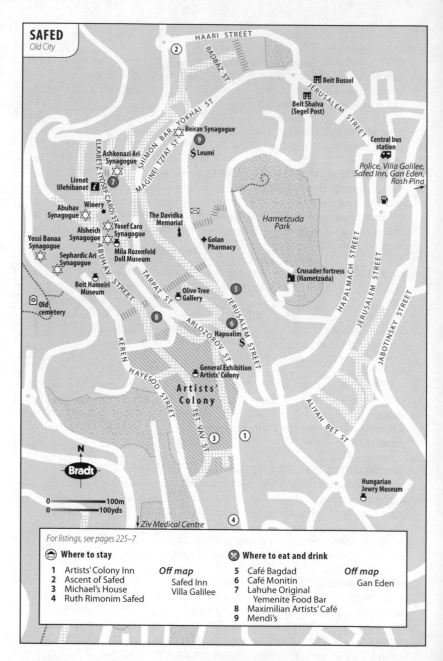

SAFED
Old City

HAARI STREET
RADBAZ ST
SHIMON BAR YOKHAI ST
MAGINEI TZFAT ST
ELKABETZ (YOSEF CARO) ST
ABUHAV STREET
KEREN HAYESOD STREET
TARPAT ST
ARLOZOROV ST
TET VAV ST
JERUSALEM STREET
HA PALMACH STREET
JERUSALEM STREET
JABOTINSKY STREET
ALIYAH BET ST

Beit Bussel
Beit Shalva (Segel Post)
Central bus station
Police, Villa Galilee, Safed Inn, Gan Eden, Rosh Pina
Beirav Synagogue
Leumi
Ashkenazi Ari Synagogue
Livnot Ulehibanot
Abuhav Synagogue
Winery
Yosef Caro Synagogue
The Davidka Memorial
Hametzuda Park
Golan Pharmacy
Alsheich Synagogue
Yossi Banaa Synagogue
Mila Rozenfeld Doll Museum
Sephardic Ari Synagogue
Crusader fortress (Hametzuda)
Beit Hameiri Museum
Old cemetery
Olive Tree Gallery
Hapoalim
General Exhibition Artists' Colony
Artists' Colony
N
Bradt
0   100m
0   100yds
Hungarian Jewry Museum
Ziv Medical Centre

For listings, see pages 225–7

Where to stay
1 Artists' Colony Inn
2 Ascent of Safed
3 Michael's House
4 Ruth Rimonim Safed

Off map
Safed Inn
Villa Galilee

Where to eat and drink
5 Café Bagdad
6 Café Monitin
7 Lahuhe Original Yemenite Food Bar
8 Maximilian Artists' Café
9 Mendi's

Off map
Gan Eden

from Russia and Perushim (disciples of Rabbi Elijah ben Solomon Zalman) did little to maintain the dwindling population.

Amid the 1929 Arab riots, Safed's Jewish quarter was attacked. Many fled, and by 1948 the Jewish population numbered just 2,000. Upon the British withdrawal, the Palestinian residents attacked, a move that was successfully countered by divisions of the Palmach (a precursor to the IDF) and resulted in most of the Arab population fleeing. Among the Arab refugees was the family of Mahmoud Abbas, the President of the Palestinian Authority and of the State of Palestine.

GETTING THERE AND AWAY There is one direct Egged bus 846 a day to and from Tel Aviv, leaving Tel Aviv's central bus station at 12.30 (*3hrs 30mins/₪42.50*) and Safed at 08.15. It is also possible to change in Netanya, Herzliya or Megiddo junction for more regular routes. From Haifa Merkazit Hamifratz, bus 361 operated by Nateev Express runs every 30 minutes (*1hr 50mins/₪22.40*). Superbus service 450 runs hourly (*1hr/₪14*) between Tiberias and Safed. Nateev Express 982 and 993 have a total of six daily departures between Jerusalem's central bus station (*3hrs 35mins/₪37.50*) and Safed, while Nateev Express bus 511 has frequent services until 16.00 between Kiryat Shmona (*45mins/₪16*) and Safed and will stop at sights along route 90. NTT bus 440 runs between Nazareth and Safed (*1hr 45mins/₪21.50*) from Tuesday to Friday.

GETTING AROUND All of Safed's sights of interest are contained inside the Old City which is easily navigable by foot (and mostly pedestrianised, so you don't have a lot of choice). If you need to get to the hospital in the south of the city, take bus 6 or 7 from the central bus station. Alternatively there are several taxi companies operating in the city, **Moniot Hamavrik** (⟍*6974222*) and **Moniot Ilan Mazuz** (m *052 2692082*), for instance.

ORIENTATION Outside the Old City, with its quaint architecture and charming environment, Safed is rather ordinary and there isn't much to see. The main commercial area is Jerusalem (Yerushalayim) Street, which separates the artists' quarter to the south and Old Town and ancient synagogues to the north. Accommodation is cheaper in the New City, but if your pocket permits, staying close to the Old City is certainly worth the extra expense. Facilities, hotels and eateries are concentrated in the east, which also has some of the best views. All galleries and shops are on Elkabetz Street in the Old City, where you can also find tourist information at **Livnot Ulehibanot** (*17 Elkabetz St;* ⟍*6924427;* w *livnot.org;* ⊕ *08.00–16.00 Sun–Thu*), which offers advice on attractions and courses, as well as tours through the underground tunnels of the city.

TOUR OPERATORS

Israel Extreme m 052 6478474; e info@ israelextreme.com; w israelextreme.com. Safed-based tour agency specialising in walking tours around the Old City as well as customised adventure excursions to the Upper & Lower Galilee & the Golan Heights.

Kabbalah Tour International Centre for Safed Kabbalah; 17 Elkabetz St; ⟍6821771. Kabbalah Tour packages including master classes, workshops, excursions, lectures & performances.

Activities & packages range from 1½hr workshops (₪500) to 5-day all-inclusive deals. Works together with the International Centre for Safed Kabbalah.

Richard Woolf m 050 5894647; e woolfr@ netvision.net.il. A well-known, highly reputable & extremely knowledgeable local tour guide, Richard can tailor trips to your preference & time constraints.

⬆ **WHERE TO STAY** *Map, page 224*

Safed has a good variety of accommodation to suit tastes and budgets – from the luxury spa hotels on Mount Canaan to mid-range and budget guesthouses. Within the Old City there are lots of rooms to be rented and it is worth visiting the Livnot Ulehibanot office (above), which also functions as a municipal information centre. Alternatively, there is a very informative website (w *safed.co.il*) with a wealth of information about the city and its attractions.

🏠 **Artists' Colony Inn** (4 rooms) 9 Simtat Yud Zayin St; ☎6041101; e benay@artcol. co.il; w artcol.co.il. Set in an idyllic Safed stone building these rooms offer a luxurious taste of the mysticism that abounds in the Old City. Jacuzzis, AC, fluffy dressing gowns & a huge rustic kosher b/fast make this the ideal romantic getaway. **$$$$**

🏠 **Ruth Rimonim Safed** (82 rooms) Artists' Colony Rd; ☎6994666; e info@rimonim.com; w rimonim.com. Built on the ruins of a 17th-century Turkish khan or inn, this elegant hotel is one of the most picturesque & well positioned in the city. Luxurious outdoor swimming pool, health club & spa set within spacious grounds with breathtaking views of the Galilee. **$$$$**

🏠 **Villa Galilee** (21 rooms) 106 Mount Canaan; ☎6999922; e info@villa-galilee.com; w villa-galilee.com/en. Luxury boutique spa hotel perched on top of Mount Canaan. Antique elegance has been twinned with excellent facilities & the intimate ambience of a small hotel. There is an unpretentious gourmet French restaurant, a choice of spectacular views from the rooms, a swimming pool & beautiful spa. **$$$$**

🏠 **Michael's House** (3 rooms) 55 Tet Vav St; m 052 6334532. Located along the steps leading up to the artists' quarter is this delightful guesthouse. 3 large, comfortable rooms have been created within the 150-year-old cottage, each on a different level of the higgledy-piggledy building. The wooden penthouse apartment sleeps 2, the Rose Courtyard sleeps 4 & the family unit can sleep up to 6. **$$$–$$**

🏠 **Safed Inn** (18 rooms) 191 Bialik St, Mount Canaan; ☎6971007; e riki@safedinn.com; w safedinn.com. Undoubtedly the best budget & mid-range option in Safed (& possibly the Upper Galilee). The building has been in the family for more than 80 years, but it opened its doors in 2008. This charming, comfortable guesthouse has everything from 'dormitories' (with just 2 beds & en-suite facilities) to standard dbls (with AC) & deluxe dbls (which also have jacuzzi bath). All are fantastic value for money, especially when you add the lovely gardens, helpful, hospitable family owners, ₪5 washing & drying machines, BBQ, table tennis, ₪10 for sauna & hot-tub use & bicycle rental. Bus 3 goes from central Safed or call for a pickup. **$$$–$$**

🏠 **Ascent of Safed** (31 rooms) 2 Haari St; ☎077 3601101; e info@ascentofsafed.com; w ascentofsafed.com. This large hostel caters for those wanting to delve more deeply into Kabbalah & participate in the many classes & workshops they organise. Trips, excursions & tours can also be arranged. Only married couples may stay in dbl rooms. **$$$–$**

✕ WHERE TO EAT AND DRINK *Map, page 224*

Most of Safed's restaurants are kosher and abide by Shabbat hours. While many do serve meat, there is also an abundance of vegetarian and fish eateries. There are also several nice bakeries around town that provide for an affordable and tasty snack, and numerous kosher falafel and shawarma stands on Jerusalem Street.

✕ **Café Monitin** 70 Jerusalem St; ☎8243638; w cafemonitin.com; ⊕ 09.00–23.00 Sun–Thu, 09.00–14.00 Fri. Kosher. Traditional dishes served in style. Indoor seating area overlooking the old city. A pleasant place to have a morning coffee & shakshooka. **$$$**

✕ **Gan Eden** Mount Canaan; ☎6972434; ⊕ 09.00–23.00 Sun–Thu, 09.00–14.00 Fri. Cosy, romantic Italian-style vegetarian & fish restaurant whose views from Mount Canaan are as exceptional as their food. The couple's b/fast, pasta selection & desserts are recommended. **$$$**

✕ **Café Bagdad** 61 Jerusalem St; ☎6974065; ⊕ 08.00–10.00 Sun–Thu. Something of a Safed institution is this little café that has been around for decades. Toasted sandwiches, fruit shakes, salads, desserts & falafel are on offer at decent prices. Outdoor seating area on the side of the street with splendid views over the Old City & the surrounding hills. **$$**

✕ **Lahuhe Original Yemenite Food Bar** 80 Elkabetz St; ⊕ 08.30–18.00 daily. A tiny eatery making only one dish – *lakhukh* – a stuffed Yemenite flat bread. Also serves homemade wine. With a seating area on busy Elkabetz St, it is a pleasant spot for a break after gallery hopping. **$$**

✕ **Maximilian Artists' Café** Hamaayan Sq; ☎077 7882887; ⊕ summer 08.00–midnight Sun–Thu, 08.00–Shabbat Fri, winter 08.00–21.00 Sun–Thu, 08.00–Shabbat Fri. Kosher. Delightful little vegetarian café in the square serving a selection of pasta, Israeli cheeses, salads, fresh fruit juices & cakes. $$

✗ Mendi's 29 Jerusalem St; ☎077 4108002; ⏱ noon–22.00 Sun–Thu, 09.30–3hrs before Shabbat Fri. Kosher. Traditional European Jewish dishes such as *chunt*, slow-cooked meats & hearty soups are served in this comfortable eatery. It is hugely popular with the yeshiva crowd, & offers Shabbat meals to be ordered in advance. Excellent value. $$

ENTERTAINMENT AND NIGHTLIFE Having a pumping night out in Safed is a distinct impossibility, unless of course you have arrived during the **Klezmer Festival** (early August) in which case concerts go on until the small hours. The alternative to an early night is an evening walk around the Old City, which is an extremely pleasant way to while away a few hours.

OTHER PRACTICALITIES The most convenient **ATMs** are **Bank Hapoalim** (*72 Jerusalem St;* ☎*03 6532407;* ⏱ *08.30–13.15 Sun & Tue–Wed, 08.30–13.00 & 16.00– 18.30 Mon & Thu*) and **Bank Leumi** (*35 Jerusalem St;* ☎*6994311;* ⏱ *08.30–14.00 Sun & Tue–Wed, 08.30–13.00 & 16.00–18.15 Mon & Thu*). **Exchange shops** are plentiful along Jerusalem Street and operate with standard opening hours (⏱ *08.30–13.30 Sun–Fri, 16.00–19.00 Sun–Mon & Wed–Thu; see map for exact locations*). Here you will also find a **post office** (*37 Jerusalem St;* ☎*6920115;* ⏱ *08.00–18.00 Sun & Thu, 08.00–12.30 & 15.30–18.00 Mon–Tue, 08.00–13.30 Wed*) and **Golan Pharmacy** (*50 Jerusalem St;* ☎ *6920472;* ⏱ *08.30–19.00 Sun–Thu, 08.30–14.00 Fri*). **Ziv Medical Centre** is 2km south of the town centre (*Harambam Rd;* ☎*6828811*) and the central **police station** is at 100 Hagalil Street (☎*6978444*).

WHAT TO SEE AND DO
Synagogues
Yosef Caro Synagogue (*Elkabetz St*) Named after the great scholar and Kabbalah follower Josef Caro, who is renowned for his authorship of the Shulchan Aruch (The Set Table), the basis of Jewish law. Upon expulsion from Spain he settled in Safed in 1536, serving as the city's chief rabbi and head of the rabbinic court.

Yossi Banaa Synagogue (*Yud Aleph St*) Housing the tomb of Yossi Banaa in a small chamber at the far end of the building, the synagogue (also known as Tzaddik Halavan) dates to the end of the 15th century and was built by Jewish exiles from Spain. Yossi Banaa, a 3rd-century Talmudic sage, was often referred to as the 'White Zaddik' after his famed miracle where he turned black chickens white on Yom Kippur. Inside the synagogue, an ancient Torah is housed in the Holy Ark, which is removed once a year on the eve of Bag La'omer for the pilgrimage to Meron (see box, page 232).

Ashkenazi Ari Synagogue (*Guri Haari St*) According to tradition this is the site of one of Safed's many miracles where, during the 1948 Arab–Israeli War, people crowded inside seeking shelter. Direct attacks on the synagogue caused much damage, but not a single member of the congregation was injured. It was founded by Spanish exiles in the 16th century and associated with Rabbi Isaac Luri (known as Ari), the revered Kabbalah master. While named after its ties with the Ashkenazi community, it is frequented by the whole spectrum of Jewish worshippers.

Sephardic Ari Synagogue (*Haari St*) Built in 1522 by North African Jews, this is the city's oldest synagogue. Throughout the 1948 Arab–Israeli War, the synagogue held an important defensive spot on the border between the Jewish and Arab quarters of the city, and was badly damaged during the conflict.

Abuhav Synagogue (*Alsheich St*) Aesthetically Abuhav Synagogue would probably take first prize, with its large, distinctive white-domed roof, whitewashed walls, blue window frames and elegant interior. Believed to be named after the 15th-century rabbi Yitzhak Abuhav, who is remembered as one of Spain's great sages, he became head of a yeshiva in Toledo where he studied philosophy and Kabbalah before moving to Safed. The Torah scroll, kept inside the ornate Ark, is not only the oldest scroll in the city, but is also the centre of numerous traditions and legends. It is taken out three times a year: on Yom Kippur, Shavuot and Rosh Hashanah.

Alsheich Synagogue (*Alsheich St*) This small synagogue, named after Rabbeinu Moshe Ben Haim Alsheich, is built in the style of 16th-century Sephardic synagogues. Tradition has it that during the severe earthquakes of 1759 and 1837 that ravaged the area, the synagogue remained totally undamaged, and this has become a legend handed down through the decades. A large blue door (with a number 10 on the doorpost) marks this rather modest synagogue, whose unkempt exterior somehow adds to its appeal. Note that this synagogue doesn't have a women's section.

Beirav Synagogue (*Meginei Tzfat St; services throughout the Sabbath & religious holidays, closed at other times*) Popular with visitors from all over the world thanks to its lively, traditional musical services, it was given a facelift a few years ago when English-speaking members of the Safed community renewed activity in the run-down 19th-century building.

Museums

Beit Hameiri Museum (*Keren Hayesod St;* e *yaniv@hameiri-cheese.co.il;* w *hameiri-cheese.co.il; guided tours noon Fri; admission adult/child ₪20/15*) Situated in a beautiful stone building, Israel's first dairy has been maintained for over 160 years. Today, the family-run dairy offers weekly tours, presentations on cheese and dairy production with some gourmet cheese tasting to finish. It's an interesting detour off the religion trail, and offers the opportunity to buy some traditional Safed specialities.

Hungarian Jewry Museum (*Haatzmaut Sq;* ✆ 6923880/1; w *hjm.org.il;* ⏱ *09.00–13.00 Sun–Fri; admission free*) Opened in 1986, the museum is still lovingly maintained by two of its original founders. It depicts Jewish life throughout Hungary, Transylvania, Slovakia, Ukraine, Bachka, Banat and Burgenland through a collection of letters, books and personal possessions.

General Exhibition Artists' Colony (*Hamaayan Sq;* ✆ 6920087; e *generalexhibition@gmail.com;* ⏱ *10.00–17.00 Sun–Thu, 10.00–14.00 Fri–Sat*) Large gallery showcasing paintings and sculptures by renowned Israeli artists. Located inside the former Red Mosque built in 1901, the centre is identified by its minaret. Above the entrance, the original plaque with an Arabic poem verse remains.

Mila Rozenfeld Doll Museum (*Kikar Sadeh, Eshtam Bldg;* ✆6972041; ⏱ *10.00– 18.00 daily*) Following the 1994 terrorist attack on the Tel Aviv Dizengoff Centre in which her daughter Alla died, Mila Rozenfeld started this museum in memory of the victims. It houses beautifully detailed porcelain dolls in various historical and ethnographic costumes.

Other sites

Artists' Colony At the heart of the Old City just off Jerusalem Street, amid a maze of cobbled lanes and ancient stone buildings, is Safed's artists' quarter. It was established in 1949 in the previously Arab part of town, following a need to centralise art within the newly formed country. It created a focal point for artists and attracted big names in the art world, both those from within Israel, and Europe's Holocaust survivors. Today about 60 artists have workshops and galleries here, ranging from paintings to ceramics to sculptures to photography, most in keeping with the underlying theme that abounds in Safed: Kabbalah. A number of galleries and shops are also based along Elkabetz (Yosef Caro) Street. An amble around the area is one of the city's highlights, where amenable artists show off their works and engage in lively chatter and debate with anyone who wishes to join in. For more information about the galleries, visit w artists.co.il.

Old cemetery According to religious tradition, it is in the ancient cemetery at Safed that some of the holiest *tzaddikim* (righteous people) rest. The custom of praying at their gravesides is age-old in Judaism, and the cemetery here is comparable only to that of the Mount of Olives in Jerusalem. The beauty of the cemetery adds to its unquestionable air of peace and spirituality, the unusual blue tombstones and burial caves dotted with brightly coloured flowers resting quietly and majestically upon the hill. Whether you're a believer or not, a mellow stroll around the cemetery to meet some of Judaism's most revered followers is the perfect way to feel the Safed vibe. In the middle of the cemetery and often crowded with worshippers rests one of the five most important *tzaddik*, **Rabbi Isaac Luria, R'Yitzchak Ben Shlomo** (or 'The Holy Arizal'), the great 16th-century Kabbalah master.

Clarinet and Klezmer in the Galilee (w *clarinet-klezmer.com*) Normally held in July, this is a week of nightly classical, jazz and klezmer performances held in a variety of venues around town. Some of the world's leading clarinettists join forces to produce this week-long festival which culminates in the Gala Final Concert. People come from far and wide to appreciate the festival, especially at the weekend, so if you are planning to stay during this time, you will need to book accommodation ahead.

Crusader fortress (Hametzuda in Hebrew) On the top of the hill at the centre of Safed stands the scanty remains of a Crusader fortress built in 1140CE to control the thoroughfare to Damascus. The castle was built on the site of an ancient citadel, the result of the 66CE Jewish revolt against the Romans. It is a bit of a hike but the views from the top of Israel's highest city and the pleasant park setting are worth the effort.

The Davidka Memorial Located just beyond Jerusalem Street is an old and rather crass cannon, which is by tradition said to have driven the last of the Arabs out of the city in the 1948 Arab–Israeli War. The handmade weapon was rather ineffectual with regards to actual firepower but made an almighty blast that had the same end result.

Beit Bussel Of historical interest in Safed is a building dating back to 1904 and known as Beit Bussel, named after Yosef Bussel, one of the founders of Kibbutz Degania. Originally opened by British missionaries to function as a hospital for Jews of the Galilee and Safed, this fine stone structure had since been used for various purposes, including a Haganah outpost in the Arab–Israeli War of 1948.

It has not been renovated since, and at present it is only possible to see it from the outside. Dating from the same period **Beit Shalva**, located across the road, has in contrast been restored and currently functions as Safed College.

ROSH PINA   *Population 2,900*

According to Jewish Kabbalah tradition, it is in Rosh Pina that the Messiah will appear, and one can certainly see why. Cottages built from local stone perch high on the slopes of Mount Canaan amid tree-lined cobbled stone lanes. A labyrinth of artists' workshops peeks out from behind spring blossoms, while gourmet restaurants lay beneath shady leaves. Even the internationally renowned Kabbalah follower Madonna was seen house hunting here, hoping to be one more of the lucky residents that call this beautiful little town home. Yet the town is not just a pretty face, holding an honourable place in Jewish history when in 1883 it became the first Jewish settlement in Palestine to come under the patronage of Baron Edmond de Rothschild (see box, page 186).

Rosh Pina has, with the obvious exception of the large and out-of-place shopping centre at its foot (in fact there are two shopping centres, the smaller and older **Galil Shopping Centre** and the newer **Chan Rosh Pina Mall**), preserved its rural heritage, and restored early pioneer houses and a synagogue commissioned by Rothschild can be visited. It was also within this tiny settlement that the first Jew to be hanged by the British Mandate authorities, Shlomo Ben Yosef, is buried. There isn't an awful lot to do here, but that's kind of the idea. Wander through the small lanes of the Old Town, appreciate the beauty of the place, peruse the artists' workshops and sip a cool drink in one of the beautiful cafés, and you'll feel it was a job well done. Over recent years, Rosh Pina has adopted a luxury tourism market, so accommodation is pricey but fantastic. Most accommodation is in luxury zimmers, and there are plenty to choose from. Guesthouses further from the old part of town are slightly cheaper, and lampposts are weighed down with signs advertising zimmers of all shapes and sizes. For all amenities and practicalities, the shopping centre is the place to go.

GETTING THERE AND AROUND Nateev Express buses 511 and 522 leave Safed every 1½ hours (*30mins/₪8.50*). Egged bus 500 leaves every 30 minutes to an hour between Rosh Pina and Kiryat Shmona (*16mins/₪16*), continuing to Acre and Haifa. Buses 541 (stopping in Tiberias) and 542 between Kiryat Shmona and Afula also stop at the central bus station in Rosh Pina. The town is tiny, albeit positioned on a rather steep slope, so walking is your only option if you haven't rented a car.

TOURIST INFORMATION You'll find the home of the **Tourist Information Centre** (\ *6801465;* ⊕ *08.00–16.00 Sun–Thu*) on the ground floor of the Galil Shopping Centre (page 231).

🏠 WHERE TO STAY

🏠 **Hameiri Estate** (9 rooms) Hahalutzim St; \6938707; w hrp.co.il/en. Identifiable by its 2 unusual palm trees standing sentry outside, this castle-like zimmer holds pride of place as the very last house at the top of Hahalutzim St. Large, beautifully maintained rooms are like something out of a medieval fairy tale. Sun terrace with views over the valley below. **$$$$$**

🏠 **Mitzpe Hayamim** [map, page 222] (83 rooms) Old Rosh Pina to Safed Rd; \6994555; e sales@mitzpe-hayamim.com; w mitzpe-hayamim.com. This is one of the most well-known & highly respected hotels & spa resorts in the country & deservedly so. Sprawling landscaped gardens, orchards & a fully operational organic farm envelop the luxury top-of-the-range hotel &

spa facilities, where the ethos is to connect guests to the magic of nature. Designed by Bauhaus architect Yehezkel Rozenberg & commissioned by German homeopath, physician & vegetarian Dr Erich Jacob Yaroslavsky (known simply as Dr Yaros), this resort is the culmination of decades of fine tuning. Needless to say, you will need to have an accumulation of US$50 bills in your pocket to fully appreciate it. **$$$$$**

🏠 **Pina Barosh** (7 rooms) 8 Hahalutzim St; ☏ 6937028, 6936582; w pinabarosh.com/en. Exceptionally attractive restaurant & zimmer with spectacular views. Stone cottage swathed in brightly coloured flowers & plants. Bright, airy

rooms decorated with elegance & imagination. They also offer a wine bar & tours of nearby wineries. **$$$$$**

🏠 **Auberge Shulamit** [map, page 222] (4 rooms) 34 David Shuv St; ☏ 6931485–94; e shulamit@shulamit.co.il; w shulamit.co.il. Wonderful views over the surrounding countryside. Classy & elegant, French-style, family-run hotel. Beautifully decorated, luxury rooms are set within a stone lodge that once housed the Israeli–Syrian armistice conference of the 1940s. B/fast terrace & evening restaurant with wonderful vista. Communal rooftop jacuzzi. In-room massages available. **$$$$**

✖️ **WHERE TO EAT AND DRINK** For budget-style eating there are several inexpensive restaurants, fast-food joints, cafés and a sushi bar in and around both the Galil and Chan shopping malls. A busy **falafel kiosk** is located opposite the mall car park, which is your best budget option.

✖️ **Muscat Restaurant** Old Rosh Pina to Safed Rd; ☏ 6994555; e sales@mitzpe-hayamim.com; w mitzpe-hayamim.com; ⏰ 13.00–midnight daily. Part of the ultra-deluxe Mitzpe Hayamim (page 230), the menu features a unique blend of the most freshly grown produce one could ever hope to find. Meals are prepared using only organic products grown on the resort's farm, quality meats & fish are cooked on open grills & wine is brought in from local wineries. **$$$$$**

✖️ **Auberge Shulamit Restaurant** 34 David Shuv St; ☏ 6931485–94; e shulamit@ shulamit.co.il; w shulamit.co.il; ⏰ 08.30–noon & 13.00–22.00 daily. Fine cuisine specialising in home-smoked fish & meats with terrific views of the Golan Mountains. Delicate hors d'oeuvres & a mouth-watering dessert tray. Pasta or soup of the day makes a good cheaper-end option. **$$$$**

✖️ **Rafa's House** Artists' quarter; ☏ 6936192; ⏰ 12.30–23.30 daily. Picturesque location. Selection of claypot dishes & prime steaks. Cool, shaded outdoor area or elegant grotto-style interior. **$$$$**

✖️ **Shiri Bistro** 8 Hahalutzim St; ☏ 6937028, 6936582; w pinabarosh.com/en; ⏰ 08.30–late daily. French-style cuisine served in a covered patio area surrounded by an abundance of plants & flowers & offering stunning views. Delicate yet unpretentious meals with southern Mediterranean gourmet influence. Adjacent to Pina Barosh (see above). **$$$**

▭ **Chocolatte** Old Rosh Pina down the steps from the synagogue; ☏ 6860219; w chocolatte. co.il; ⏰ 11.00–19.00 Tue–Wed & Sat–Sun, 11.00–23.00 Thu–Fri. A funky, comfortable décor & outdoor patio in the heart of the Old Town – this place is a chocolate lover's dream. Embrace your inner Willy Wonka & try the oh-so-rich handmade chocolate desserts, truffles & drinks. **$$**

♀ **Blues Brothers Pub** Erus St; ☏ 6935336; w villa-tehila.co.il/en; ⏰ 21.00–late Thu–Sat. Attached to the delightful Villa Tehilla Guest House (**$$$$**), this little watering hole is one of the most pleasant options in town. A leafy beer garden & conservatory make an apt setting for a few relaxing drinks, while the cave-like interior is retro & friendly.

OTHER PRACTICALITIES There are two **shopping centres** at the base of Rosh Pina. The smaller and older Galil Shopping Centre houses most practicalities, including Newpharm **pharmacy** (☏ 6860645; ⏰ 09.00–22.00 Sun–Thu) and **Bank Hapoalim** (☏ 03 6532407; ⏰ 08.30–13.00 & 16.00–18.30 Mon & Thu, 08.30–13.15 Tue–Wed, 08.15–12.30 Fri). There are also several cheap eateries, and the **police station** is just outside. The newer Chan Rosh Pina Shopping Centre has a selection of high-street shops and more places to eat.

The small moshav of Meron might for the greater part of the year appear to be a quiet and relatively insignificant village, but once a year the entire area fills with pilgrims, here to celebrate the festival of Lag Baomer. The moshav and mountain are revered as the site of the final resting place of Shimon bar Yokhai, known as the Rashbi, a 1st-century rabbi who is credited by many as having written the Zohar, the principal script in Jewish mysticism (Kabbalah), and his grave attracts tens of thousands of Jewish pilgrims every year. It was his request to his students that they should celebrate the anniversary of his death (which fell on Lag Baomer) with dancing, singing and feasting.

Lag Baomer is celebrated on the 33rd day of the Omer, which falls on the 18th day of Iyar in the Jewish calendar (usually in May in the Gregorian calendar). Its origins lay with Rabbi Akiva of whom Rabbi Shimon bar Yokhai was a dedicated disciple. According to the Talmud, 24,000 of Rabbi Akiva's students were struck down by a divine plague, punishment for not displaying respect to one another. Lag Baomer is today celebrated as the day the plague ended and also the day when it is believed Rabbi Shimon bar Yokhai passed.

The festival at Meron is a fascinating mixture of spirituality, celebration, feasting and partying, a religious Woodstock of sorts. The annual pilgrimage centres on bar Yokhai's large, domed tomb, where a huge bonfire belches out heat and smoke, and male Orthodox members dance fervently around it. Women and children dance and sing traditional songs in the courtyard below. Dozens of sheep and cattle are slaughtered in ritualistic kosher manner, and tents and caravans sprawl across the surrounding countryside, a combination of Hassidic and Sephardim families, many of whom attend with their three-year-old sons. For it is on Lag Baomer at Meron that hundreds of toddlers receive their first upsherin, the Jewish first haircut. The ceremony is a time of great happiness and pride as parents watch as their sons have payot (temple curls) shaped.

While doubtless a happy and celebratory event, it is a sacred and important part of Orthodox belief, and sightseers must ensure they adhere to customs. Visiting the impressive tombs of Rabbi Shimon bar Yokhai and other early rabbinical figures such as Rabbi Hillel and Rabbi Shammai is, at any time, worthwhile. A little further up the mountain from the tombs is one of the oldest synagogues in the Galilee, whose east wall is carved out of the steep rock cliff.

WHAT TO SEE AND DO

Artists' galleries Explore the maze of workshops at the top of the hill upon which Rosh Pina sits and watch the artists as they create leatherwork, ceramics, jewellery, pottery, paintings and anything else that takes their fancy. A wonderfully bohemian and almost spiritual atmosphere abounds, where artists happily show off their work and engage in enthusiastic chatter.

Baron Garden Flowers and plants imported from France in 1886 and planted under the care of Baron Rothschild still flourish in the small garden whose design is said to have been based on the gardens at Versailles.

Ancient cemetery Located on the hill opposite the artists' quarter, the cemetery has been untouched for decades. Here rest the remains of Rosh Pina's founding members, mainly Jewish immigrants from Romania who settled here with the aid of Baron Rothschild. A small path leads to the cemetery from behind the iron gate.

Getting there and away Nateev Express runs several services between Safed and the rest of the country. Buses 5, 361, 967, 980 and 987/8 leave Safed every 30 minutes and stop in Meron (*10mins/₪11.50*) on the way. To go up the mountain you will need to have your own vehicle or be prepared for an exerting but beautiful hike.

TRAVELLING WESTWARDS FROM SAFED AND ROSH PINA

MOUNT MERON At 1,200m above sea level, Mount Meron (Har Meron in Hebrew) was Israel's highest mountain until the 1967 Six Day War, which saw the Golan Heights and Mount Hermon brought under Israeli rule following their annexation. The mountain is heavily forested, and dense, green wooded slopes hide caves and sinkholes, a prime habitat for countless species of rare plants and animals. It is the third contender for the site of Jesus's Transfiguration (along with Mount Hermon and Mount Tavor, both of which are visible from the summit) and offers staggering views across the Sea of Galilee. Access to the mountain road is through the village of Meron and is a pleasant drive to the summit, which is a nature reserve. Several nice trails offer undemanding walks and wonderfully fresh air.

BARAM NATIONAL PARK (\ *6989301;* w *parks.org.il;* ⊕ *08.00–17.00 Sat–Thu, 08.00–16.00 Fri, closes 1hr earlier in winter; admission adult/child ₪15/7*) A Jewish village in Mishnaic and Talmudic times, Baram is now the site of one of the most beautiful ancient synagogues in the country. Many believe the village was built in this remote location because of the legend that Queen Esther was buried here. A biblical figure, Esther rose to be Queen of Persia and is famed as having saved the kingdom's Jewish population from persecution. Today, the lively and joyous Festival of Purim is celebrated in her memory, with the Megillah (Scroll of Esther) read in Baram.

That the village was affluent is indicated by the presence of two synagogues, only one of which remains today. An inscription discovered at the smaller synagogue reads 'Peace in this place and all of Israel' and is now housed in Paris's Louvre Museum. The larger of the two synagogues is the *raison d'être* of the national park, its majestic façade, large basalt blocks, sculptures and its three gates facing Jerusalem unarguably impressive.

Following the Arab conquest, Christian Arab villagers of the Maronite Church chose to leave the synagogues standing, building their own church – located next to the synagogue – which is today the spiritual centre of the Maronite faith. In 1948, the village was abandoned after the residents were evacuated by the IDF owing to its proximity to the Lebanese border.

The rare kermes oak forest of the **Baram Oaks Nature Reserve**, located near the archaeological site, makes a nice conclusion to a visit.

Getting there and away Nateev Express bus 43 leaves Safed at 06.20, 09.30 and 13.30 daily (*35mins/₪12.50*) and stops in Kibbutz Baram, from where it is a short walk to the park entrance.

PEKI'IN (AL-BUQEI'A) The small, charming village of Peki'in, with its predominantly Druze population, is rather unexpectedly one of the most notable sites in Judaism. It claims to be the only place that Jews have lived continuously for 2,000 years, and evidence of their historic presence can be seen in the form of Jewish symbols embedded in stone houses dotting the village. As the originally large Jewish population dwindled, Jews began to adopt the language and customs of their Arab neighbours, all along retaining their religious beliefs. The village was emptied of Jewish inhabitants during the Arab uprising of 1936–39. A restored synagogue dating to the Roman period is located in the centre of the village and is cared for by a member of the Zenati family, whose ancestors were some of the founding Jewish members of Peki'in. The synagogue contains a fragment of an ancient Torah scroll and stone carvings believed to have been brought by refugees escaping the Roman destruction of Jerusalem.

Peki'in is also the site where it is believed Rabbi Shimon bar Yokhai and his son Rabbi Eliezer hid in a cave to escape persecution by the Romans during the Bar Kokhba rebellion. It was during their 13 years in hiding that they compiled the Zohar, the foremost book of Kabbalah. According to the village tourist department, Peki'in, with its population of 4,200, receives 60,000 visitors a year, many of whom come to light candles and slip prayer papers into the cracks of the cave.

Besides its obvious historic and religious draw, the village is beautiful in its own right, perched high on the hill overlooking the Bet Kerem Valley below, its ancient stone houses clinging to the slopes. Olive groves and fruit trees fill the surrounding fields, a testament to its rural, agricultural roots, where Druze, Christians and Jews have lived harmoniously for thousands of years.

Getting there and away Nateev Express buses 44, 45 and 46 to and from Nahariya pass the town every 2 to 3 hours (*35mins/₪12.50*).

🏠 **Where to stay and eat** There are countless small Druze restaurants in Peki'in serving traditional, hearty meals. Pitta, hummus, labneh cheese, olives, grilled meats and salads are all extremely well priced, one of the most characteristic traits of Druze hospitality and customs. Locally produced olive oils and marinated olives are sold in plastic bottles, and make for an authentic souvenir.

🏠 **Peki'in Youth Hostel (HI)** (50 rooms) ✆ 02 5945677; e pkiin@iyha.org.il. Geared towards large groups, it is housed in a vast complex & is a good budget option, if not the most visually pleasing choice in town. Kosher b/fast included & small cinema available. Ask at reception for guided tours or Druze homestay options. Located on the outskirts of the village. **$$–$**

MONTFORT CASTLE, NAHAL KEZIV AND GOREN PARK
As the sun sets over the Nahal Keziv Valley and the dense pine forests that engulf it, **Montfort Castle** (⊕ *in daylight hrs; admission free*), rising high on a jagged ridge, remains the last thing illuminated, as though left alone on a grand stage. The area here is laden with fantastic hiking opportunities, the Keziv Stream winding its way through the deep valley providing for some Herculean but immensely rewarding walks.

The castle was built by French Crusaders during the late 12th century but was later bought by the German Teutonic Knights. Following conflicts with the Knights Templar and Knights Hospitaller in Acre, the Teutonic Knights moved to this location, declaring it their Holy Land headquarters. With papal funding, they fortified the castle, turning it into a grand fortress and the largest in the Upper Galilee. The keep that stands in the centre is probably the most indicative of the full extent and magnificence of the structure. In 1271, the Teutonic Knights surrendered to the Mamluk sultan Baibars in exchange for free passage and escaped with their treasury and archives, thus ending the short and turbulent life of Montfort Castle.

Because of its precipitous location, the castle can only be reached by a fairly arduous uphill trek. A 1km trail leads from the Hila lookout at the end of Meilia village through road. To avoid the walk, **Goren Park**, with its great picnicking opportunities and population of rather confident jackals, has a lookout terrace. It is located across the valley from the castle. A path can begin or end a lovely hike down into the Keziv Valley and up to the castle, and it offers fabulous views of both, especially at sunset. It is possible to camp unofficially in the park although the ground can be rather rough.

An alternative way to approach the castle is to embark on a truly wonderful trek along the **Keziv Stream** and valley. A 6km circular walk following the black-marked trail starting in Hila leads you through vast pine forests reminiscent of the remote wildernesses of Canada and Scandinavia.

Getting there and away Goren Park is located between Kibbutz Eilon and Moshav Goren on route 899. From Nahariya, Nateev Express buses 27 and 28 stop at Kibbutz Eilon (*20mins/₪9.60*) and the Goren junction six times a day (*07.00, 09.00, 11.00, 12.30, 14.30, 15.40*). Only bus 27 returns and leaves from the junction on route 899 three times a day (*07.15, 11.30, 14.45*). Alternatively, there are countless buses leaving every 30 minutes to Maalot Tarshiha from Nahariya, where you can hitch to Hila.

Where to stay

Travel Hotel Eilon (28 rooms) Kibbutz Eilon; ↘6883034; e orit@travelhotels.co.il; w travelhotels.co.il/eng. Excellent location for exploring the rural countryside of the region. A relaxed & affordable place to base yourself. Simple but comfortable rooms have kitchenette & AC. It is a big favourite with families as there are plenty of outdoor areas & self-catering facilities. **$$$**

YEHIAM FORTRESS NATIONAL PARK (↘ 8276600; w parks.org.il; ⊕ 08.00–17.00 Sat–Thu, 08.00–15.00 Fri, closes 1hr earlier in winter; admission adult/child ₪14/7) The massive fortress is situated within the boundary of Kibbutz Yehiam and holds a tender place in the hearts of all who live there. While the strong walls and imposing buttresses were built centuries ago, the fortress's defensive stature was used in more recent times when, during the 1948 Arab–Israeli War, residents sought refuge and protection from the surrounding conflict. The exact date of its construction is unknown, but at some point in its life it, like the nearby Montfort Castle, was sold to the Teutonic Knights upon their departure from Acre. In 1265, it was conquered by the Mamluk sultan Baibars in his rampage through the region. Much of the fortress was destroyed and remained derelict until Daher Al-Omar Al-Zaydani returned it to its former glory in the 1760s, constructing the great square defences we see today.

While there is an interesting movie presentation within the national park, the most rousing and worthwhile reason to visit (besides the impressive remains themselves) is the fabulous view of the green peaks and valleys of the Galilee offered from the top.

Getting there and away From Nahariya take route 89 heading towards Safed and turn on to route 8833 at the Gaaton junction. From Nahariya, Nateev Express bus 42 goes to and from Kibbutz Yehiam several times a day (*23mins/₪8.50*).

TRAVELLING EASTWARDS FROM SAFED AND ROSH PINA

TEL HAZOR NATIONAL PARK (↘ 6937290; w parks.org.il; ⊕ 08.00–17.00 Sat–Thu, 08.00–16.00 Fri, closes 1hr earlier in winter; admission adult/child ₪22/9) Covering 1km², UNESCO-listed Tel Hazor is the largest biblical site in Israel, whose population, at its height, reached an estimated 40,000, four-times that of David and Solomon's Jerusalem. Extensive excavations have revealed 22 phases of occupation spanning 2,700 years, stretching from the early Bronze Age to the Hellenistic period. Hazor comprises two main sections: the acropolis and the fortified enclosure. Its location along the great Via Maris trade route was surely a key factor in its abounding success, and it is the only Canaanite site mentioned in the royal documents of Mari (located in modern-day Syria) which attest to its importance in trading tin. In its prime, Hazor covered an area twice the size of Meggido (pages 201–2). Biblically, Hazor didn't pale in importance. It is written that the King of Hazor, Jabin, headed a coalition of Canaanite cities against the encroaching Israelites, led by Joshua. Hazor is described as having been the 'head of all those kingdoms' (Joshua 11:1–5, 10). When the Canaanites were defeated, Joshua had Hazor razed to the ground.

Israelite Hazor's rebuilding is attributed to Solomon, who fortified the city in order to control movement along the Via Maris. In the 9th century BCE, presumably under the rule of King Ahab, the city was developed. It was during this time that the massive water system, a major feature of this national park today, was built. Ruins from many of the significant phases of Hazor are visible in the park; a trip to the small archaeological museum in Kibbutz Ayelet Hashahar is recommended before delving into the archaeological ruins. Fortifications from the Canaanite period, a large casement wall and gate believed to be from King Solomon's time, and a late Canaanite altar shed some light on the tumultuous past of this great city.

Getting there and away The national park is located along route 90 between Kiryat Shmona (*15mins*) and Rosh Pina (*15mins*), 4km from the Mahanaim junction. Most buses heading to Kiryat Shmona or south will stop there, although some express buses coming from Tel Aviv or Haifa don't, so be sure to ask the driver before boarding.

AGAMON HULA VALLEY BIRDWATCHING RESERVE (✆ *6817137;* w *agamon-hula.co.il;* ⊕ *09.00–1hr before dusk Sun–Thu, 06.30–1hr before dusk Fri–Sat; admission ₪52 with shuttle*) South of Kiryat Shmona, Hagoshrim and Tel Dan National Park, the Hula Valley sits tucked into the northern part of the Syrian-African Rift Valley and is one of the most crucial winter stopovers for the 360 species of migratory birds who drop in on their way south. Between the months of October and March, an estimated 500 million birds jostle for space in the skies and waters of the Hula Valley, a large proportion of which is today utilised for agriculture. Up until 1950, when most of the area was drained, the Hula Valley was one of the largest wetland areas in the Middle East. Following environmental objections to the drainage, a small swampland was created in 1963 and claimed the honour of being Israel's first nature reserve. Today, the area is undoubtedly the single most important wetland in the country for waterbirds and is graced with the presence of 20 globally threatened species, including the imperial eagle, spotted eagle and marbled duck.

Lake Agamon sits at the centre of the Agamon Hula Reserve and is the stage for spotting countless species of wildfowl, including hundreds of thousands of cranes. Other wildlife is in abundance too, with water buffalo, once indigenous to the area, having been reintroduced.

A large array of eco-friendly transport methods is on offer to get out into the heart of the park, ranging from bicycles, tandems, four-person bicycles, golf carts or the safari wagon. There are two flat and fairly undemanding routes (6km and 10.5km) following a circular route around the lake. A small introductory video is presented at the entrance and can be played in English on request.

BUS TIMES

From	To	Bus no	Departure time	Journey time	Price (₪)
Kiryat Shmona	Kfar Blum	30	10.50; 15.50	7mins	9.10
		32	10.55; 14.00	13mins	
		54*	10.00; 11.15; 12.45; 14.00	7mins	
		59**	22.00**	7mins	
Kfar Blum	Kiryat Shmona	30	10.57; 15.57	36mins	
		32	11.08; 14.13	37mins	
		54*	08.09; 10.39; 11.54; 13.24	7mins	
		59**	18.42**	7mins	

* Golan Bus
** Shabbat service

Getting there and away All Kiryat Shmona-bound buses will stop along route 90, from which it is a hefty 3km walk to the park entrance. Follow directions through agricultural buildings to the large car park. There is a nature reserve run by the Israel Nature and National Parks Protection Authority a little further south along the valley which can be easily mistaken for the birdwatching centre, so look out for signs.

KFAR BLUM Founded in 1943, Kibbutz Kfar Blum was named after the Jewish socialist and former French president Leon Blum. From its founding until the present day, it has survived on an economy based primarily on agriculture, although of late, tourism seems to have snuck in and taken over, and now the kibbutz offers an array of family activities in the shape of **Kfar Blum Kayaks** (⚉ *6902616; w kayaks. co.il*). They offer two-person kayaks or six-person rafts on trips down the Jordan and Hatzbani rivers. A 75-minute circular route costs ₪79 per person, while a 150-minute 'adrenalin' trip is ₪112 per person. Children's activities, bicycle tours and a rope park complete with zip line and climbing wall are all offered for around ₪79 per person. It is highly recommended to visit midweek and out of school holidays, as come weekends it is overrun with excitable children and raucous families.

In summer, the week-long **Voice of Music Festival**, also referred to as the Kfar Blum Festival, marks the centre of all activity in and around the kibbutz. Up to 15,000 music lovers attend the fantastic mix of classical compositions and modern experimental pieces each year.

Getting there and away If you're travelling by car, turn east at Gomeh junction off route 90, then follow the road for 4km before turning left to the kibbutz. There are a few local buses, as well as Golan bus services, between Kiryat Shmona, the largest town in the area, and Kfar Blum (see box, above).

⌂ WHERE TO STAY AND EAT

⌂ **Pastoral Hotel Kfar Blum** (125 rooms) ⚉ 6836611; e pastoral@kbm.org.il; w kfarblum-hotel.co.il. Luxury hotel & spa decorated in a Mediterranean-style elegance. Bright & airy rooms overlook the kibbutz's olive orchards & outdoor swimming pool. Suites have jacuzzi baths & separate living rooms. Tennis courts, a gym, sports facilities & restaurant are open to hotel guests. **$$$$$**

Å **Kfar Blum Kayaks Campsite** Located in the grounds of the kayaking centre (page 242) next to the Jordan River. Hot showers, a cooking area, picnic tables & a kiosk are ₪50 pp.

Kiryat Shmona, the largest town in the Upper Galilee, sits amid the stunning landscape of the region, with its verdant valleys, fresh mountain peaks and its proud religious and Zionist history. The town, however, is most certainly the ugly duckling of the area, and it is showing no signs of flourishing into a beautiful swan any time soon. The centre is dilapidated and run-down, seemingly forgotten about in the midst of the tourism boom seen in recent years in the surrounding settlements. While it claims to be the centre of tourism for the region, there really is very little of interest for visitors, and it is highly recommended to stay in one of the countryside zimmers or national park campsites nearby. Large manufacturing plants scar the area directly around the town, their bright lights and incessant noise humming throughout the night. Kiryat Shmona is a major transport hub, however, and there are buses to and from the otherwise relatively inaccessible northern Golan region. In fairness, the suburbs are marginally better, some parts even passing as quaint, but overall time would best be spent in other areas.

HISTORY The city was founded in 1949 on the site of a ruined Bedouin village whose residents fled after Safed was captured by Israeli forces in the 1948 Arab–Israeli War. It was initially used as a camp for immigrants involved in agriculture in the region but has slowly developed over the years into a large, if not particularly appealing, city. The city is named in honour of Joseph Trumpeldor and his seven comrades (*shmona* translates as 'eight') who died in 1920 defending **Tel Hai** (pages 240–1). The town used to make international headline news regularly as it was a popular target for Hezbollah and PLO rockets, launched from behind the nearby Lebanese border. Throughout countless skirmishes, residents have found themselves packing their bags and temporarily relocating south or spending days or weeks in underground bunkers.

GETTING THERE AND AWAY Kiryat Shmona is the transport hub of the region and can be reached from all major cities across the country. It also has good connections with the more inaccessible parts of the northern Golan and Upper Galilee. Egged bus 541 runs regularly to and from Tiberias (*1hr 30mins/₪27*), stopping at Rosh Pina and the Hula Valley. Bus 840 makes the same journey (*1hr/₪27*) only twice a day in the evenings. Bus 963 to Jerusalem leaves at 08.30 (*3hrs 11mins/₪42.50*) and returns to Kiryat Shmona at 13.40. Direct routes 845 and 840 leave hourly from Tel Aviv (*3hrs 25mins/₪42.50*). Route 500 leaves every 45 minutes up to 16.00 to Acre (*1hr 30mins/₪34*) and Haifa Merkazit Hamifratz (*2hrs 15mins/₪37.50*).

GETTING AROUND The bus station is centrally located and within easy walking distance of shops. If you are planning on hanging around in the city then inter-city buses, sheruts and taxis all run from outside the main bus terminal. Alternatively, renting a car is possible. The two most convenient options are **Eldan Car Rental** (*4 Tzahal St;* \6903186; w *eldan.co.il/en;* ⊕ *08.00–16.45 Sun–Thu, 08.00–12.45 Fri; from ₪140/day*) and **Sixt** (*Leshem St;* \6941631; ⊕ *08.00–17.00 Sun–Thu, 08.00–noon Fri; from ₪250/day*).

WHERE TO STAY AND EAT Kiryat Shmona has no major hotels and very few eating options. You are strongly advised to take advantage of the beautiful countryside lodging, camping and restaurants on the doorstep of this unsightly city, notably Kibbutz Manara, Horshat Tal and Kibbutz Hagoshrim.

🏠 **Manara Guest House** (51 rooms)
📞6908198; e tayarot@manara.co.il; w manara.
co.il. Simply decorated but well equipped & roomy.
Facilities include TV, AC, refrigerator, microwave & en-
suite bathroom with bath & separate shower. Guests
can use the swimming pool (in summer) & the price
includes b/fast in the kibbutz cafeteria. **$$$**
🏕 **Maayan Baruch Campsite** [map, page
222]📞6954624. A pleasant campsite by the Snir
Stream & on the Israel National Trail. Paintball &
Hagoshrim kayaks provide entertainment. The
campsite is conveniently located across the road
from the service area with a petrol station, a small
supermarket & a couple of cafés. **$$**
🍴 **Nehalim** Gan Hatzafon; 📞6904875;
🕐 noon–23.00 daily. This is an extremely pleasant
restaurant specialising in meat & fish dishes with a
selection of creative sauces. Located on a delightful
spot near the convergence of the Banias, Hatzbani
& Dan rivers, 2.5km east of the Hametzudot
junction on the right (look out for the petrol
station). **$$$$$**

OTHER PRACTICALITIES There is a small **shopping centre** opposite the bus station that
has all the standard high-street chain stores and is your best bet for getting provisions.
The central branch of **Bank Hapoalim** is on Tzahal Square (📞*03 6532407;* 🕐 *08.30–
13.15 Sun & Tue–Wed, 08.30–13.00 & 16.00–18.30 Mon & Thu*).

WHAT TO SEE AND DO

The Golden Park Traversed by the Ein Zahav Stream, the park is a rather
pleasant escape from the drabness of the city centre. Green lawns, a small wood,
an Ottoman-period flour mill and a small, quaint mosque – today housing the
Kiryat Shmona History Museum (*26 Hayarden St;* 📞*6940135;* 🕐 *08.00–noon Sun–
Thu*) – are all features of the park. About 3.5km outside the town centre in the
direction of the Golan Heights is **Shehumit Hill**, a basalt formation which rises 85m
above the surrounding area and offers a bird's-eye view of both Kiryat Shmona and
the nearby Hula Valley. Alternatively, a walk through the Tel Hai historical site is
also an option. Tel Hai open-air **Sculpture Garden** (Har Apsalim in Hebrew), with
works dating between 1980 and 1994 scattered in the hills of the nearby valley, is
located behind the Tel Hai College, which was established in 1957 and effectively
incorporates the historical site, including the **Tel Hai Courtyard** (📞*04 6951333*). The
latter was used in 1948 as an army base and subsequently in 1953 reconstructed as
a cultural centre and museum. Guided tours have to be arranged in advance. The
college also has an outdoor café with a leafy terrace.

Manara Cliff and kibbutz These days Manara is most well known for its cable-car
system leading down Israel's highest cliff (888m). Zimmers have been created by the
residents and the stunning views offered by being perched high on a cliff edge are one
of its key assets (especially if you look beyond Kiryat Shmona at its foot towards the
lush greenery of the Hula Valley). The **Galilee Adventure Park** (📞*6905830;* w *cliff.co.il;*
🕐 *09.30–16.30 daily; admission w/day ₪64, w/end ₪74*) is a little kitsch and clearly
aimed mainly towards the younger (or more fearless) set, but the 1,940m-long cable
car is a novel way of getting up the cliff to the kibbutz. A 1,200m-long mountain slide
that snakes its way back down the cliff hit the headlines during the 2006 Lebanon
War when Hezbollah rockets destroyed a significant section.

Rappelling, a zip line, a trampoline bungee dome and climbing wall give thrill-
seekers a choice of extreme activities. For those less disposed to throw themselves
off cliffs, a 1-hour guided hike can be arranged providing an explanation of the area,
land and surrounding sites. Alternatively, the kibbutz's apple orchards are open to
summer fruit pickers as is the well-maintained (but often crowded) swimming
pool. Price packages can be purchased together with nearby Kibbutz Kfar Blum
activities (page 237).

The entrance to the Manara Cliff cable car is along route 90 just south ofKiryat Shmona. Buses heading to and from Kiryat Shmona will drop you at the cable-car entrance. To drive to the kibbutz, follow route 90 north and turn left at the Tel Hai turn-off. After 3km, turn left and follow the signs to Manara.

AROUND KIRYAT SHMONA

TEL HAI Straddling the border with Lebanon, the site of **Tel Hai** (✆6951331; ⊕ 08.00–16.00 Sun–Thu, 10.00–17.00 Fri; admission adult/child ₪18/15) has long since come to represent Zionist heroism and has become a pilgrimage for scores of Jewish tourists and Israeli schoolchildren. The lands upon which Tel Hai, a modest farming settlement, was built, were originally purchased in 1893 by the wealthy Jewish French baron, Edmond de Rothschild (see box, page 186). In 1907, Arab farmers from Metulla built Tel Hai (known then as Talha), but left the area in 1911. In 1916, the Hashomer group moved in and in 1918, members of the Galilee Farmers Union settled here, and it became one of only four Jewish settlements in the Galilee. The 1916 Sykes–Picot Agreement called for the division of large areas of the Middle East, where the Galilee would have been split in half. The secret agreement left the British, French and Arabs in dispute about the future of the area and, although the British conceded to allow the Upper Galilee to be under French control, the Arabs were strongly opposed. A retaliation on 1 March 1920 saw the community of Tel Hai attacked. As the story goes, a group of Arab soldiers demanded to search the premises, believing the Jews to be harbouring French soldiers. The Jewish farmers signalled for reinforcements from nearby Kfar Giladi, who arrived shortly after, led by the one-armed Joseph Trumpeldor, a Zionist from the Russian Empire and founder of the Zionist Mule Corps (a British army battalion formed of Jewish volunteers). A raging conflict ensued, and Trumpeldor and his seven comrades were killed. Remaining defenders burnt down the courtyard buildings and abandoned Tel Hai. Later the same year, members of Kibbutz Kfar Giladi returned and rebuilt the farm, a move that resulted in Tel Hai (along with Metulla and Kfar Giladi) being included in the British Mandate over Palestine and therefore, later, in the State of Israel. In 1926, Kibbutz Tel Hai merged with Kfar Giladi.

The story of Tel Hai is one that has come to represent Jewish determination and the Zionist struggle for Palestine, today acting as a poignant symbol of heroism, self-defence and sacrifice told throughout Israeli households. Trumpeldor and his seven soldiers have left a long legacy, notably the city of Kiryat Shmona (City of Eight), which was named in their memory. Claimed to be Trumpeldor's last words, the phrase 'Never mind, it is good to die for our country' became legendary in Israel, although many attribute the origin of these words to the ancient Latin phrase *Dulce et decorum est pro patria mori* (It is sweet and honourable to die for one's country). Every year, the battle at Tel Hai and the death of Joseph Trumpeldor are honoured in a memorial held on the 11th day of Adar in the Jewish calendar.

The fort that stands today provides visitors with an insight into the historical background of the site, and a monument commemorating the eight heroes stands in the form of a stone lion (Roaring Lion) erected near their graves. Initially buried in Kfar Giladi, their bodies were subsequently moved here in 1924. The site designed by sculptor Abraham Melnikov on the initiative of yishuv institutions was erected on top of a mass grave, and the monument was unveiled in 1934.

Up the road is the **Beit Hashomer Museum** (✆6941565; ⊕ 08.00–16.00 Sun–Thu, 08.00–noon Fri; admission adult/child ₪15/10) at Kibbutz Kfar Giladi. Often referred to as the precursor to the IDF, Hashomer (meaning 'Watchman') was a group of 108 men and women selected to protect Jewish settlements in the country. Until its formation in

1907, settlement protection was outsourced to Circassian and Arab guards. Hashomer was successful in its protection of Jewish interests, to the antagonism of the Arab population. Many were exiled by the Ottoman government, yet the group survived until 1920, when it was succeeded by the Haganah, a better-organised military group. The museum here displays early 20th-century clothing, buildings, photos, weapons and an audio-visual presentation. Batia Lichansky, sister-in-law of Yitzhak Ben Zvi, one of the primary members, also has a sculpture display in one of the rooms.

Getting there and away Tel Hai is located on route 90 just south of Kiryat Shmona. Head through the city and follow signs to the site and nearby Kibbutz Kfar Giladi. Bus 21 from Kiryat Shmona runs to and from Metulla every 2 hours and will drop you off at the kibbutz (*7mins/₪5*).

Where to stay

Tel-Hai Guesthouse (HI) (83 rooms) Kibbutz Tel Hai, opposite side of the junction to Kibbutz Kfar Giladi; ₪02 5945666; e tel-hai@iyha. org.il; w iyha.org.il. In keeping with the Hostelling International reputation for exceptionally clean yet uninspiring rooms, this hostel provides a good, cheap option in the area. Private rooms & dorms have AC & TV, & the price includes kosher b/fast. **$$$–$**

TEL DAN NATIONAL PARK (↖ 6951579; w parks.org.il; ◷ 08.00–16.00 Sat–Thu, 08.00–15.00 Fri; admission adult/child ₪28/14) Kill two birds with one proverbial stone at Tel Dan Nature Reserve, combining nature and archaeology. The Dan River is the most crucial source of the Jordan River, fed by meltwater from Mount Hermon. Countless streams converge in the park's grounds as they pour into the river on their way to the Jordan Valley. Vegetation and wildlife thrive in the abundance of water and the mild climate, forming a shady forest in which to explore. Four trails lead through the park's grounds, providing access to its different attractions. Follow the course of the river through the sometimes 20m-tall Syrian ash trees (*1hr 15mins*) or head to the remains of the ancient biblical city of Dan (*45mins*), which according to the Book of Judges was captured from the Caananites by the Tribe of Dan. It has been associated with Jeroboam, a biblical figure who was the first king of the northern tribe of Israel. Hilltop reconstructions of an arched Canaanite gate and Israelite-period city gateway are good accompaniments to the remains.

Getting there and away Buses 55, 58 and 158 run between Kiryat Shmona and the northern Golan Heights stop at Kibbutz Dan (1km from the park entrance – there is no camping here) several times daily (*16mins/₪9.10*), as well as Shear Yashuv and Horshat Tal (*15mins/₪9.10*) along the way.

Where to stay and eat

Shear Yashuv The quaint Shear Yashuv holiday village sits in a prime location, equidistant from the sites of the northern Golan Heights & those in the Upper Galilee. The village is small but chock-full of dainty wooden zimmers as well as a clinic, small gym, grocery store, restaurant & horseriding centre. There is also access to the Banias River from within the village. A map on the right as you enter the village will direct you to the 26 family-run zimmers & other amenities. **$$$–$$**

Kibbutz Dafna Campsite ↖ 4989070. One of the nicest camping sites in Israel. Facilities include small swimming pools (ideal for children) & a laid-back café. Outside the entrance there is a restaurant, an Italian pizza truck & even an Israeli 'Naot' shoe outlet. The kibbutz itself is idyllic & worth exploring. **$$**

Horshat Tal Campsite ↖ 6942360; w parks. org.il; ◷ 14.00–23.00, closed in winter; admission campsite child/adult ₪63/53, bungalow ₪300, cabin ₪650. Located 5km east from Kiryat Shmona & signposted on route 918. The campsite is large & staff are not too friendly. Pitch your tent next to the gushing streams flowing through manicured lawns or rent a bungalow or cabin. Clean showers & toilets & plenty of space under the shade of the oak trees (unless it's a summer w/end in which case it's peg to peg). A night in the campsite grants you access to the adjacent park for an early-bird swim in the frosty waters of the natural pools. **$**

✖ **Dag Al Hadan** North of Kibbutz Hagoshrim; ✆6950225; e dagaldan@gmail.com; w dagaldan.co.il/en; ⊕ noon–midnight daily. Kosher. Situated on the confluence of the Hatzbani & Dan rivers, this delightful open-air fish restaurant dishes up a fabulous selection of fresh- & saltwater fish, as well as offering a lovely riverside location. The local trout is highly recommended. There's a 10% discount for guests taking part in kayaking & rafting activities in the kibbutz. There is also a well-equipped campsite. **$$$$**

What to do

Hagoshrim Kayaks (✆077 2717500; w kayak.co.il) is a popular kayaking centre on the Jordan River, offering 'extreme' routes and for the more faint-hearted and families a gentler route. There is a campsite, children's paddling pool, bike rental and ATV tours also on offer – but be warned, this place is shoulder-to-shoulder during school summer holidays. Despite its name, it is not located in Kibbutz Hagoshrim, but near Maayan Baruch campsite.

METULLA *Population 1,600*

Metulla is a small, rural town located at the end of the north–south highway 90 just 8km north from Kiryat Shmona, straddling the border with Lebanon. Founded in 1896 as one of Baron Edmond de Rothschild's purchases, the land on which it stands originally belonged to a Druze landowner. In the early 20th century, the town was used as a transit point for illegal immigrants from the French Mandate in Syria and Lebanon. Until the 1980s and the construction of the Canada Centre (a vast sporting complex; page 243), the local economy depended on agriculture, namely fruit, wine and cattle. Today, the Canada Centre and the town's surrounding natural and historic attractions have created a prosperous tourist economy, although agriculture still plays a pivotal role. Several waterfalls gush through the orchard-lined valleys on their route from the snow-capped peaks of Mount Hermon to the Hula Valley, visible to the south. The Ayun River, which enters Israel from Lebanon, has carved out a small canyon on its way to the lower lands around the Jordan Valley. The town oozes tranquillity and an appreciation of the nature that surrounds it. The lovely little main street is lined with white limestone houses, restaurants and galleries, and accommodation, mainly zimmer cabins and bed and breakfast, is plentiful. Because of its proximity to the Lebanese border, the town does bustle with soldiers, particularly during times of high alert. But for the most part it is a quiet, peaceful, rural farming community.

GETTING THERE AND AWAY Bus 20 leaves every 2 hours (*last departure at 20.22*) between Kiryat Shmona and Metulla (*15mins/₪10.50*).

🏠 **WHERE TO STAY AND EAT** Accommodation options are scant and consequently can be quite pricey.

🏠 **Beit Shalom Estate** (13 rooms) 28 Harishonim St; ✆6940767; m 057 7707845; e miriam@beitshalom.co.il; w beitshalom.co.il.

Refined elegance & antique glamour exude at the luxury Beit Shalom Estate. Exquisitely decorated with no rooms alike, the family-run guesthouse offers a small spa, gourmet restaurant & a real personal touch. **$$$$$**

🏠 **Travel Hotel Metulla** (28 rooms) ✆6883040; e metula@travelhotels.co.il. A modern & cosy hotel renovated in 2013 & located a few hundred metres from the entrance to the Wadi Ayun Nature Reserve. Rooms are bright & nicely decorated. **$$$$**

✗ **Beit Shalom Restaurant** 28 Harishonim St; ✆6940767; ◷ 09.00–midnight daily. Rustic country-style dishes with a taste of the Mediterranean. Housed in a 19th-century stone mansion, this is the place to treat yourself. Mains include lamb kebab on green tahini & chicken liver in plum sauce as well as simpler pasta dishes. **$$$**

WHAT TO SEE AND DO

Canada Centre (*1 Harishonim St;* ✆*6950370;* w *canada-centre.co.il;* ◷ *10.00– 20.00 Mon–Sat; ice skating & spa 10.00–16.00 Mon–Thu, 10.00–18.00 Fri*) In rather distinct contrast to the sleepy little town in which it sits, this huge complex is a hub of sport, exercise and leisure facilities. It features the country's largest ice-skating rink, sizeable indoor and outdoor swimming pools, squash courts, table-tennis rooms, a fitness centre, bowling alley and basketball court. There is also a shooting range, and a health club offering treatment packages.

Nahal (Wadi) Ayun Nature Reserve (✆ *6951519;* ◷ *08.00–17.00 Sat–Thu, 08.00–15.00 Fri, closes 1hr earlier in winter; admission adult/child ₪28/14*) Located on the edge of Metulla is the beautiful Ayun Nature Reserve. As the Ayun Stream sweeps across the border from Lebanon, it flows through a canyon, creating in turn four waterfalls. The rest of the year, however, sees a raging flow, providing some lovely hiking opportunities. You may choose to walk either uphill or down, starting from different entrances accordingly. The hike of roughly 2.5km is pleasant and suitable for a novice.

One entrance to the reserve is located in Metulla's upper car park (signposted), and is the beginning of the longer of two trails (*1hr 30mins*). For a lovely hike, follow the path downstream, passing all the falls as you go. The *pièce de résistance* of the reserve is the 30m-high Tanur Waterfall, the last of the four. It gushes over the steep canyon shelf, spraying the wild flowers, oleander and honeysuckle with a fine mist of ice-cold water. Note that if you can't arrange for transport to pick you up at the lower car park, there is a rather hefty walk back upstream to the upper one. The shorter trail through the reserve forms a circular route, beginning and ending in the lower car park. It incorporates the Tanur Waterfall and a birdwatching post (*30mins*). To get to the Tanur Waterfall and lower car park, turn right approximately 1km before Metulla. For the Ayun and Cascade Falls (and upper car park), take the road near the border fence in the north of the town.

UPDATES WEBSITE

You can post your comments and recommendations, and read feedback and updates from other readers online at w bradtupdates.com/israel.

8

The Golan Heights

Telephone code 04

Please note that the region known as the Golan Heights is, according to UN classification, an Israeli-occupied area of land (total landmass 1,860km², of which 1,250km² is occupied by Israel) and belongs to Syria. Israel's annexation of the Golan Heights in 1981 was not recognised by the UN and as such remains a disputed zone. The Israeli Golan Law of 1980 nonetheless applies Israeli law and administration to the area. For the purposes of this guidebook and the ease of use to travellers, however, it has been included under the title of Israel. The area has no borders or checkpoints, posing few or no problems for visitors.

Conjuring images of war-torn lands, ferocious battles and heavy rocket fire, the Golan Heights (Al-Jawlan in Arabic) is often overlooked by foreign visitors to Israel, its tumultuous existence and remote location acting as deterrents to most. Yet in fact it exudes a charming peace, harmony and beauty. Culturally and geologically, it stands apart from neighbouring Galilee, its rugged, untamed landscape sparsely inhabited by Druze and Jewish communities as well as a small Arab Alawite community. Roaring rivers, jagged mountain peaks, deep canyons and gushing waterfalls have found their place in the wild 55km stretch of land that forms Israel's northern- and easternmost frontiers. The Golan Heights area is of strategic importance and provides about 30% of Israel's drinking water supply. It is an exceptionally fertile land blanketed in fruit groves and vineyards.

Life in the Golan has for years relied on agriculture, vineyards, orchards and, most significantly, cattle rearing. In recent years, however, tourism has started to creep in and now rural pursuits are being offered to those in search of solitude, nature and an escape from all things urban.

Beginning at the Sea of Galilee, the southern Golan plateau offers a tranquil environment, where rolling hills dotted with cattle and grazing horses spill into the lake below. Inhabited by Jewish communities, the southern region is characterised by its rich archaeological remains and stunning natural scenery. In contrast is the rugged northern region of the Golan Heights, the towering Mount Hermon range sitting at its northernmost point overlooking Syria and Lebanon. A few Druze communities farm the lower slopes where imposing Roman castles and grand Crusader forts guard the ancient highways.

Oak forests, blossoming wild flowers and alpine meadows combine to form an impressive and unexpected landscape and an environment that supports the country's most varied wildlife species. As a meeting point for fauna arriving from the cold steppes of Asia and Europe and the desert lands of the Syrian–African Rift Valley, its variety is immense. Gazelles, hyenas, wild boars, foxes, wolves and hundreds of species of birds including the Bonelli's eagle and Egyptian vultures roam over the lands.

The population of the Golan Heights is approximately 39,000, over half of whom are Druze. Inhabiting the four Druze villages of Majdal Shams, Masadeh, Buqata and

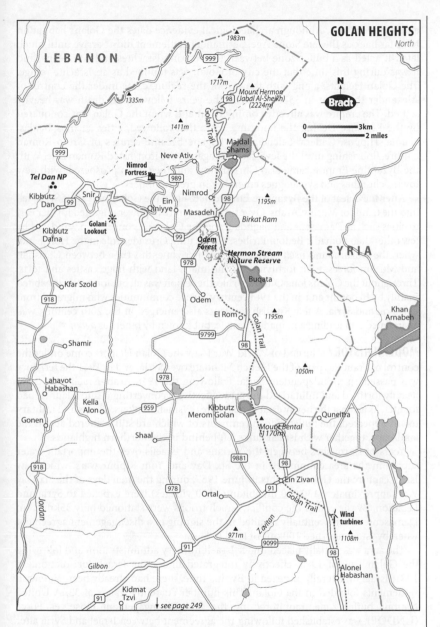

Ein Qiniyye they are famed for their hospitality, loyalty and traditional food. The 16,500 Jews who live here are spread across more than 30 tiny villages, their luxury guesthouses, rustic restaurants and laid-back lifestyle well known across the country.

HISTORY

ANCIENT–19TH CENTURY The mélange of historic, archaeological and modern battle sites that are scattered across the Golan Heights are testament to its colourful

Map labels (Golan Heights North):
LEBANON
1983m
999
1717m
98 Mount Hermon (Jabal Al-Sheikh) (2224m)
1335m
1411m
Golan Trail
999
Neve Ativ
Nimrod Fortress
989
Majdal Shams
N Bradt
0 3km
0 2 miles
Tel Dan NP
Kibbutz Dan
99
Snir
Ein Qiniyye
Nimrod
98
1195m
Masadeh
Golani Lookout
Kibbutz Dafna
Birkat Ram
99
Odem Forest
SYRIA
978
Hermon Stream Nature Reserve
Kfar Szold
Buqata
918
Odem
El Rom
1195m
Shamir
9799
Golan Trail
98
Khan Arnabeh
Lahavot Habashan
978
1050m
Kella Alon
959
Gonen
Kibbutz Merom Golan
Quneitra
Shaal
Mount Bental (1170m)
918
9881
98
Jordan
Ein Zivan
978
91
Ortal
Golan Trail
Zavitan
Wind turbines
1108m
971m
9099
98
Gilbon
91
Alonei Habashan
Kidmat Tzvi
see page 249

8

and turbulent past. Although archaeological evidence dates the Golan's habitation to as far back as the late Stone Age, permanent settlement didn't arrive until much later. It acted as a buffer zone between the warring Israelites and Arameans, and it was during this time that the city of Golan was founded as an Israelite refuge. The Golan Heights, along with the rest of the region, came under the control of Alexander the Great in 332BCE and in the years following his death was heavily settled. The empire was already coming to an end when the Golan was conquered by the Romans. During the booming years that followed, cities such as Banias, Gamla, Hippos, Gadera, Seleucia and Sogane became centres of Greco-Roman culture, flourishing until the Jewish revolt against the iron-fisted Roman rule. With the Byzantine Empire came also Christianity, and the Golan prospered, with new towns, churches and synagogues emerging in great numbers.

After the defeat of the Byzantine Empire in 636BCE the Golan, and all of Syria, fell into the hands of Muslim Arabs. Over time, the centre of power migrated further east to cities such as Damascus and Baghdad, and the Golan was once again wandered by few other than nomadic Bedouin tribes. That is until Crusader rule in the Holy Land, when the Golan found itself once again a buffer zone, this time between Christian and Muslim forces, each fortifying this no-man's-land with huge castles and forts. Throughout the Golan's long Ottoman rule, the region was all but forgotten, inhabited mainly by Bedouins and, in the 19th century, Druze communities who migrated from Lebanon and Syria. A few Kurdish residents also emerged in the 20th century, well assimilated and leading a nomadic lifestyle, but known by others as *agha*.

MODERN HISTORY The end of World War I saw the Golan Heights come under the control of France as part of the French Mandate over Syria, and in 1941 the territory was passed on to independent Syria. Following the 1948 Arab–Israeli War, Syria heavily fortified and militarised the area, effectively converting it into a launch pad for attacks against the newly established State of Israel. Bunkers, camps and military towns appeared, the bullet-ridden remnants of which are still scattered across the landscape, together with Israeli tanks left behind in the northern highlands.

Years of skirmishes between the Syrians and Israelis over the important water supply in the area culminated in the Six Day and Yom Kippur wars, which saw Israel capture the Golan Heights in June 1967, during the final days of the Six Day War; approximately 130,000 inhabitants (200 villages) were expelled to Syria and Lebanon. By the end of the conflict, Israeli troops were stationed only 35km from Damascus, which eventually resulted in the signing of a disengagement agreement whereby Israel returned 100km² of land to Syria.

The area was initially placed under Israeli military administration and following the Golan Law of 1980, effectively integrated under the Israeli jurisdiction. In 1981, Israel unilaterally annexed it. By this time, there had already been 30 Jewish settlements founded in the Golan. This number currently stands at 33. A United Nations buffer zone, monitored by the UN Disengagement Observer Force (UNDOF), was established following the agreement between Israel and Syria after the 1973 Yom Kippur War.

While Syria and Israel have on numerous occasions attempted to finalise the status of the Golan, there has been no progress since 2000, and with the war raging in Syria since 2011, it is unlikely to be settled any time soon. During the wars, most of the Druze inhabitants fled the area, while those who remained were cut off from their neighbours on the other side of the border. Back in 1981, more than 90% of the inhabitants of the Golan rejected Israeli citizenship and were instead issued with a *laissez-passer* document, whereby their nationality remained undefined

The **Golan Trail** (Shvil Golan in Hebrew) is a 125km stretch on the Israel National Trail and is suitable for avid hikers and novices alike. Hiking difficulty is moderate (especially if you're advancing from north to south), and the scenery is simply breathtaking, with the trail taking you through the cherry groves of the northern Golan, past forests, flower fields and river pools in national parks as it wends towards Hamat Gader (pages 255–6), where you can let your muscles have their well-deserved rest.

It is possible to start at any point on the trail, so after locating the first white, blue and green marker, you can easily follow the route, which would take you about six days to complete if you were doing the entire stretch. Do bear in mind that some sites, such as Nimrod Fortress, are not on the trail, so you will need extra time if you decide to veer off. Although there are minefields in some parts of the Golan Heights, these are concentrated along the demarcated border with Syria. The sections of the trail that do lead in that direction past the minefields are clearly marked with 'mines – danger' yellow signs written in three languages – Arabic, English and Hebrew – solidly attached to barbed wire fencing. The signs and the fencing are clearly visible and unmissable, and it is extremely important not to deviate from the markings.

Internet coverage is good right across the Golan Heights, and you can easily use 3G/4G networks with an Israeli number. Alternatively, there is a National Trail application (alas in Hebrew only) to show you the way. Remember to bring warm clothing and sleeping gear, since nights can be very cold. Tap water in the Golan Heights is excellent. You can always ask residents in a kibbutz to fill up your bottles. Shops are infrequent, so it is recommended to carry some supplies with you.

If you don't fancy undertaking the trail alone, contact **Eyal Gary** (m *050 4524335;* e *eyalgary@hotmail.com;* w *adam-bg.com*), a professional and very pleasant local guide who can arrange hiking and nature tours.

For additional information, visit w golantrail.com and w israel-trail.com.

and they continued travelling and trading with Syria. The number of people still carrying laissez-passer in the Golan is unknown.

ORIENTATION

Travelling in the Golan Heights is somewhat different from other areas of the country, so it is a good idea to orientate yourself with the region and what it has to offer before embarking on a trip. Firstly, the region has an extremely limited public transport network. Where possible, buses have been included, but the ideal – and sometimes only – way to travel is to rent a car from nearby Galilean towns such as Tiberias or Nazareth. Hitchhiking is possible and may be the only option besides hiking. Although rugged and sparsely populated, the Golan Heights is a small region. It is easily navigable, although roads closer to the Syrian border (which is separated by the UN Demilitarised Zone) are sometimes unpaved. Owing to its altitude, most notably in the mountainous areas of northern Golan, temperatures can plummet, and a substantial blanket of snow covers the slopes of Mount Hermon throughout the winter months. Warm clothing is essential, even in the summer months, where the air at the peak of Mount Hermon can still be fairly brisk.

For the most part, the Golan Heights are a peaceful, rural stretch of land. Yet it is important to be aware of some safety points. Unexploded landmines – unstable, dangerous relics left from the Yom Kippur and Six Day wars – are scattered across the region, both in fields and along the sides of roads. Warning signs are everywhere and barbed-wire fences surround 'no entry' zones but beware, especially when hiking. Always stick to marked trails and heed all warnings. The IDF do extensive training up in the rugged terrain of the northern Golan Heights so be on alert or you might find yourself staring down the barrel of a tank gun. It is important to adhere to 'no entry' signs for both **landmine zones** and **army training areas**. For more information call ℡04 6977224, but if in doubt, don't enter.

A stretch of no-man's land exists between the Golan Heights and Syria proper demarked by the 1974 Ceasefire Line. While this region is heavily fenced off, it is important to steer well clear of the line as mortar rounds have been launched in recent years from Syria. Government advisories recommend not to travel east of Route 98.

Katzrin is the largest urban centre in the region, and a preliminary glance will tell you that it is not exactly large. Tiny but hospitable and beautiful moshavim, kibbutzim and Druze villages that house the rest of the Golan's population provide rural-style accommodation, rustic home-cooking and activity centres such as horseriding, bicycle rental and jeep tours. **Ramot** is a good base for these activities in the south and **Merom Golan** or **Neve Ativ** are lovely options in the north. **Accommodation** in the Golan is expensive; there's no two ways about it. In summer, campsites are a good budget option, but the emergence of a couple of well-equipped hostels in the southern part of the area is a godsend to the thrifty traveller. In the north, zimmers will be your only option in winter months when it's too cold to camp. While these can be extremely pricey in peak season and at weekends, weekdays are more reasonable. They are worth the price, too, as Golan's zimmers are some of the most luxurious in the country. Several are listed in this section, but it is possible (and recommended) to drive through any of the dozens of moshavim or kibbutzim and look for vacancy signs outside. In peak seasons it is certainly advisable to book ahead.

KATZRIN *Population 7,300*

Katzrin (or Kisrin, Qasrin and Qazrin as various road signs spell it) is the only semi-major settlement in the entire Golan Heights region, and is often referred to – rather generously – as the capital. There is no real need to stay in the town, but if you are in search of a post office, supermarket, bank, police station or medical centre then it is the obvious choice. There are of course such facilities dotted around the Golan Heights' many moshavim, but Katzrin's concentration of services, centred on its nearby shopping centre, make it the most convenient. While the town itself is not unattractive, there isn't an awful lot to do. So if you do choose to stopover, then expect an early night.

GETTING THERE AND AWAY There are regular bus services connecting Katzrin with major cities in Israel, but there is no direct connection with Kiryat Shmona. If you plan to travel in the Golan Heights to or from Katzrin, you will have to change buses or hitchhike.

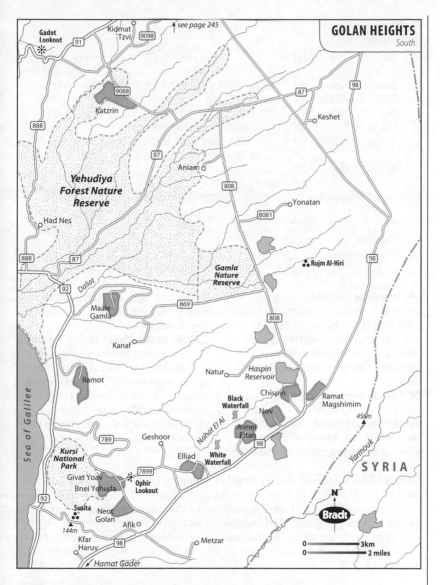

see page 245

GOLAN HEIGHTS
South

Gadot
Lookout

Kidmat
Tzvi

Katzrin

Keshet

Yehudiya
Forest Nature
Reserve

Had Nes

Aniam

Yonatan

Rujm Al-Hiri

Gamla
Nature
Reserve

Daliot

Maale
Gamla

Kanaf

Natur

Haspin
Reservoir

Ramot

Black
Waterfall

Chispin

Ramat
Magshimim

Nov

Nahat El Al

Avnei
Eitan

Geshoor

Elliad

White
Waterfall

Kursi
National
Park

Givat Yoav
Bnei Yehuda

Ophir
Lookout

Susita

Neot
Golan

Afik

Metzar

Kfar
Haruv

Hamat Gader

Sea of Galilee

Yarmouk

S Y R I A

456m

144m

N

Bradt

0 ———— 3km
0 ———— 2 miles

TOURIST INFORMATION The **Golan Heights Tourist Information Centre** (*Katzrin Shopping Centre;* ☏ *6962885;* e *info-tour@golan.org.il;* w *tourgolan.org.il;* ⊕ *08.30–16.30 Sun–Thu, 08.30–13.00 Fri*) is located in the shopping centre (page 250). It is small but there are lots of leaflets to pick up.

WHERE TO STAY, EAT AND DRINK Sleeping options are limited to small bed and breakfasts of which the tourist information centre can provide an updated list. The Golan's magic, however, most certainly isn't in Katzrin, and you are well advised to seek refuge in the beautiful rural accommodation in nearby villages. At the time of writing, the wonderful **Golan Garden Hostel** (m *053 4303677;* e *info@golangarden. com;* w *golangarden.com*) was closed for renovation but still offering adventure tours.

From	To	Bus no	Departure time	Journey time	Price (₪)
Jerusalem	Kaztrin	966	08.30; 08.40; 12.15; 17.40; 21.05**; 21.20**	4hrs	42.50
Kaztrin	Jerusalem	966	05.30; 06.00; 13.00; 17.00; 20.45**; 21.15**		
Tel Aviv	Kaztrin	843	09.45; 14.00; 17.00; 20.30**	4hrs	42.50
Kaztrin	Tel Aviv	843	04.50; 07.00; noon; 16.00**		
Tiberias	Kaztrin	52*	08.45; noon; 14.15; 22.40**	50mins	14.50
		57*	07.25; 10.30; 13.00; 15.00; 16.30	1hr	
Kaztrin	Tiberias	52*	17.05; 19.40	1hr	
		57*	06.15; 09.00; 11.45; 13.05; 13.50; 15.50; 18.00; 21.00**	1hr	
		142*	07.45	50mins	
		147*	10.30	1hr	

* Golan Bus
** Shabbat service

🏠 **SPNI Golan Field School** (34 rooms)
Zavitan Rd; ✆6961234; e rafim@spni.org.il. Has
6-bed rooms that can be rented by groups for
₪330 including b/fast per night (beds in these
rooms cannot alas be booked separately as dorms).
Often full of school groups so best to call ahead.
$$$

✗ **Golan Brewery** Katzrin Shopping Centre;
✆6961311; w beergolan.co.il; ⏱ 11.00–22.30
daily. A restaurant & brewery in one, offering a
cloudy glass of locally brewed ice-cold beer, its
location in the shopping centre is rather soulless,
but the beer (& lack of alternatives) makes it a
pleasant choice. Beer tastings can be arranged in
the restaurant itself. **$$**

🖥 **Olea Essence Olive Oil Factory** ✆6850023;
e info@oleaessence.com; w oleaessence.com;
⏱ 09.00–18.00 Sun–Fri. Located across the street
from the winery (page 251), the factory building
houses a small traditional Druze food bar (**$$–$**)
as well as a shop selling oil-based products where
you can taste various kinds of oil. For details of
stores elsewhere in Israel, see the website.

OTHER PRACTICALITIES Hutzot Hagolan Shopping Center (⏱ *08.30–21.00 Tue–
Sun; 08.30–15.00 Fri*) built on the outskirts of the town, about 2km from the
centre, contains most of Katzrin's facilities. In the town centre itself, the **Canyon
Lev Katzrin** shopping mall (*Dalyot St*) has a café, pharmacy and anything else you
may need for your journey. **Bank Leumi** (*Katzrin Shopping Centre;* ✆039 544555;
⏱ *08.30–13.00 & 16.00–18.15 Mon & Thu, 08.30–14.30 Tue–Wed, 08.30–12.30
Fri*) has an **ATM**.

WHAT TO SEE AND DO
Golan Archaeological Museum (*Katzrin;* ✆6961350; e *museum@golan.org.il;*
⏱ *09.00–16.00 Sun–Thu, 09.00–13.30 Fri, 10.30–13.30 Sat; admission adult/child
₪28/20 including entry to Katzrin Ancient Village*) The museum is located in the
town itself, next to the small commercial centre, and houses finds from prehistory
through to Talmudic times. A reconstruction Chacolithic house is one of the
museum's top attractions.

Katzrin Ancient Village (*Katzrin Rd East;* ✆6962412; ⏱ *09.00–16.00 Sun–Thu,
09.00–14.00 Fri, 10.00–16.00 Sat; admission adult/child ₪28/20 including entry to
the Golan Archaeological Museum*) Located next to the shopping centre about 2km

from town is a large-scale reconstruction of a Talmudic village and synagogue. The village was built here to commemorate the ancient village discovered and excavated nearby, whose synagogue was undoubtedly its crowning glory. After a violent earthquake in 746CE, the flourishing town was abandoned and remained deserted until the Mamluk period, when it was resettled and a mosque was erected inside the synagogue. Reconstruction wine and olive presses, traditional houses, a spring and the synagogue have been built to create an entertaining and informative experience.

Golan Magic (*Katzrin Shopping Centre;* ✆*6963625;* w *magic-golan.co.il;* ⊕ *09.00–17.00 Sun–Thu, 09.00–16.00 Fri, 09.00–17.00 Sat; admission adult/child ₪25/18*) This 180° show features the history and geography of the Golan Heights and incorporates smells, sights and sounds. It is an entertaining sensory experience and probably the least energetic activity you can do in the Golan region.

Golan Heights Winery (*Katzrin Industrial Park;* ✆ *6968435;* e *winetour@golanwines.co.il;* w *golanwines.co.il/english;* ⊕ *08.30–17.30 Sun, 08.30–18.30 Mon–Thu, 08.30–13.30 Fri*) Founded in 1984, it is the third-largest wine factory in Israel. Owned collectively by eight kibbutzim and moshavim in the Golan Heights, it enjoys access to a wide selection of grapes resulting in the production of 53 varieties of wine. You can taste three wines for ₪10, while a tour costs ₪20 and includes a tasting and a gift at the end. There is a wide range of group and individual tours offered in five languages, including English. Ring ahead to enquire about tour times. See box, page 189.

AROUND KATZRIN

YEHUDIYA FOREST NATURE RESERVE (✆ *6962817;* w *parks.org.il;* ⊕ *07.00–17.00 daily, closes 1hr earlier in winter; admission adult/child ₪22/9*) The Yehudiya reserve spreads like an outstretched hand across the southern Golan, and is characterised by its five rivers, verdant vegetation, gushing waterfalls, clear pools and steep canyons. The park's 66km² are home to wild boar, jackals, red foxes, Syrian hyrax and porcupines who live amid the huge variety of tree and plant species. It is also one of the best spots in the region to spy the Bonelli's eagle and Egyptian vulture that are often seen soaring in the skies above. Flowing through the 'fingers' of the park are the Meshoshim, Zavitan, Yehudiya, Gamla and Daliyot rivers that emerge from deep, rock-cut canyons into the Beit Zaida Valley just north of the Sea of Galilee.

Getting there and away The park has two entrances. One is 5km south of Katzrin off route 87 and entails walking along the rocky river bed. The other is the main entrance. Golan bus 52 runs between Tiberias and Katzrin (*26mins/₪6*) and will stop outside the main entrance, but the service is irregular; timetables vary from day to day, but there is generally one bus in the morning and two in the afternoon each way.

Practicalities There are innumerable hiking trails in and around the park, and the information centre can offer a wealth of advice and recommendations. Trails range from mild, family-oriented walking paths to extremely challenging routes that involve rappelling or swimming, so be sure to choose carefully before setting off. **Yehudiya Campsite** (✆ *6962817*) is located next to the information centre, midway between the Katzrin road and the Yehudiya junction on route 87. It is basic without shower facilities but will do for one night. Alternatively hitch a ride to the Sea of Galilee; there are endless camping opportunities along its shores.

MESHUSHIM POOLS The hexagonal pools in the west of the park are among the most famous features in the region, and a dip in the clear waters is an undoubted highlight. Surrounded by eight-sided columns the pools are a geological marvel, formed when mineral-rich molten rock slowly cooled. There are several ways to approach the pools, the shortest and easiest being the 1½-hour hike from the Meshushim car park. To reach the car park follow route 888 north from the Beit Zaida junction and turn left just after the village of Had Nes. The trail leads down the canyon, across the river bridge to the pools on the other side. For a longer and considerably tougher hike, start at the Yehudiya car park on route 87 and follow the trail westwards to the pools (*4hrs*). Note that this isn't a circular route, so you will need to arrange for transport to pick you up at the end.

UPPER YEHUDIYA CANYON Beginning at either the Yehudiya Campsite or car park on route 87, the trail leads to the ancient village of Yehudiya from where it continues along the top of the canyon before descending steeply to the stream below. At one of the falls the trail leads across a deep pool, so it is important to note that you will need to swim across with all your belongings or turn back at this point. The trail then continues down the canyon where you can either carry on for a further 2km (through some more pools and waterfalls) or follow the green route, which will bring you back out at the ancient village of Yehudiya. The circular route takes approximately 4 hours.

UPPER ZAVITAN CANYON A long but moderately challenging hike leads from kilometre 6.5 on the Katzrin road to the Yehudiya car park (*5hrs*). The trail follows the Black Gorge southwards, passing the Zavitan Hexagon Pools and Zavitan Waterfall along the way.

GAMLA NATURE RESERVE (✆6822282; w *parks.org.il;* ⊕ *Apr–Sep 08.00–17.00 daily, Oct–Mar 08.00–16.00 daily, on Fri the park closes 1hr earlier; admission adult/child ₪28/14*) The dramatic landscape of the Gamla Nature Reserve once provided an apt home for both the wildlife and ancient history that was within its boundaries. The steep sides of the ridge were inhabited by Israel's largest flock of griffon vultures, which made their nests on the inclines above the ravines. Unfortunately, a ferocious bush fire in May 2010 ravaged the area, and a charred scrubland posed little appeal to visitors and indeed the vultures. The situation has since stabilised, and birds of prey have returned to the area.

The park is also home to some fine archaeological remains that play a key role in the Golan's history. The ancient city of Gamla was the capital of Jewish Golan from 87BCE to 68CE, and it was here that one of the heroic stories of the Jewish revolt unfolded. Led by Josephus Flavius, Commander of the Galilee, the fortified city of Gamla was the setting for mighty battles between the Jewish army and Vespasian's Roman troops, battles that ultimately resulted in Roman victory. Thousands of Gamla's residents were slaughtered, while others chose to leap from the cliffs rather than surrender. Extensive excavations have revealed impressive and substantial remains, including a 2nd-century synagogue, Byzantine church, an aqueduct, ritual bathhouse and several public buildings.

Getting there and away Follow the Sea of Galilee road until you reach the Gamla junction, then follow route 869 to the Daliot junction. After 2km, turn north where a signposted dirt road leads to the park. Golan bus 16 (*15mins/₪5.90*) leaves Katzrin at 13.15 and stops outside the park.

RUJM AL-HIRI (Galgal Refaim in Hebrew) A few kilometres east of the Gamla Nature Reserve lies the impressive prehistoric megalithic site of Rujm Al-Hiri, believed to have been built by nomads as a place for rituals and a burial tomb. Dating back more than 2,000 years, the exact dates of its construction remain a mystery. Rujm Al-Hiri is the largest site of its nature in the Middle East and, according to some estimates, approximately 40,000 metric tons of basalt stones were used to build its concentric walls around the central burial chamber. What remains today looks spectacular when viewed from above but less so at ground level. Nevertheless, the 160m diameter of the outer circle makes the sheer size of the site pretty impressive. It lies on the Golan Trail and can also be approached from a dirt road off route 808.

RAMOT

The tiny moshav of Ramot (meaning 'heights' in Hebrew) was established in 1969 and has since developed as a hub of Golan tourism and, if your budget allows, is a beautiful, quaint little place to base yourself for exploring the area. Almost without exception every house has created luxury zimmer accommodation, each competing with its neighbour for novelty, quality and, unfortunately, high prices. Ramot is not a cheap place to stay and those on a budget are limited to camping. During peak times the moshav can get booked up so it is certainly worth making reservations during this time. There is a comprehensive list of zimmers at w zimmeril.com.

Ramot is perfectly located for exploring the landscape of the lower Golan, with its undulating green hills and views of the Sea of Galilee. Horseriding, jeep tours, cycling and hiking can all be arranged from within the moshav, and the weather in the lower lands is generally milder than the highlands of the northern stretches of the Golan Heights. There are several excellent restaurants in the village plus two simple supermarkets.

GETTING THERE AND AWAY There are a few Golan bus services per day from Katzrin, including bus 12 (*07.40 & 14.15*) and bus 16 (*13.15*), while bus 147 between Katzrin and Tiberias also stops here. Egged bus 843 has three daily departures from Tel Aviv to Katzrin (*3hr 30mins/₪39.50*) and stops at Ramot intersection.

TOURIST INFORMATION AND TOUR OPERATORS Ramot is so tiny that most establishments don't use street names. As you enter the village, myriad signs will point you to the right hotel, or just ask for directions.

Ramot Horse Ranch North Ramot; m 053 7364751; e office@ramotranch.com; w ramotranch.com. Extremely well-equipped & well-managed horseriding centre located 3km north of Ramot (signposted). Owners Justine & Uri Peleg offer guided treks ranging from a few hours to a few days. There is also a very well-equipped & nicely furnished B&B cabin (**$$$$**) to stay overnight. Advance booking is recommended.

Ofan Naim Bicycle Rental 6732524. Bicycles, helmets & maps are provided that will lead you on several self-guided tours around the area. Prices range from ₪50 for a 2hr tour to ₪60 for a longer journey down to the Sea of Galilee from where you will be picked up.

CRASH OUT OR SPLASH OUT IN THE SOUTHERN GOLAN HEIGHTS

Apart from the accommodation recommended in the villages and towns covered in this chapter, there are some other great spots that are worth considering, especially if you're looking for something a bit special, or are travelling on a tight budget.

CRASH OUT

⋏ Genghis Khan Givat Yoav; **m** 052 3715687; **w** gkhan.co.il. The best budget option in the southern Golan Heights. Yurt tents, each with their own shower & toilet, are set amid green lawns with picnic tables & BBQ area. There are excellent views over the Golan hills. **$**

⋏ The Indian Camp Avnei Eitan; ✆6762151; **e** info@tipi.co.il; **w** tipi.co.il. Budget-priced tepees are a big favourite with Israeli families. Cheapest options consist of huge tents with matting for bedding down for a communal night's sleep; less rudimentary private tents (**$$$**) are also offered. **$**

⋏ Yehudiya Campsite Yehudiya National Park; ✆6962817. Simple campsite at the entrance to the national park with no shower facilities. **$**

SPLASH OUT

🏠 **Cnaan Village** [map, page 211] (5 rooms) Had Nes; ✆6822128; **e** spa@cnaan-village. co.il; **w** cnaan-village.com. Luxury, intimate spa village in the heart of the lower Golan Heights. The 5 exquisite, romantic suites each reflect a different emotion & include king-size beds, jacuzzis & private terraces with stunning views. The spa boasts a beautiful indoor swimming pool & a range of massages & treatments. **$$$$$**

🏠 **Mitzpe Hashalom Country Lodge** [map, page 211] (27 rooms) Kfar Haruv; ✆6761767; **w** mitzpe-hashalom.co.il/english. Located next to the Peace Vista (page 257) & set within manicured grounds. While the service is homely & accommodating (they even deliver b/fast hampers to your door), here it is all about the location. The utterly spectacular views of the Sea of Galilee will take your breath away. Cabins have kitchenette, jacuzzi, AC & living room. They also offer a unique holistic experience involving calming cave pools, music & wine. **$$$$**

🏠 **Zimmers** The whole of the Golan Heights kibbutzim & moshavim are awash with luxury, romantic zimmers, whose rustic yet elegant cabins all sport jacuzzi baths, elegant décor & pretty surroundings. There are literally hundreds & while on w/ends they are extremely expensive, during the week you can get some good last-minute deals. It is also worth noting that most zimmers have a 2-night minimum stay on w/ends. For a complete list, visit **w** zimmeril.com.

🏠 WHERE TO STAY AND EAT

🏠 **Golan Rooms** (10 rooms) ✆6731814; **m** 052 3393277; **e** golanrms@ramot-bb.co.il; **w** ramot-bb.co.il/en. Stunningly located guest rooms with sweeping views over the Sea of Galilee. Rooms are bright & fresh with kitchenettes. Large swimming pool, jacuzzi, sauna & restaurant. B/fast included. **$$$$$**

🏠 **Barak Guest Rooms** (8 rooms) ✆6732525; **m** 050 2850225. Lovely wood cabins complete with jacuzzi bath, TV, kitchenette, AC & private veranda. **$$$$**

🏠 **Ramot Resort Hotel** (109 rooms) entrance to Ramot; ✆6732636; **e** ramot@ ramot-nofesh.co.il; **w** ramot-nofesh.co.il/en. This accommodation offers the best value for money in the area, with a plush hotel & cabins overlooking the Sea of Galilee. Facilities include in-room massages, a spa, gym & swimming pool. Cabins have jacuzzi baths, huge-screen TVs & patios, while rooms offer breezy balconies. The reception can arrange tours, guides & activities. **$$$**

✗ **Italkiya Beh Ramot (Italian in Ramot)** **m** 057 9443778; ⏰ 17.00–22.00 Mon–Thu, 09.00–22.30 Fri–Sat. Hearty Italian pasta & pizzas, with traditional ingredients imported from Italy. **$$**

KURSI NATIONAL PARK (✆ *6731983;* w *parks.org.il;* ☉ *Apr–Sep 08.00–17.00 daily, Oct–Mar 08.00–16.00 daily; admission adult/child ₪14/7*)

During construction of a road in 1976, workers stumbled across what was to be later identified as the largest Byzantine monastery in Israel. Measuring 123m by 145m the church contains large and highly ornate mosaics depicting animals and plants. During the Talmudic and Mishnaic periods, Kursi was a Jewish fishing village, and has long been believed to be the Christian site where Jesus performed his miracle of healing a man possessed by demons. Mark 5:1–20 tells of Jesus casting the evil spirits from the man into a nearby herd of swine, who then ran down the hill and drowned in the Sea of Galilee. Just south of the monastery and church a small chapel was discovered with an apse covering a cave, considered in Christian tradition to be the place where the miracle occurred. Although the monastery and church suffered vandalism and damage by the Persians in 614CE they were rebuilt, only to be ravaged by an earthquake in the 8th century.

Getting there and away The Kursi junction is located on route 92, which runs along the east side of the Sea of Galilee. Golan buses 51, 57, 64 and 147 depart from Tiberias (*26mins/₪8*) every 2 hours and will stop at the junction on request.

HAMAT GADER (✆ *6659964;* w *hamat-gader.com/en;* ☉ *08.30–17.00 Sat–Sun, 08.30–22.00 Mon–Fri; admission ₪99*)

The hot, mineral-rich waters of the Hamat Gader spa draw thousands of visitors every year in search of a revitalising, youth-enhancing experience. The wafts of sulphur as you enter the park grounds are as unexpected as its alligator park, the largest in the Middle East. Parrot shows, baboons and two rather ominous-looking pythons are some of the inmates of the animal park, located on the opposite side to the spa facilities. Hamat Gader's popularity is certainly not new founded. As early as the 2nd century, people were bathing in the spring's hot waters, and the site was frequented through to its abandonment in the 9th century. While the development of the park has seemed to focus on entertainment rather than history, a few structures are worth exploring. A synagogue, built during the Roman–Byzantine period, represents the Jewish sages who mention the baths in the Talmud, while the scale of the beautiful Roman bathhouses is testament to its significance in society at the time. The crowds on weekends and holidays – especially in winter, when people

---

HIKING NAHAL EL AL

Nahal El Al is one of the Golan's most southerly rivers and provides the backdrop to one of the region's most beautiful hikes. Characterised by its two waterfalls, the Black Waterfall and White Waterfall named after the basalt and limestone rocks over which they spill, the area is exceptionally fertile and home to pomegranate, olive and fruit trees. The hike begins from moshav **Avnei Eitan** and follows the course of the river, arriving first at the 8m-high Black Waterfall. From there it continues to the 20m-high White Waterfall, from the top of which is a beautiful view of the area. A small pool at its base gives a refreshing welcome in the heat of summer. The entire trek is approximately 4.5km in length (*4hrs*) and finishes in moshav Eliad. For an unusual sleeping experience, the **Indian Camp** (✆ *6762151;* e *info@tipi.co.il;* w *tipi.co.il/en; tepee ₪95 pp, yurt ₪450*) in Avnei Eitan offers budget tepees and private yurts (see box, page 254).

look for respite from the cold in the 30°C waters – can unfortunately add grey hairs rather than invigorate the spirit, so it is highly recommended to visit off-season or on weekdays. Pools have been created with, for better or worse, a variety of features including fountains and jacuzzi beds. It is best to enjoy the waters before 11.00, when it starts getting busy.

Getting there and away A daily Golan bus (24) leaves Tiberias at 09.15 and returns from Hamat Gader at 13.50 (*22mins/₪6*). By car heading north from Jerusalem or south from Tiberias along route 90, turn on to route 98 following the Jordanian border fence. The site is signposted from the main road.

🏠 **Where to stay and eat** The spa's luxury **hotel village** (📞 *6393, 6655555*; e *spavillagehotel@hamat-gader.com*; w *spavillage.co.il/en*; **$$$$$**) offers cabins, complete with mineral jacuzzi, as well as an extensive range of massages, classes and therapies. The price includes bed and breakfast, a meal in the onsite kosher Thai restaurant, Siam, massages and the spa facilities. The hotel is for over 16s only, and bookings must be for a minimum of two nights at weekends.

MOUNT BENTAL AND KIBBUTZ MEROM GOLAN

The slopes of the 1,170m Mount Bental played a key role in the 1973 Yom Kippur War that saw Israel take control of the Golan Heights. Today, the summit has been turned into a memorial site for one of the war's bloodiest battles that played out in what has been coined the Valley of Tears, the deserted village of Quneitra, sitting in its midst in the stretch of land now patrolled by the UN Disengagement Observer Force (UNDOF). Rather ironically, the view that stretches over the bloodied lands of the Valley of Tears and beyond (Damascus is but 60km away) is one of the region's most stunning, and a must on any visit. An abandoned Israeli bunker has been left as a monument to the 160 Israeli tanks that held off Syria's 1,500-strong force, a win that saw a turning point for Israel in the battle for the Golan Heights.

The mountain's facilities are run by **Kibbutz Merom Golan** at its base, the first kibbutz established in this region following the 1967 Six Day War. The settlement is a pleasant place to base yourself for some rural pursuits and Golan relaxation. Guest cabins, reputable horseriding stables, jeep and quad-bike tours, and an excellent restaurant are all located within the tiny moshav, giving it a cosy resort-like feel. Hidden amid its orchards is an old Circassian cemetery, which used to be part of the village of Mansoura, one of the 12 Circassian villages in the Golan Heights that were razed at the end of 1969. The cemetery is not marked, and you

BUS TIMES					
From	**To**	**Bus no**	**Departure time**	**Journey time**	**Price (₪)**
Katzrin	Merom Golan	14	11.30; 20.12	27mins	9.10
		87	16.28; 18.23	31mins	
Kiryat Shmona (via Kazrin)		54	10.00; 11.15; 12.45; 13.45	32mins	
		59	14.40; 15.45; 16.30; 18.25; 19.30; 22.00**	32–40mins	
		159	20.29; 21.30	32–40mins	
** Shabbat service					

The controversial little stretch of land that forms the Golan Heights bears the scars of its violent and bloody past, where long-forgotten, unexploded landmines lay in their hundreds, bullet-ridden buildings stand abandoned and memorial sites dot the landscape. To help understand its history a stop at some of its most stunning lookouts offers more than a view over the landscape. On the following sites, fierce battles unravelled that shaped this hotly contested little region of the Middle East into what it is today.

PEACE VISTA North along route 98 the Peace Vista (Mitzpe Hashalom) is signposted on the left just before the small moshav of Kfar Haruv. The view looks north and west across the shimmering waters of the Sea of Galilee edged by the green plantations of the kibbutzim along the shores.

OPHIR LOOKOUT Heading north along route 98 from the Peace Vista, turn left on to route 789 at the Kursi junction. Signposted on the left just after Givat Yoav an unpaved road follows an olive grove until reaching the car park. At 350m above the level of the Sea of Galilee the view, enjoyed from the shade of the ancient olive trees, is wonderful. A 3-hour hike to the ancient ruins of the Jewish settlement of **Bnei Yehuda** can be started from the car park. Blue markers lead the way down the winding path to Kibbutz Ein Gev on the eastern shore of the lake. Getting back to the car park can be problematic, so it is best to either hitch up and leave the car in the kibbutz or arrange to be met at the bottom.

BENTAL LOOKOUT (VALLEY OF TEARS) See page 256.

GOLANI LOOKOUT The site is a memorial to the fallen troops of the Golani Brigade in the Tel Fahr battle of the Six Day War. A 650m trail takes visitors past the abandoned Syrian outpost to the lookout point over the Hula Valley. Along the trail memorial plaques tell the story of the battle that resulted in the capture of the Syrian stronghold.

GADOT LOOKOUT Perched on the natural boundary that separates the uplands of the Golan from the valleys of the Upper Galilee, the lookout provides a view not of aesthetic beauty but of historical drama and political consequence. This site marks the spot where the pre-1967 Syrian border stood. As you stand at the lookout, there is a clear and poignant divide between the rocky, once-Syrian lands and the green valleys of Israel behind it. The no-man's-land that you see is in fact the remnants of the Syrian front line of defence during the Six Day War, and today thousands of unstable mines remain. The area is heavily fenced off and warning signs are aplenty, so be sure not to venture off any paths. Scattered eucalyptus trees grow on the vista, obviously non-native to the region and mark the site of submerged Syrian bunkers, purportedly planted on the suggestion of the legendary Israeli spy Eli Cohen who used the trees as targets for Israel's air-force planes.

The Golan Heights   MOUNT BENTAL AND KIBBUTZ MEROM GOLAN

8

need to walk through the orchards in the direction of Quneitra or ask any of the farmers for its exact location. Although overgrown, some of the tombstones are still well preserved and bear witness to bygone days.

GETTING THERE AND AWAY Golan Bus (w *golanbus.co.il*) operates several routes stopping at Merom Golan.

TOURIST INFORMATION AND TOUR OPERATORS

Z Merom Golan Tourism Office
\6960267; e hazmanot@biz-mg.co.il;
w meromgolantourism.co.il. This is located near the ranch & can arrange bookings for all the activities & accommodation on offer in the kibbutz.
Jeep Point m 052 2513482; e perry_s@merom-golan.org.il; w jeepoint.co.il. Authentic jeep tours around the Golan Heights where stops for strong coffee & BBQs allow you to be at one with nature.

Merom Golan Cattleman Ranch \6960267; m 057 8514497. Offering day treks around Mount Bental, which leave from the exceptionally well-tended stables & meander through the leafy kibbutz out into the fields.
Merom Golan Quad Bike \6960483; m 057 8514497; e tracmg@gmail.com; w tomcarsmeromgolan.co.il. Can arrange professional quad-biking & Tomcar off-road vehicle trips across the surrounding countryside, ranging from 1 to 3hrs. A driving licence is required to be able to drive quad bikes.

WHERE TO STAY The kibbutz is a good choice for somewhere to stay, with several eating options and plenty of tourist facilities. Jeep and ATV tours, horseriding treks, a swimming pool and weekend bar make this the ideal place to base yourself for a couple of days. The **tourism office** can point you in the right direction.

Merom Golan Hotel (52 rooms)
\6960267; e hazmanot@biz-mg.co.il;
w meromgolantourism.co.il. The hotel has 32 very pleasant guest rooms & 20 luxury wood
cabins set within the rustic, quiet grounds of the kibbutz. Both the stone-built rooms & enormous cabins have the full range of amenities, the cabins offering an extra veranda & eating area. **$$$**

WHERE TO EAT AND DRINK The kibbutz has a kosher dining room that serves simple meals either to the table or in buffet style.

Habokrim Restaurant \6960267; ⊕ noon–late Sun–Thu, noon–Shabbat Fri, varies on Sat so call ahead. Kosher. The name, which translates as 'the cowboy', gives a pretty good idea of the kind of meals served in this comfortable, ranch-style restaurant. Yes, this is meat heaven. Steak, prime rib & lots of potatoes. There is a huge buffet at w/ends. **$$$$**

Coffee Annan \6820664; ⊕ 09.00–17.00 Sun–Fri, 10.00–17.00 Sat. The tongue-in-cheek name not only translates as 'in the clouds', but is also a reference to the former UN secretary-general who classified the Golan Heights as military-occupied & thus belonging to Syria, not Israel. The café lies on the Golan Trail & serves an assortment of cakes & vegetarian sandwiches, quiches, pasta & salads. **$$**

MOUNT HERMON (JABAL AL-SHEIKH)

Often referred to by Israelis as 'the eyes of the nation', Mount Hermon's strategic location for the military, as it 'peers over the neighbour's walls' into Syria and Lebanon, is a crucial component in the country's early-warning system. As it is heavily patrolled by IDF forces it is difficult to forget the ever-present animosity that Israel and Syria hold towards each other over this land. Mount Hermon is Israel's highest point, rising to 2,224m, and is significantly cooler than anywhere else in the country. Together with its volcanic basalt rocks and pine forests, this produces a uniquely alpine quality. Summer snowmelts and an abundance of springs feed the rivers that roar their way down to the valleys, its plentiful and influential water source one of the factors fuelling the region's border disputes. The

From	To	Bus no	Departure time	Journey time	Price (₪)
Kiryat Shmona	Banias	58	10.37	12mins	9.10
	Buqata	158*	12.27	37mins	
	Ein Qiniyye	58**	14.17	20mins	
	El Rom		16.17	42mins	
	Majdal Shams		18.17	29mins	
	Masadeh		20.39*	34mins	
	Neve Ativ		21.39*	23mins	
	Nimrod Fortress		21.30**	17mins	
	Odem	55	noon; 17.30	32mins	
		58	10.37; 14.17	51mins	
		51**/58**	21.30**	51mins	

** Shabbat service

peak can be snow-capped year-round, and a drive up the winding forested road to the summit bestows panoramic views and a temperature drop of up to 15°C (even in the height of summer) that will take your breath away. Even throughout the stifling hot summers of the lower Golan plains and shores of the Sea of Galilee, the fresh breezes that blow off the mountain demand warmer attire.

Mount Hermon has been a sacred landmark in Hittite, Palestinian and Roman times and stood as the northwestern margin of the Israelite conquest under Moses and Joshua. According to the Gospels, it was the site where Jesus revealed to his disciples his purpose to construct his Church and go to Jerusalem to be resurrected, and it's another contender for the site of Jesus's Transfiguration.

The throngs of visitors who today make their way to the summit up the steep, snaking mountain pass are not thinking of Mount Hermon's ancestral ghosts or political tensions but are instead heading in the direction of Israel's only ski resort (6981333; w skihermon.co.il). A vast car park 2km below the summit is serviced by shuttle buses, ferrying budding alpinists to and from the resort's range of ski trails and slopes. While not exactly on a par with the Swiss Alps, a ski school, sled riding, cross-country trails, restaurants and emergency Magen David centre have been incorporated to make it an enjoyable experience and a great diversion off the history trail. Out of ski season, a ticket costs adult/child ₪49/42.

GETTING THERE AND AROUND There is no public transport up the mountain, so you will need your own transport to get to the summit and ski resort. Route 98 leads past Majdal Shams to the single road at the base of the mountain, from where it is a windy route up to the summit.

Bus services in the Mount Hermon area are run by **Golan Bus** (w golanbus.co.il) and are relatively infrequent. Above is the timetable with routes and distances to the settlements and sites described in the rest of this chapter.

WHERE TO STAY AND EAT

Neve Ativ Located 2km from Majdal Shams and 10km from Mount Hermon, the tiny moshav of Neve Ativ, built on the ruins of Jubatha Al-Zeit village, has embraced the tourism trade and not only runs the Hermon Ski Resort but is also home to countless zimmers, guest rooms and the luxury Rimonim Hermon Hotel.

In the years following the Six Day War, stories of great bravery and self-sacrifice emerged to a nation reeling in its aftermath. Among these, one man's name stood out, a name that has become legendary in households across the country and whose heroism is unparalleled in Israeli minds: Eli Cohen. An Egyptian-born Jew, Cohen was recruited by Mossad in 1960 after making aliyah and serving out his army conscription. He adopted a false Syrian identity under the alias Kamel Amin Thabet, and spent a year in Buenos Aires establishing his cover as a wealthy businessman before moving to Damascus. Over the next few years he managed to infiltrate Syrian ruling circles, gaining the confidence of military and government officials and sending classified information back to Mossad. Information gathered by Cohen on Syrian air-force pilots was allegedly used to deter fighter pilots from attacking Tel Aviv in 1967. Upon threat to their families, the fighter pilots dropped their bombs into the Mediterranean Sea, reporting back to Damascus that the targets had been hit. In 1965, one of Cohen's radio transmissions to Israel was intercepted and he was sentenced to death, despite protests from several world leaders and Pope Paul VI. He was publicly hanged in Damascus and until this day his remains have never been returned to his family in Israel. Four decades on, negotiations for Eli Cohen's remains continue to be a breaking point in peace talks between Israel and Syria. According to many, at the time of his death Eli Cohen was third in line to the presidency of Syria.

The **Neve Ativ Tourism Office** (✆ *6981333*) can help arrange rafting, trekking, horseriding, cycling, skiing and jeep tours in the area.

⌂ **Rimonim Holiday Village** (44 rooms) ✆ 6985888; w rimonim.com. Swiss Alp-style wooden cabins, complete with sloping red roofs, are nestled among pine trees & have great heating for those freezing winter nights. It also has a spa centre, heated swimming pool & restaurant. **$$$$**

Nimrod The miniature moshav of Nimrod (barely more than six families live here), located at 1,110m above sea level, has managed to get itself firmly established on the Golan tourist trail (it also lies on the Golan Trail route), mainly thanks to the acclaimed restaurant **The Witch's Cauldron and the Milkman** (✆ *6870049;* ◷ *10.00–late daily; $$$$*). From miles around big, witch-shaped signs cast their spell of intrigue, directing motorists to the large rustic cabin in the hilltop village overlooking the Birkat Ram pool. The restaurant developed out of a roaring trade in the owner's homemade goat's cheese and now includes a whole variety of dishes. Winter warmers made from the fruits of the Golan are the general theme with hearty casseroles, creative meat dishes, robust pastries and fresh salads. Here there is also a basic campsite (m *052 2821141*).

There are no direct buses to Nimrod, and it is a 5km walk from Neve Ativ, so your own transport is necessary. Watch out for signs to the Witch's Cauldron and the Milkman Restaurant on routes 98 and 989 that lead to the turn-off for the moshav.

SOUTHWARDS FROM MOUNT HERMON

MAJDAL SHAMS AND MASADEH Of Israel's 104,000 Druze residents, 18,000 live within a small area in the northern Golan Heights, distributed among four main towns: Majdal Shams, Masadeh, Ein Qiniyye and Buqata. With 10,000 residents, Majdal Shams (meaning 'tower of the sun' in Arabic) was established at the end of the 18th century and is considered the centre of the Druze community in the Golan, with Masadeh (there is a small Hotel Toscana here (m 050 7528623) right on the Golan Trail if looking for accommodation other than camping), a short distance south of it, a close second.

While the towns themselves are rather higgledy-piggledy, their small, simple restaurants are one of the Golan's true highlights. What these small eateries lack in finesse and elegance (and they certainly do), they make up for in quality, traditional dishes cooked with an expertise you cannot find elsewhere. Hummus, salads, freshly baked pitta, olives plucked straight from the surrounding groves, vegetables and meats followed by sticky baklava and strong coffee combine to form a simple, yet oh-so-memorable meal prepared from the fields of Mount Hermon. The unassuming, rudimentary **Nidal Restaurant** (*Route 98, Masadeh;* ✆*6981066;* ⊕ *07.30–23.00 daily;* **$$**) offers hospitality like no other and serves hot, fresh pitta, hummus and chips as well as grilled meat dishes and salads.

While one wouldn't call Majdal Shams and Masadeh beautiful, it is clear from the outset that they, along with most other Druze towns, are comparatively affluent. Modern houses are under constant construction, and new cars vie for space on the dusty roads alongside the timeless horse and cart. The towns are a constant buzz of agricultural fervour: tractors chug through from the fields, a shepherd on a mobile phone urges his bleating goats through the town centre, while young boys in Nike shirts trot their horses out to pasture.

Odem Forest and El Rom Odem Forest and El Rom is what remains of the once-huge forest that covered this part of the Golan Heights. Route 978 goes straight through the middle of the forest and there are plenty of lay-bys where you can park and have a wander. In little clearings on the side of the road Druze families sell freshly made flat breads and labneh cheese as well as homemade olive oil and fresh honey.

Where to stay

Golan Heights Hostel (ILH) (28 beds) m 054 2600334; e info@golanheightshostel. com; w thegolanheightshostel.com. Known as the budget place to stay in the Golan Heights, the hostel epitomises comfort in nature. Rooms & communal areas are pristine, & the cosy rustic atmosphere is all you need after a day of hiking. Often fully booked, it is advisable to make a reservation in advance. **$$**

El Rom Campsite m 050 5645800; w camping-elrom.co.il. In the relatively large kibbutz, about 1km along the main road off the Golan Trail, there is a simple but welcoming campsite set amid shady pine trees with a toilet & shower block, picnic benches, campfire & tatty sofas available. It is located on the outskirts of the quiet, pretty village. Pitching a tent costs ₪50. **$$**

BIRKAT RAM

Located just above Masadeh, at the base of Mount Hermon, is the volcanic crater pool of Birkat Ram (which translates as the 'ram pool'). According to Talmudic text, the pool opened up during the Great Flood of Noah, never to close again thereafter. The Talmud speaks of only three such places, the other two being the springs in Hamat Gader and Tiberias. The pool is approximately a 30-minute walk from Masadeh and lies on the Golan Trail. If coming by car, there are a few turn-offs towards Birkat Ram along route 98.

Following the 1967 Six Day War that left much of the Golan Heights under Israeli control, the unsuspecting Druze village of Majdal Shams found itself quite literally torn apart. The new border meant that many families were suddenly living in separate countries and completely isolated from one another. To date, Syria and Israel have no means of communication, neither telephone nor mail, although the internet has of course made some contact possible. The borders are completely closed and all ties between local people severed. As a desperate measure to catch a glimpse of their loved ones, relatives started to gather on a 1,110m-high hill within Israeli-controlled land to shout affections and wave. This hill has become known as the Shouting Hill, and provided the backdrop for the Israeli film *The Syrian Bride*. Rising above a narrow, heavily IDF-patrolled valley beginning a few metres from Majdal Shams, it is but a distance of 3km away from the hill where relatives gather on the other side of the 'border'. Yet, they seem like a hundred kilometres apart, for all know that it is the closest they will ever again get to each other. Weddings, funerals and family occasions are shared at a distance that seems nowhere near to ever being closed.

NIMROD FORTRESS (☎ *6949277; w parks.org.il; ⏰ 08.00–17.00 Sat–Thu, 08.00–16.00 Fri, closes 1hr earlier in winter; admission adult/child ₪21/9, combined ticket with the Hermon Stream Nature Reserve ₪38/19*) One of the most striking sights in the northern Golan landscape is the Crusader Nimrod Fortress (originally known as Qalat Al-Subebia). Sitting high on the slopes of Mount Hermon above the deep valley and ancient road that once connected Damascus and the Galilee, it is an eerily imposing sight.

The early phase of the fortress was built in 1228 by Al-Aziz Uthman, Saladin's nephew, as an attempt to block the march of the Sixth Crusade heading to Damascus from Acre. The fortress was later aggrandised after its capture by the Mamluk sultan Baibars to include the striking towers we see today. Inscriptions, including the carving of a cheetah, Baibars's symbol, are evidence of its ruler at the time. Not long after the Muslim conquest of Acre in the 13th century and subsequent demise of Crusader rule, Nimrod fell into disrepair. Once more brought into commission after the Ottoman Turks conquered the country, it was used as a luxury prison for exiled Ottoman aristocrats from Palestine.

It is possible to spend a few hours exploring the restored sections of the fortress. Of particular interest are the 'secret corridor', large stone brick halls, central keep and towers.

HERMON STREAM NATURE RESERVE (BANIAS) (☎ *6950272; w parks.org.il; ⏰ 08.00–17.00 Sat–Thu, 08.00–16.00 Fri, 08.00–13.00 holiday eve, closes 1hr earlier in winter; admission adult/child ₪28/14, combined ticket with Nimrod Fortress ₪38/19*) The Hermon Stream Nature Reserve, which is commonly referred to as Banias, sits on the western border with the Upper Galilee and is famed for both its impressive waterfall and dramatic history. The park has two entrances located a few kilometres from each other. Heading from Kiryat Shmona, the first entrance offers an easy 10-minute walk down to the waterfall, while the second entrance a little further along route 99 provides access to the archaeological ruins and springs. Three designated routes of differing length and ardour can be taken, but only one, approximately 90 minutes in length, will lead you from the waterfall to the ruins and springs and vice versa. Be sure not to venture off the designated trail that follows the stream, as the park sits amid several mined areas. Note that this longer route is not circular, so make sure you have enough energy to get yourself back again.

The Hermon Stream is fed by waters descending from Mount Hermon, with a series of waterfalls created as the waters cascade down the steep gradients towards the Hula Valley. The largest of these waterfalls is located here at Banias and is the *pièce de résistance* of the park. The torrent is most impressive throughout the April and May snowmelt (although it flows year-round), so be prepared to get a bit wet.

The archaeological park displays phases of the once-prosperous city's history. Scanty remnants of Greek culture, brought to the region following Alexander the Great's conquest, can be seen, while the extravagant Palace of Agrippa is a lasting legacy of the Agrippa II settlement here. Crusader remains and a steady stream of pilgrims hold testimony to the importance of the site in Christianity. According to tradition, it was here that Jesus gave Peter the 'keys to heaven' and performed the miracle of healing the bleeding woman. The Crusaders viewed Banias as a strategic point between their stronghold in Palestine and the surrounding Muslim regions, and it was strongly defended. Throughout the Crusades, power over Banias changed regularly until eventually Saladin reigned victorious, and remains of these mighty battles are left as testament across the landscape.

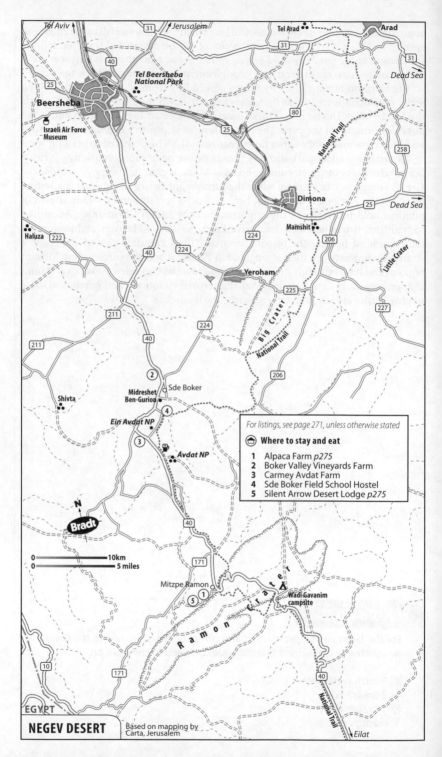

For listings, see page 271, unless otherwise stated

Where to stay and eat

1. Alpaca Farm *p275*
2. Boker Valley Vineyards Farm
3. Carmey Avdat Farm
4. Sde Boker Field School Hostel
5. Silent Arrow Desert Lodge *p275*

NEGEV DESERT   Based on mapping by Carta, Jerusalem

9

The Negev Desert

Telephone code 08

In his book *The Innocents Abroad*, Mark Twain described the Negev Desert as 'a desolation that not even imagination can grace with the pomp of life and action', an observation that 150 years on remains rather apt. The vast Negev Desert occupies half of Israel, and is characterised by the geological phenomenon that is the Ramon Crater, as well as its remarkable landscapes, waterfalls, caves, archaeological sites and rich history. The path of the ancient Nabatean Spice Route once wove its way through the peaks and troughs of the desert mountains, prosperous cities appearing along the way; Abraham built his well in the present-day city of Beersheba; and Israel's first prime minister settled and died in the remote Kibbutz Sde Boker.

Beersheba marks the gateway to the region but is little more than a through route to the wonders of the desert below. Mitzpe Ramon's isolated location teetering on the edge of the crater has made it the capital of highland tourism, where nature, active pursuits and ecotourism prevail.

Tourism in the desert is still in its infancy, and if you plan on visiting under your own steam – a highly rewarding and recommended experience – then be prepared for the harsh desert elements. While the region is big, this isn't the Sahara, and you're never too far from some sort of civilisation, but stick to marked roads, as the IDF do extensive training in the region, and make sure you have plenty of water, petrol and sunscreen. Picnics are recommended, if you are hiking, and major towns have supermarkets to replenish your provisions. Some small settlements, such as Mitzpe Ramon, have a few pleasant dining options to consider.

Public transport is extremely limited and independent travellers often have to resort to hitchhiking. Renting a car is undoubtedly the best option to get the most out of your trip and avoid standing in the sweltering desert heat on the side of a dusty road waiting for sporadic buses to pass.

BEERSHEBA *Population 215,000*

Often referred to as 'the capital of the Negev', Beersheba is (with the exception of Eilat), Israel's southernmost city. It sits on the fringes of the desert and acts as a gateway for those delving into the rural depths of the Negev Desert. The city is unsurprisingly rather dusty, run-down and sprawling, new neighbourhoods clearly defined by their white, modern apartment blocks and out-of-place greenery. Yet culturally, Beersheba is quite a treat. While there is no real need to hang around for too long, it lays claim to an interesting history and ethnographic make-up, acting as a trade centre for surrounding Bedouin settlements. A weekly market is held by these communities and it is undoubtedly worth timing your visit to coincide with one. Today Beersheba is Israel's sixth-largest city and manages to maintain a certain allure through its highly reputable Ben-Gurion University, and the campus forms

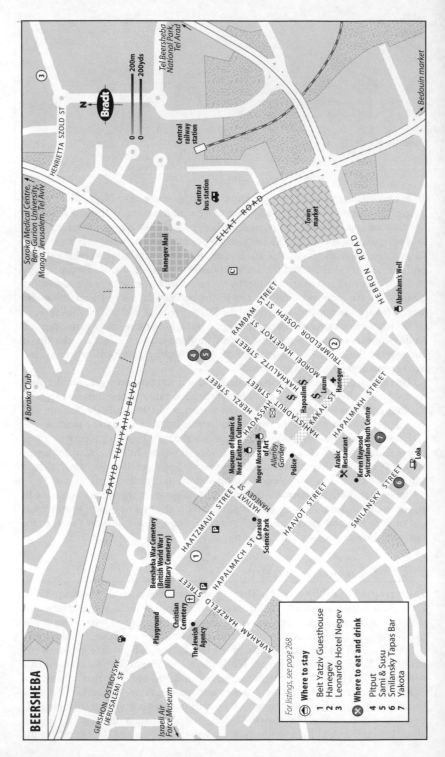

BEERSHEBA

Soroka Medical Centre, Ben-Gurion University, Manga, Jerusalem, Tel Aviv

HENRIETTA SZOLD ST

Tel Beersheba National Park, Tel Arad

Central railway station

Central bus station

Hanegev Mall

EILAT ROAD

Town market

HEBRON ROAD

Abraham's Well

Bedouin market

RAMBAM STREET

ELIEZER JOSEPH ST

MORDEI HAGETAOT ST

TRUMPELDOR STREET

HAKHALUTZ STREET

HERZL STREET

HADASSAH STREET

HAHISTADRUT STREET

KAKAL ST

Leumi

Hapoalim

Hanegev

Baraka Club

DAVID TUVYAHU BLVD

HAPALMAKH STREET

Museum of Islamic & Near Eastern Cultures

Negev Museum of Art

Allenby Garden

Police

Arabic Restaurant

Keren Hayesod Switzerland Youth Centre

SMILANSKY STREET

Lola

HAATZMAUT STREET

HATIVAT HANEGEV ST

HAAVOT STREET

Beersheba War Cemetery (British World War I Military Cemetery)

Playground

Christian Cemetery

The Jewish Agency

Carasso Science Park

HAPALMACH ST

AVRAHAM HARZFELD STREET

GERSHON OSTROVSKY ST

Israeli Air Force Museum

For listings, see page 268

Where to stay
1 Beit Yatziv Guesthouse
2 Hanegev
3 Leonardo Hotel Negev

Where to eat and drink
4 Pitput
5 Sami & Susu
6 Smilansky Tapas Bar
7 Yakota

0   200m
0   200yds

N

Bradt

266

the hub of modern life, where bars and nightlife attract the younger set. Standing in contrast is the old Turkish town (Old City), the heart of the ancient city where character, not beauty, is the main charm. In all, Beersheba can be quite a surprise and not nearly as drab and unappealing as it may appear at first sight.

HISTORY The Old Testament phrase 'from Dan to Beersheba' indicates that the city marked the southern limit of Palestine, and is associated with Abraham, Isaac, Jacob and Elijah. When in 1902 the Ottomans chose Beersheba as their administrative centre for the Negev, it was but an abandoned site, frequented only by Bedouin groups using the area's water sources. Buildings were erected along with police and train stations and train lines were opened to Ashkelon, Gaza and Damascus.

The city played an important role during the British Mandate period under which it continued to develop, and was at the time home to around 4,000 Muslim Arabs. During the 1936–39 Arab riots, many Jews fled the city, not returning until after the 1948 Arab–Israeli War. Because of the predominantly Arab population, Beersheba was given to the Arabs in the 1947 UN Partition Plan of Palestine, only to be taken by Israel the following year. Upon the Israeli conquest, the city was all but abandoned by its Arab inhabitants.

GETTING THERE AND AWAY
By bus Beersheba acts as the gateway to the south and there are subsequently good bus and rail links with the rest of the country. **Egged** buses are frequent, but **Metropoline** (\ *5900, 6232032;* w *metropoline.com*) offers a better choice of routes in the Negev. To and from Tel Aviv's central bus station, Metropoline buses 370 and 380 make the journey every 20 minutes (*1hr 7mins/₪15; less frequent in the evenings*), while buses 369 and 353 are less regular and take longer. Egged buses 470 and 446 from Jerusalem (*1hr 40 mins/₪27*) depart every 15 to 30 minutes. Metropoline bus 388 links Beersheba with Arad (*50mins/₪8.70*), from where you can connect to the Dead Sea (Egged bus 384 goes all the way to Ein Bokek and Ein Gedi). To reach Eilat, express buses 394 and 397 make the journey every 2 hours (*3hrs 40mins/₪51.50*). Metropoline buses 60, 64 and 65 frequently hurtle between Mitzpe Ramon and Beersheba (*1hr–1hr 25mins/₪15*), with buses 60 and 64 stopping at every stop along the way including Sde Boker.

By train The train links Beersheba with the rest of the country through Tel Aviv. Trains depart every hour (*1hr 15mins–1hr 48mins/₪27*).

GETTING AROUND
By bus Bus 7 starts at the central bus and train stations, heads down to the market, on to the Old City and then heads north along Yitzhak Rager Boulevard towards the Soroka Hospital and university. Bus 31 from the central station will drop you directly outside the Hatzerim Air Force Museum (*10mins*).

By car Rental is a good option in Beersheba and enables easy exploration of the surrounding landscape, including the air-force base, which is a 10-minute drive. Cars can be rented from **Avis** (*2 Amal St;* \ *6271777;* ⊕ *08.00–17.00 Sun–Thu, 08.00–13.00 Fri*) or **Sixt** (*1 Pinhas Hahozev St;* \ *6282589;* ⊕ *08.00–17.00 Sun–Thu, 08.00–noon Fri*).

TOURIST INFORMATION The **Tourist Information Office** (*1 Hebron Rd;* \ *6234613;* ⊕ *08.30–16.00 Sun–Thu*) is located at Abraham's Well museum. English-speaking staff will help with bus routes and tours of the city, and they can provide maps.

⌂ WHERE TO STAY *Map, page 266*

Beersheba is somewhat lacking in hotels as most visitors tend to merely stop in on their way south.

⌂ **Leonardo Hotel Negev** (244 rooms) 4 Henrietta Szold St; ☏ 6405444; w leonardo-hotels.com. Previously the Golden Tulip, this is Beersheba's plushest hotel option. Centrally located, it offers comfortable rooms with kitchenette as well as a swimming pool, health club & business centre. **$$$$$**

⌂ **Beit Yatziv Guesthouse** (95 rooms) 79 Haatzmaut St; ☏ 6277444; e reservation@rashi.org.il; w beityatziv.com/en. This guesthouse is a good, solid, mid-range option in town, offering basic private rooms with AC, TV & kosher b/fast. Rooms are spacious, clean & decorated in a modern style. There is also a swimming pool (summer only) & big buffet dining room. **$$$$**

⌂ **Hanegev Hotel** (22 rooms) 26 Haatzmaut St; ☏ 6277026; e liei5@actcom.co.il. The hotel needs a lick of paint & rooms are simple but comfortable. Good location in the heart of the Old City. Dbls have AC & TV. **$$**

✖ WHERE TO EAT AND DRINK *Map, page 266*

While not renowned for its fine dining, Beersheba does have a few good options. In the Old City, Smilansky Street has the bulk of the restaurants while in the New City you're best heading to the area around the central train and bus stations, around the university or to the Hanegev Mall. The Thursday **Bedouin market** offers the chance to try some traditional Bedouin cooking while the covered **town market** has a wonderful selection of shawarma, burekas, falafel and freshly baked breads.

✖ **Pitput** 122 Herzl St; ☏ 6289888; ⊕ 08.30–02.00 daily. Italian-style cuisine with an emphasis on meat & fish. They also do some wonderful big b/fasts, & in the evening it's a great place to enjoy a beer. A changing exhibition displays work from artists from the Negev Desert. **$$$$**

✖ **Yakota** 27 Mordei Hagetaot St (cnr 18 Anilevich St); ☏ 6232689; ⊕ noon–midnight Sun–Thu, 11.00–17.00 Fri. Kosher. Moroccan restaurant serving all the favourites including slow-cooked tagine, aromatic salads & succulent meats. **$$$$**

✖ **Sami & Susu** 12 Rambam St; ☏ 6652135; ⊕ 11.00–20.30 Sun–Thu, 10.30–15.30 Fri. A much-loved & raved-about Romanian meat restaurant since 1970. Kebabs & all manner of delights for carnivores from the freshest cuts. **$$$**

✖ **Smilansky Tapas Bar** 23 Smilansky St; ☏ 6654854; ⊕ 17.00–02.00 Sun–Thu, noon–02.00 Fri–Sat. Considered one of the best bars outside Tel Aviv. **$$$**

ENTERTAINMENT AND NIGHTLIFE Thanks to the large number of university students there are many places where you can go out and let your hair down. Big, raucous party nights are frequent but there is also a good selection of quieter, more relaxed places to just sit and enjoy a drink. Alternatively, the Hanegev Mall has plenty of cafés in which to sit and while away the evening over a cappuccino and a slice of cake.

☆ **Baraka Club** 70 Shloshet Bnei Harod St; ☏ 6269100; w barakalive.co.il; ⊕ 22.30–late daily. One of the most popular clubs in town, it is loud, flashy & fun. Each night sees a different theme ranging from karaoke to student nights to live music.

☆ **Manga** 85 Yitzhak Rager Bd; ☏ 6499951; ⊕ 18.00–late daily. Located near the teachers' centre, Manga is the quintessential student pick-up bar: loud, crowded & cheap, but it has a nice covered garden area, comfy sofas & decent sushi.

OTHER PRACTICALITIES In the city centre you will find everything you need around the pedestrianised Kakal Street. The central **police station** (*30 Herzl St;*

6462744) is behind Allenby Garden. For shopping, head to the **Hanegev Mall** (⊕ *09.00–22.00 Sun–Thu, 09.00–15.15 Fri, 18.00–21.30 Sat*).

Banks Around & along Haatzmaut St there are numerous exchange shops, banks & ATMs.

$ Bank Hapoalim 40 Haatzmaut St; ☎03 6532407; ⊕ 08.30–13.15 Sun & Tue–Wed, 08.30–13.00 & 16.00–18.30 Mon & Thu, 08.15–12.30 Fri
$ Bank Leumi 39 Haatzmaut St; ☎076 8859400; ⊕ 08.30–14.00 Sun & Tue–Wed, 08.30–13.00 & 16.00–18.00 Mon & Thu

Medical
✛ **Soroka Medical Centre** 151 Yitzhak Rager Bd; ☎6400111. Approximately 3km from the city centre.

✛ **Hanegev Pharmacy** 86 Mordei Hagetaot St; ☎2777016; w hanegev.co.il; ⊕ 08.00–19.00 Sun–Mon & Wed–Thu, 08.00–14.30 Tue, 08.00–13.30 Fri
✛ **Superpharm** Hanegev Mall; ⊕ 08.00–23.00 Sun–Thu, 08.00–17.00 Fri, 17.00–23.30 Sat

Post
✉ **Central post office** 51 Hadassah St; ☎6295805; ⊕ 08.00–18.00 Sun–Tue & Thu, 08.00–13.30 Wed, 08.00–noon Fri

WHAT TO SEE AND DO
Abraham's Well (*1 Hebron St;* ☎ *6234613; admission ₪5*) Within the small archaeological site is the stone well believed to have been dug by Abraham. It is recorded in the Bible that at the beginning of 2000BCE, Abraham and Isaac arrived in Beersheba where they dug wells and formed alliances with Abimelech, the King of the Philistines. The well itself has been dated to at least the 12th century BCE.

Old City The Old City dates to the end of the 19th century and owes its origins to the Turks who designed and constructed it based on a grid pattern. While it has undoubted charm, don't expect the quaint cobbled alleys of Jerusalem, Acre or Nazareth's Old City counterparts. The area is run-down and badly maintained, and the local government has done little to restore some of the more impressive Ottoman buildings. Smilansky Street has been partially remodelled and has some restored buildings that provide a glimpse of what the area would have once looked like. Today it forms the centre of the Old City and is home to several good restaurants and cheap shops.

Negev Museum of Art (*60 Haatzmaut St;* ☎ *6993535;* w *negev-museum. org.il;* ⊕ *10.00–16.00 Mon–Tue & Thu, noon–19.00 Wed, 10.00–14.00 Fri–Sat; admission adult/child ₪12/10*) The small museum is housed in a stone Ottoman building dating from 1906 and displays a range of changing exhibitions including contemporary and early Israeli art. The building first acted as Beersheba's city hall until 1953, when it was converted into a museum. The adjacent **Museum of Islamic and Near Eastern Cultures** (w *ine-museum.org.il/en*) is located in a former Ottoman mosque dating back to the reign of Sultan Abdul Hamid II.

Town market (*cnr of Hebron & Eilat roads*) The covered market is a fascinating hubbub of activity and certainly worth a visit, if only for the food stalls and bakeries. Wandering around the stalls laden with meats, cheeses, vegetables and a whole host of home wares is a great insight into real city life.

Bedouin market (*Eilat Rd;* ⊕ *Thu*) The market officially opened in 1905, although the area has long been a meeting place for groups of Bedouins, who would come to buy, sell

9

and swap pretty much everything. Today, it has become slightly more contemporary, with cheap clothes, shoes and homeware made in China standing alongside authentic Bedouin craft stalls and livestock. It is a fantastic place to buy traditional Bedouin keepsakes such as glassware, jewellery and precious stones, as well as mats, carpets and cushions. You will also find exceptionally cheap Bedouin food here.

Beersheba War Cemetery (British World War I Military Cemetery)
(*Haatzmaut St*) A little further up from the Negev Museum is Israel's largest British, Australian and New Zealand military cemetery. Beneath the rows of white tombstones lie soldiers who died in battles against the Turks during World War I.

Israeli Air Force Museum (*Kibbutz Hatzerim;* \9906888; w *iaf.org.il;* ☉ *08.00–16.00 Sun–Thu; admission adult/child* ₪30/20) The museum is located 6km west of Beersheba, just past Kibbutz Hatzerim adjacent to the IDF's southern air-force base. With the roaring drone of fighter jets above, visitors can walk around the large outdoor museum and get up close and personal with air-force jets and helicopters from the IDF's past. Guided tours in English can be arranged at the entrance and there is a rather nice audio-visual presentation displayed inside a Boeing plane. Bus 31 from the central bus station stops outside.

Tel Beersheba National Park (\6467286; w *parks.org.il;* ☉ *Apr–Sep 08.00–17.00, Oct–Mar 08.00–16.00 daily; admission adult/child* ₪14/7) East of the city, near the Bedouin settlement of Tel Sheba, is the national park at the centre of which sit the excavated remains of a fortified city dating from the Israelite period. The city was built atop a *tel* (a mound composed of the remains of successive settlements) and much of the ancient city has been restored, which adds a certain humanity and understanding to a visit. Of particular interest are the well, city streets, storehouses, public buildings and private homes, the city wall and gates, and the reservoir.

SDE BOKER AND AROUND

Founded in May 1952, the small isolated Kibbutz Sde Boker resting high in the Negev Mountains is famed across the country as being the last home, and final resting place, of Israel's first prime minister David Ben-Gurion and his wife Paula, who moved here in 1953 after Ben-Gurion resigned. His Zionist vision for the desert lands that occupy half of the country was to cultivate and settle, claiming that 'the future of Israel lies in the desert'. In honour of Ben-Gurion's love for this remote region and his passion for developing land suitable for Jews from around the world to settle in, he – and later his wife – were interred on a nearby cliff, adjacent to the *midrasha* (research academy) named after Ben-Gurion. Today, the kibbutz and surrounding farms act as a good base for exploring the surrounding Negev, most notably the Ein Avdat and Avdat national parks, and while facilities are fairly limited, Sde Boker does offer a small supermarket and a few guesthouses and hostels.

GETTING THERE AND AROUND Metropoline bus 64 runs along route 40 between Beersheba and Mitzpe Ramon (*1hr 25mins/*₪15) several times a day, stopping in the centre of the kibbutz (*43mins/*₪13).

TOURIST INFORMATION The **Sde Boker Tourist Information Centre** (\6554418; ☉ *08.00–16.00 daily*) is located in the entrance to the research academy.

WHERE TO STAY AND EAT

Boker Valley Vineyards Farm [map, page 264] (4 rooms) m 052 5786863, 052 6822930; w bokerfarm.com. The family-run winery located 8km north of Sde Boker is rustic Negev at its best. Their luxurious wood cabin is a rural retreat with all the comforts of home. There are family & dbl cabins as well as a khan tent for dormitory-style accommodation for groups. **$$$$**

Carmey Avdat Farm [map, page 264] (6 rooms) m 052 2705328; e farm@carmey-avdat. co.il; w carmey-avdat.com. Run by the Izrael family, who followed their dream into the desert & established a vineyard on the ancient Nabatean Spice Route. Luxury cabins take advantage of the natural resources & beauty of the desert & offer peaceful landscape views, natural construction materials & not a TV in sight. Plunge pools & fruit orchards complete the oasis effect. **$$$$**

Krivine's Guesthouse (14 beds) 15 Neve Tzin, Midreshet Ben-Gurion; m 052 2712304; e johnjkrivine@yahoo.com; w krivine-guesthouse.com. Well-priced, bright, sunny private apartments (for 2–10 people), a kitchen for guest use, Wi-Fi, a large shady garden & a hearty b/fast option make this an excellent choice in the region. **$$$**

Sde Boker Field School Hostel [map, page 264] (47 rooms) Midreshet Ben-Gurion; \6532016; m 050 2050569. 2 hostels attracting mainly school groups so dorms ($) are often fully booked. Rooms are clean & bright, with en-suite bathrooms, AC & b/fast. Discounted use of academy swimming pool. The field school can also organise jeep & camel tours & recommend hiking routes. **$$**

WHAT TO SEE AND DO

Ben-Gurion's home (*Sde Boker;* \ *6560320;* ⊕ *08.30–16.00 Sun–Thu, 08.30–14.00 Fri, 09.00–15.00 Sat; admission adult/child ₪10/7*) The hut in which Ben-Gurion and his wife lived until his death in 1973 stands untouched and is a fascinating insight into the humble home life of the country's first leader. The area around the hut has been converted into a small museum of sorts including displays of his famous statements, photographs of the early kibbutz and an archive of the more than 5,000 books that formed his personal library. The hut is located on the southern edge of the kibbutz.

Ben-Gurion Tomb Memorial Park In honour of his love for the desert, Ben-Gurion and his wife are buried on a cliff 3km south of the kibbutz. The tombs form a central space within a beautiful memorial park offering a staggering view of the sweeping Zin Valley. Picnic tables and public toilets make it a popular lunch spot along the route south.

Midreshet Ben-Gurion (\ *6532016;* ⊕ *08.00–16.30 Sun–Thu, 08.00–noon Fri*) Adjacent to the Ben-Gurion Tomb Memorial Park is the desert research institute. It opened in 1965 and has since established more than 12 scientific and educational institutions, including a national solar energy centre, school for environmental studies and institute for desert research. The **Desert Sculpture Museum** displays art created from desert materials, and tours can be arranged by calling in advance. You can rent bicycles from the **Geofun Desert Cycling Center** (\ *6553350;* e *info@geofun. co.il;* w *geofun.co.il;* ⊕ *09.00–18.00 Mon–Thu, 08.30–14.00 Fri*) to explore the Negev Desert.

Sde Boker Winery (*Kibbutz Sde Boker;* m *050 7579212;* e *winery@sde-boker.org. il*) Wine tastings and tours can be arranged by contacting the winery in advance.

Bedouin villages The area between Mitzpe Ramon and Sde Boker is settled by Bedouin tribes, and you can visit some of the villages to observe the traditional lifestyle.

9

One of the best examples in the region is in the settlement of **Wadi Aricha** (m *054 6001357*; e *salman.aricha@gmail.com*; w *negevtour.co.il*), where you can take part in workshops and other desert activities.

AROUND SDE BOKER
Ein Avdat National Park (↖ *6555684, 6554418*; w *parks.org.il*; ☼ *Apr–Sep 08.00–17.00 daily, Oct–Mar 08.00–16.00 daily; admission adult/child ₪28/14*) This highly picturesque national park is often overlooked, not receiving the fame (and consequent crowds) of other desert oases like the Ein Gedi Nature Reserve on the shore of the Dead Sea. The park runs along both sides of the dramatic Zin Canyon, through which trickles the Zin Stream, and extends all the way to the Avdat National Park. The park's geography is unique, characterised by pools, waterfalls and ice-cold springs, while the abundance of water and vegetation has created an oasis for wildlife. A gentle circuitous hike lasting 2 or 3 hours takes visitors along the river's edge to the palm-fringed **lower pools** known as Ein Akev, with the larger one approximately 8m deep, and a 15m-high **waterfall**. A longer 3-hour hike incorporates the **upper pools**, **Ein Maarif spring**, **poplar grove** and **caves** where monks lived during the Byzantine period. The long trail begins in either the upper or lower car park and ends in the other, meaning you will either have to walk back or arrange for transport to collect you at the other end. For those wishing

THE NABATEAN SPICE ROUTE

When the Nabateans, wealthy Arab nomads, settled in the Negev in the 4th century BCE they took control of the transport of spices, incense, herbs, gems and medicines that were crossing from the Far East and Arabian Peninsula to Gaza Port. What has become known as the 2,400km-long 'Spice Route' was the source of the Nabateans' famed affluence (frankincense in particular), and their will and passion to defend it are legendary. With the Roman conquest of Egypt came a struggle for control over the prosperous route, one that ended with the Romans creating alternate routes across the desert. The competition had its effect, however, and as the spice trade started to wane Nabatean inhabitants adopted farming, a practice in which they proved successful. In 105CE, however, the Roman emperor Trajan finally annexed the Nabatean kingdom and incorporated it into the Roman Provincia Arabia.

The route itself was paved around the 1st century BCE, linking the Nabatean capital of Petra in Jordan to Gaza's port. Along the route appeared great camps, stopovers for the mile-long camel caravans that transported their wealth across the desert. In 2005, UNESCO declared the route and the four great Nabatean cities of Avdat, Mamshit, Shivta and Haluza World Heritage Sites, compounding and protecting their historic importance and allowing visitors to follow in the footsteps of the ancient Nabateans.

AVDAT One of the most important Nabatean cities in the Negev, Avdat is at present also the easiest to visit. Its striking ruins, clearly visible from route 40, rise above the surrounding lowlands and safeguard remnants of the Nabatean and Roman presence in the area (page 273).

MAMSHIT (MEMPHIS) (↖ *6556478*; w *parks.org.il*; ☼ *Apr–Sep 08.00–17.00 daily, Oct–Mar 08.00–16.00 daily; admission adult/child ₪22/9*) The walled Nabatean city of Mamshit is the smallest yet best preserved of the Spice Route cities and the site of one of the biggest ancient treasures ever discovered in Israel, consisting of over to see both the upper and lower pools, it is recommended to begin at the entrance to the Avdat National Park and follow the signs to the Ein Akev spring. Finish at the lower car park of the Ein Avdat National Park approximately 5km south of the entrance to the Midreshet Ben-Gurion. The tiny white speck in the skies accompanying you along the hike is the airship dirigible balloon watching over the Dimona nuclear plant.

Avdat National Park (*6551511; ⊕ Apr–Sep 08.00–17.00 daily, Oct–Mar 08.00–16.00 daily, closes 1hr earlier Fri; admission adult/child ₪28/14*) When you're driving south along route 90, the ancient hilltop settlement of Avdat is unmistakable. A visit to the park is crucial to the understanding of the fascinating and unique history of the Negev and in particular the Nabatean Spice Route. The remains themselves are incredibly impressive (in particular the churches and reconstructed Roman villa) and the view from the top of the hill unparalleled.

The entrance to the national park is behind the service station off the motorway. Tickets are purchased in the well-stocked information centre that has small displays of artefacts unearthed from the site and an audio-visual presentation detailing its history. Inside there is also a souvenir shop with locally designed jewellery pieces and other memorabilia on sale. The hiking trail to the Ein Akev spring (page 272) starts behind the information centre too.

10,000 coins. Well-preserved and restored houses, streets, churches and defensive towers (one of which can be climbed for a great view over the site) provide a true insight into Nabatean culture. Mamshit's two churches, complete with highly ornate mosaics, are a particular highlight of the site and on some Jewish holidays the city's market street is recreated, providing a kitsch but enjoyable insight into Nabatean life. There are several good accommodation options within the site including a communal tent with mattresses (*₪65/40*), five-person bungalows (*₪450*) and five-person *tukuls* (thatched tents) (*₪350*). In the summer months, it is possible to live like the ancient Nabateans and camp in the city's ancient khan (inn) (*adult/child ₪50/40*).

SHIVTA (w *parks.org.il;* ⊕ *24hrs daily; admission free*) In the far west of the Negev stands the vast Nabatean city of Shivta whose remains have survived the tests of time beautifully thanks to the region's dramatically low humidity. Although the city started life as a Nabatean caravan stop, most of the remains date to the Byzantine period and include two ornate marble churches and a large baptismal font hewn from rock. A 700m trail leads north to a modern orchard which utilises ancient methods to grow desert fruits, no mean feat in one of the driest places in the country. At the Telalim junction along route 40 follow signs to Nitzana along route 211. The site is on the right after approximately 15km.

HALUZA Excavated rather hastily, the Nabatean city of Haluza (or Elusa) in the west Negev Desert cannot compete with its Spice Route counterparts for impressively preserved relics. The site, which can be accessed only by 4x4, is covered with sand, only a few of its once-impressive buildings visible above ground. Two churches, a theatre and many inscriptions have been discovered, accurately dating the site and putting it firmly on the map as an integral part of the Spice Route. At the time of writing, the site was closed to visitors.

Avdat once stood as one of the most important cities in the Negev, where great Nabatean caravans stopped on their long journeys across the desert's Spice Route (see box, pages 272–3). The city, station 62 on the Spice Route, was named after the Nabatean king Obodas III (Abdah in Arabic) who is believed to have been buried here. The king was revered as a deity and it was under him that the city's temple was built. In 106CE, the Romans annexed the Nabatean kingdom and the city moved into another phase of prosperity and prestige. The Romans incorporated Avdat and the Nabatean kingdom into their empire, Provincia Arabia, and created a series of defence fortresses stretching across their empire's southern border. As the spice trade dried up, Nabatean inhabitants adopted agriculture as their means of livelihood, in particular the production of wine. At the end of the 3rd century CE, a fortress was built on the eastern half of the acropolis hill, most likely to serve as a defence against threatening Arab tribes. The city reached its peak during the Byzantine period, by which time Christianity had taken a firm hold. During this time, the acropolis was rebuilt, complete with churches, a monastery and citadel. Today, the site encompasses the remains from the early Roman, late Roman and Byzantine periods, as well as a small Nabatean temple. St Theodore's Church, with its Greek-inscribed marble tombstones inserted in the floor, is the most interesting Byzantine relic in Avdat. At the further end of the site (and if continuing on along the Israeli National Trail) are the remains of an extensive Roman army camp. Early in the 7th century CE, the town was totally destroyed by an earthquake and was never reinhabited.

MITZPE RAMON *Population 5,500*

Built in the 1950s, Mitzpe Ramon was meant to be a temporary camp for road construction workers. At that time, the only road to Eilat ran along the border with Jordan and was not safe. It was therefore decided that a motorway should be built through the middle of the country. In the 1980s, the Israeli air force established itself in the area, so aircraft can now be regularly heard overhead.

Despite these modern developments, few towns can attest to the kind of view that Mitzpe Ramon's residents wake up to on a daily basis. On the edge of the gargantuan Ramon Crater in the heart of the Negev Desert, Mitzpe Ramon is about as remote as it gets. Small though it is, the town makes a good base for exploring the desert, and facilities have sprung up over recent years in the area's rural tourism boom. Compared with several other desert towns, Mitzpe Ramon is almost pretty, and certainly clean. Attempts have been made to liven the place up with small gardens and greenery adding a touch of colour to the otherwise brown landscape. Ibex and bicycle-mounted children cruise the quiet, dusty streets where traffic is minimal. Yet it isn't all roses as the town suffers from intensely hot summers, freezing winters, mass unemployment and a lack of entertainment. Up to the 1990s, the mining sector had created numerous jobs in the area, but the last mine closed in 2005, and today most residents here are employed in the prison service and tourism. Yet, those looking to participate in true desert adventures and ecotourism have a choice of places to stay at the end of the day. The town is tiny, which, compounded with the myriad signs pointing to all the tourist attractions and hotels, means street names are rarely used in addresses, so it is impossible to get lost. Mitzpe Ramon lies on the boundary between two deserts: the upper is cooler and the lower is hotter. Temperature changes are noticeable once you start hiking down the crater.

GETTING THERE AND AWAY Metropoline buses 60, 64 and 65 to and from Beersheba 85km away depart frequently. Bus 65 leaves Beersheba about once an hour and takes an hour to reach Mitzpe Ramon (₪9.30), while bus 60 takes 2 hours (₪16.50). Egged bus 392 (₪39.50) departs from Eilat once every 3–4 hours and takes 3 hours to reach Mitzpe Ramon, travelling along the Egyptian border, past army bases in the Negev.

TOURIST INFORMATION AND TOUR OPERATORS

i Visitors' centre ↘6588691–8; **w** negevtour.
co.il; ⊕ 08.00–16.00 Sat–Thu, 08.00–15.00 Fri.
On the precipice of the crater, this offers plenty
of local information, particularly about hiking &
rappelling, as well as a good bilingual map of the
town, which considering its diminutive size might
be a bit of an overkill. An audio-visual presentation
depicting the unique history, geology, zoology
& archaeology of the crater is shown at intervals
inside the centre.
Guide Horizon ↘6595333; **m** 052 3690805;
e manager@guidehorizon.com; **w** guidehorizon.
com. Adrenalin-fuelled buggy tours ranging from
half a day to 2 days that end with a sizzling BBQ &
a soak in the attached spa (below).

Karkom Jeep Tours **m** 054 5343797;
e negevjeep@gmail.com; **w** negevjeep.co.il/
english. Specialists in jeep tours across the Negev
& further afield to the Dead Sea, the Spice Route
& into Jordan.
Negevland ↘6595555; **m** 050 9988144;
e negevland@gmail.com; **w** negevland.co.il/en.
All-round adventure masters, the list of activities
is inexhaustible: including jeep tours, mountain
biking, rappelling, archery & paintballing.
Experienced guides & quality equipment.
Negevland's office is a few metres from the Mitzpe
Ramon visitors' centre.

⌐ WHERE TO STAY A good variety of accommodation is represented in Mitzpe Ramon, ranging from the most basic communal tents to the luxurious Isrotel Ramon Inn. Family-run zimmers make up the wide choice of mid-range accommodation and the visitors' centre can supply you with a list. When choosing a zimmer or cabin it is worth checking out the kitchen facilities, as eating options are sparse. Nights in the desert camps can be a great way of being at one with nature but are a bit rough and ready. Be sure to take some warm clothes, even in summer. There are also several campsites in the crater itself. Pitch your own tent or sleep in a communal Bedouin one.

⌂ Beresheet (111 private villas) 1 Ein Akev
St; ↘6387797; **e** info@isrotel.co.il; **w** isrotel.com.
Its name meaning 'Genesis' in Biblical Hebrew, this
hotel is truly unique & offers the complete luxury
package, including tours, spiritual workshops, spa,
indoor & outdoor swimming pool, desert activities,
top-quality restaurant &, of course, immaculate
self-catering apartments with staggering views.
This is the desert à la carte. **$$$$**
⌂ Alpaca Farm [map, page 264] (5 rooms)
↘6588047; **m** 052 8977010; **e** office@alpaca.
co.il; **w** alpacas-farm.com. The bright, spacious
cabins sleep 4–7 people, offering great value &
a unique desert experience. Guests can wander
around the farm, get involved in daily tasks &
help with the animals. Cabins have fully equipped
kitchenettes, TVs & big verandas. It is also possible
to sleep in a communal area on mats for ₪80/
night. **$$$**

⌂ Guide Horizon (8 rooms) ↘6595333;
m 052 3690805; **e** manager@guidehorizon.com;
w guidehorizon.com. Rustic wood cabin offering
characterful private rooms. A funky spa, holistic
centre & sauna plus decks scattered with cushions
are a perfect way to chill out after a rigorous day
buggying (above). **$$$**
⌂ Silent Arrow Desert Lodge [map, page
264] (50 beds) **m** 052 6611561; **e** info@
silentarrow.com; **w** silentarrow.co.il. Be at one
with nature & the wild desert by sleeping in the
private dome tents (₪170 pp), the communal
tent (₪90 pp) or in your own tent in the campsite
(₪90 pp), which has kitchen, toilet & shower
facilities. Desert activities can be arranged through
the lodge. **$$**
⌂ The Green Backpackers (5 rooms) 2/2
Nakhal Sirpad St; ↘6532319; **e** greenbmr@gmail.
com; **w** thegreenbackpackers.com. A wonderful,

cosy guesthouse with dorms as well as private rooms. There is an airy outdoor terrace, communal kitchen, extra blankets & hot water bottles for

those chilly desert nights. You will be well looked after by the attentive staff at this fabulous hostel. They also arrange tours around the area. **$$–$**

✕ WHERE TO EAT AND DRINK

✕ **Inn Sense Bistro** (formerly Chez Eugene) Spice Quarter; ✆6539595; w innsense.co.il; ⏲ 08.00–22.30 Tue–Sun. Elegant gourmet restaurant that comes as a surprise amid the rustic desert & Bedouin-style eateries. Mediterranean cuisine combines with the fruits of the desert to create fusion meals of prime ingredients & a blend of flavours. It is attached to the boutique hotel (**$$$$**) of the same name, which has 6 rooms. **$$$$**

✕ **Hahavit Restaurant and Café** 10 Nakhal Tzihor, ✆6588226; ⏲ 11.00–late Sun–Thu, after Shabbat Sat. Better on the inside than it appears on the outside, it has simple pub food, ice creams,

snacks & drinks, & what it lacks in culinary finesse it makes up for with the view. **$$**

✕ **Hakatzeh** 2 Har Ardon St; ✆6595273; m 057 9441865; ⏲ noon–20.00 daily. Rustic home-cooking where almost any meal will be accompanied by rice & potatoes. Quiches & lighter bites are a good lunch option. **$$**

✕ **Lasha Bakery** Spice Quarter; m 050 3611488; w lashabakery.com; ⏲ 09.00–19.00 Sun–Thu, 08.00–15.00 Fri. In the heart of the Spice Quarter, this tiny bakery is a gem of a place. Excellent pastries plus shakshooka on bread & good coffee. **$**

OTHER PRACTICALITIES The centre of the town is very small; the focus of the activities here is the square with a supermarket and a few eateries at the start of Ben-Gurion Boulevard off the main roundabout by the petrol station. The most central **ATM** is **Bank Hapoalim** (*1 Ben-Gurion Bd; *2407; ⏲ 08.30–13.15 Sun & Tue–Wed, 08.30–13.00 & 16.00–18.30 Mon & Thu*) just a few metres away. You'll also find a Shugersal **supermarket** and falafel stalls, and a **post office** (*4 Tzichor St; ✆6588416; ⏲ 08.00–18.00 Sun & Thu, 08.00–12.30 & 15.30–18.00 Mon–Tue, 08.00–13.30 Wed, 08.00–noon Fri*) is just around the corner. The closest **police station** is in the town of Dimona, which is 67km away.

WHAT TO SEE AND DO The word 'activity' certainly sums up the range of things to do, as most of the unusual selection of tourist attractions involve breaking a sweat. If it's horseriding, bone-shaking jeep tours, hiking, archery, riding a llama or rappelling you're looking for, then you're in luck. The town has also discovered the appeal of alternative therapies and massage centres, and apart from the Isrotel Ramon Inn spa there are countless independent therapists who work from home or a small clinic. The visitors' centre can provide you with a list and contact details. Therapies include massage, shiatsu, fortune telling, Chinese medicine, acupuncture and reflexology.

Ramon Crater Nature Reserve At 45km long, 8km wide and 500m deep, the Ramon Crater is a vast gash across the Negev Desert. The spectacularly impressive crater holds claim to being the world's largest karst erosion cirque (often referred to internationally by its Hebrew name *makhtesh*), and was formed millions of years ago as the ocean that once covered this part of the desert retreated northwards. Around five million years ago, the Arava Rift Valley was created causing great rivers to divert their course, their powerful flows eroding the land and leaving in their wake a great crater. The black rock throughout the crater is obsidian natural glass, formed by the cooling of volcanic lava. The nature reserve boasts a rich habitat, particularly vultures, which are now considered endangered in Israel, hyenas and ibex.

The entire crater and its surrounding mountains have been incorporated into the nature reserve, and it is one of the few places in the Negev where the IDF do not train, although you are likely to hear and even see military aircraft from the nearby bases flying overhead. This is nonetheless a fantastically open and free area to explore both on foot and by car. Hiking trails are exhaustive (see box, below) and the visitors' centre will gladly assist visitors and provide a free map detailing hiking opportunities, while countless organisations arrange jeep tours around the main sites (page 275).

Desert Archery Park (m *050 5344598*; w *desertarchery.co.il*) The unusual activity that is desert archery is played somewhat like a game of golf, yet instead of clubs you have bows and arrows and instead of a golf green, you have the vast expanse of the Ramon Crater. Courses of between 1km and 4km accommodate fitness levels and a half-hour archery training session is provided before setting off.

Bio Ramon (✆*6588755*; ⊕ *08.00–17.00 Sat–Thu, 08.00–16.00 Fri, closes 1hr earlier in winter; admission adult/child ₪12/6*) Located near the visitors' centre this small 'live museum' is generally aimed at children but can be fun for all ages wanting to learn about the four-legged residents of the desert.

HIKING IN THE RAMON CRATER

Hiking opportunities in the Ramon Crater are seemingly endless, but here is a selection of our favourites. For more trails, visit w negevtrails.com.

MAKHTESH PROMENADE A good place to start exploring the crater is from the Hagamal (Camel) Lookout, which is located south of the visitors' centre along the Makhtesh Promenade. While not particularly over-exerting, the trail isn't for the faint-hearted as it skims the edge of the cliff to a suspended platform providing panoramic views of the crater. From the lookout the trail continues on past a sculpture garden and takes approximately an hour.

THE PRISM From a little past the Hagamal Lookout a trail (*4km/2hrs*) leads down the sharp face of the crater to the Prism, a unique sandstone hill. The geological formation was created after the stones were baked in the roasting summer sun only to crystallise as they cooled, leaving prism-like shapes covering the hillside.

SAHARONIM STRONGHOLD This is one of the most beautiful spots in the crater, a fact that seems compounded by the groups of onager (wild ass) and ibex, which are often spotted at the natural spring here. From the Beerot campsite make your way by car to the Saharonim car park. From this point several trails fan out offering hikes of differing length and difficulty. The simplest (*0.5km/1hr*) incorporates the Nabatean stronghold at the top of the hill directly in front of the car park and then descends to Ein Saharonim (spring), which in winter flows with water. For a longer hike (*5.5km/4hrs*) continue on from Ein Saharonim across the Saharonim Ridge to the Wadi Gavanim campsite (crossing route 40). Do bear in mind that this is the only campsite in the area with facilities. Continue in a clockwise direction along Nahal Gavanim ending back in the Saharonim car park.

Alpaca Farm (☏ *6588047;* m *052 8977010;* e *office@alpaca.co.il;* w *alpacas-farm. com;* ⏲ *summer 08.30–18.30 daily, winter 08.30–16.30 daily; admission ₪30*) This lovingly run farm began with the arrival of 190 llamas and alpacas who entered Israel from South America aboard a jet plane. Today, the farm raises its 400-plus animals for their fine wool. Activities include touring the farm, feeding the animals, visiting the petting centre, horseriding into the desert, learning wool-making techniques and yoga classes. The farm is located a few kilometres out of town and is well signposted. There is no public transport, so you will need to get there under your own steam. They also offer accommodation – see page 275.

10

The Dead Sea and the Judean Desert

Telephone code 08

The eerie name of the sea that marks the lowest point on earth couldn't in fact be more apt. Shark-a-phobes be reassured, for in the salty waters of the Dead Sea nothing can live, its extreme salinity meaning all forms of organism are unable to survive, both in the water and on the shores that surround it. Yet in contrast to this rather gloomy picture of a barren and lifeless region, the Dead Sea has had a colourful religious, cultural and geological life and is today one of the country's most alluring and popular places to visit.

Biblical history abounds along the shores of the sea, with names such as John the Baptist, King David, King Herod, Sodom, Gomorrah and Lot intricately connected with its history. With the discovery of the Dead Sea Scrolls at Qumran in 1947, the sea's religious significance became unparalleled. In recent years, the phenomenon that spurred King Herod to build his majestic spa on the cliff at Masada has been tapped and the sale of Dead Sea products for their therapeutic properties has become a worldwide trade, thrusting Israel into the tourist limelight.

SAFETY

While drowning in water in which you can barely swim let alone fully submerge yourself in may seem ridiculous, the fact that it is difficult to swim in often causes the most problems for bathers. While you're bobbing around enjoying the newspaper, winds can quickly push you out to sea where you won't stop until reaching Jordan. It is therefore imperative (and the law) to only swim in designated areas where there are lifeguards.

The anecdote 'salt is good for healing wounds' couldn't be more appropriate – or painful – as at the Dead Sea. While it is said to be effective in the treatment of skin problems, the extreme salinity means it can burn excruciatingly if you have any broken skin. If you think you're free of scrapes and scratches, fear not, the sea will find a tiny one you didn't even know existed. Needless to say, splashing or putting your eyes anywhere near the water is painful and dangerous.

Danger signs along the coast – which should be strictly adhered to – warn of sinkholes. The fragile coast is prone to suddenly and dramatically dropping away and leaving a gaping hole in the ground, a geological phenomenon not so impressive if you're standing on it at the time. Ein Gedi Beach (page 281) fell victim to exactly this national event in 2015. And do remember to drink extra water, especially when hiking or spending prolonged periods of time on the beach.

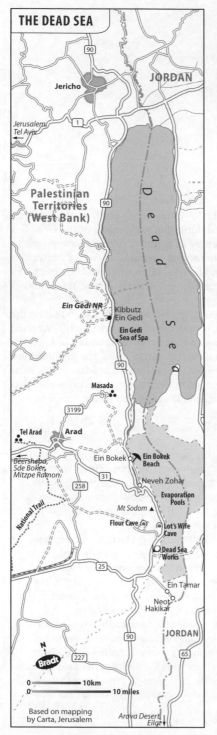

THE DEAD SEA

Jericho

JORDAN

Jerusalem/
Tel Aviv

Palestinian
Territories
(West Bank)

Dead Sea

Ein Gedi NR
Kibbutz
Ein Gedi
Ein Gedi
Sea of Spa

Masada

Tel Arad   Arad

Beersheba,
Sde Boker,
Mitzpe Ramon

Ein Bokek   Ein Bokek
Beach

Neveh Zohar

Evaporation
Pools

Mt Sodom ▲

National Trail

Flour Cave   Lot's Wife
Cave

Dead Sea
Works

Ein Tamar

Neot
Hakikar

JORDAN

Bradt

N

0   10km
0   10 miles

Based on mapping
by Carta, Jerusalem

Arava Desert,
Eilat

The incredible buoyancy of the Dead Sea makes for a fun and slightly surreal experience, bobbing up and down like a cork. Beaches have subsequently popped up along the coast, ranging from free and crowded to expensive and crowded to private and crowded. In peak seasons, finding a place to put your towel is unlikely, but out of season (especially midweek) beaches are much quieter.

GEOGRAPHY AND GEOLOGY

The Dead Sea is in fact a large, saline lake. Fed by the Jordan River that winds its way from the north forming the natural border between Jordan and Israel, the sea lays claim to being the lowest point on earth at 418m below sea level. Its inhospitable environment is due to the fact that the water comprises 30% salinity, up to nine-times saltier than other seas and oceans (that's about 300g of salt per kilogram of water). Yet this isn't just your ordinary table salt (although it does become that after a trip through the salt works at the southern end of the Dead Sea); the sea is laden with highly concentrated mineral salts. These extremely high concentrations mean its density is a lot greater than that of fresh water and is the underlying cause of both the sea's famed buoyancy and its therapeutic properties.

GETTING THERE AND ORIENTATION

Visiting the Dead Sea is relatively easy either under your own steam or as part of a coach tour. Nothing, however, can beat renting a car and cruising along the coast road at your own pace. Public transport to and from the Dead Sea and desert in general is limited, but there are regular services from Jerusalem and Tel Aviv that will drop you at the major sites.

Finding a tour going down to the Dead Sea and Masada is about as easy as finding sand in the desert, but is not always an enjoyable experience. Cramming in as much as possible, tours hurtle out of Jerusalem zooming round the sites and heading home again. If time is of the essence and this is your only option, ask at any hotel or hostel reception, and they will book you on to a tour. Flat fees of around ₪100 normally get you on the bus, and you then pay for entrance tickets separately.

Accommodation, eating options and facilities are, however, in short supply in the area, so you're best advised to book ahead, especially in summer when getting a room anywhere is unlikely at the last minute, and stock up on provisions. If you can stand the heat then camping is also an option.

EIN GEDI

The western stretch of coast known as Ein Gedi, comprising a kibbutz and a nature reserve, is one of the most popular and most visited sections of the Dead Sea. Its proximity to Jerusalem (a mere hour's drive) and the Masada archaeological site, a beautiful valley oasis and a kibbutz spa make it a top spot along the route south.

Ein Gedi has a long and unique history and countless excavations in the area have unearthed evidence of settlement here for centuries. Throughout the Chacolithic, Persian and Hasmonean periods, settlers concentrated around the springs while biblical references tell us that David sought refuge here from King Saul. During the Bar Kokhba revolt (132–135CE), Ein Gedi was an important rebel outpost and it continued to thrive throughout the Roman and Byzantine periods. The antiquities park in the nature reserve delves further into the rich history of the area.

GETTING THERE AND AROUND Buses 486 and 487 from Jerusalem make the journey several times a day (*1hr 50mins/₪34*), while bus 421 from Tel Aviv's Arlozorov bus station travels here once a day at 09.00 (*3hrs/₪42.50*), returning at 13.00. Bus 384 to and from Beersheba (*2hrs/₪37.50*) and Arad (*1hr 30mins/₪27*) makes the journey five times daily and will drop you at Masada or Ein Bokek along the way. Bus 444 passes four times daily in each direction to Eilat (*3hrs/₪42.50*). Ein Gedi is a good jumping-off point for sights in the West Bank, including Qumran National Park.

WHERE TO STAY AND EAT

Ein Gedi Resort (148 rooms) 6594220/1; e info.resort@ein-gedi.co.il; w en.ein-gedi.co.il. Nestled among the green lawns of the kibbutz, its clean, spacious rooms feature kitchenettes, AC, TV & are based on HB or FB (kosher) with meals at the Ein Gedi Botanical Garden Restaurant. Price includes entry into the Ein Gedi Spa, & there's a pool onsite. **$$$$**

Ein Gedi Youth Hostel (HI) (51 rooms) 6584165; e eingedy@iyha.org.il; w iyha.org.il. The fact that it is extremely hard to get a bed in the hostel attests to its popularity & value for money. Located a short walk from the entrance to the nature reserve it is exceptionally clean, offers dorms (**$**) & dbl rooms, AC & kosher b/fast. Some rooms come with balconies overlooking the Dead Sea. **$$$**

Khan Campsite m 054 6079175. Originally the Ein Gedi Beach campsite, it moved up to the kibbutz in 2015 when the beach closed. Services include a 24/7 bar, fridges, good Wi-Fi, beautiful views over the Dead Sea, friendly staff & free use of the Ein Gedi Resort swimming pool (⏱ 10.00–18.00 daily). **$**

Ein Gedi Botanical Garden Restaurant ⏱ 07.00–09.30, noon–14.00 & 18.00–21.00 daily. Offers a big buffet with salads & Mediterranean-style foods (*₪70 pp*). Guests at the Ein Gedi Resort get b/fast plus lunch or dinner or both, so if you're staying a few days, you might want to consider this option. **$$$**

WHAT TO SEE AND DO The beach here closed in 2015 when a hole opened up in the road. Although it is still possible to swim nearby, there are no facilities, and it would entail an arduous walk down to the shore and back up.

10

Ein Gedi Nature Reserve (☎ *6584285;* ⊕ *Apr–Sep 08.00–17.00 daily, Oct–Mar 08.00–16.00 daily; admission adult/child ₪28/14*) This 25km² reserve is a true tropical oasis, providing a lifeline for flora and fauna in an otherwise dry, barren expanse of desert landscape. Situated on the Syrian–African Rift Valley the reserve is fed year-round by four springs: David, Arugot, Shulamit and Gedi.

Historically, the reserve was an important area for growing unusual plants including therapeutic and aromatic species as well as dates, a highly sought-after commodity. To this day, it still boasts an impressive and fundamental array of plants and trees of East African origin. A large variety of mammals, birds and reptiles are also drawn to the oasis, the Nubian ibex and Syrian hyrax being the most noticeable and easily spotted residents. The local celebrities, however, are the small colony of leopards who live in the nearby hills, but these shy creatures are infrequently seen.

Marked **trails** of varying length and difficulty wind gently uphill, along (and sometimes through) rivers and streams, allowing for fantastic views over the Dead Sea and Jordan Mountains, wildlife spotting and spectacular waterfalls and Dodim Cave. The **David spring trek** can vary in length between 1.5km and 3km depending on the route chosen and detours to hidden waterfalls. Allow 90 minutes to 3 hours, which leaves time for a cooling-off swim in one of the waterfall pools. The longer, 4km **Arugot trek** is for the slightly more energetic and takes approximately 4 hours, the extra effort rewarded by an impressive waterfall.

Approximately 1km from the entrance to the reserve on the way to the kibbutz is an **ancient synagogue** (*admission adult/child ₪15/7, free with the nature reserve ticket*) dating back to the 3rd to 6th centuries CE. Built during the Byzantine period by Jewish residents of the area, this ornate synagogue was an integral part of the flourishing community. It has a beautiful mosaic floor, discovered in the 1960s by the farmers from Kibbutz Ein Gedi, situated just above the reserve.

DEAD SEA CLINICS

Renowned worldwide for its purported therapeutic properties, the Dead Sea has become a honeypot for those in search of natural relief from a whole host of ailments. Spa resorts and health clinics along the coast have harnessed the region's climate, unique conditions and medicinal products to offer a series of specialist treatments: climatotherapy, which draws on climatic elements such as humidity, pressure and temperature; balneotherapy, a treatment that uses the thick, black Dead Sea mud; and thalassotherapy, which involves bathing in the unique waters of the sea. The following are considered the best Dead Sea spas:

DMZ Medical Spa Lot Spa Dead Sea Hotel, Ein Bokek; ☎ 9973117; w lothotel.com/clinic. Treats psoriasis, asthma, orthopaedic & cardiac rehabilitation, cystic fibrosis & skin diseases.

Dead Sea Clinic Central Solarium, Ein Bokek; ☎ 6520297; e deadseaclinic@gmail.com; w deadseaclinic.com/en. Offers over 100 different treatments, specialising in respiratory diseases, joint problems, dermatological diseases & anti-stress.

Ein Gedi Spa (page 283) Renowned for treating neurological metabolic disorders, traumatic ailments, allergies, bronchial asthma & rheumatic illnesses.

While the reserve is open year-round, winter flooding of the David and Arugot rivers often results in the park's closure and hiking is prohibited. The best time to visit is spring or autumn when the summer heat relents and the park is less crowded.

Ein Gedi kibbutz and spas (✆ *6594221, 6594726;* e *eg@ein-gedi.org.il;* w *en. ein-gedi.co.il*) The beautiful, palm-fringed kibbutz has successfully cashed in on the rapidly growing international phenomenon of Dead Sea treatments. Its main economy today centres on tourism and while the flash hotels along the coast at Ein Bokek may have all the mod cons, Ein Gedi has years of experience and the added bonus of pretty, leafy surroundings and a real family atmosphere. A small supermarket here is a good place to stock up on the basics if you are planning picnics or self-catering meals, but don't expect too much. The kibbutz runs the **Nature's Creation** spa (✆ *6594220*) offering top-of-the-range holistic treatments including Ayurveda, massages, mud wraps, salt peeling and herbal saunas. Just along the coast, the **Ein Gedi Sea of Spa** (✆*6201030, 6594813;* w *eingediseaofspa.com;* ⊕ *summer 08.30–18.30 daily, winter 08.30–16.30 Sat–Thu, closes 1hr earlier on Fri; w/day ₪95, w/end ₪100*), 4km south of the kibbutz, has honed promotion of the famed Dead Sea products to the maximum. The spa is a fantastic way to experience the sea's therapeutic properties with a huge array of facilities and treatments. Six thermo-mineral water pools, massages, mud baths and an outdoor freshwater pool will leave you feeling clean, young and healthy. A meal in the spa's restaurant, which serves a selection of meat dishes, salads and desserts, is included in the entry price.

MASADA

(✆*6584207/8;* w *parks.org.il;* ⊕ *Apr–Sep 08.00–16.00 daily, Oct–Mar 08.00–17.00 daily, closes 1hr earlier on Fri; admission adult/child ₪23/14; cable car one-way/ return adult ₪56/74, child ₪28/42; NB: on exceptionally hot days, the climbing path is closed so the cable car is the only way up*) More than just one of the country's most-visited tourist destinations, the archaeological site of Masada represents Israeli patriotism at its proudest. Upon the protruding rock that towers some 400m above the western shore of the Dead Sea, IDF soldiers come to swear allegiance, repeating the mantra 'Masada shall not fall again'. For it was here, on the precipitous rock shelf, that the ancient fortress built by Herod the Great in the 1st century BCE became the 20th-century symbol of Jewish heroism. The fortress was captured by the Zealots, a Jewish sect, in 66CE in their revolt against Rome and became the last standing Jewish stronghold. After a long siege, the Romans finally stormed the fortress in 73CE, only to find that all 960 Zealots had committed suicide rather than surrender to their forces. Today, it is one of the most important stops on the Jewish pilgrimage route and in 2001 was awarded UNESCO World Heritage status. A museum complex opened in 2007 displays some of the most impressive artefacts excavated from the ruins as well as depicting the life, times and history of this fascinating site.

HISTORY Although finds date the origin of the site to the Chacolithic period 6,000 years ago, it wasn't until Herod got his hands on it that Masada really came into its own. Major fortifications between 37BCE and 31BCE included two beautiful, ornate palaces, heavy defensive walls, state-of-the-art aqueducts and water cisterns and a bathhouse complex. In 66CE, following Herod's death, the Jewish revolt against the Romans saw a group of rebels overcome the Roman garrison stationed at Masada. After the fall of Jerusalem in 70CE, the rebels were joined by Zealots, an extremist opposition group, and families fleeing the devastation, only to be stormed by the Romans three years later. They established camps at the base of the fortress and laid a complicated and arduous siege to it, one that would last many months.

GETTING THERE AND AWAY There are two ways to approach Masada: from route 90 that runs along the Dead Sea (*5mins off the main road*) or along route 3199 from Arad. The youth hostel, visitors' centre, cable cars and Snake Path are all accessed from the eastern Dead Sea entrance, while visitors arriving for the sound and light show or wishing to ascend the Roman Ramp will need to approach from the direction of Arad. There isn't a through road from the western side to the Dead Sea so be aware that if you come from this direction you will need to take the very long route back to Arad and down past Ein Bokek (*1hr drive*) to reach the coast and hostel. Buses heading to Ein Gedi from Beersheba and Arad will stop at the junction on the way (page 281), while buses coming from Jerusalem and Tel Aviv will continue on to the archaeological site from Ein Gedi (page 281).

WHERE TO STAY AND EAT

⌂ Masada Guest House (HI) (88 rooms) ☏5945622; e massada@iyha.org.il; w iyha. org.il. Located just off route 90 sits this huge, immaculate hostel offering more than just staggering views over the Dead Sea. Rooms have AC, TV & minibar, & there is a swimming pool in summer. Guests receive a 25% discount off Masada cable-car tickets. Kosher b/fast included, & other meals can be ordered for ₪45. **$$$**

WHAT TO SEE AND DO

The Snake Path The path provides the eastern entrance to the site but the walk uphill is steep and tiring, especially during the blistering summer heat. The alternative is to take the cable car, which leaves from near the car park and finishes at the top of the Snake Path. Both begin from the Dead Sea road.

The Roman Ramp The ramp that ascends to the fortress from the west side is a third option of entering and exiting the site. The ramp can be accessed only from the Arad road.

Palaces Many of the ancient structures and buildings have been restored, one of the most striking being the wall paintings inside the two Herodian palaces. The three-terraced Northern Palace acted as Herod's personal quarters, while the vast complex that comprised the Western Palace was home to servants, workshops and storehouses. Inside, it is possible to see the remains of Herod's throne room, arranged around a central courtyard. Just to the south of the Western Palace are the remains of Herod's swimming pool, another example of the luxurious lifestyle that he enjoyed at Masada.

Bathhouses Designed in a Romanesque style, the bathhouses have been well restored and show the intricate engineering that went into the creation of Herod's luxurious early spa. The bathhouses are located just south of the Northern Palace.

Roman villa With an architectural design reminiscent of the great villas of Rome, this wonderfully restored mansion is a perfect example of the level of luxury and grandeur afforded to those who resided here. After the Zealots took control of the fortress, many of the buildings were divided up to accommodate the substantial population.

Synagogue The incredible discovery of the Masada synagogue has led archaeologists and historians to believe that it may be the oldest Jewish house of prayer in the world. It is the only synagogue to be dated to the time of the Second Temple and contained fragments of scrolls from Ezekiel and Deuteronomy.

Roman camps There are a total of eight Roman camps that surround the lower reaches of the Masada cliff. It was here that Roman garrisons stationed themselves during their long and relentless siege of the fortress. Thanks to the arid climate and soil, the camps are considered the best-preserved Roman army camps ever discovered.

Byzantine church Southeast of the synagogue is another large building complex within which was discovered a 5th-century Byzantine church. A small portion of semi-restored mosaics can be seen at the rear of the building.

Storehouses On the right just through the East Gate are the semi-restored remains of 11 storehouses. Amphorae and jars containing remnants of wine, oil and flour were found in the larger rooms while it is believed valuables and weaponry may have been kept in the smaller ones.

Sound and light show (✆ *9959333; e rontal.n@npa.org.il; Mar–Oct 21.00 Tue & Thu; admission adult/child ₪45/35*) Shown against the backdrop of the western side of the mountain (reached from the Arad road), this 40-minute show depicts the history of the site in an impressive light display. The audio is in Hebrew but there are earphones for English, French, German and Spanish visitors. Tickets must be booked in advance through the Arad visitors' centre (✆ *9950190*), which also organises transport there and back (page 288).

Ahava Factory Store (✆ *6584319;* ◷ *08.00–16.00 Sun–Fri, 08.00–17.00 Sat*) Peruse the shelves laden with Dead Sea products from Israel's biggest and most famous manufacturer. They make great souvenirs and cost half what you'd pay in Europe or the US.

EIN BOKEK

All good things have to come to an end and the natural, rugged beauty of the Dead Sea does so at the resort of Ein Bokek, about 16.5km south of Masada. This conglomeration of enormous chain hotels and their attached luxury spas, souvenir shops and food kiosks are an eyesore along the wild stretch of coastline. Nevertheless, the hotels are expensive and specialist, attracting guests who come to relax and enjoy some pampering and relaxation, not to party all night. There is a definite touristy feel to the highly developed strip, but the free (if overcrowded) Ein Bokek Beach (also known as Hordus Beach) can be found nestled amid the towering buildings. And as a guest, there is no doubt that your Dead Sea therapeutic experience would be top-of-the-range, if decidedly mass-produced.

GETTING THERE AND AROUND There are seven buses a day (348 and 421) from Arad (*45mins; ₪27*) which continue to Ein Gedi, stopping at Masada along the way. By car, follow route 31 until Zohar junction, where you then turn on to route 90 running along the Dead Sea until you reach Ein Bokek. There are few roads and limited public transport in this region, so a car is a great way to get around. Route 90 runs from just outside Jerusalem through the West Bank in the Palestinian Territories

10

all the way along the coast of the Dead Sea and continues south into the Arava Desert. **Hertz car rental** (☎*6841000;* ⊕ *08.30–17.00 Sun–Thu, 08.30–14.00 Fri*) can be found in town in the Solarium Spa building opposite the Daniel Hotel, and the **Magen David Adom** emergency assistance station is right next door.

TOURIST INFORMATION The well-equipped **Tourist Information Office** (☎*9975010;* e *infocenter@ma-tamar.co.il;* ⊕ *08.00–17.30 Sun–Thu, 09.00–13.00 Fri*) is located in the Solarium Spa building across the road from the Daniel Hotel, and the friendly and knowledgeable staff can help with all manner of information, recommendations and desert and Dead Sea trivia.

WHERE TO STAY AND EAT Four star is the lowest-ranked hotel you're likely to find at Ein Bokek, and all pride themselves on quality, service and top-of-the-range facilities. All the major chains are represented, including Rimonim, Leonardo, Crowne Plaza and Fattal. Inside all the hotels are excellent fine-dining options and the resort has numerous cheap kiosks and supermarkets.

🏠 **Crowne Plaza Dead Sea** (304 rooms) ☎6591919; e ds_gmsec@hiil.co.il; w crowneplaza.com. Luxury, compliments of the Crowne Plaza chain of international hotels. Rooms are wood floored & elegant & have all mod cons. Facilities include the Asian fusion Sato Bistro (☎*6591975;* ⊕ *18.00–23.00 Sun–Thu;* ₪90), a state-of-the-art fitness & spa centre & indoor & outdoor pools. **$$$$$**

🏠 **Daniel Dead Sea Resort & Spa** (302 rooms) ☎6689999; w tamareshotels.co.il. The hotel has a cosy & relaxed atmosphere & rooms all have views of the Dead Sea with a fresh & pleasant décor. Expansive swimming pools, a top-of-the-

range spa & wealth of treatments complete the Dead Sea experience. HB & FB available. **$$$$$**

✗ **Taj Mahal** Tulip-Inn Hotel; m 053 9373341; e noach_sharon@hotmail.com; w taj-mahal. co.il; ⊕ noon–sunrise daily. Bedouin-style tent with rich-coloured cushions & twinkling lanterns. Indulge in some barefoot eating & drinking with a Middle Eastern grill & nargileh pipe. Live music & belly dancing on Fri. **$$$$**

✗ **On the Beach Restaurant** ☎6520231; ⊕ 24hrs daily. Offers standard sandwiches, grilled meats, pizza & pasta with views of the Dead Sea. **$$$**

OTHER PRACTICALITIES Ein Bokek has countless shops (particularly on the strip directly in front of Hordus Beach) selling Dead Sea products. There is a supermarket and a pharmacy, and hotel receptions can offer postal services. The Sky Blue Mall close to the Hordus Beach has cafés, fast-food restaurants, shops and an exchange kiosk.

WHAT TO SEE AND DO
Ein Bokek (Hordus) Beach (☎*6594433;* ⊕ *08.00–17.00 daily*) This free beach has several pros and cons. On the upside, the shallow waters of the evaporation pools create white sandy beaches leading down to clear, turquoise waters that gently lap against the sheltered shore. On the downside, behind you is the sprawling and unsightly mass of gigantic hotels and tourist tack. It is also one of the sea's busiest beaches, especially in peak seasons. Facilities include a 24-hour restaurant (above) and showers.

VALLEY OF SODOM

Spanning the southern portion of the Dead Sea is the area known as the Valley of Sodom, named thus for the belief that it was here that God unleashed his fury upon the city of Sodom for its 'sins'. Today, Mount Sodom marks the precise spot and is a must-stop on the tour route. The region is nowadays characterised by the mountain and its range of walks, caves, gorges and powder-like chalky sand. Also worth visiting at the base of the Dead Sea, just after the Dead Sea Works and a 20-minute drive from Ein Bokek, are the moshavim of Neot Hakikar and Ein Tamar, which offer a more low-key desert experience where nature and adventure prevail.

GETTING THERE AND AWAY There is no public transport to the moshavim so you will need to get there under your own steam. Coming from Ein Gedi and Ein Bokek on route 90, turn right just after the evaporation pools and follow the road for about 8km. If you reach the Arava junction you've gone too far.

WHERE TO STAY Many of the families have created guesthouse accommodation and visitors have a choice of campsites, simple rooms and pleasant cabins. There are also opportunities to stay in desert Bedouin tents. Pick up a copy of the moshavim leaflet in the **Ein Bokek Tourist Information Office** (page 286) or visit w ma-tamar. org.il for full listings.

Belfer's Dead Sea Cabins (3 rooms) Neot Hakikar; ☎ 6555104; e michaelbelfer@gmail.com. Split-level cabins are suitable for families & have kitchenette, large porch, outdoor BBQ facilities & free bicycles. Great location for exploring the desert. **$$$**

Cycle Inn (6 rooms) Neot Hakikar; ☎ 6552828; e esteeuzi@zahav.net.il. Family-run guesthouse offering a campsite & private rooms. It has a very communal, friendly atmosphere & is a good budget option for exploring the desert & Dead Sea region. **$$$**

WHERE TO EAT AND DRINK Home-cooking is the name of the game in Neot Hakikar, and there are a handful of rustic meals to be had in the moshavim. **Yossi's Place** (m 052 8808111), **Mothers Secrets** (m 052 8991199) and **Pnina's** (☎ 6555107) offer baked goods, hummus, grilled meats and sandwiches but they must be ordered in advance.

OTHER PRACTICALITIES Neot Hakikar has a range of facilities, small supermarkets, a swimming pool and medical centre, as well as local tour guides who can organise adventure activities, hiking and workshops.

WHAT TO SEE AND DO
Sodom Mountain and Lot's Wife Cave While there is no proof that this is the biblical site of Sodom, it has been the traditional spot. The 11km by 3km mountain range consists almost wholly of salt and is, according to the Book of Genesis, the site of the two towns of Sodom and Gomorrah that were destroyed by God with a rain of fire and brimstone (sulphur) for their wickedness. Before the destruction ensued, God sent two angels to warn all good men to leave the evil towns. The angels found only one good man, Lot, whom they saved, along with his wife and daughters, warning them not to look back. When Lot's wife disobeyed the warning, she was turned into a pillar of salt. Tour buses and signposts today point to a pillar above the entrance to a cave just off the main road as that of Lot's wife and it marks another quick stop along the pilgrimage route.

Nahal Perazim and the Flour Cave Some 3km south of Lot's Wife Cave, a small turn-off on the right between kilometre markers 193 and 194 leads to the **Flour Cave**. So named because of the fine, white powdery chalk that covers everything it touches (including your hair, clothes and face), the cave is part of **Nahal Perazim**, a beautiful, narrow, dry gorge. A 15-minute walk through the gorge will bring you to the entrance of the pitch-black cave (torches are advisable) where it is but a short walk to the other end. White floury steps lead up and out of the 18,000–20,000-year-old cave where you can return to the car park along the path above the gorge. Alternatively, more seasoned hikers can follow a blue (then black) marked trail that leads from the exit of the Flour Cave up Mount Sodom.

Jeep tours Several outfits and private guides offer jeep tours out into the heart of the desert. These include **Masa Midbar** (*Neot Hakikar;* m *052 2317371*), **Barry Hermon** (m *052 8491115*) and **Camel Lot** (m *052 8666062*). The last also offer camel and donkey treks.

Art galleries Within the two moshavim are several artists' galleries ranging from pottery and ceramic sculpting to metal arts and furniture to glass sculpting. Many offer workshops.

ARAD *Population 24,400*

The small, desert city of Arad is most well known for its ancient namesake, today located a few kilometres away at Tel Arad. Yet the city is rather pleasant, if not attractive, in its own right, and considerable efforts over recent years to improve its image have been successful. Its altitude and unique arid climate make it an ideal place for asthma sufferers, and plans to develop the city into a centre for medical treatments are under way. Public transport links with the Dead Sea (25km away), Jerusalem and Beersheba are good in desert terms and there is a modern, ethnically diverse feel to the place. The artists' quarter (Eshet Lot) in the industrial zone is worth a visit if you're in the area, and comprises works by local artists who aim to capture the beauty and ruggedness of the desert in their works.

GETTING THERE AND AWAY Direct bus 389 from Tel Aviv makes the journey twice daily at 18.00 and 20.00 (*1hr 45mins/₪34*), returning at 06.15, 08.15, 14.15 and 17.00. To Ein Bokek on the Dead Sea, bus 384 leaves daily at 06.55, 08.55, 10.15, 13.10 and 16.10 (*40mins/₪21.50*) and continues to Ein Gedi, stopping at Masada along the way. Bus 421 has two departures daily at 11.01 and 14.01 and makes a similar journey, but is a little faster (*27mins/₪21.50*). There are several buses a day to and from Beersheba (*1hr/₪16*), from where you can connect to Jerusalem, Eilat, Sde Boker and Mitzpe Ramon.

TOURIST INFORMATION AND PRACTICALITIES Located in central Arad near the mall, the **Arad Visitors' Centre** (\ *9950190;* ⏰ *Apr–Sep 08.00–17.00 daily, Oct–Mar 08.00–16.00 daily; admission adult/child ₪23/12*) houses the **Museum of Biblical Arad**. They also arrange tickets and transport to Masada's sound and light show (page 285) and can supply a list of guesthouses in the town.

🏠 **WHERE TO STAY AND EAT** There are a few small hotels, guesthouses and a selection of eateries and pubs in the town, with fare ranging from simple pizzas to Chinese. While the cuisine is most certainly not on a par with Eilat or Tel Aviv, there is something to suit every taste and pocket.

Arad Hostel (HI) (50 rooms) 4 Haatad St; 02 5945599; e arad@iyha.org.il; w iyha.org.il. Clean, simple dorms with TV, AC, bunks & kosher b/fast. The reception is closed on Shabbat & you need to call ahead if you're arriving in the afternoon. Dorm rooms not available on w/ends. **$$$**

Kfar Hanokdim (35 rooms) 9950097; e kfar@khn.co.il; w kfarhanokdim.co.il/en. Set in the desert just outside of Arad is this authentic Bedouin experience. To get there, take route 3199 out of Arad & continue for 8km; it is signposted on the right. Choose to stay in the communal tent on colourful mattresses or in the private cabins, all made from locally sourced, organic materials. Be entertained by Bedouin hospitality, enjoy traditional cooking, or embark on a donkey or camel trek into the desert. Must be reserved in advance. Packages include a trek & a night's accommodation for ₪250 pp. **$$**

Canaanite Khan (400 places) Tel Arad National Park; 6992447. A campsite (*adult/child ₪53/42*) with a wide range of sleeping options. Bring your own tent, sleep on mattresses provided, or opt for self-contained rooms for up to 5 people. Facilities include BBQ & bonfire areas. **$**

WHAT TO SEE AND DO

Tel Arad (6992444; w parks.org.il; ⊕ Apr–Sep 08.00–17.00, Oct–Mar 08.00–16.00, closes 1hr earlier on Fri; admission adult/child ₪14/7) About 10km east of Arad on the road to Beersheba are the remains of not one but two ancient settlements. In the 2nd century BCE, a huge Canaanite city was built here, its 1km² area making it the largest excavated Canaanite settlement in the country. Some of the excavated remains of houses have been fully restored, their distinctive shape and layout having coined a new archaeological term 'Aradian house'. Further up the hill, an Israelite settlement dates to about 1000BCE during the reign of King Solomon, and came into being some 1,500 years after the abandonment of the Canaanite city. Referred to as a citadel fortress, it lasted throughout the reigns of the kings of Judah until its destruction between 597BCE and 577BCE, during which time Jerusalem was under siege from the Babylonians. Inside the fortress courtyard is an Israelite temple, a smaller version of King Solomon's Temple in Jerusalem.

Artists' quarter (*Industrial Area*) Small artists' galleries display their works which reflect the beauty, barrenness and ancient traditions of the desert. Tours can be arranged through the visitors' centre.

11

The Arava Desert and Eilat

Telephone code 08

Southern Israel, stretching from the Dead Sea towards the Red Sea, is a sparsely populated area. The Arava Desert, which Israel shares with Jordan to the east, is dotted with tiny kibbutzim, national parks and holiday retreats, while the western border from the Gaza Strip in the north to the Taba border crossing in the south delineates Israel's Sinai frontier and border with Egypt. The territory beyond route 12 and 40 to the west is heavily militarised and public transport is very infrequent here, but the Arava Desert and city of Eilat make long journeys south worthwhile.

THE ARAVA DESERT

As the desert makes its way towards the city of Eilat, there appears to be a lull before the party storm. Civilisation gets sparser, the landscape more remote and facilities fewer and farther between. Yet the Arava Desert is in fact one of the most bewitching regions of Israel's south where Bedouin communities thrive, the Spice Route starts its long trek westwards and where the air is the freshest in the country. There are numerous wadis (*nakhals* in Hebrew) tucked away amid its rocky formations. Kibbutzim dot the fringes of route 90, their isolated positions and organic farming practices producing an ideal getaway for those seeking the utmost in seclusion and nature. And nature is the name of the game in the southern Arava, the Yotvata Hai Bar Reserve (page 292), Timna Park (page 293) and International Birding and Research Centre (page 302) providing a great insight into the desert's wilder strip of land.

GETTING THERE AND AROUND This is one of the most inaccessible areas of the country and travel is therefore difficult by public transport, so renting a car in Beersheba or Eilat is by far the best way to get the most out of your time in this remote region. Route 40 from Beersheba passes Sde Boker and Mitzpe Ramon and joins with route 90 coming down from the Dead Sea and Jerusalem. Route 90 then continues all the way through the Arava Desert to Eilat. Buses 394 and 397 from Beersheba stop at the junctions to the kibbutzim and parks along the Arava Desert on their way to Eilat. There are seven buses daily in each direction.

TOURIST INFORMATION AND TOUR OPERATORS The small **Yotvata Visitors' Centre** (⏱ *08.00–15.00 Sat–Thu, 08.00–13.00 Fri*) is located directly outside the mall in Kibbutz Yotvata along route 90. The **Shaharut Camel Riders** (page 292) organise camel treks in the wilds of the Arava Desert, and there are countless tour operators in Eilat (page 295) that can arrange 4x4 and birdwatching trips. When visiting individual nature reserves on your own, lectures and tours can be arranged on site, but that might require extra time and staying overnight in a tent.

WHERE TO STAY Sleeping (almost) under the stars, getting out into nature and learning to appreciate the fruits of the wild desert, is becoming hugely popular, and as a result eco-lodges and Bedouin-style khans (tents) have appeared throughout the Arava. Whether it's meditating, communal living, organic toilets or rustic, home-cooked meals over a campfire, the lodges offer them all, as well as private rooms with air conditioning and hot water so you don't have to rough it. Most of the lodges also offer campsites if you have your own tent, and there are campsites in the Timna Park and Yotvata Hai Bar Reserve as well. Some of the kibbutzim dotted along route 90 have nice, clean rooms and use of the swimming pool and dining room. For accommodation at Shaharut Camel Riders or the Kibbutz Lotan Guesthouse, see below.

Kibbutz Lotan 6356888; e office@ klotan.co.il; w kibbutzlotan.com. The bohemian kibbutz of Lotan is ideal for hippies-at-heart in search of some natural living. With the word 'eco' in front of all their activities guests are left in no doubt as to their ethos (& no, you won't be finding televisions inside any of their mud-coated guesthouses). At the kibbutz you can learn how to build your own eco-friendly house, enjoy a *watsu* (water shiatsu) massage in the spa centre, relax in the swimming pool or do a spot of birdwatching. Guesthouses are pleasant but simple, & there is also dorm accommodation (₪250). The atmosphere on the kibbutz is lovely, however, & you pay for the experience. **$$$**

Keren Kolot (22 rooms) Kibbutz Ketura; m 053 9419109; e reception@ketura.co.il; w keren-kolot.co.il. If you're not opposed to the smell of cow dung – & you get used to it rather fast – then the spacious, comfortable rooms offered on the kibbutz are a good base for visiting the area. A communal pool (in summer) is free of charge to enjoy, but simple kosher dining room,

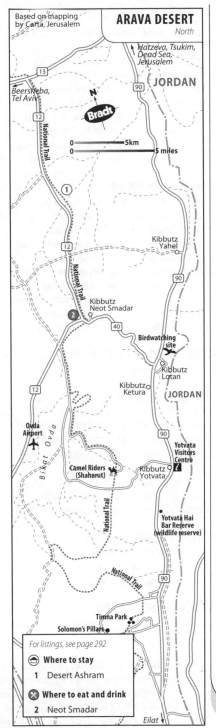

For listings, see page 292

Where to stay
1 Desert Ashram

Where to eat and drink
2 Neot Smadar

café & bicycle rental are extras as well as tours of the experimental orchards where exotic, hard-to-pronounce fruits are grown. **$$$**

🏠 **Desert Ashram** [map, page 291] (80 beds) Shittim; m 052 3824617; e ashram@desertashram.co.il; w desertashram.co.il. Located on the west side of the Arava Desert on the path of the Israel National Trail (see box, page 59) is this serene centre of meditation in the heart of the remote desert. Prices include accommodation – in rooms or wooden huts with AC, in a dorm or the campsite – FB organic, vegetarian food & meditation sessions. **$$$–$**

🏠 **Negev Eco Lodge** (40 beds) Tsukim, south of Hatzeva; m 052 6170028, call 09.00–18.00 Sun–Thu; e desertdaysmud@gmail.com; w desert-days.com. This eco-lodge is constructed from sustainable desert materials & offers 7 rooms (sleeping up to 6 people) each with an eco-toilet, hot water, coffee facilities & shared kitchen. A communal khan offers dormitory accommodation & there is a real community feel to the lodge, where people can get close to nature. A pool,

animal corner & desert tours are other attractions. **$$$–$**

🏠 **Desert Routes Inn** (also known by its Hebrew name Shvilim) (60 beds) Hatzeva, northern Arava just south of the Dead Sea; ✆ 03 5004266; e office@shvilimbamidbar.co.il; w shvilimbamidbar.co.il/en. Enjoy the isolated peaceful atmosphere of the desert with the modern comforts of home. 11 self-contained apartments have kitchenette, cable TV & AC, while a khan (tent) offers dormitory accommodation on mattresses. Internet, BBQ area & a community swimming pool. There is a small supermarket in the moshav as well as tour booking facilities. **$$–$**

🛆 **Yotvata Hai Bar Reserve Camping** ✆ 08 6373057; e haibar-yotvata@npa.org.il. This well-equipped camping site is located in the nature reserve itself & can accommodate up to 500 people. Mattresses (if required) & igloo tents can be rented for an additional fee. Tours of the reserve & lectures by a reserve inspector can be arranged at reception. **$$–$**

✖ **WHERE TO EAT AND DRINK** Dining options are sparse, so eating in the simple kibbutz dining rooms is often the only choice.

✖ **Neot Smadar** [map, page 291] ✆ 6358111; ⊙ 06.00–21.00 Sun–Thu, 06.00–15.00 Fri, 18.00–21.00 Sat. This wonderful organic farm shop at the Ketura junction offers a lovely little menu of creative dishes, which are delicious & oh-so-healthy. **$$**

✖ **Yotvata Rest Stop** Hatzeva; ✆ 6357363; ⊙ 05.30–19.00 Sun–Thu, 05.30–18.00 Fri, 07.00–20.00 Sat. Buffet-style canteen with OK

mains & a really good selection of desserts; be sure to try some of the Choco chocolate milk for which the kibbutz is famous. **$$**

✖ **Bar Bamidbar** ✆ 6581406. Simple but good restaurant in moshav Hatzeva. **$$$**

✖ **Shaharut Restaurant** Serves freshly baked Bedouin fare in a traditional atmosphere. **$$$**

OTHER PRACTICALITIES Between Beersheba in the Negev Desert and Eilat in the far south of the Arava, there is a distinct lack of any kind of facilities. The tiny Kibbutz Yotvata about 40km north of Eilat has a small supermarket and petrol station, and the kibbutzim dotted along route 90 offers minimal services.

WHAT TO SEE AND DO

Desert Ashram A spiritual and meditational haven in the depths of the desert offering a Work Meditation Programme (WOMP), festivals and workshops (above).

Camel Riders (*Shaharut*; ✆ 6373218; w *camel-riders.com*) Camel caravan trips ranging from a few hours up to eight days (₪75–1,500) are the quintessential desert experience, with roaring open fires, sleeping under the stars and a mighty sore rear end being part and parcel of the trip. They also organise jeep tours, have a restaurant and offer Bedouin-style half-board accommodation in a large communal tent (₪60) or simple, private huts ($). If you're arriving on the 397 bus that runs between Beersheba and Eilat, call ahead to get picked up from the junction.

Timna Park (↘ 6316756; w parktimna.co.il/en; ⊕ 08.00–16.00 daily, Jul–Aug until 13.00; admission adult/child ₪44/39) The 90km² Timna Valley is home to some of the country's most impressive geological formations, a rich and powerful history and a never-ending array of hiking trails. Historically Timna stands alone as the earliest, most technologically advanced and productive centre in the ancient world. From the 14th to the 12th centuries BCE, the Egyptians operated a vast copper-mining enterprise here. While this was the site's most productive period, evidence has pointed to continued mining communities operating as far back as the late Neolithic period.

The vast U-shaped valley is surrounded by mountains that appear in myriad colours over the course of a day and have hiking trails radiating in every direction over and around them. A car is a prerequisite for visiting the park as there is no public transport, though most sites can be driven to. Nevertheless, there are ample opportunities to get away from the road and into the heart of the desert. A hiking map is supplied at the entrance detailing treks of between 1 and 10 hours. Among the park's many attractions are the famous **Solomon's Pillars**, formed by years of erosion of the pink sandstone cliff face from which they protrude. Other notable sites include the rock-cut **Mushroom, Valley of Inscriptions** and the **ancient mines**. Camping is possible at the park's entrance.

EILAT   *Population 65,215*

The fourth-largest city in Israel, Eilat has also, since 1985, been acting as the country's only free-trade zone. Known under the Ottomans and the British Mandate as Umm Rash Rash, the town was conquered in March 1949 as part of the Ovda Campaign in the Arab–Israeli War. Quite ironically in the 1950s, it was also via the port of Eilat that Israel received oil from Iran, its main fuel supplier back then. Although Eilat has claims to antiquity and there have been archaeological excavations carried out in the surrounding area, today it is predominantly one vast tourist resort, where you are unlikely to encounter history and Holy Land charm. If, however, you're after some hedonistic, raucous and rather tacky seaside fun, then this is definitely the place.

After driving through the serene, staggeringly beautiful landscape of the Negev and Arava deserts, Eilat comes as quite a shock. Perched on the tiny strip of Red Sea coast that Israel lays claim to, it is something of an Israeli Las Vegas. In fact, Eilat is soon to become the only city in Israel where gambling is legal. Row upon row of big chain hotels line the coast, the glittering Red Sea water swarms with all manner of sea craft and squealing sun-seekers, and the pumping neon-lit pedestrian strip is crammed with restaurants, beach bars and shopping malls. A big favourite with boisterous Israeli teenagers enjoying their first trip away from the folks, Eilat can be rowdy and wild. Nevertheless, it has also managed to maintain a noisy family atmosphere, especially on the beaches further along the south coast. The 12km stretch of Israel's Red Sea coast means that day trips to Petra in Jordan and Egypt's Sinai coast are easily accessible, while day trips into the southern Arava Desert are welcome ways to escape the city.

Eilat enjoys almost 365 days a year of sunshine, a year-round water temperature of 21°C and a winter low of 20°C, making it the country's only beach resort that quite literally never stops. Summer temperatures can reach in excess of 40°C but because of its dry, desert atmosphere and lack of humidity, it remains rather pleasant and often more bearable than the intense, sticky humidity of the Mediterranean.

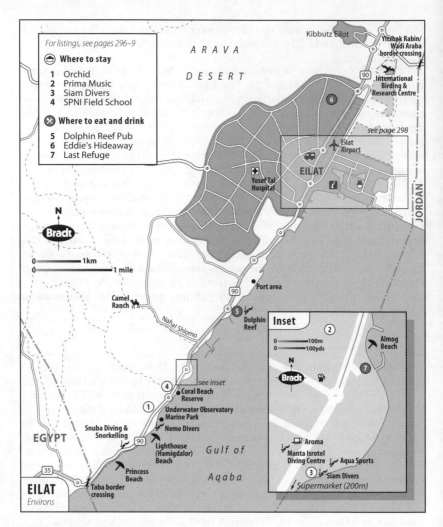

For listings, see pages 296–9

Where to stay
1 Orchid
2 Prima Music
3 Siam Divers
4 SPNI Field School

Where to eat and drink
5 Dolphin Reef Pub
6 Eddie's Hideaway
7 Last Refuge

ARAVA

DESERT

Kibbutz Eilot

Yitzhak Rabin/
Wadi Araba
border crossing

90

International
Birding &
Research Centre

see page 298

6

EILAT

JORDAN

Yosef Tal
Hospital

Eilat
Airport

N

Bradt

0   1km
0   1 mile

Camel
Ranch

90

Port area

Nahal Shlomo

5 Dolphin
Reef

Inset

0   100m
0   100yds

N

Bradt

2

Almog
Beach

7

4   see inset
Coral Beach
Reserve

1 Underwater Observatory
Marine Park

Nemo Divers

Snuba Diving &
Snorkelling

EGYPT

90

Lighthouse
(Hamigdalor)
Beach

Gulf of

Aqaba

Aroma

Manta Isrotel
Diving Centre

Aqua Sports

3 Siam Divers

Supermarket (200m)

35

Princess
Beach

EILAT
Environs

Taba border
crossing

GETTING THERE AND AWAY

By bus The central bus station [298 B2] is located on Hatmarim Boulevard and can be a somewhat disorganised and busy place. Egged bus 390 from Tel Aviv's central bus station does the journey approximately every 90 minutes (*5hrs 20mins/₪70*). Bus 394 has one evening and one late night departure (*5hrs/₪70*), while bus 393 has only one departure per day at 06.30 (*5hrs 30mins/₪70*). All three buses go via Beersheba. Bus 444 to and from Jerusalem departs in each direction at 07.00, 10.00, 14.00 and 17.00 (*5hrs/₪70*) and heads along the Dead Sea, past Ein Gedi. Bus 392 has only one departure per day and follows route 12 approaching Eilat from the Egyptian border. Transport to Eilat gets booked up in summer by hordes of loud teenagers so reserve a seat in advance.

By air At present there are two airports serving Eilat: the city airport right in the centre of Eilat and Ovda Airport around 60km north. The latter, originally built as a military airport, currently accepts a lot of charter flights including El Al, Aeroflot,

Wizz Air and Ryanair. If travelling from elsewhere in Israel, the city-centre airport is more convenient. Commercial flights to Eilat come from Haifa, Tel Aviv's Sde Dov or Ben-Gurion airports with **Arkia** (w *arkia.com*) and **Israir** (*Shalom Centre;* \6340666). Prices start at €40 and €54 one-way respectively. The airport is smack bang in the centre of town and is a 5-minute walk to the promenade or city centre.

However, in 2018, both airports will be replaced by the new and modern Ramon Airport, located just 18km from Eilat. At present more information is available from w ramon-airport.com.

By land The Taba and Arava (Yitzhak Rabin) border crossings provide overland entry into Egypt's Sinai Peninsula and Jordan respectively (see box, page 296).

GETTING AROUND Eilat's city centre is small, so walking is the easiest way to get around. There are taxis everywhere, and fares generally cost around ₪15. Bus 15 from the town centre goes through the tourist village and makes the 7km journey along the south coast to the Taba border regularly, stopping at the beaches, major hotels and the Underwater Observatory Marine Park (page 301) along the way. For the return journey, take bus 16. Alternatively, a number of car-rental companies have their offices in Eilat.

🚗 **Avis** [298 B2] Shalom Centre, 2 Hatmarim Bd; \6373164/5; w avis.co.il; ⏱ 08.00–17.00 Sun–Thu, 08.00–14.00 Fri. Min of 3 days' rental.

🚗 **Europcar** [298 B2] Shalom Centre, 2 Hatmarim Bd; \6373511; w europcar.com; ⏱ 08.00–18.00 Sun–Thu, 08.00–13.00 Fri

🚗 **Sixt** [298 B2] C-Hotel, Arava Rd; \9191156; w sixt.com; ⏱ 08.00–17.00 Sun–Thu, 08.00–noon Fri

TOURIST INFORMATION AND TOUR OPERATORS

ℹ️ **Tourist Information Office** [298 D3] 8 Beit Hagesher St; \6309111; e eilatinfo@tourism. gov.il; w eilat.city/en; ⏱ 08.30–17.00 Sun–Thu, 08.00–13.00 Fri. Sells tickets for most of Eilat's attractions & can offer help & advice on booking accommodation, especially in peak seasons, when it can be difficult to find a room.

Egged Tours [298 B2] ⏱ 08.00–16.00 daily. To the left inside the central bus station. Now work together with **Fun-Time Travel** who can arrange Ovda Airport shuttles & run Holiday Taxi (w *withflo.com*).

Issta [298 B2] \6344405. Has an office in the Shalom Shopping Centre.

Land tours

Bee Traveller (formerly Holit Desert Tours) m 052 8082020; e info@beetraveler.net; w israelpetratours.com; ⏱ 09.00–16.00 daily, for bookings 08.00–22.00. Offers several well-priced tours to sights around southern Israel, Jordan & Sinai. They also arrange cycling tours, rappelling, camel & donkey trips, paintballing & archery in the area.

Camel Ranch Wadi Shlomo; \6370022; w camel-ranch.co.il/en. Another great way to see the beautiful countryside around Eilat is to take a camel safari. A half-day tour (*₪200*) departs from here both morning & afternoon. The ranch is well signposted from the south beach road, but there is no public transport, so you will need to take a taxi from the centre or walk from Coral Beach.

Desert Eco Tours [298 A3] Zofit Centre; \6326477; e erez@desertecotours.com; w desertecotours.com/english. Has an exhaustive list of tours going as far afield as Cairo or as close as Timna Park.

Red Sea Sports Club Page 303. Offers one of the best all-round packages of excursions to get you out into the wild desert lands. Jeep safari tours include destinations such as Petra in Jordan, Timna Park & the Red Canyon.

United Tours Page 44. The national tour company also offers tours from Eilat to other parts of the country.

Eilat is sandwiched between two borders and it is possible to travel to Egypt and Jordan as part of a greater Middle East trip or simply as a short detour from Israel.

JORDAN Aqaba is clearly visible from Eilat, not only thanks to the large Jordanian flagpole, but also because it is only 15km away. This city of approximately 190,000 inhabitants makes for a worthwhile day trip from Eilat, especially if you want to explore the pristine underwater world and scuba-diving facilities. Laid-back and friendly, Aqaba is a world away from the big hotels and entertainment venues just over the border. From here, you can travel onwards to the stunning valley of **Wadi Rum**, where most of the 1962 *Lawrence of Arabia* was filmed with Peter O'Toole, as well as to the magnificent Nabatean ruins of **Petra** where you can experience the beauty of temples carved into the pink rock in the heart of the desert. Visit under your own steam by crossing the border at Eilat and hopping in a taxi (*2hrs*) or joining one of the many tours operating from Eilat.

The Israeli–Jordanian border is marked by the **Yitzhak Rabin/Wadi Araba crossing** (`\` *6300555;* ⏱ *06.30–20.00 Sun–Thu, 08.00–20.00 Fri–Sat; closed Yom Kippur & 1st day of Eid Al-Adha*), located about 6km north of Eilat. It was at this border that Israel and Jordan celebrated the signing of the peace agreement between the two states in 1994. Note that it is no longer possible – unless travelling with an Israeli tour group – to obtain a Jordanian entry visa at the border. There is unfortunately no Jordanian consulate in Eilat, so visa-related enquiries should be directed to the Jordanian embassy in Tel Aviv (*14 Abba Hillel Silver St;* `\` *03 7517722;* e *tel-aviv@fm.gov.jo;* ⏱ *09.00–15.00 Mon–Fri*).

EGYPT Egypt's northern coastline in the Sinai Peninsula is a popular tourist destination among Israelis and foreign tourists. There are numerous small tourist villages just over the Taba border crossing, but **Dahab**, 150km south from Eilat, is world famous for its freediving opportunities and competitions. The sea is impeccably blue and Egyptian hospitality is memorable. The stunning and UNESCO-listed Orthodox **Saint Catherine's Monastery** is located a further 128km inland on the road to Cairo. Visiting the monastery is worth all the effort, but will take time. Note that after the Taba crossing there is no public transport and as such you would need to arrange your own transport in Egypt (which can be expensive) or perhaps ask one of the tour buses at the border crossing to give you a lift.

The **Taba crossing** to Egypt (`\` *6370192;* ⏱ *24/7 in theory, please check in advance; closed Yom Kippur & 1st day of Eid Al-Adha*) is the terminus of Egged bus 15 from Eilat city centre. For further enquiries, contact the Egyptian consulate in Eilat (*15 Efroni St;* `\` *6376882*).

WHERE TO STAY From first appearances, Eilat might look like a mass of hotels, but on closer inspection you'll find that, um, indeed you were right. Big, small, cheap, expensive, classy, grubby – you name it, Eilat has it. Yet despite the number of places to stay, the city's continuing tourist boom means that you might have a hard time finding a room in the peak summer months. Budget accommodation isn't as well represented as the mid-range and certainly high-end establishments, and finding a decent, cheap hostel with vacancies is not always an easy task. Because of the stiff competition among higher-end establishments, however, prices are considerably lower than in Tel Aviv or Jerusalem and you get a lot more for your money. What might get you a simple room in a two- or three-star hotel elsewhere, could get you a four-star hotel in Eilat, especially midweek.

Camping on the city's beaches is illegal and the law often enforced. That said, just up from the Egyptian border, families pitch enormous tents and set up barbecue areas and settle in for the week. It has a fun atmosphere and soft white sand if you can find space. Alternatively, the campsite at the **SPNI Field School** [map, page 294] (*50 rooms; ₪243, camping ₪60 pp;* \6372021; e *eilat@spni.org.il*) opposite the Coral Beach Reserve has clean amenities and is open year-round.

Herod's Palace [298 E4] (468 rooms) North Beach; \6380000; w herods-hotels.com. With a prime beachfront location, this hotel is something of a tourist attraction in itself as passers-by stop to gawp. It oozes opulence & extravagance in every way & is the ultimate in self-indulgence & glamour. The adjacent, adults-only Vitalis Spa is the icing on the cake for those in search of some 'me' time. **$$$$$**

Orchid Hotel and Resort [map, page 294] (178 rooms) South Beach; \6360360; w orchidhotel.co.il/en. Standing like a gleaming tropical oasis cascading down the desert hills, the Orchid is a spectacular swirl of palm-fringed pools, luxury oriental cabins & exotic greenery. Facilities include a spa, health resort, gourmet & Thai (kosher) restaurants & access to the beautiful Hamigdalor Beach opposite. **$$$$$**

Queen of Sheba Hotel [298 D3] (481 rooms) 8 Antibes St; \6306655; e res.eilat@queenofshebaeilat.com; w queenofshebaeilat.com. The US$100 million spectacular that is the Hilton's first theme hotel, the Queen of Sheba has to be seen to be believed. Its jaw-dropping interior design focuses on Solomon & Sheba, & the hotel & rooms are decorated in rich, regal colours & style. A spa, swimming pool, 6,500m² shopping mall & countless restaurants combine to form Eilat's most impressive hotel. **$$$$$**

Dan Panorama [298 C3] (277 rooms) North Beach; \6389999; e panoramaeilat@danhotels.com; w danhotels.com. Located right on the beach & offering a wealth of facilities including a huge pool (heated in winter), spa, a selection of restaurants & bars & spacious, tasteful rooms. **$$$**

Prima Music [map, page 294] (144 rooms) Almog Beach; \6388555; w hotels.co.il. This unpretentious, 4-star hotel is a great family option located to the south of the city. Rooms are spacious & bright (in varying musical themes). There is a big swimming pool, plenty of outdoors areas, free bicycle rental & onsite scuba-diving centre. **$$$**

Arava Hostel [298 C1] (90 beds) 106 Almogim St; \6374687; e harava@bezeqint.net; w aravahostel.com. Founded in 1986, this hugely popular hostel has had plenty of years getting it right & now offers some of the best budget accommodation in town. Private rooms (for 2, 3 or 4 people) all have small en-suite bathrooms & AC, or there is a dormitory option. A snack bar, sun terrace, shared kitchen & BBQ are available for guest use. **$$**

Sunset Motel [298 B1] (25 rooms) 130 Retamim St; \6373817; e motelsunset@gmail.com; w sunsetmotel.co.il. An excellent mid-range option in the city centre. Rooms are located in separate semi-detached houses & are all en suite. There is a leafy & cosy inner courtyard, & staff are helpful & accommodating. **$$**

Corinne Hostel [298 B1] (70 beds) 127/1 Retamim St; \6371472; w corinnehostel.com. A well-established hostel offering good-quality budget accommodation in the city centre. The décor is a little quirky, but it has all the features of a successful backpacker hostel, from a shared kitchen to communal areas to a TV area & tour bookings (to Petra). **$**

Siam Divers [map, page 294] (10 rooms) Coral Beach; \6323636; e info@deepdivers.co.il; w en.deepdivers.co.il. Attached to the highly reputable diving centre, this newly renovated hostel has one of the best budget locations in the city away from the hubbub of central Eilat. **$**

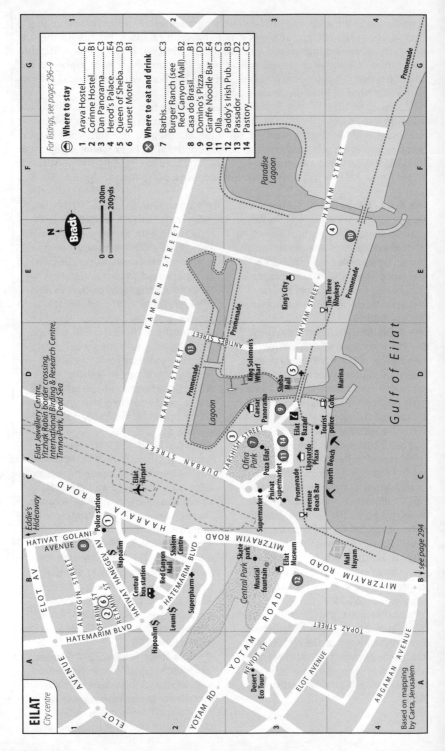

EILAT
City centre

Based on mapping
by Carta, Jerusalem

✕ WHERE TO EAT AND DRINK Eilat's restaurant options range from the sublime to slime. The city has a restaurant on every inch of space that isn't occupied by a hotel, and most are of a very high standard. Unsurprisingly, fresh fish and seafood can be found on most menus and is highly recommended. For something a bit cheaper, there are plenty of fast-food chains and kiosks selling burekas, soggy pizza and hamburgers. For something quick and cheap there is **Domino's Pizza** along the promenade [298 D3], a **Burger Ranch** in the Red Canyon Mall [294 B2] and a branch of the popular **Giraffe Noodle Bar** on Herod's promenade [298 E4] (✆ 6316583; $$). Although Eilat is Israel's only VAT-exempt city, this exemption does not extend to food prices, so the final bill in restaurants here will be the same as anywhere else in the county.

✕ Casa do Brasil [298 B1] 3 Hativat Golani St; ✆6323032; w casadobrasil.co.il; ◷ noon–midnight daily. This offers probably the best all-you-can-eat lunch or dinner anywhere in the country. It is fantastic value for money as you get the choice of pretty much any kind of meat you can imagine grilled, rotisseried or fried, as well as sides of salad, bread, pasta & pizza if you have space. $$$$$

✕ Eddie's Hideaway [map, page 294] 2 Hamasger St; ✆072 3341119; ◷ 18.00–midnight Sun–Thu, 17.00–midnight Fri, 14.00–midnight Sat. Recently reopened, the oldest restaurant in Eilat (1979) offers an eye-popping menu with treats such as Nairobi shrimp cooked in spicy pineapple sauce or honey BBQ'd ribs gracing the pages. Comfortable, well priced & deliciously different. $$$$

✕ Last Refuge [map, page 294] Coral Beach; ✆6373627; ◷ 12.30–23.30 daily. This specialises in locally caught fish & seafood & while prices are a bit steep, you do get what you pay for in terms of quality & quantity as well as a pleasant ambience. You can sit outside on the deck if the weather isn't too stifling. $$$$

✕ Olla [298 C3] 17 Tarshish St; ✆6325566; w olla-tapas.co.il; ◷ 12.30–01.00 Sun–Thu. Chic, elegant Spanish-style restaurant serving an interesting (if not very Spanish) selection of tapas (₪25–35 each) & wonderful, fresh fish & seafood mains. $$$$

✕ Passador [298 D2] Americana Hotel, 10 Kaman St; ✆6378228; e rest@passador.co.il; ◷ 12.30–midnight daily. Square wooden booths

are designed in a slightly oriental décor & the set menu offers great value. The 2-course lunch or dinner menu includes salads, carpaccio, *ceviche* or soup, followed by dishes such as lamb kebab, chicken liver, pasta or steak. Fish is available for an extra charge. There is also a good-value business lunch & dinner. $$$$

✕ Pastory [298 C3] 7 Tarshish St; ✆6345111; ◷ 13.00–23.00 daily. Popular Italian restaurant with a mouth-watering menu including fresh gnocchi, fettuccini & tortellini, as well as steaks, gluten-free pasta & homemade ice cream. There is a big wine bar in the restaurant & a good wine selection. $$$

✕ Barbis [298 C3] 19 Tarshish St; ✆6342404; w barbis.co.il; ◷ noon–01.00 daily. Succulent, juicy burgers make this a huge local favourite. With red leather booths & imaginative toppings it is American diner food with a twist. $$

✕ Dolphin Reef Pub [map, page 294] Dolphin Reef; ✆6300111; ◷ 08.30–16.00 daily, closes earlier in winter. Certainly one of the most tropical & atmospheric places in the city, where you can enjoy grilled meats, fresh fish, hamburgers, salads or lighter bar food snacks while the dolphins splash away in the background. The sandy floor, swinging music (often live) & thatched roof make it a great place to spend an afternoon. $$

✕ Paddy's Irish Pub [298 B3] 1 Yotam Rd; ✆6370921; ◷ noon–03.00 daily. A good pub with a great selection of beers. There is an outdoor seating area & numerous TV screens to catch a football game. $$

ENTERTAINMENT AND NIGHTLIFE Many of the larger hotels have discos and live music concerts, while most of Eilat's nightlife spots can be found around the North Beach area and along the hotel promenade, although there are some lively beach bars further along the coast. A good place to start is **Three Monkeys Pub** [298 E3]

$\mathbb{Q}$ *6368989;* ⏰ *20.00–late daily*) with outdoor sitting area. For something a little more tropical, the **Dolphin Reef Pub** (page 299) further south along the coast is a classic Eilat hangout, although its opening hours are not as late as one might wish. It is the city's beach bars that often form the hub of night-time activity, the balmy weather, warm sand and relaxed atmosphere (and wild parties) attracting the younger set. The tourist information centre produces the weekly *Events in Eilat*, which is certainly worth picking up when you arrive. For something a bit different, there are evening cruises that offer an open bar, dancing and jacuzzis. **Lamie Tourism** (*Eilat Marina;* $\mathbb{Q}$*6333560;* **w** *touryourway.com*) and the **Red Sea Sports Club** both have regular outings in summer.

SHOPPING Israelis love shopping and nowhere more so than in Eilat's glitzy malls, where everything is minus the 17% VAT. Eilat has been granted exemption from value-added tax and has subsequently seen a rise in designer and brand shops. For foreigners, however, prices in airport duty-free shops are probably still lower. As a souvenir from Eilat, for what it's worth, consider buying a piece of jewellery with **Eilat stone**, a beautiful green-blue colour national stone of Israel. **Eilat Jewellery Centre** ($\mathbb{Q}$*6378551*) arranges free buses to their factory and showroom.

In town, standard mall opening hours are 09.00–21.00 Sunday to Thursday, 09.00–15.00 and late-night opening on Saturdays.

Mall Hayam [298 B4] This has the biggest concentration of fashion shops as well as countless cafés, restaurants & everything-you-need-for-the-beach stores.

Poza Eilat [298 C3] Smaller but newly opened, with a range of stores, including a bookshop.

Red Canyon Shopping Centre [298 B2] Hatmarim Bd. This mega mall boasts 3 cinemas, clothes & shoe shops, bookstores & most of the city's administrative offices, including a post office.

Shalom Centre [298 B2] Home to souvenir shops, more clothes & shoes & several car-rental agencies.

Sheba Mall Queen of Sheba Promenade; **w** sheba-mall.co.il; ⏰ 10.00–midnight daily. The entrance to this is hard to miss, with its numerous boutiques located along the boardwalk.

OTHER PRACTICALITIES Eilat has excellent Wi-Fi coverage, and there is Wi-Fi on most public beaches of the city's 12km coastline. The **tourist police** [298 C3] (⏰ *10.00–15.00 Sun–Wed, 10.00–18.00 Thu–Sat*) are located across the street from the tourist office.

Banks There are commission-free currency-exchange booths everywhere, & most hotels will change money, although the commission can often be a little on the steep side. There are countless **ATMs**, especially in the city centre & malls.

$ **Bank Hapoalim** [298 B2] 3 Hativat Hanegev St; $\mathbb{Q}$ 03 6532407; ⏰ 08.30–13.30 Sun & Tue–Wed, 08.30–12.45 & 16.00–18.30 Mon & Thu

$ **Bank Leumi** [298 B2] Hatmarim Bd; $\mathbb{Q}$ 03 9545522; ⏰ 08.30–13.45 Sun & Tue–Wed, 08.30–13.00 & 16.00–18.15 Mon & Thu

Medical
✚ **Yosef Tal** Yotam Rd; $\mathbb{Q}$ 6358011. This is the central hospital in Eilat.
✚ **Superpharm** [298 B2] 9 Hatmarim Bd; ⏰ 6383000; ⏰ 08.30–22.00 Sun–Thu, 08.00–17.00 Fri, 10.30–23.00 Sat. One of several pharmacies around Hatmarim Bd.

Post
✉ **Post office** [298 B2] Red Canyon Mall; $\mathbb{Q}$ 6372348; ⏰ 08.00–18.00 Sun–Tue & Thu, 08.00–13.30 Wed, 08.00–noon Fri

WHAT TO SEE AND DO Eilat is currently awaiting the opening of the first casino in Israel, but in the meantime **Eilat Museum** [298 B3] ($\mathbb{Q}$*6340754;* ⏰ *10.00–20.00*

Mon–Thu, 10.00–14.00 Fri, noon–20.00 Sat & holidays; admission adult/child ₪10/5) can be a pleasant distraction from the beach. On display are pictures of the city from days gone by with some historical facts. Combine a visit here with an ice cream by the largest **musical fountain** [298 B3] (*20.30 & 21.30 Tue, Thu–Fri & Sat*) in Israel, which opened in 2015. Alternatively, there is a **skate park** [298 B3] (⊕ *noon–23.00 Sun–Thu, 09.00–15.00 Fri, 09.00–23.00 Sat*).

Beaches With such a small claim on the Red Sea coast, pretty much the entire stretch of Israeli land has been developed for beach activities, with the exception of the distinctly unsightly commercial port. In the midst of the city centre is **North Beach** [298 C4], which forms the hub of all things gaudy and noisy but is often a big hit for youngsters or those wanting to sip a cocktail in the sun. By far the more beautiful and relaxing beaches are found closer to the Egyptian border, namely **Princess Beach**, which is the best place to swim, snorkel and chill out on the sand. **Lighthouse (Hamigdalor) Beach** is another pleasant choice with a bar and facilities. Not far from the Princess Beach is the beautiful underwater garden reef of the **Coral Beach Reserve** (✆ *6376829*; w *parks.org.il*; ⊕ *09.00–17.00; admission adult/child ₪35/21; mask & snorkel ₪23 on ₪100 deposit*), which is a snorkeller's dream. Over 100 types of stony coral and 650 species of fish have been identified in the reserves, and marked buoy trails lead visitors past its highlights. From here, you can also swim up to the Underwater Observatory Marine Park to observe the feeding of the fish from the sea. Just north of the reserve are the free **Coral** and **Village** beaches that also offer pleasant snorkelling opportunities, shaded sun loungers and waiter-serviced bars. Village Beach in particular is known for its young atmosphere and if you're slightly self-conscious about your physique then a day here won't help things much. Coral Beach has a more wholesome, family atmosphere frequented by a whole mishmash of shapes and sizes. For a beach experience with a difference, a day at the **Dolphin Reef** (page 299) will let you share the waters of a family of bottlenose dolphins.

Underwater Observatory Marine Park (✆ *6364200*; w *coralworld.com*; ⊕ *08.30–17.00 Sat–Thu, 08.30–16.00 Fri; admission adult/child ₪109/89, with oceanarium ₪76/58*) The futuristic-looking white observatory is an Eilat landmark, jutting out into the reef along the coast. For non-divers and children, the observatory is a lovely way to see life beneath the waves with its 360°, 6m-deep observation deck. For a less natural experience there is a shark tank, aquariums and outdoor turtle and stingray pool, while the newly built **oceanarium** is an extremely enjoyable all-moving, all-shaking simulative movie theatre that takes delighted visitors on a tour of the deep blue seas. The *Coral 2000* (*₪35/29*) departs daily except Sundays from the park, but is in fact no more than a fancy-looking glass-bottomed boat. Nonetheless, it is an enjoyable way to see the reef. Various activities also include shark and turtle feeding.

Dolphin Reef (✆ *6300100*; e *info@dolphinreef.co.il*; w *dolphinreef.co.il*; ⊕ *09.00–17.00 Sun–Thu, 09.00–16.30 Fri–Sat; admission adult/child ₪67/46*) The special relationship between human and dolphin is nowhere more prevalent than at the Dolphin Reef, where a group of bottlenose dolphins, given the choice between human interaction or not, have chosen to stick around. Floating pontoons allow visitors to see the dolphins playing, feeding and interacting, while snorkelling (*adult/child ₪290/260/½hr*) or diving (*adult/child ₪339/309/½hr*) encounters provide a once-in-a-lifetime opportunity to get up close and personal. The small beach in the park is separated from the dolphins by a net allowing even swimmers to get close to the dolphins. Snorkelling and diving experiences should be booked up to two weeks in advance in peak seasons.

International Birding and Research Centre (m *050 7671290;* e *ibrce.office@ gmail.com;* w *birds.org.il/en*) While Eilat's tourism boom has soared over the past decade and people flock to its warm waters and party atmosphere, the city has long since been a holiday destination for visitors of the winged variety. Along with the Galilee's Hula Valley (page 236), this region is one of the world's best birdwatching spots as they pass on their north–south migration routes from Europe and Africa. The Birding and Research Centre offers expertly guided birdwatching tours in 4x4 jeeps (₪*150/2hrs,* ₪*400/full day*), as well as the possibility of helping in the tagging and releasing of birds for research. The birdwatching park and centre are located just north of the city near the King Hussein border crossing to Jordan. Turn right at the Eilat junction (just after the kibbutz), from where it is signposted. The park includes both salty and freshwater pools fringed with different species of vegetation, and can be accessed by a variety of picturesque walking trails perfect for wildlife spotting. Binoculars can be rented at the centre for a small charge. In March of every year the **Eilat Spring Migration Festival** (w *eilatbirdsfestival. com*) is held to coincide with one of the biggest fly-bys of migratory birds. Special all-inclusive flight, transfer, hotel and birding activity packages can be arranged through their website.

Scuba diving and snorkelling Eilat's crystal-clear waters that maintain a year-round temperature of 21°C have long been a magnet for scuba divers. Rapid and extreme over-development, however, has led to a serious decline in fish numbers and species, and today the area is rather disappointing for seasoned divers and pales in contrast to the great dive resorts along Egypt's Sinai coast. Nevertheless, its shallow, currentless waters are perfect for beginners and still certainly pretty enough to attract scores of divers from around the country.

Diving regulations in Israel are stringent. If you have forgotten your certification card or haven't dived in the last six months, expect to be asked to complete a 1-hour refresher course or be refused completely. Insurance (₪*100 for 5 days*) is a must-have and can be bought from any dive centre. Strict safety rules mean that all Eilat's dive centres now offer a high standard of equipment, tuition and facilities. Needless to say, this comes at a price, and you can expect to pay double what you would pay in Egypt. Packages offered by some centres are the most economical option and normally include day trips to the more fish-laden waters of Aqaba, Jordan and Sinai. Diving live-aboards to Sinai and Egypt proper are an amazing experience if your budget runs to it.

Diving centres
⛵ **Aqua Sports** Coral Beach; ☏6334404; e info@aqua-sport.com; w aqua-sport.com. Well-established centre offering the complete diving experience to both beginners & pros. Daily dive & snorkel trips to Sinai are one of their most popular excursions & they also offer live-aboard safaris to Egypt & PADI courses, with a good range of options for snorkellers.
⛵ **Dolphin Reef** Page 299.

⛵ **Manta Isrotel Diving Centre** Isrotel Hotel, Coral Beach; ☏*3882, 6333666; e manta@isrotel. co.il; w divemanta.com. Part of the fantastic Red Sea Sports Club, the diving club has probably the best choice of packages & dive excursions. Their 3-day dive package (*with/without equipment* ₪620/365) is great value for money as is the 1-week package (₪*1,200 without equipment*), which includes a night dive, 2 days' diving in Aqaba with overnight accommodation & a cruise to Taba or Coral Island.

Nemo Divers m 052 3515808; e nemodive@netvision.net.il; w diving-israel. com. A small, friendly dive shop that offers a comprehensive range of facilities including PADI dive courses, introductory dives & an array of 4–9-day live-aboard safaris to Sinai.

Siam Divers Coral Beach; ╲6323636; e info@deepdivers.co.il; w en.deepdivers.co.il; 8 dives ₪400, with equipment ₪750. Specialising in technical diving, this big dive resort also caters for beginners & recreational divers. Activities offered include a range of diving courses, more safari live-aboards than you can shake a snorkel at, shore & boat dives & an underwater photography lab (the photographs are underwater, not the lab).

Watersports Eilat has managed to come up with more ways to get wet than Israelis have found to eat hummus, and these days the sea is abuzz with the sound of raucous splashing and the hum of motorboats. No-one does watersports better than the **Red Sea Sports Club** (*Coral Beach*; ╲*6333666*; e *rssc@isrotel.co.il*), who operate most of their activities from Jetty C on the King Solomon's Wharf. Canoes, motorboats, waterskiing, parasailing and banana boat rides leave regularly and don't need to be booked in advance. Cruises to Coral Island (*₪280/1 day*) and Taba (*₪160/half-day*) can be combined with parasailing and scuba diving.

Appendix 1

LANGUAGE

The **Modern Hebrew alphabet** consists of 27 letters, almost all of which are consonants, although there are several letters that can function as vowels. A series of dots and dashes that represent vowels are marked beneath words in children's books and the Bible but are generally omitted from other texts. Hebrew words run from right to left and, as such, books, cards, magazines, etc, will open in reverse to what is common in many other countries. Stress is generally on the last syllable of the word. Some letters are known in Hebrew as *sofit*, or final, and are used at the end of words. They have the same pronunciation but take a different form, for example פ which is ף at the end of words. The Hebrew words below have been spelt phonetically in the alphabet although it is important to note that 'ch' should be pronounced like a throaty 'kh', not as in cheese or church.

Hebrew numerals can be written using either the Western-adapted Arabic numbers, eg: 1, 2, 5, or by means of letters of the Hebrew alphabet, as each letter carries a specific numerical value (eg: א is 1, while י is 10). This format is mainly used for religious documents.

aleph	א	used either as a silent letter or to make an 'a' sound
bet	ב	pronounced as either 'b' or 'v'
gimel	ג	like 'g' as in goat
dalet	ד	like 'd' as in duck
hey	ה	like 'h' as in harp; takes on a more 'ar' sound when used at the end of words
vav	ו	like 'v' as in volcano; like vowels 'o' as in octopus or 'u' as in tuna
zayin	ז	like 'z' as in zebra
chet	ח	like a throaty 'h' (there is no similar sound in English)
tet	ט	like 't' as in tumble
yud	י	like 'y' as in yak; also 'i' as in igloo or 'ee' as in sweet
kaf	כ	like 'k' as in kettle
lamed	ל	like 'l' as in lemon
mem	מ	like 'm' as in mountain
nun	נ	like 'n' as in notebook
samech	ס	like 's' as in summer
ayin	ע	pronounced as either a throaty 'i' or 'a' as in iron
pey	פ	pronounced as either 'p' or 'f'
tzadik	צ	like 'tz' as in 'pssst' when trying to get someone's attention
kof	ק	like the English 'k' or 'c' as in coffee
resh	ר	like a throaty 'r' as in the French *raison d'être*
sheen	ש	like either 'sh' or 's'
taf	ת	like 't' as in tea

Together with Hebrew, **Arabic** is also a national language in Israel, spoken as a mother tongue by approximately 20% of the population. The Palestinian dialect of Arabic is known as Levantine or *shami* referring to the countries of the Levant (Lebanon, Syria, Jordan and Palestine) and is essentially used for day-to-day conversations. Modern Standard Arabic *fusha* (pronounced 'fus-ha') is the language of newspapers, books and pan-Arab television channels (eg: Al-Jazeera) and represents a grammatical base for learning the language. The Arabic alphabet consists of 28 letters written from right to left. Arabic short vowels are indicated with short vowel marks above or under a relevant consonant; they are used in religious texts and language study materials only, so that the pronunciation of each word must be memorised individually, similarly to Hebrew. Below is a list of mixed Palestinian and Standard Arabic essentials that will come in handy on your trip. Arabic does not have a 'p' sound, meaning that Pakistan is pronounced as *bakistan* and Palestine as *falesteen*. The word *yalla* gets everywhere in Arabic. It's a multi-purpose word meaning 'Come on!', 'Let's go!', 'Hurry up!', etc.

aliph	ا	like 'a' in bag
ba	ب	like 'b' in bat
ta	ت	like 't' in tap
tha	ث	like 'th' in theory
jim	ج	like 'j' in jet
ha	ح	a 'huffed h', called a 'heavy h' by linguists, made by tightening the throat muscles as you pronounce the 'h' as in hob
kha	خ	like 'ch' in the Scottish word loch, or like a throat being cleared
dal	د	like 'd' in doll
dhal	ذ	a hard 'th', like in this or then
ra	ر	like 'r' in rack
za	ز	like 'z' in doze
sin	س	like 's' in sad; always a soft hissing 's', never as a hard 'z' sound as in wise
shin	ش	like 'sh' in show
sad	ص	like 's' in salt or sorry, but with more oomph; called a 'heavy s' by linguists
dad	ض	like 'd' in dog but with more oomph; in linguistics known as a 'heavy d'
ta	ط	like 't' in tart but with more oomph; in linguistics known as a 'heavy t'
tha	ظ	like 'th' in bother, a 'hard th'
'ein	ع	this is a difficult sound, a bit like the 'i' in mine but with an almost nasal stress on it – sort of like German 'nein' but the comparison only bears out if you also know how to pronounce that properly
'ghein	غ	like 'kh' but with a sound through it; not just a guttural sound but a kind of 'gargled g'
fa	ف	like 'f' in full
qaf	ق	like 'c' in car but the sound may be made further back in the throat
kaf	ك	like 'k' in kit
lam	ل	like 'l' in lot
mim	م	like 'm' in meet
nun	ن	like 'n' in nag
ha	ه	like 'h' in hat
waw	و	like 'w' in wig
ya	ي	like 'y' in yard

A1

ESSENTIALS

English	Pronunciation	Hebrew	Pronunciation	Arabic
Good morning	*boker tov*	בוקר טוב	*sabah al-khair*	صبح الخير
Good evening	*erev tov*	ערב טוב	*masaa al-khair*	مساء الخير
Goodnight	*layla tov*	לילה טוב	*tisbah ala khair*	تصبح على خير
Hello/goodbye	*shalom*	שלום	*salam / marhaba*	سلام\مرحبا
My name is …	*kor-eem li …*	… קוראים לי	*ismee*	… اسمي
What is your name?	*eich kor-eem lecha (m) / lach (f)?*	איך קוראים לך?	*shu ismak (m) / ismik (f)*	شو اسمك؟
I am from England	*ani me anglia*	אני מאנגליה	*ana min inkiltra*	آنا من إنكلترا
How are you?	*ma shlomcha (m) /shlomech (f)?*	מה שלומך?	*kifak (m) / kifik (f)*	كيفك؟
Pleased to meet you	*naim lekhair otcha (m)/othach (f)*	נעים להכיר אותך	*fursa saeeda*	فرصة سعيدة
Thank you	*toda*	תודה	*shukran*	شكرا
Please	*bevakasha*	בבקשה	*min fadhlak (m) / min fadhlik (f)*	من فدلك
Don't mention it	*al lo davar*	אל לא דבר	*la tazkar al-maudua*	لا تذكر الموضوع
Cheers!	*lechaim!*	לחיים	*sihtain!*	صحتين
Yes	*ken*	לא	*naam / aywa*	نعم \ ايوة
No	*lo*	כן	*laa*	لا
I don't understand	*ani lo mevin (m) / mevina (f)*	אני לא מבין / מבינה	*ana mish fahim (m) / fahima (f) / laa afham*	انا مش فاهم\فاهمة\لا افهم لا افهم
Please would you speak more slowly	*bevakasha daber (m)/ dabri (f) yoter le-at*	בבקשה דבר / דברי יותר לאט	*takallam bi but' min fadhlak (m) / takallamii bi but', min fadhlik (f)*	تكلم ببطء من فضلك \ تكلم ببطء من فضلك\تكلمي ببطء من فضلك
Do you understand?	*ata mevin (m) / at mevina (f)?*	אתה מבין / את מבינה	*mafhoom?*	مفهوم؟

QUESTIONS

How?	*eich?*	איך?	*keef?*	كيف؟
What?	*ma?*	מה?	*shu? / esh? / matha?*	شو \ ايش؟ \ مذا؟
Where?	*eifo?*	איפה?	*weyn? / eyn?*	وين؟ \ اين؟
What is it?	*ma ze?*	מה זה?	*ma hatha?*	ما هذا؟
Which?	*eize?*	איזה?	*ayy?*	اي؟
When?	*matai?*	מתי?	*mata? / emta?*	متى \؟ امتى؟
Why?	*lama?*	למה?	*leysh?*	ليش؟
Who?	*mee?*	מי?	*man? / meen?*	من؟ \ مين؟
How much?	*kama?*	כמה?	*addeysh? / bekkam?*	اديش؟ \ بيكم؟

NUMBERS

1	*echad*	אחד / 1	*wahad*	١ \ واحد
2	*shtaim*	שתיים / 2	*ethnain*	٢ \ إثنان
3	*shalosh*	שלוש / 3	*thalaatha*	٣ \ ثلاثة
4	*arba*	ארבע / 4	*arbaa*	٤ \ أربعة
5	*chamesh*	חמש / 5	*khamseh*	٥ \ خمسة
6	*shesh*	שש / 6	*sitteh*	٦ \ ستة

306

English	Pronunciation	Hebrew	Pronunciation	Arabic
7	sheva	שבע / 7	sab'a	٧ \ سبعة
8	shmoneh	שמונה / 8	thamanyeh	٨ \ ثمانية
9	teshah	תשע / 9	tis'a	٩ \ تسعة
10	eser	עשר / 10	ashara	١٠ \ عشرة
11	echad esreh	אחד עשרה / 11	ihda'sh	١١ \ أحد عشر
12	shteim esreh	שתים עשרה / 12	ithna'sh	١٢ \ إثنا عشر
13	shlosh esreh	שלושה עשרה/ 13	thalatta'sh	١٣ \ ثلاثة عشر
14	arba esreh	ארבעה עשרה / 14	arbata'sh	١٤ \ أربعة عشر
15	chamesh esreh	חמש עשרה / 15	khamista'sh	١٥ \ خمسة عشر
16	shesh esreh	שש עשרה / 16	sitta'sh	١٦ \ ستة عشر
17	shvah esreh	שבע עשרה / 17	sabata'sh	١٧ \ سبعة عشر
18	shmona esreh	שמונה עשרה / 18	thamanta'sh	١٨ \ ثمانية عشر
19	tsha esreh	תשע עשרה / 19	tisita'sh	١٩ \ تسعة عشر
20	esrim	עשרים / 20	ishreen	٢٠ \ عشرين
21	esrim ve echad	עשרים ואחד / 21	wahad wa'ishreen	٢١ \ واحد وعشرين
30	shloshim	שלושים / 30	thalatheen	٣٠ \ ثلاثين
40	arbaim	ארבעים / 40	arba'een	٤٠ \ أربعين
50	chamishim	חמישים / 50	khamseen	٥٠ \ خمسين
60	shishim	ששים / 60	sitteen	٦٠ \ ستين
70	shivim	שבעים / 70	saba'een	٧٠ \ سبعين
80	shmonim	שמונים / 80	thaman'een	٨٠ \ ثمانين
90	tishim	תשעים / 90	tis'een	٩٠ \ تسعين
100	meah	מאה / 100	miyya	١٠٠ \ مئة
1,000	elef	אלף / 1,000	alf	١٠٠٠ \ ألف

TIME

What time is it?	ma hashaa?	מה השעה	addeysh assaa? / assaa kam?	عديش الساعة؟ / الساعة كم؟
Today	hayom	היום	ilyom	اليوم
Tonight	halayla	הלילה	al-laila	الليلة
Tomorrow	machar	מחר	bukra / ghada	بكرا / غدا
Yesterday	etmol	אתמול	imbaarih / al-laila al-madiya	امبارح \ الليلة الماضية
Morning	boker	בוקר	masa'a	مسعاء
Evening	erev	ערב	leeil	ليل

DAYS OF THE WEEK

Sunday	yom rishon	יום ראשון	yom al-ahad	يوم الأحد
Monday	yom sheni	יום שני	yom al-ithnain	يوم الإثنين
Tuesday	yom shlishi	יום שלישי	yom al-thalaatheh	يوم الثلاثاء
Wednesday	yom reviee	יום רביעי	yom al-arbi'a	يوم الأربعاء
Thursday	yom chamishi	יום חמישי	yom al-kamees	يوم الخميس
Friday	yom shishi	יום שישי	yom al-juma'a	يوم الجمعة
Saturday	(yom) shabbat	שבת	yom al-sabt	يوم السبت

MONTHS

In both Judaism and Islam, months are lunar and vary in names and timings significantly from the common Gregorian calendar months. Lunar months are essentially used for religious and official purposes, while the names on page 308 are standard for everyday life.

A1

English	Pronunciation	Hebrew	Pronunciation	Arabic
January	yanuar	ינואר	yanayir	يناير
February	februar	פברואר	fibrayir	فبراير
March	mertz	מרץ	maris	مارس
April	april	אפריל	abreel	أبريل
May	mai	מאי	mayu	مايو
June	yuni	יוני	yunyu	يونيو
July	yuli	יולי	yulyu	يوليو
August	ogust	אוגוסט	agustus	أغسطس
September	september	ספטמבר	sibtambir	سبتمبر
October	october	אוקטובר	uktubir	أكتوبر
November	november	נובמבר	nufambir	نوفمبر
December	detzember	דצמבר	disambir	ديسمبر

GETTING AROUND
Public transport

English	Pronunciation	Hebrew	Pronunciation	Arabic
I'd like / I want ...	ani rotzeh (m) /	... אני רוצה	beddi ...	... بدي
... a one-way ticket	... cartis chad kivuni	... כרטיס חד כיווני	... tizkara zahab	... تذكرة ذهاب
... a return ticket	.... cartis du kivuni	... כרטיס דו כיווני	... tizkara zahab wa ib	... تذكرة ذهاب وإياب
... to go to ...	... lehagia le ...	... להגיע ל	... musafer ila ...	... مسافر إلى ...
How much is it?	kama ze oleh?	כמה זה עולה?	addeysh? / bekkam?	عديش؟ \ بكم؟
What time does the ... leave to ...?	be eiza shaa ha ... ozev?	באיזה שעה ה ... עוזב?	emta yatla al ... ila ...?	امتى يطلي ال ... إلى؟
The train has been delayed/cancelled	harakevet mitakevet / butlah	הרכבת מתעכבת / בוטלה	timma ilgha / takhrat al-qatar	تم إلغاء \ تأخرة القطار
Platform	ratzif	רציף	menassa	منصة
Ticket office	misrad cartisim	משרד כרטיסים	maktab al-tazaker	مكتب التذاكر
Timetable	luach zmanim	לוח זמנים	jadul muaeed	جدول مواعيد
From	meh	מ	min	من
To	le	ל	ila	إلى
Bus station	tahanat otobus	תחנת אוטובוס	mahattat al-basat	محطة الباصات
Train station	tahanat rakevet	תחנת רכבת	mahattat al-qatar	محطة القطار
Airport	namal teufah	נמל תעופה	matar	مطار
Port	namal	נמל	meena	ميناء
Bus	otobus	אוטובוס	otobis / bas	أتوبيس \ باص
Train	rakevet	רכבת	qatar	قطار
Plane	matoss	מטוס	tayara	طائرة
Boat	oneeyah	אנייה	qareb	قارب
Ferry	maaboret	מעבורת	al-abaara	العبارة
Car	mechonit	מכונית	sayara	سيارة
4x4	arba al arba	ארבע על ארבע	sayara arba bil arba	سيارة أربعة بأربعة
Taxi	monit	מונית	taksee	تاكسي
Minibus	minibus	מיניבוס	minibus	ميني باص
Motorbike	ofanoa	אופנוע	motorbike	موتوربايك
Bicycle	ofnaim	אופניים	darajah	دراجة
Arrival/departure	nichnasim / yotzim	נכנסים / יוצאים	al-qadamin al-mughadarin	القادمين \ المغادرين

English	Pronunciation	Hebrew	Pronunciation	Arabic
Here	*po*	פה	*hohn*	هن
There	*sham*	שם	*hoonak*	هناك
Bon voyage!	*derech tzlecha!*	דרך צלחה!	*rihla sayyida!*	رحلة سعيدة!

Private transport

English	Pronunciation	Hebrew	Pronunciation	Arabic
Is this the road to …?	*zot haderech le …?*	זאת הדרך ל ...	*hal hatha al-tariq ila …?*	هل هذا الطريق إلي؟ ...
Where is the service station?	*eifo hatachanat delek?*	איפה התחנת דלק?	*weyn mahattat benzeen?*	وين محطة بنزين؟
Please fill it up	*bevakasha maleh ad hasof*	בבקשה מלא עד הסוף	*mumkin itemalee / itabee al-sayaara, law samaht?*	ممكن اتملي \ اتابي الصيرة، لو سمحت!
I'd like … litres	*ani rotzeh (m) / rotzah (f)… litrim*	אני רוצה ... ליטרים	*beddi … litr, law samaht*	بدي ... ليتر، لو سمحت!
Diesel	*diesel*	דיזל	*diesel*	ديزل
Leaded petrol	*ragil*	רגיל	*betrol*	بترول
Unleaded petrol	*netul oferet*	נטול עופרת	*benzene / betrol khali min rasas*	بنزين \ بترول خالي من رصاص
I have broken down	*nitkati*	ניתקעתי	*al-sayaara a-til*	الصيرة عتيل

Road signs

English	Pronunciation	Hebrew	Pronunciation	Arabic
Give way	*zchut kdima*	זכות קדימה	*efsah al-tariq*	افسح الطريق
Danger	*sakanah*	סכנה	*khateer*	خطير
Entry	*knissah*	כניסה	*dukhul*	دخول
Detour	*maakaf*	מעקף	*ettifaf*	التفاف
One way	*chad sitri*	חד סטרי	*etteja wahida*	اتجاه واحد
Toll	*mass*	מס	*rusum*	رسوم
No entry	*ein knissah*	אין כניסה	*dukhul mamnua*	دخول ممنوع
Exit	*yetziah*	יציאה	*khuruj*	خروج

Directions

English	Pronunciation	Hebrew	Pronunciation	Arabic
Where is it?	*eifo?*	איפה?	*weyn hatha?*	وين هذا؟
Go straight ahead	*lech (m) / lechi (f) yashar*	לך / לכי ישר	*mubasharan*	مباشرا
Turn left	*pneh (m) / pni (f) smola*	פנה / פני שמאלה	*lif yasaar*	ليف يسار
Turn right	*pneh (m) / pni (f) yamina*	פנה / פני ימינה	*lif yameen*	ليف أيمن
…at the traffic lights	*… bah ramzor*	ברמזור	*ishara tauiya*	اشارة توعية
…at the roundabout	*… bah kikar*	בכיכר	*ala mafraq / dawar*	علي مفرق \ دوار
North	*tzafon*	צפון	*shamal*	شمال
South	*darom*	דרום	*junoob*	جنوب
East	*mizrach*	מזרח	*sharq*	شرق
West	*maarav*	מערב	*gharb*	غرب
Behind	*meachor*	מאחור	*wara*	وراء
In front of	*lifnei*	לפני	*amam*	أمام

English	Pronunciation	Hebrew	Pronunciation	Arabic
Near	leyad	ליד	qareeb	قريب
Opposite	mul	מול	muqabel	مقابل

Street signs

English	Pronunciation	Hebrew	Pronunciation	Arabic
Entrance	knissah	כניסה	madhkal	مدخل
Exit	yetziah	יציאה	makhraj	مخرج
Open	patuach	פתוח	maftooh	مفتوح
Closed	sagur	סגור	maghlooq / musakir	مغلق \ مسقر
Toilets	sherutim	גברים / נשים	hammam	حمام
men/women	gvarim / nashim	שירותים	rijal / nisaa	رجال \ نساء
Information	meidah	מידע	maalumat	معلومات

ACCOMMODATION

English	Pronunciation	Hebrew	Pronunciation	Arabic
Where is a cheap/ good hotel?	eifo yesh malon zol / tov?	איפה יש מלון זול / טוב?	weyn fee hotel qwais/ rakhees?	وين في هتل كويس \ رخيص؟
Could you please write the address?	bevakasha reshom et haktovet?	בבקשה רשום את הכתובת?	mumkin tiktib al-inwaan, min fadlak?	ممكن تكتب العنوان من فضلك؟
Do you have any rooms available?	yesh haderim pnuim?	יש חדרים פנויים?	fee guraf faadiyeh / faaraga?	في غرف فاضية \ فارغة؟
I'd like …	ani rotzeh (m) / rotzah (f) …	אני רוצה …	beddi / arju …	بدي \ أرجو …
… a single room	… cheder yachid	… חדר יחיד	… ghurfa mufrada	… غرفة مفردة
… a double room	… cheder zugi	… חדר זוגי	… ghurfa bi sareer muzdowg	غرفة بسرير مزدوج …
… a room with 2 beds	… cheder im shtei mitot	חדר עם שתי מיטות …	… ghurfa bi sarirayn	غرفة بسريرين …
… a room with a bathroom	… cheder im miklachat ve sherutim	חדר עם מקלחת ושירותים …	… ghurfa bi hammam	غرفة بحمام …
… to share a dorm	… cheder meshutaf	… חדר משותף	… li musharaka makan annaum	لمشاركة مكان النوم
How much is it per night/person?	kama ole lelayla / leadam?	כמה עולה ללילה / לאדם?	addeysh bel leila / lil'wahad?	عديش بليلة \ بتكليف للوحد؟
Is breakfast included?	haim kolol aruchat boker?	האם כולל ארוחת בוקר?	hal hadha maa al-futur?	هل هذا مع الفطور؟
I am leaving	ani ozev (m) / ozevet (f)	אני עוזב / עוזבת	ana musafir (m) / musafira (f) alyom	آنا مسافر \ مسافرة اليوم

FOOD

English	Pronunciation	Hebrew	Pronunciation	Arabic
Do you have a table for … people?	yesh shulchan le … anashim?	יש שולחן ל .. . אנשים?	tawlah le … (wahad / ithnain)?	طاولة ل … (وحد \ إثنين)؟
… a children's menu?	… tafrit yeladim?	תפריט ילדים? …	fee qaima lil atfal?	في قائمة للأطفال؟
I am a vegetarian	ani tzimchoni	אני צמחוני	ana nabati	أنا نباتي
Do you have any vegetarian dishes?	yesh tzimchoniot?	יש מנות צמחוניות?	hal andakum atbat nabatiya?	هل عندكوم أطباق نباتية؟
Is this restaurant kosher/halal?	hamisada zot ksherah?	המסעדה זאת כשרה?	hal hatha al-mataam halal?	هل هذا المطعم حلال؟

English	Pronunciation	Hebrew	Pronunciation	Arabic
Please may I have …	bevakasha efshar lekabel…	בבקשה אפשר לקבל …	ateeni …	أعطني
… a fork/knife / spoon/the bill	… mazleg / sakin / kaf / cheshbon	מזלג / סכין / כף / חשבון	shawka / sikkin / malaqa	شوكة \ سكين \ ملعقة
Bon appétit!	beteavon!	בתיאבון!	sahtein!	صحتين!

Basics

English	Pronunciation	Hebrew	Pronunciation	Arabic
Bread	lechem	לחם	khoubz	خبز
Butter	chem'a	חמאה	zibdeh	زبدة
Cheese	gvina	גבינה	jibneh	جبنة
Oil	shemen	שמן	zeit	زيت
Pepper	pilpel	פלפל	filfil	فلفل
Salt	melach	מלח	malh	ملح
Sugar	sukar	סוכר	sukar	سكر
With/w/out sugar	im / bli sucar	עם / בלי סוכר	disukar / bidun	بسكر \ بدون سكر

Fruit

English	Pronunciation	Hebrew	Pronunciation	Arabic
Apples	tapuchim	תפוחים	tuffah	تفاح
Bananas	bananot	בננות	mouz	موز
Grapes	anavim	ענבים	inab	عنب
Oranges	tapuzim	תפוזים	burtuqal	برتقال
Pears	agassim	אגסים	ijas	إجاص

Vegetables

English	Pronunciation	Hebrew	Pronunciation	Arabic
Carrots	gzarim	גזרים	jazzar	جزر
Garlic	shum	שום	thuum	ثوم
Onions	btzalim	בצלים	basal	بصل
Peppers	pilpelim	פלפלים	felfel	فلفل
Potatoes	tapuchei adama	תפוחי אדמה	batata	بطاطا

Protein

English	Pronunciation	Hebrew	Pronunciation	Arabic
Fish	dag	דג	sammak	سمك
Beef	baker	בקר	lahem baqar	لحم بقر
Chicken	off	עוף	dajaj	دجاج
Lamb	kevess	כבש	lahem khrouf	لحم خروف
Pork	chazir	חזיר	lahem khanzir	لحم خنزير
Turkey	tarnegol hodu	תרנגול הודו	lahem al-dik al-rumi	لحم الديك الرومي
Eggs	beytzim	ביצים	baydha	بيضة
Beans	shuit	שעועית	fuul	فول

Drinks

English	Pronunciation	Hebrew	Pronunciation	Arabic
Beer	bira	בירה	biira	بيرة
Coffee	kafeh	קפה	qahweh	قهوة
Fruit juice	mitz peyrot	מיץ פירות	asiir	عصير
Milk	chalav	חלב	haleeb	حليب
Tea	teh	תה	shay	شاي
Water	maim	מים	mai	ماء
Wine	yain	יין	nabeed	نبيذ

SHOPPING

English	Pronunciation	Hebrew	Pronunciation	Arabic
Do you have …?	yesh lachem …?	יש לכם …?	indak …?	عندك …؟
How much is it?	kama ze ole?	כמה זה עולה?	addeysh / bekkam hatha?	عديش \ بكم هذا؟
I don't want/like it	ani lo ohev (m) / ohevet (f) et ze	אני לא אוהב / אוהבת את זה	ana mish ayiz / ma biddi	أنا مش عيز \ عيزة … أنا ما بدي …
I'm just looking	ani rak mistakel (m) / mistakelet (f)	אני רק מסתכל / מסתכלת	bas bat faraj	بس بتفرج
It's too expensive	ze yakar midai	זה יקר מדי	hadha kteer ghaalee	هذا كتير غالي
I'll take it	ani ekach et ze	אני אקח את זה	bakhud ha	باخذها
Please may I have…	bevakasha efshar…	בבקשה אפשר …	fee …, min fadhlak (m) / fadhlik (f)	في … من فضلك؟
Do you accept…?	ata mekabel (m) / mekabelet (f) …?	אתה מקבל / מקבלת …?	be tiqbal …?	بتقبل … ؟
Credit cards	cartis ashrai	כרטיס אשראי	betaqa eetman	بطاقة ائتمان
More	yotair	יותר	akthar	أكثر
Less	pachot	פחות	aql	أقل
Smaller	katan yotair	קטן יותר	asghar	أصغر
Bigger	gadol yotair	גדול יותר	akbar	آكبر

COMMUNICATIONS

English	Pronunciation	Hebrew	Pronunciation	Arabic
I'm looking for …	ani mechapess (m) / mechapesset (f) et ha …	אני מחפש / מחפשת את ה …	ana abhath an …	أنا أبحث عن …
Bank	bank	בנק …	bank	بنك
Post office	sniff hadoar	סניף הדואר	maktab al-barid	مكتب البريد
Church	knessiah	כנסיה	kenissa	كنيسة
Synagogue	bet haknesset	בית הכנסת	kenis yahudiya	كنيس يهودية
Mosque	misgad	מסגד	masjid	مسجد
Embassy	shagrirut	שגרירות	safara	سفارة
Currency exchange	chalfan ksafim	חלפן כספים	sarraf	صراف
Tourist information office	merkaz meidah tayarut	מרכז מידע תיירות	maktab al-mualumat al-siyahiya	مكتب المعلومات السياحية

EMERGENCIES

English	Pronunciation	Hebrew	Pronunciation	Arabic
Help!	hatzilu!	הצילו!	sa'iduni!	ساعدني!
Call a doctor!	tikreu le rofeh!	תקראו לרופא!	ittasil ala doctor / tabeeb!	اتصال على دكتور \ طبيب!
There's an accident	haita teuna	הייתה תאונה	fee haadith	في حادث
I'm lost	halachti leibud	הלכתי לאיבוד	ana daayi'a	أنا ضائع \ ضائعة
Go away!	lech (m) / lechi (f) meepo!	לך / לכי מפה!	atrukni washani / ebtead anni!	اتركني وشأني / ابتعد عني!
Police	mishtarah	משטרה	shurta	شرطة
Fire	esh	אש	naar	نار
Ambulance	ambulance	אמבולנס	issaaf	اسعاف
Thief	ganav	גנב	sarragh	سارق
Hospital	beit cholim	בית חולים	mustashfa	مستشفي
I am ill	ani choleh (m) / cholah (f)	אני חולה	ana mareed (m) / mareeda (f)	أنا مريض \ مريضة

312

HEALTH

English	Pronunciation	Hebrew	Pronunciation	Arabic
Diarrhoea	shilshul	שלשול	ishaal	إسهال
Nausea	bchilah	בחילה	gathayaan	غثيان
Doctor	rofeh	רופאה	doktor / tabeeb	دكتور \ طبيب
Prescription	mirsham	מרשם	wafsa	وصفة .
Pharmacy	beit merkachat	בית מרקחת	saydaliya	صيدلية
Antibiotics	antibiotika	אנטיביוטיקה	mudadat hayawee	مضادات حيوية
Antiseptic	chomer mechateh	חומר מחטא	mutahir	مطهر
Contraceptive	glulot neged herayon	גלולות נגד הריון	waseela manalhaml	وسيلة لمنع الحمل
Sunblock	crem shizuf	קרם שיזוף	waqe min al-shams	واقي من الشمس
I am …	ani…	אני…	ana …	أنا …
… asthmatic	…astmati	…אסתמטי	… marbuu	… مربوع
… epileptic	…epileptic	…אפילפטי	… masrua	… مصروع
… diabetic	… ani choleh (m) cholah (f) sukeret	… חולה סכרת	… ana mareed (m) mareeda (f) bil sukkar	أنا مريض \ مريضة … بالسكر
I'm allergic to…	ani elergi le…	… אני אלרגי ל	… indee hassassi (m) / hassassiya (f)	أنا حساسي \ حساسية …
… penicillin	… penetzilin	… פניצילין	… binisileen	… بنسلين
… nuts	… egozim	… אגוזים	… al-mukassarat	… المكسرات
… bees	… dvorim	… דבורים	… al-nahl	… النحل

TRAVEL WITH CHILDREN

English	Pronunciation	Hebrew	Pronunciation	Arabic
Is there a…?	ha'im yesh…?	… האם יש	fee …?	في … ؟
… baby changing room	… pinat hachtalah	… פינת החתלה	… ghurfat tagheer lil atfal?	غرفة تغيير للأطفال …
… a children's menu	… tafrit le yeladim	… תפריט לילדים	… menu lil atfal?	… قائدة للأطفال
… infant milk formula	… tachlif chalav letinokot	… תחליף חלב לתינוקות	… laban mugafaf lil atfal / haleeb lil atfal	لبن مغفف لالطفال\حليب … للأطفال؟
Nappies	chitulim	חיתולים	hafadat	حفاضات
Potty	sir layla	סיר לילה	nooniya lil atfal	نونية للأطفال
Babysitter	shmartaf	שמרטף	jalisat atfal	جليسة إطفال
Highchair	kisseh yeladim	כיסא ילדים	kursi lil atfal	كرسي للأطفال

OTHER

English	Pronunciation	Hebrew	Pronunciation	Arabic
And/some/but	ve / kama / aval	ו / כמה / אבל	wa / baad / bass	و \ بعض \ بص
This/that	ze	זה	hadha	هذا
Expensive/cheap	yakar / zol	יקר / זול	ghaale / rakhees	غالي \ رخيص
Beautiful/ugly	yaffeh / mechoar	יפה / מכוער	hilweh / qabeeh	هلو \ قبيح
Old/new	yashan / chadash	ישן / חדש	qadeem / jadeed	قديم \ جديد
Good/bad	tov / ra	טוב / רע	qwais / mish qwais	كويس \ مش كويس
Early/late	mukdam / meuchar	מוקדם / מאוחר	bakeer / mitakhir	بكير \ متخير
Hot/cold	cham / kar	חם / קר	harr / bard	حر \ برد
Difficult/easy	kasheh / kal	קשה / קל	saib / sahal	سعب \ سحل
Boring/interesting	meshaamem / meanien	משעמם / מעניין	mumil / muthir	ممل \ مثير

Appendix 2

GLOSSARY

aliyah	meaning 'ascent' in Hebrew; wave of mass immigration of Jews from the diaspora (plural aliyot; people making aliyah are called olim)
Baha'i	the Baha'i faith was founded in 1863 in Iran and developed out of the Shi'a branch of Islam. It is one of the world's youngest religions.
Basha	alternative spelling 'pasha'; a title of a man of high rank or office in the Ottoman Empire
Bauhaus	Bauhaus art school (in Israel used essentially to refer to an architectural style) considered to be the most influential modernist art school of the early 20th century. It was founded in Weimar, Germany, in 1919. Among its notable proponents are such renowned artists as Wassily Kandinsky and Paul Klee.
effendi	Ottoman honorific title for a man of high class and social position
haapala	meaning 'immigration' in Hebrew; refers to illegal immigration of Jews to Palestine during the British Mandate period
Haganah	meaning 'defence' in Hebrew; Zionist military organisation active in Palestine between 1920 and 1948
Halakhah	body of Jewish law as a supplement to the spiritual and religious laws
hammam	name of Arabic origin, refers to a Turkish steam bath modelled on the Roman bath
haredim	devout Jews who strongly follow religious law and tradition
Haskalah	Jewish enlightenment in 18th-century Europe
IDF	Founded in 1948, the Israeli Defence Force (often referred to as 'Tzahal' for its abbreviation in Hebrew) is the army of Israel. Service is compulsory for both men and women; at present, approximately 30% of its recruits and 50% of its officers are female.
Intifada	meaning 'shaking off' in Arabic, the term essentially refers to two uprisings (1987–93 and 2000–03) by Palestinians that attempted to obtain autonomy and independence
kashrut	a set of rules and procedures for ensuring that food and drinks are kosher
khan	the historical equivalent of a bonded warehouse for the storage and transit of a specific kind of good from wholesalers to retailers. Also may be used to suggest 'inn' for travellers. In Israel it is essentially used to describe a Bedouin-style tent.
kollel	meaning 'community' in Hebrew, it is an institute for advanced Talmudic study
kosher	term describing food and drinks complying with the Jewish religious laws (kashrut)
makhtesh	a geological formation believed to be unique to the Negev Desert and the Sinai
menorah	candelabra with seven or nine lights used in Jewish religious and spiritual traditions; national emblem of Israel

mezuza	meaning 'doorpost' in Hebrew; a small parchment scroll affixed to a doorway in a Jewish household; traditionally suggests that 'the people who dwell here live Jewish lives'
mikvah	a bath for ritual ablutions in Judaism (plural mikvaot)
Palmach	meaning 'striking force' in Hebrew and pronounced 'pal-makh'; established in 1941, it was the unofficial and underground army of the yishuv in Palestine under the British Mandate. Yitzhak Rabin was its most notable member and one of the first to join.
Palyam	underground Jewish navy, division of Palmach
payot	side locks or side curls worn by observant Jewish men
Qibla	the direction for prayer, towards Mecca, usually marked in a Muslim religious building by a mihrab niche
sabil	Arabic term meaning a small public fountain often built outside mosques for ablutions
Sabra	refers to an Israeli-born Jew; the term is used to describe earlier generations of Jews born in early 20th-century Palestine. Sabra is a desert cactus that has a thorny skin but is sweet and juicy on the inside.
senjak	Ottoman administrative unit in Palestine meaning 'district'
sherut	shared taxi
Shi'a	from Arabic 'followers of Ali'; refers to those who favoured the rule of Ali, the Prophet Mohammed's cousin, after the Prophet's death in 632CE. Shi'a Muslims constitute the largest Muslim group after Sunni.
souk	Arabic for 'market'; often refers to traditional Middle Eastern-style markets. Persian equivalent is 'bazaar' and Hebrew is 'shuk'.
Sunni	from Arabic 'of the tradition/practice' of Prophet Mohammed; refers to the largest branch in Islam, whose followers believed that Mohammed's companions were to succeed the Prophet after his death in 632CE. This contradicts the bloodline approach adopted by the Shi'a branch.
tallit	large rectangular prayer shawl
tefillin	two small boxes attached to leather straps and containing excerpts from the Torah
tel	mound composed of the remains of successive settlements
tughra	Ottoman calligraphic seal carving, usually affixed at the top of a building façade
Tzahal	see IDF (page 314)
Upsheri	Jewish religious ceremony of a boy's first haircut
vilayet	Ottoman administrative unit in Palestine meaning 'province', further divided into senjaks
yarmulke	a skullcap worn by Orthodox Jewish men, usually during prayer, but by some at all times
yeshiva	Torah academy or a centre of Talmudic learning
yishuv	collective of Jewish residents and settlements in Ottoman Syria and Palestine, as opposed to the diaspora. Approximately 90% of the yishuv residents came originally from Europe.
zimmer	pronounced 'tzimeh', it refers to (usually) rural and luxurious accommodation in Israel

Appendix 3

FURTHER INFORMATION

BOOKS
Other Middle East guides For a full list of travel guides available from Bradt, visit w bradtguides.com/shop.

Darke, Diana *Eastern Turkey* 2nd ed, 2014
Darke, Diana and Walsh, Tony *Oman* 4th ed, 2016
Doyle, Paul *Lebanon* 2nd ed, 2016
French, Carole *Jordan* 1st ed, 2012
Hann, Geoff, Dabrowska, Karen and Townsend-Greaves, Tina *Iraq: the ancient sites and Iraqi Kurdistan* 2nd ed, 2015
Irving, Sarah *Palestine* 1st ed, 2011
Oleynik, Maria and Smith, Hilary *Iran* 5th ed, 2017

History
Arendt, Hannah *Eichmann in Jerusalem. A Report on the Banality of Evil* Penguin Classics, 2006
Bar-Zohar, Michael *Lionhearts: Heroes of Israel* Little, Brown & Co, 2000
Dumper, Michael *The Politics of Sacred Space: The Old City of Jerusalem in the Middle East Conflict* Lynne Rienner Publishers Inc, 2001
Emmett, Chad F *Beyond the Basilica: Christians and Muslims in Nazareth.* University of Chicago Press, 1995
Finkelstein Israel, Mazar, Amihai and Schmidt, Brian *The Quest for the Historical Israel: Debating Archaeology and the History of Early Israel* Society of Biblical Literature, 2007
Gartman, Eric *Return to Zion. The History of Modern Israel* The Jewish Publication Society, 2015
Gilbert, Sir Martin *Israel: A History* Black Swan, 2008
Keneally, Thomas *Schindler's List* Hodder and Stoughton, 1994
Maxwell Miller, J *History of Ancient Israel and Judah* SCM Press, 2006
Mayer, Arno *Ploughshares into Swords: From Zionism to Israel* Verso Books, 2008
New York Times Correspondents *Israel: The Historical Atlas* John Wiley & Sons, 1997
Said, Edward W *The Question of Palestine* Random House, 2003
Seikaly, May *Haifa: Transformation of a Palestinian Arab Society, 1918–1939* I B Tauris, 2000
Shapira, Anita *Israel: A History* W&N, 2012
Shindler, Colin *A History of Modern Israel* Cambridge University Press, 2008
Stein, Claudia *Tel Aviv Spaziergänge* Books On Demand, 2017. In German and recommended for German-speakers.

Religion
Cohen, Abraham *Everyman's Talmud* Schocken Books, 1995
Drane, John W *Introducing the Old Testament* Lion Hudson plc, 2000
Kurzweil, Arthur *Kabbalah for Dummies* John Wiley & Sons, 2006

Sarna *The Torah: The Five Books of Moses* Jewish Publication Society, 1992
Siddiqui, M *How to Read the Quran* W W Norton & Co, 2008

Fiction

Fallenberg, Evan *Light Fell* SOHO Press, 2008
Grossman, David *To the End of the Land* Jonathan Cape, 2010
Kharmi, Ghada *In Search of Fatima: a Palestinian Story* Verso, 2009
Oz, Amos *A Tale of Love and Darkness* Vintage, 2005
Oz, Amos *My Michael* Vintage, 1992

Guidebooks and general reference

Baltsan, Hayim *Hebrew Dictionary* Webster's New World, 2017
Cassidy, Cardinal Edward and Charlesworth, James H *The Millennium Guide for Pilgrims to the Holy Land* D & F Scott Publishing Inc, 2000
Hoffman, Rabbi Lawrence *Israel: A Spiritual Travel Guide, 2nd ed: A Companion for the Modern Jewish Pilgrim* Jewish Lights, 2005
Levy, Ya'acov *Oxford English–Hebrew Hebrew–English Dictionary* Kernerman Publishing, 1999
Porter, Richard and Cottridge, David *A Photographic Guide to Birds of Israel and the Middle East* New Holland Publishers Ltd, 2000

CINEMA

Beaufort (2007) Israeli-produced movie depicting Israel's withdrawal from southern Lebanon after 18 years.

Exodus (1960) Tells the story of Palestine under the British Mandate and the immigration of the Jews.

Follow Me – The Yoni Netanyahu Story (2012) Documentary about Yonatan Netanyahu, Benjamin Netanyahu's older brother, who died during the Entebbe Operation in 1976.

Gett: The Trial of Viviane Amsalem (2014) A story of an Israeli woman trying to obtain divorce (Gett in Hebrew), starring the magnificent Ronit Elkabetz.

Kippur (2000) Israeli-produced movie depicting the Yom Kippur War.

Lebanon (2010) The story of four young Israeli soldiers and their experiences during the Lebanon War.

Lemon Tree (2008) A poignant story about the Israeli–Palestinian conflict and individuals caught in the middle.

Munich (2005) Depicts the massacre of Israeli athletes at the 1972 Munich Olympics at the hands of Palestinian Black September militants.

Operation Thunderbolt (*Mivtsa Yonatan*) (1977) Re-enactment of the rescue operation undertaken by the IDF following the hijacking of a flight from Tel Aviv to Paris that was forced to land in Entebbe, Uganda.

Paradise Now (2005) A story of suicide bombings as seen through the eyes of two young Palestinian men.

Schindler's List (1993) Deals with the Holocaust in Europe and the story of Oscar Schindler, who saved his Jewish workers from death camps.

Syrian Bride (2004) Tells the story of a young Druze bride from the Golan Heights who is sent to Syria for an arranged marriage, never to return or see her family again.

The Band's Visit (2007) A tragicomedy about an Egyptian Police Orchestra band due to play at an Arab cultural centre in Israel and taking a wrong bus to a town in Negev. Starring the magnificent Ronit Elkabetz and brilliant Saleh Bakri.

The Impossible Spy (1987) Chronicles the life of Eli Cohen, Israel's most acclaimed spy.

Waltz with Bashir (2008) Animated movie depicting the director's memories of the 1982 Lebanon War.

MUSIC Modern Israeli music is a mix of ethnic beats, and includes Arabic (often Yemenite), Ethiopian and more familiar Western tunes. Below is a list of singers and bands that you may enjoy before or during your trip to Israel.

Achinoam Nini, known as Noa, is an internationally renowned singer of Yemenite descent. **Eliad** is a popular R&B singer.

Idan Amedi was a finalist in the Kokhav Nolad (Israeli version of *The Voice*) and is a popular singer with a pleasant voice and reasonably good lyrics.

The Idan Raichel Project is a group led by talented Israeli singer and songwriter Idan Raichel, creating a mixture of very good ethnic sounds that include Ethiopian and Latin influences.

Liran Danino, with an unusual and beautiful voice, is not as high-profile as he used to be a few years back, but still releases some good music.

Nathan Goshen is a very popular singer in Israel at the moment, with some of his English-language tunes even making it to radio stations across Europe.

Ofra Haza was the Hebrew-language Israeli voice of the 1980s and 90s until her death in 2000. Famous worldwide, her music is classic now.

Marina Maximilian Blumin sings in Hebrew, English and Russian and has a brilliant voice.

Rotem Cohen is a pop singer with a good voice releasing romantic and soft tunes.

Sarit Hadad is a good example of Arabic lyrics in popular music in Israel, producing a unique Arabic–Hebrew combination.

Shlomo Artzi still fills stadiums with his classics of the 1970s, 80s and 90s.

WEBSITES

w eyeonisrael.com Interactive map of the country.

w goisrael.com Israel Ministry of Tourism.

w kabbalah.com Official website of the Kabbalah Centre.

w kashrut.com Kosher and Jewish prayer time information service.

w jerusalem.muni.il Jerusalem Municipal Tourism department.

w jewishencyclopedia.com

w parks.org.il Israel Nature and National Parks Authority.

w touristisrael.com An informative and reliable source of information about tourism in Israel.

Index

Page numbers in **bold** indicate major entries; those in *italics* indicate maps

FOLLOW BRADT

For the latest news, special offers and competitions, subscribe to the Bradt
newsletter via the website w bradtguides.com and follow Bradt on:

f BradtTravelGuides
🐦 @BradtGuides
📷 @bradtguides
𝔭 bradtguides